D0185726

Good Housekeeping
NEW
STEP-*by*-STEP
COOK
BOOK

Good Housekeeping

— NEW —

STEP-*by*-STEP

COOK
BOOK

BCA

LONDON   NEW YORK   SYDNEY   TORONTO

This edition published 1993 by BCA
by arrangement with Ebury Press

CN 1101

Text and photography © Ebury Press and the
National Magazine Company Ltd 1993

All rights reserved. No part of this publication may be reproduced, stored in a
retrieval system, or transmitted in any form or by any means, electronic,
mechanical, photocopying, recording or otherwise, without the prior
permission of the copyright owners.

The expression Good Housekeeping as used in the title of this book is the trade
mark of the National Magazine Company Limited and The Hearst Corporation,
registered in the United Kingdom and USA, and other principal countries of the
world, and is the absolute property of the National Magazine Company Limited and
The Hearst Corporation. The use of this trade mark other than with the express
permission of The National Magazine Company Limited or The Hearst
Corporation is strictly prohibited.

MANAGING EDITOR: JANET ILLSLEY

DESIGN: Peter Bridgewater
SPECIAL PHOTOGRAPHY: Ken Field
TECHNIQUES PHOTOGRAPHY: Karl Adamson
FOOD STYLISTS: Lyn Rutherford, Jacqueline Clark,
Joanna Farrow, Emma-Lee Gow and Carole Handslip
PHOTOGRAPHIC STYLIST: Sue Russell
CONTRIBUTING AUTHORS: Janet Smith, Fiona Hunter,
Jacqueline Clark and Joanna Farrow
CONTRIBUTING EDITOR: Diana Artley
ADDITIONAL RESEARCH AND EDITORIAL ASSISTANCE: Helen Middleton,
Emma-Lee Gow, Helen Bonthrone, Hilary Bird and Trisha Cochrane

The publishers would like to thank Prestige and Kenwood
for lending equipment for photography.

Typeset by Textype Typesetters, Cambridge
Colour separations by Magnacraft, London
Printed and bound in Germany by
Mohndruck Gmbh, Gutersloh

FOREWORD

The *Good Housekeeping New Step-by-Step Cook Book* is a wonderful collection of more than 750 recipes and ideas for cooking in the '90s. As well as guiding the novice cook, this book will, I hope, also be an inspiration to the more accomplished cook with its excellent mix of recipes for both new, creative dishes and sophisticated classic ones. The step-by-step instructions are written in a very straightforward style and are accompanied by photographs illustrating each stage of the dish. This means that as you work through the recipe you can see clearly how the food should look - what the texture of a sauce should be, for example, how the pastry should be used, or where exactly to make cuts into meat. Preparation and cooking times are also there to help you select the most suitable recipes. All the essential techniques are described, from roasting and making sauces to pastry-making and using gelatine. But remember that the recipes are only there as a guide to help you to success in your cooking. Once all the techniques have been mastered you will feel relaxed enough to try out your own variations.

Many of the recipes are short and quick to suit today's style of everyday family cooking. You'll find plenty of new ideas for cooking pasta, fast grills and stir-fries, for instance, alongside dozens of more elaborate recipes for entertaining on special occasions and at weekends. In keeping with our change in attitude to health and diet, the book contains lots of recipes for fish and shellfish, pasta and chicken, and new ways with fresh fruit and vegetables. However, here at the Good Housekeeping Institute we firmly believe that there is no such thing as a bad food, only a bad diet. So you'll also find, and I'm sure you'll be tempted by, the selection of delicious desserts and bakes that have been included.

The book's design makes it easy to find your way around the chapters and through the colour index to pinpoint specific recipes. Pages of practical information are also there to give advice on selecting foods, from basic fruits and vegetables to unusual herbs and salad leaves. A guide to essential kitchen equipment includes new developments in processors and mixers as well as the more familiar kitchen tools.

I'm sure that the *Good Housekeeping New Step-by-Step Cook Book* is all you'll need for a lifetime of everyday cooking and entertaining.

MOYRA FRASER
Cookery Editor, Good Housekeeping

CONTENTS

INTRODUCTION

The aim of this book is to make cooking as straightforward and as pleasurable as it possibly can be. The clear step-by-step instructions and the accompanying photographs will help you to achieve impressive results. However, there are also a number of general guidelines which you should follow in order to get the best out of the recipes.

❖ Cookery Notes ❖

❖ Both metric and imperial measures are given for the recipes. Follow either metric or imperial throughout as they are not interchangeable.
❖ All spoon measures are level unless otherwise stated. Sets of measuring spoons are available in both metric and imperial sizes for accurate measurement of small quantities.
❖ Ovens should be preheated to the specified temperature. Grills should also be preheated. The cooking times given in the recipes assume that this has been done.
❖ Cooking times can vary according to the individual oven. Start checking to see whether the dish is cooked towards the end of the cooking time.
❖ Where a stage is specified in brackets under freezing instructions, the dish should be frozen at the end of that stage.
❖ Where margarine is required use either block or soft tub margarine. Otherwise use as specified in the recipe.
❖ Size 2 eggs should be used except where otherwise specified.
❖ Plain or self-raising flour can be used unless otherwise specified. Use white, brown or wholemeal flour but see individual chapters for use in pastry, bread and cake making.
❖ Brown or white breadcrumbs can be used unless one type is specified.
❖ Use freshly ground black pepper unless otherwise specified.

❖ Weights and Measures ❖

For consistently good results from a recipe, accurate measuring is essential.
❖ Balance scales are more accurate and last longer than spring scales.
❖ Make sure you read the line on the measuring jug at eye level when measuring liquids.
❖ Do not hold the measuring spoon into which you are pouring liquid over the dish you are making, in case you pour out too much.

The recipes in this book contain both metric and imperial measurements. Use the following reference charts if you need to convert or adapt any measurements yourself.

❖ Conversion Charts ❖

❖ Liquid ❖

METRIC ❖	IMPERIAL ❖
5 ml	1 tsp
15 ml	1 tbsp
25 ml	1 fl oz
50 ml	2 fl oz
150 ml	¼ pint
200 ml	7 fl oz
300 ml	½ pint
450 ml	15 fl oz
600 ml	1 pint
900 ml	1½ pints
1 litre	1¾ pints
1.1 litres	2 pints
1.7 litres	3 pints

❖ Solid ❖

METRIC ❖	IMPERIAL ❖
25 g	1 oz
50 g	2 oz
125 g	4 oz
225 g	8 oz
350 g	12 oz
400 g	14 oz
450 g	1 lb
700 g	1½ lb
900 g	2 lb
1 kg	2.2 lb

❖ Oven Temperature Scales ❖

°CELSIUS SCALE ❖	FAHRENHEIT SCALE °F ❖	GAS OVEN MARKS
110°C	225°F	¼
130	250	½
140	275	1
150	300	2
170	325	3
180	350	4
190	375	5
200	400	6
220	425	7
230	450	8
240	475	9

COOKING UTENSILS & EQUIPMENT

A well-equipped kitchen does not mean one which contains every possible gadget and appliance. The most important considerations when choosing cooking utensils and equipment are frequency of use and quality. You should concentrate on buying a small number of high-quality but very practical tools which will stand the test of time rather than a larger number of lower quality items, many of which may never be taken out of the kitchen drawer.

Pots and pans and knives are arguably the most indispensable items used in cooking. And, while they are not strictly essential as all cooking tasks can be performed by hand if necessary, food preparation machines can make such a difference when you are cooking large quantities or involved in a time-consuming task that they should be seriously considered when you are equipping your kitchen.

Following are some general guidelines on how to choose what you need:

❖ Pots and Pans ❖

The key factor here is the material from which a cooking pot or pan is made. This determines how quickly and evenly it conducts heat to the food and how easily it will burn.

❖ ALUMINIUM conducts heat evenly. Medium and heavy gauge aluminium are suitable for most types of hob but lightweight aluminium is suitable only for gas and has a short life as it tends to distort.

❖ CAST IRON conducts heat well. It is thick, heavy and good for long, slow cooking at low temperatures. Because cast iron is heavy, it is not suitable if you have problems lifting things and it is also liable to break if dropped on a hard floor surface.

❖ COPPER conducts heat very well and is preferred by many professional chefs. It must be lined with tin, nickel or aluminium to prevent the copper from reacting with very acid foods. Copper is expensive and needs regular cleaning.

❖ STAINLESS STEEL needs a layer of aluminium or copper bonded on to the base to help it conduct heat well. Pans of stainless steel are expensive, but they are also very durable and will, if looked after properly, last forever.

❖ VITREOUS ENAMEL is a coating applied to various metals to make them more attractive on the exterior and easier to clean on the interior. Painted enamel is inferior and chips easily. Look out for the trademark Vitramel (TM) which denotes good quality enamel and application.

❖ EARTHENWARE AND CERAMICS are not good conductors of heat although they do tend to retain heat well once hot. They are most suitable for use in the oven and should be set on a heat diffusing mat if used on top of the hob.

Aim for a good range of sizes in building up a collection of pans, so that you can choose the right size of pan for the task in hand. Food will not cook properly if the pan is too big or too small for what is in it.

Below is a guide to what is really essential and what you can acquire when you choose:

❖ Pan Checklist ❖

BASIC SELECTION	ADDITIONAL SELECTION
❖	❖
2 heavy-based 1.7 litre (3 pint) saucepans with lids 2 larger saucepans with lids heavy-based frying pan or sauté pan with lid milk pan	steamer omelette or crêpe pan wok preserving pan fish kettle

❖ Knives ❖

There are few cooking tasks which cannot be achieved with a sharp knife. The material from which a knife is made affects its sharpness and durability.

❖ CARBON STEEL is easy to sharpen. However, it discolours on contact with acidic food and rusts easily. Dry carbon steel knives thoroughly after washing.

❖ STAINLESS STEEL does not discolour or rust easily. However, it blunts quickly and is difficult to sharpen.

❖ HIGH CARBON STAINLESS STEEL has all the advantages. It sharpens well and does not discolour or rust easily. Inevitably, high carbon stainless steel knives are the most expensive.

Knives should be looked after well and the following guidelines will help to keep your knives in good condition:

❖ Always wash and dry them thoroughly after use.

❖ Do not keep knives all together in a drawer. Use a knife block which will prevent the blades from damaging each other.

❖ Sharpen them regularly.

As with pots and pans, aim to have a basic selection of good knives and acquire others when you can.

❖ Knife Checklist ❖

BASIC SELECTION	ADDITIONAL SELECTION
❖	❖
cook's knife, at least 20 cm (8 inches) long paring knife carving knife and fork bread knife serrated knife palette knife	filetting knife boning knife

❖ Food Preparation Machines ❖

The main point to consider when you are buying a machine is just how sophisticated you need it to be. It is easy to be tempted into thinking that you must have the most highly developed model on the market, but do stop to think whether you will really use all those functions, and remember that the machine and any attachments will have to be cleaned and stored somewhere.

Food Processors

A machine which slices vegetables, grates cheese, blends soups, mixes cakes, chops nuts, purées fruit, kneads bread and whisks cream sounds like the perfect kitchen companion. Most food processors are supplied with a metal blade, a shredder/grater and a slicer disc as standard. In general, the more you pay, the larger the capacity of the bowl and the more attachments you get. Top-of-the-range models also offer greater power and optional extras such as extra shredders, a chipper, a fruit press, a mill, an ice-cream maker, a Parmesan disc and a julienne disc. How much use you make of these clearly depends on the scale and kind of cooking you do. There are, however, a number of essential features which you should look for when buying:

* Measurements on the feed tube and bowl
* Variable speeds (although you do not need more than three) and a pulse (a short burst of high speed) for greater control
* Adjustable slicing discs
* Non-slip feet
* Flex storage
* Reversible discs, to save on storage space
* Safety-locking lid

In addition, there are some particularly useful features offered by more expensive food processors which you may consider paying more for:
* Mini chopping bowls for small quantities of food
* Drip-feed lid/feed tube which allows liquids to be added to the bowl while the processor is running (useful when making mayonnaise)
* Different feed-tube sizes – a double-feed tube is useful for foods of different sizes and a wide semi-circular feed tube is good for large items such as cabbage
* Integral storage for attachments
* Finger grips on attachments
* Dishwasher-safe attachments
* Liquidiser attachment for fine, smooth purées
* Citrus press or juice extractor
* Blade storage compartment or box

If you use your food processor a lot it can be worth buying a second bowl to save having to wash up too often during a preparation session.

Blenders

A blender, which may also be an attachment to a food processor, is generally used for puréeing and liquidising. It purées more finely than a food processor and is especially good for mayonnaise. Blenders are not recommended for dry chopping, however.

There are two types of blender to choose from:
* Goblet blenders, in which the cutting blades are at the bottom. Check the height of the blades before you buy as some are too high to cope with one-yolk mayonnaise and small quantities of food. Most goblets carry measurements down the side so you can check the quantity you are working with and add as necessary. A handle on the side of the goblet is useful for lifting it off the base when it contains hot liquid.
* Hand-held blenders, which require more effort than goblets but which are very portable.

Mini-choppers

These are useful for chopping small amounts of nuts, herbs or vegetables and can also blend small amounts of liquid. They cannot compete with full-sized food processors on larger quantities.

Food Mixers

These are particularly useful for mixing cakes, kneading dough and whisking, as food processors are not very good at incorporating air into mixtures such as egg whites, sponges or cream. They can be either hand-held or table-top models.
* Hand-held mixers may come with a bowl and stand and operate without being held. Or they may simply consist of a motorised head into which a selection of mixers, whisks and beaters can be fitted. There is little advantage in buying the type with a bowl and stand as these then have to be stored somewhere. Beaters alone can be used in a suitable bowl of your own.
* Table-top mixers are large and take up a lot of space. They can deal with large quantities of mixture such as bread dough or fruit cake, however, and can be left to operate without supervision.

❖ Other Utensils and Equipment ❖

In spite of the huge range of kitchen tools and equipment on the market, the number of utensils which are needed on a day-to-day basis is relatively small. If you are interested in a particular area of cooking, such as cake decorating or preserving, you may want, or need, to add more specialist tools to your collection to help in specific tasks. The following checklist is intended to act as a general guide to what is essential equipment for the average kitchen:

❖ Basic Selection ❖

saucepans (see above)	fish slice
knives (see above)	colander
casseroles	sieve
roasting tin	grater
mixing bowls	potato peeler
cake tins	potato masher
kitchen scales	skewers
measuring jug	rolling pin
measuring spoons	corkscrew
chopping boards	bottle opener
(ideally separate ones for	can opener
different foods, see page 433)	baking sheet
wooden spoons	wire cooling rack
slotted spoon	balloon whisk
ladle	kitchen scissors
spatulas	tongs

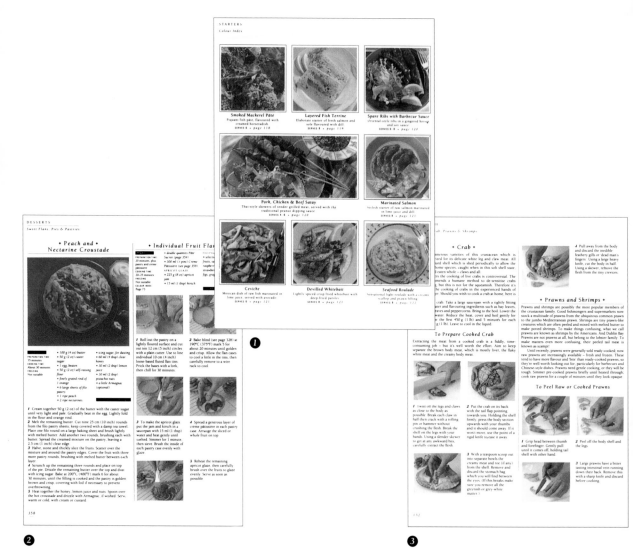

❖ How to Use This Book ❖

❶ Your starting point for choosing recipes and putting together a menu is the Colour Index. Here you will find a photograph of every recipe in the book. In addition, you will find the following information:

❖ a brief description of the dish
❖ the number of people it serves
❖ the page on which the recipe appears

❷ As well as thorough step-by-step instructions, each recipe also provides further useful information:

❖ Preparation and cooking times are listed at the top of each recipe, together with an indication of whether any extra time should be allowed, for example, in the case of marinating or soaking.
❖ Freezing notes indicate the suitability of the dish for freezing.

When the dish can be frozen at the end of a certain stage in the preparation, this stage is given in brackets.

❖ A reference to a page in the Colour Index tells you where to find a photograph of the finished dish if it does not appear with the recipe.
❖ Calorie counts are given per serving or appropriate portion of the dish. Where the calorie count ranges from a higher to a lower figure, this reflects the fact that the dish may serve a larger number of people, in which case the portion size and calorie count are reduced.

❸ At the beginning of each chapter you can find general information on the food in question and on how to choose, prepare, cook and serve it. Where appropriate, step-by-step photographs illustrate the essential techniques and you can refer back to this section from the recipes if you are unsure about a preparation or cooking method.

COLOUR INDEX

Chicken Consommé
Sparkling clear full-flavoured consommé
with classic variations.
SERVES **4** ❖ *page 98*

Cock-a-Leekie Soup
Clear light chicken and leek soup
flavoured with prunes.
SERVES **6** ❖ *page 98*

Mushroom Soup
A richly flavoured soup served with
crunchy Parmesan croûtons.
SERVES **4** ❖ *page 99*

French Onion Soup
The ever-popular French classic, served with toasted
Gruyère-topped croûtes.
SERVES **4** ❖ *page 99*

Roquefort & Watercress Soup
Deliciously rich, creamy soup, equally
good served hot or chilled.
SERVES **4** ❖ *page 100*

Spinach Soup
Pretty green-flecked soup served hot,
with cream and croûtons.
SERVES **4** ❖ *page 100*

Lettuce & Watercress Soup
Refreshing summer soup, ideal for
slimmers. Serve hot or chilled.
SERVES 6 ❖ *page 100*

Vegetable Soup with Pasta
Lightly spiced soup flavoured with chilli
and fresh coriander.
SERVES 4 ❖ *page 101*

Pea & Chervil Soup
A light, summery soup which acquires
its flavour from empty pea pods.
SERVES 6 ❖ *page 101*

Carrot & Coriander Soup
A smooth, creamy soup, spiced with
coriander.
SERVES 6 ❖ *page 102*

Spiced Leek & Potato Soup
A smooth-textured creamy soup with a
hint of curry flavour.
SERVES 6 ❖ *page 102*

Parsnip & Apple Soup
The characteristic flavour of parsnips is blended with a
hint of tart cooking apple in this velvety-textured soup.
SERVES 6 ❖ *page 102*

Cream of Celeriac Soup
Velvety-textured soup, with a hint of
lemon and chopped dill.
SERVES 3 - 4 ◆ *page 103*

Cream of Jerusalem Artichoke Soup
Smooth, delicately flavoured soup
enhanced with cream and croûtons.
SERVES 4 ◆ *page 103*

Mixed Bean & Vegetable Soup
This hearty, nourishing soup can be
served as a main course.
SERVES 6 ◆ *page 104*

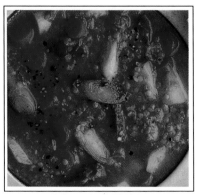

Winter Lentil Soup
Comforting winter vegetable and lentil
potage, ideal as a main meal.
SERVES 4 ◆ *page 104*

Minestrone
Classic Italian main-course soup
enriched with Pesto and Parmesan.
SERVES 6 - 8 ◆ *page 105*

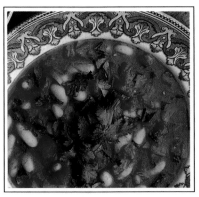

Bean & Coriander Potage
Substantial bean and vegetable soup,
liberally flavoured with coriander.
SERVES 4 ◆ *page 105*

Tuscan Bean Soup
Thick, wholesome soup, which can be
served as a meal in itself.
SERVES 6 ◆ *page 106*

Scotch Broth
Nourishing beef and vegetable main-
course soup to serve in winter.
SERVES 4 ◆ *page 106*

Hot & Sour Prawn Soup
Oriental-style soup, flavoured with
prawns, chilli and lemon grass.
SERVES 4 ◆ *page 106*

Bouillabaisse
The renowned Mediterranean mixed fish
and shellfish soup, flavoured with saffron.
SERVES 6 ✦ *page 107*

Mixed Fish Chowder
Chunky soup, featuring smoked
haddock, prawns and potatoes.
SERVES 4 ✦ *page 107*

Vichyssoise
Classic chilled creamy leek soup, served
topped with chives.
SERVES 4 ✦ *page 108*

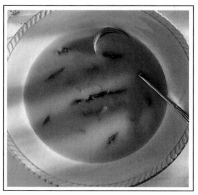

Chilled Asparagus Soup
A delicious summer soup, perfect as an
elegant starter.
SERVES 6 ✦ *page 108*

Iced Tomato & Basil Soup
This refreshing chilled soup is best made when tomatoes are at their
cheapest and most flavoursome. Serve with croûtons or crusty bread.
SERVES 4 ✦ *page 109*

Gazpacho
This famous Spanish chilled soup is traditionally served with
bowls of finely chopped cucumber, onion and green pepper.
SERVES 6 ✦ *page 109*

Minted Melon & Cucumber Soup
Wonderfully refreshing chilled soup for
a hot summer's day.
SERVES 4 ✦ *page 109*

Canapés
Oriental parcels, wholewheat blinis, mini croissants and mini pizzas: ideal party food.
SERVES 20-25 ◆ *page 112*

Smoked Salmon & Prawn Bites
Piquant seafood-topped mini scones – attractive party finger foods.
MAKES 120 ◆ *page 113*

Dips: Tzaziki, Hummus & Herbed Cheese Dip
Tasty dips are the perfect way to start a casual, relaxed meal. Serve these with colourful crudités, warm pitta bread and bread sticks.
SERVES 4-8 ◆ *page 115*

Prawn & Feta Purses
Crisp, light low-calorie filo parcels with a delicious filling.
MAKES 25 ◆ *page 114*

Spicy Crab Dip
Tangy seafood dip, served well chilled with crudités.
SERVES 4 ◆ *page 115*

Taramasalata
A flavoursome homemade version of this popular Greek starter.
SERVES 6 ◆ *page 115*

Guacamole with Crudités
Tasty Mexican avocado dip, flavoured with lime, fresh coriander
and spices, served with an assortment of crudités.
SERVES 6-8 ◆ *page 115*

**Olives with Garlic; Spiced
Cashews; Toasted Seed & Nut
Mix; Gruyére & Peanut Sablés**
SERVES 10-12 ◆ *page 113-4*

Pâté de Campagne
Coarse-textured traditional French pâté
with olives and garlic.
SERVES 10-12 ◆ *page 116*

Peppered Chicken Liver Pâté
Smooth-textured pâté, spiked with green
peppercorns.
SERVES 8 ◆ *page 116*

Smoked Salmon Pâté
A very quick and easy pâté made with
smoked salmon trimmings.
SERVES 6 ◆ *page 116*

Mushroom & Cashew Nut Pâté
Protein-rich pâté, best served with toast
or granary bread.
SERVES 8 ◆ *page 117*

Spinach Ricotta Terrine
Delicate terrine served with toasted
walnuts and a tomato coulis.
SERVES 6 ◆ *page 117*

Salmon Mousse
The ultimate seafood mousse, made with
freshly poached salmon.
SERVES 8 ◆ *page 118*

Smoked Mackerel Pâté
Piquant fish pâté, flavoured with
creamed horseradish.
SERVES 6 ✦ *page 118*

Layered Fish Terrine
Elaborate starter of fresh salmon and
sole flavoured with dill.
SERVES 8 ✦ *page 119*

Spare Ribs with Barbecue Sauce
Oriental-style ribs in a gingered hoisin
and soy sauce.
SERVES 6-8 ✦ *page 120*

Pork, Chicken & Beef Satay
Thai-style skewers of tender grilled meat, served with the
traditional peanut dipping sauce.
SERVES 4-6 ✦ *page 120*

Marinated Salmon
Stylish starter of raw salmon marinated
in lime juice and dill.
SERVES 8 ✦ *page 121*

Ceviche
Mexican dish of raw fish marinated in
lime juice, served with avocado.
SERVES 6 ✦ *page 121*

Devilled Whitebait
Lightly spiced crisp fried whitebait with
deep-fried parsley.
SERVES 8 ✦ *page 121*

Seafood Roulade
Sensational light roulade with a creamy
scallop and prawn filling.
SERVES 8 ✦ *page 122*

Smoked Salmon Rolls

Attractive starter with a cream cheese,
prawn and dill filling.

SERVES 8 ◆ *page 123*

Prawn Cocktail

Ever-popular, quick and easy starter
suitable for any occasion.

SERVES 4 ◆ *page 123*

Salad with Thai Crab Cakes

Luxury fish cakes served warm on a
colourful mixed leaf salad.

SERVES 6 ◆ *page 124*

Roasted Peppers with Yogurt & Pistachio Nuts

For this simple attractive starter use a colourful mixture of
peppers. Serve with warm crusty bread.

SERVES 4 ◆ *page 124*

Grilled Chicory with Pears

Caramelised chicory perfectly
complemented by pears and hazelnuts.

SERVES 4 ◆ *page 124*

Warm Scallop & Basil Salad

Irresistible salad, containing sun-dried
tomatoes and lots of basil.

SERVES 6 ◆ *page 125*

Minted Citrus Salad

Refreshing low-calorie starter of pomelo,
ugli fruit, melon and papaya.

SERVES 4 ◆ *page 125*

Avocado with Raspberry Vinegar

Fanned avocado slices perfectly offset by
the sharpness of raspberries.

SERVES 4 ◆ *page 126*

Asparagus with Coriander Hollandaise
A deliciously different way of serving
this prize vegetable.
SERVES **4** ◆ *page 126*

Baked Tomatoes with Cheese
Mozzarella and goat's cheese stuffed
tomatoes on crisp toast rounds.
SERVES **6** ◆ *page 127*

Deep-fried Potato Skins
More-ish deep-fried skins, served with
two contrasting tasty dips.
SERVES **2-3** ◆ *page 127*

Warm Salad of Mushrooms
Guaranteed to impress, this warm salad of assorted mushrooms,
tender spinach leaves and crisp bacon is quick to prepare.
SERVES **6-8** ◆ *page 128*

Filo Purses with Vegetables
Crisp light filo parcels filled with stir-
fried vegetable julienne.
SERVES **6** ◆ *page 128*

Salade Tiède
Frisée in a creamy vinaigrette with hot
crisp bacon and croûtons.
SERVES **4** ◆ *page 128*

Baked Mushroom Croûtes
Mixed wild and cultivated mushrooms
on baked baguette slices.
SERVES **6** ◆ *page 129*

Artichoke & Spinach Salad
Char-grilled Jerusalem artichokes and
young spinach flavoured with lemon.
SERVES **6** ◆ *page 129*

Dressed Crab
An impressive way of serving crab for a special lunch or supper.
SERVES 2-3 ◆ *page 135*

Avocado with Crab
This tempting starter with its rich blend of flavours is quick to prepare.
SERVES 4 ◆ *page 135*

Grilled Lobster
A simple dish which brings out the fine delicate taste of lobster.
SERVES 4 ◆ *page 135*

Chilli Prawns with Cashews
Delicious stir-fry of prawns, spring onions and cashew nuts.
SERVES 2-3 ◆ *page 136*

Prawns Fried in Garlic
Dublin Bay prawns are the variety used in this superb dish.
SERVES 2 ◆ *page 136*

Prawns with Fennel & Rice
Large succulent prawns, tossed with fennel, courgettes and rice.
SERVES 4 ◆ *page 136*

Scallops in Creamy Basil Sauce
Pretty scallops served in a wine and cream sauce with basil.
SERVES 4 ◆ *page 137*

Scallops with Ginger
Tasty spiced seafood dish, with ginger, chilli and coriander.
SERVES 3 ◆ *page 137*

Scallops au Gratin
Scallops in a delicate sauce with a crunchy topping – served in their shells.
SERVES 4 ◆ *page 137*

Mussels & Clams with Tomatoes
Delicious steamed shellfish in a tasty
tomato and garlic broth.
SERVES 2-3 ✦ *page 138*

Mussels with Garlic & Parsley
Baked mussels, coated in garlic and
Parmesan-flavoured breadcrumbs.
SERVES 4-6 ✦ *page 138*

Monkfish & Mussel Skewers
Brochettes of firm white monkfish and
yellow mussels on a salad.
SERVES 4 ✦ *page 138*

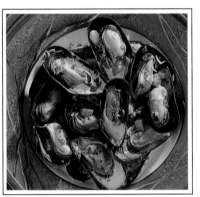

Mussels in White Wine
Mussels on their half-shell in a rich
cream and wine sauce.
SERVES 4-6 ✦ *page 139*

Oysters au Gratin
Mouthwatering oysters with bacon and
artichoke hearts.
SERVES 4-6 ✦ *page 139*

Seafood Pilaki
Delicious mixture of monkfish, squid
and mussels in a tomato sauce.
SERVES 8 ✦ *page 140*

Glazed Seafood Platter
Sumptuous mixture of shellfish and fish
with a cheese topping.
SERVES 6 ✦ *page 140*

Mixed Seafood Brochettes
Seafood selection, marinated, then
grilled and served on rice.
SERVES 4 ✦ *page 141*

Italian Seafood Salad
A stunning salad of assorted shellfish in
a lemon dressing.
SERVES 6 ✦ *page 141*

Grilled Turbot with Chervil
Delicious turbot steaks served with a
chervil and tomato sauce.
SERVES 4 ♦ *page 146*

Sole with Mousseline Sauce
Delicate fillets of lemon sole in a lemon
cream sauce.
SERVES 8 ♦ *page 146*

Haddock with Parsley & Lemon
Baked haddock served with a traditional
parsley sauce.
SERVES 4 ♦ *page 146*

Monkfish with Lemon & Dill
Firm-fleshed monkfish, marinated and
grilled to perfection.
SERVES 4 ♦ *page 147*

Parchment Baked Fish
Fish steaks baked in parcels with
cucumber and fennel seeds.
SERVES 4 ♦ *page 147*

Rolled Plaice with Pesto
Piquant plaice rolls served on a bed of
colourful vegetables.
SERVES 4 ♦ *page 148*

Grilled Plaice with Mushrooms
Tasty, nutritious dish, ideal for a low-
calorie supper.
SERVES 4 ♦ *page 148*

Golden Crumbed Plaice
Quick and easy fish dish with a crunchy
breadcrumb and nut topping.
SERVES 4 ♦ *page 148*

Seafood Kebabs
Skewered monkfish, prawns and cucumber,
served with a garlic vinaigrette.
SERVES 4 ♦ *page 149*

Monkfish with Mustard Seeds
Nutritious fish in a low-calorie lemon
and mustard yogurt sauce.
SERVES 6 ◆ *page 149*

Sweet & Sour Monkfish Kebabs
Skewers of bacon-wrapped fish,
aubergine and red onion.
SERVES 4 ◆ *page 150*

Haddock & Soured Cream Gratin
Tasty fish supper, with a tomato and
herb creamy sauce.
SERVES 2 ◆ *page 150*

Cod & Crab Gratin
Cod, mushrooms and crabmeat with a
cheesy potato topping.
SERVES 4 ◆ *page 150*

Sweet & Sour Fish
Stir-fried fish with green beans, red pepper
and mushrooms.
SERVES 4 ◆ *page 151*

Trout in Riesling
Succulent trout braised in wine on a bed
of leeks.
SERVES 4 ◆ *page 152*

Lemon & Mustard Mackerel
Grilled mackerel flavoured with a tangy
lemon and mustard butter.
SERVES 6 ◆ *page 152*

Salmon Steaks in Citrus Dressing
Grilled salmon enhanced with lime,
orange and a hint of cardamom.
SERVES 4 ◆ *page 152*

Salmon & Thyme Parcels
Deliciously moist salmon cutlets baked
in paper with herbs.
SERVES 4 ◆ *page 153*

Salmon Steaks with Hollandaise
Simply baked salmon portions with a
smooth Hollandaise sauce.
SERVES 8 • *page 153*

Dill-glazed Salmon
This cold poached whole salmon makes an impressive centrepiece
for a special occasion. It is served with a lemon mayonnaise.
SERVES 8 • *page 154*

Salmon Trout with Herb Sauce
Delicate cold salmon trout, served with a
watercress and herb sauce.
SERVES 4 • *page 154*

Salmon en Croûte
Delicious whole salmon with a spinach
filling, encased in melting puff pastry.
SERVES 8 • *page 155*

Spinach & Seafood Pasties
A tasty melangé of cod, prawns and
spinach in puff pastry.
SERVES 4 • *page 155*

Crispy Layered Fish Pie
Light, crisp filo pastry enveloping a
haddock and rice filling.
SERVES 6 • *page 156*

Golden Topped Fish Pie
Mixed seafood in a creamy sauce with a
crisp potato topping.
SERVES 4 • *page 156*

Smoked Haddock Soufflé
Light, airy hot soufflé flavoured with
watercress and Parmesan.
SERVES 4 • *page 157*

Spiced Fish Stir-fry

Scallops and monkfish stir-fried with
spices and colourful vegetables.

SERVES **4** ✦ *page 158*

Curried Fish with Lemon

Fillets of sole in a creamy curried sauce
with ginger and coconut.

SERVES **6** ✦ *page 158*

Italian Fish Stew

A variety of fish and shellfish cooked
with saffron, garlic and tomatoes.

SERVES **8** ✦ *page 161*

Fritto Misto

Assorted seafood deep-fried until crisp
and golden.

SERVES **8** ✦ *page 159*

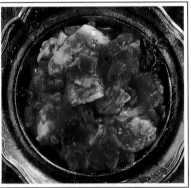

Greek-style Fish Casserole

A quick fish dish, flavoured with
marjoram and garlic.

SERVES **4** ✦ *page 159*

Smoked Haddock Casserole

Rich, creamy mixture of prawns,
haddock and vegetables.

SERVES **6** ✦ *page 160*

Paella

Colourful Spanish dish of mixed
seafood, rice and peppers.

SERVES **4** ✦ *page 160*

Fish Cakes with Herbs

Tasty fish and potato cakes, coated with
breadcrumbs.

SERVES **4** ✦ *page 158*

Kedgeree

Flavourful mixture of smoked haddock,
rice and hard-boiled egg.

SERVES **4** ✦ *page 161*

Roast Beef & Yorkshire Pudding
Traditional roast with gravy and
individual Yorkshire puddings.
SERVES 4-8 ✦ *page 168*

Fillet of Beef with Mushrooms
Prime fillet stuffed with mushrooms and
sweet peppers, with a tasty sauce.
SERVES 8 ✦ *page 168*

Beef Wellington
Tender fillet flavoured with pâté and
mushrooms, in puff pastry.
SERVES 8 ✦ *page 169*

Boeuf Bourguignon
Rich beef casserole with button onions
and mushrooms in red wine.
SERVES 8 ✦ *page 170*

Peppered Rib of Beef
Boned and rolled rib, flavoured with
herbs, garlic and coriander.
SERVES 6 ✦ *page 170*

Boiled Beef & Carrots
Boneless salted silverside or brisket
simmered with vegetables.
SERVES 6 ✦ *page 170*

Spiced Beef Casserole
Slow-cooked beef and mushroom casserole
flavoured with horseradish and ginger.
SERVES 6 ✦ *page 171*

Italian Braised Beef
Beef casseroled in wine, with artichoke
hearts, mushrooms and olives.
SERVES 6 ✦ *page 171*

Oxtail & Lentil Casserole
Hearty, nourishing winter dish with root
vegetables and lentils.
SERVES 6 ✦ *page 172*

Beef Casserole with Kumquats
Chuck steak cooked with celery, leeks
and kumquat slices.
SERVES **4** ◆ *page 172*

Beef Hotpot
Stewing steak cooked with root
vegetables, with a crisp potato topping.
SERVES **4** ◆ *page 173*

Steak & Kidney Pie
Tender cubes of braising steak and oxtail
with a pastry crust.
SERVES **4** ◆ *page 173*

Steak au Poivre
Prime steaks encrusted with peppercorns
in a brandy cream sauce.
SERVES **4** ◆ *page 174*

Grilled Steaks with Madeira
Grilled fillet steaks served with a
Madeira flavoured demi-glace.
SERVES **4** ◆ *page 174*

Peppered Beef Sauté
Sautéed strips of tender beef and red
onion in a creamy sauce.
SERVES **2-3** ◆ *page 174*

Steak & Stilton Parcels
Stilton-topped steaks encased in crisp,
light filo pastry.
SERVES **4** ◆ *page 175*

Steak & Kidney Kebabs
Skewers of rump steak, lamb's kidneys,
mushrooms and button onions.
SERVES **4** ◆ *page 175*

Stir-fried Beef & Vegetabls
Rump steak stir-fried with baby corn,
mangetouts and broccoli.
SERVES **4** ◆ *page 176*

Chilli Beef with Noodles
Stir-fried beef with red pepper, broccoli
and thin noodles.
SERVES **4** ◆ *page 176*

Beef Burgers
Moist oaty burgers flavoured with herbs,
served in baps.
SERVES **4** ◆ *page 176*

Beef & Potato Moussaka
Minced beef and aubergine chunks in
tomato, with a cheesy potato topping.
SERVES **4** ◆ *page 177*

Chilli Tacos
Spicy mince and kidney beans in taco
shells, topped with cheese.
SERVES **4** ◆ *page 177*

Italian-style Veal Kebabs
Tender strips of veal wrapped in Parma ham
and grilled on skewers.
SERVES **4** ◆ *page 178*

Basil & Citrus Veal Escalopes
Meltingly tender veal liberally flavoured
with basil, orange and lemon.
SERVES **4** ◆ *page 178*

Veal Goulash
ustaining casserole, spiced with paprika
and topped with soured cream.
SERVES **8** ◆ *page 179*

Calf's Liver with Grapes
An unusual but delicious combination,
served with a Madeira sauce.
SERVES **4** ◆ *page 179*

Liver with Sage & Apple
Tender calf's liver sautéed with leeks,
apple slices and sage.
SERVES **4** ◆ *page 179*

Crown Roast of Lamb
Traditional celebration roast with a tasty
apricot stuffing.
SERVES **6** ✦ *page 180*

Thyme Roasted Loin of Lamb
Boned loins rolled around a tasty
spinach, thyme and mushroom stuffing.
SERVES **6** ✦ *page 180*

Garlic & Rosemary Rack of Lamb
Spectacular 'guard of honour' liberally
flavoured with garlic.
SERVES **4** ✦ *page 181*

Lamb with Peppers & Aubergines
Roast half leg with red peppers,
aubergines and oregano.
SERVES **4** ✦ *page 181*

Roast Lamb Fillets with Garlic
Tender stuffed fillets of lamb with a
piquant mustard sauce.
SERVES **4** ✦ *page 182*

Lamb & Courgette Pilaf
Lean lamb with courgettes, dried
apricots and brown rice.
SERVES **4** ✦ *page 182*

Lamb Casserole with Almonds
Creamy lamb casserole with ground
almonds, cumin and ginger.
SERVES **8** ✦ *page 182*

Country Lamb Casserole
Lamb, cooked with swede, carrots,
celery and barley.
SERVES **6** ✦ *page 183*

Irish Stew
Lamb neck cutlets layered with potatoes,
onions and herbs.
SERVES **4** ✦ *page 183*

Grilled Lamb Chops with Mint
Chump chops marinated in wine vinegar,
honey and mint, then grilled.
SERVES 4 ◆ *page 184*

Lamb Cutlets with Apricots
Tender cutlets braised with dried
apricots and cinnamon.
SERVES 4 ◆ *page 186*

Lamb Noisettes with Mushrooms
Lamb cooked with button mushrooms
and onions in white wine.
SERVES 4 ◆ *page 186*

Lamb Kebabs in a Spicy Dressing
Skewers of lamb, courgettes, corn and
tomatoes in a yogurt dressing.
SERVES 4 ◆ *page 184*

Lamb Fillet & Pepper Stir-fry
Stir-fried lamb with peppers, carrots,
mangetouts and courgette.
SERVES 4 ◆ *page 185*

Spiced Lamb Meatballs
Bite-sized meatballs spiced with chilli
and cumin.
SERVES 4 ◆ *page 185*

Lamb Escalopes in Oatmeal
Leg steaks flavoured with mustard,
crisply coated with oatmeal.
SERVES 4 ◆ *page 186*

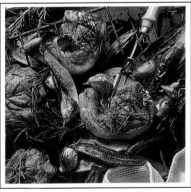

Grilled Lamb with Courgettes
Loin chops spiked with rosemary, grilled
with courgettes.
SERVES 4 ◆ *page 184*

Spicy Cinnamon Lamb
Slices of lamb cooked with ginger,
cinnamon and nutmeg.
SERVES 4 ◆ *page 187*

Lamb Chops & Leeks with Lentils

Loin chops braised on a bed of leeks and
red lentils.

SERVES **4** ◆ *page 187*

Spiced Lamb with Spinach

Spicy casserole of lamb with turnips and
spinach.

SERVES **6** ◆ *page 187*

Spiced Lamb Escalopes

Tender escalopes marinated in a spicy
paste, then baked.

SERVES **4** ◆ *page 188*

Shepherd's Pie

Favourite family meal, with its
characteristic potato topping.

SERVES **4** ◆ *page 188*

Lamb & Aubergine Bake

Topped with golden, cheesy gnocchi,
this has a delicious taste.

SERVES **6** ◆ *page 189*

Minted Lamb Burgers

Flavoursome burgers, cooked with
cucumber and spring onions.

SERVES **4** ◆ *page 189*

Pan-fried Liver with Tomatoes

Wafer-thin slices of lamb's liver
marinated and cooked in Marsala.

SERVES **4** ◆ *page 190*

Kidneys Provençale

Delicate lamb's kidneys cooked with
tomatoes, courgettes and basil.

SERVES **4** ◆ *page 190*

Pork Loin with a Fruit Crust

Roast loin of pork encrusted with a
mixture of dried fruits.

SERVES **4** ◆ *page 191*

Roast Pork Loin with Rosemary
Succulent roast with a Dijon mustard
and rosemary glaze.
SERVES 6-8 ◆ *page 191*

Lemon-roasted Pork with Garlic
Tender roast fillets with a lemon, basil
and garlic stuffing.
SERVES 6 ◆ *page 192*

Pork with Celeriac Stuffing
Pork fillets with a tasty bacon, celeriac
and bulgar wheat stuffing.
SERVES 6 ◆ *page 192*

Quick Pork Cassoulet
Streaky pork rashers and kidney beans
in a spicy tomato stock.
SERVES 4 ◆ *page 192*

Pork & Herb Bean Pot
Slow-cooked casserole of pork, garlic
sausage and pinto or black-eye beans.
SERVES 8 ◆ *page 193*

Pork with Prunes
Thin pork chops cooked in white wine
with large prunes.
SERVES 4 ◆ *page 194*

Pork & Pasta Sauté
Quick, easy sauté of pork fillet,
vegetables and pasta.
SERVES 4 ◆ *page 194*

Stir-fried Pork with Baby Corn
Tasty stir-fry of pork, baby corn, carrots
and sugar snap peas.
SERVES 4 ◆ *page 195*

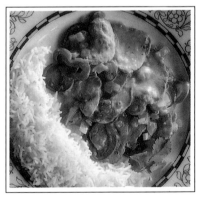

Pork in Wine & Coriander
Pan-fried fillet with green pepper and
ground coriander.
SERVES 4 ◆ *page 195*

Toad in the Hole
Whole sausages baked in a crisp
Yorkshire pudding.
SERVES **4** ✦ *page 196*

Golden Grilled Pork Steaks
Loin steaks, marinated and served with a
tangy citrus sauce.
SERVES **4** ✦ *page 196*

Sausages with Lentils
Chunky French-style sausages cooked
with green lentils and parsnips.
SERVES **4** ✦ *page 196*

Sausage & Bean Casserole
Herby sausages with chick peas and
kidney beans in tomato stock.
′SERVES **6** ✦ *page 197*

Sausage & Potato Skewers
Tasty kebabs of spicy pork sausages and
new potatoes.
SERVES **4-6** ✦ *page 197*

Glazed Baked Gammon
Celebration joint with a delicious honey
and orange glaze.
SERVES **8** ✦ *page 198*

Gammon with a Crunchy Glaze
Whole gammon joint with an almond
and sesame seed coating.
SERVES **8** ✦ *page 198*

Bacon Chops in Cider Sauce
Bacon chops baked with mustard, served
with a cider sauce.
SERVES **4** ✦ *page 199*

Boiled Bacon with Parsley Sauce
Whole bacon joint simmered with
vegetables, served with parsley sauce.
SERVES **6-8** ✦ *page 199*

Traditional Roast Chicken
Succulent chicken with a tasty parsley and lemon stuffing,
served with roast potatoes and seasonal vegetables.
SERVES 4-6 ◆ *page 206*

Pot Roast Chicken with Peppers
Whole chicken cooked with peppers and
garlic in wine and stock.
SERVES 4 ◆ *page 207*

Saffron Chicken with Spinach
Spinach-stuffed chicken supremes,
served with a creamy saffron sauce.
SERVES 6 ◆ *page 207*

Chicken & Gorgonzola Parcels
Gorgonzola-stuffed chicken breasts
wrapped in sage and Parma ham.
SERVES 4 ◆ *page 208*

Chicken Fillets with Pesto
Low-calorie dish of baked chicken filled
with soft cheese and pesto.
SERVES 4 ◆ *page 208*

Chicken Casserole with Apricots
Chicken cooked with bacon rolls,
apricots and thyme in Marsala.
SERVES 4 ◆ *page 208*

Chicken Parmigiana
Chicken baked with aubergines, tomato,
mozzarella and Parmesan.
SERVES 6 • *page 209*

Chicken with Lemon & Sage
Braised chicken breast fillets with sage,
garlic and lemon.
SERVES 4 • *page 210*

Chicken & Artichoke Bake
Chicken and artichoke hearts in a cheesy
sauce, topped with filo pastry.
SERVES 4 • *page 210*

Chicken with Spicy Tomato Sauce
Chicken thighs flavoured with cumin,
coriander, chilli and tomatoes.
SERVES 4 • *page 210*

Chicken with Mushrooms & Cognac
Chicken cooked in white wine and
enriched with cream and egg yolks.
SERVES 4 • *page 211*

Spicy Chicken with Cashews
Chicken thighs coated with nuts, garlic
and ginger, in a yogurt sauce.
SERVES 4 • *page 211*

Coq au Vin
Famous French casserole in red wine,
served with bread croûtes.
SERVES 8 • *page 212*

Chicken with Corn & Peppers
Chicken thighs with sweetcorn, green
pepper and brown rice.
SERVES 4 • *page 212*

Chicken Curry with Coconut
Creamy curry, flavoured with ginger,
creamed coconut and cashews.
SERVES 8 • *page 213*

Spring Chicken Fricassée
Chicken fillets flavoured with garlic
soft cheese, with baby vegetables.
SERVES 4 ♦ *page 214*

Sesame Chicken Stir-fry
Chicken strips stir-fried with broccoli,
baby corn and peanuts.
SERVES 4 ♦ *page 214*

Chicken with Oyster Sauce
Stir-fried chicken with flat mushrooms
and mangetouts.
SERVES 4 ♦ *page 215*

Stir-fried Chicken & Courgettes
Tasty stir-fry of chicken, red pepper and
courgette strips.
SERVES 4 ♦ *page 215*

Chicken with Nuts & Mushrooms
Chicken sautéed with walnuts,
mushrooms and cucumber.
SERVES 4 ♦ *page 216*

Chicken with Tarragon
Breasts of chicken braised in wine,
enhanced with juniper and tarragon.
SERVES 4 ♦ *page 216*

Chicken Chow Mein
Chicken and prawns with bean sprouts
and noodles in an oriental sauce.
SERVES 4 ♦ *page 216*

Chicken & Avocado Stroganoff
Chicken, mushrooms and avocado
chunks in a mustardy yogurt sauce.
SERVES 4 ♦ *page 217*

Honey Barbecued Drumsticks
Grilled or barbecued drumsticks in a
soy, citrus and honey marinade.
SERVES 8 ♦ *page 217*

Lemon Chicken Kebabs
Chicken and mixed vegetable skewers,
served with rice.
SERVES 4 ◆ *page 217*

Chicken with Spiced Butter
Grilled chicken breasts flavoured with a
chilli and coriander butter.
SERVES 4 ◆ *page 218*

Cider Roast Poussins
Poussins flavoured with soft cheese,
garlic, herbs and apple slices.
SERVES 4 ◆ *page 218*

Devilled Poussins
Tasty poussins marinated in a spice
paste and baked until crisp.
SERVES 8 ◆ *page 219*

Poussins with Pepper Stuffing
Young poussins stuffed with a tasty mixture of peppers, breadcrumbs,
celery and sun-dried tomatoes, served with a herb sauce.
SERVES 8 ◆ *page 219*

Ballottine of Turkey
An impressive special occasion meal: boned turkey stuffed with
smoked loin of pork and a tasty forcemeat. Serve hot or cold.
SERVES 18-20 ◆ *page 222*

Roast Stuffed Turkey
Traditional roast with festive stuffing,
forcemeat balls and seasonal vegetables.
SERVES 10-12 ◆ *page 220*

Turkey with Cashew Nuts
Turkey escalopes with mushrooms and
cashews in a soured cream sauce.
SERVES 4 ♦ *page 224*

Turkey Sauté with Lemon & Nuts
Strips of turkey with green pepper,
walnuts and lemon.
SERVES 4 ♦ *page 223*

Turkey Escalopes with Asparagus
Tender escalopes with asparagus and
sage in a cream sauce.
SERVES 4 ♦ *page 224*

Turkey & Watercress Roulades
Turkey escalopes rolled around a creamy
watercress and nut filling.
SERVES 4-6 ♦ *page 223*

Turkey Curry
The ideal recipe for using up leftover
Christmas turkey.
SERVES 4 ♦ *page 224*

Guinea Fowl with Grapes
Guinea fowl casseroled in wine and
Madeira with grapes.
SERVES 6 ♦ *page 225*

Roast Goose with Apples & Prunes
Celebration goose with a prune, sage and onion stuffing,
cooked with apple wedges and prunes.
SERVES 8 ♦ *page 225*

Traditional Roast Duckling
Duckling roast with stuffing balls,
served with an apple sauce.
SERVES 4-6 ♦ *page 226*

Crispy Duck with Mangetouts
Duck strips stir-fried with mangetouts,
water chestnuts and onions.
SERVES 6 ❖ *page 226*

Duck with Redcurrant Sauce
Crisp duck breasts flavoured with
cinnamon and redcurrant jelly.
SERVES 6 ❖ *page 226*

Blueberry Duck
Duck breasts with a blueberry sauce
enriched with crème de cassis.
SERVES 8 ❖ *page 227*

Roast Duckling with Grapefruit
Tender duck complemented by a
grapefruit and honey sauce.
SERVES 4 ❖ *page 227*

Casserole of Grouse with Wine
Grouse cooked with shallots, celery and
bay leaves in red wine.
SERVES 4 ❖ *page 225*

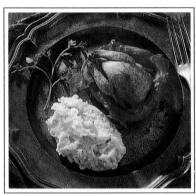

Roast Quails in Peppers
Quails baked in red peppers, served with
herb polenta.
SERVES 4 ❖ *page 229*

Honeyed Pigeons with Kumquats
Bacon-wrapped pigeons casseroled with
baby onions and kumquats.
SERVES 6 ❖ *page 229*

Pheasant with Apples & Pecans
Pheasant breasts, cooked with vegetables,
topped with apples and pecan nuts.
SERVES 6 ❖ *page 230*

Pheasant Casserole with Chestnuts
Joints of pheasant cooked with whole
chestnuts in red wine.
SERVES 4 ❖ *page 230*

Rabbit with Prunes
Rabbit fillets cooked with shallots,
carrots and prunes.
SERVES 4 ◆ *page 231*

Rabbit with Mustard & Marjoram
Rabbit joints marinated in wine with herbs, then casseroled
with button onions, garlic, marjoram and mustard.
SERVES 6 ◆ *page 231*

Hare with Wild Mushrooms
Casserole of hare in red wine with
juniper, herbs and mushrooms.
SERVES 6 ◆ *page 232*

Venison with Pomegranate
Lean venison fillets cooked briefly with
pomegranate and mushrooms.
SERVES 4 ◆ *page 232*

Venison Escalopes in Red Wine
Venison marinated in wine with herbs,
then cooked with redcurrant jelly.
SERVES 6 ◆ *page 233*

Venison Casserole
Venison and stewing beef cooked with
vegetables and dried apricots.
SERVES 8 ◆ *page 233*

Omelette

The classic French folded omelette, with
flavouring and filling variations.

SERVES 1 ◆ *page 238*

Spinach & Mushroom Omelette

Spinach-flavoured omelette with a
creamy mushroom filling.

SERVES 2 ◆ *page 239*

Frittata

Delicious Italian-style omelette flavoured with prawns, salmon,
new potatoes, courgettes and broad beans.

SERVES 6 ◆ *page 238*

Chicken & Mushroom Pancakes

Buckwheat pancakes with a chicken
filling, topped with Gruyère.

SERVES 6 ◆ *page 240*

Ratatouille Pancakes

Buckwheat pancakes rolled around a
tasty ratatouille filling.

SERVES 4 ◆ *page 241*

Omelette Rolls

Thin omelettes rolled around savoury fillings,
served cold as an alternative to sandwiches.

MAKES 8 ◆ *page 239*

Mediterranean Egg Grill
Grilled eggs nestling in a bed of
Mediterranean vegetables with herbs.
SERVES **4** ♦ *page 241*

Smoked Haddock & Egg Pancakes
Crisp pancakes with a creamy smoked
haddock and hard-boiled egg stuffing.
SERVES **3-4** ♦ *page 241*

Cheese Soufflé
An impressive classic hot soufflé with
variations.
SERVES **4** ♦ *page 243*

Baked Eggs with Chorizo
Tasty eggs baked with chorizo,
asparagus, pimentos and prosciutto.
SERVES **4** ♦ *page 242*

Cauliflower Soufflés
Individual hot soufflés baked in ramekins, flavoured with
cauliflower and Cheddar cheese.
SERVES **8** ♦ *page 244*

Spanish Tortilla
A classic tortilla cooked with onions and
potatoes, served cut into wedges.
SERVES **6** ♦ *page 242*

Spinach & Gruyère Soufflé
Attractive green-flecked soufflé with an
excellent flavour.
SERVES **3-4** ♦ *page 244*

Asparagus Scramble
Creamy scrambled eggs with asparagus
and paprika.
SERVES **3** ♦ *page 244*

Walnut, Bacon & Roquefort Roulade
Light, airy spinach roulade, enclosing a
tasty walnut, bacon and Roquefort filling.
SERVES 4-6 ❖ *page 245*

Cheese Fondue
Classic Swiss fondue, made with
Emmental, Gruyère and dry white wine.
SERVES 4 ❖ *page 246*

Pan Haggerty
Pan-fried potatoes layered with onions
and grated cheese.
SERVES 4 ❖ *page 247*

Cheesy Potato, Bacon & Onion Bake
Tempting bake, featuring caramelised
onions, bacon and potatoes in fromage frais.
SERVES 4 ❖ *page 247*

Macaroni Cheese
Popular, simple supper dish with a
crunchy breadcrumb topping.
SERVES 4 ❖ *page 248*

Golden Cheese Pudding
Deliciously rich dish, flavoured with
Gruyère, Parmesan and spices.
SERVES 4 ❖ *page 246*

Ricotta & Spinach Gnocchi
Low-calorie version of this tempting
Italian speciality, topped with Parmesan.
SERVES 4 ❖ *page 249*

Three Cheese Macaroni
Luxury macaroni cheese, flavoured with
Fontina, mozzarella and Parmesan.
SERVES 4 ❖ *page 248*

Three Cheese Aubergine Tart
Savoury flan with a cheesy aubergine,
tomato, spinach and herb filling.
SERVES 6 ❖ *page 247*

Spinach & Feta Puffs
Quick and easy puff pastry parcels, with a spinach, feta and nutmeg filling.
SERVES 4 ◆ *page 249*

Cheese & Potato Cake
Pan-fried potatoes, flavoured with bacon, spring onions, parsley and cheese.
SERVES 3 ◆ *page 250*

Soufflé Welsh Rarebits
Poppy seed toasts with a piquant, cheesy soufflé topping.
SERVES 4 ◆ *page 250*

Mozzarella & Tomato Toasts
Toast rounds topped with olive paste and mozzarella wrapped in salami with tomato.
SERVES 6 ◆ *page 251*

Cheese & Vegetable Croûtes
Croûtes piled high with aubergine, courgette, fennel, peppers and cheese.
SERVES 4 ◆ *page 251*

Chèvre en Croûte
Baked slices of baguette, flavoured with hazelnut oil and garlic – topped with chèvre, paprika and thyme – on a bed of salad leaves.
SERVES 6 ◆ *page 251*

Baked Artichokes

Tender young purplish globe artichokes
baked in extra-virgin olive oil.

SERVES 6 ◆ *page 256*

Jerusalem Artichoke & Chive Bake

Light, tasty bake enriched with eggs and
topped with grated cheese.

SERVES 4 ◆ *page 256*

Asparagus with Beurre Blanc

Perfectly cooked asparagus spears, accompanied by a classic herb-
flavoured butter sauce. Serve as an elegant accompaniment or starter.

SERVES 6 ◆ *page 257*

Spiced Aubergines with Yogurt

Tender-cooked aubergines, flavoured
with chilli, coriander and mustard seeds.

SERVES 4-6 ◆ *page 258*

Broccoli Stir-fry

Broccoli florets cooked in a soy sauce
mixture, with garlic and sesame seeds.

SERVES 6 ◆ *page 258*

Sautéed Aubergines & Courgettes

Batons of aubergines and courgettes
flavoured with toasted sesame seeds.

SERVES 8 ◆ *page 257*

Broad Beans with Artichokes
Young broad beans with artichoke
hearts, raw cured ham and saffron.
SERVES 6 ❖ *page 258*

French Beans with Tomatoes & Herbs
French beans with fresh tomatoes, basil,
parsley, garlic and onion.
SERVES 6 ❖ *page 259*

Chestnut & Brussels Sprout Sauté
Whole chestnuts cooked with onion
wedges, celery and brussels sprouts.
SERVES 8 ❖ *page 259*

French Beans with Feta
Fine beans tossed with crumbly feta
cheese and sun-dried tomatoes.
SERVES 4 ❖ *page 259*

Cauliflower with Olives & Capers
Cauliflower florets with anchovy fillets,
black olives, capers and parsley.
SERVES 6 ❖ *page 260*

Spring Green Sauté
Coarsely shredded spring greens sautéed
with garlic and topped with pine nuts.
SERVES 6 ❖ *page 260*

Cabbage with Juniper Berries
Shredded cabbage cooked with onion,
garlic and juniper berries.
SERVES 4 ❖ *page 261*

Braised Red Cabbage with Pine Nuts
Red cabbage flavoured with ginger,
balsamic vinegar and toasted pine nuts.
SERVES 8 ❖ *page 260*

Chinese Braised Vegetables
Colourful assortment of vegetables,
flavoured with ginger, garlic and soy sauce.
SERVES 8 ❖ *page 261*

Glazed Carrots with Lemon
Fine carrot slices, flavoured with lemon,
garlic, butter and a little sugar.
SERVES 4 ◆ *page 262*

Courgettes with Sesame Seeds
Stir-fried courgettes with spring onion,
garlic and toasted sesame seeds.
SERVES 6 ◆ *page 262*

Celery Gratin
Celery in soured cream with a crisp
breadcrumb and cheese topping.
SERVES 6 ◆ *page 263*

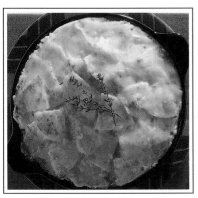

Celeriac with Gruyère
Celeriac baked in cream with garlic and
topped with Gruyère.
SERVES 6 ◆ *page 263*

Fennel with Beans & Mangetouts
Fennel slices stir-fried with French beans
and mangetouts, flavoured with lemon.
SERVES 6 ◆ *page 263*

Stir-fried Mixed Vegetables
Carrot ribbons stir-fried with beans, Chinese
leaves, spring onions and mangetouts.
SERVES 4 ◆ *page 261*

Marrow with Tomato & Onion
Marrow cubes braised with onions, herbs
and fresh tomatoes.
SERVES 4-6 ◆ *page 264*

Citrus Leeks with Sugar Snaps
Leeks and sugar snap peas tossed in a
tangy citrus dressing.
SERVES 6 ◆ *page 264*

Baby Carrots in Spiced Dressing
Tender, young carrots with flaked
almonds, cumin, coriander and chives.
SERVES 4 ◆ *page 262*

Baked Mushrooms with Parsley
Flavourful flat mushrooms enhanced
with garlic and parsley.
SERVES 4-6 ⋄ *page 264*

Mushrooms Sautéed with Thyme & Garlic
A mouthwatering mixture of mushrooms with thyme, garlic
and a hint of lemon, in a mustardy crème fraîche sauce.
SERVES 4-6 ⋄ *page 265*

Spinach & Mushroom Bhaji
A delicious spicy accompaniment best
served with curries.
SERVES 8 ⋄ *page 265*

Parsnip & Ginger Bake
A delicious baked purée of parsnips, enriched
with cream, eggs and flaked almonds.
SERVES 4 ⋄ *page 266*

Golden Parsnip Galette
Finely sliced parsnips layered with garlic
and baked until golden and tender.
SERVES 4-6 ⋄ *page 266*

Roast Potatoes with Garlic
Potatoes roasted with whole garlic
cloves until crisp and golden.
SERVES 8 ⋄ *page 266*

Gratin of Potatoes
Irresistible creamy potato gratin with a
crunchy breadcrumb topping.
SERVES 6-8 ◆ *page 266*

Fantail Roast Potatoes
Fanned whole roast potatoes coated with
sesame seeds.
SERVES 8 ◆ *page 267*

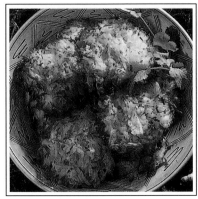

Coriander Rosti
Shredded potato cakes flavoured with
onions and chopped coriander.
SERVES 6-8 ◆ *page 267*

Swede & Orange Purée
A tasty purée, ideal served with a roast
or hearty casserole.
SERVES 4 ◆ *page 268*

Sweet Potatoes Dauphinoise
Sweet potato slices layered with garlic
and nutmeg, baked in cream.
SERVES 6 ◆ *page 268*

Glazed Shallots
Tender shallots braised in butter and
tossed in chopped parsley.
SERVES 4 ◆ *page 268*

Ratatouille
An authentic Provençale ratatouille,
liberally flavoured with herbs.
SERVES 6 ◆ *page 269*

Turnips Stir-fried with Leeks
Fine slices of turnip with leeks, bacon
and a hint of lemon.
SERVES 3-4 ◆ *page 269*

Herb-glazed Tomatoes
Beefsteak tomatoes baked with cream,
lemon juice and basil.
SERVES 8 ◆ *page 269*

Crab Salad
Delicious crab meat tossed in a lemon dressing and served on a
bed of cucumber, tomatoes, pasta shells and shredded lettuce.
SERVES 2 ◆ *page 274*

Tuna Bean Salad
Flaked tuna with red onion rings and
cannellini beans in a tangy dressing.
SERVES 4-6 ◆ *page 275*

Warm Seafood Salad
Scallops, prawns, artichokes and bacon
on a bed of salad leaves.
SERVES 2 ◆ *page 276*

Salad Niçoise
Superb Mediterranean main-course salad of
tuna, anchovies, eggs, olives and vegetables.
SERVES 4 ◆ *page 275*

Chicken & Spiced Wheat Salad
Spiced bulgar wheat, topped with chicken,
spring onions and cherry tomatoes.
SERVES 6 ◆ *page 277*

Chicken & Pasta Salad
Tricolour pasta tossed in a pesto dressing
with chicken, ham, fennel and tomatoes.
SERVES 4 ◆ *page 276*

Coronation Chicken
Bite-sized chicken pieces tossed in a
creamy curried mayonnaise.
SERVES 4 ◆ *page 276*

Oriental Chicken Salad
Grilled chicken breasts on a bed of
salad, with a citrus soy dressing.
SERVES 4 ◆ *page 277*

Duckling Salad

Crisp cooked duck breast slices in a
ginger dressing on a bed of salad leaves.

SERVES 6 ❖ *page 278*

Peasant Salad

Hearty, colourful vegetarian salad, which
makes a meal in itself.

SERVES 8 ❖ *page 278*

Greek Salad

Refreshing salad of cucumber, tomatoes,
olives and feta cheese.

SERVES 4-6 ❖ *page 278*

Grilled Vegetable Salad

Delicious salad of grilled Mediterranean
vegetables in a balsamic vinaigrette.

SERVES 4-6 ❖ *page 279*

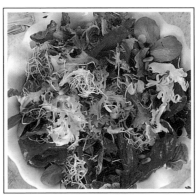

Mixed Leaf Salad

Crisp salad leaves, alfafa sprouts and
pine nuts in a light dressing.

SERVES 4 ❖ *page 280*

Summer Leafy Herb Salad

Assorted salad leaves and herbs,
enhanced with edible flowers.

SERVES 8 ❖ *page 280*

French Bean & Fennel Salad

Beans, fennel and cucumber tossed with
avocado slices and olives.

SERVES 8 ❖ *page 281*

Cauliflower, Broccoli & Pepper Salad

Crisp colourful salad in a tahini and
lemon dressing, with sesame seeds.

SERVES 6 ❖ *page 281*

Summer Salad Bowl

Versatile salad, which can be adapted
according to availability of ingredients.

SERVES 6 ❖ *page 280*

Spinach, Watercress & Bacon Salad
Tender young spinach leaves and watercress with crisp snippets of bacon.
SERVES **4** ✦ *page 281*

Mangetout & Mushroom Salad
Mangetouts and button mushrooms tossed in a herb mayonnaise dressing.
SERVES **4** ✦ *page 282*

Watercress, Croûton & Feta Salad
Simple, crunchy salad which can be assembled in minutes.
SERVES **4-6** ✦ *page 283*

Pepper, Mangetout & Corn Salad
A quick and easy salad in a tangy lemon dressing.
SERVES **6** ✦ *page 282*

Roasted Pepper Salad
Vividly colourful sweet pepper and chilli salad with a ginger and onion dressing.
SERVES **4** ✦ *page 283*

Tomato & Basil Salad
Simple, classic summer salad enhanced with a garlic vinaigrette.
SERVES **6** ✦ *page 284*

Fennel, Pear & Parmesan Salad
Wafer-thin fennel slices with pears and finely pared Parmesan.
SERVES **6** ✦ *page 282*

Avocado & Cucumber Salad
Slices of avocado and cucumber with crushed coriander seeds.
SERVES **8** ✦ *page 282*

Flageolet & Artichoke Salad
Tasty combination of beans, artichoke hearts, olives and parsley.
SERVES **6** ✦ *page 284*

Tomato & Artichoke Salad
Tomato wedges and artichoke hearts in
a garlic and lemon dressing.
SERVES 4 ✦ *page 284*

Three Bean Salad
Colourful mixed bean and pepper salad
with coriander and a spicy dressing.
SERVES 6 ✦ *page 285*

Spinach & Baby Corn Salad
Light spinach salad with alfafa, chicory
and baby corn cobs.
SERVES 6-8 ✦ *page 284*

Bulgar Wheat Salad
Tasty salad with crisp vegetables, liberally
flavoured with herbs and hazelnuts.
SERVES 6 ✦ *page 285*

Mustardy Potato Salad
Small tender potatoes tossed in a
piquant creamy dressing.
SERVES 4 ✦ *page 286*

Pasta Salad
Small pasta, courgette julienne and thin
asparagus with feta and Gruyère.
SERVES 6 ✦ *page 286*

Spiced Potato Salad
New potatoes tossed with coriander in
a spiced yogurt dressing.
SERVES 6 ✦ *page 287*

Wild Rice & Thyme Salad
Pretty rice salad with broad beans,
French beans and mushrooms.
SERVES 6-8 ✦ *page 287*

Roasted New Potato Salad
Rosemary flavoured potatoes in a tasty
dressing with bacon and mushrooms.
SERVES 6 ✦ *page 286*

Jerusalem Artichoke Gratin
Crisp topped gratin of Jerusalem
artichokes, leeks, peas and baby onions.
SERVES **4** ◆ *page 291*

Mixed Lentil Casserole
A nutritious combination of lentils, carrots, leeks, mooli and button mushrooms,
flavoured with ginger, garlic and coriander.
SERVES **6** ◆ *page 292*

Vegetable Bake with Cheese
Root vegetables baked with a Cheddar
cheese topping.
SERVES **6** ◆ *page 291*

Root Vegetable & Tahini Stew
Chunky vegetable stew with an unusual
flavour.
SERVES **4** ◆ *page 293*

Winter Vegetable Casserole
A sustaining root vegetable mixture,
enriched with a little cream.
SERVES **6** ◆ *page 292*

Red Kidney Bean Hot Pot
Tasty combination of kidney beans and
vegetables with a crunchy topping.
SERVES **4 - 6** ◆ *page 293*

Vegetable Chilli
Spicy vegetarian chilli, delicious topped
with soured cream or yogurt.
SERVES 8 ◆ *page 294*

Bean Goulash
Based on the Hungarian classic, this
version uses a mixture of different beans.
SERVES 6 ◆ *page 294*

Vegetable Couscous
Steamed couscous topped with a spicy
mixture of vegetables.
SERVES 4 ◆ *page 295*

Vegetable Curry
A versatile curry which can be varied
according to the vegetables available.
SERVES 4-6 ◆ *page 296*

Vegetable Korma
Traditional southern Indian dish, enriched
with cream and ground almonds.
SERVES 4-6 ◆ *page 296*

Boston Baked Beans
Haricot beans cooked in a dark, rich
sauce, flavoured with treacle.
SERVES 6-8 ◆ *page 295*

Spinach Dhal
Spicy dish, best served as part of
an Indian-style meal.
SERVES 6 ◆ *page 297*

Savoury Nut Burgers
Grilled nut burgers, flavoured with
onion, parsley and soy sauce.
SERVES 8 ◆ *page 297*

Hot Spiced Chick Peas
A quick and easy supper dish. Serve with
rice, baked potatoes or bread.
SERVES 4 ◆ *page 295*

Vegetable Tempura
Japanese-style crisp vegetables, quickly
fried in a light batter.
SERVES 4 ◆ *page 298*

Stir-fried Vegetables
Any combination of vegetables can be
used for this tasty stir-fry.
SERVES 4-6 ◆ *page 298*

Glazed Vegetable Pastries
Crisp filo baskets filled with baby
vegetables, topped with a creamy dressing.
SERVES 4 or 8 ◆ *page 299*

Curried Tofu Burgers
Moist low-calorie burgers, with
coriander, nuts and garlic.
SERVES 4 ◆ *page 297*

Quorn Kebabs with Tomato Salsa
Grilled Quorn and corn kebabs, served
with a tomato and chilli salsa.
SERVES 4 ◆ *page 300*

Vegetable Kebabs with Tofu Sauce
Skewers of courgette, baby corn, mushrooms
and tomatoes, with a tasty sauce.
SERVES 2-4 ◆ *page 299*

Potato Gnocchi
Classic Italian dish, traditionally served
with pesto and Parmesan.
SERVES 4 ◆ *page 301*

Aubergine & Tomato Gratin
Aubergine slices baked with tomato,
herbs and mozzarella.
SERVES 4-6 ◆ *page 300*

Peppers with Goat's Cheese & Lentils
Grilled peppers with a tasty cheese,
lentil and olive stuffing.
SERVES 4 ◆ *page 301*

Tian de Courgettes
A simple supper dish of rice and
courgettes baked with a cheese topping.
SERVES 3-4 ❖ *page 302*

Vegetable & Nut Roast
Any type of chopped nuts can be used for
this loaf, which can be served hot or cold.
SERVES 4-6 ❖ *page 303*

Aubergine Cannelloni
Aubergine slices rolled around a tasty
ricotta filling, baked in a tomato sauce.
SERVES 6 ❖ *page 302*

Lentil Loaf
A soft-textured mildly flavoured loaf,
best served with a crisp salad.
SERVES 4-6 ❖ *page 303*

Stuffed Peppers
Red peppers baked with a mushroom,
rice and pine nut stuffing.
SERVES 6 ❖ *page 304*

Imam Bayildi
Traditional Turkish dish of stuffed aubergines
served warm or cold with crusty bread.
SERVES 6 ❖ *page 304*

Jacket Potatoes
Baked potatoes with a spicy hot chilli
bean filling.
SERVES 4 ❖ *page 305*

Bulgar-stuffed Tomatoes
Beefsteak tomatoes with a tasty bulgar
wheat, nut, olive and pesto stuffing.
SERVES 4 ❖ *page 305*

Catalan Red Peppers
Cold peppers stuffed with a mixture of wild
and white rice, tomatoes, olives and capers.
SERVES 4 ❖ *page 305*

Spaghetti alla Carbonara
Spaghetti tossed in a creamy egg and
bacon sauce, with parsley.
SERVES 4 ◆ *page 310*

Seafood Spaghetti
Spaghetti with a superb mixture of mussels, large prawns, scallops
and leeks in a delicious creamy saffron and wine sauce.
SERVES 4 - 6 ◆ *page 311*

Spaghetti with Garlic
Simple, yet intensely flavoured pasta,
with garlic, chilli and herbs.
SERVES 4 - 6 ◆ *page 311*

Pasta with Bacon Sauce
Pasta tossed in a tasty bacon, olive and
tomato sauce with plenty of herbs.
SERVES 4 ◆ *page 310*

Tagliatelle with Tomato Sauce
Pasta topped with a tasty sun-dried tomato
sauce, Parmesan and crème fraîche.
SERVES 4 ◆ *page 312*

Fettucine with Gorgonzola Sauce
A very rich creamy dish, flavoured with
Gorgonzola and basil.
SERVES 4 - 6 ◆ *page 312*

Pasta with Spicy Sausage & Tomato
Substantial pasta dish flavoured with a fresh tomato sauce
and Kabanos spicy sausages.
SERVES 6 ◆ *page 313*

Linguine with Clams & Smoked Salmon
An elegant pasta starter of fine noodles
tossed with seafood.
SERVES 6 ◆ *page 312*

Pappardelle with Parma Ham
Broad noodles with asparagus, leeks,
Parma ham and a creamy Parmesan sauce.
SERVES 4 ◆ *page 313*

Cappelletti with Mushroom Sauce
Pasta in a deliciously rich sauce,
enhanced with dried porcini mushrooms.
SERVES 4 ◆ *page 313*

Spring Vegetable Pasta
Penne with a colourful assortment of
vegetables in a creamy herb sauce.
SERVES 4-6 ◆ *page 314*

Pasta, Veal & Rosemary Gratin
Giant pasta shells baked with a tasty veal
stuffing and a cheese topping.
SERVES 6 ◆ *page 315*

Pasta with Mushroom & Leek Sauce
Creamy pasta dish flavoured with bacon,
mushrooms and leeks.
SERVES **4** ❖ *page 314*

Lasagne
Traditional recipe featuring layers of pasta, Bolognese
sauce and Béchamel, with a Parmesan crust.
SERVES **4 - 6** ❖ *page 316*

Pasta & Aubergine Gratin
Mediterranean-style bake with
courgettes, aubergine and tomatoes.
SERVES **4** ❖ *page 315*

Prawn & Leek Pasta Shells
Giant pasta shells filled with leeks,
prawns and cottage cheese.
SERVES **4** ❖ *page 317*

Spinach & Ricotta Cannelloni
Sheets of lasagne rolled around a tasty
filling, then baked in a tomato sauce.
SERVES **4 - 6** ❖ *page 316*

Vegetable Lasagne
Vegetarian lasagne well flavoured with
Mediterranean vegetables and herbs.
SERVES **6** ❖ *page 317*

Special Fried Rice
Tasty combination of stir-fried rice,
prawns and vegetables.
SERVES 4 ✦ *page 320*

Fragrant Saffron Pilaf
Basmati rice flavoured with cloves, cardamom, cinnamon
and saffron, cooked with button mushrooms.
SERVES 6 ✦ *page 321*

Egg Fried Rice
Fried rice flavoured with vegetables,
nuts and scrambled eggs.
SERVES 6 ✦ *page 320*

Fragrant Coconut Rice
Lemon grass lends a unique flavour to
this rice accompaniment.
SERVES 4-6 ✦ *page 320*

Mixed Rice Pilaf
Wild and brown rice mixture, with
toasted pine nuts and chopped parsley.
SERVES 6 ✦ *page 321*

Thai Fried Rice
Thai-style rice with spring onions,
spiced with hot red chilli.
SERVES 4 ✦ *page 322*

Asparagus Risotto
Traditional creamy risotto, with fine
asparagus and shredded Parmesan.
SERVES 4 ◆ *page 322*

Mushroom Risotto
Tasty combination of mushrooms,
broccoli, French beans and rice.
SERVES 4 ◆ *page 323*

Buttered Saffron Couscous
Steamed couscous flavoured with
saffron, pine nuts and parsley.
SERVES 6 ◆ *page 324*

Basmati Pilaf
The perfect complement to authentic Indian curries, this delicious pilaf
is flavoured with an assortment of spices, pistachio nuts and raisins.
SERVES 4 ◆ *page 322*

Lemon Couscous with Mushrooms
Quick-cook couscous flavoured with
lemon and topped with flat mushrooms.
SERVES 2 ◆ *page 324*

Hot Noodles with Sesame Dressing
Chinese egg noodles tossed in a spicy
dressing with sesame seeds.
SERVES 6 ◆ *page 324*

Singapore Noodles
Serve this tasty mixture of stir-fried
vegetables and noodles as a light meal.
SERVES 4 ◆ *page 325*

Toasted Polenta
Grilled polenta, ideal as an accompaniment
to casseroles or grilled meat.
SERVES 6 ◆ *page 325*

Vegetable Pie

Assorted vegetables in a cheesy sauce
topped with Parmesan-flavoured pastry.
SERVES 4 - 6 ❖ *page 331*

Quiche Lorraine

Classic quiche with a creamy cheese,
bacon and parsley filling.
SERVES 4 ❖ *page 332*

Rich Leek Tart

Rich, moist, deep flan with plenty of
leeks, cream and cheese.
SERVES 6 - 8 ❖ *page 332*

Tarte Provençale

This delicious tart combines all the classic flavours of Provence –
aubergine green pepper, tomatoes, garlic, olives and herbs.
SERVES 6 - 8 ❖ *page 333*

Spinach and Garlic Tart

Rich savoury tart flavoured with spinach,
garlic, ground almonds and pine nuts.
SERVES 4 - 6 ❖ *page 332*

Mediterranean Tartlets

Individual flans filled with sun-dried
tomatoes, feta, onions and basil.
SERVES 6 ❖ *page 334*

Goat's Cheese & Watercress Tart
Delicious savoury flan with a creamy
filling, best served with a salad.
SERVES **4 - 6** ❖ *page 334*

Spanakhopitas
Squares of filo pastry with a tasty
spinach and feta cheese filling.
SERVES **4 - 6** ❖ *page 335*

Sweet Pepper & Basil Flan
Grilled red peppers and herbs in a
creamy cheese mixture.
SERVES **4** ❖ *page 333*

Plaice & Spinach Flan
An unusual filling of rolled plaice
fillets and spinach.
SERVES **4 - 6** ❖ *page 334*

Smoked Salmon Quiche
Olive pastry flan case with a deliciously
rich smoked salmon filling.
SERVES **6** ❖ *page 335*

Raised Game Pie
Impressive hot water crust pie encasing
a mixture of game, herbs and dried fruit.
SERVES **8 - 10** ❖ *page 336*

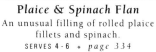

Sausage Rolls
Homemade sausage rolls – ideal for
parties and picnics.
MAKES **28** ❖ *page 338*

67

Gougère
Crisp, light savoury choux pastry with a
colourful filling of stir-fried vegetables.
SERVES 4 • *page 338*

Mushroom & Pepper Vol-au-Vents
Individual vol-au-vents filled with a mixture of
mushrooms, sweet peppers and shallots in a creamy sauce.
MAKES 8 • *page 337*

Pizza Niçoise
Tasty pizza topped with tuna, anchovies,
olives and mozzarella.
SERVES 4 • *page 340*

Wild Mushroom & Hollandaise Pizza
Luxurious topping of assorted wild
mushrooms in a rich hollandaise sauce.
SERVES 4 • *page 340*

Smoked Salmon & Avocado Pizza
Special occasion pizza with a creamy
salmon, avocado and dill topping.
SERVES 4 • *page 341*

Chorizo, Feta & Aubergine Pizza
Ready-made pizza bases with a quick
and easy Mediterranean-style topping.
SERVES 2 • *page 341*

Peaches in Spiced Wine
Luscious ripe peaches soaked in wine
flavoured with cinnamon and cloves.
SERVES 6 ◆ *page 344*

Pears in Red Wine
Whole pears, gently simmered in wine
flavoured with cloves, until tender.
SERVES 4 ◆ *page 345*

Oranges in Caramel
Classic inexpensive dessert with a
crunchy caramel topping.
SERVES 6 ◆ *page 344*

Fragrant Fruit Salad
Refreshing mixture of lychees,
pineapple, mangoes and kiwi fruit.
SERVES 8 ◆ *page 345*

Red Fruit Terrine
Ripe red fruit and delicate mint leaves
set in a splendid wine jelly.
SERVES 6 ◆ *page 346*

Soft Fruit in Summer Sauce
Mouthwatering summer fruits in a red
sauce, lightly flavoured with kirsch.
SERVES 8 ◆ *page 345*

Strawberry & Champagne Jelly
Full-flavoured frais du bois set in a delicate pink
champagne jelly.
SERVES 6 ◆ *page 346*

Summer Pudding
Ever-popular soft fruit dessert, which
can be made with frozen fruit too.
SERVES 8 ◆ *page 346*

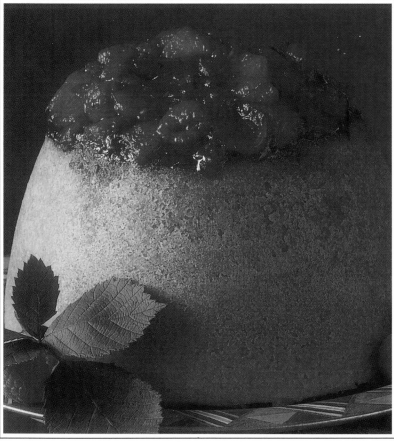

Steamed Fruit Pudding
Delicious sponge pudding with a fruit topping, plus
variations for all kinds of steamed puddings.
SERVES 4 ◆ *page 349*

Baked Stuffed Apples
Tasty cooking apples baked with a
mincemeat filling.
SERVES 4 ◆ *page 348*

Christmas Pudding
Traditional rich plum pudding, served
with brandy butter.
SERVES 10 ◆ *page 350*

Cinnamon Fruit Wafers
Wafer-thin sponge rounds layered with
spiced cream and poached fruits.
SERVES 8 ◆ *page 348*

Gooseberry Fool
Soft, creamy dessert, best served with
crisp biscuits for a contrast in texture.
SERVES 4-6 ◆ *page 347*

Bread & Butter Pudding

Traditional household favourite, laden with fruit and flavoured with cinnamon.

SERVES **6** ◆ *page 352*

St Clement's Pudding

During baking this pudding separates into a custard layer with a sponge topping.

SERVES **4** ◆ *page 351*

Old-fashioned Rice Pudding

An all-time winter favourite, popular with adults and children alike.

SERVES **4 - 6** ◆ *page 351*

Queen of Puddings

An ever-popular old English pudding, with a light meringue topping.

SERVES **4** ◆ *page 351*

Lemon Caramel Rice

Light, creamy textured pudding with a caramelized lemon topping.

SERVES **4** ◆ *page 351*

Bakewell Tart

A traditional flan with an almond filling, equally good hot or cold.

SERVES **6** ◆ *page 355*

Rich Pear Sponge

An impressive flan with a rich almond sponge filling, studded with pear halves.

SERVES **10 - 12** ◆ *page 352*

Blueberry Crumble

An irresistible warming crumble, with a crunchy oat and nut topping.

SERVES **6 - 8** ◆ *page 353*

Rhubarb & Orange Crumble Cake

An orange-flavoured sponge, topped with rhubarb and a crunchy crumble topping.

SERVES **8** ◆ *page 353*

Pineapple Tarte Tatin
A delicious adaptation of the classic
French tarte tatin.
SERVES 6 ◆ *page 356*

Apple Pie
A traditional apple pie, flavoured with brown sugar,
sultanas, nutmeg, cinnamon and orange rind.
SERVES 6 ◆ *page 355*

Pear Tart
Luscious tart with a pear purée filling,
topped with pear slices.
SERVES 6 ◆ *page 357*

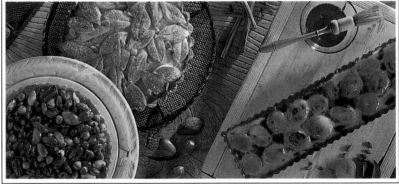

Mille Feuilles
Featherlight layers of puff pastry, inter-
leaved with spiced plums and cream.
SERVES 4 ◆ *page 357*

Glazed Nut Flan; Deep-dish Apple Flan; Apricot & Cardamom Flan
Attractive glazed flans with tempting fillings – good
enough to rival the best shop-bought patissèrie.
SERVES 6-8 ◆ *page 355-7*

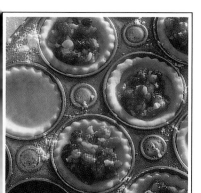

Mince Pies
Traditional festive mince pies, with a
sugar glaze.
MAKES 18 ◆ *page 354*

Peach & Nectarine Croustade
Crisp filo pastry encasing a creamy
filling, with peach and nectarine slices.
SERVES 8 ◆ *page 358*

Profiteroles
Crisp light choux buns, filled with
cream in a rich chocolate sauce.
SERVES 4 ◆ *page 359*

Baked Cheesecake with Red Fruit Sauce
Creamy, velvety smooth baked cheesecake with a crisp
base and topping, served with a fruit sauce.
SERVES 8 ◆ *page 360*

Individual Fruit Flans
Attractive glazed fresh fruit flans with a
crème patissière filling.
MAKES 10 ◆ *page 358*

Hot Chocolate Cheesecake
Tempting rich cheesecake, served warm
from the oven.
SERVES 8-10 ◆ *page 360*

Raspberry Cheesecake
Chilled raspberry yogurt cheesecake,
rippled with raspberry purée.
SERVES 10-12 ◆ *page 361*

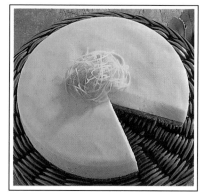

Lemon Cheesecake
Light chilled cheesecake, with a
refreshing citrus tang.
SERVES 8 ◆ *page 361*

Meringue Basket
This impressive basket is the ideal way
to serve fruits in season.
SERVES 6-8 ❖ *page 363*

Meringues with Chocolate Sauce
Meringues with a Grand Marnier cream
filling, topped with a rich dark sauce.
SERVES 8 ❖ *page 362*

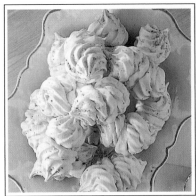

Brown Sugar & Hazelnut Meringues
Golden meringues with a delicious
flavour, filled with cream or ice cream.
MAKES 18 ❖ *page 362*

Snow Eggs
Light fluffy poached meringues, floating
on a smooth coffee custard.
SERVES 6 ❖ *page 363*

Pavlova
Colourful assortment of fruits nestling
in cream on a luscious deep meringue.
SERVES 8 ❖ *page 364*

Lemon Meringue Pie
Ever-popular dessert with a tangy lemon
filling and meringue topping.
SERVES 6-8 ❖ *page 364*

Hazelnut Meringue Gâteau
Nutty meringue rounds sandwiched with
raspberries and whipped cream.
SERVES 6-8 ❖ *page 365*

Chocolate Chestnut Vacherin
Layers of hazelnut meringue interleaved with a deliciously
rich mixture of chestnut purée, chocolate and cream.
SERVES 10 ❖ *page 365*

Hot Chocolate Soufflé
An impressive soufflé with a hint of
cinnamon in its rich flavour.
SERVES **4** ❖ *page 366*

Kirsch & Almond Soufflés
Delicious individual soufflés, with a
hidden fresh plum filling.
SERVES **6** ❖ *page 366*

Summer Fruit Mousse
Superb soft fruit mousse, which can be
adapted according to available fruit.
SERVES **6-8** ❖ *page 368*

Chocolate Orange Soufflé
A velvety smooth, rich dessert topped with
whipped cream and grated chocolate.
SERVES **6-8** ❖ *page 368*

Lemon Mousse
Mouthwatering refreshing dessert with
a sharp tang of citrus.
SERVES **4-6** ❖ *page 368*

Chilled Lemon Soufflé
Topped with slices of star fruit, this light creamy
soufflé has a crunchy pistachio caramel side coating.
SERVES **6-8** ❖ *page 367*

75

Dark & Light Chocolate Terrine
Dark and light chocolate mousses,
marbled together and coated with praline.
SERVES 6 - 8 ❖ *page 369*

Crêpes Suzette
Flambéed crêpes, flavoured with Grand
Marnier and orange.
SERVES 4 - 6 ❖ *page 370*

Crème Caramel
Light silken baked custard with a rich
caramel sauce – a perennial favourite.
SERVES 4 - 6 ❖ *page 371*

Crème Brûlée
Heavenly pots of rich baked custard,
with a crisp caramelized sugar topping.
SERVES 6 ❖ *page 371*

Petits Pots de Crème au Chocolat
Deliciously rich, smooth chocolate
creams set in individual pots.
SERVES 6 - 8 ❖ *page 373*

Vanilla Bavarois
Elegant smooth, creamy dessert served
with a contrasting fruit purée.
SERVES 8 ❖ *page 372*

Coeurs à la Crème
Light, delicate dessert, best served with
soft summer fruit.
SERVES 4 - 6 ❖ *page 372*

Zabaglione
This classic rich Italian dessert should
be served as soon as it is made.
SERVES 6 ❖ *page 372*

Old-English Syllabub
Smooth, creamy dessert, flavoured with
spices and ratafias.
SERVES 6 ❖ *page 372*

Trifle
Sherry-soaked sponge layered with fresh
fruit, egg custard and cream.
SERVES 8 ❖ *page 374*

Tiramisu
Wickedly rich Italian dessert flavoured
with coffee and kahlua.
SERVES 8 ❖ *page 374*

Mango, Raspberry & Lemon Sorbets
Mouthwatering fruity sorbets,
guaranteed to refresh the palate.
SERVES 3-8 ❖ *page 376*

Vanilla Ice Cream & Variations
Superb homemade ice cream with a rich
flavour and creamy texture.
SERVES 4-6 ❖ *page 375*

Raspberry Rose Ice Cream
An unusual raspberry ice cream, scented
with the fragrance of rose petals.
SERVES 6 ❖ *page 376*

Marsala Macaroon Parfait
Irresistible quick and easy ice cream,
flavoured with Marsala.
SERVES 8 ❖ *page 377*

Individual Coffee Bombes
Impressive iced bombes with a surprise
truffle filling.
SERVES 6 ❖ *page 377*

Gingernuts

Popular biscuits with a crisp texture and
extra gingery flavour.

MAKES 36 ❖ *page 381*

**Peanut & Raisin Cookies; Chocolate Nut Cookies;
Coconut & Cherry Cookies; Oat & Cinnamon Cookies**

Irresistible crunchy cookies, with a melt-in-the-mouth texture.

EACH MAKES 30 ❖ *page 381*

Caraway Biscuits

Crisp and light, these thin biscuits are
topped with caraway seeds.

MAKES 24 ❖ *page 381*

Coconut Macaroons

Almond and coconut flavoured biscuits
with a moist, chewy texture.

MAKES 24 ❖ *page 382*

Shrewsbury Biscuits

Light, lemony biscuits with an optional
inclusion of dried fruit.

MAKES 24 ❖ *page 381*

Easter Biscuits

These spicy, fruited biscuits were
originally baked around Eastertime.

MAKES 30 ❖ *page 382*

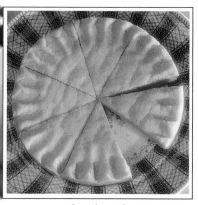

Shortbread
Rich shortbread triangles with a buttery flavour and meltingly short texture.
MAKES 8 ◆ *page 382*

Florentines
Elegant Italian fruit and almond biscuits, coated with chocolate.
MAKES 20-24 ◆ *page 383*

Brandy Snaps
Crisp fine-flavoured biscuits – ideal as an accompaniment to desserts.
MAKES 12-16 ◆ *page 384*

Pistachio Rings
Pretty biscuits, glazed with a lime glacé icing and pistachio nuts.
MAKES 20 ◆ *page 384*

Gingerbread Men
A children's favourite. You will need figure cutters to make these.
MAKES 10-12 ◆ *page 383*

Fruit & Nut Bars
Deliciously moist, chewy bars – ideal for lunch boxes.
MAKES 12 ◆ *page 385*

Madeleines
Delicate sponges, with a hint of lemon, baked in shell-shaped tins.
MAKES 24 ◆ *page 387*

Queen Cakes
Quick, easy-to-make individual buns, with variations.
MAKES 16 ◆ *page 387*

Chocolate Brownies
These irresistible American favourites have a characteristic soft, gooey texture.
MAKES 24 ◆ *page 387*

**Cherry & Coconut Crumble Bars; Lemon & Almond Bars; Date
& Banana Bars; Chocolate Pecan Bars; Vanilla Crumble Bars**
Quick, easy selection of cakes – ideal for all occasions.
EACH MAKES 25 SLICES ◆ *pages 385-6*

Scones
Traditional scones, best served split and
filled with jam and cream.
MAKES 8 ◆ *page 388*

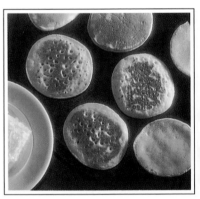

Drop Scones
Quick and easy griddle pancakes, best
eaten hot as soon as they're ready.
MAKES 15-18 ◆ *page 388*

Mixed Fruit Teabread
A very moist, well-flavoured teabread
which keeps well.
14 SLICES ◆ *page 389*

Pecan & Raisin Muffins
American-style muffins, perfect served
warm for a brunch.
MAKES 12 ◆ *page 388*

Marmalade Teabread
A moist, spicy teabread best served
thickly sliced and buttered.
8-10 SLICES ◆ *page 389*

Marbled Chocolate Teabread
Feathery swirls of chocolate and orange-
flavoured cake mixtures.
14 SLICES ✦ *page 390*

Sticky Gingerbread
Well-flavoured gingerbread, topped with
lemon glacé icing and stem ginger.
10 SLICES ✦ *page 389*

Madeira Cake
Versatile plain cake with a firm, but
light texture.
12 SLICES ✦ *page 391*

Orange & Poppy Seed Cake
An unusual cake speckled with poppy
seeds and flavoured with orange.
12 SLICES ✦ *page 391*

Victoria Sandwich Cake
Traditional English plain cake, with
flavoured variations.
8 SLICES ✦ *page 390*

Spiced Apple Cake
This really moist cake is equally good
served with cream as a pudding.
10 SLICES ✦ *page 392*

Honey Cake
Lovely moist cake, with mixed spice,
glacé cherries and chopped peel.
12-16 SLICES ✦ *page 391*

Carrot Cake
Moist cake, with a tangy cream cheese,
lemon and honey topping.
10-12 SLICES ✦ *page 392*

Lemon Syrup Cake
Mouthwatering lemon cake, soaked in a
lemon-flavoured syrup.
12 SLICES ✦ *page 392*

Dundee Cake
Traditional, rich buttery fruit cake with
its characteristic topping of almonds.
16 SLICES ◆ *page 393*

Raspberry & Apple Cake
A stunning, moist cake packed with
apples and raspberries.
8-10 SLICES ◆ *page 393*

Whisked Sponge
Classic light fatless sponge, best eaten
on the day it is made.
8 SLICES ◆ *page 394*

Genoese Cake
Delicate sponge cake, with a moist texture and a
delicious rich buttery flavour.
12-14 SLICES ◆ *page 395*

Black Forest Gâteau
Famous chocolate gâteau with a cherry
filling, cream and chocolate caraque.
SERVES 10 ◆ *page 396*

Chocolate Mousse Gâteau
Sumptuous rich gâteau, covered in a
mass of chocolate curls.
SERVES 12-16 ◆ *page 396*

Dark Chocolate Cake
Sinfully rich, dark chocolate cake
– especially for chocoholics!
SERVES 10 ◆ *page 395*

Chocolate Roulade
Temptingly rich roulade with a soft fruit and creamy yogurt
filling – perfect served with a fruit coulis as a dessert.
SERVES 8-10 ◆ *page 397*

Lemon Gâteau
Feather-light sponge filled with a
refreshing tangy lemon mousse.
SERVES 8 ◆ *page 399*

Coffee Gâteau
Splendid concoction of whisked sponge
layered with coffee crème au beurre.
SERVES 8 ◆ *page 398*

Red Fruit Gâteau
A melt-in-the-mouth sponge filled with soft fruits in a
sauce, and topped with cream and frosted fruits.
SERVES 10 ◆ *page 398*

Sachertorte
Renowned rich, moist chocolate cake
with a shiny chocolate coating.
SERVES 8-10 ◆ *page 397*

Celebration Cake
Simple, effective iced cake which can be
adapted to suit any occasion.
20 SLICES ✦ *page 400*

Teddy Bear Cake
A delightful novelty cake, guaranteed to
appeal to young children.
20 SLICES ✦ *page 400*

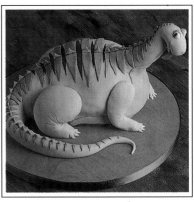

Dinosaur Cake
Impressive novelty cake which is easier
to make than it looks!
16 SLICES ✦ *page 402*

White Christmas Cake
This delicious alternative to the rich, dark
fruit cake has a moist, crumbly texture.
16-20 SLICES ✦ *page 405*

Traditional Christmas Cake
Fondant and almond paste topped fruit
cake, decorated with sugar roses and holly.
25-30 SLICES ✦ *page 404*

Simnel Cake
Traditional Easter cake with an almond
paste filling and topping.
20 SLICES ✦ *page 403*

Christening Cake
Formal christening cake, topped with
swans made from royal icing.
50 SLICES ✦ *page 406*

Wedding Cake
Elegant three-tiered fondant-iced cake,
garlanded with delicate sugar flowers.
125 SLICES ✦ *page 408*

Olive Sourdough Bread
Made from a fermented yeast starter, this olive bread has a distinctive taste.
MAKES 1 LOAF ◆ *page 418*

Cornbread
Moist, close-textured bread, made with cornmeal.
MAKES 2 LOAVES ◆ *page 418*

Wholemeal Bread & Soft White Bread
Easy, everyday bread recipe with variations for flavoured breads, shaped loaves and rolls.
MAKES 1 LOAF ◆ *pages 417-8*

Potted Herb Bread
Baked in small terracotta pots, these loaves have a delicious herby flavour.
MAKES 6 ◆ *page 419*

Soda Bread
A moist, close-textured loaf with a distinctive flavour.
MAKES 1 LOAF ◆ *page 419*

Rustic Walnut Bread
An Italian-style bread with a delicious flavour and texture.
MAKES 2 LOAVES ◆ *page 420*

Quick Cheese & Apple Bread
Non-yeast bread flavoured with mature
Cheddar, apple and peanuts.
8 SLICES ✦ *page 421*

Schiacciata
Flat pizza-type bread liberally coated with rosemary
and extra-virgin olive oil.
12 SLICES ✦ *page 420*

Mini Hot Cross Buns
Tempting moist, spicy fruit buns
traditionally made around Eastertime.
MAKES 25 ✦ *page 422*

Stollen
Irresistible fruity yeast bread, with a
marzipan filling.
SERVES 10 ✦ *page 422*

Brioche
Rich yeast bread, shaped in a
characteristic fluted mould.
SERVES 10 ✦ *page 421*

Chelsea Buns
Old-fashioned buns with a spicy fruit
and nut filling, and a shiny glaze.
MAKES 12 ✦ *page 423*

Savarin
Ring-shaped yeast bread with a redcurrant glaze, filled
with strawberries.
SERVES 6 ✦ *page 423*

Gooseberry Jam; Strawberry Conserve
Full-flavoured preserves to make during
the early summer months.
page 426; page 427

Raspberry Jam
Excellent homemade jam with an intense
flavour and a superb texture.
page 426

Blackberry Jam
Ideal recipe for using this abundant
hedgerow fruit to optimum effect.
page 426

Strawberry Jam
Mouthwatering jam made from this
popular summer fruit.
page 427

Apricot Jam
Vividly coloured jam, with a fine flavour
and a good texture.
page 427

Apple & Mint Jelly
Clear herb-flavoured jelly, best served
with roast lamb or pork.
page 428

Rosehip Jelly
A delicious jelly made from the ripe
dark red fruits of the wild rose.
page 428

Lime Marmalade
Tangy marmalade, made with whole
slices of thin-skinned limes.
page 428

Seville Orange Marmalade
The traditional marmalade, made from
bitter Seville oranges.
page 429

Lemon Curd
Luscious, smooth, rich preserve with a
refreshing, tangy flavour.
page 429

Mincemeat
A rich fruity, spicy mincemeat with more
than a dash of alcohol.
page 430

Pickled Pears with Ginger
Delicious accompaniment to cold meats.
Ideal as an unusual gift.
page 430

Brandied Cherries
Plump fresh cherries preserved in a cinnamon and brandy
flavoured syrup; best served with thick yogurt or cream.
page 430

Mustard Pickle
A colourful medley of vegetables in a
sweet-sour mustardy sauce.
page 431

Summer Pickle
This tasty pickle is the perfect
companion to a Ploughman's lunch.
page 431

Mango Chutney; Marrow & Tomato Chutney
Dark, fruity chutneys – ideal served with
cold meats or cheese.
page 432

Green Tomato Chutney
A delicious way of using unripened
homegrown tomatoes.
page 432

RECIPES

STOCKS & SAUCES

Flavourful stocks form the basis of good soups, sauces, stews and a host of other savoury dishes. Sauces – on the other hand – provide the finishing touch to many dishes, complementing and enhancing their flavour.

❖ Stocks ❖

Homemade stocks lend a superb flavour, so it's well worth making your own stock from leftover bones, poultry carcasses and fresh vegetables. You will also find that most fishmongers are only too happy to let you have fish bones, while many butchers will supply meat bones and chicken carcasses. Make up a good quantity of stock and freeze any that is not required, in manageable quantities. To save freezer space, boil the stock to reduce the volume; cool, then freeze in ice cube trays.

The characteristics of a good stock are a fine flavour and clarity. Guard against over-seasoning, as boiling concentrates the flavour and saltiness. Fat and impurities will make a stock cloudy, so these should always be removed. For successful stock-making follow these guidelines:
❖ Don't cover your stock pot completely; the stock needs to reduce by boiling and evaporation.
❖ Skim frequently to remove scum and fat.
❖ Use a conical sieve for straining if possible. Allow the stock to drip through; if you squeeze the vegetables in the sieve you will lose clarity.
❖ Allow the stock to cool, then refrigerate until the fat forms a solid layer on the surface; remove.
❖ Use fish stock on the day it is made, or within 2 days. Meat and chicken stocks can be kept in the refrigerator for up to 4 days, but they should be boiled up each day.

If you haven't time to make your own stock, use one of the ready-made alternatives. The range of stock products available has increased and improved in recent years and you can now buy a wide range of flavours. Most are inclined to be strong and salty, so use sparingly. Some products, including a range of stocks sold fresh in cartons, have no added salt, sugar or artificial additives.

❖ Sauces ❖

Sauces are intended to enhance the foods with which they are served; they should never be so over-powering as to disguise the intrinsic flavours of a dish. A great deal of mystique is attached to sauce-making, but all that is required is a little time and your undivided attention. Once the basic techniques have been mastered, you can create your own variations.

Roux-based sauces are the most common type. For a white sauce, the butter and flour mixture – known as the roux – is cooked, but not coloured. Béchamel is the classic white sauce. For a brown sauce, such as Espagnole, the roux is cooked until it is brown.

The classic emulsified sauces, including Hollandaise and Béarnaise are more difficult to make than roux-based sauces because of their tendency to separate. They are therefore prepared in a double saucepan over a gentle heat.

Other sauces included in this chapter are tomato sauces; curry and barbecue sauces; and dessert sauces. Salad dressings are to be found in the Salads chapter, while recipes for classic pasta sauces are in the Pasta chapter. Whatever type of sauce you are making, consider the texture and consistency, as well as the flavour. These characteristics are all-important to a successful sauce.

❖ Beef Stock ❖

MAKES 900 ML (1½ PINTS)	• 450 g (1 lb) shin of beef, cut into pieces	• 1 onion, peeled and sliced
PREPARATION TIME 15–40 minutes	• 450 g (1 lb) marrow bones or knuckle of veal, chopped	• 1 carrot, peeled and sliced
COOKING TIME 4–5 hours		• 1 celery stick, sliced
FREEZING Suitable	• 1 bouquet garni	• 2.5 ml (½ tsp) salt

1 To give a good flavour and colour, brown the meat and bones in the oven before using them. Place in a roasting tin and cook at 220°C (425°F) mark 7 for 30–40 minutes until well browned.
2 Put the bones and meat in a saucepan with 1.7 litres (3 pints) water, the bouquet garni, vegetables and salt. Bring to the boil and remove any scum.
3 Partially cover and simmer for 4–5 hours.
4 Strain the stock and, when cold, remove any trace of fat from the surface using a large spoon.

PRESSURE COOKER METHOD: Follow steps 1 and 2 as above, using the pressure cooker instead of a saucepan but reduce the amount of liquid to 1.4 litres (2½ pints). Bring to HIGH (15 lb) pressure and cook for 1–1¼ hours. Reduce pressure at room temperature. After cooking, finish as above.

Variation
Replace the shin of beef with fresh or cooked meat bones.

❖ Chicken Stock ❖

MAKES 1.1 LITRES (2 PINTS)	• 1 chicken carcass, bones and trimmings from a roast chicken	• 1 celery stick, sliced
PREPARATION TIME 5 minutes		• 1 bouquet garni
COOKING TIME 2–3 hours	• 1 onion, peeled and sliced	• 1 bay leaf
FREEZING Suitable	• 1 carrot, peeled and sliced	• salt

1 Break up the chicken carcass and put in a large saucepan with any skin and meat attached, plus other bones and trimmings.
2 Add 1.7 litres (3 pints) water, the onion, carrot, celery, bouquet garni, bay leaf and a little salt. Bring to the boil, then skim.
3 Partially cover and simmer for 2–3 hours.
4 Strain the stock and, when cold, remove all traces of fat.

PRESSURE COOKER METHOD: Follow steps 1 and 2 as above, using the pressure cooker instead of a saucepan but reduce the amount of liquid to 1.4 litres (2½ pints). Bring to HIGH (15 lb) pressure and cook for 45 minutes to 1 hour. After cooking, finish as above.

❖ Fish Stock ❖

MAKES 900 ML (1½ PINTS)	• 450–750 g (1–1½ lb) fish bones and trimmings	• 1 bouquet garni
PREPARATION TIME 10 minutes		• 1 onion, peeled and sliced
COOKING TIME 20 minutes	• salt	
FREEZING Suitable		

1 Put the fish bones and trimmings into a saucepan, cover with 900 ml (1½ pints) water and add a little salt. Bring to the boil, then skim.
2 Reduce the heat and add the bouquet garni and onion. Cover and simmer for 20 minutes.
3 Strain and leave to cool. Use on the same day, or store in the refrigerator for not more than 2 days.

❖ Court Bouillon ❖

MAKES 1.1 LITRES (2 PINTS)	• 1 carrot, peeled and sliced	• 6 peppercorns
PREPARATION TIME minutes	• 1 onion, peeled and sliced	• 100 ml (3½ fl oz) white wine vinegar
COOKING TIME 30 minutes	• 1 bouquet garni (thyme, parsley, bay leaf)	• 2.5 ml (½ tsp) salt
FREEZING Not suitable		

Place all the ingredients in a saucepan. Bring to the boil, lower the heat and simmer gently for 30 minutes. Strain if required before use.

NOTE: A court bouillon is a flavouring liquid used for cooking delicately flavoured fish.

❖ Vegetable Stock ❖

MAKES 1.1 LITRES (2 PINTS)	• 30 ml (2 tbsp) oil	• 4 celery sticks, chopped
PREPARATION TIME 15 minutes	• 1 onion, peeled and finely chopped	• vegetable trimmings, such as celery tops, cabbage leaves, mushroom peelings, tomato skins
COOKING TIME 1¼ hours	• 1 carrot, peeled and diced	
FREEZING Suitable	• 50 g (2 oz) turnip, peeled and diced	• 1 bouquet garni
	• 50 g (2 oz) parsnip, peeled and diced	• 6 black peppercorns
		• salt

1 Heat the oil in a saucepan, add the onion and fry gently for about 5 minutes until soft and lightly coloured.
2 Add the other vegetables to the pan with the trimmings and 1.7 litres (3 pints) water. Add the bouquet garni and peppercorns. Season with a little salt.
3 Bring to the boil, partially cover and simmer for 1½ hours, skimming occasionally.
4 Strain the stock and leave to cool. Cover and store in the refrigerator. Use within 1–2 days.

❖ Brown Onion Stock ❖

MAKES 900 ML (1½ PINTS)	• 30 ml (2 tbsp) vegetable oil	• a few sage leaves, thyme stalks and parsley stalks or 10 ml (2 tsp) dried mixed herbs
PREPARATION TIME 15 minutes	• 2 large onions, peeled and roughly chopped	
COOKING TIME 45 minutes	• 2 garlic cloves, peeled and halved	• 2 bay leaves
FREEZING Suitable	• 2 celery sticks, chopped	• 5 ml (1 tsp) yeast extract (optional)
	• 2 carrots, peeled and chopped	• salt

1 Heat the oil in a large heavy-based saucepan. Add the onions and cook, stirring all the time, for about 10 minutes or until they turn a dark golden brown. Be careful not to let the onions burn.
2 Add the remaining vegetables, herbs and yeast extract, if using. Cook over a high heat for 4–5 minutes or until the vegetables are lightly browned.
3 Add 1.1 litres (2 pints) water to the pan and bring to the boil. Season with a little salt, lower the heat and simmer gently for 30 minutes.
4 Strain through a fine sieve into a jug or bowl. The stock is now ready to use, or it can be returned to a clean saucepan and boiled rapidly to reduce the quantity and intensify the flavour. Cool and store in the refrigerator for up to 2–3 days.

NOTE: Caramelising the onions before adding the other ingredients produces a stock with a strong, slightly sweet flavour and a good brown colour.

❖ Béchamel Sauce ❖

MAKES 300 ML (½ PINT)	

PREPARATION TIME
5 minutes, plus
standing
COOKING TIME
5 minutes
FREEZING
Suitable

- *300 ml (½ pint) milk*
- *1 slice of onion*
- *1 bay leaf*
- *6 peppercorns*
- *1 blade of mace*
- *15 g (½ oz) butter or margarine*
- *15 g (½ oz) plain flour*
- *salt and pepper*
- *freshly grated nutmeg*

180 CALS/150 ML (¼ PINT)

1 Pour the milk into a sauce-pan. Add the onion, bay leaf, peppercorns and mace. Bring to scalding point, remove from heat, cover and infuse for 10–30 minutes. Strain.

2 To make the roux, melt the butter in a saucepan. Stir in the flour and cook, stirring, for 1 minute.

3 Remove from the heat and gradually pour on the warm milk, whisking constantly. Season lightly with salt, pepper and nutmeg.

4 Return to the heat and bring to the boil, whisking constantly until the sauce thickens and is smooth. Simmer for 2–3 minutes.

Variations

THICK BÉCHAMEL SAUCE: Increase the butter and flour to 25 g (1 oz) each. This thick sauce is used to bind mixtures.

SIMPLE WHITE SAUCE: Omit the infusing stage, simply stirring the cold milk into the roux.

CHEESE (MORNAY) SAUCE: Off the heat, stir in 50 g (2 oz) finely grated mature Cheddar or Gruyère cheese and a large pinch of mustard powder.

PARSLEY SAUCE: Add about 30 ml (2 tbsp) chopped parsley.

ONION (SOUBISE) SAUCE: Finely dice 1 onion, then sauté in a little butter for 10–15 minutes until softened. Stir into the Béchamel. Purée in a blender or food processor, if preferred.

MUSHROOM SAUCE: Thinly slice 75 g (3 oz) mushrooms; sweat gently in a little butter until tender. Stir into the Béchamel.

❖ Espagnole Sauce ❖

MAKES 300 ML (½ PINT)	

PREPARATION TIME
20 minutes
COOKING TIME
1¼ hours
FREEZING
Suitable

- *25 g (1 oz) butter or margarine*
- *1 rasher streaky bacon, derinded and chopped*
- *1 shallot, peeled and chopped*
- *60 ml (4 tbsp) mushroom stalks, chopped*
- *1 small carrot, peeled and chopped*
- *30–45 ml (2–3 tbsp) plain flour*
- *450 ml (¾ pint) brown beef stock*
- *1 bouquet garni*
- *30 ml (2 tbsp) tomato purée*
- *salt and pepper*
- *15 ml (1 tbsp) sherry (optional)*

250 CALS/150 ML (¼ PINT)

1 Melt the butter in a saucepan, add the bacon and fry for 2–3 minutes. Add the vegetables and fry for a further 3–5 minutes, until lightly browned. Stir in the flour, mix well and continue cooking until it turns brown.

2 Remove from the heat and gradually add the stock, stirring after each addition.

3 Bring to the boil, stirring constantly, and continue to cook, stirring, until the sauce thickens. Add the bouquet garni, tomato purée, salt and pepper. Reduce the heat and allow to simmer very gently for 1 hour, skimming occasionally.

4 Strain the sauce, reheat and skim the surface. Adjust the seasoning and add the sherry, if using, just before serving.

NOTE: This classic brown sauce is traditionally served with red meat and game. This quantity is sufficient to serve 4.

❖ Demi-glace Sauce ❖

MAKES 300 ML (½ PINT)	

PREPARATION TIME
20 minutes
COOKING TIME
About 1 hour
FREEZING
Suitable

- *1 small onion, peeled*
- *1 small carrot, peeled*
- *½ celery stick*
- *30 ml (2 tbsp) oil*
- *15 ml (1 tbsp) plain flour*
- *5 ml (1 tsp) tomato purée*
- *15 ml (1 tbsp) mushroom peelings*
- *600 ml (1 pint) brown beef stock*
- *1 bouquet garni*
- *salt and pepper*

270 CALS/150 ML (¼ PINT)

1 Finely dice the onion, carrot and celery. Heat the oil in a heavy-based saucepan. Add the finely diced vegetables. Reduce the heat and cook for about 8 minutes, or until the vegetables begin to crinkle and shrink; do not allow them to colour.

2 Mix in the flour and cook over a low heat, stirring occasionally, until it turns brown; this may take as long as 15 minutes.

3 Off the heat, stir in the tomato purée, mushroom peelings and three quarters of the cold stock. Add the herbs and seasoning. Bring to the boil, stirring. Partially cover the pan and simmer gently for about 35–40 minutes, skimming occasionally.

4 Strain the sauce into a clean pan. Boil up and add one third of the remaining cold stock. Bring the sauce to the boil and remove the scum from the surface. Repeat twice more with the remaining cold stock. Adjust the seasoning, as necessary. The sauce should be thin and syrupy.

NOTE: An ideal accompaniment to steaks; this quantity serves 4

❖ Tomato Sauce ❖

SERVES 4	• 450 g (1 lb) ripe tomatoes	• 1 bay leaf
PREPARATION TIME 20 minutes	• 1 onion, peeled	• 15 ml (1 tbsp) tomato purée
COOKING TIME 15–30 minutes	• 50 g (2 oz) carrot, peeled	• 150 ml (¼ pint) dry white wine or vegetable stock
FREEZING Suitable	• 125 g (4 oz) celery	
	• 15 ml (1 tbsp) olive oil	• salt and pepper
	• 1 large garlic clove, crushed	
	• 15 ml (1 tbsp) chopped mixed herbs, such as parsley, thyme, basil and marjoram, or 5 ml (1 tsp) dried	**65 CALS/SERVING**

1 Peel the tomatoes and chop finely, discarding the seeds.
2 Finely chop the onion, carrot and celery. Heat the oil in a saucepan and sauté the onion, carrot and celery with the garlic and mixed herbs for 4–5 minutes until softened.
3 Stir in the tomatoes, bay leaf, tomato purée, wine or stock, and seasoning. Bring to the boil, cover and simmer for 15–20 minutes, or until the vegetables are tender.
4 Uncover the sauce and continue to simmer for a further 4–5 minutes to reduce and thicken slightly. Adjust the seasoning and discard the bay leaf. The sauce is now ready to use, or if preferred it can be puréed in a blender or food processor for a smooth texture.

NOTE: It is essential to use full-flavoured tomatoes for this fresh sauce. Serve with pasta, beef burgers or other grilled meats; or use as a pizza topping.

❖ Quick Tomato Sauce ❖

SERVES 4	• 400 g (14 oz) can chopped tomatoes	• pinch of sugar
PREPARATION TIME 5 minutes	• 15 ml (1 tbsp) chopped mixed herbs, such as parsley, thyme, basil and marjoram, or 5 ml (1 tsp) dried	• 150 ml (¼ pint) dry white wine or vegetable stock
COOKING TIME 15–20 minutes		• salt and pepper
FREEZING Suitable		• 1 large garlic clove, crushed
	• 15 ml (1 tbsp) tomato purée	**50 CALS/SERVING**

Place all the ingredients in a saucepan. Bring to the boil, then simmer, uncovered, for 15–20 minutes or until the mixture has reduced and thickened.
Adjust the seasoning. Serve as above.

❖ Tomato Coulis ❖

SERVES 4–6	• 450 g (1 lb) tomatoes	• pinch of sugar
PREPARATION TIME 15 minutes, plus standing	• salt and pepper	
FREEZING Not suitable	• 30 ml (2 tbsp) chopped herbs, such as basil or chervil (optional)	**25–20 CALS/SERVING**

1 Peel the tomatoes: immerse in a bowl of boiling water for 15–30 seconds, then remove with a slotted spoon and peel off the skins. Alternatively spear on a fork and turn over a gas flame until blistered, then peel.
2 Quarter the tomatoes, deseed, then finely chop the flesh and place in a nylon sieve. Leave to drain for 10–15 minutes, then transfer to a bowl.
3 Season lightly with salt and pepper and stir in the herbs if using, with the sugar. Chill before serving.

NOTE: This uncooked fresh tomato sauce is delicious served with vegetable and fish terrines.

❖ Curry Sauce ❖

MAKES 600 ML (1 PINT)	• 30 ml (2 tbsp) oil	• 10 ml (2 tsp) turmeric
PREPARATION TIME 5 minutes	• 1 large onion, peeled and chopped	• 50 g (2 oz) split red lentils
COOKING TIME 40 minutes	• 1 garlic clove, crushed	• 450 ml (¾ pint) vegetable stock
FREEZING Not suitable	• 10 ml (2 tsp) ground coriander	• salt and pepper
	• 5 ml (1 tsp) fenugreek seeds	• 150 ml (¼ pint) Greek yogurt
	• 5 ml (1 tsp) ground cumin	**165 CALS/SERVING**

1 Heat the oil in a heavy-based saucepan. Add the onion and garlic and fry for 5 minutes or until softened. Add the spices and fry for 2 minutes, stirring.
2 Add the lentils and stock, bring to the boil, then reduce the heat, cover and simmer for 30 minutes or until the lentils are very soft. Season with salt and pepper. Stir in the yogurt and reheat gently before serving.

NOTE: This is ideal served with vegetables, pulses and hard-boiled eggs. The quantities are sufficient to serve 4–6.

❖ Barbecue Sauce ❖

SERVES 4	• 50 g (2 oz) butter or margarine	• 10 ml (2 tsp) mustard powder
PREPARATION TIME 5 minutes	• 1 large onion, peeled and chopped	• 30 ml (2 tbsp) Worcestershire sauce
COOKING TIME 20 minutes	• 5 ml (1 tsp) tomato purée	• 30 ml (2 tbsp) vinegar
FREEZING Suitable	• 30 ml (2 tbsp) demerara sugar	**150 CALS/SERVING**

1 Melt the butter in a saucepan, add the onion and fry for 5 minutes, until soft. Stir in the tomato purée and continue cooking for a further 3 minutes.
2 Mix together the remaining ingredients with 150 ml (¼ pint) water until smooth, then stir into the onion mixture. Bring to the boil and boil, uncovered, for a further 10 minutes.

NOTE: This is an excellent accompaniment for barbecued chicken, burgers, chops and sausages.

❖ Hollandaise Sauce ❖

SERVES 4

PREPARATION TIME
20 minutes
COOKING TIME
2–3 minutes
FREEZING
Not suitable

- 45 ml (3 tbsp) white wine vinegar
- 6 peppercorns
- 1 small bay leaf
- 1 blade of mace

- 75–100 g (3–4 oz) butter, at room temperature
- 2 egg yolks
- salt

215 CALS/SERVING

1 Place the vinegar, peppercorns, bay leaf and mace in a small pan and boil rapidly until reduced to only 10 ml (2 tsp); strain. Soften the butter until it is creamy.

2 In a small heatproof bowl, whisk the egg yolks with a pinch of salt and the flavoured vinegar until thoroughly combined.

3 Set the bowl over a pan of gently simmering water on a low heat and whisk for about 3 minutes, until the mixture is thick enough to leave a trail when the whisk is lifted.

4 Gradually add the butter, a little at a time, whisking constantly. When 75 g (3 oz) has been added, season lightly with salt. If still too sharp, add a little more butter.

5 The sauce should be lightly piquant and have a smooth pouring consistency. If too thick, add a little water or vinegar. Serve warm.

NOTE: Hollandaise is traditionally served with asparagus, but it makes an excellent accompaniment to many vegetables.

It is a sauce which curdles easily. If this begins to happen, add an ice cube and whisk well; the sauce should come back together.

❖ Beurre Blanc Sauce ❖

SERVES 4–6

PREPARATION TIME
20 minutes
COOKING TIME
12–15 minutes
FREEZING
Not suitable

- 50 g (2 oz) shallots, peeled
- 150 ml (¼ pint) white wine vinegar
- 300 ml (½ pint) dry white wine
- 275 g (10 oz) unsalted butter, chilled and diced

- 45 ml (3 tbsp) double cream
- 10 ml (2 tsp) chopped chervil, tarragon or dill
- salt and pepper

515–345 CALS/SERVING

1 Finely chop the shallots. Place in a saucepan with the vinegar and wine. Bring to the boil and boil, uncovered, for 10–12 minutes or until the liquid is reduced to about 90 ml (6 tbsp).
2 Strain the liquid into a small saucepan. Over a very low heat, whisk in the butter a piece at a time, making sure each piece is thoroughly incorporated before adding the next.
3 When all the butter has been added, whisk in the cream, herbs and seasoning to taste. Serve warm.

NOTE: This sharp buttery sauce is ideal for serving with poached or steamed fish.

❖ Béarnaise Sauce ❖

SERVES 4

PREPARATION TIME
20 minutes
COOKING TIME
2–3 minutes
FREEZING
Not suitable

- 1 shallot, peeled and finely chopped
- 20 ml (4 tsp) chopped tarragon
- 10 ml (2 tsp) chopped chervil
- 75 ml (3 fl oz) dry white wine
- 75 ml (3 fl oz) tarragon vinegar

- pinch of crushed white peppercorns
- pinch of salt
- 3 egg yolks
- 225 g (8 oz) butter, melted
- freshly ground pepper

480 CALS/SERVING

1 Put the shallot, 5 ml (1 tsp) of the tarragon, 2.5 ml (½ tsp) of the chervil, the white wine and tarragon vinegar in a saucepan. Add the peppercorns and salt and boil until reduced by two thirds. Allow to cool.
2 Transfer the mixture to a small heatproof bowl, set over a saucepan of gently simmering water. Add the egg yolks and whisk over a gentle heat for about 3 minutes to form an emulsion.
3 Gradually add the tepid melted butter, whisking well after each addition. Strain the sauce through a muslin-lined sieve or a fine strainer.
4 Adjust the seasoning and stir in the remaining tarragon and chervil. Serve warm.

NOTE: Béarnaise is an enriched version of Hollandaise sauce, with a more pungent flavour. It is traditionally served as an accompaniment to grilled meats.

❖ Crème Anglaise ❖

This 'real' custard is the classic accompaniment to many hot and cold desserts.

SERVES 4		
PREPARATION TIME 10 minutes, plus standing COOKING TIME 10 minutes FREEZING Not suitable	• ½ vanilla pod or few drops of vanilla essence • 300 ml (½ pint) milk	• 3 egg yolks • 20 ml (4 tsp) caster sugar

115 CALS/SERVING

1 If using a vanilla pod, split open and scrape out the seeds into a heavy-based saucepan. Add the vanilla pod and the milk. Bring slowly to the boil, take off the heat, cover and leave to infuse for 30 minutes. Remove the vanilla pod.
2 Place the egg yolks and sugar in a bowl. Using a balloon whisk, electric whisk or wooden spoon, beat the egg yolks and sugar together until they lighten in colour and thicken slightly.
3 Pour the infused milk on to the mixture, whisking or stirring until evenly mixed. Add vanilla essence to the milk at this stage, if using. Rinse the saucepan, then return the mixture to the pan.
4 Place the saucepan over a low heat and cook the custard for about 10 minutes, stirring all the time, until it thickens slightly and begins to coat the back of the spoon. Do not boil or the custard will curdle. (Watch for the froth: when it begins to disappear on the surface, the custard is starting to thicken.)
5 Immediately strain the custard through a sieve into a cold bowl to stop it cooking further. Whisk to reduce the temperature. To serve warm, pour into a jug. To serve cold, place damp greaseproof paper on the surface of the hot custard to prevent a skin forming, leave to cool, then chill.

NOTE: To rescue a custard which is beginning to separate and curdle, immediately strain it into a cold bowl, add a few ice cubes and whisk vigorously to reduce the temperature – it should smooth out again quite quickly.

If you are nervous of curdling the custard, beat 5 ml (1 tsp) cornflour with the egg yolks in step 2; this helps thicken the custard. Make sure you taste it after cooking to ensure that the taste of cornflour has disappeared; if necessary, stir over a gentle heat for a little longer, but do not boil.

Variations

CHOCOLATE: Omit the vanilla pod. Break up 50 g (2 oz) plain chocolate and add to the milk. Bring slowly to the boil, whisking until smooth. Finish as above, using 15 ml (1 tbsp) sugar only.

ORANGE, LEMON OR MINT: Omit the vanilla pod. Add the pared rind of ½ lemon or ½ orange, or a handful of mint leaves, to the milk and bring to the boil. Complete as above, straining the milk onto the whisked egg yolks and sugar.

NUTMEG: Omit the vanilla pod. Prepare the custard as above, adding a dash of freshly grated nutmeg, and 15–30 ml (1–2 tbsp) sherry if desired, at the end.

EXTRA CREAMY CUSTARD: Replace half or all of the milk with single cream, or half single and half double cream.

❖ Chocolate Custard Sauce ❖

SERVES 4		
PREPARATION TIME 5 minutes COOKING TIME 5 minutes FREEZING Not suitable	• 15 ml (1 tbsp) cocoa powder • 25 ml (1½ tbsp) cornflour	• about 25 ml (1½ tbsp) caster sugar, or to taste • 300 ml (½ pint) milk

110 CALS/SERVING

1 Blend the cocoa powder, cornflour and sugar to a smooth paste with a little of the milk.
2 In a heavy-based, preferably non-stick saucepan, heat the remaining milk until almost boiling. Pour on to the cornflour mixture, stirring all the time.
3 Return the mixture to the saucepan and bring to the boil, stirring continuously. Continue cooking for 2 minutes after the sauce has boiled. Add a little extra sugar to taste, if desired. Serve hot, with steamed and baked puddings, pies and tarts.

Variation

COFFEE CUSTARD: Replace the cocoa powder with instant coffee granules.

❖ Chocolate Fudge Sauce ❖

SERVES 4–6		
PREPARATION TIME 5 minutes COOKING TIME 7 minutes FREEZING Suitable	• 75 ml (5 tbsp) single cream • 25 g (1 oz) cocoa powder • 125 g (4 oz) caster sugar • 175 g (6 oz) golden syrup	• 25 g (1 oz) butter or margarine • pinch of salt • 2.5 ml (½ tsp) vanilla essence • 15 ml (1 tbsp) rum or brandy (optional)

365–245 CALS/SERVING

1 Combine all the ingredients, except the vanilla essence and rum, in a saucepan over a low heat, and mix well. Slowly bring to the boil, stirring occasionally. Boil for 5 minutes, then add the vanilla essence, and rum if using.
2 Let cool slightly before serving, with ice cream or bananas.

❖ Raspberry Coulis ❖

SERVES 4		
PREPARATION TIME 10 minutes FREEZING Suitable	• 225 g (8 oz) raspberries • icing sugar, to taste	• dash of liqueur, such as kirsch or framboise (optional)

50 CALS/SERVING

1 Purée the raspberries in a blender or food processor, then push through a nylon sieve to remove the seeds. If the raspberries are very ripe, simply press them through a sieve.
2 Add icing sugar to taste, then stir in a little liqueur, if using. Serve cold, with ices, sorbets, mousses or gâteaux.

Variations

Replace the raspberries with strawberries, redcurrants, blackcurrants, mango, papaya, apricots or kiwi fruit.

SOUPS

Plenty of it, piping hot or thoroughly chilled and packed with the goodness of endless combinations of vegetables, meat, fish, beans, rice – that's the secret of a good soup. Infinitely superior to canned and packet varieties, homemade soups are well worth making. Homemade stock lends a depth and quality of flavour that's hard to match with stock cubes or bouillon. It's the most important ingredient in consommé, bisques, and French onion soup; for these, substitutes just will not do. Robust soups thick with pulses or vegetables, or spicy soups, can be made successfully with stock cubes, but season with caution as they tend to be salty. The quality of these stocks, sold as cubes or tubs of concentrate, has improved dramatically in recent years, and it's worth experimenting until you find the brand you prefer. Canned chicken or beef consommé is a good alternative too.

Serving quantities vary according to the type of soup and ensuing courses. For a starter allow about 250–300 ml (8–10 fl oz). If serving soup as a main course allow about 350–400 ml (12–14 fl oz), although similarly this will depend on how substantial the soup is.

Freezing Soups

Most soups freeze well. It makes sense to add less liquid than the recipe states to reduce bulk – make a note of how much you need to add when reheating. Freeze soup in large shallow containers for speediest thawing, not forgetting to leave some headspace to allow for expansion. Even with the help of a microwave, soups seem to take forever to thaw. They're best thawed overnight at cool room temperature; attempts to speed up defrosting by mashing inevitably ruin the texture of chunky soups. Don't add cream, yogurt, fromage frais or eggs before freezing because they will curdle when the soup is reheated.

Garnishes

Choose a garnish that's appropriate to the soup and the occasion. Wholesome, chunky soups need nothing more than a sprinkling of roughly chopped herbs or a few shavings of Parmesan. Smooth purées or creamy soups are enhanced by a sprinkling of crispy bacon, toasted nuts or decorative vegetable shapes (cut with aspic cutters). Sophisticated soups call for a swirl of cream, a delicate herb sprig or perhaps a sprinkling of fleurons. These small decorative shapes are cut from puff pastry, glazed with egg and baked until golden; sprinkle with poppy seeds, Parmesan or herbs for extra interest.

Croûtons are irresistible, adding texture and flavour. Cut lightly stale bread into cubes and fry in butter or olive oil. Add crushed garlic for extra flavour or toss croûtons in chopped herbs. For theme parties, cut appropriate shapes using pastry cutters. Croûtons are best served separately for guests to add at the table since they go soft very quickly once added to the soup.

A julienne of colourful vegetables can transform plain soups. Cut matchstick-thin strips from carrots, courgettes or peppers and blanch in salted water. Drain thoroughly and float on the soup just before serving. You can prepare a julienne of finely pared lemon, lime or orange rind in much the same way (omitting the salt from the water); apply to soups sparingly.

Herb-filled ice cubes add colour and interest to chilled soups. Choose herbs that complement the flavour of the soup.

Likewise a chiffonade of salad leaves adds a summery freshness to chilled soup. Shred rocket, baby spinach or delicate lettuce leaves. Add a tiny pile to each bowl just before serving.

Accompaniments

Whether you're serving soup as a starter or a meal in itself, warm bread is the obvious but perfect accompaniment. If possible bake your own bread (see pages 414–424). Potted Herb Bread (page 419) is good with chunky vegetable soups, while something lighter and more delicate like small rolls are better with subtly flavoured soups. Poppadums are delicious with spiced or curried soups.

If you haven't the time to bake a loaf from scratch, take advantage of the wonderful range of delicious breads now available in the shops. Partly baked loaves and rolls are particularly useful, or you can liven up an uninteresting loaf with a flavoured butter. Garlic is the most popular choice; but following the same principle try flavouring the butter with grated lemon rind; chopped fresh herbs; chopped fresh chillies; a little curry paste; pesto sauce or wholegrain mustard.

CONSOMMÉ

A consommé is a concentrated clarified stock made by reducing chicken, beef or veal stock until it is concentrated, and clarifying it by cooking with egg whites. A consommé may be served as a soup, with other flavourings added if desired, or it may be used as the basis of another dish. If a consommé is garnished it takes its name from the garnish (see below). To ensure the garnish does not cloud the soup, it should be added to the hot consommé just before serving.

❖ Chicken Consommé ❖

3 Gradually pour in the stock, whisking all the time, then bring to the boil, still whisking. Immediately boiling point is reached, stop whisking, lower the heat and simmer very gently for 1 hour.

4 Carefully make a hole in the scum on the surface of the liquid and ladle the liquid out into a sieve lined with muslin over a large bowl. Reheat the consommé, check seasoning and flavour with a little sherry if desired.

Variations

BEEF CONSOMME: Use well-flavoured fat-free beef stock and lean minced steak in place of chicken.

CONSOMMÉ WITH HERBS: Flavour the consommé with 30–45 ml (2–3 tbsp) chopped tarragon, parsley, chives or mint.

CONSOMMÉ JULIENNE: Cut small quantities of vegetables such as carrot, turnip and celery into thin strips and boil separately; rinse well and add to the soup before serving.

JELLIED CONSOMMÉ: Cold consommé should be lightly jellied. Leave the consommé to cool, then chill until set. Chop roughly and serve in individual dishes.

SERVES 4	• 1.7 litres (3 pints) well-flavoured fat-free chicken stock	• 2 eggs whites, lightly whisked
PREPARATION TIME 30 minutes	• 2 leeks	• 2 egg shells, crushed
COOKING TIME 1¼ hours	• 2 celery sticks	• salt and pepper
FREEZING Suitable	• 2 carrots, peeled	• dash of sherry or Madeira (optional)
	• 2 shallots, peeled	
	• 350 g (12 oz) chicken meat, minced	56 CALS/SERVING

1 Heat the stock gently in a large pan. Meanwhile thinly slice the leeks, celery and carrots. Dice the shallots.

2 Mix the chicken and vegetables together in a large saucepan, then mix in the egg whites and shells.

❖ Cock-a-leekie Soup ❖

SERVES 6	• 15 g (½ oz) butter or margarine	• 1 bouquet garni
PREPARATION TIME 15 minutes	• 275–350 g (10–12 oz) chicken (1 large or 2 small portions)	• salt and pepper
COOKING TIME 1 hour 10 minutes		• 6 prunes, stoned
FREEZING Not suitable	• 350 g (12 oz) leeks	• parsley sprigs, to garnish
COLOUR INDEX Page 14	• 1.1 litres (2 pints) chicken stock	95 CALS/SERVING

1 Melt the butter in a large saucepan and fry the chicken quickly until golden on all sides.
2 Cut the white part of the leeks into four lengthways and chop into 2.5 cm (1 inch) pieces; reserve the green parts. Add the white parts to the pan and fry for 5 minutes until soft.
3 Add the stock, bouquet garni and salt and pepper to taste. Bring to the boil and simmer for 30 minutes or until the chicken is tender.
4 Shred the reserved green parts of the leeks, then add to the pan with the prunes. Simmer for a further 30 minutes.
5 To serve, remove the chicken and cut the meat into large pieces, discarding the skin and bones. Place the meat in a warmed soup tureen and pour over the soup. Serve hot, garnished with parsley.

✦ French Onion Soup ✦

SERVES 4

PREPARATION TIME
20 minutes
COOKING TIME
50–55 minutes
FREEZING
Not suitable

- 3 onions, peeled
- 50 g (2 oz) butter or margarine
- 15 ml (1 tbsp) flour
- 900 ml (1½ pints) beef stock
- salt and pepper
- 1 bay leaf
- ½ medium French loaf
- 75 g (3 oz) Gruyère cheese, grated

245 CALS/SERVING

1 Slice the onions thinly. Melt the butter in a saucepan, add the onions and cook gently for 15–20 minutes until dark golden brown.

2 Stir in the flour and cook, stirring, for 1 minute. Stir in the stock, seasoning and bay leaf. Bring to the boil, cover and simmer for 30 minutes.

3 Cut the loaf diagonally into 1 cm (½ inch) slices and toast lightly on both sides. Place two slices in each ovenproof soup bowl. Ladle the hot soup over the bread, discarding the bay leaf.

4 Sprinkle liberally with the cheese to form a thick layer over the bread. Place under a hot grill until the cheese is melted and bubbling. Serve immediately.

✦ Mushroom Soup ✦
with Parmesan Croûtons

SERVES 6

PREPARATION TIME
20 minutes, plus soaking
COOKING TIME
1 hour
FREEZING
Suitable

- 25 g (1 oz) dried mushrooms (ceps)
- 4 shallots, peeled
- 45 ml (3 tbsp) olive oil
- 2 garlic cloves, crushed
- 900 g (2 lb) chestnut mushrooms
- 900 ml (1½ pints) vegetable stock
- salt and pepper
- 20 ml (1½ tbsp) wholegrain mustard

PARMESAN CROÛTONS:
- 3 slices white bread, crusts removed
- oil for shallow frying
- 25 g (1 oz) freshly grated Parmesan cheese
TO SERVE:
- 60 ml (4 tbsp) double cream

275 CALS/SERVING

1 Soak the dried mushrooms in enough water to cover for 30 minutes. Drain, reserving half of the liquid. Rinse well under running water. Chop roughly and set aside.

2 Chop the shallots. Heat the olive oil in a large saucepan. Add the shallots and garlic and fry gently until softened. Add the soaked mushrooms and cook for 5 minutes. Roughly chop the chestnut mushrooms and add to the pan. Cook, stirring, for about 10 minutes.

3 Pour in the stock, season and bring to the boil. Cover and simmer gently for 45 minutes, or until the dried mushrooms are tender.

4 Meanwhile make the croûtons. Cut the bread into small cubes. Heat a 2.5 cm (1 inch) depth of oil in a deep frying pan. When a piece of bread dropped into the oil sizzles, it will be hot enough. Fry the bread cubes in the oil until golden. Remove with a slotted spoon and drain on kitchen paper. While still warm, toss the croûtons in Parmesan cheese.

5 Purée the soup in a blender or food processor, in two batches if necessary, until smooth. Return to the pan, stir in the mustard and reserved mushroom liquid; check seasoning. Serve hot with a little cream swirled in and accompanied by the croûtons.

❖ Roquefort and Watercress Soup ❖

SERVES 4

PREPARATION TIME
20 minutes
COOKING TIME
30 minutes
FREEZING
Suitable (stage 5)
COLOUR INDEX
Page 14

- *8 large garlic cloves*
- *2 onions, peeled*
- *175 g (6 oz) old potatoes*
- *30 ml (2 tbsp) oil*
- *1.1 litres (2 pints) vegetable stock*
- *2 bunches watercress*
- *175 g (6 oz) Roquefort cheese, crumbled*
- *pepper*

TO SERVE:
- *60 ml (4 tbsp) single cream*
- *crumbled Roquefort cheese*

340 CALS/SERVING

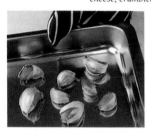

1 Put the unpeeled garlic cloves in a roasting pan and bake at 200°C (400°F) mark 6 for 25 minutes until charred. Allow to cool.

2 Meanwhile chop the onions; peel and dice the potatoes. Heat the oil in a pan, add the onions and cook for 5 minutes or until beginning to soften.

3 Add the potatoes and stock, cover and simmer for about 20 minutes or until the potatoes are soft.

4 Remove the stalks from the watercress. Stir the watercress sprigs into the soup, bring to the boil and simmer for 1 minute.

5 Peel the garlic and add to the soup. Allow to cool slightly, then purée in a blender or food processor. Return the soup to the pan.

6 Whisk in the Roquefort. Reheat gently and season with pepper. Do not boil. Serve hot or chilled with cream and extra Roquefort.

❖ Spinach Soup ❖

SERVES 4

PREPARATION TIME
10 minutes
COOKING TIME
15 minutes
FREEZING
Suitable

- *450 g (1 lb) spinach leaves*
- *900 ml (1½ pints) vegetable stock*
- *15 ml (1 tbsp) lemon juice*
- *salt and pepper*
- *few drops of Tabasco*
- *450 ml (¾ pint) buttermilk*

TO SERVE:
- *60 ml (4 tbsp) double cream*
- *croûtons (page 97)*

140 CALS/SERVING

1 Place the spinach, stock and lemon juice in a large saucepan. Season with salt and pepper and bring to the boil, then reduce the heat and simmer for 10 minutes.
2 Allow to cool slightly, then purée in a blender or food processor until smooth. Pass through a sieve and return to the pan.
3 Reheat gently with the Tabasco and buttermilk. Serve hot with a little cream swirled in and accompanied by croûtons.

❖ Lettuce and Watercress Soup ❖

SERVES 6

PREPARATION TIME
15 minutes
COOKING TIME
30–35 minutes
FREEZING
Not suitable
COLOUR INDEX
Page 15

- *1 medium cos lettuce*
- *1 bunch watercress*
- *1 bunch spring onions*
- *1 bunch chives*
- *25 g (1 oz) butter*
- *15 ml (1 tbsp) flour*
- *1.1 litres (2 pints) chicken stock*
- *150 ml (¼ pint) Greek-style yogurt*
- *salt and pepper*
- *julienne strips of spring onion or snipped chives, to garnish*

90 CALS/SERVING

1 Roughly chop the lettuce, watercress, spring onions and chives. Melt the butter in a large saucepan. Add the chopped vegetables and chives and sauté for about 2–3 minutes or until just beginning to soften.
2 Stir in the flour. Cook, stirring gently, for 1–2 minutes, then gradually stir in the chicken stock. Bring to the boil, cover and simmer gently for 25–30 minutes until the vegetables are very soft. Allow to cool slightly.

3 Purée the vegetable mixture in a blender or food processor until very smooth. Pass through a sieve into a bowl, then whisk in the yogurt. Season to taste.
4 Return the soup to a clean pan and warm through over a low heat; do not allow to boil or the soup will curdle. Serve sprinkled with a few julienne strips of spring onion or snipped chives.

NOTE: This soup is equally delicious served chilled. Refrigerate for at least 2 hours or preferably overnight, before serving.

❖ Vegetable Soup with Pasta ❖

3 Heat the oil in a saucepan. Add the onion, carrot, garlic and oregano and sauté for 2–3 minutes.

4 Add the tomato purée, French beans, tomatoes and chicken stock. Bring to the boil, cover and simmer gently for about 35 minutes or until the vegetables are just tender.

5 Meanwhile, halve, deseed and finely chop the chilli (wearing rubber gloves to avoid skin irritation). Stir the chilli into the soup with the pasta, coriander and parsley.

6 Simmer for 10–15 minutes or until the pasta is cooked. Check the seasoning and garnish with coriander to serve.

SERVES 4

PREPARATION TIME
20 minutes
COOKING TIME
50–55 minutes
FREEZING
Suitable

• 175 g (6 oz) French beans
• 1 red onion, peeled
• 2 carrots
• 125 g (4 oz) tomatoes
• 15 ml (1 tbsp) olive oil
• 1 garlic clove, crushed
• 5 ml (1 tsp) dried oregano
• 15 ml (1 tbsp) tomato purée
• 1.4 litres (2½ pints) chicken stock

• 1 green chilli
• 50 g (2 oz) dried pasta shapes
• 30 ml (2 tbsp) chopped coriander
• 30 ml (2 tbsp) chopped parsley
• salt and pepper
• coriander, to garnish

155 CALS/SERVING

1 Halve the French beans. Thinly slice the onion and carrots.

2 Peel the tomatoes: immerse in boiling water for 10–15 seconds; cool slightly, then peel away the skins. Halve, deseed and roughly chop.

❖ Pea and Chervil Soup ❖

SERVES 6

PREPARATION TIME
15 minutes
COOKING TIME
30–35 minutes
FREEZING
Not suitable
COLOUR INDEX
Page 15

• 225 g (8 oz) spring onions
• 450 g (1 lb) empty pea pods or mangetouts
• 30 ml (2 tbsp) oil
• 2 garlic cloves, crushed
• 10 ml (2 tsp) plain flour
• 1.4 litres (2½ pints) vegetable stock

• 20 ml (4 tsp) chopped chervil
• salt and pepper
• 60 ml (4 tbsp) single cream or crushed ice, to serve

120 CALS/SERVING

1 Roughly chop the spring onions and pea pods or mangetouts. Heat the oil in a large saucepan and stir in the spring onions, pea pods and garlic. Cook for 2–3 minutes, stirring constantly, until slightly softened.
2 Stir in the flour, then gradually stir in the stock and bring to the boil. Reduce the heat, cover and simmer gently for 25–30 minutes.
3 Allow the mixture to cool slightly, then purée in a blender or food processor until quite smooth.
4 Pass the soup through a sieve and return to the pan. Stir in the chopped chervil and season the soup with salt and pepper. Serve hot with a little cream stirred in, or chilled with crushed ice.

❖ Carrot and Coriander Soup ❖

SERVES 6

PREPARATION TIME
15 minutes
COOKING TIME
25–30 minutes
FREEZING
Suitable (stage 3)
COLOUR INDEX
Page 15

- *175 g (6 oz) leeks*
- *450 g (1 lb) carrots, peeled*
- *40 g (1½ oz) butter or margarine*
- *10 ml (2 tsp) ground coriander*
- *5 ml (1 tsp) plain flour*
- *1.1 litres (2 pints) vegetable stock*
- *salt and pepper*
- *150 ml (¼ pint) natural yogurt or soured cream*

TO GARNISH:
- *coriander leaves*
- *croûtons (page 97)*

105 CALS/SERVING

1 Slice the leeks and carrots. Heat the butter in a large saucepan. Add the vegetables, cover the pan and cook gently for 5–10 minutes or until the vegetables begin to soften but not colour.

2 Stir in the coriander and flour and cook for 1 minute. Add the stock and bring to the boil, stirring. Season, reduce the heat, cover and simmer for 20 minutes or until all the ingredients are quite tender.

3 Leave the soup to cool slightly, then purée in a blender or food processsor until quite smooth.

4 Return the soup to the pan and stir in the yogurt. Check seasoning and reheat gently; do not boil. Serve garnished with coriander and croûtons.

❖ Parsnip and Apple Soup ❖

SERVES 6

PREPARATION TIME
15 minutes
COOKING TIME
45 minutes
FREEZING
Suitable (stage 4)
COLOUR INDEX
Page 15

- *700 g (1½ lb) parsnips, peeled*
- *1 cooking apple*
- *25 g (1 oz) butter or margarine*
- *1.1 litres (2 pints) vegetable stock*
- *4 sage leaves or 2.5 ml (½ tsp) dried sage*
- *2 cloves*
- *150 ml (¼ pint) single cream*
- *salt and pepper*

TO GARNISH:
- *sage leaves or parsley*
- *croûtons (page 97)*

175 CALS/SERVING

1 Roughly chop the parsnips. Peel, core and roughly chop the apple.
2 Melt the butter in a large saucepan, add the parsnips and apple, cover and cook gently for 10 minutes, stirring occasionally.
3 Pour in the stock, and add the sage and cloves. Bring to the boil, cover, then simmer for 30 minutes or until the parsnips are very soft.
4 Remove the sage leaves, if using, and cloves; leave the soup to cool slightly, then purée in a blender or food processor.
5 Return the soup to the saucepan, add the cream and reheat gently. Season with salt and pepper. Serve hot, garnished with the sage or parsley and croûtons.

❖ Spiced Leek and Potato Soup ❖

SERVES 3–4

PREPARATION TIME
15 minutes
COOKING TIME
50 minutes
FREEZING
Suitable

- *225 g (8 oz) leeks*
- *1 onion, peeled*
- *225 g (8 oz) potato, peeled*
- *25 g (1 oz) butter or margarine*
- *7.5 ml (1½ tsp) mild curry paste*
- *600 ml (1 pint) brown onion stock (see page 91)*
- *salt and pepper*
- *150 ml (¼ pint) single cream*
- *chopped coriander, to garnish*

250–190 CALS/SERVING

1 Roughly chop the leeks, onion and potato. Melt the butter in a saucepan and sauté the vegetables with the curry paste for 2–3 minutes or until they start to soften and colour.
2 Add the stock and bring to the boil. Reduce the heat, cover and simmer for 45 minutes or until all the vegetables are soft. Allow to cool slightly.
3 Purée the mixture in a food processor or blender until smooth. If time allows, push through a nylon sieve for a really smooth result. Season with salt and pepper.
4 Serve hot or cover and chill for 2 hours or preferably overnight. Either stir in the cream or swirl it on top of the soup as a garnish with the coriander.

❖ Cream of Celeriac Soup ❖

SERVES 3–4

PREPARATION TIME
5 minutes
COOKING TIME
45 minutes
FREEZING
Suitable (stage 3)
COLOUR INDEX
Page 16

- 225 g (8 oz) celeriac
- 1 onion
- 25 g (1 oz) butter or margarine
- 750 ml (1¼ pints) vegetable stock
- salt and pepper
- 45 ml (3 tbsp) single cream
- dash of lemon juice
- 10 ml (2 tsp) chopped dill

120–90 CALS/SERVING

1 Peel and slice the celeriac and onion. Melt the butter in a saucepan, add the celeriac and onion, and cook gently for 1–2 minutes, stirring constantly.

2 Cover with a piece of damp greaseproof paper pressed down on to the vegetables, and a tight–fitting lid. Cook for about 10 minutes.

3 Remove the greaseproof paper and pour in the stock. Season with salt and pepper and bring to the boil. Reduce the heat, cover and simmer for about 30 minutes or until tender. Allow to cool slightly, then purée in a blender or food processor until very smooth.

4 Return the soup to the pan and reheat, then remove from the heat and stir in the cream, a dash of lemon juice and the chopped dill. Taste and adjust the seasoning, if necessary, before serving in warmed soup bowls, accompanied by warm crusty bread.

❖ Cream of ❖ Jerusalem Artichoke Soup

SERVES 4

PREPARATION TIME
20 minutes
COOKING TIME
30–35 minutes
FREEZING
Not suitable

- 900 g (2 lb) Jerusalem artichokes
- 2 lemon slices
- 1 onion, peeled
- 25 g (1 oz) butter or margarine
- 450 ml (¾ pint) milk
- 25 ml (1½ tbsp) lemon juice
- 30 ml (2 tbsp) chopped parsley
- 150 ml (¼ pint) single cream
- salt and pepper

TO SERVE:
- chopped parsley, to garnish
- croûtons (page 97)

250 CALS/SERVING

1 Put the artichokes in a large saucepan with the lemon slices. Cover with 900 ml (1½ pints) cold water. Bring to the boil, cover and cook for about 20 minutes or until tender. Drain off the water, reserving 600 ml (1 pint), and leave the artichokes to cool.

2 Peel the artichokes, then mash them roughly.

3 Chop the onion. Melt the butter or margarine in a saucepan, add the onion and cook gently for 5–10 minutes or until soft but not coloured. Stir in the reserved artichoke cooking water, the artichokes and milk. Bring to the boil, stirring, then simmer for 2–3 minutes.

4 Allow to cool slightly, then purée in a blender or food processor.

5 Return to the rinsed–out pan and stir in the lemon juice, parsley, cream, and plenty of salt and pepper. Reheat gently and serve hot, sprinkled with parsley and croûtons.

❖ Mixed Bean ❖ and Vegetable Soup

SERVES 6
PREPARATION TIME
20 minutes
COOKING TIME
40–45 minutes
FREEZING
Suitable

- 1 onion
- 450 g (1 lb) mixed root vegetables, including carrots, potatoes and parsnips
- 450 g (1 lb) mixed vegetables, such as peppers, celery and fennel
- 15 ml (1 tbsp) olive oil
- 1 garlic clove, crushed
- 10 ml (2 tsp) mild curry powder

- 2 bay leaves
- about 1.1 litres (2 pints) vegetable stock
- 425 g (15 oz) can red kidney beans
- 425 g (15 oz) can black-eyed beans
- 2 courgettes, sliced
- 45 ml (3 tbsp) chopped parsley or coriander
- salt and pepper

185 CALS/SERVING

3 Pour in the stock: there should be enough to cover the vegetables; if not, add a little more. Bring to the boil, then reduce the heat, cover and simmer for 20 minutes.

4 Drain and rinse the beans, then add to the soup and cook for a further 10 minutes. Remove the bay leaves. Purée about half of the soup in a blender.

5 Return the puréed soup to the saucepan and bring to the boil, then add the courgettes and herbs. Season to taste with salt and pepper and simmer gently for 3–4 minutes or until the courgettes are just tender. Add a little extra stock, if necessary, to thin the soup. Serve as a main course.

NOTE: Use this basic recipe to make soup from any mixture of vegetables and beans available. If time, use freshly cooked rather than canned beans. Cut the vegetables into generous chunks to give the soup a good, hearty texture.

1 Peel and roughly chop the onion and root vegetables. Prepare the other vegetables and roughly chop them.

2 Heat the oil in a large heavy–based saucepan. Add all the vegetables, except the beans and courgettes, and cook over a high heat for 4–5 minutes, stirring all the time. Add the garlic, curry powder and bay leaves and continue cooking for 2–3 minutes.

❖ Winter Lentil Soup ❖

SERVES 4
PREPARATION TIME
20 minutes
COOKING TIME
30 minutes
FREEZING
Not suitable
COLOUR INDEX
Page 16

- 225 g (8 oz) carrots, peeled
- 225 g (8 oz) parsnips, peeled
- 450 g (1 lb) leeks
- 125 g (4 oz) streaky bacon, derinded
- 30 ml (2 tbsp) oil
- 225 g (8 oz) red lentils
- 1.7 litres (3 pints) vegetable stock

- 15 ml (1 tbsp) tomato purée
- salt and pepper
- juice of 1 large orange
- grated cheese, to serve (optional)

450 CALS/SERVING

1 Cut the carrots and parsnips into small chunks. Slice the leeks. Cut the bacon into pieces.
2 Heat the oil in a large saucepan. Add the bacon and cook until lightly browned, stirring occasionally.
3 Mix in the carrots, parsnips, leeks and lentils. Fry for 1–2 minutes, stirring occasionally.
4 Pour in the stock, adding the tomato purée and seasoning. Bring to the boil, cover and simmer for about 25 minutes or until the lentils and vegetables are tender.
5 Stir in the orange juice and adjust the seasoning. If wished, add a sprinkling of grated cheese. Serve as a main course.

❖ Minestrone ❖

3 Heat the oil in a large saucepan, add the onions and garlic and fry for 5–10 minutes or until golden brown. Add the carrots and celery and cook for 2 minutes.

4 Stir in the beans, tomatoes, stock, potatoes, pasta and fresh peas, if using. Bring to the boil, then reduce the heat, half–cover and simmer for 1 hour.

5 Add the frozen peas, if using, French beans, cabbage, parsley and pesto. Season with salt and pepper and simmer for 30 minutes or until the vegetables are all tender. Serve immediately, as a main course, with the pesto and cheese in separate bowls for guests to stir into their soup.

SERVES 6–8

PREPARATION TIME
30 minutes, plus
soaking
COOKING TIME
2¼ hours
FREEZING
Suitable

- 175 g (6 oz) dried cannellini beans, soaked overnight in cold water
- 2 onions, peeled
- 2 carrots, peeled
- 2 celery sticks
- 350 g (12 oz) floury potatoes (such as King Edward or Maris Piper), peeled
- 175 g (6 oz) French beans
- 225 g (8 oz) dark green cabbage
- 60 ml (4 tbsp) olive oil
- 3 garlic cloves, crushed
- 400 g (14 oz) can chopped tomatoes

- 2.3 litres (4 pints) vegetable stock or brown onion stock (page 91)
- 125 g (4 oz) small pasta shapes
- 125 g (4 oz) shelled fresh or frozen peas
- 75 ml (5 tbsp) chopped parsley
- 60 ml (4 tbsp) pesto sauce (page 310)
- salt and pepper
TO SERVE:
- pesto (page 310)
- freshly grated Pecorino or Parmesan cheese

425–320 CALS/SERVING

Drain the beans, put them in a very large saucepan and cover with fresh water. Bring to the boil and boil rapidly for 10 minutes, then cover and simmer for 50 minutes; drain.

2 Meanwhile prepare the vegetables. Dice the onions, carrots, celery and potatoes. Slice the French beans and roughly chop the cabbage, discarding the tough stalks.

❖ Bean and Coriander Potage ❖

SERVES 4

PREPARATION TIME
15 minutes
COOKING TIME
45 minutes
FREEZING
Suitable
COLOUR INDEX
Page 16

- 1 small bunch coriander
- 2 small onions, peeled
- 350 g (12 oz) fennel
- 30 ml (2 tbsp) oil
- 10 ml (2 tsp) ground coriander
- 1.4 litres (2½ pints) chicken or vegetable stock
- 400 g (14 oz) can chopped tomatoes

- 30 ml (2 tbsp) tomato purée
- 1 garlic clove, crushed
- salt and pepper
- 400 g (14 oz) can cannellini beans
- coriander sprigs, to garnish

205 CALS/SERVING

1 Tie the coriander stalks into a bundle; chop the leaves, cover and refrigerate. Chop the onions and fennel.
2 Heat the oil in a saucepan. Add the onion and fennel and fry over a moderate heat until starting to brown.
3 Stir in the ground coriander and cook for 1 minute. Mix in the stock, tomatoes, tomato purée, garlic and seasoning. Add the coriander stalks and bring to the boil. Cover and simmer for 30 minutes.
4 Drain the beans, then stir into the soup. Cover and simmer for about 10 minutes or until the vegetables are tender and the beans heated through.
5 Remove the coriander stalks and discard. Stir about 45 ml (3 tbsp) chopped coriander leaves into the soup. Taste and adjust the seasoning. Serve garnished with coriander and accompanied by crusty bread as a main course.

❖ Tuscan Bean Soup ❖

SERVES 6

PREPARATION TIME
20 minutes, plus
soaking
COOKING TIME
1½ hours
FREEZING
Suitable

- 350 g (12 oz)
cannellini beans, soaked
overnight in cold water
- 2 large onions, peeled
- 6 celery sticks
- 450 g (1 lb) tomatoes
- 60 ml (4 tbsp) olive oil
- 2 garlic cloves, crushed
- 1.4 litres (2½ pints)
vegetable stock

- 15 ml (1 tbsp) chopped
thyme or sage
- salt and pepper
- freshly grated
Parmesan cheese, to
serve

260 CALS/SERVING

1 Drain the beans and put them in a saucepan. Cover with fresh water, bring to the boil and boil rapidly for 10 minutes. Lower the heat, cover and simmer for about 50 minutes or until the beans are tender. Drain, reserving the cooking liquor.
2 Put half the beans in a blender or food processor. Add 300 ml (½ pint) of the reserved cooking liquor and purée until smooth.
3 Roughly chop the onions and celery. Peel and chop the tomatoes. Heat the oil in a large saucepan. Add the onions, celery and garlic and cook over a moderate heat for 5–10 minutes or until beginning to brown.
4 Stir in the tomatoes, stock, whole beans and bean purée with the thyme or sage. Season with salt and pepper and bring to the boil. Reduce the heat, cover and simmer for about 40 minutes or until all the ingredients are tender. Serve hot, sprinkled with Parmesan cheese and accompanied by crusty bread.

❖ Scotch Broth ❖

SERVES 4

PREPARATION TIME
15 minutes
COOKING TIME
2½ hours
FREEZING
Suitable
COLOUR INDEX
Page 16

- 700 g (1½ lb) shin of
beef
- salt and pepper
- 1 carrot, peeled
- 1 turnip, peeled
- 1 onion, peeled
- 2 leeks

- 45 ml (3 tbsp) pearl
barley
- 15 ml (1 tbsp) chopped
parsley, to garnish

510 CALS/SERVING

1 Remove any fat from the meat and cut the meat into bite-sized pieces. Put the meat in a saucepan, cover with 2.3 litres (4 pints) water, then add salt and pepper. Bring slowly to the boil, cover and simmer for 1½ hours.
2 Chop the vegetables and add to the pan with the barley. Cover and simmer for a further 1 hour or until the vegetables and barley are soft.
3 Remove any fat that has formed on the surface with a spoon or absorbent kitchen paper.
4 Serve hot, sprinkled with parsley.

NOTE: If possible, make the soup the day before required. Allow to cool, then chill. The fat will solidify on the surface and can be removed easily. Reheat the soup thoroughly to serve.

❖ Hot and Sour Prawn Soup ❖

SERVES 4

PREPARATION TIME
10 minutes
COOKING TIME
20 minutes
FREEZING
Not suitable
COLOUR INDEX
Page 16

- 1 onion, peeled
- 1 small green chilli
- 2.5 cm (1 inch) piece
fresh root ginger
- 15 ml (1 tbsp) oil
- 50 g (2 oz) small
oyster mushrooms
- 1.1 litres (2 pints)
chicken stock
- 1 lemon grass stalk

- 15 ml (1 tbsp) white
wine vinegar
- 1 small bunch
watercress
- 350 g (12 oz) large
cooked peeled prawns
- salt and pepper

140 CALS/SERVING

1 Chop the onion. Halve, deseed and finely chop the chilli. Peel and finely chop the ginger.

2 Heat the oil in a large saucepan, add the onion, chilli and ginger and fry, stirring, for 4–5 minutes. Add the mushrooms and sauté for 1–2 minutes.

3 Stir in the stock, lemon grass and wine vinegar. Bring to the boil, cover and simmer for 10–12 minutes. Meanwhile roughly chop the watercress, discarding the stalks. Add to the soup with the prawns and simmer for 2 minutes. Remove the lemon grass and adjust the seasoning before serving.

Variation
Replace the watercress with 60 ml (4 tbsp) chopped coriander.

❖ Bouillabaisse ❖

4 Arrange the fish in a layer over the vegetables, pour over the saffron liquid and just enough stock to cover the fish. Bring to the boil and simmer uncovered for about 8 minutes.

5 Add the shellfish and cook for a further 5–8 minutes, until the fish pieces are cooked but still hold their shape. Serve garnished with parsley, and accompanied by French bread, as a main course.

NOTE: An authentic bouillabaisse is made with a variety of Mediterranean fish, some of which are only available in the south of France. However, regional variations use whatever fish is available locally. After cooking, the fish is usually removed from the soup and served on a separate plate.

SERVES 6

PREPARATION TIME
25 minutes, plus soaking
COOKING TIME
20–25 minutes
FREEZING
Not suitable

• 900 g (2 lb) mixed fish and shellfish, eg monkfish, red mullet, John Dory, bass, prawns, crab, cleaned
• few saffron strands
• 2–3 onions, peeled
• 1 celery stick
• 150 ml (¼ pint) olive oil
• 225 g (8 oz) tomatoes
• 2 garlic cloves, crushed
• 1 bay leaf

• 2.5 ml (½ tsp) dried thyme or fennel
• few parsley sprigs
• finely shredded rind of ½ orange
• salt and pepper
• about 1.1 litres (2 pints) fish stock
• parsley sprigs, to garnish

365 CALS/SERVING

1 Skin and fillet the fish if necessary, then cut into fairly large, thick pieces. Remove shellfish from their shells.

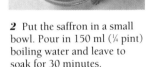

2 Put the saffron in a small bowl. Pour in 150 ml (¼ pint) boiling water and leave to soak for 30 minutes.

3 Slice the onions; chop the celery. Heat the oil in a large saucepan, add the onions and celery and fry gently for 5 minutes, until beginning to soften. Skin the tomatoes and slice. Add to the pan with the garlic, herbs, orange rind and seasoning.

❖ Mixed Fish Chowder ❖

SERVES 4

PREPARATION TIME
15 minutes
COOKING TIME
35–40 minutes
FREEZING
Not suitable
COLOUR INDEX
Page 17

• 450 g (1 lb) smoked haddock fillet
• 25 g (1 oz) desiccated coconut
• 175 g (6 oz) onion, peeled
• 6 celery sticks
• 350 g (12 oz) old potatoes
• 1 small green pepper

• 50 g (2 oz) butter or margarine
• salt and pepper
• 300 ml (½ pint) milk
• 125 g (4 oz) cooked peeled prawns
• chopped parsley or dill, to garnish

385 CALS/SERVING

1 Skin the haddock and cut into bite-sized pieces. Place the coconut in a measuring jug and make up to 300 ml (½ pint) with boiling water.
2 Roughly chop the onion and celery. Peel the potatoes and cut into small chunks. Chop the green pepper, discarding the core and seeds.
3 Melt the butter in a large pan. Add the onion and celery, cover and cook for about 5 minutes until starting to soften. Add the potatoes and pepper and cook for 1–2 minutes.
4 Strain the coconut liquid and add to the pan with a further 600 ml (1 pint) water. Bring to the boil, season, cover and simmer for about 20 minutes or until the vegetables are tender.
5 Add the haddock and milk to the soup. Bring to the boil, cover and simmer for 5–10 minutes, or until the fish is flaking apart. Mix in the prawns, warm gently and adjust the seasoning. Garnish with chopped herbs to serve.

❖ Vichyssoise ❖

SERVES 4

PREPARATION TIME
10 minutes, plus
chilling
COOKING TIME
45 minutes
FREEZING
Suitable (stage 3,
without cream)

- 4 leeks
- 1 onion, peeled
- 50 g (12 oz) butter or
margarine
- 350 g (2 oz) potatoes
- 1 litre (1¾ pints)
vegetable stock
- salt and pepper

- 200 ml (7 fl oz) single
cream
TO GARNISH:
- 60 ml (4 tbsp) yogurt
- snipped chives

270 CALS/SERVING

1 Slice the leeks and onion.
Melt the butter in a heavy-
based saucepan, add the leeks
and onion and cook gently for
about 10 minutes.

2 Thinly slice the potatoes
and add to the pan with the
stock. Bring to the boil, lower
the heat and season. Cover
and simmer for 30 minutes.

3 Allow to cool slightly, then
purée the soup in a blender or
food processor. Pour into a
bowl and stir in the cream.

4 Chill for at least 4 hours.
Taste and adjust the seasoning,
if necessary. Serve topped with
yogurt and chives.

❖ Chilled Asparagus Soup ❖

SERVES 6

PREPARATION TIME
15 minutes, plus
chilling
COOKING TIME
40–55 minutes
FREEZING
Suitable
COLOUR INDEX
Page 17

- 700 g (1½ lb)
asparagus
- salt and pepper
- 2 onions, peeled
- 25 g (1 oz) butter or
margarine
- 1.4 litres (2½ pints)
chicken stock

- 150 ml (¼ pint) single
cream
- finely pared lemon
rind, to garnish

125 CALS/SERVING

1 Cut the tips from the
asparagus stalks and simmer
them very gently in salted
water for 3–5 minutes, until
just tender. Drain well and
refresh with cold water.

2 Scrape the asparagus stalks
with a potato peeler or knife
and cut off the woody ends;
thinly slice the stalks. Chop
the onions.

3 Melt the butter in a large
saucepan. Add the asparagus
stalks and onions, cover and
cook for 5–10 minutes, until
beginning to soften.

4 Add the stock and seasoning to taste. Bring to the boil,
cover and simmer for 30–40
minutes, until the asparagus
stalks and onions are tender.

5 Allow to cool slightly, then
purée in a blender or food
processor until smooth. Pass
through a sieve into a bowl,
then stir in the cream.

6 Chill in the refrigerator for
2–3 hours. Serve garnished
with the reserved asparagus
tips and finely pared
lemon rind.

❖ Iced Tomato and Basil Soup ❖

SERVES 4

PREPARATION TIME
10 minutes, plus
chilling

COOKING TIME
1 minute

FREEZING
Suitable

COLOUR INDEX
Page 17

- 450 g (1 lb) tomatoes
- 1 small onion, peeled
- 15 ml (1 tbsp) tomato purée
- 15 ml (1 tbsp) chopped basil
- 600 ml (1 pint) vegetable or chicken stock
- salt and pepper
- basil sprigs, to garnish

35 CALS/SERVING

1 Roughly chop the tomatoes and onion and place in a blender or food processor with the tomato purée and basil. Purée until smooth.

2 Pass through a sieve into a saucepan, then stir in the stock and heat gently to remove froth. Season with salt and pepper.

3 Remove from the heat and leave to cool, then chill in the refrigerator for at least 2 hours or overnight. Serve garnished with basil.

❖ Gazpacho ❖

SERVES 6

PREPARATION TIME
20 minutes, plus
chilling

FREEZING
Suitable (stage 3)

- 1.1 kg (2½ lb) ripe red tomatoes
- 2 onions, peeled
- 2 green peppers
- 1 large cucumber
- 45 ml (3 tbsp) red wine vinegar
- 30 ml (2 tbsp) olive oil
- 2.5 ml (½ tsp) sugar
- 2–3 garlic cloves, crushed
- two 180 ml (6 fl oz) bottles tomato juice cocktail, or 350 ml (12 fl oz) tomato juice
- 30 ml (2 tbsp) tomato purée
- salt and pepper
- crushed ice, to serve

100 CALS/SERVING

1 Roughly chop 900 g (2 lb) tomatoes and one of the onions. Halve, core and deseed the peppers; cut one of them into large pieces. Peel three quarters of the cucumber and roughly chop.

2 Place these prepared ingredients in a food processor with the vinegar, oil, sugar, garlic, tomato juice, tomato purée and seasoning. Blend until almost smooth.

3 Strain the soup through a nylon sieve, pushing through as much as possible. Adjust the seasoning, cover and chill well.

4 To prepare the garnish, dice the remaining green pepper, cucumber and onion. Place in separate bowls. Peel, quarter, deseed and dice the remaining tomatoes; place in a small bowl. Cover and refrigerate.

5 Serve the soup, well chilled, accompanied by the bowls of diced vegetables and crushed ice.

NOTE: Served chilled in summer, this is a wonderfully refreshing soup. The tomatoes must be very ripe and bright red – canned chopped tomatoes are a good substitute. Use two 400 g (14 oz) cans in place of fresh tomatoes for the soup, but always chop some fresh ones for the garnish.

❖ Minted Melon ❖ and Cucumber Soup

SERVES 4

PREPARATION TIME
15 minutes, plus
chilling

COOKING TIME
15 minutes

FREEZING
Suitable

- 2 ripe medium cantaloupe or rock melons
- ½ cucumber, about 175 g (6 oz)
- finely pared rind of 1 lemon
- 25 g (1 oz) caster sugar
- 3 large mint stems, crushed
- salt and pepper
- lemon juice, to taste (optional)
- mint sprigs, to garnish

55 CALS/SERVING

1 Halve and deseed the melons, then roughly chop the flesh. Peel, halve, deseed and roughly chop the cucumber.

2 Place the melon flesh and the chopped cucumber in a large saucepan with the pared lemon rind, sugar and 150 ml (¼ pint) water. Stir well.

3 Heat, stirring continuously, until the sugar has dissolved, then simmer for about 10 minutes. Add the crushed mint stems and allow to cool.

4 Discard the mint and lemon rind. Transfer the mixture to a blender or food processor and purée until smooth. Season with salt and pepper. Push through a nylon sieve into a bowl. Cover and chill for at least 2 hours, preferably overnight.

5 Add a little lemon juice to taste, if wished. Adjust the seasoning and serve in chilled bowls, garnished with mint sprigs.

STARTERS

The perfect starter is something attractive and delicious which sets the tone of the meal and tempts guests' appetites for the food that is to follow. There's no point in planning a spectacular main course and pudding and then serving an uninteresting first course. It is at the beginning of the meal that appetites are keenest and most appreciative, so choose carefully. Get a casual supper for friends off to a relaxed start by serving a fun 'hands on' starter like a tasty dip with crudités, Deep-fried Potato Skins (page 127) or a selection of savoury finger foods. Smart formal affairs call for something rather more elegant like a Layered Fish Terrine (page 119) or Avocado with Raspberry Vinegar (page 126).

Choosing a Starter

Aim to achieve a balance and contrast of flavours, textures and colours throughout the meal. If you're serving a substantial main course – a hearty stew or a roast with all the trimmings – then a small portion of a fruit or vegetable based starter is adequate. In fact the 'wet and dry' rule is as good as any when choosing your courses. That is, a 'wet' course such as a soup or dip should precede a 'dry' course such as grilled meat or fish. Aim too for balance in 'weight' of the courses. A chunky soup, followed by steak and kidney pie and a steamed dessert may be traditional country fare, but is far too filling for most appetites.

Pay attention to the variety and balance of flavours throughout the courses, and avoid repetition both of ingredients and 'heavy' cooking methods such as deep-frying. A delicate short-crust pastry tartlet or a filo parcel starts any meal in style but precludes a tart or pie for pudding. If fish is the main course then obviously fish is inappropriate as a starter. A salad or meat course would be better instead. If you're planning a 'themed' meal, then the starter should hint at what is to come.

Bear in mind how health-conscious many people are today and avoid putting together a meal that consists of several rich cream or butter based courses. If your main course is heavy and filling, serve a very light and refreshing starter. Most people are cutting down on their meat consumption, so don't plan a menu with meat in both the first and second courses.

Consider too, the time of year. Food in season will always be the cheapest, freshest and most appropriate. Homegrown asparagus makes a short appearance in the shops in the summer so it's a shame not to take advantage of this. Try serving it lightly steamed with coriander hollandaise (see page 126).

Plan the menu so that you leave plenty of time to be with your guests. For very large numbers, cold starters like pâtés, terrines, mousses or salads that can be laid out on the table in advance are easiest. Warm salads and hot soufflés are best for smaller affairs or where the main course requires little last minute attention.

For informal supper parties or speedy pre-theatre suppers you may find it more convenient to serve a selection of canapés or savoury finger foods with drinks rather than a sit-down starter. These can be prepared beforehand, warmed through if necessary, and handed round as guests arrive.

For impromptu after-work suppers or when preparation time and energy are limited, simple hors d'oeuvres are best. Smoked salmon with brown bread and lemon; Parma ham with figs; salami with olives; grilled vegetables drizzled with olive oil; tomato, basil and mozzarella salad; these unpretentious combinations never fail.

Having made your choice, it really is worth adding a garnish no matter how simple. A wedge of lemon or lime adds colour to fish and seafood starters while a sprinkling of chopped fresh herbs brings most foods to life.

Party Food

Included in this chapter are plenty of ideas for delicious savoury finger foods to serve at drinks parties. Cocktail eats are notoriously time-consuming to prepare, but we've cut corners to enable you to prepare party food in half the time it usually takes. For quick and easy canapés, try Wholewheat Blinis, savoury Mini Croissants and Oriental Parcels (page 112).

Other ideas for party nibbles include Spiced Cashews, Toasted Seed and Nut Mix, and Olives with Garlic and Lemon (page 114). You can also dress up sausage rolls by glazing with egg, then sprinkling with grated cheese or sesame seeds before baking. Or try tossing cooked chicken nuggets in Parmesan and serving with a Herbed Cheese Dip (page 115). A colourful platter of crudités and a selection of dips always look attractive. Allow 8–10 'bites' per head, with nuts, olives, dips and 'dunks' as extras.

CANAPÉS

These time-saving canapés are ideal party food. Serve about 8–10 bites per person and freeze the rest for another occasion.

❖ Wholewheat Blinis ❖

MAKES 100	

PREPARATION TIME
20 minutes, plus rising
COOKING TIME
About 20 minutes
FREEZING
Suitable (without topping)

- 125 g (4 oz) plain wholewheat flour
- 125 g (4 oz) plain white flour
- 7 g (¼ oz) sachet easy-blend yeast
- 5 ml (1 tsp) salt
- 375 ml (13 fl oz) tepid milk
- 2 eggs, size 1
- oil, for frying

TOPPING:
- soured cream
- lumpfish roe or smoked salmon
- chives, to garnish

40 CALS/BLINI

1 In a warmed large bowl, mix the flours with the yeast and salt. Beat in the tepid milk, 1 whole egg plus 1 yolk, until evenly blended. Cover and leave to rise in a warm place for 1 hour.
2 Lightly whisk the remaining egg white; fold into the batter.
3 Lightly oil a griddle or frying pan and cook small spoonfuls of batter, in batches, until golden brown underneath; turn and cook the other side. Serve warm or cold, topped with soured cream and lumpfish roe or smoked salmon. Garnish with chives.

❖ Mini Croissants ❖

MAKES 48	

PREPARATION TIME
30 minutes
COOKING TIME
8–10 minutes
FREEZING
Suitable (stage 1)

- 240 g (8½ oz) can mini-croissant dough
- beaten egg, to glaze

FILLING:
- soft cheese
- smoked salmon

50 CALS/CROISSANT

1 Unroll the croissant dough, separate and cut into about 24 triangles; cut each in half and roll into croissants.
2 Place on a baking sheet, brush with egg and bake at 200°C (400°F) mark 6 for 8–10 minutes. Cool slightly on a wire rack. Serve warm, split and filled with soft cheese and smoked salmon.

❖ Oriental Parcels ❖

MAKES 60	

PREPARATION TIME
30 minutes
COOKING TIME
10–12 minutes
FREEZING
Suitable (stage 2)
COLOUR INDEX
Page 18

- 225 g (8 oz) filo pastry
- 4 spring onions
- 225 g (8 oz) cooked peeled prawns
- 30 ml (2 tbsp) light soy sauce
- 5 ml (1 tsp) grated fresh root ginger
- 1.25 ml (¼ tsp) garlic salt
- melted butter, for brushing
- sesame seeds, for sprinkling

20 CALS/PARCEL

1 Cut the filo pastry into 5×30 cm (2×12 inch) strips. Cover with a damp cloth and set aside. Finely chop the spring onions. Chop the prawns and mix with the spring onions, soy sauce, ginger and garlic salt.

2 Spread a filo pastry strip with melted butter. Place about 2.5 ml (½ tsp) filling at one end and fold the end diagonally into a triangle, enclosing the filling. Continue folding over and over to the end of the strip. Repeat with remaining filo strips and filling.

3 Place the filo parcels on a greased baking sheet, brush with melted butter and sprinkle with sesame seeds. Bake at 220°C (425°F) mark 7 for 10–12 minutes until crisp and golden. Serve warm.

❖ Mini Pizzas ❖

MAKES 40	

PREPARATION TIME
20 minutes
COOKING TIME
8 minutes
FREEZING
Suitable

- two 20 cm (8 inch) ready-to-cook pizza bases

TOPPING:
- tomato slices
- chopped spring onions
- feta cheese, crumbled

25 CALS/MINI PIZZA

1 Stamp out 4 cm (1½ inch) rounds from the uncooked pizza bases, using a small pastry cutter.
2 Top each with a slice of tomato, a little chopped spring onion and crumbled feta cheese.
3 Bake at 220°C (425°F) mark 7 for about 8 minutes until golden brown and bubbling. Serve warm.

❖ Smoked Salmon ❖ and Prawn Bites

3 Brush with beaten egg. Bake at 220°C (425°F) mark 7 for about 12 minutes or until well risen and brown.

4 Allow to cool. Separate the scone bites, splitting them in half with a knife.

5 Drain and dry the prawns, then chop finely. Mix with the mayonnaise, Tabasco, lemon juice and seasoning to taste. Spread onto about half of the scone bases. Garnish with lemon and dill.

6 Top the remaining scones with soured cream and tiny pieces of smoked salmon. Squeeze over lemon juice and grind over some black pepper, if wished.

MAKES 120	
PREPARATION TIME 40 minutes	• 275 g (10 oz) white self-raising flour
COOKING TIME 12 minutes	• 5 ml (1 tsp) baking powder
FREEZING Suitable (scone bases only)	• salt and pepper

MAKES 120
PREPARATION TIME
40 minutes
COOKING TIME
12 minutes
FREEZING
Suitable (scone bases only)

- 275 g (10 oz) white self-raising flour
- 5 ml (1 tsp) baking powder
- salt and pepper
- 2.5 ml (½ tsp) dried dill
- 50 g (2 oz) butter or margarine
- 2 eggs
- 150 ml (¼ pint) milk
- 175 g (6 oz) cooked peeled prawns
- 45 ml (3 tbsp) mayonnaise

- few drops of Tabasco
- lemon juice to taste
- 90 ml (3 fl oz) soured cream
- 50 g (2 oz) smoked salmon, chopped

TO GARNISH:
- dill sprigs
- lemon pieces

20 CALS/'BITE'

1 Sift the flour with the baking powder and 2.5 ml (½ tsp) salt into a large bowl. Stir in the dill. Rub in the butter until the mixture resembles bread-crumbs. Beat 1 egg with the milk and use to bind the mixture to a soft dough.

2 Knead the dough lightly until just smooth. Roll out to a 20 cm (8 inch) square and place on a baking sheet. Mark into six strips, then mark across into 10 to give 60 'bites'.

❖ Gruyère and Peanut Sablés ❖

MAKES 72
PREPARATION TIME
20 minutes
COOKING TIME
20 minutes
FREEZING
Suitable
COLOUR INDEX
Page 19

- 450 g (1 lb) packet shortcrust pastry
- 1 egg, beaten
- 75 g (3 oz) Gruyère cheese, grated

- cayenne pepper
- 75 g (3 oz) salted peanuts, roughly chopped

40 CALS/SABLÉ

1 Divide the pastry in half and roll each piece out to a 23 cm (9 inch) square. Place each square on a baking sheet and brush with beaten egg.
2 Sprinkle the cheese over one of the squares. Press down firmly and sprinkle with cayenne pepper. Cut the pastry into six strips and separate slightly.
3 Sprinkle a little cayenne over the second piece of pastry. Scatter with the peanuts and press down firmly. Cut into strips and separate as above.
4 Bake at 200°C (400°F) mark 6 for about 20 minutes or until crisp and golden brown. Cool slightly on the baking sheet, then cut into squares or triangles.

❖ Spiced Cashews ❖

SERVES 8

PREPARATION TIME
5 minutes
COOKING TIME
15–20 minutes
FREEZING
Not suitable
COLOUR INDEX
Page 19

215 CALS/SERVING

- 275 g (10 oz) unsalted cashew nuts
- 25 g (1 oz) butter, melted
- 2.5 ml (½ tsp) salt
- 10 ml (2 tsp) soy sauce
- few drops of Tabasco

1 In a medium bowl, mix together all the ingredients. Spread out evenly on edged baking sheets.
2 Bake at 150°C (300°F) mark 2 for 15–20 minutes, stirring halfway through. Allow to cool.

NOTE: These tasty nuts can be stored in an airtight container for up to 2 weeks.

❖ Toasted Seed and Nut Mix ❖

SERVES 10

PREPARATION TIME
5 minutes
COOKING TIME
5 minutes
FREEZING
Not suitable
COLOUR INDEX
Page 19

90 CALS/15 ML (1 TBSP)

- 75 g (3 oz) pumpkin seeds
- 75 g (3 oz) sunflower seeds
- 75 g (3 oz) pine nuts
- 175 g (6 oz) salted peanuts
- mild paprika

1 Place the seeds and nuts in a large roasting tin. Grill under a moderate heat until tinged with colour, stirring and turning occasionally.
2 While still warm, sprinkle the seeds and nuts liberally with the paprika, mixing well. Serve warm or cold.

❖ Olives with Garlic and Lemon ❖

SERVES 12

PREPARATION TIME
15 minutes
FREEZING
Not suitable
COLOUR INDEX
Page 19

150 CALS/SERVING

- 450 g (1 lb) mixed black and green olives
- 3 small red chillies
- 3 garlic cloves, sliced
- 30 ml (2 tbsp) chopped oregano, thyme or parsley
- 30 ml (2 tbsp) citrus pepper
- 3 lemon slices, halved
- 100 ml (3½ fl oz) olive oil

1 Press each olive with the end of a rolling pin, but do not crush; place in a bowl.
2 Lightly crush the chillies between sheets of greaseproof paper, then mix with the garlic, herbs, citrus pepper, lemon slices and oil. Pour over the olives and stir well.
3 Cover and leave to marinate for 24 hours before serving.

NOTE: These olives can be stored in a covered bowl in the refrigerator for up to 2 weeks if completely covered with oil.

❖ Prawn and Feta Purses ❖

MAKES 25

PREPARATION TIME
25 minutes
COOKING TIME
10–15 minutes
FREEZING
Not suitable

80 CALS/'PURSE'

- 125 g (4 oz) cooked peeled prawns
- 225 g (8 oz) feta cheese, crumbled
- 1 cm (½ inch) piece fresh root ginger, peeled and grated
- salt and pepper
- 30 ml (2 tbsp) chopped chives or dill
- pinch of ground nutmeg
- 400 g (14 oz) packet filo pastry
- melted butter
- chives, to garnish

1 If the prawns have been frozen, make sure they are thawed and thoroughly drained. Roughly chop the prawns and mix with the feta cheese, ginger, seasoning, chives and nutmeg.

2 Cut the filo pastry into 75 10 cm (4 inch) squares. Brush each square of pastry with butter and lay three on top of each other to make 25 piles. Place a teaspoonful of filling in the middle of each pile.

3 Draw the pastry up around the filling, pinching to form a money bag shape. Pull out and arrange frilly tops. Place on greased baking sheets and brush lightly with melted butter. Bake at 200°C (400°F) mark 6 for 10–15 minutes until golden brown. Cool slightly. Serve garnished with chives.

DIPS WITH CRUDITÉS

Serve an assortment of crudités with these dips. Choose a selection to appeal to the eye as well as the taste buds. Baby vegetables, such as carrots, baby corn, cherry tomatoes and button mushrooms can be served whole. Celery, fennel, cucumber, courgettes, peppers and carrots need to be cut into strips or trimmed to a manageable size. Radishes, spring onions and cauliflower florets can also be used.

Sliced fresh fruit, such as apples, pears, nectarines, grapes, mangoes, star fruit and fresh dates, make good crudités too.

❖ Herbed Cheese Dip ❖

SERVES 6–8

PREPARATION TIME
5 minutes
FREEZING
Not suitable
COLOUR INDEX
Page 18

- 300 g (10 oz) carton full-fat soft cheese with garlic and parsley
- 60 ml (4 tbsp) mayonnaise
- 30 ml (2 tbsp) chopped parsley
- 30 ml (2 tbsp) chopped chives
- salt and pepper
- chives, to garnish
- crudités, to serve

230–170 CALS/SERVING

1 In a small bowl, beat the soft cheese with the mayonnaise, parsley and chives until evenly mixed. Season to taste.
2 Transfer to a serving dish and garnish with chives. Serve with a colourful selection of crudités.

❖ Tzaziki ❖

SERVES 4

PREPARATION TIME
10 minutes
FREEZING
Not suitable
COLOUR INDEX
Page 18

- ½ medium cucumber
- 150 ml (5 fl oz) natural yogurt (preferably firm-set)
- 10 ml (2 tsp) olive oil
- 15 ml (1 tbsp) chopped mint
- 1 garlic clove, crushed
- salt and pepper
TO SERVE:
- warm pitta bread
- crudités

45 CALS/SERVING

1 Dice the cucumber, discarding the seeds; place in a bowl.
2 Add the yogurt and olive oil. Add the chopped mint and garlic. Stir well, adding salt and pepper to taste. Cover and chill before serving. Serve with warm pitta bread and crudités.

❖ Hummus ❖

SERVES 8

PREPARATION TIME
10 minutes
FREEZING
Not suitable
COLOUR INDEX
Page 18

- two 400 g (14 oz) cans chick peas, drained
- juice of 2 large lemons
- 150 ml (¼ pint) light tahini
- 60 ml (4 tbsp) olive oil
- 2 garlic cloves, crushed
- salt and pepper
TO SERVE:
- black olives, to garnish
- warm pitta bread

290 CALS/SERVING

1 Put the chick peas in a blender or food processor with the lemon juice and work to a smooth purée.
2 Add the tahini paste, all but 10 ml (2 tsp) of the oil, the garlic and seasoning. Blend until smooth.
3 Spoon into a serving dish and sprinkle with the reserved oil. Garnish with olives and serve with warm pitta bread.

❖ *Taramasalata* ❖

SERVES 6

PREPARATION TIME
10 minutes
FREEZING
Not suitable
COLOUR INDEX
Page 18

- 225 g (8 oz) smoked cod's roe, skinned
- 1 garlic clove, crushed
- 50 g (2 oz) fresh breadcrumbs
- 1 small onion, peeled and chopped
- grated rind and juice of 1 lemon
- 150 ml (¼ pint) olive oil
- pepper

40 CALS/SERVING

1 Break up the cod's roe, place in a blender or food processor and work to a purée. Add the garlic with the breadcrumbs, onion, lemon rind and juice; blend for a few more seconds.
2 Gradually add the oil, blending well after each addition until smooth. Blend in 90 ml (6 tbsp) hot water with the pepper.
3 Spoon into a serving dish and chill for at least 1 hour. Serve with warm pitta bread or toast.

❖ *Guacamole* ❖

SERVES 6–8

PREPARATION TIME
10 minutes
FREEZING
Not suitable
COLOUR INDEX
Page 19

- 1 small onion, peeled
- 2–3 garlic cloves
- 2.5 cm (1 inch) piece fresh root ginger, peeled
- 4 large ripe avocados
- finely grated rind and juice of 2 small limes
- 60 ml (4 tbsp) chopped coriander
- 10 ml (2 tsp) ground coriander
- 10 ml (2 tsp) ground cumin
- 5 ml (1 tsp) chilli powder
- 2 ripe tomatoes
- salt and pepper
- crudités, to serve

140–85 CALS/SERVING

1 Put the onion, garlic and ginger in a food processor and process until finely chopped.
2 Halve, stone and peel the avocados, then chop roughly.
3 Add the chopped avocados to the mixture in the processor with all the remaining ingredients, except the tomato and seasoning. Process until almost smooth. Transfer to a bowl.
4 Roughly chop the tomatoes, discarding the seeds, then stir into the guacamole. Season with salt and pepper. Cover and chill in the refrigerator for 30 minutes. Serve with crudités.

❖ *Spicy Crab Dip* ❖

SERVES 4

PREPARATION TIME
10 minutes
FREEZING
Not suitable
COLOUR INDEX
Page 18

- 225 g (8 oz) white crab meat, flaked
- 225 g (8 oz) soft cheese
- 45 ml (3 tbsp) canned pimiento, finely chopped
- juice of ½ lemon
- 10 ml (2 tsp) Worcestershire sauce
- 5 ml (1 tsp) anchovy essence
- 1.25 ml (¼ tsp) cayenne pepper
- salt and pepper
- crudités, to serve

135 CALS/SERVING

1 Fold the crab meat into the soft cheese until evenly mixed.
2 Fold in the pimiento, then stir in the lemon juice, Worcestershire sauce, anchovy essence, cayenne and seasoning. Turn into a serving bowl; chill for at least 2 hours. Serve with crudités.

❖ Pâté de Campagne ❖

SERVES 10–12

PREPARATION TIME
20 minutes, plus
chilling
COOKING TIME
2 hours
FREEZING
Suitable

• 275 g (10 oz) streaky
bacon rashers
• 450 g (1 lb) belly of
pork
• 275 g (10 oz) diced pie
veal
• 175 g (6 oz) lamb's
liver
• 1 onion, peeled
• 1 garlic clove, crushed
• 50 g (2 oz) black
olives, stoned and
chopped

• salt and pepper
• 5 ml (1 tsp) chopped
sage
• 30 ml (2 tbsp) olive oil
• 15 ml (1 tbsp) lemon
juice
• 30 ml (2 tbsp) brandy

380–310 CALS/SERVING

1 Derind the bacon, then
stretch, using the back of a
knife. Finely mince the pork,
veal, liver and onion. Mix with
the remaining ingredients.

2 Layer the bacon and minced
ingredients in a 1.1 litre
(2 pint) terrine, topping with
a layer of bacon rashers.

3 Cover with foil or a lid and
place in a roasting tin, half-
filled with boiling water. Cook
at 170°C (325°F) mark 3 for
about 2 hours. Weight down
the pâté and allow to cool,
then refrigerate overnight.
Leave at room temperature for
30 minutes before serving.
Cut into slices to serve.

❖ Peppered Chicken Liver Pâté ❖

SERVES 8

PREPARATION TIME
15 minutes, plus
chilling
COOKING TIME
15 minutes
FREEZING
Suitable

• 1 onion, peeled
• 50 g (2 oz) butter
• 450 g (1 lb) chicken
livers, trimmed
• 1 garlic clove, crushed
• 2.5 ml (½ tsp) dried
marjoram
• 5 ml (1 tsp) lemon
juice

• 15 ml (1 tbsp) brandy
or sherry
• salt and pepper
• 10 ml (2 tsp) green
peppercorns in brine,
drained

200 CALS/SERVING

1 Chop the onion. Melt the butter in a sauté pan, add the onion
and cook until softened. Add the livers, garlic and marjoram.
Cook over a moderate heat, stirring occasionally, for 10 minutes.
2 Remove from the heat and stir in the lemon juice and brandy
or sherry. Allow to cool slightly.
3 Transfer the mixture to a blender or food processor and work
until smooth. Season with salt to taste and a little pepper.
4 Chop the green peppercorns and stir into the pâté. Spoon into
a serving dish, cover and chill in the refrigerator for at least
2 hours, until firm. Serve with toast or granary bread.

❖ Smoked Salmon Pâté ❖

SERVES 6

PREPARATION TIME
10 minutes, plus
chilling
FREEZING
Suitable
COLOUR INDEX
Page 19

• 175 g (6 oz) smoked
salmon scraps
• 75 g (3 oz) unsalted
butter or margarine
• 20 ml (4 tsp) lemon
juice

• 60 ml (4 tbsp) single
cream
• pepper
• cucumber slices, to
garnish

155 CALS/SERVING

1 Cut up the smoked salmon pieces, reserving a few for garnish,
and place in a blender or food processor.
2 Melt the butter and mix with the lemon juice and cream. Pour
into the blender or food processor.
3 Blend the mixture until smooth, then season with pepper.
4 Spoon into a 300 ml (½ pint) dish and refrigerate until set.
5 Leave at room temperature for 30 minutes before serving.
Garnish the pâté with twists of smoked salmon and cucumber.

❖ Mushroom and Cashew ❖ Nut Pâté

SERVES 8

PREPARATION TIME
15 minutes
COOKING TIME
15 minutes
FREEZING
Not suitable
COLOUR INDEX
Page 19

- 45 ml (3 tbsp) oil
- 50 g (2 oz) unsalted cashew nuts
- 700 g (1½ lb) medium open-cup mushrooms
- 2 garlic cloves, crushed
- 5 ml (1 tsp) dried thyme
- 1.25 ml (¼ tsp) cayenne pepper
- 2.5 ml (½ tsp) ground allspice
- 200 g (7 oz) silken tofu
- 30 ml (2 tbsp) chopped parsley (optional)
- salt and pepper

200 CALS/SERVING

1 Heat the oil in a large, heavy-based frying pan and fry the cashews for 2–3 minutes or until browned on all sides. Remove from the oil with a slotted spoon and leave to cool.
2 Chop the mushrooms and add to the pan with the garlic, thyme, cayenne and allspice. Cook for about 10 minutes or until the mushrooms are very soft, stirring all the time. Cool slightly.
3 Meanwhile, put the nuts in a food processor and process until very finely chopped. Tip them into a bowl. Put the tofu in the food processor and process until smooth. Add the mushrooms and process until finely chopped.
4 Add to the nuts with the parsley, if using, and stir until mixed. Season with salt and pepper and a little extra cayenne and allspice, if liked. Spoon the pâté into a serving dish, cover and chill. Remove from the refrigerator 30 minutes before serving. Serve with toast or warm granary bread.

❖ Spinach Ricotta Terrine ❖

SERVES 6

PREPARATION TIME
20 minutes, plus chilling
COOKING TIME
1½–2 hours
FREEZING
Not suitable

- 225 g (8 oz) spinach leaves
- 3 spring onions, trimmed
- 15 ml (1 tbsp) olive oil
- 2 garlic cloves, crushed
- 350 g (12 oz) ricotta cheese
- 3 eggs
- 300 ml (½ pint) double cream
- salt and pepper

TO GARNISH:
- watercress sprigs
- toasted walnut pieces

TO SERVE:
- tomato coulis (page 95)

405 CALS/SERVING

1 Lightly oil a 1.4 litre (2½ pint) ovenproof terrine. Line the base and sides with non-stick baking parchment and lightly brush with oil.

2 Roughly chop the spinach. Finely chop the spring onions. Heat the oil in a large saucepan, add the spring onions and garlic, and cook for 2–3 minutes. Add the spinach and continue to cook, stirring, until the spinach has wilted and all excess liquid has evaporated. Remove from the heat.

3 Put the spinach mixture in a blender or food processor and add the ricotta cheese, eggs and double cream. Add salt and pepper to taste and blend until smooth.

4 Pour the mixture into the prepared terrine and cover with oiled foil. Stand in a roasting tin and pour in enough boiling water to come about halfway up the sides of the terrine.

5 Cook in the oven at 180°C (350°F) mark 4 for 1½–2 hours or until a skewer inserted into the centre of the terrine comes out clean. Leave to cool in the roasting tin.

6 Pour any excess liquid off the terrine, then chill in the refrigerator for at least 2 hours. Turn the terrine out on to a plate and cut into thick slices. Garnish with sprigs of watercress and toasted walnuts. Serve with the tomato coulis.

❖ Salmon Mousse ❖

SERVES 8

PREPARATION TIME
30 minutes, plus
chilling
COOKING TIME
10–15 minutes
FREEZING
Not suitable
COLOUR INDEX
Page 19

- 350 g (12 oz) tail-end piece salmon or sea trout fillet
- 1 small onion, peeled and sliced
- 1 medium carrot, peeled and sliced
- 2 bay leaves
- 4 black peppercorns
- salt and pepper
- 75 ml (5 tbsp) white wine
- 15 ml (1 tbsp) gelatine
- 300 ml (½ pint) milk

- 25 g (1 oz) butter or margarine
- 30 ml (2 tbsp) flour
- 75 ml (5 tbsp) lemon mayonnaise (page 273)
- 150 ml (¼ pint) whipping cream
- 1 egg white
TO GARNISH:
- cucumber slices
- dill sprigs

295 CALS/SERVING

5 Fold the mayonnaise into the salmon mixture. Whip the cream until soft peaks form, then fold into the mousse; adjust the seasoning. Whisk the egg white until stiff and fold lightly into the mousse until no traces of egg white are visible.

6 Spoon the mousse into an oiled 15 cm (6 inch) soufflé dish, smooth the surface, cover and refrigerate for at least 2 hours, until set. Leave at room temperature for 30 minutes before serving. Garnish with cucumber slices and dill sprigs.

1 Place the salmon in a small shallow pan. Add half the onion and carrot slices, 1 bay leaf, 2 peppercorns and a good pinch of salt. Spoon over the wine and add 75 ml (5 tbsp) water. Bring slowly to the boil, then cover and simmer gently for 10–15 minutes, until the fish flakes easily when tested with a knife.

2 Flake the fish, discarding the skin, and place in a bowl. Boil the cooking liquid until reduced by half, strain and reserve. Sprinkle the gelatine over 45 ml (3 tbsp) water in a bowl and leave to soak for 5 minutes until sponge-like. Bring the milk to the boil with the remaining onion, carrot, bay leaf and peppercorns. Remove from heat and infuse for 10 minutes; strain.

❖ Smoked Mackerel Pâté ❖

SERVES 6

PREPARATION TIME
15 minutes
FREEZING
Suitable

- 275 g (10 oz) smoked mackerel fillets
- 50 g (2 oz) butter or margarine, softened
- 45 ml (3 tbsp) creamed horseradish

- 30 ml (2 tbsp) single cream
- pepper

195 CALS/SERVING

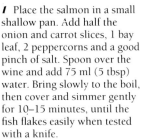

3 Melt the butter in a pan, stir in the flour and cook, stirring, for 1 minute. Remove from the heat and gradually stir in the strained milk. Bring to the boil slowly and cook, stirring, until the sauce thickens. Pour into a bowl, add gelatine and stir until dissolved. Let cool.

4 Stir the fish into the cooled sauce with the reserved cooking juices. Spoon into a blender or food processor and switch on for a few seconds only; the fish should retain a little of its texture. Transfer to a large bowl.

1 Remove the skin from the smoked mackerel and tweeze out any small bones. Flake into a bowl.
2 Add the butter, creamed horseradish and cream. Mash with a fork until evenly blended. Season with pepper; salt is not usually needed.
3 Spoon the mixture into a serving dish, cover tightly and refrigerate until required. Leave the pâté at room temperature for 30 minutes before serving. Serve with toast or crispbreads.

NOTE: Make sure the type of smoked mackerel you buy for this recipe does not need further cooking.

❖ Layered Fish Terrine ❖

SERVES 8	

PREPARATION TIME
30 minutes, plus chilling
COOKING TIME
45 minutes
FREEZING
Not suitable

- 700 g (1½ lb) whiting, sole, plaice or hake, skinned and chilled
- 3 egg whites, chilled
- salt and white pepper
- 15 ml (1 tbsp) lemon juice
- 30 ml (2 tbsp) chopped dill
- 30 ml (2 tbsp) chopped tarragon
- 300 ml (½ pint) double cream, chilled

- 25 g (1 oz) butter
- 450 g (1 lb) tail-end piece salmon, filleted and skinned
- 15 ml (1 tbsp) green peppercorns in brine, drained
- dill, to garnish

380 CALS/SERVING

5 Cut the salmon into chunky strips, about 1 cm (½ inch) square and the length of the loaf tin or terrine. Cover and chill in the refrigerator until required.

6 Carefully stir the green peppercorns into the fish mixture. Spoon a third of the fish mixture into the terrine and spread evenly to cover the base. Lay half of the salmon strips on top, leaving a 1 cm (½ inch) border all the way round. Cover with half of the remaining fish mixture, levelling it carefully.

7 Repeat the salmon layer, using the remaining salmon strips. Finally cover with the remaining fish mixture and smooth the top.

8 Cover the terrine with buttered foil. Stand in a roasting tin and pour in enough boiling water to come halfway up the sides of the terrine. Bake at 180°C (350°F) mark 4 for 45 minutes or until a skewer inserted into the centre comes out clean.

1 Remove any bones from the white fish, then cut into pieces. Work in a blender or food processor until finely minced.

2 Add the egg whites and pepper; process until evenly mixed. Turn into a bowl, cover and chill for 30 minutes.

3 Add the lemon juice, dill, and tarragon; process slowly adding the cream. Add salt to taste, cover and chill for at least 30 minutes.

4 Meanwhile liberally grease a 1.2 litre (2 pint) terrine or loaf tin with the butter; line base with greaseproof paper.

9 Transfer the terrine to a wire rack and leave to cool, then cover with cling film and chill in the refrigerator for at least 4 hours.

10 When ready to serve turn the terrine out onto a plate and wipe with absorbent kitchen paper to remove any butter or liquid. Cut into thick slices and serve garnished with dill.

❖ Seafood Roulade ❖

3 Place the haddock in a small saucepan with the milk and seasoning. Bring to the boil, cover and simmer for 8 minutes or until the fish is tender. Strain and reserve the liquor; there should be about 200 ml (7 fl oz). Flake the fish, discarding skin and bone.

4 Melt 50 g (2 oz) butter in a saucepan. Stir in 50 g (2 oz) flour followed by the reserved milk. Bring to the boil and cook for 1 minute, stirring all the time to make a very thick sauce. Let cool slightly, then mix in the flaked haddock and the egg yolks. Adjust seasoning.

SERVES 8

PREPARATION TIME
35 minutes
COOKING TIME
12 minutes
FREEZING
Not suitable

- 350 g (12 oz) cooked prawns in shells
- 200 ml (7 fl oz) dry white wine
- onion slices and a bay leaf, for flavouring
- 225 g (8 oz) shelled scallops
- 225 g (8 oz) haddock fillet
- 200 ml (7 fl oz) milk
- salt and pepper

- 75 g (3 oz) butter or margarine
- 65 g (2½ oz) plain flour
- 4 eggs, separated
- 30 ml (2 tbsp) single cream
- 10 ml (2 tsp) chopped dill
- dill sprigs, to garnish

250 CALS/SERVING

5 Whisk the egg whites until stiff but not dry. Stir one large spoonful into the haddock mixture, then lightly fold in the remainder and pour gently into the paper case. Push the mixture out carefully to fill the case to the edges. Bake at 200°C (400°F) mark 6 for about 12 minutes or until lightly browned and just firm to touch. Remove paper clips.

6 Meanwhile, add the scallops to the fish stock and simmer for 1–2 minutes. Take off the heat. Melt 25 g (1 oz) butter in a saucepan and stir in 30 ml (2 tbsp) flour, followed by the stock mixture. Bring to the boil stirring, and cook for 1 minute. Take off the heat and mix in the prawns, cream and dill. Adjust the seasoning and keep warm in a bain-marie.

1 First prepare the paper case. Cut a sheet of strong non-stick baking parchment into a rectangle measuring 40×30 cm (16×12 inches). Fold up 2.5 cm (1 inch) around the edges, then snip in at the corners and secure with paper clips or staples. Place on a baking sheet and brush the paper case generously with melted butter.

2 To prepare the fish stock, remove the heads and shells from the prawns, reserving the flesh, and place in a small saucepan with the wine, 200 ml (7 fl oz) water and the flavouring ingredients. Bring to the boil and simmer for 10 minutes. Strain the stock into a food processor, add the scallop coral and blend until smooth. Strain into a jug. Cut the white scallop flesh into small pieces and reserve.

7 Flip the cooked roulade onto a large sheet of damp grease-proof paper. Carefully ease off the paper case. Make a shallow cut along one short edge – this helps to start rolling.

8 Spread thinly with the sauce and fish mixture and roll up from the short edge. Serve immediately, accompanied by the remaining sauce.

❖ Smoked Salmon ❖ and Cream Cheese Rolls

SERVES 8

PREPARATION TIME
25 minutes, plus
chilling
FREEZING
Not suitable
COLOUR INDEX
Page 21

- 275 g (10 oz) cream cheese, at room temperature
- 30 ml (2 tbsp) mayonnaise
- finely grated rind of 1 lime or lemon
- 225 g (8 oz) cooked peeled prawns (thawed and thoroughly dried if frozen)
- 15 ml (1 tbsp) powdered gelatine
- 30 ml (2 tbsp) lime or lemon juice
- 8 large thin slices smoked salmon
- 60–75 ml (4–5 tbsp) finely chopped dill
- pepper

TO GARNISH:
- lime or lemon twists
- dill sprigs

355 CALS/SERVING

1 Put the cream cheese in a bowl with the mayonnaise and lime or lemon rind and beat until evenly mixed. Chop the prawns finely.

2 Sprinkle the gelatine over 60 ml (4 tbsp) cold water in a small heatproof bowl. Leave for about 5 minutes until spongy, then stand the bowl in a saucepan of gently simmering water until the gelatine has dissolved. Remove and allow to cool for a few minutes.

3 Stir the dissolved gelatine into the cream cheese mixture until evenly blended, then stir in the lime or lemon juice. Cover the bowl and chill in the refrigerator for about 30 minutes, or until the mixture is just firm enough to hold its shape.

4 Divide the cream cheese mixture evenly between the salmon slices, and spread evenly, then scatter over the chopped dill. Sprinkle the chopped prawns over the dill and press down gently with your fingertips. Grind black pepper over the top.

5 Carefully roll up the salmon slices from a short end, then place seam side down on a plate. Cover with cling film and chill in the refrigerator for at least 2 hours, until firm.

6 To serve, cut each salmon roll on the diagonal into 8 neat slices, then arrange the slices, slightly overlapping, on individual plates. Garnish with lime or lemon twists and dill. Serve at room temperature, with crusty granary or wholewheat rolls.

❖ Prawn Cocktails ❖

SERVES 4

PREPARATION TIME
10 minutes
FREEZING
Not suitable

- 60 ml (4 tbsp) mayonnaise
- 60 ml (4 tbsp) single cream
- 10 ml (2 tsp) tomato purée
- 10 ml (2 tsp) lemon juice
- dash of Worcestershire sauce
- dash of dry sherry
- salt and pepper
- 225 g (8 oz) cooked peeled prawns
- few lettuce leaves, shredded
- lemon slices, to garnish

200 CALS/SERVING

1 In a small bowl, mix together the mayonnaise, cream, tomato purée, lemon juice, Worcestershire sauce and sherry. Season to taste. Add the prawns and stir well to coat.

2 Place the shredded lettuce in four glasses and top with the fish mixture.

3 Garnish each prawn cocktail with lemon slices. Serve with thinly sliced brown bread.

❖ Avocado with ❖ Raspberry Vinegar

SERVES 4
PREPARATION TIME
20 minutes, plus
chilling
FREEZING
Not suitable

- 125 g (4 oz) raspberries
- 75 ml (5 tbsp) white wine vinegar
- 90 ml (6 tbsp) sunflower oil
- 45 ml (3 tbsp) olive oil
- salt and pepper
- 2 firm, ripe avocados
- 1 small head radicchio

395 CALS/SERVING

1 Put half of the raspberries in a small bowl. Heat the vinegar until bubbling, then pour over the raspberries. Leave for at least 1 hour or overnight.

2 Turn the raspberries into a nylon sieve, pressing gently to extract all juices but not the pulp. Whisk in the oils and seasoning.

3 Halve, stone and peel each avocado. Slice the flesh and add to the dressing. Stir gently to coat in the dressing. Cover tightly and chill for 2 hours.

4 To serve, place a few radicchio leaves on each serving plate. Spoon on the avocado mixture and garnish with the remaining raspberries.

❖ Asparagus with ❖ Coriander Hollandaise

SERVES 4
PREPARATION TIME
25 minutes
COOKING TIME
10 minutes
FREEZING
Not suitable

- 450 g (1 lb) asparagus
- salt
- 15 ml (1 tbsp) lemon juice
  SAUCE:
- 125 g (4 oz) unsalted butter, diced
- 25 ml (1½ tbsp) coriander seeds, crushed and lightly toasted
- 25 ml (1½ tbsp) lemon juice
- 10 ml (2 tsp) white wine vinegar
- 2 egg yolks
- pinch of sugar
- pinch of salt
  TO GARNISH:
- blanched lemon rind strips
- chervil sprigs

295 CALS/SERVING

1 To make the sauce, melt the butter, add the coriander seeds and warm gently until the butter just begins to bubble. Remove from the heat, cover and leave to infuse for 20 minutes.
2 Meanwhile scrape the asparagus stalks and remove the woody ends. Tie the asparagus in two equal bundles. Stand them in a saucepan of boiling salted water, to which the lemon juice has been added, so that they stand upright; the tips should be out of the water.
3 Cover with a lid or dome of foil and cook gently for about 10 minutes or until tender, depending on the size of the spears.
4 For the sauce, put the lemon juice and vinegar in a saucepan and bring to the boil. Gently reheat the coriander butter until just beginning to foam.
5 Put the egg yolks, sugar and salt in a blender and blend briefly, then, with the motor running, slowly pour in the lemon juice and vinegar mixture. When it has all been absorbed, slowly pour in the coriander butter, with the motor still running.
6 Drain the asparagus well and arrange on warmed serving plates. Spoon the coriander hollandaise over the asparagus. Garnish with strips of lemon rind and sprigs of chervil.

❖ Baked Tomatoes ❖ with Cheese and Basil

SERVES 6

PREPARATION TIME
20 minutes
COOKING TIME
20–25 minutes
FREEZING
Not suitable
COLOUR INDEX
Page 22

- 6 large tomatoes
- 125 g (4 oz) mozzarella cheese
- 30 ml (2 tbsp) finely chopped basil
- 175 g (6 oz) rindless soft goat's cheese
- salt and pepper

- 6 thick slices of bread
TO SERVE:
- salad leaves
- Vinaigrette Dressing (page 273)

380 CALS/SERVING

1 Cut a thin slice from the bottom of each tomato and discard. Using a small, sharp knife or a teaspoon, carefully scoop out the seeds and most of the flesh, keeping the tomato shells whole. Strain the scooped-out tomato pulp and reserve the juices.

2 Coarsely grate or finely chop the mozzarella cheese and mix with the basil, goat's cheese and enough reserved tomato juice to form a thick, creamy mixture. Season, then spoon into the tomato shells.

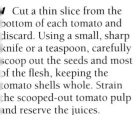

3 Using a plain, round 9 cm (3½ inch) pastry cutter, stamp out six rounds from the bread slices. Toast the rounds on both sides, then place in a single layer in a lightly oiled ovenproof dish.

4 Place a tomato on top of each toasted bread round. Cook the tomatoes, uncovered, in the oven at 180°C (350°F) mark 4 for 20–25 minutes or until the cheese mixture looks melted and golden and the tomatoes are lightly cooked but not too soft. Serve with salad leaves and vinaigrette.

NOTE: If preferred, use any soft creamy cheese instead of the goat's cheese.

❖ Deep-fried Potato Skins ❖

SERVES 2–3

PREPARATION TIME
15 minutes
COOKING TIME
1 hour
FREEZING
Not suitable

- 8 potatoes, each about 125 g (4 oz)
- 30 ml (2 tbsp) oil
- salt and pepper
- 350 g (12 oz) juicy ripe tomatoes
- 2 spring onions
- 15 ml (1 tbsp) chilli sauce
- 150 ml (¼ pint) soured cream

- 30 ml (2 tbsp) chopped chives
- oil for deep-frying
TO GARNISH:
- spring onions
- coriander sprigs

720–480 CALS/SERVING

1 Scrub the potatoes clean and dry them with absorbent kitchen paper. Thread the potatoes on skewers, then brush them with the oil and sprinkle with salt. Place directly on the oven shelf and bake at 200°C (400°F) mark 6 for 45–55 minutes or until the potatoes feel soft when squeezed.

2 Meanwhile, make the dips: finely chop the tomatoes and spring onions and mix with the chilli sauce; season with salt and pepper. In a separate bowl, mix the soured cream with the chives and season with salt and pepper. Cover the dips and chill in the refrigerator.

3 When the potatoes are tender, remove them from the oven and cut them in half lengthways. Scoop out the flesh, leaving a layer of potato about 1 cm (½ inch) thick on the skin. Cut each skin in half lengthways.

4 Heat the oil in a deep-fat fryer to 190°C (375°F). Deep-fry the potato skins, a few at a time, for 30–60 seconds or until crisp. Remove with a slotted spoon and drain upside-down on absorbent kitchen paper.

5 As soon as all the potato skins are fried, sprinkle them with a little salt and serve immediately. Place the bowls of dip in the centre of a large platter and arrange the potato skins around them. Garnish with spring onions and coriander.

NOTE: Serve a few vegetable crudités as well, if liked, to scoop up any excess dip.

❖ Warm Salad of Mushrooms ❖

SERVES 6–8
PREPARATION TIME
15 minutes
COOKING TIME
10–12 minutes
FREEZING
Not suitable
COLOUR INDEX
Page 22

- selection of mixed salad leaves
- 175 g (6 oz) young spinach leaves
- 175 g (6 oz) smoked streaky bacon
- 700 g (1½ lb) mushrooms (see note)

- 90 ml (6 tbsp) olive oil
- 1 garlic clove, crushed (optional)
- salt and pepper
- 25 ml (1½ tbsp) tarragon vinegar

280–210 CALS/SERVING

1 Arrange the salad leaves and spinach on individual plates. Remove the rind from the bacon, then cut the bacon into thin strips. Cut the mushrooms into thick slices.

2 Heat a heavy-based frying pan and fry the bacon until the fat runs. Increase the heat and fry for 2–3 minutes until crisp. Add the oil and mushrooms and cook over a high heat for 3–4 minutes until the mushrooms are just tender. Add the garlic, if using, and pepper, and cook for a minute longer.

3 Using a slotted spoon, remove the mushrooms from the pan and scatter over the salad leaves. Quickly add the vinegar to the juices remaining in the pan and boil rapidly for 2 minutes. Season with salt and pepper. Pour the warm dressing over the salads and serve immediately.

NOTE: If possible, use a mixture of wild mushrooms for this salad. Otherwise a mixture of cultivated oyster, shiitake and cup mushrooms works well.

❖ Filo Purses with Stir-fried Vegetables ❖

SERVES 6
PREPARATION TIME
20 minutes
COOKING TIME
25 minutes
FREEZING
Not suitable
COLOUR INDEX
Page 22

- 2 celery sticks
- 1 large carrot, peeled
- 4 spring onions
- 75 g (3 oz) butter or margarine
- 2.5 cm (1 inch) piece fresh root ginger, peeled and chopped
- 125 g (4 oz) bean sprouts

- juice of 1 small lemon
- salt and pepper
- 5 large sheets filo pastry, each about 45 × 30 cm (18 × 12 inches)

155 CALS/SERVING

1 Cut the celery, carrot and spring onions into thin shreds.

2 Heat 25 g (1 oz) of the butter in a large frying pan. Add the ginger, vegetables and bean sprouts, and stir-fry over a high heat for 3–4 minutes or until beginning to soften.

3 Add the lemon juice and continue to stir-fry briskly until the vegetables are tender and most of the moisture has evaporated. Season and leave to cool.

4 Melt the remaining butter. Cut the pastry sheets in four to make a total of 20 rectangles. Layer the pieces in six stacks of three, using up the two spare rectangles on any thin or split pastry stacks and brushing each layer with melted butter.

5 Divide the vegetable mixture between the six stacks and draw the pastry edges up around the filling, pinching the tops together to form little 'money bags'. Place the pastries on a greased baking sheet.

6 Brush the filo purses again with melted butter. Bake in the oven at 200°C (400°F) mark 6 for about 20 minutes or until well browned and crisp. If necessary, cover the pastries lightly with greaseproof paper to prevent over-browning towards the end. Serve warm.

❖ Salade Tiède ❖

SERVES 4
PREPARATION TIME
10 minutes
COOKING TIME
10 minutes
FREEZING
Not suitable
COLOUR INDEX
Page 22

- 1 small head frisée
- 135 ml (9 tbsp) olive oil
- 30 ml (2 tbsp) wine vinegar
- 2 garlic cloves, crushed
- 5 ml (1 tsp) French mustard
- salt and pepper

- 125 g (4 oz) thick-cut unsmoked streaky bacon
- 4 thick slices white bread, crusts removed
- 30 ml (2 tbsp) single cream

530 CALS/SERVING

1 Separate the salad leaves and put them in a salad bowl.

2 To make the dressing, put 90 ml (6 tbsp) of the oil in a bowl with the wine vinegar, garlic, mustard and salt and pepper to taste. Whisk with a fork until thick.

Remove the rind from the bacon and cut into strips. Cut the bread into small cubes. Heat the remaining oil in a frying pan, add the bacon and fry over brisk heat until crisp and browned. Remove with a slotted spoon and drain on absorbent kitchen paper. Fry the bread cubes in the fat remaining in the pan until crisp and golden on all sides.

Stir the cream into the dressing, then pour over the frisée. Add the warm bacon and croûtons, toss quickly to combine the ingredients and serve immediately.

❖ Baked Mushroom Croûtes ❖

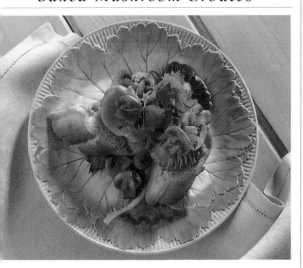

SERVES 6

PREPARATION TIME
0 minutes
COOKING TIME
hour
REEZING
ot suitable

- 225 g (8 oz) button mushrooms
- 225 g (8 oz) wild mushrooms, such as chanterelles, ceps, etc
- 75 g (3 oz) butter
- 30 ml (2 tbsp) chopped coriander
- 30 ml (2 tbsp) lemon juice

- 30 ml (2 tbsp) olive oil
- salt and pepper
- 1 baguette
- 1 garlic clove, halved
- 90 ml (6 tbsp) single cream (optional)
- coriander sprigs, to garnish

230 CALS/SERVING

Thinly slice the button mushrooms and any large wild ones. Place in an ovenproof dish and dot with half the butter. Sprinkle with the chopped coriander, lemon juice and olive oil. Season with salt and pepper.

Cover the dish with foil and bake at 200°C (400°F) mark 6 for about 40 minutes, stirring once, halfway through cooking.

Thickly slice the baguette. Rub the slices with the garlic clove. Thinly spread one side with the remaining butter. Place six slices, butter side uppermost, on an edged ovenproof dish. Place in the oven for 10 minutes. Wrap the remaining slices in foil.

Spoon the hot mushrooms and juices over the six bread slices. Drizzle over the single cream if wished. Place in the oven, uncovered, with the foil-wrapped bread, for 10 minutes.

Serve immediately, accompanied by the hot bread and garnished with coriander sprigs.

❖ Artichoke and Spinach Salad ❖

SERVES 6

PREPARATION TIME
15 minutes, plus marinating
COOKING TIME
15–20 minutes
FREEZING
Not suitable
COLOUR INDEX
Page 22

- 450 g (1 lb) Jerusalem artichokes
- salt and pepper
- 2 lemons

- 60 ml (4 tbsp) olive oil
- 1 garlic clove, crushed
- 175 g (6 oz) young spinach leaves

110 CALS/SERVING

1 Scrub the artichokes, then cut into 5 mm (¼ inch) slices. Place in a large saucepan of boiling salted water. Add the pared rind and juice from 1 lemon. Simmer for about 12–15 minutes or until the artichokes are just tender.

2 Meanwhile, make the dressing. In a medium bowl, whisk together the olive oil, garlic, juice from the remaining lemon and seasoning.

3 Drain the artichokes, then toss in the dressing. Cool, then cover and leave in the refrigerator for 2–3 hours.

4 Remove tough stalks from the spinach; tear into small pieces if necessary.

5 Spoon the artichokes into a grill pan with any remaining marinade. Grill on both sides for 3–4 minutes until browned.

6 Toss the grilled artichokes and any pan juices with the spinach. Adjust the seasoning and serve immediately.

129

SHELLFISH

Fresh, perfectly cooked shellfish is prized the world over for its delicate flavour and stunning appearance. There's nothing that quite compares with a plateful of juicy prawns; a bowl of steaming mussels; or a magnificent platter of fruits de mer. Shellfish can be divided into three types: crustaceans, molluscs and cephalopods. Crustaceans include the prized lobster, crabs, shrimps, prawns and freshwater crayfish. They have hard external skeletons which are segmented to allow for movement. Molluscs live inside one or two hard shells (valves). The bivalves include oysters, mussels, clams and scallops. Cephalopods, namely squid, octopus and cuttlefish, belong to the mollusc family but have no shells.

All shellfish is highly perishable, so freshness should be the main consideration. Get to know a good local fishmonger – look for a shop with a fast turnover and a clean, well presented display. Avoid anywhere that has lots of fish left at the end of the day.

Choosing Shellfish

Look for tightly closed, undamaged shells. Lobsters and crabs should feel heavy for their size. Fresh shellfish has a clean, unnoticeable smell – don't buy if it has a strong smell of any kind. Prawns develop a strong chlorine-like smell if past their best.

When buying frozen shellfish, choose firm, thoroughly frozen and undamaged packets. Buy more than the recipe calls for to allow for weight loss after thawing. Cook quickly once thawed.

Refrigerate shellfish as soon as possible after purchase. It will deteriorate rapidly if stored in warm conditions. All shellfish really should be eaten on the day of purchase, particularly oysters, mussels and prawns, but if this is impractical, it can be stored in the refrigerator for up to 1 day. Frozen shellfish will deteriorate and lose its flavour after 2–3 months.

❖ Lobster ❖

There is much controversy surrounding the cooking of live lobsters. The RSPCA recommends putting them in a freezer for 2 hours, to render them unconscious before cooking. But for many cooks there is still something inhumane about this. If you have the choice it is preferable to get your fishmonger to cook the lobster for you. If you haven't, here is our method:

Weigh the lobster. Take a large saucepan with a tightly fitting lid; fill with water and flavourings such as onion, carrot, celery, bouquet garni and peppercorns. Bring the water to a rapid boil then holding the lobster by its back lower it in. Cover, reduce the heat and boil gently for 10 minutes for the first 450 g (1 lb) and 5 minutes for each additional 450 g (1 lb). Leave to cool in the liquid.

Some classic lobster dishes call for raw, cut-up pieces of lobster. This is another job that's best left to your fishmonger.

To Prepare Cooked Lobster

1 Twist off the claws and pincers. Crack open the large claws using the back of a heavy knife, being careful not to crush the meat inside. Reserve the smaller claws to use as a garnish.

2 Put the lobster, back upwards, on a flat surface and using a sharp knife split the lobster cleanly in two, piercing through the 'cross' at the centre of the head.

3 Remove and discard the intestine which runs through the centre of the tail, the stomach (which lies near the head) and the spongy looking gills or 'dead man's fingers', which are inedible.

4 Using a teaspoon, scoop out the edible soft grey liver (tomalley) and red roe (if any). Carefully lift the tail meat from the shell, pulling it out neatly and in one piece if you can. Cut into thick slices (or as directed in the recipe).

5 Using a skewer, carefully remove the meat from each rear leg, in a whole piece.

❖ Crab ❖

There are numerous varieties of this crustacean which is particularly prized for its delicate white leg and claw meat. All crabs have a hard shell which is shed periodically to allow the crab to grow. Some species, caught when in this soft shell state, are cooked and eaten whole – claws and all.

Like lobsters the cooking of live crabs is controversial. The RSPCA recommends a humane method to de-sensitise crabs before cooking, but this is not for the squeamish. Therefore it's best to leave the cooking of crabs in the experienced hands of your fishmonger. Should you wish to cook a crab at home, here is our method:

Weigh the crab. Take a large saucepan with a tightly fitting lid; fill with water and flavouring ingredients such as bay leaves, onion, celery leaves and peppercorns. Bring to the boil. Lower the crab into the water. Reduce the heat, cover and boil gently for 15 minutes for the first 450 g (1 lb) and 5 minutes for each additional 450 g (1 lb). Leave to cool in the liquid.

To Prepare Cooked Crab

Extracting the meat from a cooked crab is a fiddly, time-consuming job – but it's well worth the effort. Aim to keep separate the brown body meat, which is mostly liver, the flaky white meat and the creamy body meat.

1 Twist off the legs and claws as close to the body as possible. Break each claw in half then crack with a rolling pin or hammer without crushing the flesh. Break the shell on the legs with your hands. Using a slender skewer to get at any awkward bits, carefully extract the flesh.

2 Put the crab on its back with the tail flap pointing towards you. Holding the shell firmly, press the body section upwards with your thumbs and it should come away. If it won't move, use the point of a rigid knife to ease it away.

3 With a teaspoon scoop out into separate bowls the creamy meat and roe (if any) from the shell. Remove and discard the stomach bag which you will find between the eyes. (If this breaks make sure you remove all the greenish or grey-white matter.)

4 Pull away from the body and discard the inedible feathery gills or 'dead man's fingers'. Using a large heavy knife, cut the body in half. Using a skewer, remove the flesh from the tiny crevices.

❖ Prawns and Shrimps ❖

Prawns and shrimps are possibly the most popular members of the crustacean family. Good fishmongers and supermarkets now stock a multitude of prawns from the ubiquitous common prawn to the jumbo Mediterranean prawn. Shrimps are tiny prawn-like creatures which are often peeled and mixed with melted butter to make potted shrimps. To make things confusing, what we call prawns are known as shrimps by the Americans. And Dublin Bay prawns are not prawns at all, but belong to the lobster family. To make matters even more confusing, their peeled tail meat is known as scampi!

Until recently, prawns were generally sold ready-cooked; now raw prawns are increasingly available – fresh and frozen. These tend to have more flavour and 'bite' than ready-cooked prawns, so they're well worth looking out for, particularly for barbecues and Chinese-style dishes. Prawns need gentle cooking, or they will be tough. Simmer pre-cooked prawns briefly until heated through; cook raw prawns for a couple of minutes until they look opaque.

To Peel Raw or Cooked Prawns

1 Grip head between thumb and forefinger. Gently pull until it comes off, holding tail shell with the other hand.

2 Peel off the body shell and the legs.

3 Large prawns have a bitter tasting intestinal vein running down their back. Remove this with a sharp knife and discard before cooking.

❖ Scallops ❖

Scallops are best bought live in the shell. However, they are kept tightly closed by a strong muscle which makes them really difficult to prise out – especially if you aren't practised at it. It's advisable to get your fishmonger to open them because it can be very frustrating! Don't forget to ask for the shells for serving.

Large scallops are usually sliced for cooking, while smaller ones are left whole. Like prawns they need only brief cooking or they will be tough. The really delicate orange coral takes a matter of seconds to cook so this is usually separated and added last.

To Prepare Scallops in the Shell

To open them yourself, follow the method below, but if they still refuse to open, heat them in a low oven for about 10 minutes. Don't leave them in the oven for too long or the delicate flesh will be overcooked.

1 Scrub the shells under cold running water to remove as much sand as possible. Give any that are open a sharp tap with the back of a knife. Discard any that do not close.

2 Put a scallop flat side up on a board or hold it level in the palm of your hand. Insert the point of a strong knife (with a blade that's about 10 cm (4 inches) long) between the shells at about 45° to the hinge. It probably won't go straight in but be patient and continue pushing and twisting until it does.

3 When the shells have opened slightly, slide your finger in between the shells (it's a good idea to wear a sturdy glove for this) then with the knife in your other hand quickly cut round the top shell to detach the muscle and allow the shells to be parted.

4 Push the top shell backwards until the hinge at the back snaps. Rinse the scallop (still attached to the lower shell) under cold running water to remove any sand.

5 Using a small knife and being careful not to tear the flesh, cut away all the grey coloured beard-like fringe.

6 Slide the point of a knife under the black thread on the side of the scallop. Gently pull it off with the attached intestinal bag. Ease the scallop away from the bottom shell.

❖ Mussels ❖

Mussels are usually sold live in the shell although they are also available ready-cooked and frozen in 450 g (1 lb) bags (which is roughly equivalent to 900 g (2 lb) mussels in the shell). They are at their best in the cold winter months although farmed or imported species often make their way into the shops at other times throughout the year.

The process of cleaning and preparing mussels puts a lot of people off, but it's very straightforward. Once the mussels are prepared they take only minutes to cook.

To Prepare Mussels in the Shell

1 Put the mussels in the sink and under cold running water scrape off any mud or barnacles with a small sharp knife. Pull away the hair-like beard that protrudes from the shell.

2 Tap any mussels that remain open with the back of the knife. If they refuse to close, throw them away. Rinse again in cold water until there is no trace of sand.

❖ Oysters ❖

The delicately flavoured oyster is praised the world over. To be appreciated fully they are best eaten raw from the half shell seasoned simply with lemon juice or black pepper, so freshness is of upmost importance. Choose oysters with tightly closed shells and refrigerate quickly after purchase, covered with a damp cloth. Always eat oysters on the day that you buy them.

To Open Oysters

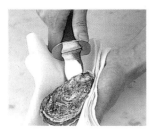 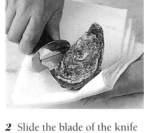

1 Put the oyster, wrapped in a clean tea towel, on a firm surface with the flattest shell uppermost and the hinge pointing towards you. Gripping the oyster firmly, insert an oyster knife into the small gap in the hinge and twist to snap the shells apart.

2 Slide the blade of the knife along the inside of the upper shell to sever the muscle that keeps the shells together.

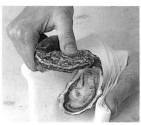 

3 Lift off the top shell, being careful not to spill any juice. Clean away any bits of broken shell from the lower shell.

4 Run the blade of the knife under the oyster to loosen it from the shell.

❖ Squid ❖

In this country squid enjoys an undeserved reputation for being tough and rubbery. This is invariably due to bad cooking; squid should be cooked very quickly or very slowly to make it tender. Cooked properly, it is delicious and amazingly versatile. Try it deep-fried, stuffed and baked, or stewed in its own ink.

Squid is not difficult to prepare, but you may find the procedure slightly unpleasant. Look out for ready prepared squid in the fishmongers or follow these instructions. It's best to do the whole operation in the sink under cold running water.

To Prepare Squid

1 Holding the body firmly in one hand, grip the head and tentacles with the other hand, pull gently and they will come away along with the contents of the body.

2 Cut off the tentacles, just in front of the eyes. Remove the ink sac from the head if required for the recipe, otherwise throw the head and body contents away. Remove and discard the squid's beak which can be found where the tentacles are joined.

3 Peel off the thin layer of skin that covers the body and discard.

4 Pull out the plastic-like quill, then turn the body inside out and wash thoroughly.

❖ Dressed Crab ❖

SERVES 2-3
PREPARATION TIME
30 minutes
FREEZING
Not suitable

- 1 cooked crab, about 900 g (2 lb), cleaned
- salt and pepper
- 15 ml (1 tbsp) lemon juice
- 30 ml (2 tbsp) fresh white breadcrumbs
- 1 egg, hard-boiled
- 15 ml (1 tbsp) chopped parsley
- frisée, to serve

195-130 CALS/SERVING

1 Using two forks, flake all the white meat from the crab. Season and add about 5 ml (1 tsp) lemon juice.

2 Pound the brown meat in a bowl and work in the bread-crumbs with the remaining lemon juice and seasoning.

3 Using a small spoon, put the white meat in both ends of the cleaned crab shell, making sure that it is well piled up in the shell. Spoon the brown meat in a neat line down the centre between the two sections of white crab meat.

4 Chop the egg white; sieve the yolk. Hold a blunt knife between the white and brown crab meat and carefully spoon lines of parsley, sieved yolk and chopped egg white across the crab, moving the knife as you go. Serve on a bed of frisée.

❖ Avocado with Crab ❖

SERVES 4
PREPARATION TIME
15 minutes
COOKING TIME
5 minutes
FREEZING
Not suitable
COLOUR INDEX
Page 23

- 1 small onion, peeled
- 30 ml (2 tbsp) oil
- 10 ml (2 tsp) garam masala
- 150 ml (¼ pint) mayonnaise (page 273)
- 10 ml (2 tsp) tomato purée
- finely grated rind and juice of ½ lemon
- salt and pepper
- 225 g (8 oz) white crab meat, flaked
- 2 ripe avocados
- lemon twists and paprika, to garnish

500 CALS/SERVING

1 Chop the onion very finely. Heat the oil in a small saucepan, add the onion and garam masala and fry gently, stirring, for 5 minutes until the onion is soft. Turn into a bowl and cool.
2 Add the mayonnaise to the cold onion with the tomato purée, lemon rind and juice, salt and pepper. Fold in the crab meat.
3 Halve the avocados lengthways and remove stones. Place an avocado half on each serving plate. Spoon in the filling. Garnish with lemon twists and a sprinkling of paprika. Serve, as a starter or lunch.

❖ Grilled Lobster with ❖ Beurre Blanc

SERVES 4
PREPARATION TIME
20 minutes
COOKING TIME
12 minutes
FREEZING
Not suitable

- 4 lobsters, about 450–550 g (1–1¼ lb) each
- about 3 litres (5 pints) court bouillon (page 91) (optional)
- salt and pepper
- 50 g (2 oz) butter, melted
- lemon slices and parsley sprigs, to garnish
- Beurre Blanc (page 94), to serve

305 CALS/SERVING

1 Simmer the lobsters in court bouillon or salted water until three-quarters cooked (see page 131); drain.
2 Split each lobster in half lengthways and remove the inedible parts (see page 131).
3 Sprinkle the flesh with salt and pepper to taste and brush with melted butter. Cook under a medium grill for about 5 minutes.
4 Transfer to a warmed platter. Add the claws and garnish with lemon slices and parsley. Serve the Beurre Blanc separately.

❖ Chilli Prawns with Cashews ❖

SERVES 2–3

PREPARATION TIME
20 minutes, plus
marinating
COOKING TIME
1–2 minutes
FREEZING
Not suitable

- 450 g (1 lb) large
cooked prawns in shells
(about 24)
- 1 bunch spring onions
- 1 garlic clove, crushed
- 45 ml (3 tbsp) soy
sauce
- 45 ml (3 tbsp) dry
sherry

- pepper
- 2 dried red chillies
- 40 g (1½ oz) salted
cashew nuts
- 30 ml (2 tbsp) oil
- coriander leaves, to
garnish

405–270 CALS/SERVING

1 Peel the prawns and discard
the heads. Split down the back
of each prawn to open slightly
and remove the black
intestinal vein. Slice the spring
onions into short lengths.

2 In a bowl, mix together the
garlic, soy sauce, sherry,
pepper and 45 ml (3 tbsp)
water. Gently stir in the
chillies, prawns, spring onions
and nuts. Cover tightly and
leave to marinate in the
refrigerator for several hours,
turning occasionally.

3 Drain, reserving marinade.
Heat the oil in a large wok or
frying pan. Add the prawn
mixture and stir-fry over a
high heat for 1–2 minutes.
Pour in any remaining
marinade, bubble up and
adjust seasoning. Serve at
once, garnished with coriander
and accompanied by rice.

❖ Prawns Fried in Garlic ❖

SERVES 2

PREPARATION TIME
5 minutes
COOKING TIME
5 minutes
FREEZING
Not suitable

- 50 g (2 oz) butter
- 30 ml (2 tbsp) olive oil
- 12 raw Dublin Bay
prawns in shells
- 3 garlic cloves, crushed
- 60 ml (4 tbsp) brandy

- salt and pepper
- lemon wedges, to
garnish

460 CALS/SERVING

1 Melt the butter with the oil in a large heavy-based pan. Add
the prawns and garlic and fry over a high heat for 5 minutes,
tossing the prawns constantly.
2 Sprinkle the brandy over the prawns with salt and pepper to
taste. Serve immediately, garnished with lemon wedges.

❖ Prawns with Rice and Fennel ❖

SERVES 4

PREPARATION TIME
20 minutes
COOKING TIME
40 minutes
FREEZING
Not suitable
COLOUR INDEX
Page 23

- 175 g (6 oz) long-grain
brown rice
- salt and pepper
- 450 g (1 lb) raw
prawns in shells
- 1 large bulb fennel
- 2 large courgettes
- 30 ml (2 tbsp) oil

- 150 ml (¼ pint) fish or
vegetable stock
- 25 g (1 oz) butter
- 30 ml (2 tbsp) chopped
dill
- 1 garlic-clove, crushed

410 CALS/SERVING

1 Cook the rice in boiling salted water for about 30 minutes or
until tender. Rinse with boiling water and drain well.
2 Meanwhile, peel the prawns, discarding the heads, then cut
down their backs and remove the black intestinal vein. Wash well
and dry on kitchen paper. Halve, or divide into three if large.
3 Thinly slice the fennel. Cut the courgettes into dice.
4 Heat 15 ml (1 tbsp) of the oil in a large frying pan. Add the
prawns and stir-fry quickly until they turn pink; remove.
5 Heat the remaining oil in the pan. Add the fennel and stir-fry
for 2–3 minutes until slightly softened. Mix in the courgettes
and stir-fry briefly. Stir in the rice and seasoning; heat through.
6 Return the prawns to the pan with the stock and bring to the
boil. Cover and cook gently for 3–4 minutes or until the prawns
are cooked and just firm. Stir in the butter, dill and garlic. Adjust
the seasoning and serve immediately.

✤ Scallops in Creamy Basil Sauce ✤

SERVES 4

PREPARATION TIME
10 minutes
COOKING TIME
10 minutes
FREEZING
Not suitable
COLOUR INDEX
Page 23

- 900 g (2 lb) shelled scallops
- 1 small onion
- 30 ml (2 tbsp) oil
- 15 g (½ oz) butter
- 2 garlic cloves, crushed
- 150 ml (¼ pint) dry white wine

- 20 ml (4 tsp) chopped basil
- salt and pepper
- 150 ml (¼ pint) double cream
- basil sprigs, to garnish

535 CALS/SERVING

1 Cut the scallops, including the coral, into fairly thick slices. Finely chop the onion. Heat the oil and butter in a large frying pan, add the onion and garlic, and fry gently for 5 minutes or until soft and lightly coloured.

2 Add the scallops to the pan and toss to coat in the oil and butter. Stir in the wine and basil and season to taste. Cook over a moderate heat for 2–3 minutes or until the scallops are tender, turning them constantly so that they cook evenly on all sides. Do not overcook or they will become tough and rubbery.

3 Remove the scallops from the liquid with a slotted spoon and set aside on a plate. Boil the liquid until reduced by about half, then stir in the cream, a little at a time, and simmer until the sauce is thick.

4 Return the scallops to the pan and heat gently. Taste and adjust the seasoning and serve garnished with basil.

✤ Scallops with Ginger ✤

SERVES 3

PREPARATION TIME
5 minutes
COOKING TIME
5 minutes
FREEZING
Not suitable

- 450 g (1 lb) shelled large scallops
- 4 celery sticks
- 1 bunch spring onions
- 25 g (1 oz) piece fresh root ginger
- 2 large garlic cloves
- 30 ml (2 tbsp) oil
- 1.25 ml (¼ tsp) chilli powder

- 30 ml (2 tbsp) lemon juice
- 30 ml (2 tbsp) soy sauce
- 45 ml (3 tbsp) chopped coriander
- salt and pepper

280 CALS/SERVING

1 Cut the scallops into 5 mm (¼ inch) slices. Slice the celery and onions diagonally. Peel and slice the ginger and garlic.

2 Heat the oil in a large wok or frying pan. Add the prepared ingredients with the chilli powder and stir-fry over a high heat for 2 minutes or until just tender.

3 Pour in the lemon juice and soy sauce, allow to bubble up, then stir in about 30 ml (2 tbsp) chopped coriander and seasoning. Serve immediately, topped with more coriander.

✤ Scallops au Gratin ✤

SERVES 4

PREPARATION TIME
20 minutes
COOKING TIME
10 minutes
FREEZING
Not suitable
COLOUR INDEX
Page 23

- 8 large scallops
- 300 ml (½ pint) Mornay Sauce (page 92)
- 60 ml (4 tbsp) dry white wine
- salt and pepper
- 125 g (4 oz) mushrooms, sliced

- 175 g (6 oz) fresh white breadcrumbs
- 125 g (4 oz) butter, melted
- juice of ½ lemon
- lemon slices, to garnish

515 CALS/SERVING

1 Open each scallop by inserting a knife between the shells and severing the muscle. Pull shells apart.

2 Slide the knife under the grey outer rim of flesh to free the scallop. Take out the white meat and coral.

3 Scrub the rounded shells and sterilize in boiling water; dry.

4 Coat the base of each shell with sauce; sprinkle with wine. Lay scallop in the shell.

5 Season with salt and pepper. Surround with mushrooms and cover with the remaining sauce. Sprinkle with the breadcrumbs and butter. Bake at 200°C (400°F) mark 6 for about 10 minutes. Sprinkle with a little lemón juice. Garnish with lemon slices to serve.

❖ Mussels and ❖ Clams with Tomatoes

SERVES 2–3

PREPARATION TIME
10 minutes
COOKING TIME
10 minutes
FREEZING
Not suitable
COLOUR INDEX
Page 24

- 1 small onion, peeled
- 225 g (8 oz) ripe tomatoes
- 25 g (1 oz) butter
- 1–2 large garlic cloves, crushed
- 150 ml (¼ pint) dry white wine
- finely grated rind of 1 lemon
- 30 ml (2 tbsp) chopped parsley
- 1 kg (2¼ lb) mussels, cleaned
- 450 g (1 lb) small clams, cleaned
- pepper

560–375 CALS/SERVING

1 Finely chop the onion. Chop the tomatoes roughly. Melt the butter in a saucepan and cook the garlic and onion until soft. Add the wine, tomatoes, lemon rind and half the parsley. Bring to the boil.
2 Add the mussels and clams to the pan, cover and cook over a high heat for about 5 minutes or until the mussels and clams are open, shaking the pan frequently. Discard any mussels or clams which have not opened.
3 Season with pepper to taste. Transfer to large bowls or soup plates and sprinkle with the remaining parsley. Serve at once.

NOTE: Venus clams are ideal for this recipe. If you cannot obtain fresh clams, use extra mussels instead.

❖ Mussels with ❖ Garlic and Parsley

SERVES 4–6

PREPARATION TIME
20 minutes
COOKING TIME
15 minutes
FREEZING
Not suitable

- 1.1–1.4 kg (2½–3 lb) mussels, cleaned
- 150 ml (10 tbsp) fresh white breadcrumbs
- 150 ml (10 tbsp) chopped parsley
- 2 garlic cloves, finely chopped
- pepper
- 100 ml (3½ fl oz) olive oil
- 30 ml (2 tbsp) freshly grated Parmesan cheese
- lemon wedges, to serve

435–290 CALS/SERVING

1 Place the mussels in a large saucepan containing 1 cm (½ inch) boiling water. Cover and cook over a high heat for about 5 minutes until the mussels are open, shaking the pan frequently. Discard any mussels that do not open.

2 Discarding the empty half-shell from each mussel. Strain the cooking liquid through a sieve lined with absorbent kitchen paper and reserve. Place the mussels in their half-shells on two baking sheets.

3 Mix together the breadcrumbs, parsley, garlic and plenty of pepper. Add the oil and 60 ml (4 tbsp) of the strained cooking liquid. Mix well, then adjust the seasoning.

4 With your fingers, pick up a good pinch of the breadcrumb mixture and press it down on each mussel, covering it well and filling the shell. Sprinkle with the Parmesan and bake at 230°C (450°F) mark 8 for 10 minutes, swapping the baking sheets over halfway through cooking. Serve with lemon wedges and French bread.

❖ Monkfish and Mussel Skewers ❖

SERVES 4

PREPARATION TIME
20 minutes
COOKING TIME
10 minutes
FREEZING
Not suitable
COLOUR INDEX
Page 24

- 12 streaky bacon rashers
- 700 g (1½ lb) monkfish fillet, skinned
- 24 shelled mussels
- 25 g (1 oz) butter or margarine
- 60 ml (4 tbsp) chopped parsley
- finely grated rind and juice of 1 large lemon
- 4 garlic cloves, crushed
- pepper
- shredded lettuce, to serve
- lemon slices, to garnish

415 CALS/SERVING

1 Halve the bacon rashers and roll up neatly. Cut the monkfish into 2.5 cm (1 inch) cubes. Thread the cubed fish, mussels and bacon alternately on to 12 oiled skewers.

Melt the butter in a saucepan, remove from the heat, then add the parsley, lemon rind and juice, and garlic. Season with pepper; the mussels and bacon should provide sufficient salt.

Place the skewers on an oiled grill rack and brush with the parsley mixture. Cook under a medium grill for 10 minutes, turning frequently during cooking and brushing with the parsley mixture with each turn.

Arrange the hot skewers on a serving platter lined with shredded lettuce. Garnish with lemon slices and serve immediately.

❖ Mussels in White Wine ❖

SERVES 4–6
PREPARATION TIME
5 minutes
COOKING TIME
minutes
FREEZING
Not suitable

- *1 shallot, peeled*
- *25 g (1 oz) celery*
- *100 ml (4 fl oz) dry white wine*
- *1.4 kg (3 lb) mussels, cleaned*
- *15 ml (1 tbsp) chopped parsley*
- *100 ml (3½ fl oz) double cream*
- *pepper*

225–150 CALS/SERVING

Finely chop the shallot and celery. Put into a saucepan with the wine and bring to the boil. Add the mussels and cover the pan with a close-fitting lid. Cook over a high heat for about minutes, shaking the pan frequently, until the mussel shells are open.

Remove from the heat and discard any mussels which have not opened. Discard the one loose shell from each mussel. Put the mussels on their half-shell into a warmed dish or individual cocottes. Keep warm.

Strain the cooking liquid through a sieve lined with absorbent kitchen paper. Return to the pan and add the parsley, cream and pepper to taste. Bring just to boiling point, then pour over the mussels.

Serve immediately, as a starter or light meal accompanied by warm crusty bread.

❖ Oysters au Gratin ❖

SERVES 4–6
PREPARATION TIME
20 minutes
COOKING TIME
10 minutes
FREEZING
Not suitable

- *50 g (2 oz) streaky bacon*
- *75 g (3 oz) celery*
- *200 g (7 oz) can artichoke hearts, drained*
- *12 large oysters*
- *200 g (7 oz) mozzarella cheese, thinly sliced*

220–150 CALS/SERVING

1 Finely chop the bacon, celery and artichokes. In a small pan, fry the bacon until the fat begins to run. Add the celery and artichokes; cook, stirring, for 2 minutes. Cool.

2 Scrub the oyster shells well. Open the oysters by inserting an oyster knife into the hinge linking the shells and cutting through the muscle. Prise shells apart; discard flatter ones.

3 Spoon a little of the bacon and artichoke mixture over each oyster.

4 Top with cheese. Cook under a medium grill for 10 minutes. Serve as a starter or light meal.

❖ *Seafood Pilaki* ❖

SERVES 8

PREPARATION TIME
15 minutes
COOKING TIME
40 minutes
FREEZING
Not suitable
COLOUR INDEX
Page 24

- *1 large onion, peeled*
- *2 celery sticks*
- *3 large carrots, peeled*
- *30 ml (2 tbsp) olive oil*
- *2 garlic cloves, crushed*
- *finely grated rind and juice of 1 lemon*
- *400 g (14 oz) can chopped tomatoes*
- *700 g (1½ lb) monkfish fillet, skinned*
- *450 g (1 lb) cleaned squid*
- *900 g (2 lb) mussels, cleaned*
- *30–45 ml (2–3 tbsp) chopped parsley*
- *salt and pepper*
- *chopped celery leaves, to garnish*

190 CALS/SERVING

1 Chop the onion and celery; slice the carrots. Heat the oil in a large heavy-based pan. Add the garlic, onion, celery, carrots and lemon rind and cook for about 5 minutes, stirring all the time.
2 Add the lemon juice and the tomatoes with their juice. Cover and cook over a low heat for 25 minutes or until the vegetables are very tender; stir occasionally and add a little water if needed.
3 Cut the monkfish into chunks. Slice the squid into rings. Add the monkfish to the pan with a little water. Cover and cook for 3–5 minutes, then add the squid.
4 Arrange the mussels on the top, cover and cook for about 5 minutes or until the fish is just tender, stirring occasionally. Discard any unopened mussels. Stir in parsley and seasoning to taste. Serve hot or cold, garnished with celery leaves.

❖ *Glazed Seafood Platter* ❖

SERVES 6

PREPARATION TIME
20 minutes
COOKING TIME
15 minutes
FREEZING
Not suitable

- *225 g (8 oz) haddock fillet, skinned*
- *450 g (1 lb) halibut fillet, skinned*
- *75 g (3 oz) fennel*
- *300 ml (½ pint) dry white wine*
- *150 ml (¼ pint) fish stock*
- *1 bay leaf*
- *225 g (8 oz) queen scallops, shelled*
- *125 g (4 oz) cooked shelled mussels*
- *125 g (4 oz) cooked peeled prawns*
- *40 g (1½ oz) butter*
- *40 g (1½ oz) plain flour*
- *1 egg yolk*
- *150 ml (¼ pint) double cream*
- *salt and pepper*
- *50 g (2 oz) Emmenthal cheese, coarsely grated*

440 CALS/SERVING

1 Cut the haddock and halibut fillets into bite-sized pieces. Remove the feathery tops from the fennel, finely chop and reserve. Cut the fennel into wafer-thin slices.

2 Place the fish and fennel in a sauté pan or frying pan and pour on the wine and stock. Add the bay leaf. Bring to the boil, cover and simmer for 7–8 minutes or until the fish i just cooked.

3 With a slotted spoon, remove the fish and fennel from the cooking liquor and arrange in a single layer in a large gratin dish.

4 Add the scallops and mussels to the liquid, return to the boil and immediately remove with a slotted spoon. Scatter over the fish with the prawns. Cover the platter with foil and keep warm in the over at 170°C (325°F) mark 3.

5 Melt the butter in a saucepan. Stir in the flour and cook, stirring, for 1–2 minutes. Strain in the cooking liquor, bring to the boil, stirring all the time, then simmer for 2–3 minutes until thickened. Beat in the egg yolk, cream and seasoning.

6 Spoon the sauce evenly ove the seafood and sprinkle with the cheese. Place the platter under a hot grill until golden brown. Serve immediately, garnished with the reserved fennel tops.

❖ Mixed Seafood Brochettes ❖

SERVES 4

PREPARATION TIME
15 minutes, plus
marinating
COOKING TIME
10 minutes
FREEZING
Not suitable

- 100 ml (4 fl oz) olive oil
- pared rind of ½ lemon
- 1 thyme sprig
- 1 bay leaf
- 6 parsley stalks
- salt and pepper

- 125 g (4 oz) each turbot and salmon steak
- 450 g (1 lb) shelled scallops
- 125 g (4 oz) shelled scampi

490 CALS/SERVING

1 For the marinade, mix the olive oil with the lemon rind, herbs and seasoning. Cut the turbot and salmon into pieces equal in size to the scallops.

2 Skewer the fish alternately on four metal skewers and place in a shallow dish. Pour over the marinade and leave for 2 hours, turning frequently.

3 Remove the brochettes from the marinade and drain, reserving marinade.

4 Grill for 10 minutes, turning and basting with the marinade frequently. Serve on a bed of rice, with lemon wedges.

❖ Italian Seafood Salad ❖

SERVES 6

PREPARATION TIME
20 minutes, plus
chilling
COOKING TIME
about 12 minutes
FREEZING
Not suitable

- 600 g (1¼ lb) mussels, cleaned
- 1 onion, peeled and chopped
- 1 bay leaf
- salt and pepper
- 350 g (12 oz) cleaned squid
- 1 small green pepper
- 1 small red pepper
- 1 carrot, peeled
- 350 g (12 oz) shelled scallops

- 350 g (12 oz) cooked peeled prawns
- 150 ml (¼ pint) olive oil
- 60 ml (4 tbsp) lemon juice
- 30 ml (2 tbsp) capers
- 45 ml (3 tbsp) chopped parsley
- 1 garlic clove, crushed
- black olives, to garnish

430 CALS/SERVING

1 Put the mussels in a large saucepan containing a 1 cm (½ inch) depth of water. Bring to the boil, cover and cook over a high heat for about 5 minutes until the shells are open, shaking the pan frequently. Remove the mussels from the pan with a slotted spoon; discard any that remain closed.

2 Add 1.75 litres (3 pints) water to the reserved cooking liquid. Add the onion, bay leaf and a pinch of salt and bring to the boil. Add the squid and simmer gently for 5 minutes or until tender.

3 Meanwhile halve, core and deseed the peppers, then cut into fine strips. Pare the carrot into fine ribbons, using a potato peeler.

4 Remove the squid from the cooking liquid and set aside. Bring the liquid back to the boil, add the scallops and poach gently for 2–3 minutes, then remove with a slotted spoon and set aside.

5 Using a sharp knife, cut the squid into 1 cm (½ inch) thick rings. Cut the scallops into four, removing the tough muscle near the coral.

6 Reserve a few mussels in their shells for garnish. Shell the remaining mussels and put in a large serving bowl with the squid, prawns and scallops. Add the peppers and carrot.

7 Mix together the oil, lemon juice, capers, parsley and garlic with pepper to taste. Pour over the seafood. Mix lightly but thoroughly. Taste and add salt if necessary.

8 Chill for at least 2 hours. Serve garnished with black olives and the reserved mussels in shells.

FISH

No wonder fish is regaining popularity. It is a rich source of protein, vitamins and minerals, and it's relatively low in calories too.

As more and more exotic species find their way to our shops, the choice of fresh fish has never been better. Most fishmongers are only too willing to clean and fillet fish and to act as cookery advisors too. They will suggest which fish to try as alternatives to your favourites and how to cook them to get the best results.

In general fish requires little cooking; its delicate flavour and texture is easily spoilt. Freezing doesn't do most cooked fish dishes any good either; sauces dry up and the fish itself becomes mushy, so we rarely recommend doing this. Frozen raw fish keeps well for 2–3 months after which it begins to lose its flavour. Ideally buy and cook fresh fish on the same day, but if this is impossible, remove it from the original wrappings, rinse and dry, then rewrap and store in the refrigerator for up to 1 day.

Choosing Fish

Really fresh fish is unmistakable. It will look bright and fresh with vivid markings, clean shiny scales, bright eyes and bright red gills. The flesh should be soft and spring back when pressed – ask your fishmonger for permission before you check this!

Fillets and steaks should look translucent rather than opaque. Avoid fillets and steaks if they look dry and shrivelled. If buying fish pre-packed from a supermarket, check the sell-by date. If buying frozen fish choose solidly frozen fillets in undamaged packets. With the exception of skate and shark, fresh fish does not smell 'fishy'.

❖ Preparing Fish ❖

Most fishmongers will willingly and expertly prepare fresh fish for you. There's no point in attempting to do this at home if you find the prospect daunting or unpleasant. However, it is quite simple providing you remember that for preparation purposes, fish is divided into two basic categories: flat fish such as plaice, sole, brill; and round fish such as mackerel, cod, bream, whiting.

All fish, with the exception of whitebait, must have their scales and insides removed before cooking. Scaling is definitely a job for the fishmonger. If there are a few scales still attached when you get the fish home, simply scrape them off using the blunt side of a large knife, working from tail to head.

Before gutting, remove the fins with kitchen scissors to make the fish look neater. If you're going to bone the fish, remove the dorsal fin completely by cutting down each side of the fin into the bony structure that connects the fin to the flesh. The fin can then be pulled away along with the underlying bones. Trim the tail and cut off the head behind the gills, if desired.

Gutting Fish

The easiest way to gut a fish is through the belly. If gutting a round fish, cut along the belly as far as you can and pull out the innards. Rinse thoroughly to remove all traces of blood. To gut a flat fish, make a small incision below the gills and pull the innards out.

If you wish to preserve the shape of the fish or keep it whole for stuffing, you will need to gut the fish through the gills. To do this, push your finger through the gills to open them out, then keeping the gills open with one hand, grip the innards with the other hand and pull them out in one piece. Reach into the body cavity to make sure that you have removed everything. Rinse thoroughly.

Skinning Fish

Once gutted, fish can be grilled, barbecued, baked, steamed or fried, but many recipes call for skinned fish fillets. If you're intending to cook whole flat fish, remove the dark skin only; the white skin will help keep the fish in one piece during cooking. Flat fish that are to be filleted should be skinned completely. Round fish and very large flat fish, such as turbot, are easier to skin after filleting or cooking.

To Skin Flat Fish

1 Lay the fish on a board, dark side uppermost and make an incision across the skin where the tail joins the body. Starting at the cut, use the point of the knife to lift a flap of skin until you can get a firm grip.

2 Salt your fingers. Grasping the flap of skin with your salted fingers (the salt should help you to grip) and holding down the tail in the other hand, pull the skin away. It should come away cleanly in one piece. Turn the fish over and remove the white skin in the same way, if desired.

✢ Boning and Filleting ✢

In order to fillet fish at home, you must have a proper sharp filleting knife with a long flexible blade which will glide over the bones as you cut. If your knife is blunt or too short you will inevitably end up leaving a lot of flesh attached to the bones. You will get four fillets from a flat fish, which should be skinned before filleting. Round fish yield two fillets and are skinned after filleting. Cook fillets as soon as they have been prepared, or wrap in cling film and store in the refrigerator until required, or they will dry out.

To Fillet Flat Fish

1 Lay the fish on a board with its tail pointing towards you and its eyes facing up. Cut down the centre of the fish from the head to the tail along the backbone.

2 Starting at the head end, insert the blade of the knife between the flesh and the bones. Aiming to skim the blade over the bones, cut down along the flesh. When the head end of the fillet is detached, lift it and continue cutting until the whole fillet is removed.

3 Repeat this procedure to remove the second fillet.

4 Turn the fish over and cut two more fillets from the other side. If there is any orange roe, save it for stock. When all the fillets are removed you should be left with a clean skeleton (which can also go in the stockpot) and four neat fillets.

To Fillet Round Fish

1 Lay the fish on its side with the tail pointing towards you. Cut along the backbone from the head to the tail, cutting right through to the backbone.

2 Cut through behind the gills to separate the fillet from the head. Starting at head end, insert knife between fillet and bones. Aiming to skim the knife over the bones, cut the fillet to detach completely.

3 Holding the fish by the exposed bones and with the tail still towards you, cut the remaining fillet from the ribs. Check fillets in case any bones are still attached; remove with tweezers or your fingers.

4 To skin fillets, lay skin side down with the tail end towards you. Make a cut at the tail end so the fillet can be lifted slightly from the skin. With salted fingers press on exposed skin to keep it on the board. Insert the knife at a slight angle beneath the fillet and cut away from you to separate the fillet.

Boning Whole Round Fish

Small round fish like herrings are often cooked whole because they are fiddly to fillet. Sometimes you may need to bone a large round fish if you are cooking it whole.

1 Scale and gut the fish in the usual way (see page 143). Cut off the head and tail or leave them on if preferred. Extend the cut along the belly (used for gutting) so that it goes right to the tail.

2 Open the fish out, then lay it on its side on a board. Carefully cut the rib bones free from the flesh on the upperside.

3 Turn the fish over and repeat on the other side, working through to the backbone, being careful not to cut through the flesh.

4 With a pair of kitchen scissors, cut through the backbone as close to the head as possible. Hold the backbone at the head end and carefully pull it free. Snip it at the tail end so that it can be removed completely.

5 Check the flesh for any remaining bones, removing any small bones with tweezers.

NOTE: If it is a small fish, simply open it out, then lay it on a board cut side down. Press firmly along the backbone with your fingers to loosen it. Turn the fish over and you should now be able to pull the backbone away with the ribs attached. Remove any fine bones that don't come away, using tweezers.

❖ Cooking Fish ❖

Because white fish is lacking in fat, it is easily dried out during cooking. If you're cooking fish by a 'dry' method such as grilling or barbecuing then it's important to baste frequently with butter, oil or a marinade. For moist methods of cooking like poaching it's vital to cook the fish gently; if the cooking liquid boils vigorously the fish will disintegrate during cooking.

Bear in mind that the subtle flavour is easily masked or overpowered by strong flavours, so choose accompanying sauces carefully. Similarly, choose a cooking method that's appropriate to the fish. Chunky steaks of firm or oily fish or sturdy whole fish can withstand fierce treatments which would ruin less robust fillets. Here are a few basic methods of cooking; refer to individual recipes for more detailed instructions.

Deep-frying

Coat the prepared fish with seasoned flour, batter or egg and breadcrumbs. Half fill a deep saucepan or deep-fat fryer with vegetable oil and heat to 190°C (375°F). Fry the fish, a few pieces at a time, until golden brown. The cooking time will depend on the density and size of the fish. Obviously tiny whitebait will cook very quickly, while larger fish will take several minutes. The most accurate way to determine whether it is cooked is to cut a piece open and try it. Drain thoroughly on absorbent kitchen paper.

Shallow-frying

Coat the fish in seasoned flour or egg and breadcrumbs and fry in vegetable oil or a mixture of vegetable oil and butter. Test whether the fish is cooked as above. Drain as above.

Fillets or steaks, brushed with olive oil, will cook on a hot oiled griddle in a matter of minutes.

Grilling

Before you start cooking, line the grill pan with foil to prevent lingering fish smells. If cooking whole fish or thick fillets with skin on, slash the skin so that the heat can penetrate. Brush generously with melted butter, oil or a marinade, season with salt and pepper and cook under a preheated hot grill until the flesh looks opaque. Turn large fillets or fish occasionally. Cut into the fish at the thickest point to check whether it's cooked.

Barbecued fish is cooked in much the same way. Choose robust tuna, monkfish, mackerel, shark or sardines in preference to delicate fish like plaice and sole. To make turning easier and to help prevent the fish breaking up, put it in a fish rack or thread it onto skewers. Brush frequently with marinade or oil.

Baking

Put the fish in a shallow dish with a few herbs, seasoning and a splash of wine, fish stock or milk. Cover and bake at 180°C (350°F) mark 4. Alternatively, bake en papillote – wrapped in a foil or greaseproof paper parcel – at the same temperature. Whole fish will take about 30–40 minutes while fillets and steaks will take anything from 15–25 minutes depending on their size.

Poaching

Heat a well flavoured court bouillon or fish stock or some dry white wine or milk flavoured with aromatics such as parsley, onion, bay, celery and a few peppercorns. Add the fish and simmer very gently until the fish is just opaque. Don't let the liquid boil or the fish will break up.

Steaming

Season thoroughly before cooking and sprinkle with a few herbs, a squeeze of lemon juice or a knob of butter. Wrap in foil and steam over boiling water until the fish is opaque. This will take about 10 minutes but will depend on the thickness of the fillets. Delicate thin plaice and sole fillets will cook very quickly.

Fillets of uniform thickness can also be cooked in the microwave, flavoured as above.

❖ Grilled Turbot with ❖
Chervil and Tomato Sauce

SERVES 4

PREPARATION TIME
20 minutes
COOKING TIME
10–12 minutes
FREEZING
Not suitable
COLOUR INDEX
Page 25

- 300 ml (½ pint) milk
- 1 onion slice
- 1 mace blade
- 4–6 black peppercorns
- 2 tomatoes
- 25 g (1 oz) butter
- scant 15 g (½ oz) plain flour
- salt and pepper

- 5 ml (1 tsp) tomato purée
- 1 large bunch chervil
- 4 turbot steaks, about 175 g (6 oz) each
- lemon juice, to taste

280 CALS/SERVING

1 Put the milk in a small pan with the onion, mace and peppercorns. Bring to the boil and remove from heat. Leave to infuse for 10 minutes; strain.

2 Immerse the tomatoes in boiling water for 15–30 seconds, then remove and peel away the skins. Cut the flesh into strips, discarding seeds.

3 Melt 15 g (½ oz) butter in a small pan. Stir in the flour and cook for 1 minute. Off the heat, gradually stir in the strained milk. Season.

4 Bring to the boil, stirring constantly. Simmer gently for a few minutes. Whisk in the tomato purée and about 60 ml (4 tbsp) chopped chervil.

5 Meanwhile, melt the remaining butter. Halve the turbot steaks, brush with melted butter and grill for about 5–6 minutes each side.

6 Add the tomato strips to the sauce. Reheat gently, stirring in lemon juice to taste. Garnish the turbot with chervil and serve with the sauce.

❖ Lemon Sole ❖
with Mousseline Sauce

SERVES 6

PREPARATION TIME
15 minutes
COOKING TIME
4–6 minutes
FREEZING
Not suitable
COLOUR INDEX
Page 25

- 2 egg yolks
- 10 ml (2 tsp) lemon juice
- salt and pepper
- 50 g (2 oz) unsalted butter, softened

- 12 single lemon sole fillets
- melted butter, for brushing
- 50 ml (2 fl oz) whipping cream

260 CALS/SERVING

1 To make the mousseline sauce, place the egg yolks in a small bowl. Add 5 ml (1 tsp) of the lemon juice, salt and pepper and a knob of the softened unsalted butter. Place the bowl in a bain-marie over a gentle heat and whisk well until the mixture is quite thick.
2 Remove the bowl from the bain-marie and whisk in the rest of the softened butter, a small piece at a time. Add the remainder of the lemon juice. Keep the sauce warm by returning the bowl to the bain-marie over a low heat.
3 Brush the sole fillets with melted butter and grill for 2–3 minutes on each side.
4 Lightly whip the cream and fold into the sauce. Serve the grilled sole fillets immediately, with the mousseline sauce spooned over.

❖ Haddock with ❖
Parsley and Lemon

SERVES 4

PREPARATION TIME
15 minutes
COOKING TIME
20–25 minutes
FREEZING
Not suitable

- 450 g (1 lb) haddock fillet, skinned
- 45 ml (3 tbsp) lemon juice
- 90 ml (6 tbsp) chopped parsley
- salt and pepper

- 50 g (2 oz) butter or margarine
- 45 ml (3 tbsp) plain flour
- 300 ml (½ pint) milk

260 CALS/SERVING

1 Divide the fish into about 8 even-sized pieces and place in a shallow ovenproof dish. Sprinkle with the lemon juice and half of the parsley. Season with salt and pepper. Add 60 ml (4 tbsp) water, then cover tightly.

2 Bake the fish at 180°C (350°F) mark 4 for about 20–25 minutes, or until it starts flaking apart.

3 Meanwhile, melt the butter in a small pan. Stir in the flour and cook for 1 minute. Gradually stir in the milk and bring to the boil, stirring. Cook, stirring, for 1–2 minutes until thickened and smooth. Stir in the remaining parsley.

4 Using a fish slice, lift the fish onto a serving platter, draining slightly; cover and keep warm. Add the cooking juices to the sauce and reheat gently without boiling. Adjust the seasoning.

5 Spoon some of the sauce over the fish to serve, and accompany with creamed potatoes and glazed carrots. Serve the remaining sauce separately.

❖ Grilled Monkfish ❖ with Lemon and Dill

SERVES 4	
PREPARATION TIME 10 minutes, plus marinating COOKING TIME 12 minutes FREEZING Not suitable	• 700 g (1½ lb) monkfish tail, or other firm white fish • 45 ml (3 tbsp) lemon juice • 15 ml (1 tbsp) chopped dill or 2.5 ml (½ tsp) dried • 2 garlic cloves, sliced • 45 ml (3 tbsp) olive oil • salt and pepper • lemon slices, to garnish

200 CALS/SERVING

1 Remove all membrane from the fish and cut out the backbone to give two long fillets. Cut these in half to give four 'steaks'. Place in a non-metallic dish.

2 Whisk the lemon juice with the dill, garlic and olive oil; season well. Pour over the fish, cover and leave in a cool place to marinate for at least 4 hours, turning occasionally.

3 Drain the fish, arrange on a wire rack in a grill pan and grill for about 6 minutes on each side, basting regularly with the marinade. Serve immediately, garnished with lemon slices and accompanied by French beans and fennel.

❖ Parchment Baked Fish ❖

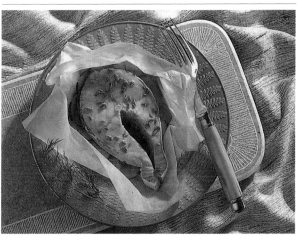

SERVES 4		
PREPARATION TIME 15 minutes, plus soaking COOKING TIME 15 minutes FREEZING Not suitable	• 50 ml (2 fl oz) dry white wine • 125 g (4 oz) cucumber, thinly sliced • 4 fish steaks (cod, halibut, turbot or salmon), about 150 g (5 oz) each	• 5 ml (1 tsp) fennel seeds • 25 g (1 oz) butter or margarine • salt and pepper • fennel sprigs, to garnish

170 CALS/SERVING

1 Cut 4 pieces of non-stick baking parchment or greaseproof paper, each about 28 cm (11 inches) square, and crumple them together into a small bowl. Pour over the wine and leave to soak for 1 hour; push down into the wine occasionally.

2 Separate and open out the parchment sheets. Arrange a circle of cucumber rounds in the centre of each sheet. Place a fish steak on top. Sprinkle with fennel seeds and dot with a small piece of butter. Season with salt and pepper. Drizzle over any remaining wine.

3 Lift up opposite sides of the parchment and fold together. Twist and tuck under the two shorter ends. Place the parcels on a baking sheet. Bake at 200°C (400°F) mark 6 for about 15 minutes. Serve at once, garnished with fennel.

❖ Rolled Plaice with Pesto ❖

SERVES 4

PREPARATION TIME
20 minutes
COOKING TIME
10 minutes
FREEZING
Not suitable

- 8 small plaice fillets, about 550 g (1¼ lb) total weight
- 3 spring onions
- 125 g (4 oz) fine asparagus or French beans
- 1 carrot, peeled
- 15 ml (1 tbsp) pesto
- 30 ml (2 tbsp) lemon juice
- 100 ml (4 fl oz) fish stock
- salt and pepper
- 75 g (3 oz) oyster or button mushrooms
- 125 g (4 oz) baby corn cobs, halved
- 125 g (4 oz) mangetouts
- 30 ml (2 tbsp) oil (optional)

225 CALS/SERVING

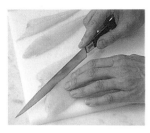

1 Skin the plaice fillets and divide each one along the centre line into 2 fillets. Roll up loosely (skinned side in).

2 Cut the spring onions, asparagus and carrot into 6 cm (2½ inch) lengths.

3 Place the fish in a shallow pan. Mix the pesto with the lemon juice and stock. Pour over the fish and season. Bring to the boil, cover tightly with damp greaseproof paper and the lid. Simmer gently for 10 minutes or until cooked. Meanwhile, steam the vegetables or sauté in oil until tender. Serve topped with the fish and juices.

❖ Grilled Plaice with Mushrooms ❖

SERVES 4

PREPARATION TIME
20 minutes
COOKING TIME
10 minutes
FREEZING
Not suitable
COLOUR INDEX
Page 25

- 225 g (8 oz) button mushrooms
- 125 g (4 oz) eating apple
- 25 g (1 oz) butter or margarine
- 25 g (1 oz) fresh brown breadcrumbs
- 5 ml (1 tsp) wholegrain mustard
- 30 ml (2 tbsp) chopped parsley
- salt and pepper
- 4 plaice fillets, about 125 g (4 oz) each, skinned
- 60 ml (4 tbsp) dry cider
- apple slices, to garnish

215 CALS/SERVING

1 Finely chop the mushrooms. Peel, core and chop the apple. Melt the butter in a small pan and sauté the mushrooms and apple for 2–3 minutes. Increase the heat and cook, stirring, for 1–2 minutes, until most of the excess liquid has evaporated.
2 Off the heat, stir in the breadcrumbs, half the wholegrain mustard and the chopped parsley. Season with salt and pepper.
3 Divide the mixture between the plaice fillets and roll up, skinned side inside. Secure with wooden cocktail sticks. Place the rolled plaice fillets, seam side down, in a small shallow flameproof dish.
4 Whisk together the remaining mustard and the cider. Spoon over the fish. Grill for about 10 minutes, turning occasionally and brushing with the mustard mixture.
5 Remove the cocktail sticks. Serve the fish immediately, garnished with apple slices. Accompany with steamed potatoes and a green salad or steamed broccoli.

❖ Golden Crumbed Plaice ❖

SERVES 4

PREPARATION TIME
10 minutes
COOKING TIME
10 minutes
FREEZING
Not suitable
COLOUR INDEX
Page 25

- 450 g (1 lb) plaice fillets, skinned
- dash of lemon juice
- 1 bay leaf
- salt and pepper
- 40 g (1½ oz) butter or margarine
- 50 g (2 oz) fresh brown breadcrumbs
- 3 celery sticks, roughly chopped
- 25 g (1 oz) chopped walnuts
- 30 ml (2 tbsp) chopped parsley
- parsley sprigs, to garnish

255 CALS/SERVING

1 If necessary, divide each fish fillet in half, then roll up with the skinned side inside; secure with a cocktail stick.
2 Place the fish in a sauté pan, and add water to barely cover. Add the lemon juice, bay leaf and seasoning. Bring slowly to the boil, cover and simmer very gently until tender, about 5 minutes.
3 Meanwhile melt the butter in a frying pan. Add the breadcrumbs and fry, stirring occasionally, until beginning to brown. Mix in the celery and walnuts and cook until the crumbs are golden. Stir in the parsley and seasoning.
4 Drain the fish on absorbent kitchen paper. Remove the cocktail sticks. Serve immediately, topped with the golden crumbs and garnished with parsley. Grilled tomatoes make an ideal accompaniment.

❖ Seafood Kebabs ❖

SERVES 4

PREPARATION TIME
20 minutes
COOKING TIME
8–10 minutes
FREEZING
Not suitable

- 450 g (1 lb) monkfish or cod fillet
- 125 g (4 oz) cucumber
- 50 g (2 oz) large cooked prawns in shells
- 1 lime or lemon, thinly sliced
- 75 ml (3 fl oz) Garlic Vinaigrette (page 273)
- 15 ml (1 tbsp) chopped dill or 2.5 ml (½ tsp) dried
- salt and pepper
- salad leaves and dill sprigs, to garnish

130 CALS/SERVING

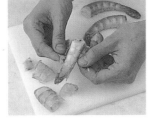

1 Skin the fish if necessary, then cut into 2.5 cm (1 inch) cubes. Halve the cucumber lengthways and thickly slice.

2 Peel the prawns, leaving the tail shell on.

3 Thread the prawns and lime slices onto four wooden skewers, alternating with the cubes of fish and cucumber. Place the kebabs in a flameproof dish.

4 Spoon the vinaigrette and dill over the kebabs. Grill for about 8–10 minutes, turning and basting occasionally. Season and serve immediately on a bed of salad leaves. Garnish with dill.

❖ Monkfish with Mustard Seeds ❖

SERVES 6

PREPARATION TIME
10 minutes
COOKING TIME
18–20 minutes
FREEZING
Not suitable

- 45 ml (3 tbsp) black mustard seeds
- 30 ml (2 tbsp) plain flour
- 900 g (2 lb) monkfish fillet, skinned
- 1 onion, peeled
- 30 ml (2 tbsp) oil
- 300 ml (½ pint) natural yogurt
- 1 garlic clove, crushed
- 15 ml (1 tbsp) lemon juice
- salt and pepper
TO GARNISH:
- cooked whole prawns
- coriander sprigs

220 CALS/SERVING

1 Finely grind 30 ml (2 tbsp) of the mustard seeds in a small electric mill or with a pestle and mortar. Mix them with the flour.

2 Cut the monkfish into 2.5 cm (1 inch) cubes and toss in the flour and ground mustard seeds.

3 Thinly slice the onion. Heat the oil in a large heavy-based frying pan and fry the onion for about 5 minutes until golden.

4 Add the remaining mustard seeds to the pan with the monkfish. Fry over moderate heat for 3–4 minutes, turning very gently once or twice.

5 Gradually stir in the yogurt with the garlic, lemon juice and seasoning. Bring to the boil, lower the heat and simmer gently for about 10 minutes or until the fish is tender.

6 Taste and adjust the seasoning. Turn the fish mixture into a warmed serving dish and garnish with the prawns and coriander. Serve immediately.

❖ Sweet and Sour ❖ Monkfish Kebabs

SERVES 4

PREPARATION TIME
25 minutes, plus
marinating
COOKING TIME
10–12 minutes
FREEZING
Not suitable
COLOUR INDEX
Page 26

- 450 g (1 lb) monkfish fillet, skinned
- 12 streaky bacon rashers
- 1 small aubergine, about 125 g (4 oz), thinly sliced
- 2 small red onions, peeled
- 2 lemons or limes, sliced
- 15 ml (1 tbsp) lemon juice
- 30 ml (2 tbsp) clear honey
- 15 ml (1 tbsp) soy sauce
- 15 ml (1 tbsp) tomato purée
- salt and pepper
- frisée, to garnish

355 CALS/SERVING

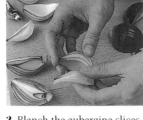

1 Cut the monkfish into 2.5 cm (1 inch) cubes. Stretch the bacon rashers with the back of a knife and cut in half. Wrap a piece of bacon around each fish cube.

2 Blanch the aubergine slices in boiling water, drain and dry on absorbent kitchen paper. Quarter the onions, then separate each quarter into two, to give thinner pieces.

3 Thread the fish, onions, aubergines and lemon or lime slices on to 8 wooden skewers. Place the kebabs side by side in a non-metallic dish.

4 Whisk together the lemon juice, honey, soy sauce, tomato purée and seasoning. Spoon over the kebabs.

5 Cover and leave to marinate in the refrigerator for at least 12 hours, turning once. Place the kebabs in a grill pan. Brush with a little of the marinade and grill for 10–12 minutes, turning occasionally, until all ingredients are tender. Serve the kebabs garnished with frisée.

❖ Haddock and ❖ Soured Cream Gratin

SERVES 2

PREPARATION TIME
10 minutes
COOKING TIME
10 minutes
FREEZING
Not suitable
COLOUR INDEX
Page 26

- 350 g (12 oz) haddock fillet
- knob of butter
- 2 medium firm tomatoes
- 150 ml (¼ pint) soured cream
- 15 ml (1 tbsp) chopped chives
- 15 ml (1 tbsp) chopped parsley
- 25 g (1 oz) Gruyère cheese, grated
- salt and pepper

380 CALS/SERVING

1 Skin the haddock if necessary and chop roughly. Choose a shallow flameproof serving dish just large enough to take the fish in a single layer. Put the knob of butter in the dish and place under a hot grill to melt.

2 Add the fish to the dish and turn in the butter. Grill for 10 minutes, turning occasionally, until cooked.

3 Chop the tomatoes and mix with the soured cream, herbs, grated cheese and seasoning. Spoon over the fish and cook under the grill until bubbling. Serve immediately, with boiled new potatoes and spinach.

❖ Cod and Crab Gratin ❖

SERVES 4

PREPARATION TIME
15 minutes
COOKING TIME
15 minutes
FREEZING
Not suitable

- about 700 g (1½ lb) medium new potatoes
- 450 g (1 lb) cod fillet
- 300 ml (½ pint) milk
- salt and pepper
- 225 g (8 oz) small button mushrooms
- 25 g (1 oz) butter or margarine
- 25 g (1 oz) flour
- 25 g (1oz) each white and dark crab meat
- 10 ml (2 tsp) Dijon mustard
- 75 g (3 oz) Cheddar cheese, grated

445 CALS/SERVING

1 Scrub the potatoes and boil in their skins until tender. Drain, then slice thickly.

2 Meanwhile, skin the cod fillet and cut the flesh into 2.5 cm (1 inch) pieces.

3 Place the fish in a saucepan with the milk and seasoning. Bring to the boil, cover and simmer for 5 minutes. Add the mushrooms, re-cover and simmer for a further 5 minutes, or until the fish is tender. Strain off and reserve the milk. Place the fish and mushrooms in a shallow flameproof dish, cover and keep warm.

4 Melt the butter in a small saucepan. Stir in the flour and cook for 1 minute. Off the heat, gradually stir in the reserved milk. Cook, stirring, for 2–3 minutes until thickened and smooth. Stir in the crab meat, mustard and seasoning and heat through gently.

5 Pour the sauce over the cod and mushrooms, stirring gently to mix. Level the surface with a knife.

6 Top with thick slices of potato and scatter over the grated cheese. Grill until golden and bubbling. Serve immediately, accompanied by a crisp green salad.

❖ Sweet and Sour Fish ❖

SERVES 4

PREPARATION TIME
10 minutes
COOKING TIME
10–12 minutes
FREEZING
Not suitable

- 4 cod fillets, about 150 g (5 oz) each, skinned
- 15 ml (1 tbsp) soy sauce
- 30 ml (2 tbsp) lemon juice
- 10 ml (2 tsp) white wine vinegar
- 15 ml (1 tbsp) clear honey
- 10 ml (2 tsp) tomato ketchup
- 1 garlic clove, crushed
- 1.25 ml (¼ tsp) paprika
- 1 red pepper
- 125 g (4oz) spring onions
- 125 g (4 oz) button mushrooms
- 15 ml (1 tbsp) oil
- 125 g (4 oz) frozen green beans
- pepper

200 CALS/SERVING

1 Divide each cod fillet in half lengthwise. Roll up neatly with the skinned side inside.
2 Mix together the soy sauce, lemon juice, vinegar, honey, tomato ketchup, garlic and paprika. Place in a large sauté pan, add the fish and baste with the sauce. Bring to a very gentle simmer, cover and cook for 10–12 minutes, or until tender.
3 Meanwhile halve the pepper, remove the core and seeds, and cut into strips. Slice the spring onions; halve the mushrooms.
4 Heat the oil in another sauté pan and stir-fry the vegetables over a high heat for 3–4 minutes until just tender. Season well with pepper.
5 Serve the fish with the sauce spooned over and accompanied by the stir-fried vegetables.

Variation
If you like fresh root ginger, grate a little into the pan as you stir-fry the vegetables.

❖ Trout in Riesling ❖

SERVES 4		
PREPARATION TIME 20 minutes COOKING TIME 25 minutes FREEZING Not suitable	• 4 small gutted trout, about 200 g (7 oz) each • 125 g (4 oz) trimmed leeks, finely sliced • salt and pepper	• 225 ml (8 fl oz) Riesling wine • 5 ml (1 tsp) cornflour • 75 g (3 oz) butter

390 CALS/SERVING

1 Butter a shallow, medium ovenproof dish just large enough to hold the trout in a single layer. Rinse, drain and dry the fish.

2 Spread the leeks over the base of the dish. Place the fish on top and season. Pour on the wine; cover with buttered foil. Bake at 200°C (400°F) mark 6 for 25 minutes or until tender.

3 With a slotted spoon transfer the trout and leeks to a warmed serving dish; cover with foil. Boil the cooking liquid in a small saucepan until reduced by half.

4 Mix cornflour with a little cold water. Stir into the sauce. Bring to the boil, stirring, until thickened slightly. Gradually whisk in the butter. Serve the trout with the sauce.

❖ Lemon and Mustard Mackerel ❖

SERVES 6		
PREPARATION TIME 10 minutes, plus marinating COOKING TIME 20 minutes FREEZING Not suitable COLOUR INDEX Page 26	• 4 mackerel, about 350 g (12 oz) each, cleaned • 15 ml (1 tbsp) mustard seeds • 50 g (2 oz) butter, softened • grated rind and juice of 1 lemon • 15 ml (1 tbsp) Dijon mustard • 5 ml (1 tsp) paprika	• salt and pepper • 450 g (1 lb) cucumber • 30 ml (2 tbsp) olive oil • 60 ml (4 tbsp) chopped parsley TO GARNISH: • parsley sprigs • lemon wedges • paprika

700 CALS/SERVING

1 Make several deep slashes along the length of each fish on both sides. Arrange in a non-metallic dish.
2 Crush the mustard seeds with a rolling pin, then beat into the butter. Add the grated lemon rind, 15 ml (1 tbsp) lemon juice, the mustard, half the paprika and seasoning, mixing well.
3 Spread this butter into the slashes in the fish. Spread any remainder over the fish. Pour any remaining lemon juice over the fish, cover and leave to marinate in the refrigerator for at least 1 hour.
4 Transfer the mackerel to a wire rack in a grill pan and grill for 10 minutes on each side or until cooked through.
5 Meanwhile, finely dice the cucumber. Heat the oil in a frying pan and add the cucumber. Sauté for 2–3 minutes, then stir in the remaining paprika and parsley. Cook for a further 1 minute.
6 Serve the grilled mackerel with the cucumber. Garnish with parsley and lemon wedges dipped in paprika.

❖ Grilled Salmon ❖ Steaks in Citrus Dressing

SERVES 4		
PREPARATION TIME 15 minutes, plus marinating COOKING TIME 8 minutes FREEZING Not suitable COLOUR INDEX Page 26	• 75 ml (3 fl oz) oil • grated rind and juice of 1 lime • 30 ml (2 tbsp) orange juice • 5 ml (1 tsp) clear honey • 1 green cardamom pod	• 4 salmon steaks, about 175 g (6 oz) each TO GARNISH: • lime slices • salad leaves

495 CALS/SERVING

1 Whisk together 50 ml (2 fl oz) of the oil, the grated lime rind, 30 ml (2 tbsp) lime juice, the orange juice and honey. Extract the seeds from the cardamom pod and crush them, then add to the dressing.
2 Place the salmon steaks in a shallow, non-metallic dish and pour over the lime and honey dressing. Cover and leave to marinate in the refrigerator overnight.
3 Remove the salmon steaks from the marinade and brush with the remaining oil. Cook under a hot grill for about 8 minutes, turning halfway through cooking.
4 Meanwhile, put the marinade in a small saucepan and bring to the boil; keep warm over a low heat.
5 Serve the salmon steaks with the marinade as a warm dressing. Garnish with lime slices and salad leaves.

❖ Salmon and ❖ Thyme Butter Parcels

SERVES 4

PREPARATION TIME
20 minutes
COOKING TIME
15–20 minutes
FREEZING
Not suitable
COLOUR INDEX
Page 27

- 4 salmon cutlets
- 30 ml (2 tbsp) oil
- 50 g (2 oz) butter, softened
- 1 garlic clove, crushed
- 10 ml (2 tsp) mustard seeds

- 30 ml (2 tbsp) chopped thyme
- salt and pepper
- 4 tomatoes
- thyme sprigs, to garnish

350 CALS/SERVING

1 Carefully remove the centre bone from each cutlet. Curl each half cutlet around to form a medallion and tie with string.

2 Heat the oil in a sauté pan and briefly brown the salmon on both sides, cooking in batches, if necessary. Drain on absorbent kitchen paper and leave to cool.

3 Blend together the butter, garlic, mustard seeds, thyme and seasoning.

4 Skin, deseed and chop the tomatoes.

5 Cut 8 pieces of greaseproof paper, each about 25 cm (10 inches) square. Place a salmon medallion in the centre of each and top with some herb butter and tomato.

6 Draw up the corners of the paper and tie with string to form bundles. Place on a baking sheet. Bake at 200°C (400°F) mark 6 for 10–15 minutes or until the salmon is cooked. Serve garnished with thyme.

❖ Baked Salmon Steaks ❖ with Hollandaise Sauce

SERVES 8

PREPARATION TIME
15 minutes
COOKING TIME
20–30 minutes
FREEZING
Not suitable

- 8 salmon steaks, about 175 g (6 oz) each
- 50 g (2 oz) butter
- salt and pepper
- lemon juice, to taste
- HOLLANDAISE SAUCE:
- 45 ml (3 tbsp) wine or tarragon vinegar
- 15–30 ml (1–2 tbsp) water

- 3 egg yolks
- 350 g (12 oz) unsalted butter, softened
- salt and white pepper
TO GARNISH:
- tarragon sprigs

540 CALS/SERVING

1 Line two baking sheets with buttered foil. Place the salmon on the foil, dot each steak with butter and season with salt, pepper and lemon juice.

2 Wrap loosely and bake in the oven at 180°C (350°F) mark 4 for 20–30 minutes, according to the thickness of the fish.

3 Meanwhile, to make the sauce, put the vinegar and water in a saucepan. Boil gently until reduced by half, then cool.

4 Put the egg yolks and reduced vinegar liquid in a double saucepan or bowl over a pan of gently simmering water and whisk until thick and fluffy.

5 Gradually add the butter, a tiny piece at a time, whisking briskly after each addition until the piece has been absorbed. The final sauce should be the consistency of mayonnaise. Season to taste. If the sauce is too sharp, add a little more butter.

6 Serve the salmon garnished with tarragon and accompanied by the hollandaise sauce and seasonal vegetables.

❖ Crispy Layered Fish Pie ❖

SERVES 6

PREPARATION TIME
40 minutes
COOKING TIME
30 minutes
FREEZING
Not suitable

- 350 g (12 oz) spinach leaves, stalks removed
- 75 g (3 oz) long-grain rice
- salt and pepper
- 1 hard-boiled egg
- 225 g (8 oz) fresh haddock fillet
- 225 g (8 oz) smoked haddock fillet
- 225 ml (8 fl oz) milk
- 125 g (4 oz) butter
- 30 ml (2 tbsp) plain flour
- 400 g (14 oz) packet filo pastry, each sheet 19 × 38 cm (7½ × 15 inches)

335 CALS/SERVING

1 Place the spinach in a sauce-pan with only the water that adheres after washing. Cover tightly and cook for 5–6 minutes, or until tender. Drain, squeezing out excess liquid; chop roughly. Leave to cool. Cook the rice in boiling salted water; drain and cool.

2 Roughly chop the hard-boiled egg. Put the fresh and smoked haddock in a shallow pan. Pour on the milk and bring to a simmer. Poach gently for about 10 minutes until just cooked. Strain and reserve cooking liquor. Flake the fish into large pieces, discarding skin and bones.

3 Melt 40 g (1½ oz) butter in a saucepan, add the flour and cook for 1–2 minutes. Gradually stir in the reserved liquor. Bring to the boil and cook, stirring, for 1–2 minutes or until thickened. Carefully stir in the fish and chopped egg. Season with salt and pepper, then leave to cool.

4 Melt the remaining butter. Cut off a third of the filo pastry and freeze for future use, to leave 25 × 19 cm (10 × 7½ inch) rectangles.

5 Place one pastry sheet on a greased baking sheet. Brush lightly with butter and continue layering the filo sheets, brushing each with butter, until half the pastry has been used.

6 Spoon the rice onto the pastry, leaving a 2.5 cm (1 inch) border all round. Cover the rice with spinach and then top with the fish mixture.

7 Place a sheet of filo pastry on top of the filling, brush with butter then complete the layering as above. Seal the edges well and brush the top with butter. Bake at 200°C (400°F) mark 6, covering lightly with foil if necessary, for about 30 minutes or until the pie is crisp and golden brown in colour.

❖ Golden Topped Fish Pie ❖

SERVES 4

PREPARATION TIME
40 minutes
COOKING TIME
40–45 minutes
FREEZING
Not suitable
COLOUR INDEX
Page 27

- 900 g (2 lb) old potatoes, peeled
- salt and pepper
- 350 g (12 oz) fennel
- squeeze of lemon juice
- 450 g (1 lb) haddock fillet
- 150 ml (¼ pint) dry white wine
- 225 g (8 oz) shelled scallops, cleaned
- 150 g (5 oz) cooked peeled prawns
- 75 g (3 oz) butter
- 40 g (1½ oz) plain flour
- 75 ml (5 tbsp) single cream
- 15 ml (1 tbsp) chopped dill or 2.5 ml (½ tsp) dried
- about 100 ml (3½ fl oz) hot milk
- 30 ml (2 tbsp) fresh white breadcrumbs
- dill sprigs, to garnish

605 CALS/SERVING

Cut the potatoes into large chunks, then cook in boiling salted water until just tender; drain well.

Thinly slice the fennel, removing core and stems; reserve these. Blanch the fennel slices in boiling salted water with the lemon juice added, for 5 minutes or until just tender. Drain well.

Place the haddock in a sauté pan and pour over the wine together with 350 ml (12 fl oz) water; season and add the fennel core and stems. Bring slowly to the boil; cover and simmer until just tender – about 10 minutes. Add the scallops for the last minute of the cooking time.

Remove the haddock and scallops from the pan; strain liquor and reserve. Flake the haddock flesh, discarding any skin and bone. Slice each scallop into two or three pieces, discarding any membrane. Place the haddock and scallops in a 2.3 litre (4 pint) shallow ovenproof dish with the fennel slices and prawns.

Melt 50 g (2 oz) butter in a saucepan. Add the flour and cook for 1 minute, then stir in the strained cooking liquor. Bring to the boil, stirring, and cook for 1–2 minutes. Off the heat, mix in the cream and dill; adjust seasoning and pour over the fish.

Mash the potatoes. Beat in the hot milk, with the remaining butter and plenty of seasoning. Cover the fish mixture with spoonfuls of potato. Sprinkle with the breadcrumbs. Bake at 190°C (375°F) mark 5 for about 40–45 minutes or until lightly browned and bubbling hot. Garnish with dill.

✤ Smoked Haddock ✤ and Watercress Soufflé

PREPARATION TIME
15 minutes
COOKING TIME
40–50 minutes
FREEZING
Not suitable

- 400 g (14 oz) smoked haddock fillets
- about 375 ml (12 fl oz) milk
- 2 bay leaves
- few peppercorns
- 30 ml (2 tbsp) freshly grated Parmesan cheese
- 1 bunch watercress
- 50 g (2 oz) butter
- 45 ml (3 tbsp) plain flour
- 3 eggs, separated
- 1.25 ml (¼ tsp) ground nutmeg
- 30 ml (2 tbsp) lemon juice
- pepper

400 CALS/SERVING

1 Place the fish in a large sauté pan, add 300 ml (½ pint) milk, the bay leaves and peppercorns. Cover and poach for about 12 minutes or until the fish is just cooked.

2 Meanwhile, lightly grease a 1.2 litre (2 pint) soufflé dish, then dust out with 15 ml (1 tbsp) of the Parmesan. Roughly chop the watercress.

3 Flake the fish, discarding any skin and bones. Strain the milk into a jug and make up to 300 ml (½ pint) with extra milk.

4 Melt the butter in a saucepan, add the flour and cook for 1–2 minutes. Stir in the milk, then cook, stirring, for 2–3 minutes or until thickened. Cool slightly, then stir in the fish, watercress, egg yolks, nutmeg, lemon juice and plenty of black pepper.

5 Whisk the egg whites until stiff, but not dry. Lightly fold into the fish mixture. Pour into the prepared soufflé dish and run a knife around the edge of the dish to achieve the classic 'hat' effect.

6 Sprinkle the remaining cheese over the top. Bake at 180°C (350°F) mark 4 for 40–45 minutes or until well risen, golden brown and just firm to the touch. Serve immediately, with a green salad and French bread.

❖ Spiced Fish Stir-fry ❖

SERVES 4

PREPARATION TIME
15 minutes
COOKING TIME
5–7 minutes
FREEZING
Not suitable
COLOUR INDEX
Page 28

- 225 g (8 oz) monkfish fillet
- 225 g (8 oz) shelled scallops, cleaned
- 5 ml (1 tsp) flour
- 10 ml (2 tsp) ground coriander
- 10 ml (2 tsp) ground cumin
- 1 small green pepper
- 1 small yellow pepper
- 1 onion, peeled
- 225 g (8 oz) tomatoes
- 30 ml (2 tbsp) oil
- 125 g (4 oz) bean sprouts
- 75 ml (5 tbsp) dry white wine
- chopped coriander or parsley, to taste
- salt and pepper

180 CALS/SERVING

1 Slice the monkfish into thin strips and the scallops into thin rounds, removing their coral to cook separately.

2 On a plate, mix the flour and spices together. Lightly coat all the fish in this mixture.

3 Halve, deseed and finely slice the peppers. Slice the onion thinly. Skin the tomatoes and cut into wedges.

4 Heat 15 ml (1 tbsp) oil in a large frying pan. Add the fish and stir-fry for 2–3 minutes or until tender. Remove from the pan and set aside. Add the peppers and onion to the pan and stir-fry over a high heat until beginning to brown.

5 Add the tomatoes and bean sprouts to the vegetables and cook for 2–3 minutes or until the tomatoes begin to soften. Return the fish to the pan. Mix in the wine with the coriander or parsley and seasoning to taste and allow to bubble up. Serve immediately, with rice or noodles.

❖ Curried Fish ❖ with Lemon and Ginger

SERVES 6

PREPARATION TIME
20 minutes, plus marinating
COOKING TIME
20–25 minutes
FREEZING
Not suitable
COLOUR INDEX
Page 28

- 5 ml (1 tsp) garam masala
- 5 cm (2 inch) piece fresh root ginger, peeled and finely chopped
- 2 garlic cloves, crushed
- 12 sole fillets, skinned, about 1.1 kg (2½ lb) total weight
- 175 g (6 oz) spring onions
- 45 ml (3 tbsp) chopped coriander
- finely grated rind and juice of 1 lemon
- salt and pepper
- 50 g (2 oz) creamed coconut
- 2.5 ml (½ tsp) saffron strands
- 25 g (1 oz) salted cashew nuts
- 15 ml (1 tbsp) oil
- 150 ml (¼ pint) single cream
- chopped coriander, to garnish

275 CALS/SERVING

1 Mix together the garam masala, ginger and garlic. Place the sole fillets in a flat, non-metallic dish and rub with the spice mixture. Cover tightly and leave to marinate in the refrigerator overnight.
2 Chop the spring onions. Mix half of them with the coriander, lemon rind, 45 ml (3 tbsp) lemon juice and seasoning.
3 Place the fillets, skinned side up, on a plate and spoon a little of the onion mixture into the centre of each one. Roll up and secure with cocktail sticks.
4 Put the creamed coconut, saffron and cashew nuts in a blender or food processor with 200 ml (7 fl oz) water. Work until smooth.
5 Heat the oil in a large shallow flameproof casserole and sauté the remaining spring onions for 2–3 minutes. Add the coconut liquid and fish with any remaining marinade. Bring to the boil and cover. Simmer very gently, or cook in the oven at 180°C (350°F) mark 4, for 15 minutes, or until the fish is tender.
6 Add the cream and heat gently without boiling for a further 2–3 minutes. Adjust seasoning. Remove cocktail sticks. Serve garnished with chopped coriander. Accompany with saffron rice.

❖ Fish Cakes with Herbs ❖

SERVES 4

PREPARATION TIME
15 minutes
COOKING TIME
10 minutes
FREEZING
Not suitable
COLOUR INDEX
Page 28

- 275 g (10 oz) haddock fillet, skinned
- 15 ml (1 tbsp) lemon juice
- 15 ml (1 tbsp) Worcestershire sauce
- 15 ml (1 tbsp) creamed horseradish
- 100 ml (4 fl oz) milk
- 15 ml (1 tbsp) snipped chives
- 15 ml (1 tbsp) chopped parsley
- 350 g (12 oz) cooked potatoes, mashed
- 50 g (2 oz) fresh wholemeal breadcrumbs

175 CALS/SERVING

1 Purée the fish in a blender or food processor with the lemon juice, Worcestershire sauce and horseradish. Transfer to a bowl and stir in the milk, herbs and potatoes until evenly blended.
2 Shape the mixture into 4 fish cakes; coat with breadcrumbs.
3 Grill under a moderate heat for 5 minutes on each side, until browned. Serve with a fresh tomato sauce and crisp leafy salad.

❖ Fritto Misto ❖

SERVES 8

PREPARATION TIME
30 minutes
COOKING TIME
10–15 minutes
FREEZING
Not suitable

- 700 g (1½ lb) squid, cleaned
- 6 small red mullet, cleaned and filleted
- 350 g (12 oz) firm, white fish fillets (cod, haddock or sole), skinned
- 12–18 large raw prawns
- 350 g (12 oz) whitebait
- 90 ml (6 tbsp) seasoned flour
- oil, for deep-frying

TO GARNISH:
- parsley sprigs
- lemon wedges

440 CALS/SERVING

1 Slice the body of the squid into rings 5 mm (¼ inch) thick and the tentacles into 1 cm (½ inch) pieces.

2 Slice the red mullet. Cut the white fish fillets into long thin strips. Peel the prawns.

3 Toss all the fish in seasoned flour. Heat the oil in a deep fat fryer to 190°C (375°F). Add the fish pieces a few at a time and fry until crisp and golden brown.

4 Drain on absorbent kitchen paper and keep each batch warm while frying the remainder. Divide the fish between eight warmed plates. Garnish with parsley and lemon.

❖ Greek-style Fish Casserole ❖

SERVES 4

PREPARATION TIME
20 minutes
COOKING TIME
30 minutes
FREEZING
Not suitable

- 350 g (12 oz) onion, peeled
- 1 large green pepper
- 45 ml (3 tbsp) oil
- 1 garlic clove, crushed
- 15 ml (1 tbsp) flour
- 400 g (14 oz) can chopped tomatoes with herbs
- 15 ml (1 tbsp) tomato purée
- 2.5 ml (½ tsp) dried marjoram
- salt and pepper
- 550 g (1¼ lb) thick-cut cod fillet or monkfish tail, skinned

235 CALS/SERVING

1 Roughly chop the onion. Halve the green pepper, remove the seeds, then chop roughly.
2 Heat the oil in a medium casserole. Add the onion and sauté for 3–4 minutes until beginning to brown. Stir in the green pepper and garlic and sauté for a further 2–3 minutes.
3 Mix in the flour, cook for 1 minute, then stir in the tomatoes, tomato purée, marjoram and plenty of seasoning. Bring to the boil, stirring.
4 Cut the fish into eight even pieces and add to the casserole. Baste with the sauce mixture.
5 Cover tightly and bake at 180°C (350°F) mark 4 for about 30 minutes or until the fish is just beginning to flake apart. Serve with pasta tossed in pesto, or with crusty bread.

❖ Smoked Haddock Casserole ❖

SERVES 6

PREPARATION TIME
20 minutes
COOKING TIME
40 minutes
FREEZING
Not suitable

- 450 g (1 lb) fresh haddock fillet
- 225 g (8 oz) smoked haddock fillet
- 350 g (12 oz) onion, peeled
- 350 g (12 oz) old potatoes
- 175 g (6 oz) courgettes
- 175 g (6 oz) carrots, peeled
- 25 g (1 oz) butter or margarine
- 600 ml (1 pint) light stock
- 125 g (4 oz) cooked peeled prawns
- 15 ml (1 tbsp) cornflour
- 150 ml (¼ pint) single cream
- 30–45 ml (2–3 tbsp) chopped parsley
- pepper

240 CALS/SERVING

1 Skin the haddock and cut the flesh into large pieces. Slice the onion. Peel the potatoes and cut into large chunks. Thickly slice the courgettes and carrots.

2 Melt the butter in a 4 litre (7 pint) flameproof casserole. Add the onion, courgettes and carrots and sauté gently, stirring, for 3–4 minutes.

3 Add the stock and potatoes and bring to the boil. Cover and simmer gently on the hob or cook in the oven at 170°C (325°F) mark 3 for 30 minutes or until all the vegetables are tender.

4 Add the haddock and prawns; bring back to the boil. Cover and simmer gently on the hob or return to the oven for a further 5 minutes until the fish is cooked.

5 Mix the cornflour to a smooth paste with a little water. Stir into the casserole and cook for 1 minute until slightly thickened, stirring all the time.

6 Just before serving, stir in the cream and parsley. Warm gently and season to taste with pepper. Serve in soup bowls, accompanied by crusty white bread.

❖ Paella ❖

SERVES 4

PREPARATION TIME
20 minutes
COOKING TIME
30 minutes
FREEZING
Not suitable
COLOUR INDEX
Page 28

- 700 g (1½ lb) haddock fillet
- good pinch of saffron strands
- 450 g (1 lb) tomatoes
- 1 yellow pepper
- 1 green pepper
- 2 onions, peeled
- 90 ml (6 tbsp) olive oil
- 450 g (1 lb) long-grain white rice
- about 600 ml (1 pint) light stock
- 300 ml (½ pint) white wine
- 30 ml (2 tbsp) chopped thyme
- 1 garlic clove, crushed
- salt and pepper
- 225 g (8 oz) cooked shelled mussels
- 225 g (8 oz) cooked peeled prawns
- cooked prawns in shells, to garnish

450 CALS/SERVING

1 Skin the fish and cut into 5 cm (2 inch) pieces. Place the saffron in a jug, pour on 150 ml (¼ pint) boiling water and leave for 10 minutes.

2 Skin, quarter and deseed the tomatoes, reserving the juices. Halve, core and deseed the peppers, then cut into pieces. Chop the onion.

3 Heat the oil in a large flame-proof casserole. Add the onion and fry until just brown. Stir in the rice, then the stock, wine and strained saffron liquid. Bring to the boil.

4 Gently mix in the haddock pieces, peppers, tomatoes and strained juices, thyme, garlic and seasoning. Cover tightly and bake at 180°C (350°F) mark 4 for 20 minutes.

5 Carefully stir in the cooked shelled mussels and prawns. Re-cover and bake for a further 10 minutes or until the rice is quite tender and all the liquid is absorbed. Adjust the seasoning and serve the paella immediately, garnished with whole prawns and accompanied by crusty bread

❖ Italian Fish Stew ❖

3 Heat the oil in a large heavy-based saucepan, add the onion, garlic and pimiento and fry gently for 5 minutes.

4 Add the tomatoes and anchovies and stir to break them up. Add the wine and stock, bring to the boil, lower heat and add the bay leaves and half the basil. Simmer, uncovered, for 20 minutes.

5 Add the firm fish to the tomato mixture, then strain in the saffron water and season to taste. Cook for 10 minutes, then add any delicate-textured fish and cook for a further 5 minutes.

6 Add the prawns and mussels, cover and cook for 5 minutes or until the mussels open. Discard the bay leaves and any unopened mussels. Put a slice of toast in each serving bowl and spoon over the stew.

SERVES 8

PREPARATION TIME
25 minutes
COOKING TIME
45 minutes
FREEZING
Not suitable

- 900 g (2 lb) tomatoes
- good pinch of saffron strands
- about 1.1 kg (2½ lb) mixed fish fillets (red mullet, bream, brill, monkfish, plaice or cod), skinned
- 20–24 large cooked whole prawns in shells
- 100 ml (3½ fl oz) olive oil
- 2 large onions, peeled and finely chopped
- 4 garlic cloves, crushed
- 4 slices canned pimiento, cut into strips
- 4 anchovy fillets, drained
- 300 ml (½ pint) dry white wine
- 300 ml (½ pint) fish stock or water
- 4 bay leaves
- 90 ml (6 tbsp) chopped basil
- salt and pepper
- 20–24 mussels, cleaned
- 8 slices of toast, to serve

420 CALS/SERVING

1 Skin, deseed and chop the tomatoes. Soak the saffron strands in a little boiling water for 30 minutes.

2 Meanwhile, cut the fish into chunky bite-sized pieces. Peel the prawns.

❖ Kedgeree ❖

SERVES 4

PREPARATION TIME
10 minutes
COOKING TIME
20–25 minutes
FREEZING
Not suitable
COLOUR INDEX
Page 28

- 175 g (6 oz) long-grain rice
- salt
- 450 g (1 lb) smoked haddock fillets
- 2 hard-boiled eggs, shelled
- 50 g (2 oz) butter or margarine
- cayenne pepper, to taste
- chopped parsley, to garnish

425 CALS/SERVING

1 Cook the rice in fast boiling salted water until tender. Drain and rinse under cold water. Drain well and spread out on a tray to dry.
2 Meanwhile, put the smoked haddock in a large frying pan with just enough water to cover. Bring to simmering point, then simmer for 10–15 minutes, until tender. Drain, skin and flake the fish, discarding any bones.
3 Chop one hard-boiled egg; slice the other and set aside. Melt the butter in a saucepan, add the cooked rice, fish, chopped egg and cayenne pepper to taste. Stir over a moderate heat for about 5 minutes, until hot. Pile on to a warmed serving dish and garnish with parsley and hard-boiled egg slices.

MEAT

The current desire for a healthier, lower-fat diet means that our consumption of meat is decreasing. Thankfully, meat producers are gradually responding to this and producing new leaner cuts. The increased demand for fast food means that they're also developing new tender cuts which cook quickly. In fact meat is highly nutritious, and for a lot of people it's still their major source of protein, B vitamins and iron. If you are worried about your fat consumption, or on a diet, choose the lean cuts without too much visible fat. Alternatively, make a small amount of meat go further by serving it with lots of vegetables or by mixing it with pulses in casseroles and stews.

Choosing Meat

Meat should look and smell fresh. As for colour, a lurid red doesn't necessarily indicate freshness. Instead look for a good clear colour; the colour of meat will darken naturally on exposure to the air. A greyish tinge is certainly a bad sign. Any fat should be creamy white; if it's yellow – except for some specialist breeds such as Jersey and Guernsey beef – the meat is probably past its prime. Look for a smooth outer layer of fat, if appropriate to the cut, and a fair amount of 'marbled' fat distributed throughout the meat; this will keep it moist during cooking and add flavour.

Always look for a neat, generally well trimmed piece of meat. Splinters of bone and ragged edges indicate poor butchery. Cuts should be trimmed of sinew. Joints and steaks should be of uniform thickness so that they cook evenly. Offal should look fresh and moist, and it should not smell.

A good butcher is invaluable; a shop run by helpful knowledgeable staff inevitably means that they care about their meat and will have treated it properly. It is also likely that they will be able to advise you about cooking times and methods as well as prepare joints, steaks and the like to your specific requirements.

Storing Meat

All meat should be stored loosely wrapped in the coldest part of the refrigerator. It's advisable to remove meat from its original wrapping and place it, freshly wrapped, on a plate to prevent any blood dripping through the refrigerator shelves. Always store raw meat well away from cooked foods.

Offal, minced meat and small cuts of veal are best eaten on the day of purchase. Larger joints, chops and steaks will keep for 2–3 days. Lean cuts will keep for longer than fatty cuts since the fat turns rancid first. 'Off' or bad meat will have an unpleasant smell, slimy surface and possibly even a greenish tinge. Because of the possibility of food poisoning it's not worth taking a risk with meat that you suspect of being past its best.

Marinades

A good marinade will make all the difference to the taste and texture of a piece of meat. Usually based on oil or wine or something acidic, like fruit juice or yogurt, it will tenderise tough cuts and lend a subtle aroma and flavour. Oil and wine based marinades tend to soak into the meat adding moisture to dry cuts while yogurt will tenderise and form a soft crust on the food as it cooks. Aromatics like lemon rind, bay leaves, thyme, garlic and onion add fragrance as well as flavour.

Put the food in a shallow non-metallic dish and pour over the marinade. Leave in a cool place for at least 1 hour but preferably overnight. When ready to cook, brush or strain off excess marinade and cook as directed in the recipe. If you're cooking on a barbecue or under the grill baste the meat frequently with the marinade as it cooks. Any remaining marinade can be brought to the boil in a small pan, strained if necessary, and served poured over accompanying vegetables or salad leaves. The exception to this is any yogurt based marinade which would curdle.

❖ Cooking Methods ❖

To get the most from a cut or joint of meat it is vital to cook it appropriately. Lean, fine-grained cuts respond well to quick cooking while tougher cuts with more connective tissue need long, slow cooking to make them tender.

Roasting

Only good quality tender joints are suitable for roasting. Opinions differ about roasting times and temperatures because there is a great deal of variation in the way people like their meat cooked. We found that high temperature roasting, at 230°C (450°F) mark 8, was only suitable for really top quality cuts, such as beef fillet.

However you decide to cook your roast, it's important to weigh the joint and bring it to room temperature before cooking. Put the meat, fat side up, on a roasting rack and smear with mustard or stud with slivers of garlic. Pork should be rubbed with oil and salt to make a nice crisp crackling. With the exception of pork with crackling, baste all roasts frequently during cooking to keep them moist; if the joint is very lean add moisture in the form of dripping or oil. Refer to the chart overleaf for roasting times.

To determine accurately whether the meat is cooked, insert a meat thermometer into the thickest part to ascertain the internal temperature. Alternatively and much less accurately, push a skewer right into the middle of the joint. If the juices run clear the meat is thoroughly cooked; if they run pink, the meat is medium; if bloody, it's rare or undercooked.

❖ Roasting Meat ❖

MEAT ❖	COOKING TIME AT 180°C (350°F) MARK 4 ❖	INTERNAL TEMPERATURE ❖
BEEF		
Rare	• 20 minutes per 450 g (1 lb) plus 20 minutes	60°C (140°F)
Medium	• 25 minutes per 450 g (1 lb) plus 25 minutes	70°C (160°F)
Well Done	• 30 minutes per 450 g (1 lb) plus 30 minutes	80°C (175°F)
VEAL		
Well Done	• 25 minutes per 450 g (1 lb) plus 25 minutes	70°C (160°F)
LAMB		
Medium	• 25 minutes per 450 g (1 lb) plus 25 minutes	70–75°C (160–170°F)
Well Done	• 30 minutes per 450 g (1 lb) plus 30 minutes	75–80°C (170–175°F)
PORK		
Well Done	• 35 minutes per 450 g (1 lb) plus 35 minutes	80–85°C (175–180°F)

Stewing and Casseroling

These cooking methods are almost identical except one is cooked on the hob and the other in the oven. For a good colour, brown the meat thoroughly, in batches if necessary, before adding any liquid. If you are reducing your fat intake the fat can be skimmed off the stew or casserole before serving. The most effective way of removing fat is to prepare the dish ahead and allow it to cool completely until the fat solidifies on the surface; it can then be removed easily.

Choose a good heavy-based saucepan or casserole to prevent the contents burning or sticking to the bottom and make sure that it has a tightly fitting lid so that the liquid will not evaporate too rapidly. Keep the liquid at a gentle simmer just below boiling point; if it boils the meat is likely to be tough. All the less tender, more economical cuts of meat can be used. Any meat labelled 'stewing' will take longer to cook than meat labelled 'braising'. If you're making stews or casseroles for the freezer, add flavourings such as garlic sparingly.

Braising

Braising is similar to the above methods although, generally speaking, it tends to involve less liquid. The browned meat is set on a bed of vegetables with sufficient liquid to create steam, covered tightly and cooked very gently. Slightly tenderer cuts are used. Read the labels in the supermarket or ask your butcher for advice on suitable cuts for braising.

Frying, Grilling and Barbecuing

These methods are only suitable for tender cuts. Marinating the meat before cooking helps to add flavour and keeps it moist. Ensure that the frying pan, grill or barbecue is hot before you begin cooking so that the meat is sealed and browned. If cooking thicker pieces, or pork or sausages which must be cooked right through, reduce the heat once the meat has browned or if barbecuing move it away from the heat source.

If frying, use a good heavy-based pan and a fat that can withstand the high temperature: olive or vegetable oil; clarified butter rather than pure butter; dripping; some vegetable margarines (avoid low fat brands which contain water and therefore splatter).

For stir-frying, cut the meat into small evenly sized pieces across the grain. A marinade of soy sauce, garlic and a dash of dry sherry will ensure that the meat is tasty and tender if nothing is suggested in your recipe. Heat the wok and a little vegetable oil until very hot. Add the meat, drained of marinade if necessary and keep turning and stirring as the meat cooks.

❖ COOKING STEAKS Professional chefs determine when a steak is cooked as required by pressing it with their fingertips – they can tell by the degree of resistance. For inexperienced cooks this is impractical. In fact cooking steaks to perfection is difficult. The only really reliable way is to cut the steak open and look at it. The timing depends on the thickness rather than the size of the piece of meat. As a rough guide, a 2 cm (¾ inch) thick steak will take about 2 minutes' grilling or frying each side for rare; 3–4 minutes each side for medium; and 6–7 minutes to be cooked through.

Boiling

This is a misnomer since boiling produces tough and tasteless meat. Meat for boiling is usually salted, so it should be soaked overnight in several changes of cold water before cooking. Cover the meat with fresh water and a tightly fitting lid and simmer gently for about 25 minutes per 450 g (1 lb) plus 30 minutes for large joints and about 1½ hours minimum for small joints; do not boil. Add vegetables, spices and herbs to the cooking liquid if you intend using it as stock. Pressure cookers greatly reduce the cooking time. Refer to the manufacturer's handbook, but in general allow about two thirds of the cooking time.

❖ Carving Meat ❖

Regardless of the cut or type of meat here are a few golden rules which make carving much easier:

❖ A decent-sized, really sharp knife is essential. It's worth keeping a knife sharpener to hand to re-sharpen the knife half way through.

❖ A proper carving fork with two long prongs and a finger guard helps keep the meat firmly in place.

❖ Leave the joint to stand on an edged dish in a warm place for 5–15 minutes before you start. This allows the meat to 'relax' and makes carving much easier. Pour off any juices that collect in the dish and add them to the gravy.

❖ Always put the joint on a firm, flat, non-slip surface. A board is ideal, but some people prefer to use a spiked metal dish.

❖ Remove any string or skewers which will get in the way as you carve.

❖ Before starting to carve, loosen the cooked meat from any outer, exposed bones.

❖ Cut across the grain of the meat, which usually means cutting at a right angle to the main bone.

A GUIDE TO MEAT CUTS

Cuts of meat and their names vary enormously across Britain and throughout Europe and the United States. Some butchers and supermarkets in this country now stock a good range of Continental cuts. If you are unsure of a particular description it's best to ask. The following cuts are most commonly available:

❖ Beef ❖

Beef is still the first choice for roasting, but influences from abroad and changes in our eating patterns are encouraging us to use it in many other ways too.

❖ TOPSIDE A very lean cut with little fat, so it is usually sold with a layer of fat tied around it. Great for roasting and braising. Also sold sliced for making beef olives.

❖ RIB Both fore rib (the end of the ribs) and rib are sold on the bone or boned and rolled. Rib is more fatty than topside. It is usually roasted and served hot or cold.

❖ SIRLOIN This is another tender cut, sold either on the bone or boned and rolled for roasting. Sometimes it is sold with the fillet still attached, otherwise this is removed and sold separately as fillet steak.

Porterhouse steak is cut from the thick end of the sirloin and can weigh as much as 800 g (1½ lb). When it is cooked on the bone it is called T-bone steak. Minute steak is very thin steak from the upper part of the sirloin.

❖ FILLET OR TENDERLOIN The ultimate joint for roasting and making Beef Wellington, fillet is the small 'eye' on the inside of the rib bone. It is extremely expensive, but very lean and tender. Fillet is best served rare. Chateaubriand is a thick slice or steak cut from the middle of the fillet, that serves 2 people. Tornedos or filet mignon steaks are also cut from the fillet.

❖ ENTRECÔTE By definition, this is the part of the meat between the ribs. However, a slice cut from the sirloin or rump is sometimes sold by this name.

❖ RUMP STEAK A lean tender cut, taken from the hind quarter. Suitable for grilling and frying.

❖ FLASH FRY STEAKS Cut from the thick flank, topside or silverside, these steaks are beaten and passed between spiked rollers to make them tender.

❖ SILVERSIDE Another lean, boneless joint sold for roasting, but it can be dry and tough if cooked in this way. Traditionally it is salted and boiled. Uncooked salted beef is an unpalatable shade of grey, but it soon becomes pink when cooked.

❖ BRISKET Sometimes sold on the bone, but more commonly boned and rolled; it may also be salted. Brisket is best braised or pot roasted, but it can be roasted.

❖ CHUCK AND BLADE STEAK A lean cut which is usually sold sliced or cubed for braising, stewing and pie fillings. Look for some marbling of fat throughout.

❖ THICK FLANK (TOP RUMP) Another lean boneless cut for pot roasting and braising. If thinly sliced it can be fried.

❖ THIN FLANK Suitable for braising and stewing.

❖ NECK AND CLOD For stewing or mince.

❖ SHIN AND LEG Lean meat with lots of connective tissue. Needs slow, moist cooking such as stewing or casseroling.

Carving Beef

If you buy a joint of fore rib ask the butcher to chine the backbone. After cooking, remove the backbone and cut down between the meat and the bones. Carve the meat downwards, on to and between the rib bones.

Boned and rolled joints are simply laid on their side and carved through. Do not attempt to slice one standing on its end.

❖ Veal ❖

Veal comes from young calves so it is a very tender, lean meat. The palest (and most desired by some) comes from baby milk-fed calves; as the animals get older they supplement their diet with grass and the meat darkens. Veal production is a dubious and at times inhumane practice. If you are happy to eat veal you should at least try to buy it from a butcher who uses a reliable supplier.

Despite its tenderness veal does not roast well; because it is so lean it tends to dry out. The most common cuts are as follows:

❖ LEG A prime cut, sold sliced as escalopes.

❖ FILLET The most expensive cut, generally sold in a piece for roasting. Follow recipes carefully because it tends to dry out. If possible, ask your butcher to lard it for you or marinate for about 1 hour before cooking.

❖ KNUCKLE OR OSSO BUCO Meat and bone ready sawn into 5 cm (2 inch) pieces for stews and of course the Italian speciality, Osso Buco.

❖ LOIN Usually sold as cutlets and chops. It may also be boned and sold as entrecôte steak, or rolled for roasting.

❖ BREAST This is usually the cheapest cut. Sold boned and rolled and sometimes ready stuffed for roasting.

❖ PIE VEAL Diced trimmings. Needs long slow cooking.

❖ LIVER AND KIDNEYS Calf's liver and kidneys are considered to be superior to all others. Calf's liver is mild and tender. It can be thinly sliced and sautéed or grilled.

❖ Lamb ❖

Think of lamb and you'll probably think of Spring; new potatoes, young peas and mint from the garden. Although home-produced lamb is at its best in the Spring, there is a good supply all year round, owing to imported New Zealand lamb. Today's lamb is leaner than ever thanks to new ways of dividing the carcass, many influenced by French butchers. Shoulders and legs of lamb are now cut into steaks, and minced lamb is more widely available.

❖ LEG Probably the most popular cut for roasting, the leg has plenty of lean meat. It is usually sold with the bone in, but some butchers now sell ready boned legs. After boning it can also be 'butterflied' – spread flat for grilling or barbecuing – so that it cooks quickly and easily.

❖ SHOULDER Sold whole or halved for roasting. Chops or steaks can also be cut from the shoulder for grilling or braising.

❖ LOIN The loin consists of both chump and loin chops. Chump chops have a small round bone in the centre, and loin chops a small T bone. Loin steaks are simply loin chops with the bone removed. The whole loin can also be roasted in one piece either on or off the bone.

❖ SADDLE OF LAMB OR DOUBLE LOIN This is a really large joint for roasting consisting of the whole loin from both sides of the lamb. It is sometimes sold sliced into butterfly or Barnsley chops.

❖ FILLET OF LAMB This is also cut from the loin; it is very lean and can be roasted, or cooked en croûte rather like a fillet of beef.

❖ RACK OF LAMB Formerly known as best end of neck, this is sold as a whole roasting joint consisting of 6–8 chops or cutlets. Usually chined by the butcher to make serving easier, the tips of the cutlet bones are then scraped of all fat and meat to look attractive. The cut used for Guard of Honour and Crown Roast.

❖ LAMB CUTLETS Individual cutlets are popular for grilling and frying. Boned and rolled cutlets are called noisettes; these neat portions of lean meat are excellent grilled or fried.

❖ SCRAG AND MIDDLE NECK These are usually sold as neck cuts on the bone for stewing and braising in dishes like Lancashire Hotpot and Irish Stew. The main 'eye' of the middle neck is sold as neck fillet for grilling and frying.

❖ BREAST OF LAMB Generally sold ready boned and rolled and sometimes stuffed, breast of lamb is tender enough to roast, but because it contains a lot of connective tissue it is best cooked slowly and thoroughly. Riblets are cut from the breast for grilling.

❖ LIVER Suitable for frying or braising. To tone down the strong flavour, soak in milk for 1 hour before cooking, if wished.

❖ KIDNEY Lamb's kidney is darker than calf's and smaller. It is best quickly fried or grilled.

❖ HEART Whole hearts can be stuffed and braised or casseroled. Before cooking, wash thoroughly, trim away any fat and tubes and snip the cavity walls. Leave to soak for 1 hour in clean salted water. Rinse and drain.

❖ BRAINS Lamb's brains have a delicate flavour. They are usually sold in sets (one portion). Before cooking, soak for 2 hours in cold water or milk to remove all traces of blood.

❖ SWEETBREADS These are part of the lamb's thymus gland. Soak as above before cooking.

Carving Lamb

To carve a leg of lamb, put the joint on a board with the meatier side uppermost and the carving fork firmly in the knuckle end to steady it. Cut a narrow wedge-shaped piece of meat from the top middle of the joint, cutting right down to the bone. Carve slices from either side of the first cut, gradually slanting the knife as you go to get larger slices. Do not try to cut the slices too thinly. Turn the joint over and cut off the fat. Carve slices along the joint.

To carve a shoulder of lamb, hold the joint at the shank end with the crisp skin uppermost. Cut a wedge-shaped slice through the middle of the joint in the angle between the shoulder blade and the leg bone. Carve slices from each side of the cut until the shoulder and shank bones are reached. Turn the joint over and carve horizontal slices from the underside.

❖ Pork ❖

The pork of today is leaner than it has ever been and it's available in a variety of quick cooking cuts. Pork must always be well cooked: it should never be served rare or medium. Use a meat thermometer to check the internal temperature of roast pork; a reading of 85°C (180°F) indicates that it's well cooked. Alternatively, insert a skewer into the thickest part of the joint and the juices should run clear.

Part of the attraction of roast pork is the crackling. For good, crisp crackling score the rind, pat it dry, then rub it with oil and a generous amount of salt. Don't baste the rind as it cooks or it will not crisp. For moist methods of cooking like stews and casseroles it's best to remove the rind.

❖ LOIN A popular joint for roasting either on the bone or boned, stuffed and rolled. It usually has a good layer of crackling. It may also be cut into loin chops which sometimes have the kidney attached, or loin steaks (boned loin chops).

❖ LEG This large joint is usually sold divided into the fillet end and the knuckle or shank end. Both are good for roasting. The fillet end is sometimes cut into leg steaks for grilling or frying.

❖ SHOULDER OR HAND SPRING Another joint for roasting, or using diced in pie fillings, curries and casseroles.

❖ TENDERLOIN OR PORK FILLET This lean and really versatile cut is excellent for cubing and making kebabs for grilling. When thinly sliced it is perfect for pan-frying. Escalopes are thin, batted-out slices cut across the grain from the fillet or the leg.

❖ SPARE RIBS These are cut from the belly or the ribs. Spare rib chops can be casseroled or braised, while trimmed American or Chinese spare ribs are less meaty and are typically cooked in barbecue sauce.

❖ BELLY A long thin cut streaked with fat. It may also be sold as a boned and rolled joint.

❖ LIVER Pig's liver has a strong flavour, which can be toned down slightly by soaking in milk for 1–2 hours before cooking. It is really only suitable for inclusion in pâtés and terrines – mixed with other meats and well flavoured with herbs and spices.

Carving Pork

If you are roasting a pork loin, ask the butcher to chine the bone when you buy the joint. To carve, sever the chined bone from the rib bones. Cut the crackling off all in one piece and divide into portions. Cut down between the rib bones to divide the joint into chops. Alternatively, cut along the length of the joint between the meat and the rib bones then carve off slices without bone.

To carve a leg of pork (shank end), remove some of the crackling. Cut thin slices down to and around the bone as far as possible. When the shank bone is reached, carve at an angle over the top of the bone. Turn the whole joint over and cut down towards the thin end of the bone at an angle.

To carve a leg (fillet end) carve slices through to the bone on either side of it.

❖ Bacon and Ham ❖

Bacon is quite simply pork that has been preserved or cured. But, as a meat, bacon is almost in a category of its own. For some, the smoky flavour and aroma as it cooks are irresistible. Moreover bacon is highly versatile. Use it grilled until crisp in salads, to top baked potatoes, or in sandwiches. Cook it until the fat runs, and toss with vinaigrette and lentils, or use it to flavour pasta dishes, stews and casseroles.

There are several methods of curing bacon which all produce different flavours. Basically the meat is injected with brine solution which colours, flavours and preserves the meat. A side of bacon may be cured whole or cuts – such as the middle – may be cured separately. After curing it may be smoked. Unsmoked bacon is known as 'green' bacon.

Ham, strictly speaking, is the hind leg of a pig cut from the whole side, then cured and matured separately. Gammon is the name given to whole hind legs cut from a side of bacon after it has been cured. Cooked gammon is now frequently described as ham.

Cuts of Bacon, Ham and Gammon

Throughcut (middle) rashers are the back and streaky joined together. Back, streaky and throughcut rashers are virtually interchangeable in recipes, although streaky is obviously much more fatty. If you are trying to reduce your fat consumption look out for 'fat reduced' bacon. Always drain grilled or fried bacon on kitchen paper after cooking.

Check whether the recipe states smoked or unsmoked bacon. Smoked bacon will lend a smoky flavour to foods it is cooked with and in some dishes this may be too strong.

Ham has a subtler more delicate flavour than bacon, but it is equally versatile. Hams are usually sold ready cooked; if not, cook as bacon. Some of the best known cures are York, Suffolk, Honey-roast, Cumberland and Virginia. Some hams, such as the Italian Parma ham, French *Bayonne* and Spanish *Serrano* are eaten raw.

❖ COLLAR OF BACON Taken from the shoulder, then boned and rolled, this is a good joint for boiling or braising. It may need to be soaked before cooking.

❖ FOREHOCK OF BACON This cheap cut is sold with the bone in or, more conveniently, boned and rolled. It has a good flavour and is fairly lean. Use in pot roasts, braise with lentils and vegetables or simmer it.

❖ GAMMON Buy gammon raw as a whole or half gammon or as smaller cuts which are known as middle, corner and gammon hock. Most are sold boned, ready to boil, braise or bake.

Gammon steaks and rashers are cut after boning and are suitable for grilling or frying.

Cooking Bacon and Gammon Joints

To remove excess salt, soak large smoked joints overnight in frequent changes of cold water. Green or mild cure joints need only 4–6 hours' soaking or none at all – ask your butcher's advice. Simmer in water, with a few vegetables for flavour, for 20–25 minutes per 450 g (1 lb) plus 20 minutes. For joints over 4.5 kg (10 lb) allow 15–20 minutes per 450 g (1 lb) plus 15 minutes.

❖ Boeuf Bourguignon ❖

SERVES 8

PREPARATION TIME
20 minutes
COOKING TIME
2¼ hours
FREEZING
Suitable (stage 2)

- 225 g (8 oz) piece bacon, rinded
- 1.8 kg (4 lb) braising steak or topside
- 50 g (2 oz) butter
- 60 ml (4 tbsp) oil
- 2 garlic cloves, crushed
- 60 ml (4 tbsp) plain flour
- salt and pepper
- bouquet garni
- 300 ml (½ pint) beef stock
- 600 ml (1 pint) red Burgundy wine
- 24 button onions, peeled
- 350 g (12 oz) button mushrooms
- chopped parsley, to garnish

510 CALS/SERVING

1 Dice the bacon. Cut the meat into 4 cm (1½ inch) pieces. Heat half the butter and oil in a flameproof casserole and fry the bacon for 5 minutes. Drain. Fry the meat in batches for about 8 minutes or until browned.

2 Return the bacon to the casserole with the garlic. Stir in the flour and add seasoning, the bouquet garni, stock and wine, then bring to the boil, stirring. Cover and cook at 170°C (325°F) mark 3 for 1½ hours.

3 Meanwhile, heat remaining butter and oil in a frying pan and sauté the onions for 10 minutes or until golden brown; remove. Add mushrooms and fry for 5 minutes. Add the mushrooms and onions to the casserole. Cook for a further 30 minutes or until the meat is tender. Garnish with parsley.

❖ Peppered Rib of Beef ❖

SERVES 6

PREPARATION TIME
20 minutes, plus
marinating
COOKING TIME
50–60 minutes,
plus standing
FREEZING
Not suitable
COLOUR INDEX
Page 29

- 300 ml (½ pint) brown ale
- 75 ml (3 fl oz) olive oil
- 15 ml (1 tbsp) dried herbes de Provence
- 2 garlic cloves, sliced
- 1.1 kg (2½ lb) boned and rolled rib of beef or silverside
- 15 ml (1 tbsp) coriander seeds
- 15 ml (1 tbsp) each black, dried green and white peppercorns
- salt and pepper

300 CALS/SERVING

1 Mix together the ale, olive oil, herbs and garlic. Add the meat, turning well to coat. Cover and leave to marinate in the refrigerator overnight, turning occasionally.
2 Crush the coriander seeds and peppercorns using a pestle and mortar or in a strong bowl with the end of a rolling pin.
3 Remove the meat from the marinade; pat dry. Press the peppers and coriander all over the meat.
4 Place the meat in a roasting tin and pour round the marinade. Roast at 230°C (450°F) mark 8 for 10 minutes to seal, then lower the oven temperature to 200°C (400°F) mark 6 and roast for 15 minutes per 450 g (1 lb) for rare or 20 minutes per 450 g (1 lb) for medium-rare.
5 Turn off the oven and transfer the meat to a serving dish; leave to rest in the oven for 15–20 minutes. Skim the pan juices. Place over a medium heat and bring to the boil, adding water if the sauce is too strong. Season and strain into a warm sauceboat.
6 Remove the string, then slice the meat thickly. Serve with the sauce and accompanied by carrots and potatoes or noodles.

❖ Boiled Beef and Carrots ❖

SERVES 6

PREPARATION TIME
15 minutes, plus
soaking
COOKING TIME
2½ hours
FREEZING
Not suitable
COLOUR INDEX
Page 29

- 1.6 kg (3½ lb) lean salted silverside or brisket of beef
- 2 small onions, peeled
- 8 cloves
- 2 small turnips, peeled
- 2 celery sticks
- 1 leek
- bouquet garni
- 6 black peppercorns, lightly crushed
- 18 small carrots

505 CALS/SERVING

1 If necessary, soak the meat in cold water for several hours or overnight, then rinse. (The length of time the meat should be soaked for depends on how salty it is; check with the butcher.) Tie the meat into a neat joint.
2 Quarter the onions and press a clove into each quarter. Cut the turnips into quarters. Chop the celery and leek.
3 Place the beef in a large saucepan, add just enough water to cover and bring slowly to the boil. Skim the surface, then add the bouquet garni, peppercorns, onions, turnips, celery and leek. Lower the heat and simmer very gently for about 2 hours.
4 Add the carrots and simmer gently for a further 20–30 minutes or until the carrots are tender.
5 Carefully transfer the beef and carrots to a warmed serving plate and keep warm. Skim the fat from the surface of the cooking liquor, then strain. Boil to reduce slightly, then pour into a warmed sauceboat. Serve the beef surrounded by the carrots; hand the sauce round separately.

❖ Spiced Beef Casserole ❖ with Horseradish

SERVES 6

PREPARATION TIME
20 minutes
COOKING TIME
2¼ hours
FREEZING
Suitable (stage 4)

- 1.1 kg (2½ lb) stewing beef
- 450 g (1 lb) onions
- about 45 ml (3 tbsp) oil
- 1 garlic clove, crushed
- 225 g (8 oz) button mushrooms
- 25 g (1 oz) plain flour
- 2.5 ml (½ tsp) ground ginger
- 5 ml (1 tsp) medium-hot curry powder
- 5 ml (1 tsp) dark muscovado sugar
- 600 ml (1 pint) beef stock
- 30 ml (2 tbsp) Worcestershire sauce
- salt and pepper
- 30 ml (2 tbsp) creamed horseradish
- 45 ml (3 tbsp) chopped parsley

`395 CALS/SERVING`

1 Trim the beef of any excess fat and cut into 4 cm (1½ inch) pieces. Slice the onions.

2 Heat 30 ml (2 tbsp) oil in a 4 litre (7 pint) flameproof casserole and brown the meat, one third at a time. Drain on absorbent kitchen paper.

3 Lower the heat, add the onions, garlic and mushrooms, with a little more oil if necessary. Sauté, stirring occasionally, for 3–4 minutes. Stir in the flour, spices and sugar and cook, stirring, for a further 1–2 minutes. Add the stock, Worcestershire sauce and seasoning.

4 Return all the meat to the casserole, bring to a gentle simmer, then cover and cook at 170°C (325°F) mark 3 for about 2 hours or until the meat is tender.

5 Stir in the horseradish, adjust the seasoning and sprinkle with parsley. Serve with Brussels sprouts, carrots and mashed potato.

❖ Italian Braised Beef ❖

SERVES 6

PREPARATION TIME
20 minutes, plus marinating
COOKING TIME
2¼ hours
FREEZING
Suitable (stage 3)
COLOUR INDEX
Page 29

- 1.1 kg (2½ lb) braising steak
- 350 g (12 oz) onions, peeled
- 2 large garlic cloves, crushed
- 750 ml (1¼ pint) bottle Chianti
- about 105 ml (7 tbsp) olive oil
- 30 ml (2 tbsp) tomato purée
- 15 ml (1 tbsp) wine vinegar
- salt and pepper
- small bunch thyme sprigs or 10 ml (2 tsp) dried thyme
- 50 g (2 oz) plain flour
- 300 ml (½ pint) beef stock
- 175 g (6 oz) brown cap or button mushrooms
- 400 g (14 oz) can artichoke hearts, drained
- about 18 pitted black olives

`475 CALS/SERVING`

1 Cut the beef into large cubes, discarding any excess fat. Roughly chop the onions. Place the beef, onions and garlic in a bowl with the wine, 45 ml (3 tbsp) olive oil, the tomato purée, vinegar and seasoning. Add the thyme. Stir thoroughly to mix, then cover and leave to marinate in the refrigerator for at least 24 hours.

2 Strain off the marinade and reserve. Heat about 60 ml (4 tbsp) olive oil in a large flameproof casserole. Brown the meat, in batches, adding a little more oil if necessary. Remove all the meat from the casserole using a slotted spoon.

3 Stir the flour into the oil remaining in the casserole and cook for about 1 minute. Whisk in the marinade and stock and bring to the boil, stirring. Replace the meat, cover the casserole tightly, then cook at 170°C (325°F) mark 3 for 2 hours or until tender.

4 Ten minutes before serving, halve or quarter the mushrooms and artichoke hearts. Stir the mushrooms, artichokes and olives into the casserole, then simmer on top of the cooker for about 5 minutes. Check the seasoning before serving.

❖ Oxtail and Lentil Casserole ❖

4 Stir in the lentils, re-cover and cook for a further 1 hour or until the meat is quite tender. Cool the casseroles, then refrigerate overnight. Skim all fat off the surface and reheat on top of the stove. Adjust the seasoning and serve with braised red cabbage and mashed potato.

NOTE: This casserole is best made a day ahead to allow the fat to set on the surface of the liquor. It can then be skimmed away easily to give delicious rich, almost fatless juices on reheating.

❖ Beef Casserole with Kumquats ❖

SERVES 6	
PREPARATION TIME 20 minutes, plus chilling	• 2.3 kg (5 lb) oxtail, cut up
	• 60 ml (4 tbsp) seasoned flour
COOKING TIME 3¼ hours	• 450 g (1 lb) carrots, peeled
FREEZING Suitable	• 450 g (1 lb) parsnips, peeled
	• 450 g (1 lb) onions, peeled
	• 30–45 ml (2–3 tbsp) oil

• 2.3 litres (4 pints) beef stock
• 30 ml (2 tbsp) tomato purée
• 15 ml (1 tbsp) dried mixed herbs
• salt and pepper
• 125 g (4 oz) red lentils

585 CALS/SERVING

1 Toss the chunks of oxtail in seasoned flour to coat evenly. Cut the carrots and parsnips into large fingers; cut the onions into chunks.

2 Heat a little oil in each of two large flameproof casseroles and brown the oxtail pieces in batches evenly on all sides. Remove with a slotted spoon.

3 Add the vegetables to the casseroles and brown lightly, then remove. Add the stock, tomato purée, dried mixed herbs and seasoning to the casseroles. Bring to the boil. Replace the meat, then the vegetables. Cover the dishes tightly and cook at 170°C (325°F) mark 3 for 2 hours.

SERVES 4	
PREPARATION TIME 20 minutes	• 900 g (2 lb) chuck steak
COOKING TIME 2½ hours	• salt and pepper
	• 40 g (1½ oz) flour
FREEZING Not suitable	• 1 tangerine
	• 45 ml (3 tbsp) oil
	• 1 garlic clove, crushed
	• 1 bay leaf

• 300 ml (½ pint) beef stock
• 150 ml (¼ pint) red wine
• 225 g (8 oz) celery
• 350 g (12 oz) leeks
• 125 g (4 oz) kumquats

595 CALS/SERVING

1 Trim the meat of any excess fat and cut into 5 cm (2 inch) pieces. Toss in the seasoned flour.
2 Finely pare the rind from the tangerine and cut into fine shreds; set aside. Squeeze the juice from the tangerine.
3 Heat the oil in a flameproof casserole and fry the meat, a few pieces at a time, until browned and sealed on all sides.
4 Return the meat to the casserole, adding any remaining flour. Add the garlic, bay leaf, stock, wine, 45 ml (3 tbsp) tangerine juice and seasoning. Bring to a simmer. Cover and cook at 170°C (325°F) mark 3 for about 1 hour.
5 Thickly slice the celery, reserving any leaves for garnish; slice the leeks. Cut the kumquats into thin slices. Add these ingredients to the casserole. Re-cover, stir and return to the oven for a further 1½ hours or until the meat is tender.
6 Adjust the seasoning and serve garnished with the tangerine shreds and celery leaves. Serve with rice and broccoli.

❖ Steak and Kidney Pie ❖

SERVES 4

PREPARATION TIME
35 minutes
COOKING TIME
About 2 hours
FREEZING
Suitable
COLOUR INDEX
Page 30

- 700 g (1½ lb) braising steak
- 175 g (6 oz) ox kidney
- 25 g (1 oz) seasoned flour
- 1 large onion, peeled
- 125 g (4 oz) button mushrooms
- 30 ml (2 tbsp) oil
- 1–2 garlic cloves, crushed
- 150 ml (¼ pint) beef stock
- 150 ml (¼ pint) brown ale
- 1 bay leaf
- 1 thyme sprig or 2.5 ml (½ tsp) dried
- 15 ml (1 tbsp) Worcestershire sauce
- 15 ml (1 tbsp) tomato purée
- Shortcrust Pastry made with 175 g (6 oz) flour (page 329)
- milk, to glaze

`780 CALS/SERVING`

1 Trim the braising steak and cut into 2.5 cm (1 inch) pieces. Remove the white core from the kidney and cut into 2.5 cm (1 inch) chunks. Toss the steak and kidney in the seasoned flour, shaking off any excess. Chop the onion; halve the mushrooms if large.

2 Heat the oil in a large saucepan and fry the garlic, onion and mushrooms for 3 minutes. Add the steak, kidney and any remaining coating flour and cook for 5 minutes, until lightly browned. Gradually stir in the remaining filling ingredients. Cover and simmer gently for about 1¼ hours.

3 Spoon the mixture into a 1.7 litre (3 pint) pie dish. Roll out the pastry on a lightly floured work surface to an oval or circle, 5 cm (2 inches) wider than the pie dish. Cut a 2.5 cm (1 inch) wide strip from the outer edge and place on the dampened rim of the dish; brush with water.

4 Cover with the pastry lid; press the edges lightly to seal. Trim off excess pastry and flute the edges. Garnish with pastry leaves cut from the trimmings and brush with milk. Bake at 200°C (400°F) mark 6 for about 40–45 minutes.

❖ Steak and Kidney Pudding ❖

Make a suetcrust pastry by mixing 225 g (8 oz) self-raising flour, 75 g (3 oz) beef suet and a pinch of salt. Add about 120–150 ml (4–5 fl oz) cold water to mix to a soft dough. Roll out two thirds of the dough on a lightly floured surface and use to line a 1.7 litre (3 pint) pudding basin. Leave any extra pastry hanging over the sides. Complete steps 1, 2 and 3 of Steak and Kidney Pie (left) spooning the steak and kidney mixture into the lined pudding basin. Brush the top edge of the pastry with water. Roll out the remaining pastry to make the lid and lay over the pudding. Press the edges together and trim off extra pastry. Cover the top with a pleated double layer of greaseproof paper. Tie in place with string. Put into a large pan containing enough boiling water to come halfway up the sides of the basin. Cover and simmer gently for 2 hours.

`885 CALS/SERVING`

❖ Beef Hot Pot ❖

SERVES 4

PREPARATION TIME
20 minutes
COOKING TIME
2–2¼ hours
FREEZING
Suitable (stage 3)

- 175 g (6 oz) onions
- 225 g (8 oz) carrots
- 225 g (8 oz) swede
- 225 g (8 oz) celery
- 450 g (1 lb) lean stewing steak
- 30 ml (2 tbsp) oil
- 125 g (4 oz) button mushrooms
- 75 g (3 oz) red lentils
- 600 ml (1 pint) beef stock
- salt and pepper
- 225 g (8 oz) potatoes

`360 CALS/SERVING`

1 Peel and roughly chop the onions, carrots, swede and celery. Trim the beef and cut into 5 cm (2 inch) chunks.
2 Heat 15 ml (1 tbsp) oil in a large deep flameproof casserole. Sauté the beef with the onions over a high heat for 3–4 minutes. Stir in the carrots, swede, celery and mushrooms. Add the lentils and stock.
3 Bring to a simmer, cover and cook at 170°C (325°F) mark 3 for 1½ hours, or until the meat is tender. Adjust the seasoning.
4 Peel and thinly slice the potatoes and arrange in overlapping layers on top of the meat mixture. Brush with remaining oil.
5 Return to the oven at 200°C (400°F) mark 6 for 25–30 minutes or until the potatoes are cooked; brown under a hot grill, if necessary. Serve with steamed broccoli.

❖ Steak au Poivre ❖

SERVES 4

PREPARATION TIME
10 minutes
COOKING TIME
6–12 minutes
FREEZING
Not suitable

- 4 sirloin, rump or fillet steaks
- 30 ml (2 tbsp) black or green peppercorns, coarsely crushed
- 25 g (1 oz) butter or margarine
- 15 ml (1 tbsp) oil
- salt
- 30 ml (2 tbsp) brandy
- 150 ml (¼ pint) double cream

515 CALS/SERVING

1 Trim excess fat from the steaks, then place on the crushed peppercorns and press hard to encrust the surface of the meat. Turn to encrust the other side.

2 Heat the butter and oil in a frying pan and fry the steaks for 2 minutes on each side. Reduce the heat and continue cooking until cooked to taste. Season with salt.

3 Remove the steaks from the pan and keep warm. Add the brandy to the pan, remove from the heat and set it alight.

4 When the flames have died down, stir in the cream; reheat gently. Pour over the steaks and serve immediately.

❖ Grilled Steaks ❖ with Madeira Sauce

SERVES 4

PREPARATION TIME
20 minutes
COOKING TIME
8–10 minutes
FREEZING
Not suitable
COLOUR INDEX
Page 30

- 300 ml (½ pint) Demi-Glace sauce (page 91)
- 10 ml (2 tsp) tomato purée
- 50 ml (2 fl oz) good brown stock
- 50 ml (2 fl oz) Madeira
- 15 g (½ oz) butter
- salt and pepper
- 4 thick fillet steaks
- oil, for brushing

415 CALS/SERVING

1 Heat the demi-glace sauce. Add the tomato purée to the sauce and simmer for about 5 minutes. Mix in the stock and simmer for a further 10 minutes, skimming as necessary, until the sauce is syrupy in consistency. Whisk in the Madeira and butter. Adjust the seasoning.
2 Season the steaks with pepper and brush with a little oil. Grill for about 4–5 minutes each side, or until cooked to your liking.
3 Gently reheat the sauce. Serve the steaks with the sauce, and accompanied by asparagus or courgettes, and sautéed potatoes.

❖ Peppered Beef Sauté ❖

SERVES 2–3

PREPARATION TIME
10 minutes
COOKING TIME
10 minutes
FREEZING
Not suitable

- 350 g (12 oz) sirloin steaks
- 10 ml (2 tsp) green peppercorns in brine, drained
- 175 g (6 oz) red onion, peeled
- 30 ml (2 tbsp) olive oil
- 90 ml (6 tbsp) single cream
- 15 ml (1 tbsp) lemon juice
- salt
- lemon slices, to garnish

640–425 CALS/SERVING

1 Cut the steaks into thin strips. Finely chop the peppercorns. Thinly slice the onion.
2 Heat the oil in a sauté pan. Add the onion and fry until just beginning to soften.
3 Stir in the beef and peppercorns and cook, stirring, over a high heat for about 2–3 minutes or until the meat is tender.
4 Lower the heat and stir in the cream and lemon juice, with salt to taste. Garnish with lemon slices to serve, and accompany with noodles.

❖ Steak and Stilton Parcels ❖

SERVES 4

PREPARATION TIME
25 minutes, plus
chilling
COOKING TIME
15–20 minutes
FREEZING
Not suitable
COLOUR INDEX
Page 30

- 2 quick-fry steaks, about 450 g (1 lb) total weight
- 30 ml (2 tbsp) oil
- 75 g (3 oz) blue Stilton cheese
- 15 ml (1 tbsp) chopped tarragon or 2.5 ml (½ tsp) dried
- 60 ml (4 tbsp) single cream
- pepper
- 5 large sheets filo pastry, about 45×25 cm (18×10 inch) each
- 50 g (2 oz) butter, melted
- lemon juice, to serve

605 CALS/SERVING

1 Halve each steak. Heat the oil in a frying pan, then seal the meat quickly in the hot oil; allow to cool.

2 Grate the cheese or soften with a fork. Mix with the tarragon, cream and black pepper (the Stilton should add sufficient salt). Spread the mixture over the top of the cold steaks.

3 Brush one sheet of filo pastry with butter and wrap around one steak to enclose it completely like a parcel.

4 Place on a baking sheet and brush with butter. Repeat with the other steaks. Brush the last sheet of filo with butter and fold it over and over to form a strip 2.5 cm (1 inch) wide. Cut into diamond shapes.

5 Use the pastry diamonds to decorate the parcels. Brush with melted butter. Chill for about 20 minutes. Bake at 220°C (425°F) mark 7 for 15–20 minutes. Squeeze lemon juice over the parcels and serve accompanied by a salad.

❖ Steak and Kidney Kebabs ❖

SERVES 4

PREPARATION TIME
25 minutes, plus
marinating
COOKING TIME
10–15 minutes
FREEZING
Not suitable

- 225 g (8 oz) button onions
- salt and pepper
- 225 g (8 oz) lamb's kidneys, skinned
- 450 g (1 lb) rump steak
- 125 g (4 oz) button mushrooms
- 12 bay leaves
- 300 ml (½ pint) red wine
- 30 ml (2 tbsp) brandy
- 2 large garlic cloves, sliced
- olive oil, for brushing
- 150 ml (¼ pint) beef stock
- 15 ml (1 tbsp) cornflour
- watercress sprigs, to garnish

350 CALS/SERVING

1 Put the button onions in a saucepan, cover with cold salted water, bring to the boil and cook until almost tender, about 10–15 minutes. Drain and refresh under cold running water.

2 Meanwhile halve the kidneys and cut out the cores. Cut the rump steak and kidneys into bite-sized pieces.

3 Thread the steak, kidney, onions, mushrooms and bay leaves on to wooden skewers – don't pack the ingredients too tightly together. Place the skewers in a large non-metallic dish.

4 Pour over the wine and brandy and add the garlic and plenty of pepper. Cover tightly and leave to marinate for several hours if possible, turning occasionally.

5 Lift the skewers out of the marinade and place on a grill rack. Protect the ends of the skewers with foil to prevent them burning. Brush the kebabs with oil and grill, turning occasionally, until cooked through.

6 Pour the stock and marinade into a saucepan and simmer for about 10 minutes. Mix the cornflour to a smooth paste with a little water. Off the heat, stir into the pan, then bring to the boil, stirring all the time. Cook for 1 minute, then adjust the seasoning.

7 Garnish the kebabs with watercress and serve with the sauce. Accompany with rice and broad beans.

❖ Stir-fried Beef ❖ with Mixed Vegetables

SERVES 4

PREPARATION TIME
25 minutes, plus
marinating
COOKING TIME
4–5 minutes
FREEZING
Not suitable
COLOUR INDEX
Page 30

- 550 g (1¼ lb) rump steak
- 60 ml (4 tbsp) soy sauce
- 90 ml (6 tbsp) oil
- 1 large garlic clove, crushed
- 15 g (½ oz) fresh root ginger
- 3–4 medium green chillies
- salt and pepper

- 125 g (4 oz) baby corn cobs
- 175 g (6 oz) mangetouts
- 125 g (4 oz) small cup mushrooms
- 1 bunch spring onions
- 175 g (6 oz) broccoli
- 75–100 ml (3–4 fl oz) vegetable stock

460 CALS/SERVING

1 Cut the steak into thin strips, about 5 cm (2 inches) long and 5 mm (¼ inch) thick, discarding any fat.

2 In a bowl, whisk the soy sauce with 30 ml (2 tbsp) oil and the garlic. Peel and finely chop the ginger; stir into the bowl.

3 Wearing rubber gloves to avoid skin irritation, split open the chillies and rinse away the seeds. Finely chop the flesh and add half to the bowl. Tightly cover the remainder and refrigerate.

4 Add the beef to the bowl with plenty of pepper; the soy sauce should add sufficient salt. Cover and refrigerate for several hours, preferably overnight.

5 Slice the corn cobs lengthwise into fine strips. Top and tail the mangetouts; thinly slice the mushrooms. Cut each spring onion into three.

6 Divide the broccoli into small florets; trim the stalks and slice lengthwise into thin pieces. Blanch the baby corn and broccoli separately in boiling salted water for about 1 minute each; drain thoroughly.

7 Heat 30 ml (2 tbsp) oil in each of two large frying pans. Add the beef and marinade to one and the vegetables to the other. Stir-fry both over a high heat for 2–3 minutes only.

8 Combine the contents of both pans, add the stock and allow to bubble up. Adjust seasoning, adding extra chillies to taste. Serve immediately, with noodles.

NOTE: This stir-fry can be made as spicy as you like by simply adding more chillies. Use sparingly to start with as some chillies can be very hot. It's a good idea to use two frying pans to allow room for the ingredients to fry quickly and not stew. If you use a large wok, stir-fry the beef first.

❖ Chilli Beef with Noodles ❖

SERVES 4

PREPARATION TIME
10 minutes
COOKING TIME
10 minutes
FREEZING
Not suitable
COLOUR INDEX
Page 31

- 450 g (1 lb) rump steak
- 225 g (8 oz) red pepper
- 225 g (8 oz) broccoli
- 1 onion, peeled
- 30 ml (2 tbsp) oil
- 2.5 ml (½ tsp) chilli powder or few drops of Tabasco
- 10 ml (2 tsp) dried oregano

- 30 ml (2 tbsp) sherry or medium white wine
- 300 ml (½ pint) beef stock
- 15 ml (1 tbsp) soy sauce
- 50 g (2 oz) fresh or dried tagliarini (thin pasta noodles)
- pepper

270 CALS/SERVING

1 Trim the steak of any excess fat. Cut into bite-sized pieces. Halve, core and deseed the pepper and cut into similar-sized pieces. Divide the broccoli into small florets; thinly slice the stalks. Chop the onion.

2 Heat the oil in a large sauté pan and brown the beef well on all sides for about 2–3 minutes. Remove with a slotted spoon. Add the vegetables, chilli powder and oregano. Sauté, stirring, for 1–2 minutes.

3 Mix in the sherry, stock and soy sauce, then add the tagliarini. Cover and simmer for 5 minutes or until the noodles and broccoli are tender. Return the beef to the pan. Bring to the boil and simmer for 1 minute to heat through. Adjust seasoning, adding pepper as necessary.

❖ Beef Burgers ❖

SERVES 4

PREPARATION TIME
15 minutes
COOKING TIME
8 minutes
FREEZING
Suitable (stage 2)

- 450 g (1 lb) lean minced beef
- 50 g (2 oz) rolled oats
- 5 ml (1 tsp) dried mixed herbs
- 45 ml (3 tbsp) tomato chutney
- salt and pepper
- 1 egg, beaten

- flour, for dusting
- vegetable oil, for brushing
TO SERVE:
- warm burger baps
- salad
- onion rings

380 CALS/SERVING

1 In a medium bowl, mix together the beef, oats, herbs, chutney and seasoning, adding sufficient beaten egg to bind the mixture.
2 With lightly floured hands, shape into 4 or 8 flat burgers.
3 Brush each one lightly with oil, and grill until golden and cooked through, about 4 minutes on each side, depending on the thickness of the burgers.
4 Serve in warm baps on a salad base, topped with onion rings.

❖ Beef and Potato Moussaka ❖

3 Add the tomatoes, tomato purée, aubergine and seasoning; mix well. Spread evenly in a 1.7 litre (3 pint) shallow flameproof casserole. Arrange the slices of potato neatly over the top to cover the beef mixture completely.

4 For the topping, beat together the egg yolks, yogurt and grated cheese. Pour over the potatoes to cover completely. Bake uncovered at 190°C (375°F) mark 5 for about 1 hour. Brown under a hot grill if necessary.

NOTE: This is a delicious, virtually oil-free moussaka that uses blanched aubergines, rather than the more usual fried ones. Serve it with a crisp green salad.

Variation
Replace the yogurt topping with 300 ml (½ pint) cheese sauce (page 92).

SERVES 4	
PREPARATION TIME 0 minutes	

COOKING TIME –1¼ hours
FREEZING
Not suitable

- 350 g (12 oz) aubergine
- salt and pepper
- 800 g (1¾ lb) potatoes
- 450 g (1 lb) lean minced beef
- 2 onions, peeled and chopped
- 2.5 ml (½ tsp) dried thyme
- 45 ml (3 tbsp) chopped parsley
- 1.25 ml (¼ tsp) ground cinnamon

- 400 g (14 oz) can chopped tomatoes
- 15 ml (1 tbsp) tomato purée
- 2 egg yolks
- 350 g (12 oz) natural yogurt
- 50 g (2 oz) Cheddar cheese, grated

480 CALS/SERVING

1 Cut the aubergine into large chunks; blanch in boiling salted water for 2 minutes; drain well. Peel and thickly slice the potatoes and blanch in boiling salted water for 5–6 minutes; drain well.

2 In a medium sauté pan (preferably non-stick), fry the minced beef with the onions, thyme, parsley and cinnamon until the meat begins to brown; stir frequently to prevent sticking.

❖ Chilli Tacos ❖

SERVES 4	

PREPARATION TIME
10 minutes
COOKING TIME
30 minutes
FREEZING
Not suitable
COLOUR INDEX
Page 31

- 1 onion, peeled
- 1 green pepper
- 450 g (1 lb) lean minced beef
- 1 garlic clove, crushed
- 400 g (14 oz) can chopped tomatoes
- 400 g (14 oz) can red kidney beans, drained and rinsed
- 15 ml (1 tbsp) tomato purée

- 2.5 ml (½ tsp) chilli powder
- 15 ml (1 tbsp) ground cumin
- salt and pepper
- 8 taco shells
- 125 g (4 oz) Cheddar cheese, grated
- soured cream, to serve

470 CALS/SERVING

1 Chop the onion; halve, deseed and chop the green pepper. Place the minced beef, onion, garlic and green pepper in a large non-stick saucepan and heat gently, stirring, until the mince begins to brown and the vegetables soften.
2 Add the tomatoes, kidney beans, tomato purée, spices and seasoning, with 300 ml (½ pint) water and stir well. Simmer for 20–25 minutes or until well reduced.
3 Just before serving, heat the taco shells in the oven at 150°C (300°F) mark 2 for 2–3 minutes, until crisp. Spoon a little of the spiced mince into each taco shell.
4 Serve topped with grated cheese and accompanied by soured cream. Serve with a crisp leafy salad.

NOTE: The mince mixture also makes a good filling for pancakes or a tasty sauce for pasta.

❖ Italian-style Veal Kebabs ❖

5 Cook the kebabs under a moderate grill for about 12 minutes, turning frequently and basting with the marinade.

6 Sprinkle with the cheese. Grill for 1 minute or until just melted. Serve immediately, garnished with lemon wedges, on a bed of rice.

❖ Basil and Citrus Veal Escalopes ❖

SERVES 4

PREPARATION TIME
15 minutes, plus
marinating
COOKING TIME
13 minutes
FREEZING
Not suitable

• 4 veal escalopes, about 350 g (12 oz) total weight
• 4 slices Parma ham
• 60 ml (4 tbsp) olive oil
• 30 ml (2 tbsp) white wine vinegar
• 15 ml (1 tbsp) chopped rosemary

• 25–50 g (1–2 oz) freshly grated Parmesan cheese
• lemon wedges, to garnish

280 CALS/SERVING

1 Place the veal escalopes between sheets of greaseproof paper and bat out thinly, using a rolling pin. Cut each escalope into 4 or 5 strips.

2 Cut each slice of Parma ham into 4 or 5 strips. Place one on each piece of veal and roll up. Place in a non-metallic dish.

3 Mix together the oil, vinegar and rosemary and pour over the meat rolls. Leave to marinate for 2 hours.

4 Lift out the veal rolls, reserving the marinade, and thread them onto wooden skewers.

SERVES 4

PREPARATION TIME
10 minutes
COOKING TIME
5 minutes
FREEZING
Not suitable

• 4 veal escalopes
• 25 g (1 oz) butter
• 15 ml (1 tbsp) olive oil
• 120 ml (4 fl oz) orange juice
• 30 ml (2 tbsp) lemon juice

• 15 g (½ oz) basil leaves, shredded
• salt and pepper
• basil sprigs, to garnish

255 CALS/SERVING

1 Place the veal escalopes between two sheets of greaseproof paper and pound with a wooden rolling pin until about 3 mm (⅛ inch) thick. If very large, cut them into manageable neat pieces
2 Heat the butter and oil in a heavy-based frying pan or sauté pan. Fry the veal, in two batches if necessary, for 1 minute on each side. Add the orange and lemon juices and let bubble for a few seconds, turning the veal in the juice.
3 Add the shredded basil and seasoning. Serve immediately, garnished with basil and accompanied by noodles.

NOTE: For optimum flavour use freshly squeezed orange juice.

❖ Veal Goulash ❖

1 Finely chop the onion. Peel and halve the grapes; remove the pips.
2 Melt half the butter in a frying pan and fry the onion until golden. Add the stock and Madeira, season and bring to the boil. Boil rapidly for 4–5 minutes or until reduced to a slightly syrupy consistency. Add the grape halves and warm through gently.
3 Meanwhile melt the remaining butter in a large frying pan. Season the liver and fry, with the sliced sage leaves, for 3–5 minutes turning once.
4 Remove the liver from the pan and serve at once, with the Madeira sauce. Garnish with sage sprigs.

❖ Sautéed Liver ❖ with Sage and Apple

SERVES 4
PREPARATION TIME
5 minutes
COOKING TIME
10 minutes
FREEZING
Not suitable
COLOUR INDEX
Page 31

- 450 g (1 lb) thinly sliced calf's liver
- 25 g (1 oz) plain flour
- 45 ml (3 tbsp) oil
- 125 g (4 oz) leeks
- 1 eating apple
- 5 ml (1 tsp) dried sage
- 15 ml (1 tbsp) wholegrain mustard
- 150 ml (¼ pint) double cream
- 300 ml (½ pint) apple juice
- salt and pepper

510 CALS/SERVING

SERVES 8
PREPARATION TIME
5 minutes
COOKING TIME
hours
FREEZING
Suitable (stage 3)

- 1.4 kg (3 lb) stewing veal
- 50 g (2 oz) butter or margarine
- 700 g (1½ lb) onions, peeled
- 450 g (1 lb) carrots, peeled
- 30–45 ml (2–3 tbsp) paprika
- 30 ml (2 tbsp) plain flour
- 900 ml (1½ pints) veal or chicken stock
- 60 ml (4 tbsp) dry white wine
- salt and pepper
- 150 ml (¼ pint) soured cream

395 CALS/SERVING

Cut the veal into 4 cm (1½ inch) pieces. Melt the butter in a frying pan and fry the veal, a little at a time, until browned. Remove with a slotted spoon and place in a casserole dish.

Thinly slice the onions and carrots and fry in the fat remaining in the pan for about 5 minutes until lightly browned. Add the paprika and flour and fry for 2 minutes. Gradually stir in the stock, wine and seasoning. Bring to the boil, then pour over the veal.

Cover tightly and cook at 150°C (300°F) mark 2 for 2¼ hours. Pour the soured cream over the goulash and sprinkle with paprika to serve. Accompany with noodles.

❖ Calf's Liver ❖ with Grapes and Madeira

SERVES 4
PREPARATION TIME
minutes
COOKING TIME
0 minutes
FREEZING
Not suitable
COLOUR INDEX
age 31

- 50 g (2 oz) onion or shallot
- 24 large green grapes
- 50 g (2 oz) butter or margarine
- 175 ml (6 fl oz) veal or chicken stock
- 100 ml (4 fl oz) Madeira
- salt and pepper
- 4 slices calf's liver, each about 75–100 g (3–4 oz)
- 4 sage leaves, thinly sliced
- sage sprigs, to garnish

330 CALS/SERVING

1 Cut the liver into slightly smaller pieces. Sprinkle the flour onto a flat plate and coat the liver slices well on all sides.

2 Heat 30 ml (2 tbsp) oil in a large sauté pan (preferably non-stick) and brown the liver well for about 30 seconds on each side. Remove with a slotted spoon.

3 Slice the leeks. Thinly slice the apple, discarding the core. Heat the remaining oil in the pan. Add the leeks, apple and sage and sauté, stirring well, for 2–3 minutes.

4 Mix in the mustard, cream and apple juice. Bring to the boil and simmer for 5 minutes or until reduced by half. Return the liver to the pan, season and heat through for 1 minute. Serve immediately.

❖ Crown Roast of Lamb ❖

SERVES 6

PREPARATION TIME
30 minutes
COOKING TIME
About 1¼ hours
FREEZING
Not suitable
COLOUR INDEX
Page 32

- 2 best end necks of lamb, chined, about 1.4 kg (3 lb) total weight
- 1 large onion, peeled
- 4 celery sticks
- 1 large eating apple
- 50 g (2 oz) no-soak dried apricots
- 40 g (1½ oz) butter or margarine
- 150 g (5 oz) fresh breadcrumbs
- 30 ml (2 tbsp) chopped parsley
- finely grated rind of ½ large lemon
- 25 ml (5 tsp) lemon juice
- 1 egg, beaten
- salt and pepper
- 15–30 ml (1–2 tbsp) olive oil
- 15 ml (1 tbsp) plain flour
- 300 ml (½ pint) lamb stock

700 CALS/SERVING

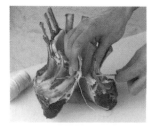

1 Cut between the tips of each cutlet bone to a depth of 2.5 cm (1 inch). Scrape these bone tips clean. Bend the joints around, fat side inwards, and sew together using strong cotton or fine string to form a crown.

2 Chop the onion and celery. Peel, core and chop the apple. Chop the apricots. Melt the butter in a saucepan and cook the onion, celery and apple until brown. Stir in the apricots, breadcrumbs, parsley, lemon rind and juice, egg and seasoning. Allow to cool.

3 Fill the centre of the joint with the stuffing and weigh. Place in a small roasting tin and spoon over the oil. Cover exposed bones with foil. Roast at 200°C (400°F) mark 6 for 20 minutes per 450 g (1 lb) plus 20 minutes, basting occasionally and covering with foil if necessary.

4 Remove foil and transfer the crown roast to a warmed serving dish; keep warm. Drain off as much fat as possible from the roasting tin, add the flour and blend well. Cook for 1 minute, stirring, then stir in the stock and cook for 2–3 minutes. Season to taste and serve hot with the joint.

❖ Thyme Roasted Loin ❖ of Lamb

SERVES 6

PREPARATION TIME
20 minutes
COOKING TIME
50 minutes
FREEZING
Not suitable

- 225 g (8 oz) button mushrooms
- 75 g (3 oz) butter or margarine
- 1 garlic clove, crushed
- 125 g (4 oz) spinach leaves
- salt and pepper
- 2 boned and rolled loins of lamb, about 700 g (1½ lb) each
- freshly grated nutmeg
- 15 ml (1 tbsp) chopped thyme or 10 ml (2 tsp) dried
- grated rind and juice of 1 lemon
- thyme sprigs, to garnish

700 CALS/SERVING

1 Finely chop the mushrooms. Melt 25 g (1 oz) butter in a sauté pan and add the mushrooms and garlic. Cook, stirring, over a high heat for 4–5 minutes or until the mushrooms are well reduced and all the excess liquid has evaporated. Leave to cool.
2 Blanch the spinach in boiling salted water for 10–15 seconds or until just beginning to wilt. Drain well. Separate the leaves out on to absorbent kitchen paper, then leave to cool.
3 Unroll the loins of lamb and line the insides with cold spinach. Spoon the mushroom mixture along the middle of each joint. Season with salt, pepper and nutmeg, then re-roll the joints and tie securely with fine string. Beat the remaining butter with the thyme, lemon rind and 30 ml (2 tbsp) lemon juice. Spread all over the lamb.
4 Place the lamb joints in a roasting tin and cook at 220°C (425°F) mark 7 for 20 minutes. Reduce the oven temperature to 180°C (350°F) mark 4 and cook for a further 30 minutes. Serve the lamb carved into thin slices, garnished with thyme sprigs.

NOTE: The timing given here produces a moist, tender joint with just a hint of pink in the middle. If you like your lamb well done, allow an additional 10 minutes.

❖ Garlic and ❖
Rosemary Rack of Lamb

SERVES 4

PREPARATION TIME
30 minutes
COOKING TIME
About 1¼ hours
FREEZING
Not suitable
COLOUR INDEX
Page 32

- 8 large garlic cloves
- 2 best end necks of lamb, chined, about 1.1–1.4 kg (2½–3 lb) total weight
- 8 long rosemary sprigs
- salt and pepper
- olive oil, for basting
- 15 ml (1 tbsp) redcurrant, mint or apple jelly, warmed

- 15 ml (1 tbsp) plain flour
- 300 ml (½ pint) lamb stock
- 15 ml (1 tbsp) crème de cassis, framboises or mûres

250 CALS/SERVING

1 Peel the garlic and place 7 cloves in a pan of cold water. Bring to the boil and boil for 2 minutes. Drain and set aside. Slice the remaining garlic clove.

2 Place one best end of lamb fat side down on a clean work surface. Cut between each rib, about 2.5 cm (1 inch) from the tips of the bones.

3 Trim away all meat and skin from these tips. Lay two sprigs of rosemary along the length of the 'eye' of the meat and place the sliced garlic on top. Season with pepper.

4 Lay the other best end on top, fat side uppermost, and interlace the bones to form a 'guard of honour'. Using fine string, tie the lamb at regular intervals.

5 Place the rack of lamb in a roasting tin on top of the remaining rosemary. Push the blanched garlic along the top of the lamb underneath the bones. Drizzle with olive oil. Rub the outside of the lamb with a little oil and score lightly with a sharp knife.

6 Roast at 200°C (400°F) mark 6 for about 20 minutes per 450 g (1 lb) plus 20 minutes for pink lamb; longer for well-done meat. About halfway through cooking, brush with the redcurrant jelly to glaze. When the lamb is cooked turn off the oven and transfer the meat to a warmed serving dish. Leave to rest in the oven for at least 15 minutes, before carving.

7 Heat the juices in the roasting tin. Skim off any fat, then stir in the flour. Cook for 1 minute, stirring, then whisk in the stock and liqueur. Bring to the boil and bubble rapidly for 2 minutes or until syrupy. Season to taste, then strain into a warm sauceboat. Remove the string from the meat. Serve the lamb cut into double cutlets with the garlic, sauce and vegetables.

NOTE: Don't be put off by the generous amount of garlic used in this recipe – the cloves literally melt and can be spread on each mouthful of lamb. Ask the butcher to remove the chine bone – the long bone that runs along the base of the 'eye' of the meat.

❖ Roast Lamb with ❖
Peppers and Aubergines

SERVES 4

PREPARATION TIME
20 minutes
COOKING TIME
About 1¼ hours
FREEZING
Not suitable
COLOUR INDEX
Page 32

- 50 g (2 oz) butter, softened
- 15 ml (1 tbsp) wholegrain mustard
- 15 ml (1 tbsp) chopped oregano or marjoram or 5 ml (1 tsp) dried
- 1.1 kg (2½ lb) half leg of lamb

- 450 g (1 lb) red peppers
- 450 g (1 lb) aubergines
- 100 ml (4 fl oz) olive oil
- 30 ml (2 tbsp) chopped oregano or parsley, to garnish (optional)

600 CALS/SERVING

1 Beat the butter with the mustard and oregano or marjoram. Trim the lamb and cut slits, about 2 cm (¾ inch) deep, at regular intervals over the surface.

2 Spread the butter all over the meat, pushing it into the slits. Place the lamb on a wire rack that will fit over a roasting tin.

3 Halve, core and deseed the red peppers, then cut into large chunks. Cut the aubergines into similar-sized chunks. Pour the olive oil into the roasting tin and stir in the vegetables.

4 Place the wire rack and lamb on top and roast at 200°C (400°F) mark 6 for 20 minutes per 450 g (1 lb) plus 20 minutes for medium lamb. Stir the vegetables twice during cooking.

5 Transfer the meat to a serving dish and leave to rest in the turned-off oven for 15 minutes. If necessary, brown the vegetables over a high heat, stirring all the time. Stir in the oregano or parsley and spoon the vegetables around the lamb. Serve immediately accompanied by potatoes.

❖ Roast Lamb ❖
Fillets with Garlic

SERVES 4

PREPARATION TIME
20 minutes
COOKING TIME
30–35 minutes
FREEZING
Not suitable
COLOUR INDEX
Page 32

- *450 g (1 lb) lamb neck fillet*
- *2 large garlic cloves, peeled and thinly sliced*
- *20 ml (4 tsp) chopped rosemary or 5 ml (1 tsp) dried*
- *salt and pepper*
- *8 rashers streaky bacon*

- *15–30 ml (1–2 tbsp) oil*
- *10 ml (2 tsp) plain flour*
- *300 ml (½ pint) lamb stock*
- *10 ml (2 tsp) Dijon mustard*
- *lime wedges and herbs, to garnish*

575 CALS/SERVING

1 Trim the lamb fillet and divide into four pieces. Split horizontally, without cutting right through, and open out like a book. Sprinkle with the garlic, rosemary and pepper. Close the fillets.

2 Derind the bacon rashers, then stretch with the back of a knife. Wrap around the fillets. Heat the oil in a small roasting tin. Add the lamb and bake at 200°C (400°F) mark 6 for 30–35 minutes or until tender. Transfer to a serving dish, cover and keep warm.

3 Pour all but 30 ml (2 tbsp) juice out of the tin. Stir in the flour and cook until lightly browned. Add the stock, mustard and seasoning and let bubble for a few minutes. Slice the lamb and serve with the sauce. Garnish with lime wedges and herbs. Accompany with potatoes and a salad.

❖ Lamb and Courgette Pilaf ❖

SERVES 4

PREPARATION TIME
15 minutes
COOKING TIME
45–50 minutes
FREEZING
Not suitable
COLOUR INDEX
Page 32

- *450 g (1 lb) lean boneless lamb*
- *45 ml (3 tbsp) olive oil*
- *15 ml (1 tbsp) dried rosemary*
- *2 onions, peeled*
- *225 g (8 oz) long-grain brown rice*
- *large pinch of powdered saffron (optional)*

- *750 ml (1¼ pints) vegetable stock*
- *salt and pepper*
- *225 g (8 oz) courgettes*
- *75 g (3 oz) no-soak dried apricots*
- *lemon slices, to garnish*

660 CALS/SERVING

1 Cut the meat into 2.5 cm (1 inch) cubes. Heat the oil in a flameproof casserole. Add the meat and rosemary and fry over a high heat until the meat is beginning to brown. Remove from the pan with a slotted spoon.
2 Slice the onion and lightly brown in the fat remaining in the casserole. Rinse and drain the rice then stir into the casserole with the saffron if using, stock and seasoning.
3 Replace the meat, cover and simmer gently for about 25 minutes. Cut the courgettes into broad sticks and the apricots into slices, then stir into the casserole.
4 Cover and simmer for a further 15–20 minutes, or until most of the liquid is absorbed and the meat is quite tender. Adjust the seasoning and serve garnished with lemon slices.

❖ Lamb Casserole ❖
with Almonds and Ginger

SERVES 8

PREPARATION TIME
20 minutes
COOKING TIME
1¼ hours
FREEZING
Suitable (stage 4)

- *1.5 kg (3¼ lb) leg of lamb*
- *450 g (1 lb) onions*
- *25 g (1 oz) piece fresh root ginger, peeled*
- *1 orange*
- *60 ml (4 tbsp) olive oil*
- *20 ml (4 tsp) ground ginger*
- *10 ml (2 tsp) ground cumin*
- *30 ml (2 tbsp) plain flour*

- *600 ml (1 pint) lamb stock*
- *125 g (4 oz) ground almonds*
- *1 large garlic clove, crushed*
- *salt and pepper*
- *150 ml (¼ pint) single cream*
- *25 g (1 oz) toasted flaked almonds*

620 CALS/SERVING

1 Trim the lamb of any excess fat and cut into 4 cm (1½ inch) cubes. Finely chop the onions and root ginger. Grate the rind from the orange; squeeze the juice from one half.
2 Heat the olive oil in a large flameproof casserole. Add about a quarter of the lamb and brown well on all sides; remove with a slotted spoon. Brown the remaining lamb in batches.
3 Add the onions to the pan with a little more oil if necessary and brown lightly. Stir in the root ginger, ground ginger, cumin and flour and cook for 1–2 minutes, stirring occasionally.

4 Pour in the stock. Stir in the ground almonds, garlic, grated orange rind and juice. Replace the meat, season lightly and bring to a simmer. Cover tightly and cook at 170°C (325°F) mark 3 for about 1½ hours or until the lamb is very tender.
5 Take the casserole out of the oven and stir in the cream. Reheat gently on the hob without boiling. Adjust the seasoning and serve garnished with the flaked almonds. Accompany with a rice pilaf and a green salad.

❖ Country Lamb Casserole ❖

SERVES 6	• 1.1 kg (2½ lb) boned leg or shoulder of lamb
PREPARATION TIME 30 minutes	• 2 onions, peeled
COOKING TIME 2¼ hours	• 350 g (12 oz) carrots, peeled
FREEZING Suitable	• 550 g (1¼ lb) swede, peeled

- 1.1 kg (2½ lb) boned leg or shoulder of lamb
- 2 onions, peeled
- 350 g (12 oz) carrots, peeled
- 550 g (1¼ lb) swede, peeled
- 4 celery sticks
- salt and pepper
- 25 g (1 oz) plain flour
- 30 ml (2 tbsp) olive oil
- 50 g (2 oz) butter or margarine
- 1 garlic clove, crushed
- 50 g (2 oz) pearl barley
- 150 ml (¼ pint) red wine
- 2 rosemary sprigs or 10 ml (2 tsp) dried
- 450–600 ml (¾–1 pint) lamb stock
- 30 ml (2 tbsp) chopped parsley, to garnish

500 CALS/SERVING

1 Trim the lamb of any excess fat and cut into large pieces, about 4 cm (1½ inches) square. Chop the onion, carrots, swede and celery into similar-sized pieces.

2 Toss the lamb in seasoned flour to coat. Heat the oil and butter in a large flameproof casserole and brown the lamb in batches. Remove with a slotted spoon and drain.

3 Lower the heat, add all the vegetables and the garlic with a little more oil if necessary, and sauté for 4–5 minutes. Return the lamb to the casserole. Add the pearl barley, wine, rosemary and just enough stock to cover.

4 Bring to the boil, stir thoroughly, cover and cook at 170°C (325°F) mark 3 for about 2 hours or until the lamb is very tender. Adjust the seasoning. Stir in the parsley just before serving.

❖ Irish Stew ❖

SERVES 4	• 700 g (1½ lb) middle neck lamb cutlets
PREPARATION TIME 15 minutes	• 2 onions, peeled
COOKING TIME 2 hours	• 450 g (1 lb) old potatoes, peeled
FREEZING Suitable	• 15 ml (1 tbsp) chopped parsley

- 700 g (1½ lb) middle neck lamb cutlets
- 2 onions, peeled
- 450 g (1 lb) old potatoes, peeled
- 15 ml (1 tbsp) chopped parsley
- 5 ml (1 tsp) dried thyme
- salt and pepper
- 300 ml (½ pint) lamb stock or water
- chopped parsley, to garnish

490 CALS/SERVING

1 Trim excess fat from the meat. Thinly slice the onions and potatoes.
2 Layer the meat, onions and potatoes in a deep casserole, sprinkling each layer with the herbs and seasoning.
3 Finish with an overlapping layer of potato. Pour in the stock or water. Cover with greaseproof paper, then the lid.
4 Cook at 170°C (325°F) mark 3 for about 2 hours or until the meat and vegetables are tender. Uncover and place under a hot grill to brown the top, if desired. Sprinkle with parsley to serve.

❖ Lamb Cutlets with Apricots ❖

SERVES 4

PREPARATION TIME
10 minutes
COOKING TIME
20 minutes
FREEZING
Not suitable

- ½ onion, peeled
- 75 g (3 oz) no-soak dried apricots
- 15 g (½ oz) butter
- 15 ml (1 tbsp) oil
- 8 lamb cutlets
- 2.5 ml (½ tsp) ground cinnamon
- 150 ml (¼ pint) lamb stock
- salt and pepper

325 CALS/SERVING

1 Thinly slice the onion. Cut the dried apricots into slivers.
2 Heat the butter and oil in a heavy-based frying pan. Add the lamb cutlets and brown on both sides; remove and set aside.
3 Add the onion to the pan and cook until softened. Stir in the apricots and cinnamon. Return the lamb cutlets to the pan and pour over the stock. Season and bring to the boil. Cover and simmer gently for 15 minutes, or until the meat is tender.
4 Transfer the cutlets to a warmed serving dish and pour the sauce over them. Serve with courgettes and carrots.

❖ Lamb Escalopes in Oatmeal ❖

SERVES 4

PREPARATION TIME
15 minutes, plus chilling
COOKING TIME
12 minutes
FREEZING
Not suitable
COLOUR INDEX
Page 33

- 2 lamb leg steaks, about 550 g (1¼ lb) total weight (bone in) and 2–2.5 cm (¾–1 inch) thick
- Dijon mustard, for spreading
- 150 g (5 oz) medium oatmeal
- 15 ml (1 tbsp) dried sage
- salt and pepper
- 1 egg, beaten
- 150 ml (¼ pint) soured cream
- large pinch of paprika
- 45–60 ml (3–4 tbsp) oil
- 25 g (1 oz) butter

550 CALS/SERVING

1 Trim any excess fat from the lamb and cut out the bone. Place the meat between sheets of greaseproof paper and, using a rolling pin, bat out thinly to a 5 mm (¼ inch) thickness. Divide each steak into 4 pieces.
2 Spread a little mustard over one side of each piece of lamb. Mix the oatmeal, sage and seasoning together.

3 Brush the meat with beaten egg and coat with the oatmeal mixture; cover and chill for about 30 minutes.
4 Mix the soured cream and 15 ml (1 tbsp) mustard together in a small bowl. Sprinkle with paprika; cover and chill.
5 Heat a little oil in a frying pan. Mix in the butter and, when foaming, add about half the meat. Fry over a moderate heat until browned and tender, about 3 minutes each side. Drain on absorbent kitchen paper. Keep warm, covered, while frying the remaining lamb, adding more oil if necessary.
6 Serve the lamb accompanied by the cream sauce and a salad.

❖ Lamb Noisettes ❖ with Mushrooms and Onions

SERVES 4

PREPARATION TIME
10 minutes
COOKING TIME
30–40 minutes
FREEZING
Not suitable

- 8–12 noisettes of lamb
- plain flour, for coating
- 15 g (½ oz) butter
- 30 ml (2 tbsp) oil
- 350 g (12 oz) button onions, peeled
- 1 garlic clove, finely chopped
- 350 g (12 oz) small button mushrooms
- 300 ml (½ pint) dry white wine
- 2 rosemary sprigs or 2.5 ml (½ tsp) dried
- salt and pepper

555 CALS/SERVING

1 Coat the lamb noisettes in flour. Heat the butter and oil in a large frying pan and brown the noisettes on both sides. Remove from the pan.

2 Add the onions and garlic to the pan and fry for about 5 minutes or until lightly browned. Add the mushrooms and fry for 2–3 minutes.

Stir in the wine, rosemary and seasoning. Replace the noisettes in the pan, then cover and simmer for 20–30 minutes until tender, turning once.

4 Remove the string from the noisettes. Put the lamb and vegetables in a warmed serving dish; keep warm. Boil the remaining liquid rapidly until reduced by half. Pour over the noisettes and serve.

❖ Spicy Cinnamon Lamb ❖

SERVES 4	
PREPARATION TIME 10 minutes	• 2 onions, peeled • 2.5 cm (1 inch) piece fresh root ginger • 700 g (1½ lb) lamb fillet or leg of lamb • 15 ml (1 tbsp) oil • 2 garlic cloves, crushed • 225 g (8 oz) can chopped tomatoes • 30 ml (2 tbsp) dark soy sauce	• 10 ml (2 tsp) dark muscovado sugar • 1.25 ml (¼ tsp) freshly grated nutmeg • 5 ml (1 tsp) ground cinnamon • pepper • spring onion shreds, to garnish

COOKING TIME 25 minutes

FREEZING Not suitable

510 CALS/SERVING

Finely chop the onions; peel and chop the ginger. Cut the lamb into thin slices.

Heat the oil in a large sauté pan, add the onions, garlic and ginger and cook for 2–3 minutes until softened. Add the meat to the pan and cook over a high heat for 4–5 minutes or until the meat is well browned.

Stir in the remaining ingredients, with 150 ml (¼ pint) water. Bring to the boil, cover and simmer gently for about 20 minutes or until the meat is tender. Serve immediately, garnished with spring onion shreds.

❖ Lamb Chops ❖ and Leeks with Lentils

SERVES 4	
PREPARATION TIME 10 minutes, plus marinating	• 4 lamb loin chops, about 450 g (1 lb) total weight and 2.5 cm (1 inch) thick • 1 small onion, peeled • 100 ml (4 fl oz) orange juice • salt and pepper • 15 ml (1 tbsp) oil • 450 g (1 lb) leeks	• 125 g (4 oz) split red lentils • 5 ml (1 tsp) paprika • 300 ml (½ pint) lamb stock • coriander sprigs, to garnish

COOKING TIME 25 minutes

FREEZING Not suitable

COLOUR INDEX Page 34

390 CALS/SERVING

1 Trim the chops of fat; place in a non-metallic dish. Finely chop the onion and sprinkle over the lamb. Pour over the orange juice and season with pepper. Cover and leave to marinate in a cool place for at least 2 hours or preferably overnight, turning once.
2 Lift the chops out of the marinade; pat dry on absorbent kitchen paper. Heat the oil in a sauté pan and brown the chops on both sides. Drain on absorbent kitchen paper.
3 Cut the leeks into 1 cm (½ inch) slices and add to the pan with the lentils and paprika. Stir over a moderate heat for 1 minute. Place the chops on top of the lentils. Add the marinade and stock.
4 Bring to the boil, cover and simmer for 20 minutes or until the lamb is tender. Adjust the seasoning. Serve garnished with coriander and accompanied by steamed or boiled potatoes.

❖ Spiced Lamb with Spinach ❖

SERVES 6	
PREPARATION TIME 15 minutes	• 900 g (2 lb) lean boned leg of lamb • 45 ml (3 tbsp) mustard oil • 1 onion, peeled • 5 cm (2 inch) piece fresh root ginger • 2 garlic cloves, crushed • 1.25 ml (¼ tsp) chilli powder • 5 ml (1 tsp) turmeric • salt and pepper	• 225 g (8 oz) turnip, peeled • 450 g (1 lb) spinach leaves • 125 g (4 oz) tomato • pinch each of ground cloves, ground cardamom and ground mace • 5 ml (1 tsp) dried dill

COOKING TIME 1½ hours

FREEZING Suitable

COLOUR INDEX Page 34

400 CALS/SERVING

1 Trim the lamb of any excess fat. Cut into 4 cm (1½ inch) pieces. Heat the mustard oil in a large flameproof casserole and brown the lamb evenly on all sides. Remove with a slotted spoon and drain on absorbent kitchen paper.
2 Roughly chop the onion and sauté in the fat remaining in the pan for about 5 minutes, until golden. Peel and grate the ginger; add to the pan with the garlic. Cook, stirring, for 1 minute. Add the chilli powder, turmeric and seasoning; cook for 1 minute.
3 Roughly chop the turnip and shred the spinach. Add to the pan with the lamb. Stir in 300 ml (½ pint) water. Bring to a simmer, cover and cook at 170°C (325°F) mark 3 for about 1¼ hours or until the lamb is almost tender.
4 Peel, deseed and chop the tomato. Add to the casserole with the cloves, cardamom, mace and dill. Return to the oven for 15–20 minutes, until the lamb is tender. Serve with rice.

NOTE: Use sunflower oil if you do not have any mustard oil.

❖ Spiced Lamb Escalopes ❖

SERVES 4

PREPARATION TIME
20 minutes, plus
marinating
COOKING TIME
30 minutes
FREEZING
Suitable (stage 4)
COLOUR INDEX
Page 34

- *12 lamb escalopes, about 550 g (1¼ lb) total weight*
- *1 onion, peeled*
- *30 ml (2 tbsp) ghee or oil*
- *2.5 cm (1 inch) piece fresh root ginger*
- *2 garlic cloves, peeled*
- *pinch of ground cloves*

- *30 ml (2 tbsp) chopped mint*
- *pinch of chilli powder*
- *salt and pepper*
- *thinly sliced onions, lemon wedges and mint sprigs, to garnish*

435 CALS/SERVING

1 Place the lamb escalopes between two sheets of greaseproof paper and bat them out slightly with a rolling pin.

2 Finely chop the onion. Heat 15 ml (1 tbsp) ghee or oil in a small saucepan and sauté the onion for about 10 minutes or until soft and golden brown. Set aside to cool.

3 Peel and chop the ginger. Place in a blender or food processor with the garlic and 50 ml (2 fl oz) water. Blend to a smooth paste. Mix with the cloves, mint, chilli powder and cooled onion. Season with salt and pepper to taste.

4 Place the lamb escalopes in a large shallow container and spread with the onion mixture. Cover and leave to marinate for 1 hour.

5 Heat 15 ml (1 tbsp) ghee or oil in a large sauté pan and brown the lamb escalopes well on both sides. Transfer to a shallow ovenproof casserole, cover with foil and a lid, and cook at 180°C (350°F) mark 4 for 20 minutes. Serve garnished with onion slices, lemon and sprigs of mint.

❖ Shepherd's Pie ❖

SERVES 4

PREPARATION TIME
20 minutes
COOKING TIME
50–55 minutes
FREEZING
Suitable (stage 2)

- *1 large onion, peeled*
- *50 g (2 oz) mushrooms*
- *2 carrots, peeled*
- *450 g (1 lb) lean minced lamb*
- *1 bay leaf*
- *30 ml (2 tbsp) plain flour*
- *300 ml (½ pint) lamb stock*
- *15 ml (1 tbsp) tomato purée*

- *700 g (1½ lb) potatoes, peeled and chopped*
- *salt and pepper*
- *25 g (1 oz) butter*
- *60 ml (4 tbsp) milk*
- *50 g (2 oz) Lancashire or Cheddar cheese, crumbled (optional)*

445 CALS/SERVING

1 Chop the onion; slice the mushrooms and carrots. Dry-fry the lamb in a non-stick frying pan with the onion, mushrooms, carrots and bay leaf, for 8–10 minutes, stirring frequently.
2 Add the flour and cook, stirring, for 1 minute. Gradually blend in the stock and tomato purée. Cook, stirring, until thickened. Cover and simmer gently for 25 minutes.
3 Meanwhile, cook the potatoes in boiling salted water for 20 minutes, until tender. Drain well, then mash with the butter and milk until smooth.
4 Spoon the lamb mixture into a 1.7 litre (3 pint) pie dish, discarding the bay leaf. Adjust the seasoning.
5 Cover with the mashed potato and sprinkle with the cheese, if using. Bake at 200°C (400°F) mark 6 for 15–20 minutes. Serve hot, with a green vegetable.

❖ Lamb ❖
and Aubergine Bake

SERVES 6

PREPARATION TIME
minutes, plus
illing
OKING TIME
hours
EEZING
itable
LOUR INDEX
ge 34

- 600 ml (1 pint) milk
- salt and pepper
- 1.25 ml (¼ tsp) grated nutmeg
- 125 g (4 oz) semolina
- 75 g (3 oz) freshly grated Parmesan cheese
- 1 egg, size 4 or 5, beaten
- 450 g (1 lb) aubergines
- olive oil, for brushing
- 2 red peppers
- 700 g (1½ lb) lean minced lamb
- 1 large onion, peeled

- 2 garlic cloves, peeled
- 1.25 ml (¼ tsp) ground allspice
- 15 ml (1 tbsp) mild chilli seasoning
- 225 ml (8 fl oz) dry white or red wine
- 30 ml (2 tbsp) chopped coriander or parsley
- 400 g (14 oz) can chopped tomatoes
- 45 ml (3 tbsp) tomato purée

480 CALS/SERVING

5 Heat a frying pan and brown the meat in batches, adding a little oil if necessary. Transfer the meat to a large saucepan. Chop the onion and garlic, and brown in the oil remaining in the pan. Add the allspice and chilli seasoning and cook for 1 minute. Add to the lamb with the wine, herbs, tomatoes and tomato purée; season well. Simmer, uncovered, for 1 hour or until well reduced and thickened. Stir in the red peppers.

6 Spoon the spicy lamb mixture over the aubergines. Arrange the rounds of gnocchi overlapping around the edge of the dish. Loosely cover with foil and bake at 200°C (400°F) mark 6 for about 1¼ hours until golden brown and bubbling, removing the foil 30 minutes before the end of the cooking time. Serve with a salad.

First make the gnocchi. ring the milk to the boil with 25 ml (¼ tsp) salt and the utmeg added. Turn down the eat and steadily pour in the molina, stirring all the time. mmer, stirring, for 2–3 inutes until the mixture is ally thick. Beat in the cheese d egg.

2 Spread the gnocchi mixture evenly in an oiled shallow 27 × 23 cm (13 × 9 inch) baking tin. Cool and chill for 1 hour until firm. Turn out and stamp out as many rounds as possible with a 5 cm (2 inch) cutter. Cover and set aside.

❖ Minted Lamb ❖
Burgers with Cucumber

SERVES 4

PREPARATION TIME
15 minutes
COOKING TIME
25–30 minutes
FREEZING
Not suitable
COLOUR INDEX
Page 34

- 1 small onion, peeled
- 450 g (1 lb) lean minced lamb
- 125 g (4 oz) fresh breadcrumbs
- finely grated rind of ½ lemon
- 45 ml (3 tbsp) chopped mint
- 1 egg, beaten
- salt and pepper

- 30 ml (2 tbsp) plain flour
- 15 ml (1 tbsp) oil
- ½ cucumber
- 6 spring onions
- 200 ml (7 fl oz) lamb stock
- 15 ml (1 tbsp) dry sherry
- mint sprigs, to garnish

375 CALS/SERVING

Meanwhile, cut the bergines into ½–1 cm ¼–½ inch) rounds. Brush the ut sides lightly with olive oil d place in the grill pan. Grill r 3–4 minutes on each side ntil golden brown. Arrange overlapping circles in a 6 litre (4½ pint) ovenproof rving dish.

4 Halve, core and deseed the red peppers, then place, skin side up, under a hot grill until well blackened and charred. Rinse under cold water and peel off the skins. Roughly chop the peppers.

1 Finely chop the onion. Mix the lamb, onion, breadcrumbs and lemon rind with 15 ml (1 tbsp) of the chopped mint and the egg. Season with salt and pepper.
2 Shape the mixture into 8 burgers with floured hands, then coat evenly with the flour.
3 Heat the oil in a large heavy-based non-stick frying pan and fry the burgers for about 3 minutes on each side, until lightly browned.
4 Meanwhile cut the cucumber into 5 cm (2 inch) long wedges. Cut the spring onions into 1 cm (½ inch) pieces. Add the cucumber and spring onions to the pan and sauté briefly.
5 Pour in the stock and sherry, then add the remaining mint and salt and pepper to taste. Bring to the boil, cover and simmer gently for about 20 minutes or until the meat is tender. Skim off any excess fat before serving and adjust the seasoning. Garnish with mint and serve with new potatoes.

❖ Pan-fried ❖
Liver with Tomatoes

SERVES 4	• 450 g (1 lb) lamb's liver, sliced	• 2 onions, peeled
PREPARATION TIME 15 minutes, plus marinating	• 30 ml (2 tbsp) Marsala or sweet sherry	• 30 ml (2 tbsp) oil
COOKING TIME 10 minutes	• salt and pepper	• pinch of ground ginger
FREEZING Not suitable	• 225 g (8 oz) tomatoes	• 150 ml (¼ pint) lamb stock

300 CALS/SERVING

1 Using a very sharp knife, cut the liver into wafer-thin strips. Place in a shallow bowl with the Marsala or sweet sherry. Sprinkle with pepper. Cover and leave to marinate for several hours.

2 Skin the tomatoes, then cut into quarters and remove the seeds, reserving the juice. Slice the flesh into fine strips and set aside. Finely slice the onions. Heat the oil in a sauté pan or non-stick frying pan. Add the onions and ginger and cook gently for about 5 minutes. Remove with a slotted spoon; set aside.

3 Add a quarter of the liver to the pan and shake briskly for about 30 seconds. Turn slices and cook for 30 seconds. Remove with a slotted spoon; cook the remainder in batches. Return onions and liver to pan. Add the stock, tomatoes and juice, and seasoning; heat through. Serve with noodles.

❖ Kidneys Provençale ❖

SERVES 4	• 12–16 lamb's kidneys	• 100 ml (4 fl oz) red wine or stock
PREPARATION TIME 20 minutes	• 1 large onion, peeled	• 10 ml (2 tsp) chopped
COOKING TIME 15–20 minutes	• 3 medium courgettes	basil or 5 ml (1 tsp) drie
FREEZING Not suitable	• 4 large tomatoes	• salt and pepper
	• 30 ml (2 tbsp) olive oil	• 12 black olives
	• 1–2 garlic cloves, crushed	

210 CALS/SERVING

1 Skin the kidneys, then cut each one in half and snip out the cores with kitchen scissors. Cut each half in two.
2 Chop the onion; slice the courgettes. Skin and roughly chop the tomatoes.
3 Heat the oil in a large heavy-based frying pan, add the onion and garlic to the pan and fry gently for 5 minutes until soft but not coloured. Add the kidneys and fry over a low heat for 3 minutes until they change colour, tossing them and shaking the pan frequently.
4 Add the courgettes, tomatoes and wine or stock and bring to a simmer, stirring. Add the chopped basil. Simmer gently for 8 minutes or until the kidneys are tender. Add the olives and heat through for 1–2 minutes. Adjust the seasoning. Serve immediately, with rice.

❖ Roast Pork Loin ❖ with a Fruit Crust

3 Pour the remaining prune juice around the meat. Roast at 180°C (350°F) mark 4 for about 40 minutes per 450 g (1 lb) or until the meat is thoroughly cooked, basting the meat with the prune juice after 20 minutes and occasionally throughout cooking. Cover with a piece of foil if it appears to be over-browning.

4 Transfer the roast to a warm serving dish and keep warm in the switched-off oven for 15 minutes before carving. Skim the fat off the pan juices, add 300 ml (½ pint) water and bring to the boil. Boil steadily until well reduced. Adjust the seasoning; strain. Serve the meat cut into thick slices with the pan juices spooned over. Mashed potatoes and braised fennel or cabbage would be good accompaniments.

SERVES 4	
PREPARATION TIME	• 175 g (6 oz) mixed dried fruit, such as prunes, apricots, peaches, pears
minutes	
COOKING TIME	• 30 ml (2 tbsp) medium or fine oatmeal
¼–1¼ hours	• finely grated rind of 1 orange
FREEZING	
Not suitable	• 2.5 ml (½ tsp) ground coriander

• 2.5 ml (½ tsp) ground allspice
• salt and pepper
• 525 ml (18 fl oz) prune juice
• 1.1 kg (2½ lb) pork loin

400 CALS/SERVING

Chop the dried fruits quite finely, stoning the prunes if necessary. Mix with the oatmeal, orange rind, coriander, allspice and seasoning. Use about 60 ml (4 tbsp) of the prune juice to bind the mixture.

2 Trim off the skin and as much excess fat from the loin as possible. Place the pork, bone side down, in a roasting tin and press the fruit mixture evenly over the skinned surface of the meat.

❖ Roast Pork Loin ❖ with Rosemary and Mustard

SERVES 6–8	
PREPARATION TIME	• 1.4 kg (3 lb) pork loin
20 minutes	• 30 ml (2 tbsp) chopped rosemary
COOKING TIME	
About 1½ hours	• 60 ml (4 tbsp) Dijon mustard
FREEZING	
Not suitable	• 50 ml (2 fl oz) lemon juice
COLOUR INDEX	
Page 35	• 50 g (2 oz) light soft brown sugar

• 175 g (6 oz) thin honey
• 15 ml (1 tbsp) soy sauce
TO GARNISH:
• rosemary sprigs
• lemon slices

345–230 CALS/SERVING

1 Remove the chine bone (backbone) from the pork and cut off the rib bones. Separate these into individual ribs.
2 In a small bowl mix together the rosemary, mustard, lemon juice, sugar, honey and soy sauce; set aside.
3 Place the pork loin in a roasting tin. Cook at 200°C (400°F) mark 6 for 40 minutes.
4 Add the ribs to the roasting tin and cook for a further 40 minutes.
5 Drain off any fat and brush the pork with the rosemary and mustard glaze. Return to the oven for about 15 minutes, basting occasionally with the glaze, until well browned and tender. Serve hot or cold, garnished with rosemary and lemon.

NOTE: If possible, ask your butcher to chine the pork and separate the rib bones for you.

❖ Lemon-roasted Pork ❖ with Garlic and Basil

SERVES 6

PREPARATION TIME
20 minutes, plus
marinating
COOKING TIME
40 minutes
FREEZING
Not suitable
COLOUR INDEX
Page 35

- 2 pork fillets, about 350 g (12 oz) each
- finely grated rind and juice of 4 lemons
- 90 ml (6 tbsp) chopped basil or parsley
- 12 garlic cloves, peeled and blanched

- salt and pepper
- 2–3 bay leaves
- 30 ml (2 tbsp) oil

TO GARNISH:
- herbs
- lemon slices

170 CALS/SERVING

1 Trim the pork fillets and split lengthwise, without cutting right through. Open each out flat. Sprinkle with the lemon rind and basil.

2 Halve any large garlic cloves. Lay the garlic cloves evenly along the middle of each fillet and season with salt and pepper.

3 Close the pork fillets and tie loosely at 2.5 cm (1 inch) intervals with string. Place in a shallow, non-metallic dish with the bay leaves and strained lemon juice. Cover and leave to marinate in the refrigerator overnight.

4 Remove the pork and reserve the marinade. Heat the oil in a sauté pan and brown the meat. Transfer to a shallow roasting tin with the marinade. Season and cook at 200°C (400°F) mark 6 for 35 minutes, basting frequently. Serve sliced, garnished with herbs and lemon slices and accompanied by sautéed shallots.

❖ Pork with Celeriac Stuffing ❖

SERVES 6

PREPARATION TIME
20 minutes, plus
soaking
COOKING TIME
1 hour 10 minutes
FREEZING
Not suitable
COLOUR INDEX
Page 35

- 75 g (3 oz) bulgar wheat or fresh brown breadcrumbs
- 125 g (4 oz) rindless streaky bacon
- 50 g (2 oz) onion or shallot, peeled
- 45 ml (3 tbsp) olive oil
- 2 garlic cloves, crushed
- 350 g (12 oz) celeriac
- finely grated rind and juice of 1 lemon
- 10 ml (2 tsp) chopped thyme

- salt and pepper
- 125 g (4 oz) butter, plus 10 ml (2 tsp)
- 2 pork fillets, about 350 g (12 oz) each
- 200 ml (7 fl oz) light stock
- 300 ml (½ pint) cider
- 10 ml (2 tsp) plain flour

330 CALS/SERVING

1 Soak the bulgar wheat in 100 ml (4 fl oz) water for 20 minutes until all the water is absorbed. (If using breadcrumbs, do not soak.) Dice the bacon; finely chop the onion.
2 Heat 30 ml (2 tbsp) oil in a frying pan and add the bacon, onion and garlic. Cook gently until the fat starts to run from the bacon. Increase the heat and brown the bacon, garlic and onion. Remove from the heat.
3 Peel and grate the celeriac and add to the bacon mixture with the lemon rind, thyme and seasoning. Stir in the soaked bulgar wheat or breadcrumbs, 50 g (2 oz) melted butter and 30 ml (2 tbsp) lemon juice.
4 Trim the pork fillets and split lengthways, not quite all the way through. Open each out like a book and bat out between damp greaseproof paper until very thin. Be careful not to split the meat. Spread the stuffing over each fillet, fold in the narrow ends and roll up. Tie at regular intervals with string.
5 Heat the remaining 15 ml (1 tbsp) oil and 50 g (2 oz) butter in a roasting tin and brown the pork. Pour in the stock and bake at 170°C (325°F) mark 3 for 1 hour or until tender.
6 Transfer the pork to a warmed dish and keep warm. Skim the fat from the juices, strain and add the cider. Mix the flour with 10 ml (2 tsp) softened butter to make a thick paste. Whisk a little at a time into the hot juices, bring to the boil and simmer for 1–2 minutes. Adjust the seasoning.
7 Serve the pork sliced, with the sauce. Accompany with mashed potato and green vegetables.

❖ Quick Pork Cassoulet ❖

SERVES 4

PREPARATION TIME
15 minutes
COOKING TIME
1 hour
FREEZING
Not suitable
COLOUR INDEX
Page 35

- 450 g (1 lb) streaky pork rashers, about 2 cm (¾ inch) thick
- 3 onions, peeled
- 6 celery sticks
- 1 green pepper
- 15–30 ml (1–2 tbsp) oil
- 2.5 ml (½ tsp) chilli powder
- 5 ml (1 tsp) dried mixed herbs
- 400 g (14 oz) can chopped tomatoes

- 450 ml (¾ pint) light stock
- salt and pepper
- 425 g (15 oz) can red kidney beans, drained
- fried breadcrumbs, for topping
- chopped parsley, to garnish

550 CALS/SERVING

Cut the rind and any excess fat off the pork rashers, then cut the flesh into bite-sized pieces. Slice the onions and celery. Halve, core and deseed the pepper, then chop roughly. Heat a little oil in a flameproof casserole and lightly brown the pork. Remove from the casserole. Add the vegetables, with a little more oil if necessary, and stir-fry for about 2–3 minutes.

Add the chilli powder and cook for 1 minute before mixing in the herbs, tomatoes and juice, stock and seasoning. Return the meat to the casserole and bring to the boil. Cover tightly and simmer for about 45 minutes or until the meat is tender.

Uncover, stir in the kidney beans and simmer to reduce and thicken slightly. Adjust the seasoning before serving, topped with fried breadcrumbs. Garnish with chopped parsley.

❖ Pork and Herb Bean Pot ❖

1 Drain the beans. Trim the pork of any excess fat and cut into 4 cm (1½ inch) pieces. Cut the rind and any excess fat from the streaky pork rashers, then slice thickly. Cut the garlic sausage into similar-sized pieces. Slice the onions and celery.

2 Heat 15 ml (1 tbsp) oil and the butter in a 5 litre (9 pint) deep flameproof casserole. Sauté the pork and streaky pork, about one third at a time, until golden brown. Remove from the casserole with a slotted spoon and drain on absorbent kitchen paper.

3 Lower the heat and add the onions, celery and garlic with a little more oil if necessary. Sauté, stirring continuously, for 3–4 minutes until the vegetables are beginning to soften and colour slightly.

4 Set aside half of the chopped herbs for the topping. Spoon a third of the beans in a layer over the vegetables. Add a pork and garlic sausage layer, then a layer of herbs and tomatoes. Continue these layers until all the ingredients are used.

5 Season the stock lightly and stir in the juniper berries; pour over the mixture in the casserole. Bring slowly to the boil, cover and cook at 170°C (325°F) mark 3 for 2 hours.

6 Mix the breadcrumbs with the reserved herbs and sprinkle over the top. Cook, uncovered, at 190°C (375°F) mark 5 for about 30 minutes, or until the topping is crisp and the meat and beans are tender. Serve with a mixed salad and crusty bread.

SERVES 8

PREPARATION TIME
20 minutes, plus soaking

COOKING TIME
2½ hours

FREEZING
Not suitable

- 275 g (10 oz) pinto, black-eye or white haricot beans, soaked overnight in cold water
- 550 g (1¼ lb) boned leg of pork
- 550 g (1¼ lb) streaky pork rashers
- 225 g (8 oz) piece garlic sausage
- 450 g (1 lb) onions, peeled
- 3 celery sticks
- 15–30 ml (1–2 tbsp) oil
- 25 g (1 oz) butter or margarine
- 2 garlic cloves, crushed
- 30 ml (2 tbsp) each chopped thyme and rosemary or 10 ml (2 tsp) dried
- 30 ml (2 tbsp) chopped parsley
- 400 g (14 oz) can chopped tomatoes
- salt and pepper
- 700 ml (1¼ pints) light stock
- 4 juniper berries, lightly crushed
- 175 g (6 oz) fresh wholemeal breadcrumbs

760 CALS/SERVING

❖ Pork with Prunes ❖

SERVES 4

PREPARATION TIME
10 minutes, plus
marinating
COOKING TIME
40 minutes
FREEZING
Not suitable

- *12 large prunes, pitted*
- *300 ml (½ pint)
Vouvray or similar
fruity, dry white wine*
- *8 thin pork chops or
steaks, about 1.4 kg
(3 lb) total weight*
- *seasoned flour, for
coating*

- *25 g (1 oz) butter*
- *300 ml (½ pint) light
stock*
- *10 ml (2 tsp)
redcurrant jelly*
- *salt and pepper*
- *thyme sprigs, to garnish*

600 CALS/SERVING

1 Place the prunes and wine in a bowl, cover and leave to marinate overnight.

2 Dip the pork chops in seasoned flour to coat. Melt the butter in a flameproof casserole and brown the chops in two batches. Return all chops to the pan. Pour in the stock, wine and prunes. Bring to the boil, cover and simmer gently for about 30 minutes or until the pork is tender, turning the meat once.

3 Transfer the pork and prunes to a warmed platter, cover and keep warm.

4 Whisk the redcurrant jelly into the cooking liquid. Bring to the boil and boil for about 4–5 minutes until the sauce has reduced slightly. Taste and adjust the seasoning, then pour over the meat. Garnish with thyme and serve immediately.

❖ Pork and Pasta Sauté ❖

SERVES 4

PREPARATION TIME
15 minutes, plus
marinating
COOKING TIME
15–20 minutes
FREEZING
Not suitable
COLOUR INDEX
Page 35

- *450 g (1 lb) pork fillet*
- *4 rashers streaky
bacon*
- *2 red onions, peeled*
- *15 ml (1 tbsp)
wholegrain mustard*
- *100 ml (4 fl oz) dry
cider*
- *1 garlic clove, crushed*
- *45–60 ml (3–4 tbsp) oil*
- *salt and pepper*

- *1 green pepper*
- *175 g (6 oz) green
beans, halved*
- *75 g (3 oz) dried pasta
shells or bows*
- *15 ml (1 tbsp) soy
sauce*
- *60 ml (4 tbsp) light
stock*

445 CALS/SERVING

1 Trim the pork and cut into strips, about 5 cm×5 mm (2×¼ inch), discarding any excess fat. Derind and chop the bacon. Finely slice the onions.

2 Put the pork, bacon and onions in a bowl. Add the mustard, cider, garlic, 15 ml (1 tbsp) oil and seasoning. Stir well. Cover and leave to marinate in the refrigerator for at least 1 hour, preferably overnight.

3 Halve, core and deseed the pepper, then cut into strips. Blanch the green beans and pepper together in boiling salted water for 2 minutes, drain; rinse under running cold water; let cool.

4 Cook the pasta in boiling salted water until just cooked about 7–10 minutes. Drain and toss in a little oil to prevent the pasta sticking.

5 Remove the pork, bacon and onions from the marinade, reserving the marinade. Heat 30 ml (2 tbsp) oil in a large sauté pan or frying pan. Add the meat and onions and sauté over a high heat for 3–4 minutes or until lightly browned.

6 Stir in the beans and green pepper with the marinade, soy sauce and stock. Season to taste with pepper. Bring to the boil, stirring, then simmer gently for about 4 minutes. Add the pasta and cook for 1 minute or until piping hot. Serve immediately.

❖ Stir-fried Pork ❖ with Baby Corn

3 Add the vegetables and continue stirring over a high heat for 2–3 minutes until piping hot.

4 Mix in the remaining ingredients and bring to the boil, stirring well. Adjust the seasoning and serve, garnished with chives and parsley. Accompany with noodles tossed in oil and fresh herbs.

NOTE: Bottled chilli and tomato sauce is available from delicatessens and larger supermarkets.

SERVES 4	
PREPARATION TIME	
minutes	
OKING TIME	
minutes	
EEZING	
ot suitable	

- 450 g (1 lb) pork fillet
- 175 g (6 oz) carrots, peeled
- 175 g (6 oz) baby corn cobs
- 175 g (6 oz) sugar-snap peas
- salt and pepper
- 45 ml (3 tbsp) sunflower oil
- 60 ml (4 tbsp) stir-fry chilli and tomato sauce

- 5 ml (1 tsp) caster sugar
- 30 ml (2 tbsp) wine vinegar
- 60 ml (4 tbsp) light soy sauce

TO GARNISH:
- chives
- parsley sprigs

380 CALS/SERVING

Trim the pork fillet and cut cross into 5 mm (¼ inch) ick slices. Cut the carrots to sticks. Blanch the egetables in boiling salted ater for 2 minutes; drain and fresh under cold water, then ain thoroughly.

2 Heat the oil in a large wok or frying pan (preferably non-stick). Add the pork and stir-fry over a high heat for 2–3 minutes or until well browned and almost tender.

❖ Pork Fillet ❖ in Wine and Coriander

SERVES 4	
PREPARATION TIME	
15 minutes	
COOKING TIME	
20 minutes	
FREEZING	
Not suitable	
COLOUR INDEX	
Page 35	

- 700 g (1½ lb) pork fillet
- 1 small green pepper
- 1 onion, peeled
- 15 g (½ oz) butter or margarine
- 15 ml (1 tbsp) oil
- 15 g (½ oz) plain flour
- 15 ml (1 tbsp) coriander seeds, ground

- 150 ml (¼ pint) light stock
- 150 ml (¼ pint) dry white wine
- salt and pepper
- coriander sprigs, to garnish

365 CALS/SERVING

1 Trim the pork and cut into 1 cm (½ inch) slices. Place the pork slices between two sheets of greaseproof paper and flatten with a mallet or rolling pin until thin. Slice the pepper into rings, discarding the core and seeds. Chop the onion.
2 Heat the butter and oil in a large saucepan, add the pork and brown on both sides. Add the pepper and onion and cook gently for 8–10 minutes, until softened.
3 Stir in the flour and coriander and cook for 1 minute. Gradually add the stock and wine; cook, stirring, until the sauce is thickened and smooth. Season with salt and pepper. Simmer gently for 5 minutes, or until the pork is tender and cooked through. Serve garnished with coriander.

❖ Toad in the Hole ❖

SERVES 4

PREPARATION TIME
15 minutes
COOKING TIME
40–45 minutes
FREEZING
Not suitable

- 30 ml (2 tbsp) oil
- 450 g (1 lb) sausages
- 125 g (4 oz) plain flour
- pinch of salt
- 1 egg
- 300 ml (½ pint) milk and water mixed

660 CALS/SERVING

1 Heat the oil in a small roasting tin and add the sausages. Cook at 220°C (425°F) mark 7 for about 5 minutes until browned.
2 Meanwhile, sift the flour and salt into a bowl and make a well in the centre. Add the egg and half the liquid.
3 Gradually draw the flour into the liquid ingredients until evenly incorporated. Add the remaining liquid and beat to give a smooth batter.
4 Pour the batter around the sausages in the roasting tin and bake for 35–40 minutes, until the batter is well risen and golden. Serve immediately.

❖ Golden Grilled Pork Steaks ❖

SERVES 4

PREPARATION TIME
15 minutes, plus marinating
COOKING TIME
15 minutes
FREEZING
Not suitable
COLOUR INDEX
Page 36

- 8 pork loin steaks, about 75 g (3 oz) each
- finely grated rind and juice of 1 large orange
- 45 ml (3 tbsp) dry sherry
- 2 bay leaves
- salt and pepper
- 1 bunch spring onions
- 4 no-soak dried apricots
- 2 garlic cloves, sliced
- oil, for brushing
- 300 ml (½ pint) light stock
- 5 ml (1 tsp) cornflour
- dash of soy sauce (optional)
- orange slices and herbs, to garnish

560 CALS/SERVING

1 Trim the pork steaks and shape into rough rounds, securing each with a cocktail stick. Place in a non-metallic dish.
2 Add the orange rind with the strained juice, sherry, bay leaves and seasoning.
3 Cut the spring onions into 1 cm (½ inch) lengths. Cut the apricots into slivers. Add to the dish with the garlic and stir well. Cover and refrigerate for at least 2 hours, preferably overnight.

4 Lift the pork onto a grill rack, reserving the marinade. Brush lightly with oil and grill for about 7 minutes each side or until tender and well browned. Remove the cocktail sticks.
5 Meanwhile simmer the marinade ingredients in a saucepan with the stock for 10 minutes. Mix the cornflour to a smooth paste with a little water then, off the heat, stir into the pan. Return to the heat and boil for 1–2 minutes, stirring all the time. Adjust the seasoning, and add a dash of soy sauce, if desired.
6 To serve, spoon the sauce over the pork steaks and garnish with orange slices and herbs.

❖ French-style ❖ Sausages with Lentils

SERVES 4

PREPARATION TIME
5 minutes
COOKING TIME
25 minutes
FREEZING
Not suitable
COLOUR INDEX
Page 36

- 450 g (1 lb) good quality chunky sausages
- 30 ml (2 tbsp) oil
- 6 large garlic cloves, peeled
- 350 g (12 oz) small brown or green lentils
- 225 g (8 oz) parsnips
- about 900 ml (1½ pints) chicken or vegetable stock
- salt and pepper
- chopped spring onion to garnish (optional)

770 CALS/SERVING

1 Skin the sausages and cut into large chunks. Heat the oil in a saucepan, preferably non-stick, and fry the sausage and garlic until golden, about 3–4 minutes.

2 Meanwhile, rinse and drain the lentils. Peel the parsnips and cut into large chunks.

3 Add the lentils and parsnips to the saucepan with the stock; bring to the boil. Cover and simmer for 20 minutes or until the lentils are tender and much of the liquid is absorbed, adding a little more stock during cooking if the mixture appears dry.

4 Adjust the seasoning. Serve sprinkled with the spring onions if desired, and accompanied by crusty bread and a tomato and onion salad.

❖ Sausage and Bean Casserole ❖

❖ Spiced Sausage ❖ and Potato Skewers

SERVES 6

PREPARATION TIME
0 minutes
COOKING TIME
1–2 hours
FREEZING
Suitable

- 225 g (8 oz) onions, peeled
- 225 g (8 oz) carrots, peeled
- 30 ml (2 tbsp) oil
- 450 g (1 lb) pork and herb sausages
- 400 g (14 oz) can chick peas
- 400 g (14 oz) can red kidney beans
- 400 g (14 oz) can tomatoes

- 15 ml (1 tbsp) cornflour
- 350 ml (12 fl oz) light stock
- 5 ml (1 tsp) Tabasco
- 30 ml (2 tbsp) tomato purée
- salt and pepper
- 30 ml (2 tbsp) chopped parsley
- sage sprigs, to garnish

495 CALS/SERVING

Slice the onions and carrots. Heat the oil in a flameproof casserole. Add the sausages and fry until evenly browned, about minutes. Remove from the casserole and cut each one into 2 or pieces.

Lower the heat, and add the onions and carrots. Cook, stirring, until beginning to soften.

Return the sausages to the casserole. Drain and rinse the chick peas and kidney beans and add to the casserole with the tomatoes. Blend the cornflour with a little of the stock, then add to the casserole with the remainder of the stock, the Tabasco, tomato purée and seasoning. Stir.

Bring to the boil, cover and cook at 170°C (325°F) mark 3 for about 1 hour, or longer if possible to increase the depth of flavour. Sprinkle with chopped parsley and garnish with sage. Serve with lots of crusty bread to soak up the juices.

SERVES 4–6

PREPARATION TIME
10 minutes, plus marinating
COOKING TIME
30 minutes
FREEZING
Not suitable

- 450 g (1 lb) spicy Italian pork sausages
- 45 ml (3 tbsp) olive oil
- grated rind and juice of 1 large lemon
- 1 garlic clove, crushed

- salt and pepper
- 900 g (2 lb) small new potatoes
- chopped rosemary, for sprinkling

375–250 CALS/SERVING

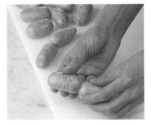

1 Twist the sausages to make short lengths. Place in a bowl with the oil, grated lemon rind and 60 ml (4 tbsp) juice, garlic and seasoning. Cover and leave to marinate in the refrigerator for 2–3 hours or overnight, stirring occasionally.

2 Scrub the potatoes; halve any large ones. Cook in boiling salted water for 10 minutes or until just tender. Drain well and cool. Thread the potatoes and sausages alternately on to wooden satay sticks.

3 Brush with the remaining marinade and sprinkle with a little rosemary. Grill for about 15 minutes, turning and basting occasionally, until the sausages are cooked through. Serve with a crisp green salad and crusty bread.

❖ Glazed Baked Gammon ❖

4 Stud with cloves and place in a baking dish. Pour the remaining wine and orange juice into the dish.

5 Spoon one third of the glaz[e] over the gammon. Bake at 200°C (400°F) mark 6 for 45 minutes, basting with the pan juices and glaze 3–4 times during cooking. Discard the pan juices and serve the gammon hot or col[d] carved into slices.

SERVES 8

PREPARATION TIME
15 minutes, plus
soaking
COOKING TIME
1¼ hours
FREEZING
Not suitable

• 1.8 kg (4 lb) smoked middle cut gammon joint
• 1 onion
• about 16 cloves
• 1 bay leaf
• 6 peppercorns
• 300 ml (½ pint) dry white wine
• 40 g (1½ oz) dark soft brown sugar

• 125 ml (4 fl oz) orange juice
• 15 ml (1 tbsp) clear honey
• 2.5 ml (½ tsp) ground ginger
• 15 ml (1 tbsp) Dijon mustard

435 CALS/SERVING

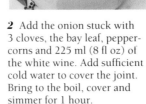

1 Soak the gammon in sufficient cold water to cover for 3 hours, then discard the water. Place the gammon in a saucepan.

2 Add the onion stuck with 3 cloves, the bay leaf, peppercorns and 225 ml (8 fl oz) of the white wine. Add sufficient cold water to cover the joint. Bring to the boil, cover and simmer for 1 hour.

3 Meanwhile, make the glaze. Place the brown sugar, 30 ml (2 tbsp) of the orange juice, the honey, ginger and mustard in a bowl and mix well. Drain the gammon and discard the onion, peppercorns and bay leaf. Remove the skin from the gammon and score the fat into a diamond pattern.

❖ Gammon with ❖ Crunchy Nut Glaze

SERVES 8

PREPARATION TIME
10 minutes
COOKING TIME
15 minutes
FREEZING
Not suitable

• 60 ml (4 tbsp) thin honey
• 15 ml (1 tbsp) Dijon mustard
• 1.6–1.8 kg (3½–4 lb) precooked corner gammon joint (see note)
• about 10 cloves
• 30 ml (2 tbsp) sesame seeds

• 15 ml (1 tbsp) white mustard seeds
• 25 g (1 oz) flaked almonds
• pickled pears, to garnish (optional)

395 CALS/SERVIN[G]

1 Mix together the honey and Dijon mustard.
2 With a sharp knife, carefully strip the rind from the cooked gammon joint and score the fat. Place in a roasting tin. Press the cloves into the scored fat and brush with half the honey and mustard glaze.
3 Add the sesame seeds, mustard seeds and almonds to the glaze and press onto the fat. Cook at 200°C (400°F) mark 6 for about 15 minutes. Serve hot or cold carved into slices, with pickled pears, if desired.

NOTE: If you prefer to cook the gammon at home rather than buy it precooked, place the joint in a roasting tin on a bed of bay leaves. Season well with black pepper. Add 300 ml (½ pint) water and cover with foil. Cook at 180°C (350°F) mark 4 for 20 minutes per 450 g (1 lb), turning the gammon over once during cooking. Continue as above.

Pickled Pears

To pickle pears, poach 450 g (1 lb) peeled firm pears in 300 ml (½ pint) water, with 60 ml (4 tbsp) honey and 15 ml (1 tbsp) white wine vinegar until tender.

❖ Bacon Chops ❖ in Cider Sauce

SERVES 4	• 4 bacon chops, about 175 g (6 oz) each	• 15 g (½ oz) butter or margarine
PREPARATION TIME 15 minutes, plus marinating	• 15 ml (1 tbsp) English mustard	• 25 ml (1½ tbsp) plain flour
COOKING TIME 45 minutes	• 25 g (1 oz) demerara sugar	• pepper
FREEZING Not suitable	• 300 ml (½ pint) dry cider	• chopped parsley, to garnish
COLOUR INDEX Page 36		365 CALS/SERVING

1 Put the chops side by side in a large ovenproof dish. Mix the mustard and sugar with 15–30 ml (1–2 tbsp) cider to make a smooth paste. Spread over the chops. Leave to marinate for 30 minutes in a cool place.
2 Bake, uncovered, at 200°C (400°F) mark 6 for 15 minutes.
3 Meanwhile, melt the butter in a saucepan, stir in the flour and cook for 1 minute. Gradually stir in the remaining cider and heat, stirring continuously, until the sauce is thickened and smooth. Simmer for 1–2 minutes. Season to taste with pepper.
4 Pour the cider sauce over the chops and bake for a further 15 minutes, or until cooked through. Serve garnished with parsley and accompanied by seasonal vegetables.

❖ Boiled Bacon ❖ with Parsley Sauce

SERVES 6–8	• 1.4 kg (3 lb) gammon, collar or forehock bacon joint	• 4 black peppercorns
PREPARATION TIME 10 minutes		TO GARNISH: • parsley sprigs
COOKING TIME 1¼–1½ hours	• 2 onions, peeled and quartered	TO SERVE:
FREEZING Not suitable	• 2 carrots, peeled and quartered	• 300 ml (½ pint) Parsley Sauce (page 92)
	• 2 celery sticks, chopped	
	• 1 bay leaf	515–385 CALS/SERVING

1 Weigh the joint and calculate the cooking time, allowing 20 minutes per 450 g (1 lb) plus 20 minutes.
2 To remove the salt, place the joint in a large saucepan with enough cold water to cover. Slowly bring to the boil, then discard the water.
3 Place the joint in a large saucepan with the vegetables, bay leaf and peppercorns. Cover with cold water and bring slowly to the boil. Skim the surface with a slotted spoon. Cover and simmer gently for the calculated cooking time.
4 When the bacon is cooked, ease off the rind and remove any excess fat. Carve into slices and serve hot, garnished with parsley and accompanied by the parsley sauce.

POULTRY & GAME

Poultry is the general name given to all domesticated birds bred for the table: chickens, ducks, geese, turkeys and guinea fowl. Strictly speaking, game is any wild bird or beast which is hunted for food, but the term is now used rather loosely to include some farmed animals, such as rabbit and venison. Guinea fowl, which used to be regarded as game, is now farmed extensively so it is classified as poultry.

Choosing Poultry and Game

A grain diet and the freedom to roam in the open air produces the best flavoured poultry. At last consumers are realising this and some farmers are being encouraged to move away from intensive battery farming methods to produce free-range birds. In response to this the EC has introduced a set of guidelines stipulating free-range farming conditions such as the maximum number of birds per square metre; feed content; and the degree of open air access allowed. The aim is to ensure that birds labelled as such really are free-range.

True free-range chickens can be identified by callouses on their feet – unfortunately most birds are sold ready trimmed so this is impossible to check. Rely on your butcher or read supermarket labels instead. With all birds look for a moist, unbroken skin with no dark patches, and a nice plump breast. When choosing duck look for a plump bird with a good light-coloured skin. Poultry that's past its best rapidly develops an 'off' smell. It should not be eaten if it smells anything other than fresh. If buying from a supermarket, check the sell-by date.

When choosing game look for soft, plump breast meat and unscarred feet. Badly calloused feet indicate an old bird. A flexible breastbone and short spurs are also signs of youth. Young pheasants and partridges have a large pointed tail feather; in older birds it is rounded. Avoid any bird that has been badly damaged by shot.

Handling and Storing Poultry

It is vital that poultry is handled, stored and cooked correctly, because most, if not all, raw poultry contains low levels of salmonella and campylobacter, the bacteria responsible for food poisoning. Provided that poultry is correctly stored these bacteria will remain at low levels. As long as it is then cooked thoroughly they will be killed by the heat and rendered harmless. Always use the following guidelines:

❖ If buying frozen poultry, check that it's frozen solid. If buying fresh, ensure that it's well chilled and within the sell-by date.
❖ Transfer poultry to the refrigerator or freezer as soon as possible after purchase. In warm weather it's advisable to carry it home in an insulated cool bag.
❖ Remove the giblets from fresh poultry, put the bird on a plate to catch any drips then cover and store in the refrigerator for up to 2 days.
❖ Frozen poultry will keep for up to 3 months. Frozen chicken should be thawed at cool room temperature, not in the refrigerator. Pierce the wrappings and put the chicken on a plate to catch any drips. Remove the giblets as soon as they are loose.
❖ Always check that poultry is completely thawed before cooking: make sure that there are no ice crystals in the body cavity and that the legs are quite flexible. Once thawed, cover and refrigerate, but cook as soon as possible. For turkey thawing times, refer to the chart on page 220. Never re-freeze raw poultry.
❖ To avoid cross-contamination, always wash your hands before and after preparing poultry. NEVER use the same utensils for preparing raw and cooked poultry without first washing them thoroughly in hot soapy water. It's advisable to keep a separate chopping board for preparing raw poultry.
❖ Stuff the neck end only. Do not stuff the body cavity or the heat may not penetrate fully to kill the salmonella bacteria.
❖ Always cook poultry thoroughly until the juices run clear. Cool leftovers quickly, refrigerate and use within 2 days.

❖ Chicken ❖

For taste, versatility and nutritional value, chicken is hard to beat. It's full of protein and B vitamins and once the skin is trimmed away, it has very little fat. It is therefore not surprising that this white meat is so popular and available in so many different shapes and sizes, both fresh and frozen. All of the chickens and cuts described below are also available as free-range birds.
❖ Oven-ready chickens range in weight from 1.4–3.2 kg (3–7 lb). Allow at least 375 g (12 oz) per person. These are suitable for roasting, casseroling, braising and barbecuing.
❖ Corn-fed chickens are a distinctive yellow colour because they are reared on a diet of maize. They can be cooked in the same way as oven-ready chickens.
❖ Poussins are 4–6 week old chickens. They weigh about 450–575 g (1–1½ lb). One poussin will serve 1–2 people. If serving 2 the bird is usually halved along the breastbone.

❖ Spring chickens are 12 week old birds weighing about 1.1 kg (2½ lb). One chicken will serve 2–3 people.

❖ Boiling fowl are older tougher birds weighing 2.3–3.2 kg (5–7 lb). Only really suitable for casseroling or for making stock, they are not as widely available as they used to be.

❖ Guinea fowl are lean golden-coloured birds weighing about 900 g – 1.8 kg (2–4 lb). They are interchangeable with oven-ready or corn-fed chickens.

❖ Chickens are also available ready jointed into halves, quarters, breasts, thighs and wings. Chicken breast fillets are the lean white breast meat sold with or without the skin. When skinned and flattened they are known as escalopes. With the wing bone attached they are known as supremes. Cook carefully; if overcooked the lean meat becomes very dry.

❖ Turkey ❖

Once limited to Christmas, turkey is now available all year round both whole and as a boned roast; you can also buy turkey breast as escalopes, and even thighs and drumsticks for roasting. Free-range turkeys are also becoming more commonly available.

❖ Oven-ready turkeys are available fresh and frozen in sizes ranging from 2.3 kg (5 lb) to an enormous 13.5 kg (30 lb). For a guide to thawing and roasting turkey see page 220.

❖ Self-basting turkeys have a basting ingredient such as butter injected under the skin to keep them moist during cooking.

❖ Jointing and Boning Poultry ❖

All types of chicken and turkeys are treated in much the same way; size being the only difference. Poussins and spring chickens are best left to your butcher to bone because they're a bit fiddly.

Before you start jointing or boning, thoroughly wash your hands and make sure that the work surface or chopping board is scrupulously clean. Use a very sharp knife or poultry shears.

Jointing

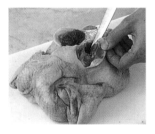

1 Put the bird breast side down and with the tip of a knife cut round the two portions of oyster meat (which lie against the backbone).

2 Turn the bird over and cut through the skin where the thigh joins the body. Cut right down between the ball and socket joint, being careful to keep the oyster meat attached to the leg. Repeat with the other leg.

3 If liked, separate the thighs from the drumsticks by cutting through at the joints. Trim off the bone end from the drumsticks.

4 Turn the chicken over again, breast side down, and using poultry shears, cut down firmly through the back into the body cavity between the backbone and one shoulder blade, leaving the wing attached to the breast.

5 Repeat on the other side. Then cut right the way through the ribcage, parallel to the backbone on both sides. Pull the back section away.

6 Turn the breast with the wings still attached, skin side up. Remove the wing portion by cutting through at a slight diagonal so that some of the breast is attached to the wing. Cut the breast into two or four portions.

Spatchcocking

Small chickens, poussins and game birds can be spatchcocked, split and flattened so that they can be grilled, barbecued or baked quickly and evenly. Using poultry shears, cut the bird along the back, each side of the backbone, then remove the backbone. Snap the wishbone in half and open out the bird. Push down on the breastbone with the heel of your hand to break the bone and flatten the bird. Thread a skewer through one leg and out through the other side, then thread a second skewer through the wings.

Boning Whole Birds

Choose a bird with a skin that's intact. A good sharp boning knife makes things easier. This method is the one used in Ballottine of Turkey (page 222); use it for chickens, ducks and turkeys. As with jointing it is vital that your hands, work surface and knife are scrupulously clean. If boning a frozen bird, make sure that it is thoroughly thawed before you start. Use the carcass and bones for making stock.

1 Remove the giblets if necessary. Cut off the wings at the second joint. Remove the parson's nose. Cut out the wishbone.

2 Put the bird breast side down and cut straight down the middle to the backbone. Carefully pull and cut the flesh away from the carcass on each side of the cut until you get to the joints.

3 Holding one leg in each hand, press firmly outwards to release the ball and socket joints. Cut through the tendons and scrape the meat back from the bone. Pull out the bone, using the knife to help free it as you pull.

4 Cut through the ball and socket joints connecting the wings. Holding the outside of the wing bone in one hand, cut through the tendons and scrape the meat from the bone. Pull the bone free.

5 Cut the meat away from both sides of the breast until you reach the point where the skin and bones meet without any flesh in between. Being very careful not to puncture the skin, pull the carcass away (you may have to use the knife to help you but take care as the skin is very delicate).

❖ Stuffing Poultry ❖

A well-seasoned stuffing mixture adds flavour and moisture and helps keep the bird in a neat shape. Ensure that the bird is thoroughly thawed before stuffing. Loosely stuff the neck end only; stuffing the cavity can inhibit heat penetration and pose a health risk. Fill the bird with cold stuffing; if it is warm the bird must be cooked at once. Do not be tempted to overfill with stuffing; remember that it will swell as it absorbs fat and moisture from the bird during cooking. Bake any excess stuffing in a separate dish. Roast the bird soon after stuffing.

❖ Trussing Poultry ❖

Trussing keeps the bird in a neat compact shape for even roasting. It also keeps in the stuffing and makes carving easier. You will need a trussing needle threaded with fine cotton string.

1 Remove giblets. Remove the wishbone, if desired (it makes carving the breast easier). Fold the neck skin under the body, then fold the wing tips back and under so that they hold it in position. Put the bird on its back and push the legs well into the sides.

2 Push the trussing needle into the bird through the second joint of one wing right through the body and out through the corresponding joint on the opposite side.

3 Insert the needle again in the first joint of the wing, pushing it through the flesh at the back of the body (catching the wing tips and the neck skin) and out through the opposite side. You should be back near where you started in step 2. Cut the string. Tie the two ends together.

4 Re-thread the needle. To truss the legs, push the needle in through the gristle at the right side of the parson's nose. Pass string over the right leg, over the left leg, then through gristle at the left side of the parson's nose. Take it behind the parson's nose and tie ends together. The bird should sit upright in a compact shape.

❖ Carving Poultry ❖

Chickens and turkeys are carved in much the same way, although with large turkeys the breast is usually carved first (right through the stuffing) and the legs are removed afterwards and carved separately. Leave the bird to stand in a warm place for about 10–20 minutes before carving, then remove the trussing string.

1 Put the bird, breast side up, on a carving board and cut down between the leg and breast on one side.

2 With a carving fork, spear the bird through the thigh (on the opposite side to the cut) and use this to help tilt it cut side upwards. Cut round the oyster meat on the underside.

3 Cut right through the leg joint, keeping the oyster meat attached. Halve the leg by cutting through the joint.

4 If the wishbone was not removed before cooking, cut it out. Make a horizontal cut above the wing joint and along through the breast – this makes it easier to carve complete slices off the breast.

5 Carve slices from the breast, parallel to the breastbone. Repeat on the other side. Serve each person with portions of dark leg meat and white breast meat.

❖ Duck ❖

Duck is much fattier than chicken or turkey with a high proportion of bone to meat. Commercially produced duckling is generally sold for eating when it is around 8 weeks old; after this time it is known as duck (although in most recipes the terms duck and duckling are interchangeable). Wild duck (mallard) has a much richer flavour than the farmed species.

Ducklings are generally sold whole, both fresh and frozen, for roasting, although portions are becoming more widely available. Breast fillets or *magrets de canard* are suitable for roasting, or for grilling or frying rather like steak. They are generally served cooked until just pink (medium or even rare), while roast duck is more commonly served thoroughly cooked. To serve a roasted duck cooked medium-rare the breast can be carved and served first and the legs returned to the oven for further cooking.

❖ Goose ❖

Goose is even richer and fattier than duck. It is usually roasted on a rack so that the fat can drain off as it cooks. Before cooking, check the cavity for any fatty deposits and remove them but don't throw them away; save them, along with any fat collected during cooking, for roasting potatoes – they will be absolutely delicious!

When buying goose, avoid any with deep yellow fat as this indicates an old bird. Instead look for a light skin and a good plump breast. Allow about 700 g (1½ lb) per person.

❖ Game ❖

To protect some species of game their sale is restricted to certain seasons (see below), although hare, rabbit and wood pigeon are considered such pests that they may be hunted at any time. As game becomes more readily available, both fresh and frozen, it is regaining popularity. Many supermarkets now stock a good selection and prices are reasonably stable.

Most game needs hanging to tenderise the flesh and develop its characteristic 'gamey' flavour. The length of time depends on the species of bird or animal, weather conditions and personal preference. Always check with your butcher or game dealer as to the age of the game and how well it has been hung. A bird that has been hung and is ready for cooking can be stored for 1–2 days in the refrigerator, or it can be frozen.

If you are given game, you can hang it yourself in a cool, dry, airy place. Hang the bird by the neck without plucking or drawing it. Check it frequently and cook it as soon as the tail feathers will pluck out easily. In warm or damp weather check it more frequently and watch for signs of deterioration – a strong smell and a greenish tinge.

Purists say that young tender game is best roasted, then served with the traditional accompaniments (see page 228), but it can also be barbecued and grilled. Game birds lack fat so to keep them moist they are barded before roasting, or the breast is covered with streaky bacon and basted frequently with butter. Large game birds are carved in the same way as chicken. Smaller birds are generally cut in half or served whole. Older game is usually much tougher and is therefore best marinated and casseroled or stewed or made into game pâté or pie.

Grouse

Grouse are small so one bird is usually served per person. Too small to carve, grouse are usually served whole or split down the middle. The young birds make the best eating. These can be distinguished by the soft, downy feathers under the wings. Ptarmigan (white grouse) and capercaille are members of the grouse family. Season: 12 Aug–10 Dec; except capercaille: 1 Oct–31 Jan.

Pheasant

Pheasant is regarded by some to be the most delicious of all the game birds. A brace of roast pheasant (one male and one female) served garnished with the tail feathers makes a spectacular centrepiece. For eating, the hen bird is considered to be the best. Although it is usually served roasted, pheasant also makes a good casserole. Oven-ready pheasants are also available frozen. Season: 1 Oct–1 Feb.

Partridge

Partridge are smaller than pheasant and are considered to be superior in flavour by some, though they are less widely available. Season: 1 Oct–1 Feb.

Quail

Quail has a good though not particularly gamey flavour. It is now a protected species, so all the quail for sale in the shops is farmed. It's a tiny bird, so two are usually served per person. It can be roasted whole or spatchcocked (see page 202) and grilled, barbecued or fried.

Woodcock

Woodcock are generally cooked whole (without drawing) with their heads still on. Traditionally, they are barded with bacon, roasted and served on toast. Because they are so small this is the best method of cooking. Season: 1 Oct–31 Jan.

Wood Pigeon

Farmed pigeon meat is rich, dark, well flavoured and suitable for roasting. Wild pigeon is tough with a very strong flavour, so it's best in a casserole or pie.

Venison

Venison is a lean, very dark, fine textured meat with a good flavour. The meat from mature deer aged about 2 years is considered to have the best flavour, although this is a matter of personal preference. Some like their venison well hung with a strong gamey flavour while others prefer the milder tasting farmed venison.

Cuts of venison are similar to lamb. Loin, saddle, fillet and leg (haunch) are prime cuts for roasting and braising. Roast venison is usually served rare, in thick slices. Tenderloin chops, escalopes and medallions are cut from the boned loin or the haunch and are suitable for grilling and frying. The other cuts – shoulder, neck and breast – are only really suitable for stewing or braising. Smoked venison is also available. Because venison is such a lean meat, all cuts benefit from being marinated, before cooking. Strongly flavoured red wine marinades spiced with juniper and cloves work best.

Rabbit and Hare

Although rabbit and hare belong to the same family, there is a good deal of difference in their flavour. Hare is usually hung for a few days to develop a strong gamey flavour, while rabbit is generally not hung and has a much milder flavour – rather like chicken. Wild rabbits can be more strongly flavoured.

Both hare and rabbit can be roasted. Very young hares (leverets) are often roasted whole. Like other game, they benefit from marinating and need constant basting during cooking to keep the flesh moist.

❖ Traditional Roast Chicken ❖

1 Wash the bird and dry thoroughly. Weigh the bird to calculate the cooking time. Ease up the breast skin of the chicken and spread a little of the butter under it, taking care to avoid puncturing the skin.

2 Put the herbs in the body cavity. Spread the rest of the butter all over the bird and season well.

SERVES 4-6

PREPARATION TIME
15 minutes
COOKING TIME
1¼–1¾ hours
FREEZING
Not suitable

- *1.4–1.8 kg (3–4 lb) oven-ready chicken*
- *about 175 g (6 oz) stuffing or sausagemeat (optional)*
- *½ onion, peeled*
- *1 lemon wedge*
- *melted butter or oil, for brushing*
- *salt and pepper*
- *few streaky bacon rashers (optional)*

305 CALS/SERVING

1 Wash the bird, dry thoroughly and put the sausagemeat or stuffing in the neck end before folding the neck skin over. Put the onion and lemon in the body cavity. Truss the bird with the wings folded under the body and the legs tied together.
2 Weigh the bird and calculate the cooking time, allowing 20 minutes per 450 g (1 lb) plus 10–20 minutes. Put in a roasting tin, brush with melted butter or oil and season.
3 Lay a few strips of bacon over the breast to prevent it from becoming dry, if preferred. Roast at 200°C (400°F) mark 6, basting occasionally; cover the breast with foil if it shows signs of over-browning. Test the thickest part of the thigh with a fine skewer; when cooked, the juices will run clear. Serve with gravy.

Parsley and Lemon Stuffing
Sauté 1 finely chopped onion and 1 finely chopped celery stick in 15 g (½ oz) butter until softened. Off the heat, add 125 g (4 oz) fresh breadcrumbs, 30 ml (2 tbsp) chopped parsley and the finely grated rind of 1 lemon. Season and mix in sufficient beaten egg to bind the stuffing.

❖ French-style Roast Chicken ❖

SERVES 4-6

PREPARATION TIME
15 minutes
COOKING TIME
1¼–1¾ hours
FREEZING
Suitable

- *1.4–1.8 kg (3–4 lb) oven-ready chicken*
- *50–75 g (2–3 oz) butter or margarine, softened*
- *5–6 tarragon or parsley sprigs*
- *salt and pepper*
- *300 ml (½ pint) chicken stock or 150 ml (¼ pint) chicken stock and 150 ml (¼ pint) white wine*

220 CALS/SERVING

3 Truss or tie the chicken and place in a roasting tin, in which it fits quite snugly. Pour the stock around to a depth of 5 mm–1 cm (¼–½ inch). Roast at 200°C (400°F) mark 6, allowing about 20–25 minutes per 450 g (1 lb), basting every 15–20 minutes; cover with foil once the chicken is well browned.

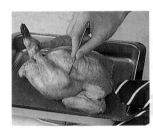

4 Test the thickest part of the thigh with a fine skewer; when cooked, the juices will run clear. Bubble up the cooking juices, skim off the fat and use to make gravy.

Variations
SOFT CHEESE WITH GARLIC: Spread 125 g (4 oz) full-fat soft cheese with garlic and herbs under the breast skin and all over the breast of the chicken. Grind plenty of black pepper over the chicken and put a few garlic cloves in the cavity. Roast with 150 ml (¼ pint) each white wine and water.

MUSTARD AND CIDER: Beat 50–75 g (2–3 oz) butter or margarine with 30 ml (2 tbsp) wholegrain mustard, 1 crushed garlic clove and seasoning. Spread under the breast skin and all over the chicken. Roast with 300 ml (½ pint) dry cider.

SPICED BUTTER: Beat 50–75 g (2–3 oz) butter or margarine with 10 ml (2 tsp) each ground coriander and cumin, 1.25 ml (¼ tsp) chilli powder, 1 crushed garlic clove and seasoning. Spread under the breast skin and all over the chicken. Place a sliced lemon in the cavity of the bird. Roast with 300 ml (½ pint) either stock or water.

❖ Pot Roast ❖
Chicken with Peppers

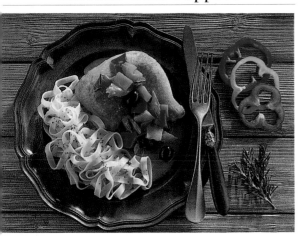

SERVES 4

PREPARATION TIME
20 minutes
COOKING TIME
1–1¼ hours
FREEZING
Not suitable

- 15 ml (1 tbsp) olive oil
- 25 g (1 oz) butter or margarine
- 1.6 kg (3½ lb) oven-ready chicken
- 1 each red, green and yellow pepper
- 3 celery sticks
- 1 whole bulb of garlic cloves
- 1 lemon
- 10 ml (2 tsp) paprika
- 12 black olives
- 1 or 2 thyme or rosemary sprigs
- 150 ml (¼ pint) white wine
- 150 ml (¼ pint) chicken stock
- salt and pepper
- 45 ml (3 tbsp) crème fraîche or single cream

320 CALS/SERVING

1 Heat the oil and butter in a flameproof casserole over a moderate heat. Add the chicken and fry, turning, until browned on all sides.

2 Meanwhile, chop the peppers, discarding the core and seeds. Roughly slice the celery. Halve the bulb of garlic and the lemon, cutting them through the middle.

3 Lift the chicken out of the casserole and add the peppers and celery with the garlic, lemon and paprika. Stir over a moderate heat for 1–2 minutes.

4 Replace the chicken and add the olives and herbs. Pour the wine and stock around the chicken and season lightly. Bring to the boil, cover tightly and cook at 180°C (350°F) mark 4 for 1–1¼ hours or until the chicken is quite tender.

5 Lift the chicken out of the casserole with a slotted spoon and cut into portions. Place on a serving dish, together with the vegetables; cover and keep warm. Discard the garlic and lemon.

6 Add the crème fraîche to the juices in the casserole and let bubble over a moderate heat until slightly thickened. Adjust the seasoning. Spoon a little of the sauce over the chicken; serve the remainder separately. Accompany the chicken with peppered noodles.

NOTE: Keep the chicken tightly covered so that it steams in the moisture trapped in the casserole.

❖ Saffron Chicken ❖
with Spinach Stuffing

SERVES 6

PREPARATION TIME
20 minutes
COOKING TIME
40 minutes
FREEZING
Not suitable
COLOUR INDEX
Page 37

- 75 g (3 oz) spinach leaves or 225 g (8 oz) frozen chopped spinach, thawed and well drained
- 25 g (1 oz) freshly grated Parmesan cheese
- juice of 2 lemons
- 2.5 ml (½ tsp) freshly grated nutmeg
- 3 garlic cloves, peeled
- salt and pepper
- 6 skinned chicken supremes (breast with wing bone), 200 g (7 oz) each
- 60 ml (4 tbsp) olive oil
- 1 onion, peeled and finely chopped
- 1.25 ml (¼ tsp) powdered saffron
- 600 ml (1 pint) chicken stock
- 150 ml (¼ pint) single cream

400 CALS/SERVING

1 Place the spinach in a food processor or blender with the cheese, 30 ml (2 tbsp) lemon juice, nutmeg, garlic and seasoning; blend until smooth. Spread the mixture over the inner side of the chicken.

2 Roll up the supremes towards the bone. Secure each with a cocktail stick.

3 Place the chicken, with the join face down, in a roasting tin. Squeeze over lemon juice and sprinkle with 15 ml (1 tbsp) oil. Cover with foil and bake at 200°C (400°F) mark 6 for about 40 minutes. Test with a fine skewer; the juices should run clear.

4 Meanwhile, heat 45 ml (3 tbsp) oil in a small pan and sauté the onion until softened. Add saffron, cook for 1 minute, then add the stock and 75 ml (3 fl oz) of the pan juices. Bring to the boil, then stir in the cream. Cook until the sauce is reduced to a thin coating consistency. Season. Remove cocktail sticks from the chicken and serve with the sauce spooned over.

❖ Chicken and ❖ Gorgonzola Parcels

SERVES 4

PREPARATION TIME
20 minutes
COOKING TIME
25 minutes
FREEZING
Not suitable
COLOUR INDEX
Page 37

- *4 skinless chicken breast fillets, about 700 g (1½ lb) total weight*
- *10 ml (2 tsp) olive paste*
- *125 g (4 oz) Gorgonzola cheese, sliced*
- *12 sage leaves*
- *4 slices Parma ham or prosciutto*
- *75 g (3 oz) shallots, peeled*
- *25 g (1 oz) butter*
- *150 ml (¼ pint) dry vermouth or white wine*
- *pepper*

450 CALS/SERVING

1 Starting at the thick side, cut a deep horizontal pocket in each chicken breast. Spread a little olive paste inside each pocket, then stuff with the sliced cheese.

2 Lay three sage leaves on top of each breast; wrap in a slice of Parma ham. Tie with fine cotton string.

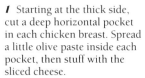

3 Finely chop the shallots. Heat the butter in a sauté pan or heavy-based frying pan, add the shallots and cook gently for 5 minutes or until beginning to soften.

4 Place the chicken on top of the shallots and pour in the vermouth or wine. Bring to the boil, cover and simmer gently for about 20 minutes or until the chicken is tender. Season with pepper. Remove the string from the chicken and serve immediately with a little sauce poured over.

NOTE: Use finely chopped black olives if olive paste is not available.

Variations

Most blue cheeses can be used in this dish: the creamier ones – such as Dolcelatte and St. Agur – are especially delicious. For a less expensive version, wrap the chicken in rindless streaky bacon instead of Parma ham.

❖ Baked ❖ Chicken Fillets with Pesto

SERVES 4

PREPARATION TIME
20 minutes
COOKING TIME
25–30 minutes
FREEZING
Not suitable

- *4 skinless chicken breast fillets, about 450 g (1 lb) total weight*
- *125 g (4 oz) low-fat soft cheese*
- *30 ml (2 tbsp) pesto sauce*
- *salt and pepper*
- *4 thin slices ham*
- *shredded basil leaves, to garnish*

255 CALS/SERVING

1 Starting at the thicker side, make a deep cut horizontally in each chicken fillet to form a pocket.
2 Mix together the soft cheese and pesto; season with salt and pepper to taste. Spoon most of the mixture into the chicken pockets. Wrap each fillet in a slice of ham.
3 Place the chicken fillets on individual pieces of foil, spoon over the remaining cheese mixture and fold each piece of foil to make a parcel.
4 Place on a baking sheet and bake at 200°C (400°F) mark 6 for 25–30 minutes or until the chicken is tender.
5 Serve garnished with shredded basil, and accompanied by baked potatoes and a mixed side salad.

❖ Chicken ❖ Casserole with Apricots

SERVES 4

PREPARATION TIME
20 minutes, plus marinating
COOKING TIME
30–35 minutes
FREEZING
Suitable
COLOUR INDEX
Page 37

- *575 g (1¼ lb) skinless chicken breast fillets*
- *10 ml (2 tsp) chopped thyme or 2.5 ml (½ tsp) dried*
- *pinch of ground cloves*
- *1 garlic clove, crushed*
- *50 g (2 oz) no-soak dried apricots*
- *10 ml (2 tsp) thin honey*
- *15 ml (1 tbsp) white wine vinegar*
- *150 ml (¼ pint) dry cider*
- *1 clove*
- *25 g (1 oz) back bacon rashers, derinded*
- *1 small onion, peeled*
- *20 ml (1½ tbsp) oil*
- *grated rind and juice of ½ orange*
- *75 ml (5 tbsp) Marsala*
- *75 g (3 oz) spinach leaves*
- *about 7.5 ml (1½ tsp) cornflour*
- *salt and pepper*

330 CALS/SERVING

1 Cut the chicken into chunks and place in a bowl with the thyme, ground cloves and garlic. Mix well, cover and leave to marinate overnight in the refrigerator. Put the apricots, honey, vinegar, cider and clove in a small saucepan and heat gently. Transfer to a bowl, cover and leave overnight, then discard the clove.

2 Cut the bacon rashers in half and form into small rolls. Chop the onion.

3 Heat the oil in a large flameproof casserole and sauté the chicken until evenly browned; remove from the pan. Add the onion, bacon and orange rind and sauté for 2–3 minutes.

4 Return the chicken to the pan and stir in 25 ml (1½ tbsp) orange juice, the Marsala, apricots and liquid. Cover and simmer for 20–25 minutes or until the chicken is tender.

5 Meanwhile cook the spinach, with just the water clinging to its leaves after washing, for about 5 minutes until tender. Drain well, finely chop, then stir into the casserole.

6 Mix the cornflour with a little cold water and stir into the casserole to thicken the juices. Cook for a few minutes, adjust the seasoning and serve.

❖ Chicken Parmigiana ❖

1 Slice the aubergines lengthwise. Blanch in batches in boiling salted water for 2 minutes. Drain and refresh under cold water; pat dry with absorbent kitchen paper.

2 Brush each side of the aubergine slices with a little oil and brown under a hot grill for a few minutes on each side. Allow to cool.

3 Dip the chicken fillets in the beaten egg, then in Parmesan cheese to coat evenly.

4 Heat 30 ml (2 tbsp) oil in a sauté pan and quickly brown the chicken fillets on both sides. Drain on absorbent kitchen paper.

5 Thinly slice the onion. Heat a further 15 ml (1 tbsp) oil in the sauté pan and sauté the onion with the garlic until softened and golden. Stir in the tomatoes, nutmeg, oregano, sugar and seasoning.

6 Spoon the tomato mixture into a 2 litre (3½ pint) shallow ovenproof dish. Arrange overlapping rows of chicken, aubergine and mozzarella on the tomato mixture. Top with any remaining Parmesan. Bake, uncovered, at 190°C (375°F) mark 5 for about 35–40 minutes, or until the chicken is cooked and golden brown. Serve with hot garlic bread and a mixed salad.

SERVES 6

PREPARATION TIME
20 minutes
COOKING TIME
40–45 minutes
FREEZING
Not suitable

- 900 g (2 lb) aubergines
- salt and pepper
- about 60 ml (4 tbsp) oil
- 700 g (1½ lb) skinless chicken breast fillets
- 1 egg, beaten
- 50 g (2 oz) freshly grated Parmesan cheese
- 225 g (8 oz) onion, peeled
- 1 garlic clove, crushed
- 400 g (14 oz) can chopped tomatoes
- pinch of freshly grated nutmeg
- 5 ml (1 tsp) dried oregano
- pinch of sugar
- 175 g (6 oz) mozzarella cheese, sliced

415 CALS/SERVING

❖ Chicken with Lemon and Sage ❖

SERVES 4

PREPARATION TIME
10 minutes
COOKING TIME
35–40 minutes
FREEZING
Not suitable

- 30 ml (2 tbsp) flour
- freshly grated rind and juice of 1 lemon
- 2 garlic cloves, crushed
- 4 skinless chicken breast fillets, about 450 g (1 lb) total weight
- 45 ml (3 tbsp) olive oil
- 300 ml (½ pint) chicken stock
- 30 ml (2 tbsp) chopped sage
- salt and pepper
- 2 egg yolks

TO GARNISH:
- lemon slices
- sage sprigs

305 CALS/SERVING

1 Mix together the flour, grated lemon rind and garlic. Use to lightly coat the chicken pieces.
2 Heat the oil in a flameproof casserole. Add the chicken pieces and cook until lightly browned, turning once or twice.
3 Stir in any remaining flour, then stir in the stock, sage and seasoning. Bring to the boil.
4 Cover and bake at 180°C (350°F) mark 4 for 25–30 minutes or until the chicken is tender and the juices run clear when the flesh is pierced with a fine skewer.
5 Mix the egg yolks with 30 ml (2 tbsp) lemon juice. Off the heat, stir into the pan juices, then return to the heat and warm gently until the sauce thickens, stirring frequently; do not boil. Adjust the seasoning.
6 Serve garnished with lemon slices and sage. Serve with rice and a mixed salad.

❖ Chicken and ❖ Artichoke Filo Bake

SERVES 4

PREPARATION TIME
15 minutes
COOKING TIME
30 minutes
FREEZING
Not suitable
COLOUR INDEX
Page 38

- 700 g (1½ lb) cooked boneless chicken
- 50 g (2 oz) butter
- 60 ml (4 tbsp) plain flour
- 450 ml (¾ pint) milk
- 75 g (3 oz) Cheddar cheese, grated
- 400 g (14 oz) can artichoke hearts, drained and halved
- finely grated rind and juice of 1 lemon
- 30 ml (2 tbsp) chopped herbs (parsley, chervil or chives)
- salt and pepper
- 4 sheets filo pastry
- melted butter, for brushing
- 25 g (1 oz) sesame seeds

600 CALS/SERVING

1 Cut the cooked chicken into bite-sized chunks, discarding the skin.
2 Melt the butter in a saucepan, add the flour and cook, stirring, for 1–2 minutes. Gradually stir in the milk and simmer, stirring, for 2–3 minutes. Add the cheese, chicken, artichoke hearts, lemon rind, 15–30 ml (1–2 tbsp) lemon juice to taste, and the herbs. Season.
3 Spoon the chicken mixture into a 1.4 litre (2½ pint) ovenproof dish.
4 Brush the sheets of filo pastry with melted butter and layer on top of the chicken mixture, overlapping the sheets as necessary. Alternatively, cut the brushed pastry into thin strips and scatter roughly over the surface of the chicken.
5 Sprinkle with the sesame seeds and bake at 220°C (425°F) mark 7 for 25 minutes, or until golden brown and cooked through. Serve immediately.

❖ Chicken with ❖ Spicy Tomato Sauce

SERVES 4

PREPARATION TIME
10 minutes
COOKING TIME
40 minutes
FREEZING
Suitable
COLOUR INDEX
Page 38

- 1 onion, peeled
- 15 g (½ oz) butter or margarine
- 15 ml (1 tbsp) oil
- 1 garlic clove, crushed
- 5 ml (1 tsp) ground cumin
- 5 ml (1 tsp) ground coriander
- large pinch of chilli powder
- 8 chicken thighs
- 400 g (14 oz) can tomatoes
- 15 ml (1 tbsp) tomato purée
- salt and pepper
- 30 ml (2 tbsp) chopped parsley

275 CALS/SERVING

1 Finely chop the onion. Heat the butter and oil in a large frying pan, add the onion and garlic, cover and cook for 4–5 minutes or until the onion is softened. Add the cumin, coriander and chilli powder and cook for 1 minute, stirring continuously.
2 Push the onion to one side of the pan, then add the chicken and brown on both sides. Stir in the tomatoes, tomato purée and seasoning.
3 Bring to the boil, stirring. Cover and simmer gently for about 30 minutes or until the chicken is tender. Stir in the parsley and serve immediately.

❖ Chicken with ❖ Mushrooms and Cognac

3 Add the mushrooms to the chicken. Cook for a further 15 minutes or until the chicken is tender. With a slotted spoon, transfer the chicken and vegetables to a warm serving dish; cover and keep warm.

4 Mix the cream with the egg yolks. Add a spoonful of cooking liquid, then pour into the pan. Cook gently for about 5 minutes or until slightly thickened. Pour some of the sauce over the chicken and vegetables. Garnish with parsley and serve immediately, with the rest of the sauce handed separately.

SERVES 4	
PREPARATION TIME 10 minutes	
COOKING TIME 1 hour	
FREEZING Not suitable	

- *350 g (12 oz) shallots or baby onions*
- *25 g (1 oz) butter*
- *1.6 kg (3½ lb) chicken, jointed*
- *1 garlic clove, crushed*
- *45 ml (3 tbsp) Cognac*
- *15 ml (1 tbsp) plain flour*
- *150 ml (¼ pint) dry white wine*
- *450 ml (¾ pint) chicken stock*

- *salt and pepper*
- *450 g (1 lb) button or wild mushrooms, or a mixture*
- *150 ml (¼ pint) double cream*
- *2 egg yolks*
- *chopped parsley, to garnish*

535 CALS/SERVING

Peel the shallots. Melt the butter in a large heavy-based frying pan, add the chicken joints and fry gently until golden brown on all sides. Add the garlic and shallots and sauté for a further 5 minutes.

2 Remove the pan from the heat. Warm the Cognac in a ladle, set alight and pour over the chicken to flame. Shake the pan to burn off all the alcohol. Sprinkle in the flour, cook for 1 minute, then stir in the wine and stock. Bring to the boil, season, cover tightly and simmer for 30 minutes.

❖ Spicy Chicken with Cashews ❖

SERVES 4	
PREPARATION TIME 15 minutes	
COOKING TIME 35–40 minutes	
FREEZING Not suitable	
COLOUR INDEX Page 38	

- *25 g (1 oz) fresh root ginger*
- *4 garlic cloves, peeled*
- *50 g (2 oz) unsalted cashew nuts*
- *150 g (5 oz) natural yogurt*
- *30 ml (2 tbsp) oil*
- *700 g (1½ lb) chicken thighs, skinned*
- *125 g (4 oz) onion, peeled*
- *2 bay leaves*

- *10 ml (2 tsp) ground cumin*
- *small pinch of cayenne pepper*
- *200 ml (7 fl oz) chicken stock*
- *salt and pepper*
- *30 ml (2 tbsp) chopped coriander or parsley*
- *coriander or parsley sprigs, to garnish*

360 CALS/SERVING

1 Peel and slice the ginger and place in a food processor or blender with the garlic, nuts, and 30 ml (2 tbsp) yogurt. Work to a rough paste.

2 Heat the oil in a large shallow flameproof casserole and brown the chicken evenly on all sides; remove from the pan with a slotted spoon.

3 Finely chop the onion and add to the casserole with the nut paste, bay leaves and spices. Cook, stirring, for 2–3 minutes. Pour in the remaining yogurt, stock and seasoning. Bring to the boil.

4 Replace the chicken in the casserole, cover and simmer, stirring occasionally, for 25–30 minutes, or until the chicken is quite tender.

5 Stir in the chopped coriander and adjust the seasoning. Garnish with sprigs of coriander or parsley and serve with rice and green beans.

❖ Coq au Vin ❖

SERVES 8

PREPARATION TIME
30 minutes
COOKING TIME
1¼–1½ hours
FREEZING
Not suitable

- *1 large chicken, jointed, or 8 chicken joints*
- *30 ml (2 tbsp) plain flour*
- *salt and pepper*
- *125 g (4 oz) butter*
- *125 g (4 oz) lean bacon, diced*
- *1 onion, peeled and quartered*
- *1 carrot, quartered*
- *60 ml (4 tbsp) brandy*
- *600 ml (1 pint) red wine*

- *1 garlic clove, crushed*
- *1 bouquet garni*
- *1 sugar lump*
- *30 ml (2 tbsp) oil*
- *450 g (1 lb) button onions, peeled*
- *pinch of sugar*
- *5 ml (1 tsp) wine vinegar*
- *225 g (8 oz) button mushrooms*
- *6 slices of white bread, crusts removed*

510 CALS/SERVING

1 Coat the chicken pieces with 15 ml (1 tbsp) of the flour, liberally seasoned with salt and pepper. Melt 25 g (1 oz) of the butter in a flameproof casserole, add the chicken pieces and fry gently until they are golden brown on all sides. Add the bacon, onion and carrot and fry until softened.

2 Heat the brandy in a small saucepan, pour over the chicken and ignite, shaking the pan so that all the chicken pieces are covered in flames. Pour on the wine and stir to loosen any sediment from the bottom of the casserole. Add the garlic, bouquet garni and sugar lump. Bring to the boil, cover and simmer gently for 1–1¼ hours or until tender.

3 Meanwhile, melt another 25 g (1 oz) of the butter with 10 ml (2 tsp) of the oil in a frying pan. Add the button onions and fry until they begin to brown. Add the sugar and vinegar, together with 15 ml (1 tbsp) water. Cover and cook for 10–15 minutes or until just tender. Keep warm.

5 Heat the remaining oil in a frying pan and fry the bread until crisp and golden brown on both sides. Cut into triangles.

4 Melt 25 g (1 oz) butter with 10 ml (2 tsp) oil in a frying pan and sauté the mushrooms for a few minutes until tender; keep warm. Remove chicken and vegetables from casserole; place in a serving dish with the onions and mushrooms; keep hot. Discard bouquet garni. Skim off excess fat, then boil the liquid briskly for 3–5 minutes to reduce it.

6 Work remaining flour and butter together to make a beurre manié. Off the heat, whisk into the cooking liquid in small pieces. Cook, stirring until the sauce is thick and shiny. Adjust the seasoning and pour over the chicken. Garnish with the fried bread.

❖ Chicken with Rice, ❖ Sweetcorn and Green Pepper

SERVES 4

PREPARATION TIME
10 minutes
COOKING TIME
40 minutes
FREEZING
Not suitable
COLOUR INDEX
Page 38

- *275 g (10 oz) brown rice*
- *salt and pepper*
- *30 ml (2 tbsp) oil*
- *25 g (1 oz) butter*
- *8 chicken thighs*
- *225 g (8 oz) onion, peeled*
- *1 green pepper, about 175 g (6 oz)*
- *300 ml (½ pint) chicken stock*

- *10 ml (2 tsp) tomato purée*
- *350 g (12 oz) can sweetcorn kernels, drained*
- *25 g (1 oz) toasted salted peanuts*
- *chopped parsley, to garnish*

720 CALS/SERVING

Cook the rice in boiling salted water according to packet instructions until tender – about 30 minutes. Drain.

Meanwhile, heat the oil in a flameproof casserole. Add the butter and when foaming add the chicken and fry until golden on both sides. Remove from the pan.

Slice the onion, add to the casserole and cook gently for about minutes or until soft but not coloured. Slice the green pepper, discarding the core and seeds. Add to the casserole with the stock, tomato purée and seasoning. Replace the chicken in the casserole, cover and cook gently for about 20–30 minutes or until the chicken is tender.

Stir in the rice and sweetcorn and cook for a few minutes until thoroughly heated through, stirring occasionally. Adjust the seasoning. Sprinkle with the toasted peanuts and plenty of chopped parsley. Serve with a mixed green salad.

Variation

If preferred use chicken breasts or quarters in place of the thighs, adjusting the cooking time accordingly.

❖ Chicken Curry with Coconut ❖

SERVES 8

PREPARATION TIME
0 minutes, plus
marinating
COOKING TIME
0–35 minutes
FREEZING
Not suitable

- 5 cm (2 inch) piece fresh root ginger
- 1.25 ml (¼ tsp) chilli powder
- 2.5 ml (½ tsp) garam masala
- 2 garlic cloves, crushed
- 8 skinless chicken breast fillets
- 150 g (5 oz) onion, peeled
- 45 ml (3 tbsp) chopped coriander
- grated rind and juice of 1 lemon

- salt and pepper
- 25 g (1 oz) cashew nuts
- 2.5 ml (½ tsp) saffron strands
- 50 g (2 oz) creamed coconut, grated
- 25 g (1 oz) ghee or butter
- 120 ml (4 fl oz) natural yogurt or single cream

225 CALS/SERVING

1 Peel and finely grate the ginger. Mix the chilli powder with half the garam masala, half the ginger and 1 garlic clove. Put the chicken breasts between two sheets of dampened greaseproof paper and bat out thinly with a rolling pin. Rub in the spice mixture, cover and leave to marinate in the refrigerator for at least 15 minutes, preferably 1 hour.

3 Place the chicken breasts skinned side down on a flat surface. Divide the onion mixture between them and carefully roll the breasts up around the mixture to enclose the filling. Place in a greased small roasting tin. Cook, uncovered, at 180°C (350°F) mark 4 for 20–25 minutes until golden and tender; the juices should run clear when tested with a skewer.

2 Finely chop the onion and mix two thirds of it with half the remaining grated ginger and 30 ml (2 tbsp) chopped coriander. Add the grated lemon rind, 30 ml (2 tbsp) lemon juice and seasoning. Stir until evenly blended.

4 Meanwhile place the cashew nuts, saffron and coconut in a blender or food processor with 100 ml (3½ fl oz) water. Blend for 2–3 minutes. Heat the ghee in a large shallow flameproof casserole. Add the remaining onion and sauté for 3–4 minutes until golden. Add the remaining garam masala, ginger and garlic and the nut liquid. Cook, stirring, for 1–2 minutes before adding the yogurt.

5 Using a slotted spoon, transfer the roasted chicken breasts carefully to the yogurt sauce. Cover the casserole tightly with foil, then a lid. Simmer very gently for about 10 minutes. Adjust the seasoning and garnish with the remaining chopped coriander. Serve with rice.

❖ Spring Chicken Fricassée ❖

3 Heat the oil in a shallow flameproof casserole. Brown the chicken pieces a few at a time, adding more oil as necessary. Remove with a slotted spoon. Add the carrots and onions to the casserole and brown lightly.

4 Return the chicken to the pan and pour in the vermouth and stock. Bring to the boil, stirring in the tarragon, garlic and seasoning.

5 Cover tightly and simmer gently for about 10 minutes. Stir in the cauliflower and broccoli and cook for another 10 minutes or until the chicken is quite tender.

6 Stir in the cream and simmer for 1–2 minutes. Adjust the seasoning and serv garnished with carrot tops. Accompany with rice.

SERVES 4	

PREPARATION TIME
20 minutes
COOKING TIME
30 minutes
FREEZING
Not suitable

- 225 g (8 oz) carrots, preferably baby ones
- 225 g (8 oz) button onions
- 225 g (8 oz) cauliflower florets
- 225 g (8 oz) broccoli florets
- salt and pepper
- 225 g (8 oz) full-fat soft cheese with garlic and herbs
- 8 chicken breast fillets with skin, about 800 g (1¾ lb) total weight
- 15 ml (1 tbsp) plain flour

- about 30 ml (2 tbsp) oil
- 100 ml (3½ fl oz) dry vermouth
- 300 ml (½ pint) chicken stock
- 30 ml (2 tbsp) chopped tarragon or 2.5 ml (½ tsp) dried
- 1 garlic clove, crushed
- 60 ml (4 tbsp) single cream
- carrot tops, to garnish

650 CALS/SERVING

❖ Sesame Chicken Stir-fry ❖

SERVES 4	

PREPARATION TIME
10 minutes
COOKING TIME
10–12 minutes
FREEZING
Not suitable
COLOUR INDEX
Page 39

- 450 g (1 lb) skinless chicken breast fillets
- 225 g (8 oz) broccoli
- 225 g (8 oz) baby corn cobs
- 60 ml (4 tbsp) sesame oil
- 30 ml (2 tbsp) soy sauce

- 200 ml (7 fl oz) orang juice
- salt and pepper
- 30 ml (2 tbsp) toasted sesame seeds
- 50 g (2 oz) unsalted peanuts in skins

540 CALS/SERVING

1 Cut the chicken into thin strips. Divide the broccoli into sma florets and cut each baby corn into two or three pieces.
2 Heat the sesame oil in a wok or large frying pan. Add the chicken and stir-fry over a high heat for 5–6 minutes, until browned.
3 Stir in the broccoli and baby corn. Cook, stirring, for a furthe 1–2 minutes.
4 Pour over the soy sauce and orange juice and allow the juices to bubble for about 3–4 minutes. Adjust the seasoning.
5 Stir in the sesame seeds and peanuts. Serve with egg noodles.

1 Cut the carrots into short fingers. Peel and halve the onions. Blanch the cauliflower and broccoli in salted water for 1–2 minutes only; drain.

2 Push a little of the soft cheese underneath the skin of each chicken breast and tuck the ends of the breast under to form small, neat rounds. Toss in the flour.

❖ Chicken with Oyster Sauce ❖

SERVES 4

PREPARATION TIME
10 minutes
COOKING TIME
15 minutes
FREEZING
Not suitable
COLOUR INDEX
Page 39

- 450 g (1 lb) skinless chicken breast fillets
- 90 ml (6 tbsp) oil
- 45 ml (3 tbsp) oyster sauce
- 15 ml (1 tbsp) dark soy sauce
- 100 ml (3½ fl oz) chicken stock
- 10 ml (2 tsp) lemon juice
- 6–8 large flat mushrooms, about 250 g (9 oz) total weight
- 1 garlic clove, finely sliced
- 125 g (4 oz) mangetouts
- 5 ml (1 tsp) cornflour
- 15 ml (1 tbsp) sesame oil
- salt and pepper

410 CALS/SERVING

1 Slice the chicken into bite-sized pieces. Heat 45 ml (3 tbsp) oil in a wok or frying pan. Add the chicken and cook over a high heat, stirring continuously, for 2–3 minutes, until lightly browned. Remove the chicken with a slotted spoon; drain on absorbent kitchen paper.

2 In a bowl, mix together the oyster sauce, soy sauce, chicken stock and lemon juice. Add the chicken and stir until thoroughly combined.

3 Slice the mushrooms. Heat the remaining oil in the wok and stir-fry the garlic over a high heat for about 30 seconds. Add the mushrooms and stir-fry for 1 minute. Add the chicken mixture, cover and simmer for 8 minutes.

4 Stir in the mangetouts and cook for a further 2–3 minutes. Mix the cornflour with 15 ml (1 tbsp) water. Remove the wok or frying pan from the heat and stir in the cornflour mixture. Return to the heat, add the sesame oil and stir until the sauce has thickened. Adjust the seasoning and serve immediately.

❖ Stir-fried ❖ Chicken with Courgettes

SERVES 4

PREPARATION TIME
10 minutes
COOKING TIME
7–10 minutes
FREEZING
Not suitable

- 450 g (1 lb) courgettes
- 1 red pepper
- 450 g (1 lb) skinless chicken breast fillets
- 30 ml (2 tbsp) oil
- 1 garlic clove, crushed
- 45 ml (3 tbsp) dry sherry
- 15 ml (1 tbsp) light soy sauce
- pepper

250 CALS/SERVING

1 Cut the courgettes into long thin strips. Cut the pepper into strips, discarding the core and seeds.

2 Slice the chicken into thin strips. Heat the oil in a wok or a large frying pan and fry the garlic for 1 minute. Add the chicken and cook for 3–4 minutes, stirring continuously.

3 Add the courgettes and pepper and continue to cook for 1–2 minutes, until the chicken is cooked and the vegetables are tender but still crisp. Stir in the sherry and soy sauce and cook for 1 minute. Season to taste with pepper. Serve immediately, with boiled rice or noodles.

❖ Advice on Roasting Turkey ❖

❖ THAWING Frozen turkeys must be thoroughly thawed before cooking. They should be left in their bags and thawed at cool room temperature, not in the refrigerator. Remove giblets as soon as they are loose – these can be used to make stock for the gravy. To check that the bird is thawed, make sure there are no ice crystals in the cavity and that the legs are quite flexible. Once it is thoroughly thawed, cover and store in the refrigerator. Cook as soon as possible.

❖ STUFFING Loosely stuff the neck end only of the bird to ensure heat penetrates the centre more quickly. Extra stuffing can be baked separately in a covered dish for about 1 hour. Allow about 225 g (8 oz) stuffing for each 2.3 kg (5 lb) dressed weight of turkey and stuff the bird just before cooking. Sew up the neck skin or use skewers; truss the bird.

❖ COOKING Weigh the bird and calculate the cooking time, to be ready 20 minutes before carving. The flesh is easier to slice after standing. Spread the turkey with butter or margarine and grind over black pepper. Wrap the turkey loosely in foil or put it straight into a roasting tin. Preheat the oven to 180°C (350°F) mark 4 and put the turkey in. Fold back the foil about 45 minutes before the end of the calculated cooking time to brown the bird. Baste regularly.

❖ TESTING Insert a fine skewer into a thigh. If the juices run clear, it is cooked. If not, return to the oven for a little longer.

❖ NOTE Leftover turkey should be cooled quickly, then refrigerated. Do not leave it standing in a warm room.

OVEN-READY WEIGHT ❖	THAWING TIME (AT ROOM TEMPERATURE) ❖	NUMBER OF SERVINGS ❖
550 g–1.4 kg (1¼–3 lb)	*4–10 hr*	2–4
1.4–2.3 kg (3–5 lb)	*10–15 hr*	4–6
2.3–3.6 kg (5–8 lb)	*15–18 hr*	6–10
3.6–5 kg (8–11 lb)	*18–20 hr*	10–15
5–6.8 kg (11–15 lb)	*20–24 hr*	15–20
6.8–9 kg (15–20 lb)	*24–30 hr*	20–30
9–11.3 kg (20–25 lb)	*30–36 hr*	30–40
11.3–13.5 kg (25–30 lb)	*36–48 hr*	40–50

OVEN-READY WEIGHT ❖	COOKING FOIL-WRAPPED ❖	COOKING WITHOUT FOIL ❖
550 g–1.4 kg (1¼–3 lb)	*1¾–2 hr*	*1½–1¾ hr*
1.4–2.3 kg (3–5 lb)	*2–2½ hr*	*1¾–2 hr*
2.3–3.6 kg (5–8 lb)	*2½–3½ hr*	*2–2½ hr*
3.6–5 kg (8–11 lb)	*3½–4 hr*	*2½–3¼ hr*
5–6.8 kg (11–15 lb)	*4–5 hr*	*3¼–3¾ hr*
6.8–9 kg (15–20 lb)	*5–5½ hr*	*3¾–4¼ hr*
9–11.3 kg (20–25 lb)	*not recommended*	*4¼–4¾ hr*
11.3–13.5 kg (25–30 lb)	*not recommended*	*4¾–5½ hr*

❖ Roast Stuffed Turkey ❖

SERVES 10–12

PREPARATION TIME
20 minutes
COOKING TIME
Depends on size
FREEZING
Not suitable

- *1 quantity stuffing (see right)*
- *4.5–5.4 kg (10–12 lb) oven-ready turkey*
- *45 ml (3 tbsp) thick honey*
- *50 g (2 oz) butter*
- *salt and pepper*
- *30 ml (2 tbsp) plain flour*
- *about 450 ml (¾ pint) turkey or chicken stock*
- *45 ml (3 tbsp) dry sherry*
- *finely grated rind and juice of 1 orange*
- *herbs, holly or watercress, to garnish*

550–460 CALS/SERVING

1 Prepare the chosen stuffing.

2 Spoon the stuffing into the neck end of the turkey only and truss the bird (see page 203). Place remaining stuffing in a greased ovenproof dish to bake later. Weigh the turkey and calculate the cooking time (see chart).

3 Place the turkey on a large strong sheet of foil, then lift into a large roasting tin. Spread the breast and legs thinly with the honey. Dot liberally with butter and grind over some black pepper. Fold the foil loosely around the turkey to enclose completely.

4 Bake at 180°C (350°F) mark 4. About 45 minutes before the end of the estimated cooking time, fold the foil back, baste well and return to the oven until cooked. (Bake extra stuffing for about 1 hour.) The turkey should be a rich, dark brown colour. Test the thickest part of the leg with a fine skewer; the juices should run clear when the bird is cooked. Return to the oven for a little longer if necessary, laying a sheet of foil over the turkey once well browned. Lift the turkey onto a serving dish, cover and keep warm.

5 Skim all fat from the cooking juices, then pour off all but 45 ml (3 tbsp) juices from the roasting tin. Stir the flour into the pan residue and cook, stirring, over a low heat until golden. Gradually pour in the stock, sherry, orange rind and juice, stirring all the time. Bring to the boil, and let bubble for 2–3 minutes. Adjust the seasoning, adding a little more sherry if wished. Garnish the turkey with herbs, holly or watercress.

Variation

To make wine gravy, replace the sherry and orange rind and juice with 90 ml (3 fl oz) dry red wine.

❖ Festive Stuffing ❖

SERVES 12

PREPARATION TIME
5 minutes
FREEZING
Not suitable

- 3 onions, peeled
- 6 celery sticks
- 45 ml (3 tbsp) oil
- 50 g (2 oz) butter or margarine
- 2 eating apples
- 175 g (6 oz) fresh breadcrumbs
- 125 g (4 oz) coarse oatmeal

- 50 g (2 oz) suet
- 45 ml (3 tbsp) chopped sage or 5 ml (1 tsp) dried
- finely grated rind of 2 oranges
- juice of 1 orange
- salt and pepper
- 1 egg, beaten

160 CALS/SERVING

1 Roughly chop the onions and celery. Heat the oil and butter in a frying pan and fry the vegetables until beginning to brown.
2 Meanwhile quarter, core and roughly chop the apples. Stir into the pan and fry for 1–2 minutes. Turn out into a large bowl to cool.
3 Stir in the breadcrumbs, oatmeal, suet and sage. Add the orange rind with 45 ml (3 tbsp) orange juice. Season well, add the egg and mix thoroughly.

❖ Apricot and Celery Stuffing ❖

SERVES 10

PREPARATION TIME
10 minutes
FREEZING
Not suitable

- 125 g (4 oz) no-soak dried apricots
- 125 g (4 oz) celery
- 175 g (6 oz) fresh breadcrumbs
- 2.5 ml (½ tsp) dried sage
- 1.25 ml (¼ tsp) ground mixed spice
- 25 g (1 oz) butter, softened

- salt and pepper
- 1 egg
- 15 ml (1 tbsp) Dijon mustard
- a little chicken or vegetable stock (optional)

115 CALS/SERVING

1 Finely chop the apricots; finely slice the celery. Place in a bowl with the breadcrumbs, sage, spice, butter and seasoning; mix well.
2 Lightly beat the egg and mustard together and use to bind the stuffing. If necessary, moisten with a little stock.

❖ Forcemeat Balls ❖

SERVES 10–12

PREPARATION TIME
20 minutes, plus chilling
COOKING TIME
45 minutes
FREEZING
Not suitable

- 175 g (6 oz) onions, peeled
- 50 g (2 oz) walnut pieces
- 50 g (2 oz) butter
- 2.5 ml (½ tsp) chilli powder
- 900 g (2 lb) pork sausagemeat
- 60 ml (4 tbsp) chopped parsley

- salt and pepper
- flour, for dusting
- about 30 ml (2 tbsp) oil
- chopped parsley, to garnish

385–320 CALS/SERVING

1 Roughly chop the onions and nuts. Heat the butter in a frying pan. Add the onions and fry until beginning to brown. Add the nuts and chilli powder and stir-fry for 1 minute. Cool.
2 Place the sausagemeat in a bowl. Stir in the onion mixture and parsley. Season well. With floured hands shape the sausagemeat into about 32 balls. Place on a flat baking sheet, cover and chill for 20 minutes.
3 Heat a thin film of oil in a large roasting tin. Add the sausagemeat balls. Bake at 180°C (350°F) mark 4 for about 45 minutes, turning occasionally. Drain on absorbent kitchen paper. Toss in chopped parsley and serve as a traditional accompaniment to roast turkey.

❖ Bacon-wrapped Chipolatas ❖

SERVES 12–15

PREPARATION TIME
20 minutes
COOKING TIME
40 minutes
FREEZING
Not suitable

- 700 g (1½ lb) pork chipolata sausages

- 450 g (1 lb) streaky bacon rashers

570–300 CALS/SERVING

1 Separate and halve the sausages. Derind and halve the bacon rashers. Wrap each sausage in bacon.
2 Lay the sausages out on a baking tray or in an ovenproof dish, with the ends of the bacon tucked underneath.
3 Roast with the turkey (or other poultry) at 180°C (350°F) mark 4 for about 30 minutes or until the bacon and sausages are golden; turn over and bake for a further 10 minutes.

❖ Bread Sauce ❖

SERVES 8

PREPARATION TIME
5 minutes, plus standing
COOKING TIME
15 minutes
FREEZING
Suitable

- 4 whole cloves
- 1 onion, peeled
- 1 small bay leaf
- 600 ml (1 pint) milk
- 125 g (4 oz) fresh white breadcrumbs

- salt and white pepper
- 15 g (½ oz) butter
- 45 ml (3 tbsp) single cream (optional)

160 CALS/SERVING

1 Stick the cloves into the onion and place in a small heavy-based pan with the bay leaf and milk.
2 Bring slowly to the boil, remove from the heat, cover and leave to infuse for 10 minutes.
3 Remove the onion and bay leaf, then add the breadcrumbs and seasoning to the milk. Return to the heat and simmer gently for 10–15 minutes, stirring occasionally. Stir in the butter, and cream if using, before serving.

❖ Ballottine of Turkey ❖

SERVES 18–20

PREPARATION TIME
1 hour
COOKING TIME
3½ hours
FREEZING
Recommended
only if serving cold

- 5.5 kg (12 lb) oven-ready turkey
- 2 onions, peeled
- 225 g (8 oz) button mushrooms
- 125 g (4 oz) butter or margarine
- 2 large garlic cloves, crushed
- 700 g (1½ lb) pork sausagemeat
- 125 g (4 oz) fresh white breadcrumbs
- 90 ml (6 tbsp) chopped parsley

- 60 ml (4 tbsp) Dijon mustard
- finely grated rind of 2 lemons
- 30 ml (2 tbsp) lemon juice
- 1 egg, beaten
- salt and pepper
- 450 g (1 lb) smoked loin of pork

TO SERVE:
- bacon rolls
- chipolata sausages

500–450 CALS/SERVING

1 First bone the turkey. Place the bird breast side down on a large chopping board. Using a small sharp knife, cut straight along the backbone. Gradually fillet the flesh away from the carcass, keeping the knife as close to the bones as possible. Take care not to puncture the skin as it has to act as a 'case' for the turkey roast – if the skin is split, the stuffing will burst out during cooking.

2 Loosen the leg and wing ball and socket joints with the point of the knife. Push these joints away from the carcass until they loosen and partially come away. Carefully split the leg flesh and ease out the bones and sinews. Ease out the large wing joint, reserving the small wing tips for the stock pot. Run your fingers all over the turkey flesh to ensure no bones or sinews remain.

3 You should have a large oblong of skin covered with turkey meat. Remove the parson's nose. To give the ballottine a better shape, fillet most of the leg and thigh meat from one side of the bird and trim off any fat (you should have about 900 g (2 lb) trimmed meat to freeze for another use). Cover and refrigerate the boned turkey while preparing the stuffing.

5 Lay the boned turkey flat on a board, flesh side up. Spread with the stuffing mixture. Place the smoked loin (halved if necessary) on top.

7 Spread the turkey generously with butter and season liberally with pepper. Wrap in foil and place in a roasting tin. Bake at 180°C (350°F) mark 4 for 2½ hours. Fold back the foil and return to the oven for about 1 hour or until well browned.

4 Roughly chop the onions and mushrooms. Heat 50 g (2 oz) butter in a sauté pan. Add the onion and fry until beginning to brown. Increase heat, add the mushrooms and garlic and fry, stirring, until all excess liquid has evaporated. Turn into a bowl and cool. Stir in the sausagemeat, breadcrumbs, parsley, mustard, lemon rind and juice, egg and seasoning. Mix thoroughly.

6 Fold the turkey skin around to enclose the stuffing completely. Secure with fine skewers or cocktail sticks, or sew the skin together.

8 Test with a fine skewer; if it is cooked, the juices should run clear. Lift the ballottine onto a serving plate. Let stand for about 20 minutes before slicing thickly. Serve with bacon rolls and chipolatas. Any leftovers can be eaten cold the next day with salads.

❖ Turkey and ❖ Watercress Roulades

SERVES 4–6

PREPARATION TIME
| minutes
COOKING TIME
| minutes
FREEZING
ot suitable
COLOUR INDEX
Page 41

- 75 g (3 oz) Brazil nuts
- 1 bunch watercress
- 50 g (2 oz) butter or margarine
- 7.5 ml (1½ tsp) ground cumin
- 1 garlic clove, crushed
- 225 g (8 oz) full-fat soft cheese
- finely grated rind and juice of 1 lemon
- salt and pepper
- 700 g (1½ lb) skinless turkey escalopes

- 30 ml (2 tbsp) plain flour
- 15 ml (1 tbsp) oil
- 300 ml (½ pint) turkey or chicken stock
- 100 ml (3½ fl oz) dry vermouth
- 30 ml (2 tbsp) single cream
- watercress sprigs, to garnish

650–435 CALS/SERVING

5 Stir any remaining flour into the pan juices. Pour in the stock and vermouth and bring to the boil. Season and stir in 15 ml (1 tbsp) lemon juice. Pour over the turkey rolls in the casserole. Cover the casserole and cook at 180°C (350°F) mark 4 for about 35 minutes or until the meat is tender.

6 Lift the rolls out of the casserole and remove the cocktail sticks. Cover and keep warm. Strain the cooking juices and boil to reduce slightly. Take off the heat, stir in the cream and adjust the seasoning. Halve the turkey rolls and spoon over a little of the sauce. Serve the remaining sauce separately. Garnish with watercress.

Roughly chop the Brazil nuts; finely chop the watercress. Heat half of the butter in a frying pan. Add the nuts, cumin and garlic and stir-fry until beginning to brown. Mix in the watercress and stir-fry until all excess moisture has been driven off. Turn into a bowl and leave to cool.

2 Beat the watercress mixture together with the cheese and lemon rind. Season, cover and chill. Meanwhile, place the turkey escalopes between sheets of dampened greaseproof paper and bat out until very thin. Cut them into 10–12 even-sized pieces.

❖ Turkey Sauté ❖ with Lemon and Walnuts

SERVES 4

PREPARATION TIME
10 minutes
COOKING TIME
20 minutes
FREEZING
Not suitable
COLOUR INDEX
Page 41

- 450 g (1 lb) skinless turkey breast fillets
- 30 ml (2 tbsp) cornflour
- 1 green pepper
- 45 ml (3 tbsp) oil
- 40 g (1½ oz) walnut halves or pieces
- 60 ml (4 tbsp) chicken stock
- 30 ml (2 tbsp) lemon juice

- 45 ml (3 tbsp) lemon marmalade
- 5 ml (1 tsp) white wine vinegar
- 1.25 ml (¼ tsp) soy sauce
- salt and pepper
TO GARNISH:
- lemon wedges
- parsley sprigs

345 CALS/SERVING

1 Cut the turkey flesh into 5 cm (2 inch) pencil-thin strips. Add to the cornflour and toss until coated. Thinly slice the pepper, discarding the core and seeds.

2 Heat half the oil in a large sauté or deep frying pan, add the pepper strips and walnuts and fry for 2–3 minutes. Remove from the pan with a slotted spoon.

3 Add the remaining oil to the pan and fry the turkey strips for 10 minutes or until golden. Add the stock and lemon juice, stirring well to scrape up any sediment at the bottom of the pan. Add the lemon marmalade, vinegar and soy sauce. Season with salt and pepper to taste.

4 Return the walnuts and green pepper to the pan. Cook gently for a further 5 minutes or until the turkey is tender. Taste and adjust the seasoning and serve immediately, garnished with lemon wedges and parsley.

Divide the stuffing mixture between the turkey pieces. Roll up and secure with wooden cocktail sticks. Sprinkle the turkey rolls with seasoned flour, reserving any excess.

4 Heat the oil with the remaining butter in a frying pan. Brown the turkey rolls in two batches. Remove from the pan and transfer to a casserole.

❖ Turkey Escalopes ❖ with Asparagus

SERVES 4

PREPARATION TIME
15 minutes
COOKING TIME
20 minutes
FREEZING
Not suitable
COLOUR INDEX
Page 41

- 225 g (8 oz) thin asparagus spears
- 2 skinless turkey escalopes, about 225 g (8 oz) each
- 30 ml (2 tbsp) plain flour
- salt and pepper
- 15 g (½ oz) butter
- 15 ml (1 tbsp) oil
- 300 ml (½ pint) chicken stock

- 5 ml (1 tsp) chopped sage or 2.5 ml (½ tsp) dried
- 60 ml (4 tbsp) dry white wine
- 150 ml (¼ pint) soured cream

370 CALS/SERVING

1 Snap off the tough ends of the asparagus spears and trim the spears to equal lengths. Cut off the tips and set aside; cut the stalks into 3 pieces.

2 Halve each turkey escalope and bat out slightly with a rolling pin or meat mallet. Coat in the flour seasoned with salt and pepper, shaking off any excess.

3 Heat the butter and oil in a large frying pan and fry the turkey until lightly browned on both sides. Add the stock, asparagus stalks, sage and wine. Cover and cook gently for 10 minutes. Add the asparagus tips, cream and seasoning. Cook for a further 5 minutes. Serve at once.

❖ Turkey with ❖ Cashew Nuts and Mushrooms

SERVES 4

PREPARATION TIME
10 minutes
COOKING TIME
10 minutes
FREEZING
Not suitable
COLOUR INDEX
Page 41

- 450 g (1 lb) skinless turkey breast fillets
- 350 g (12 oz) button mushrooms
- 50 g (2 oz) shallots or onion, peeled
- 30 ml (2 tbsp) oil
- 60 ml (4 tbsp) dry sherry
- 1 garlic clove, crushed

- 25 g (1 oz) salted cashew nuts, toasted
- 150 ml (¼ pint) soured cream
- salt and pepper
- lemon slices, to garnish

290 CALS/SERVING

1 Cut the turkey into small, thin escalopes. Bat out slightly between sheets of dampened greaseproof paper. Thinly slice the mushrooms; chop the shallots.

2 Heat the oil in a large sauté pan (preferably non-stick). Fry the turkey escalopes with the shallots in two batches, until lightly browned on both sides.

3 Return all the turkey and shallot mixture to the pan and add the sherry, mushrooms, garlic, cashew nuts and soured cream. Bring to the boil, stirring, then simmer gently for 3–4 minutes or until the turkey is tender. Season.

4 Garnish with lemon slices and serve with rice or mixed white and wild rice flavoured with chopped parsley.

❖ Turkey Curry ❖

SERVES 4

PREPARATION TIME
15 minutes
COOKING TIME
35 minutes
FREEZING
Suitable

- 1 onion, peeled
- 2 garlic cloves
- 30 ml (2 tbsp) oil
- 5 ml (1 tsp) turmeric
- 5 ml (1 tsp) black mustard seeds
- 2.5 ml (½ tsp) chilli powder
- 2.5 ml (½ tsp) ground cardamom
- 7.5 ml (1½ tsp) ground cumin
- 7.5 ml (1½ tsp) ground coriander

- 400 g (14 oz) can chopped tomatoes
- salt
- 500 g (1¼ lb) cooked turkey
- 5 ml (1 tsp) garam masala
- 150 ml (5 fl oz) natural yogurt
- chopped coriander, to garnish

325 CALS/SERVING

1 Chop the onion; finely chop the garlic. Heat the oil in a heavy based pan, add the onion and garlic and fry until golden.

2 Add the turmeric, mustard seeds, chilli powder, cardamom, cumin and coriander; cook, stirring, for 1 minute.

3 Add the tomatoes and season with salt. Bring to the boil, cover and simmer for 20 minutes. Meanwhile, chop the turkey into large chunks, discarding any bones and skin.

4 Stir the garam masala and 60 ml (4 tbsp) of the yogurt into the tomato mixture. Add the turkey, stir well, cover and cook gently for 10 minutes. Stir in the remaining yogurt and sprinkle with coriander before serving. Accompany with rice.

❖ Guinea Fowl ❖ with Grapes and Madeira

3 Return the guinea fowl to the casserole, bring to the boil, cover and cook at 170°C (325°F) mark 3 for 1 hour. Stir in the grapes, cover and cook for a further 30 minutes or until the guinea fowl are tender. Remove and trim the joints; keep warm.

4 Blend the cornflour to a smooth paste with a little water. Add to the casserole and bring to the boil, stirring; cook until the juices are slightly thickened. Return the guinea fowl. Stir in the parsley and adjust the seasoning. Serve with roast parsnips.

❖ Roast Goose ❖ with Apples and Prunes

SERVES 6

PREPARATION TIME
5 minutes
COOKING TIME
½–1¼ hours
FREEZING
Suitable (without grapes)

- 2 small guinea fowl, about 1.1–1.4 kg (2½–3 lb) each
- 2 shallots, peeled
- 15 ml (1 tbsp) oil
- 50 g (2 oz) butter or margarine
- grated rind and juice of 2 oranges
- 150 ml (¼ pint) dry white wine
- 50 ml (2 fl oz) Madeira

- 600 ml (1 pint) chicken stock
- 125 g (4 oz) walnut halves, toasted
- salt and pepper
- 350 g (12 oz) seedless white grapes
- 45 ml (3 tbsp) cornflour
- 45 ml (3 tbsp) chopped parsley

440 CALS/SERVING

1 Using sharp scissors, halve, then quarter the guinea fowl (discarding the backbones). Finely chop the shallots. Heat the oil and butter in a flameproof casserole and brown the guinea fowl in two batches. Drain on absorbent kitchen paper.

2 Lower the heat and add the shallots to the pan. Sauté, stirring, until soft. Add the orange rind and juice, the wine, Madeira, stock, walnuts and seasoning.

SERVES 8

PREPARATION TIME
35 minutes
COOKING TIME
Depends on size
FREEZING
Not suitable
COLOUR INDEX
Page 41

- 4–5 kg (9–11 lb) oven-ready goose, with giblets
- salt and pepper
- 1 large onion, peeled
- 15 g (½ oz) butter
- 450 g (1 lb) no-soak prunes
- 60 ml (4 tbsp) port
- 15 ml (1 tbsp) chopped sage or 5 ml (1 tsp) dried

- 125 g (4 oz) fresh wholemeal breadcrumbs
- 6 Cox's Orange Pippin apples
- 300 ml (½ pint) dry white wine

500 CALS/SERVING

1 Prick the skin of the goose all over with a sharp skewer or fork; pull the inside fat out of the bird and reserve. Rub seasoning over the skin.

2 To make the stuffing, chop the onion; finely chop the goose liver. Melt the butter in a large frying pan, add the onion and cook for 5–6 minutes, until softened. Add the goose liver and cook gently for 2–3 minutes.

3 Stone half of the prunes, then chop roughly and stir into the onion with the port. Cover and cook gently for 5 minutes. Add the sage, breadcrumbs and seasoning; mix thoroughly.

4 Spoon the stuffing into the neck end of the goose, then truss with strong cotton or fine string. Weigh the bird to calculate the cooking time. Put on a wire rack placed in a roasting tin. Cover the breast with the reserved fat, then with foil. Roast at 200°C (400°F) mark 6 for 15 minutes per 450 g (1 lb) plus 15 minutes, basting frequently.

5 Thirty minutes before the end of the cooking time, remove the goose and rack, then drain off the fat from the roasting tin and discard. Core the apples and cut into eighths, then add to the tin with the remaining prunes and wine. Replace the goose on the rack over the roasting tin, discarding the foil and fat. Cook, uncovered, for the last 30 minutes.

6 Serve the roast goose with the cooking juices, apples and prunes. Accompany with potatoes and braised red cabbage.

❖ Traditional Roast Duckling ❖

SERVES 4–6

PREPARATION TIME
25 minutes
COOKING TIME
Depends on size
FREEZING
Not suitable

- 1 oven-ready duckling (see note)
- salt and pepper
- 1 onion, peeled
- 25 g (1 oz) butter
- 1 small eating apple
- 100 g (4 oz) fresh wholemeal breadcrumbs
- 15 ml (1 tbsp) chopped sage or 5 ml (1 tsp) dried
- 1 egg
- 450 g (1 lb) cooking apples
- a little sugar (optional)

330 CALS/SERVING

1 Weigh the duckling to calculate the cooking time. Prick the skin all over with a skewer or sharp fork and sprinkle with salt. (This helps to draw out the fat and crisp the skin.)
2 To make the stuffing, finely chop the onion. Melt half the butter in a saucepan and cook the onion gently until softened, but not browned. Peel, core and grate the eating apple. Stir into the onion with the breadcrumbs, sage, egg and seasoning. Shape the stuffing into small balls and place in a roasting tin.
3 Place the duckling on a wire rack or trivet in a roasting tin. Roast at 180°C (350°F) mark 4 for 30–35 minutes per 450 g (1 lb). Cook the stuffing balls for the last 30 minutes of the calculated time.
4 Meanwhile, make the apple sauce. Peel, core and slice the apples. Put in a heavy-based saucepan with 15 ml (1 tbsp) water. Cover tightly and cook for about 10 minutes, until the apples are tender, shaking the pan occasionally. Stir in the remaining butter and beat with a wooden spoon until smooth. Stir in a little sugar, if liked. Carve the duckling and serve with the apple sauce and thin gravy.

NOTE: Make sure you buy a large enough duckling – there is much less flesh on a duck than on a chicken of the same weight. Allow at least 450 g (1 lb) dressed weight per person.

❖ Crispy Duck with Mangetouts ❖

SERVES 6

PREPARATION TIME
15 minutes
COOKING TIME
35 minutes
FREEZING
Not suitable
COLOUR INDEX
Page 42

- 4 duckling breast fillets, 175 g (6 oz) each
- salt
- 25 ml (1½ tbsp) thin honey
- 1 bunch spring onions
- 1 large green pepper
- 225 g (8 oz) mangetouts
- 45 ml (3 tbsp) oil
- 2 garlic cloves, crushed
- 2–3 good pinches five-spice powder
- 45 ml (3 tbsp) caster sugar
- 45 ml (3 tbsp) dark so sauce
- 45 ml (3 tbsp) wine vinegar
- 16 water chestnuts, sliced
- 40 g (1½ oz) toasted cashew nuts

325 CALS/SERVING

1 Prick the duckling breast skin all over with a skewer or fork and rub well with salt to help crisp the skin. Place, skin side uppermost, on a rack or trivet in a roasting tin.
2 Bake in the oven at 180°C (350°F) mark 4 for 15 minutes. Brush the skin with the honey and cook for a further 15 minute or until cooked through. Leave to cool, then cut into strips.
3 Cut the spring onions into 2.5 cm (1 inch) lengths. Cut the green pepper into thin strips, discarding the core and seeds. To and tail the mangetouts.
4 Heat the oil in a wok or large frying pan. Add the spring onions, green pepper, mangetouts, garlic and five-spice powder and stir-fry for 2 minutes. Add the sugar, soy sauce, vinegar and duckling strips and toss in the sauce to heat through and glaze. Add the water chestnuts and heat through.
5 Serve at once, sprinkled with toasted cashew nuts and accompanied by rice.

❖ Cinnamon Duck ❖ with Redcurrant Sauce

SERVES 6

PREPARATION TIME
10 minutes
COOKING TIME
40 minutes
FREEZING
Not suitable
COLOUR INDEX
Page 42

- 6 duckling breast fillets, about 175 g (6 oz) each
- 2 cinnamon sticks
- 175 g (6 oz) onion, peeled
- 15 ml (1 tbsp) olive oil
- 1 garlic clove, crushed
- 300 ml (½ pint) chicken stock
- 300 ml (½ pint) red wine
- 5 ml (1 tsp) dried marjoram
- 15 ml (1 tbsp) Dijon mustard
- 1.25 ml (¼ tsp) ground cinnamon
- 30 ml (2 tbsp) redcurrant jelly
- salt and pepper
- watercress, to garnish

370 CALS/SERVING

1 Brown the duckling breast skin side down first, in a larg non-stick sauté pan, two or three at a time, with the cinnamon sticks. Transfer to large roasting tin. Cook at 200°C (400°F) mark 6 for 30 minutes or until crisp and golden and just cooked through.

✤ Roast Duckling ✤ with Honey and Grapefruit

2 Meanwhile, roughly chop the onion. Heat the olive oil in a saucepan and sauté the onion with the garlic until golden. Add the remaining ingredients, bring to the boil and let bubble until reduced by half; strain and reheat.

3 Drain the fat from the duck. Serve thickly sliced with a little of the sauce spooned over. Garnish with watercress and serve the remaining sauce separately.

✤ Blueberry Duck ✤

SERVES 8	
PREPARATION TIME 20 minutes	
COOKING TIME 20–30 minutes	
FREEZING Sauce only	
COLOUR INDEX Page 42	

- 8 duckling breast fillets, about 175 g (6 oz) each
- salt and pepper
BLUEBERRY SAUCE:
- 300 g (11 oz) blueberries
- 150 ml (¼ pint) dry white wine
- 10 ml (2 tsp) caster sugar, or to taste
- 90 ml (6 tbsp) freshly squeezed orange juice
- 60 ml (4 tbsp) crème de cassis
- 30 ml (2 tbsp) wine vinegar, preferably blackcurrant
- 25 g (1 oz) unsalted butter, at room temperature
- 30 ml (2 tbsp) chopped mint
- mint sprigs, to garnish

280 CALS/SERVING

1 Lay the duckling fillets, skin side down, on a board. Cover with greaseproof paper and pound with a rolling pin to flatten slightly. Turn the fillets skin side up and score the skin on the diagonal with a sharp knife. Sprinkle with salt and pepper.
2 Place the duckling fillets, skin side up, in a single layer on a rack in a large roasting pan. Cook at 200°C (400°F) mark 6 for 20–30 minutes, according to how well cooked you like duck.
3 Meanwhile make the blueberry sauce. Set aside one quarter of the blueberries. Put the remainder in a heavy-based saucepan with the white wine and 10 ml (2 tsp) sugar. Bring to the boil, stirring, then cover and simmer for 10 minutes until the blueberries are soft, stirring occasionally. Work through a sieve.
4 Return the puréed blueberries to the pan and add the orange juice, cassis, wine vinegar and seasoning. Bring to the boil, then whisk in the butter a little at a time until incorporated. Simmer until the sauce is reduced and thickened, stirring constantly. Adjust the seasoning, adding more sugar if the sauce seems too tart. Keep warm over a low heat, stirring occasionally.
5 Cut the duckling into thin slices, diagonally across the grain, discarding the skin, if you prefer. Arrange on warmed plates.
6 Add the reserved blueberries and chopped mint to the sauce. Spoon a little of the sauce next to the duckling and garnish with mint. Serve any remaining blueberry sauce separately.

SERVES 4	
PREPARATION TIME 20 minutes	
COOKING TIME 1½ hours	
FREEZING Not suitable	

- 1.8 kg (4 lb) duckling
- 3 grapefruit
- 50 g (2 oz) butter
- 5 ml (1 tsp) Dijon mustard
- 60 ml (4 tbsp) thin honey
- 15 ml (1 tbsp) chopped rosemary or 5 ml (1 tsp) dried
- 30 ml (2 tbsp) brandy
- salt and pepper
- 2.5–5 ml (½–1 tsp) cornflour
- rosemary sprigs, to garnish

375 CALS/SERVING

1 Prick the duckling skin all over with a fork. Slice one of the grapefruit. Place 2 grapefruit slices in the neck cavity; reserve the remainder for garnish. Place the duck, breast side down, on a rack in a roasting tin.
2 Pare the rind of another grapefruit and cut into fine strips. Melt the butter in a pan, add the grapefruit rind with 120 ml (8 tbsp) grapefruit juice, the mustard, honey, rosemary, brandy and seasoning. Bring to the boil, stirring, then pour over the duck.
3 Roast at 220°C (425°F) mark 7 for 15 minutes. Turn the duckling breast side uppermost and baste with the mixture. Continue to roast, basting occasionally, at 190°C (375°F) mark 5 for about 1½ hours or until the duckling is tender, covering with foil if necessary.
4 Transfer the duckling to a warmed serving dish and return to the switched-off oven to keep warm. Skim the fat from the roasting juices. Add the juice from the remaining grapefruit, about 120 ml (8 tbsp). Mix the cornflour to a smooth paste with a little cold water, add to the juices in the roasting tin and bring to the boil. Simmer, stirring, for 2–3 minutes until slightly thickened; strain.
5 Carve the duckling, spoon a little of the juices over and serve the remainder of the sauce separately. Garnish with rosemary sprigs and the reserved grapefruit slices.

❖ Casserole of Hare ❖ with Wild Mushrooms

SERVES 6

PREPARATION TIME
20 minutes, plus
marinating
COOKING TIME
2¼–3 hours
FREEZING
Suitable

- 1 onion, peeled
- 2 carrots, peeled
- 1 celery stick
- 1 garlic clove, crushed
- 450 ml (¾ pint) red wine
- 6 juniper berries, crushed
- 30 ml (2 tbsp) olive oil
- few parsley stalks
- few thyme and rosemary sprigs or 5 ml (1 tsp) each dried
- 6 black peppercorns
- 1 small hare, jointed, or about 1.6 kg (3½ lb) selected hare joints

- 175 g (6 oz) smoked streaky bacon, preferably in one piece, derinded
- 450 g (1 lb) mixed mushrooms, (flat, button and wild)
- salt and pepper
- 50 g (2 oz) plain flour
- 15 ml (1 tbsp) oil
- 75 g (3 oz) butter or margarine
- 225 g (8 oz) button onions, peeled
- 600 ml (1 pint) beef stock

490 CALS/SERVING

1 First prepare the marinade. Roughly chop the onion, carrots and celery and place in a non-metallic bowl. Stir in the garlic, wine, juniper berries, olive oil, herbs and peppercorns.
2 Trim the hare joints and add to the marinade. Cover and leave to marinate in the refrigerator for 24 hours, stirring occasionally.
3 Cut the bacon into thick strips. Quarter any large mushrooms.
4 Remove the hare joints from the marinade with a slotted spoon and pat dry. Toss in the seasoned flour. Strain the marinade and reserve.
5 Heat the oil and butter in a 5 litre (9 pint) flameproof casserole and brown the hare evenly on all sides. Remove with a slotted spoon and drain on absorbent kitchen paper.
6 Lower the heat and add the onions and bacon to the casserole. Sauté, stirring, until the onions are golden brown and the bacon quite crisp. Add any flat or button mushrooms and cook, stirring, for a further 2 minutes. Stir in any remaining flour, then return the hare to the casserole. Add the stock, reserved marinade and a few more herb sprigs if available. Bring to a simmer, cover and cook at 170°C (325°F) mark 3 for 2 hours.
7 Add any wild mushrooms and cook for 30–50 minutes or until the hare is tender. Adjust the seasoning before serving.

❖ Venison with Pomegranate ❖

SERVES 4

PREPARATION TIME
15 minutes
COOKING TIME
15 minutes
FREEZING
Not suitable

- 1 pomegranate
- 350 g (12 oz) venison fillet
- salt and pepper
- 15 ml (1 tbsp) plain flour

- 45 ml (3 tbsp) oil
- 50 g (2 oz) mushrooms, thickly sliced
- 200 ml (7 fl oz) stock

320 CALS/SERVING

1 Using a sharp knife, halve the pomegranate. Scoop out and reserve the seeds and juice. Discard the membrane.

2 Slice the venison fillet into 5 mm (¼ inch) thick pieces. Place between sheets of dampened greaseproof paper and bat out until quite thin. Toss in the seasoned flour to coat.

3 Heat the oil in a large sauté pan and brown the venison on both sides, in batches. Return all meat to the pan, adding any remaining flour.

4 Add the mushrooms, stock and pomegranate seeds and juice. Bring to a simmer and cook for 2–3 minutes or until heated through.

❖ Venison Escalopes ❖ with Red Wine

SERVES 6

PREPARATION TIME
15 minutes, plus marinating

COOKING TIME
6–8 minutes

FREEZING
Not suitable

COLOUR INDEX
page 43

- 6 venison escalopes, cut from the haunch, about 175 g (6 oz) each
- 1 small onion, peeled
- 1 bay leaf
- 2 parsley sprigs
- 8 juniper berries
- 300 ml (½ pint) dry red wine
- 15 g (½ oz) butter or margarine
- 15 ml (1 tbsp) oil
- 30 ml (2 tbsp) redcurrant jelly
- salt and pepper

TO SERVE:
- Game Chips (page 228)

435 CALS/SERVING

1 Put the venison escalopes in a large shallow dish. Finely chop the onion and sprinkle over the meat. Add the bay leaf, parsley and juniper berries. Pour on the wine, cover and leave to marinate in the refrigerator for 3–4 hours if possible or overnight, turning the escalopes occasionally.

2 Remove the escalopes from the marinade, reserving the marinade. Heat the butter and oil in a large frying pan and fry the escalopes for 3–4 minutes on each side. Transfer to a warmed serving dish and keep warm while making the sauce.

3 Strain the reserved marinade into the frying pan and stir to loosen any sediment. Increase the heat and boil rapidly for 3–4 minutes, until reduced. Stir in the redcurrant jelly and season the mixture to taste. Cook, stirring, for 1–2 minutes.

4 Pour the sauce over the escalopes to serve. Accompany with Game Chips, Brussels sprouts and carrots.

❖ Venison Casserole ❖

SERVES 8

PREPARATION TIME
20 minutes

COOKING TIME
2¾ hours

FREEZING
Suitable (stage 3)

- 700 g (1½ lb) lean casserole or haunch of venison
- 700 g (1½ lb) lean stewing beef
- 450 g (1 lb) onions, peeled
- 350 g (12 oz) carrots, peeled
- 350 g (12 oz) celery
- about 45 ml (3 tbsp) oil
- 50 g (2 oz) butter
- 2 large garlic cloves, crushed
- 60 ml (4 tbsp) plain flour
- 1.1 litres (2 pints) beef stock
- 300 ml (½ pint) dry sherry
- finely pared rind and juice of 1 lemon
- 2 bay leaves
- salt and pepper
- 175 g (6 oz) no-soak dried apricots
- 30 ml (2 tbsp) brandy
- chopped parsley, to garnish

420 CALS/SERVING

1 Trim the venison and beef, then cut into 4 cm (1½ inch) chunks. Chop the onions; slice the carrots and celery.
2 Heat the oil and butter in a large flameproof casserole. Brown the meat in batches, adding more oil if necessary. Lift the meat out of the pan using a slotted spoon.
3 Add the onions, carrots and celery to the pan with the garlic and brown lightly. Mix in the flour and cook for 1 minute, then stir in the stock, sherry, lemon rind and strained juice, and the bay leaves. Bring to the boil, replace the meat and season. Cover tightly and cook at 170°C (325°F) mark 3 for 1½ hours.
4 Stir in the apricots, re-cover and cook for a further 1 hour, or until the meat is quite tender.
5 Stir in the brandy and simmer for 5 minutes. Adjust the seasoning and serve garnished with chopped parsley.

EGGS & CHEESE

Eggs are one of our most familiar, versatile foods with endless culinary uses. What's more they are a good source of protein and the vitamins A, D, E and K; they also contain iron. Eggs are quite low in calories too – the average egg provides about 80–90 calories. However, they are relatively high in cholesterol so nutritionists currently recommend that we restrict our consumption to about 3 per week.

In cooking we take their unique properties for granted. Apart from making tasty, fast food when simply poached, boiled or scrambled, eggs will lighten, thicken, bind, set and emulsify. However you are using them, it's vital to remember that they are extremely sensitive to temperature. Very cold eggs will curdle mayonnaise, so bring them to room temperature first. Similarly, eggs whisk to a greater volume if they are at room temperature. In cooked dishes they overcook or curdle very easily, so they must be heated slowly and gently.

When choosing eggs for cooking, remember that sizes do vary. Eggs are now graded following EC guidelines: size 1 is the biggest, weighing over 70 g, and size 7 is the smallest, weighing less than 45 g. It's always advisable to use the size specified in a recipe – it can mean the difference between success and failure! Unless otherwise specified, size 2 or 3 eggs should be used for Good Housekeeping recipes.

Although supermarkets and shops now stock a wide range of eggs – free-range, barn eggs, eggs from grain-only fed hens (the 'vegetarian' egg), brown eggs (which are intrinsically no different from white) – most of the eggs sold in this country are produced by 'battery hens' which are raised by intensive farming methods. Hopefully, consumers will continue to increase the demand for free-range eggs to herald a decline in this less than humane method of farming.

Although when we talk about eggs we generally mean hen's eggs, there are alternatives. However these are nowhere near as widely available, and for one reason or another they're not interchangeable in recipes. Quails are now farmed extensively so quail's eggs are becoming more widely available. Because of their size they are not suitable for everyday egg cookery but they are perfect for use as a garnish or in salads and canapés. They take about 2 minutes to soft boil; crack the shells under cold running water as soon as they are cooked to make them easier to peel.

Duck, goose and turkey eggs are larger and richer than hen's eggs. They must be thoroughly cooked as they are particularly susceptible to salmonella. Allow at least 10 minutes boiling time. Do not use them raw – in mousses, for example – or in dishes cooked at low temperatures, like egg custard.

Eggs and Salmonella

Eggs are susceptible to salmonella, one of the bacteria responsible for food poisoning. Since the great salmonella scare of the early nineties, we've all been advised to reappraise the way we store, handle and cook eggs at home.

For most of us, providing that the usual food hygiene rules are followed (see page 433) there is only minor cause for concern. However, certain groups of the population should not eat lightly cooked eggs and, to be really safe, they should only eat eggs when cooked so that the yolk is set. This means that dishes containing raw eggs, like mousses, cold soufflés, royal icing, ice creams, sorbets and mayonnaise, as well as those made with very lightly cooked eggs like scrambled eggs, lightly poached eggs, hollandaise sauce, lightly cooked meringues and egg custards, should be avoided. People in the 'at risk' group are the elderly, pregnant women, babies and young children, those suffering from immune deficiency diseases, or anyone that has or is recovering from any serious illness.

Buying and Storing Eggs

When buying and storing eggs, note the following points:
- Always store eggs in the refrigerator (in the egg box) or in a cool room. Never store them in a warm room or one that fluctuates in temperature. Keep them, pointed end down, to centre the yolk within the white.
- Buy eggs from a reputable source with a fast turnover. Never buy cracked or damaged eggs. Open the box in the supermarket and check each egg for cracks and the box for tell-tale wet patches.
- Check the date marked on the box and use eggs by the use-by date or within 2 weeks of purchase if there isn't one.
- If the egg is dirty, wipe it with a dry piece of kitchen paper and wash it just before use. However don't wash eggs and then store them for any length of time; washing destroys the natural protective coating and makes the shells more permeable.
- Test for freshness just before cooking: put the egg in a bowl of water; if it floats to the surface it is likely to be old (and possibly bad), because the size of the natural air pocket in the egg increases as it ages. If it stays at the bottom it is fresh.
- Do not keep foods that contain raw egg, such as mayonnaise, for more than 3 days.
- Keep eggs well away from strong-smelling foods; they quickly absorb flavours and smells.

235

❖ Cooking with Eggs ❖

It is often said that a sign of a good cook is someone who can boil an egg to perfection. Although this is relatively simple, the more skilful techniques used in egg cookery need some explanation. Many recipes call for separated eggs. Confident, experienced cooks will do this with a flourish, in one hand; but generally it is advisable to follow the method below.

Separating Eggs

1 Crack the egg against the rim of a bowl. With your thumbs, crack open the shell, letting some of the white run out into the bowl.

2 Over the bowl, tip the yolk from one half of the shell into the other until all the white is separated.

3 If the yolk breaks and a little of it falls into the bowl, scoop it out with a teaspoon. If it gets mixed in the whites will not whisk. If you're separating several eggs, it's a good idea to transfer the whites to a different bowl as you go in case you accidentally break a yolk.

Whisking Egg Whites

Professional cooks use an unlined copper bowl and a large balloon whisk for whisking egg whites. This creates maximum volume because the copper reacts with the whites to form a dense, stable foam. If you use a copper bowl always clean the inside of the bowl with a cut lemon to remove any accumulated toxic copper carbonate before you start. If a copper bowl is unavailable, opt for a balloon whisk or a hand-held electric whisk for the next best volume. Don't use a food processor with a whisk attachment because these rarely give as good results.

Bowls and whisks should be scrupulously clean; any trace of grease, water or egg yolk will hinder whisking and result in a poor volume. A pinch of salt or cream of tartar will stabilize the egg foam. Only whisk until the egg whites stand in soft peaks. Overwhisking makes the eggs dry and granular; eggs whisked to this stage will not fold in evenly and tend to lose volume quickly. Once egg whites are whisked, immediately incorporate them into the other ingredients because otherwise they will collapse if left to stand in the bowl.

Folding in

Having whisked egg whites to a peak of perfection, don't waste all that time and energy with heavy-handed mixing. Use a large metal spoon (not a wooden spoon) and add a good spoonful to the mixture you're folding into to 'let it down' or lighten it slightly. Then add the egg white, using a cutting and folding action, until the whites are evenly incorporated. Allow a hot mixture to cool a little until it is just warm, before folding in the egg whites, or the delicate structure of the whites will collapse. Similarly, let a chilled mixture stand at room temperature until it is soft enough to fold into.

1 If you are whisking egg whites to be folded into a mixture such as a soufflé or sponge, whisk only until they stand in soft peaks. The tips of the peaks should flop over gently when held up on the whisk.

2 Always fold in whisked egg whites as lightly as possible, using a large metal spoon. Cut through the centre of the mixture and turn the spoon to scoop up the mixture and turn it in a rolling action.

Boiling Eggs

This is a misnomer since vigorous boiling produces a rubbery white. For best results, lower the egg(s) into a pan of simmering water using a slotted spoon. Ensure that the water covers the eggs completely or they will cook unevenly. A small pan is best so that the eggs don't move around too much. To centre the yolk (especially if you're using the egg as a garnish), spin the egg in the pan as it cooks.

Cooking times really do depend on personal preference, the freshness of the egg and whether it's being cooked straight from the refrigerator or from room temperature. As a rough guide allow a minimum of 3½ minutes and a maximum of about 5½ minutes for soft-boiled eggs. If the egg does crack while it's cooking, add a little salt or vinegar to the water to coagulate the white and stop it all running out.

Hard-boiled eggs take about 10–12 minutes. As soon as they are cooked, drain and rinse under cold running water then crack the shell on the side of the pan to cool the egg quickly and prevent an unsightly black line forming around the yolk. To peel hard-boiled eggs roll them firmly across the work surface a couple of times and the shell should come off easily.

Eggs mollet have soft yolks and firm whites. To cook these, simmer for about 6 minutes, plunge into cold water, cool slightly and peel.

To coddle an egg, put it into a pan of boiling water, cover with a lid then remove from the heat and leave for about 8–10 minutes. It should be lightly set.

Poached Eggs

Poached eggs are really easy to cook if you have an egg poacher. If you haven't, poach eggs in a deep frying pan filled with simmering water. Add 5–10 ml (1–2 teaspoons) vinegar to help the egg set. Use really fresh eggs; stale eggs will run all over the pan. As soon as you have dropped the egg in, swirl the water around it in a circular motion to contain the shape. Simmer gently until cooked, 3–5 minutes. Because poaching can be quite tricky until you get the hang of it, it's best to cook only one egg at a time. Drain thoroughly before serving. Some cooks like to trim the edges with kitchen scissors to make a neater shape.

Fried Eggs

Use the freshest eggs possible or they will run all over the pan. Heat the fat of your choice – dripping, bacon fat, olive or vegetable oil – until very hot before you add the egg to get a nice crisp base. To help the thicker middle set, carefully 'splash' a little of the hot fat over as it cooks. Turn the eggs over or cook on one side only, depending on personal preference.

Making Omelettes and Pancakes

Vital to the success of both omelette and pancake making is a good heavy-based pan. Ideally it should be kept solely for pancake or omelette making and should never be washed or scrubbed, just carefully wiped out with kitchen paper after use. When buying a pan choose one that measures about 18–20 cm (7–8 inches) across the base with sloping sides and a non-stick coating. With a larger pan it is difficult to spread out the batter evenly. For best results, a new pan should be 'seasoned' before use. If available follow the manufacturer's instructions, otherwise fill the pan with oil and heat it gently until hot. Repeat this once or twice to seal the surface of the pan.

Before cooking, heat the pan; slow cooking makes pancakes and omelettes tough. Add a small amount of fat to the pan, heat again then tip out any excess – too much fat will fry the omelette or pancake. Don't forget to reheat and grease the pan between each one. Keep pancakes warm while you cook the remainder by stacking them on a hot plate, covering with foil and putting it in the oven or over a pan of simmering water.

* Cheese *

Like eggs, cheese is amazingly versatile either as an ingredient or as a course or meal on its own. Although there are literally hundreds of cheeses they are all produced from milk – usually cow's milk but also goat's and ewe's milk. In fact during recent years goat's cheese has become somewhat ubiquitous on restaurant menus which in turn has encouraged supermarkets and delicatessens to offer a wider range of goat's cheeses.

Although many cheeses are interchangeable in recipes as long as they are similar in texture, some cheeses have a particular property or flavour which is specifically required for certain recipes. Think of fondue made without the unique creaminess of Emmental or Gruyère; pizza without a mozzarella topping; risotto or pasta without a sprinkling of freshly grated Parmesan.

In cooking, it is important to realise that if semi-hard cheese is overheated it separates and the fat runs out. When adding cheese to a hot sauce remove the sauce from the heat before stirring in the cheese. When making cheese scones and breads use a well-matured Farmhouse cheese to get a good depth of flavour.

Because there are so many cheeses it is impossible to categorise them all, but for culinary purposes they can be divided into four groups: hard cheeses such as Parmesan and Pecorino; semi-hard cheeses including traditional favourites like Cheddar, Stilton, Edam, Cheshire and Lancashire; soft cheeses such as mould-ripened Brie and Camembert as well as the blue-veined Danish Blue; and finally fresh soft cheese including cottage cheese, cream cheese, quark and curd cheese. Vegetarian cheeses made with non-animal rennet are now available in these categories.

In general, when choosing hard or semi-hard cheeses avoid pieces that look sweaty or dried at the edges or those that are badly cracked or mis-shapen. If you're buying for a cheeseboard look for a nicely shaped piece. Soft cheeses, like Brie and Camembert, should be slightly springy to the touch and soft in the middle (or very soft verging on runny if for immediate consumption). Fresh soft cheeses, particularly goat's cheeses, should be eaten as fresh as possible. Check for signs of discolouration and a rancid smell.

When you get the cheese home, store it wrapped in greaseproof paper or foil in the refrigerator. Bring the cheese to room temperature before serving. Cheese can also be frozen but some varieties, notably the higher fat ones, freeze better than others.

Although in general cheese is high in calories and fat, it is a good source of protein, vitamins and minerals, particularly calcium. Lower-fat hard cheeses are produced from semi-skimmed milk and are ideal for those who are cutting down on fat in their diet. There are currently no legal requirements for the fat content of these cheeses but lower-fat Cheddar contains about half as much fat and approximately two thirds the calories of traditional Cheddar. Bear in mind though that the low-fat varieties tend to be milder in flavour. Skimmed milk soft cheeses are very low in fat – less than 2% compared with about 45% fat in cream cheese.

Cheese and Listeria

Following recent outbreaks of listeriosis, soft mould-ripened cheeses, such as Brie, Camembert and blue-veined soft cheeses, and all goat's and sheep's cheeses should be avoided by pregnant women and people with decreased resistance to infection.

❖ Omelette ❖

SERVES 1

PREPARATION TIME
5 minutes
COOKING TIME
1–1½ minutes
FREEZING
Not suitable
COLOUR INDEX
Page 44

• 2–3 eggs
• salt and pepper
• 15 ml (1 tbsp) milk or water

• butter or margarine for frying

390 CALS/SERVING

1 Whisk the eggs just enough to break them down; over-beating spoils the texture of the omelette. Season with salt and pepper and add the milk or water.

2 Place an omelette or non-stick frying pan over a gentle heat and, when it is hot, add a generous knob of butter and heat until it is foaming but not brown.

3 Add the beaten eggs. Stir gently with a fork or wooden spatula, drawing the mixture from the sides to the centre as it sets and letting the liquid egg in the centre run to the sides. When the eggs have set, stop stirring and cook for a further 30 seconds–1 minute until the omelette is golden brown underneath and still creamy on top. Don't over-cook or it will be tough.

4 If making a filled omelette, add the filling at this point. Tilt the pan away from you slightly and use a palette knife to fold over a third of the omelette to the centre, then fold over the opposite third. Slide the omelette out on to a warmed plate, letting it flip over so that the folded sides are underneath. Serve at once, with a salad and warm bread.

Omelette Fillings

FINES HERBES: Add 15 ml (1 tbsp) finely chopped chervil, chives and tarragon or a large pinch of dried mixed herbs to the beaten egg mixture before cooking.

TOMATO: Skin and chop 1–2 tomatoes and fry in a little butter for 5 minutes or until soft and pulpy. Put in the centre of the omelette before folding.

CHEESE: Grate 40 g (1½ oz) cheese. Sprinkle half on the omelette before folding. Sprinkle the rest over the finished omelette.

MUSHROOM: Thickly slice about 50 g (2 oz) mushrooms and cook in butter until soft. Put in the centre of the omelette before folding. (When available, use wild mushrooms.)

CURRIED VEGETABLE: Roughly chop leftover vegetables, such as potato, green beans, broad beans or parsnips. Fry in oil with about 2.5 ml (½ tsp) curry powder and a little crushed garlic. Put in the centre of the omelette before folding.

LOVAGE AND BLUE CHEESE: Add 10 ml (2 tsp) finely chopped lovage to the beaten egg mixture. Cut 25–50 g (1–2 oz) Blue Cheshire, Blue Stilton or Blue Wensleydale cheese into thin slices and scatter over the omelette before folding.

GOAT'S CHEESE: Soften about 25 g (1 oz) mild goat's cheese and blend with a little fromage frais. Season with salt and pepper and put in the centre of the omelette before folding.

PRAWN: Allow 50 g (2 oz) cooked peeled prawns per omelette. Sprinkle the prawns and a little chopped tarragon in the centre of the omelette before folding.

SMOKED SALMON: Combine 25 g (1 oz) chopped smoked salmon with a little chopped dill and 15 ml (1 tbsp) soured cream. Put in the centre of the omelette before folding over.

❖ Frittata ❖

SERVES 6

PREPARATION TIME
20 minutes
COOKING TIME
6–8 minutes
FREEZING
Not suitable

• 125 g (4 oz) small new potatoes
• 125 g (4 oz) shelled broad beans
• salt and pepper
• 1 onion, peeled
• 225 g (8 oz) courgettes
• 50 g (2 oz) soft cheese, preferably fresh goat's cheese
• 4 eggs

• 30 ml (2 tbsp) chopped thyme
• 30 ml (2 tbsp) olive oil
• 125 g (4 oz) cooked peeled prawns
• 125 g (4 oz) lightly cooked salmon, flaked
• whole cooked prawns, to garnish

215 CALS/SERVING

1 Cook the potatoes and broad beans separately in boiling salted water until just tender; drain thoroughly. Roughly chop the onion. Slice the courgettes.

2 In a bowl, whisk together the cheese, eggs, thyme and seasoning.

3 Heat the oil in a large shallow flameproof pan. Add the onion, courgettes, potatoes and beans. Cook, stirring, for 2–3 minutes, then add the prawns and salmon. Pour in the egg mixture.

4 As the eggs cook, push the mixture into the centre to allow the raw egg to flow down to the edge of the pan. When the frittata is lightly set, place the pan under a hot grill for 2–3 minutes until golden. Garnish with prawns and serve immediately.

Variations

Substitute fresh sorrel for the thyme. The broad beans can be skinned for extra colour.

❖ Spinach and ❖ Mushroom Omelette

SERVES 2		
PREPARATION TIME 5 minutes COOKING TIME 7 minutes FREEZING Not suitable COLOUR INDEX Page 44	• *225 g (8 oz) freshly cooked, or frozen chopped spinach, thawed* • *4 eggs* • *1.25 ml (¼ tsp) freshly grated nutmeg* • *salt and pepper* • *40 g (1½ oz) butter or margarine*	• *125 g (4 oz) button mushrooms, thinly sliced* • *10 ml (2 tsp) wholegrain mustard* • *150 ml (¼ pint) soured cream*

490 CALS/SERVING

1 Press the spinach in a sieve or colander to remove excess liquid. Place in a blender with the eggs, nutmeg and seasoning. Blend until smooth.

2 Heat 25 g (1 oz) butter in a large non-stick frying pan. When foaming, add the spinach mixture. Cook until the base is set, drawing the mixture from the sides to the centre as it sets and allowing the liquid egg to run to the edge of the pan. Once the base is firm, place under a hot grill for 1–2 minutes.

3 Meanwhile, heat the remaining butter in a pan and sauté the mushrooms with the mustard. Add the soured cream and seasoning and bring to the boil.

4 Spoon the mushroom mixture over one half of the omelette, then flip over to enclose the filling. Serve immediately.

❖ Omelette Rolls ❖

MAKES ABOUT 6 OMELETTES	• *8 eggs* • *salt and pepper*	• *chopped mixed herbs (optional)* • *butter*
PREPARATION TIME 5 minutes COOKING TIME 10 minutes FREEZING Not suitable COLOUR INDEX Page 44		

85 CALS/OMELETTE PLUS FILLING

1 Lightly whisk the eggs with the seasoning and 60 ml (4 tbsp) water. Add some fresh herbs if wished.

2 Heat a little butter in a large non-stick frying pan. Add a small ladle of the egg mixture and swirl around the pan to give a thin layer. Leave to set and brown for about 30 seconds.

3 Loosen around the edges, then turn out the omelette onto a sheet of greaseproof paper. Cook all the omelettes similarly. Stack interleaved with greaseproof paper; cover and cool.

4 Once cool, roll the omelettes up with one or more of the savoury fillings suggested below. Cover tightly and refrigerate until required. Serve thickly sliced on a bed of parsley, as a delicious alternative to sandwiches.

Savoury Fillings

• Mix chopped cooked chicken with roughly chopped watercress and a little mayonnaise. Season and add a little Dijon mustard.

• Mix small cooked peeled prawns with garlic mayonnaise, chopped cucumber and a little grated lemon rind and juice. Season to taste.

• Use thinly sliced salami or ham. Top with a little soft cheese and some shredded salad leaves.

• Coarsely grate some carrot, fennel and celery. Mix together with a little yogurt, lemon juice and wholegrain mustard. Add chopped parsley and grated cheese to taste.

• Roughly chop tomatoes and radishes and roll inside the omelettes with salad leaves and a dash of lemon mayonnaise or Greek yogurt.

• Flake smoked trout or mackerel fillet and mix with mayonnaise, a dash of lemon or lime juice, and a generous dollop of creamed horseradish. Add some finely chopped cucumber or apple.

❖ Pancakes ❖

MAKES 8

PREPARATION TIME
10 minutes, plus
standing
COOKING TIME
15–20 minutes
FREEZING
Suitable
COLOUR INDEX
Page 44

- 125 g (4 oz) plain white flour
- pinch of salt
- 1 egg

- about 300 ml (½ pint) milk
- 15 ml (1 tbsp oil)
- oil for frying

105 CALS/PANCAKE

1 Sift the flour and salt into a bowl and make a well in the centre. Break the egg into the well and add a little of the milk. Mix the liquid ingredients together, then gradually beat in the flour until smooth.

2 Beat in the oil and the remaining milk to obtain the consistency of thin cream. (Alternatively, the batter can be mixed in a blender.) Cover the batter and leave to stand in the refrigerator for about 20 minutes.

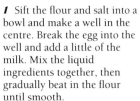

3 Heat a pancake pan; when hot, brush with the minimum of oil. Add a little extra milk to the batter if it is thick. Pour a small amount of batter into the pan and swirl around until it is evenly and thinly spread over the bottom of the pan.

4 Cook over a moderate to high heat for about 1 minute or until the edges are curling away from the pan and the underside is golden. Flip the pancake over using a palette knife and cook the second side.

5 Turn the pancake out on to a sheet of greaseproof paper (or non-stick baking parchment if the pancakes are to be frozen). Loosely fold a clean tea towel over the top. Repeat until all the pancake batter has been used, lightly oiling the pan between pancakes.

Variations

WHOLEWHEAT PANCAKES: Use a mixture of half white, half wholemeal flour.

BUCKWHEAT PANCAKES: Use a mixture of half white, half buckwheat flour. Don't sift the buckwheat flour.

SPICED CHICK PEA PANCAKES: Use chick pea (gram) flour. Toast 10 ml (2 tsp) cumin seeds under the grill, then grind to a powder. Add to the flour with 1.25 ml (¼ tsp) turmeric. Replace 150 ml (¼ pint) of the milk with water. Make slightly thicker pancakes. Use more oil if necessary.

Fillings

Almost any mixture of cooked vegetables, fish or chicken, and herbs or nuts – moistened with a little white sauce, cream or cream cheese – can be used as a pancake filling.

❖ Chicken and ❖ Mushroom Pancakes

SERVES 6

PREPARATION TIME
40 minutes
COOKING TIME
25 minutes
FREEZING
Not suitable

- 350 g (12 oz) cooked chicken
- 225 g (8 oz) button mushrooms
- 50 g (2 oz) butter or margarine
- 25 g (1 oz) plain flour
- 300 ml (½ pint) chicken stock

- salt and pepper
- 12 Buckwheat Pancakes (see above)
- 125 g (4 oz) Gruyère cheese, grated

460 CALS/SERVING

1 Roughly shred the chicken; slice the mushrooms. Melt the butter in a saucepan. Add the mushrooms and cook for 2–3 minutes. Stir in the flour and cook, stirring, for 1 minute, then stir in the stock. Bring to the boil, stirring, then simmer for 2–3 minutes. Stir in the chicken and seasoning to taste.

2 Spoon some of the chicken and mushroom mixture on to a quarter of each pancake. Fold in half, and then in half again to form neat pockets. Arrange in a lightly greased ovenproof dish.

3 Sprinkle liberally with the grated cheese and bake at 190°C (375°F) mark 5 for 25 minutes or until golden and bubbly.

❖ Ratatouille Pancakes ❖

SERVES 4
PREPARATION TIME
5 minutes
COOKING TIME
20 minutes
FREEZING
Not suitable

- ½ quantity Ratatouille (page 269)
- 8 Buckwheat Pancakes (see left)
- about 50 g (2 oz) freshly grated Parmesan or Cheddar cheese
- chervil or parsley sprigs, to garnish

375 CALS/SERVING

1 Divide the ratatouille between the pancakes. Roll up to enclose the filling, then arrange in a single layer, seam-side down, in a lightly greased gratin dish. Sprinkle with the cheese.
2 Cover with foil and bake at 200°C (400°F) mark 6 for 20 minutes or until the pancakes are heated through. Serve immediately, garnished with herbs, accompanied by a salad.

❖ Mediterranean ❖ Vegetable and Egg Grill

SERVES 4
PREPARATION TIME
20 minutes
COOKING TIME
10 minutes
FREEZING
Not suitable
COLOUR INDEX
Page 45

- 1 onion, peeled
- 350 g (12 oz) courgettes
- 1 medium green pepper
- 30 ml (2 tbsp) olive oil
- 1 garlic clove, crushed
- salt and pepper
- 10 ml (2 tsp) chopped rosemary or 2.5 ml (½ tsp) dried
- 400 g (14 oz) can chopped tomatoes
- 4 eggs
- 50 g (2 oz) Cheddar or Gruyère cheese, grated

280 CALS/SERVING

1 Slice the onion and courgettes; roughly chop the pepper, discarding the core and seeds. Heat the oil in a large flameproof sauté pan. Add the courgettes, pepper and onion and cook until beginning to soften and brown, stirring occasionally.
2 Stir in the garlic, seasoning, rosemary and tomatoes. Simmer, uncovered, until the vegetables are tender and the liquid is well reduced.

3 Make four slight hollows in the vegetable mixture and carefully break an egg into each. Season the eggs with salt and plenty of pepper and top with the grated cheese.
4 Cook under a preheated grill for about 10 minutes, depending on how well cooked you like your eggs.

NOTE: Protect the sauté pan handle with foil if necessary. Alternatively, use individual flameproof dishes for this recipe if you have them.

❖ Smoked Haddock ❖ and Egg Pancakes

SERVES 3-4
PREPARATION TIME
30 minutes
COOKING TIME
20 minutes
FREEZING
Not suitable

- 350 g (12 oz) smoked haddock fillet
- 2 eggs
- 40 g (1½ oz) butter or margarine
- 25 g (1 oz) plain flour
- 200 ml (7 fl oz) milk
- 150 ml (¼ pint) soured cream
- 15 ml (1 tbsp) snipped chives
- pepper
- 6 Pancakes (see left)
- 50 g (2 oz) fresh brown breadcrumbs

720-540 CALS/SERVING

1 Poach the fish in enough water to cover for about 5–7 minutes until tender. Drain, skin and flake into large pieces, removing any bones. Hardboil the eggs for 7 minutes, then shell and chop roughly.
2 Melt 25 g (1 oz) butter in a saucepan, add the flour and cook, stirring, for 1 minute. Remove from the heat and gradually stir in the milk and soured cream. Bring to the boil, stirring constantly, then lower the heat and cook gently, stirring, for 2–3 minutes.
3 Add the flaked fish and roughly chopped eggs to the sauce. Stir in the chives and season with plenty of black pepper; the fish adds sufficient salt. Divide the mixture among the prepared pancakes and roll up.
4 Place in a shallow ovenproof dish and sprinkle with the breadcrumbs. Melt the remaining butter and drizzle over the top. Bake at 190°C (375°F) mark 5 for about 20 minutes or until bubbling and thoroughly heated through.

❖ Spanish Tortilla ❖

SERVES 6

PREPARATION TIME
15 minutes
COOKING TIME
40 minutes
FREEZING
Not suitable
COLOUR INDEX
Page 45

- 350 g (12 oz) onions, peeled
- about 100 ml (4 fl oz) olive oil
- 700 g (1½ lb) old potatoes, peeled
- 6 eggs
- salt and pepper

355 CALS/SERVING

1 Thinly slice the onions. Heat the oil in a large non-stick frying pan, about 23–25 cm (9–10 inches) in diameter. Add the onions and cook gently for about 10 minutes or until quite soft.

2 Meanwhile thinly slice the potatoes, using a food processor if possible. Add to the pan and cook over moderate heat, stirring frequently, for 10–15 minutes until the potatoes are golden and almost tender.

3 Lift the potatoes and onions into a colander, draining and reserving the oil. In a large bowl, whisk the eggs with plenty of seasoning. Stir in the potatoes and onions.

4 Heat the reserved oil in the clean frying pan, adding a little more if necessary to give a good film. Add the potato, onion and egg mixture, pressing it down gently.

5 Cook over a moderate heat for about 6–8 minutes or until well browned underneath and the top is nearly set. Place under a hot grill for about 3 minutes to brown the top. Serve either warm or cold, cut into wedges and accompanied by a tomato, olive and onion salad and crusty bread.

NOTE: When cooking the tortilla, you need to use plenty of oil otherwise it will refuse to come out of the pan. Remember to protect the pan handle with foil if necessary, when grilling.

❖ Baked Eggs ❖ with Chorizo

SERVES 4

PREPARATION TIME
20 minutes
COOKING TIME
15–20 minutes
FREEZING
Not suitable
COLOUR INDEX
Page 45

- 1 large onion, peeled
- 30 ml (2 tbsp) olive oil
- 1 garlic clove, crushed
- 2.5 ml (½ tsp) paprika
- 400 g (14 oz) can chopped tomatoes
- salt and pepper
- 225 g (8 oz) thin asparagus spears
- 50 g (2 oz) fresh or frozen peas
- 185 g (6½ oz) can pimientos, drained
- 75 g (3 oz) prosciutto or other raw ham
- 125 g (4 oz) ready-to-eat chorizo sausage
- 4 eggs

370 CALS/SERVING

1 Chop the onion. Heat the oil in a small saucepan, add the onion and garlic and cook over a moderate heat until beginning to brown. Stir in the paprika, then cook for 1 minute. Mix in the chopped tomatoes and seasoning. Simmer for about 5 minutes.

2 Meanwhile, trim the asparagus and cut into 5 cm (2 inch) lengths. Cook the asparagus and peas separately in boiling salted water until tender; drain. Shred the pimientos into fine strips. Cut the ham and chorizo sausage into small pieces.

3 Divide the tomato sauce between four 300–450 ml (½–¾ pint) shallow ovenproof dishes. Make a well in the centre of the sauce and break an egg into each one.

4 Arrange the asparagus, peas, pimiento, ham and chorizo sausage around the egg. Season with pepper. Bake at 220°C (425°F) mark 7 for 15–20 minutes. Serve immediately.

NOTE: Spicy chorizo is the most typical Spanish sausage. It is sold raw for use in cooked dishes or cured ready to slice and serve.

❖ Cheese Soufflé ❖

3 Stir the cheese into the sauce until evenly blended. Using a hand or electric mixer, whisk the egg whites until they stand in soft peaks.

4 Mix one large spoonful of egg white into the sauce to lighten it. Gently pour the sauce over the remaining egg whites and carefully fold the ingredients together, using a metal spoon; do not overmix.

SERVES 4

PREPARATION TIME
20 minutes, plus
standing
COOKING TIME
30 minutes
FREEZING
Not suitable

- 15 ml (1 tbsp) freshly grated Parmesan cheese
- 200 ml (7 fl oz) milk
- few onion and carrot slices
- 1 bay leaf
- 6 black peppercorns
- 25 g (1 oz) butter or margarine
- 30 ml (2 tbsp) plain flour

- 10 ml (2 tsp) Dijon mustard
- salt and pepper
- cayenne pepper
- 4 eggs, separated, plus 1 egg white
- 75 g (3 oz) mature Cheddar cheese, finely grated

295 CALS/SERVING

5 Pour the soufflé mixture gently into the prepared dish; it should come about three-quarters of the way up the side of the dish.

6 Sprinkle with the reserved cheese and run a knife around the edge of the mixture. Stand the dish on a baking sheet and bake at 180°C (350°F) mark 4 for about 30 minutes, until golden brown on the top, well risen and just firm to the touch. Serve immediately. There should be a hint of softness in the centre of the soufflé.

NOTE: Use a proper straight-sided soufflé dish to get the best rise. Running a knife around the edge of the mixture before it goes into the oven helps to achieve the classic 'hat' effect. If necessary, the soufflé can be prepared ahead to the end of stage 2 and left to stand for several hours before completing.

Variations

Don't use too great a weight of flavouring ingredient or the soufflé will be heavy. Replace the Cheddar cheese with one of the following:

BLUE CHEESE: Use a semi-hard blue cheese, such as Stilton or Wensleydale.

MUSHROOM: Add 125 g (4 oz) mushrooms, chopped and sautéed in butter.

SMOKED HADDOCK: Add 75 g (3 oz) finely flaked cooked smoked haddock.

1 Grease a 1.3 litre (2¼ pint) soufflé dish with butter. Sprinkle the Parmesan into the dish and tilt the dish, knocking the sides gently until they are evenly coated with cheese. Put the milk in a saucepan with the onion and carrot slices, bay leaf and peppercorns. Bring slowly to the boil, remove from the heat, cover and leave to infuse for 30 minutes; strain.

2 Melt the butter in a saucepan and stir in the flour and mustard. Season with salt, pepper and cayenne, and cook for 1 minute, stirring. Remove from the heat and gradually stir in the milk. Bring to the boil slowly and cook, stirring, until the sauce thickens. Cool a little, then beat in the egg yolks, one at a time. Sprinkle the Cheddar cheese over the sauce, reserving 15 ml (1 tbsp) for the topping.

❖ Spinach and ❖ Gruyère Soufflé

SERVES 3–4
PREPARATION TIME
20 minutes
COOKING TIME
30 minutes
FREEZING
Not suitable

- 450 g (1 lb) spinach, leaves, cooked, or 225 g (8 oz) frozen leaf spinach, thawed
- 50 g (2 oz) butter or margarine
- 45 ml (3 tbsp) plain flour
- 200 ml (7 fl oz) milk
- salt and pepper
- 3 eggs, separated, plus 1 egg white
- 125 g (4 oz) Gruyère cheese, grated

520–400 CALS/SERVING

1 Grease a 1.3 litre (2¼ pint) soufflé dish. Put the spinach in a sieve and press to remove all moisture. Chop finely.
2 Melt the butter in a saucepan, add the spinach and cook for a few minutes to drive off any remaining moisture.
3 Add the flour and cook gently for 1 minute, stirring. Remove the pan from the heat and gradually stir in the milk. Season with salt and pepper and bring to the boil slowly. Reduce the heat and cook, stirring, until thickened. Cool slightly, then beat in the egg yolks, one at a time, and 75 g (3 oz) grated cheese.
4 Whisk the egg whites until stiff, then fold into the mixture. Spoon into the soufflé dish and sprinkle with remaining cheese.
5 Stand the dish on a baking sheet and bake at 190°C (375°F) mark 5 for about 30 minutes or until well risen and just set. Serve immediately.

❖ Cauliflower Soufflés ❖

SERVES 8
PREPARATION TIME
20 minutes
COOKING TIME
20–25 minutes
FREEZING
Not suitable
COLOUR INDEX
Page 45

- 225 g (8 oz) small cauliflower florets
- salt and pepper
- 40 g (1½ oz) butter or margarine
- 45 ml (3 tbsp) plain flour
- 200 ml (7 fl oz) milk
- 15 ml (1 tbsp) wholegrain mustard
- 4 eggs, separated
- 100 g (4 oz) mature Cheddar cheese, grated

175 CALS/SERVING

1 Grease 8 ramekin dishes. Put the cauliflower in a saucepan and just cover with boiling salted water. Cover and simmer until tender, then drain.
2 Meanwhile, melt the butter in a saucepan and stir in the flour, cook for 1 minute, stirring. Remove from the heat and gradually stir in the milk. Bring to the boil and cook, stirring, until thickened. Add mustard and seasoning.
3 Turn the sauce into a blender or food processor. Add the cauliflower and work to an almost smooth purée.
4 Turn into a large bowl and leave to cool slightly, then beat in the egg yolks, one at a time. Stir in the cheese.
5 Whisk the egg whites until stiff but not dry and lightly fold into the sauce mixture. Spoon into the ramekin dishes.
6 Bake at 180°C (350°F) mark 4 for 20–25 minutes or until browned and just firm to the touch. Serve at once.

❖ Asparagus Scramble ❖

SERVES 3
PREPARATION TIME
5 minutes
COOKING TIME
3–4 minutes
FREEZING
Not suitable

- 350 g (12 oz) asparagus, steamed, or a 285 g (10 oz) can asparagus spears, well drained
- 1 small French loaf
- about 50 g (2 oz) butter
- paprika to taste
- 6 eggs
- 60 ml (4 tbsp) milk
- salt and pepper

455 CALS/SERVING

1 Cut off the asparagus tips and reserve; roughly chop the stalks.
2 Cut the bread into 1 cm (½ inch) slices and toast on both sides. Spread with a little butter and sprinkle with paprika. Keep warm in a low oven.
3 Whisk together the eggs, milk and seasoning with a pinch of paprika.
4 Melt 25 g (1 oz) butter in a heavy-based saucepan. Add the eggs and stir over a moderate heat until beginning to set. Mix in the chopped asparagus, stirring until the eggs are lightly set.
5 Transfer the toast and egg mixture to warmed plates and top with asparagus tips. Sprinkle with paprika if wished, to serve.

❖ Toasted Walnut, Bacon ❖ and Roquefort Roulade

3 Remove from the heat and stir in the Roquefort cheese until melted; add the bacon and nuts. Season with pepper. Cover the surface with a piece of damp greaseproof paper to prevent a skin forming.

4 To make the roulade, cook the fresh spinach, with just the water clinging to the leaves after washing, for about 4–5 minutes or until wilted. Drain and chop very finely. If using frozen spinach, drain thoroughly.

SERVES 4–6

PREPARATION TIME
20 minutes
COOKING TIME
25 minutes
FREEZING
Not suitable

- 6 lean streaky bacon rashers, derinded
- 75 g (3 oz) walnut halves, toasted
- 25 g (1 oz) butter or margarine
- 25 g (1 oz) plain flour
- 300 ml (½ pint) milk
- 50 g (2 oz) Roquefort cheese, crumbled
- salt and pepper
- 700 g (1½ lb) fresh spinach, stalks removed, or 300 g (10 oz) packet frozen chopped spinach, thawed

- 1 garlic clove, crushed
- 45 ml (3 tbsp) freshly grated Parmesan cheese
- freshly grated nutmeg
- 4 eggs, separated
TO GARNISH:
- finely chopped toasted walnuts
- Parmesan cheese

575–380 CALS/SERVING

5 Put the spinach in a bowl with the garlic and 30 ml (2 tbsp) of the Parmesan. Stir well, seasoning with salt, pepper and plenty of nutmeg. Beat in the egg yolks.

6 Whisk the egg whites until stiff. Fold into the spinach mixture. Pour into the prepared tin, then quickly spread out evenly. Bake at 200°C (400°F) mark 6 for about 15 minutes or until well risen and firm to the touch.

1 Grease a 33×23 cm (13×9 inch) Swiss roll tin and line with non-stick baking parchment. Grill the bacon until crisp, then chop into large pieces. Roughly chop the walnuts.

2 To make the filling, melt the butter in a saucepan, stir in the flour and cook for 1 minute. Remove from the heat and gradually stir in the milk. Return to the heat and bring to the boil, stirring continuously. Cook, stirring, for 2–3 minutes.

7 While the roulade is in the oven, spread out a sheet of non-stick baking parchment on the work surface and sprinkle with the remaining Parmesan. Reheat the filling when the roulade is almost cooked – it should be piping hot when spread on the roulade.

8 Turn the roulade out onto the sheet of paper and peel away the lining paper. Quickly spread with the hot filling. Roll up the roulade, gently lifting the paper. Transfer to a heated serving dish and sprinkle with a few walnuts and shavings of Parmesan. Serve immediately, with a tomato salad.

❖ Golden Cheese Pudding ❖

SERVES 4

PREPARATION TIME
15 minutes, plus
standing
COOKING TIME
30 minutes
FREEZING
Not suitable

- *600 ml (1 pint) milk*
- *3 eggs*
- *60 ml (4 tbsp) freshly grated Parmesan cheese*
- *2.5 ml (½ tsp) chilli seasoning (not powder)*
- *freshly grated nutmeg*
- *salt and pepper*
- *5 large thick slices white crusty bread, about 255 g (8 oz) in total*
- *225 g (8 oz) Gruyère or Emmental cheese, grated*

620 CALS/SERVING

1 Whisk together the milk, eggs, 45 ml (3 tbsp) Parmesan, the chilli seasoning and nutmeg. Season. Halve the bread slices if very large.

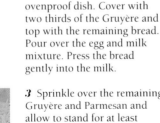

2 Place half of the bread in a well buttered 2 litre (3½ pint) ovenproof dish. Cover with two thirds of the Gruyère and top with the remaining bread. Pour over the egg and milk mixture. Press the bread gently into the milk.

3 Sprinkle over the remaining Gruyère and Parmesan and allow to stand for at least 30 minutes to absorb most of the liquid.

4 Place the dish in a roasting tin and pour in enough boiling water to come halfway up the sides of the dish. Bake at 220°C (425°F) mark 7 for about 30 minutes or until puffed, lightly set and well browned, covering loosely with foil if necessary. Serve with a tomato salad.

NOTE: For this recipe we used Gruyère de Beaufort, which you may find simply called Beaufort. Swiss Gruyère and Emmental are equally suitable.

❖ Cheese Fondue ❖

SERVES 4

PREPARATION TIME
10 minutes
COOKING TIME
About 10 minutes
FREEZING
Not suitable

- *200 g (7 oz) Gruyère cheese*
- *200 g (7 oz) Emmental cheese*
- *1 large garlic clove, halved*
- *10 ml (2 tsp) cornflour*
- *45 ml (3 tbsp) Kirsch*
- *200 ml (7 fl oz) dry white wine*
- *15 ml (1 tbsp) lemon juice*
- *pepper*
- *crusty bread, to serve*

455 CALS/SERVING

1 Grate the cheeses. Rub the halved garlic clove around the inside of a fondue pan (or a heavy-based saucepan).
2 Blend the cornflour to a smooth paste with the Kirsch. Put the wine, lemon juice and grated cheeses in the pan with the blended cornflour and bring slowly to the boil, stirring all the time. Simmer gently for 3–4 minutes, stirring frequently. Season with pepper; the cheeses add sufficient salt.
3 Set the pan over the fondue burner at the table. Serve with plenty of bite-size chunks of crusty bread for dipping.

NOTE: If you do not own a fondue set, transfer the fondue to a warmed serving dish and keep warm over a heated serving tray at the table.

❖ Pan Haggerty ❖

SERVES 4

PREPARATION TIME
5 minutes
COOKING TIME
0 minutes
FREEZING
Not suitable
COLOUR INDEX
Page 46

- 450 g (1 lb) potatoes
- 2 onions, peeled
- 25 g (1 oz) butter
- 15 ml (1 tbsp) oil
- 125 g (4 oz) Cheddar or Lancashire cheese, grated
- salt and pepper

`285 CALS/SERVING`

Peel the potatoes and slice thinly. Slice the onions thinly.

Heat the butter and oil in a large heavy-based frying pan. Remove from the heat and cover the base with a layer of potatoes. Add a layer of onions and another of grated cheese, seasoning well with salt and pepper. Continue these layers, ending with a top layer of cheese.

Cover and cook gently for about 30 minutes or until the potatoes and onions are almost cooked.

Uncover and place under a hot grill to brown. Serve straight from the pan.

NOTE: Use firm fleshed potatoes such as Desirée, Romano or Maris Piper as they will keep their shape during cooking.

❖ Three Cheese ❖ Aubergine Tart

SERVES 6

PREPARATION TIME
0 minutes
COOKING TIME
1 hour
FREEZING
Not suitable
COLOUR INDEX
Page 46

- 350 g (12 oz) packet shortcrust pastry
- 450 g (1 lb) aubergines
- 450 g (1 lb) fresh ripe tomatoes
- 45 ml (3 tbsp) olive oil
- 45 ml (3 tbsp) chopped basil or marjoram
- salt and pepper
- 450 g (1 lb) frozen leaf spinach, thawed
- pinch of mace
- 175 g (6 oz) ricotta cheese
- 200 g (7 oz) mozzarella cheese
- 45 ml (3 tbsp) freshly grated Parmesan cheese

`540 CALS/SERVING`

Roll out the pastry and use to line a 5 cm (2 inch) deep, 23 cm (9 inch) fluted flan tin. Bake blind (see page 328) for about 10 minutes until set and lightly browned. Cool.

Dice the aubergines and tomatoes. Heat the oil in a pan, add the aubergines and cook gently for 10 minutes or until beginning to soften, stirring occasionally. Add the tomatoes and basil; season.

Meanwhile, place the spinach in a frying pan and cook over a high heat for about 3–5 minutes or until all excess moisture has been driven off; season well and add the mace.

Spread the ricotta over the base of the tart. Top with the spinach, then the aubergine and tomato mixture. Dice the mozzarella and scatter over the tart. Sprinkle over the Parmesan.

Stand the flan tin on a baking sheet and bake at 190°C (375°F) mark 5 for about 40 minutes or until golden brown and heated through. Serve with salad leaves.

NOTE: If ricotta is unobtainable, use curd cheese, full-fat soft cream cheese or soft goat's cheese instead.

❖ Cheesy Potato, ❖ Bacon and Onion Bake

SERVES 4

PREPARATION TIME
40 minutes
COOKING TIME
45 minutes
FREEZING
Not suitable
COLOUR INDEX
Page 46

- 225 g (8 oz) sweetcure rindless streaky bacon rashers
- a little olive oil (optional)
- 700 g (1½ lb) onions, peeled
- 15 ml (1 tbsp) soft brown sugar
- 900 g (2 lb) medium old potatoes
- salt and pepper
- 200 ml (7 fl oz) fromage frais or soured cream
- 15 ml (1 tbsp) chopped thyme or 5 ml (1 tsp) dried
- 225 g (8 oz) Gruyère or Emmental cheese
- 300 ml (½ pint) light stock or water

`850 CALS/SERVING`

1 Chop the bacon and fry it in its own fat in a non-stick frying pan until crispy, adding a little oil if necessary. Remove with a slotted spoon; drain on absorbent kitchen paper.

2 Slice the onions. Add to the residual fat in the pan, with the sugar. Cover and cook over a moderate heat for about 20 minutes, stirring occasionally, until they are soft and caramelised.

3 Meanwhile peel the potatoes. Cover with cold salted water, bring to the boil and cook for about 10 minutes; drain. Leave until cool enough to handle, then cut into 5 mm (¼ inch) slices. (Don't leave the potatoes until cold or they might discolour.) Gently mix with the fromage frais or soured cream and thyme. Season with salt and pepper.

4 Butter a 2 litre (3½ pint) shallow ovenproof dish and cover the bottom evenly with half the potatoes. Layer over the onions, then the bacon and two thirds of the grated Gruyère. Cover evenly with the remaining potatoes in a smooth layer. Pour in the stock. Scatter over the remaining grated cheese. Stand the dish on a baking sheet and cook at 200°C (400°F) mark 6 for 45 minutes or until golden brown and the potatoes are tender.

❖ Macaroni Cheese ❖

SERVES 4

PREPARATION TIME
10 minutes
COOKING TIME
15–40 minutes
FREEZING
Not suitable

• 225 g (8 oz) short-cut macaroni or small pasta shapes
• salt and pepper
• 65 g (2½ oz) butter or margarine
• 65 g (2½ oz) plain flour
• 900 ml (1½ pints) milk

• pinch of freshly grated nutmeg or 2.5 ml (½ tsp) mustard
• 225 g (8 oz) mature Cheddar cheese, grated
• 45 ml (3 tbsp) fresh wholemeal breadcrumbs
• parsley, to garnish

790 CALS/SERVING

1 Cook the macaroni in boiling salted water for about 10 minutes or until just tender. Drain well.

2 Meanwhile, melt the butter in a saucepan, stir in the flour and cook gently for 1 minute. Remove from the heat and gradually stir in the milk. Bring to the boil and cook, stirring, until the sauce thickens.

3 Remove from the heat, season with salt and pepper and add the nutmeg or mustard, most of the cheese and the macaroni. Pour into an ovenproof dish.

4 Sprinkle with the remaining cheese and the breadcrumbs. Brown under a hot grill or place on a baking sheet and bake at 200°C (400°F) mark 6 for 25–30 minutes or until golden and bubbling. Serve immediately, garnished with parsley.

Variation

CAULIFLOWER CHEESE: Omit the macaroni. Trim one large cauliflower and cut into florets (you will need about 800 g/1¾ lb florets). Cook the cauliflower florets in fast boiling salted water for about 10 minutes or until just tender, then drain thoroughly. Place in an ovenproof dish. Pour the cheese sauce over the cauliflower. Sprinkle with the remaining cheese and breadcrumbs and grill or bake as above.

❖ Three Cheese Macaroni ❖

SERVES 4

PREPARATION TIME
10 minutes
COOKING TIME
20 minutes
FREEZING
Not suitable
COLOUR INDEX
Page 46

• 225 g (8 oz) short-cut macaroni
• salt and pepper
• 225 g (8 oz) Fontina cheese (see note)
• 125 g (4 oz) mozzarella cheese
• 50 g (2 oz) butter or margarine
• 40 g (1½ oz) plain flour
• 1 bay leaf
• 900 ml (1½ pints) milk, preferably semi-skimmed

• 10 ml (2 tsp) Dijon mustard
• large pinch of freshly grated nutmeg
• 50 g (2 oz) freshly grated Parmesan cheese
• 15 g (½ oz) fresh white breadcrumbs
• flat-leaf parsley, to garnish

770 CALS/SERVING

1 Cook the macaroni in boiling salted water for about 10 minutes or until just tender; drain well. Meanwhile coarsely grate the Fontina cheese. Roughly chop the mozzarella.
2 Melt the butter in a saucepan, stir in the flour and bay leaf. Cook, stirring, for 1–2 minutes, then gradually stir in the milk. Bring to the boil, stirring, and cook, stirring, until slightly thickened. Discard the bay leaf.
3 Off the heat, beat in the Fontina and mustard. Season with a little salt, pepper and the nutmeg. Fold in the cooked macaroni, mozzarella and 25 g (1 oz) Parmesan. Stir over a gentle heat until piping hot.
4 Spoon into a lightly greased, shallow 1.75 litre (3 pint) flameproof dish. Sprinkle with the remaining grated Parmesan and the breadcrumbs.
5 Flash under a hot grill to brown. Serve immediately, garnished with parsley.

NOTE: This is a delicious, luxurious version of macaroni cheese. Fontina is a mild, buttery Italian cheese. Substitute Gouda or Edam if it's difficult to find.

❖ Ricotta and Spinach Gnocchi ❖

SERVES 4

PREPARATION TIME
5 minutes
COOKING TIME
10 minutes
FREEZING
Not suitable

- 15 g (½ oz) butter
- 65 g (2½ oz) plain flour
- 450 ml (¾ pint) semi-skimmed milk
- 90 g (3½ oz) freshly grated Parmesan cheese
- 400 g (14 oz) fresh spinach leaves

- 150 g (5 oz) ricotta cheese
- 1 egg yolk
- salt and pepper
- freshly grated nutmeg
- parsley sprigs, to garnish

330 CALS/SERVING

First make the cheese sauce. Melt the butter in a pan, stir in 15 g (½ oz) flour and cook for 1 minute. Off the heat, stir in the milk. Bring to the boil, stirring, until thickened. Simmer for 1–2 minutes. Stir in 25 g (1 oz) Parmesan. Keep warm.

2 Cook the spinach in a covered pan, with just the water clinging to the leaves after washing, over a low heat for 1 minute. Drain well and chop. Beat into the ricotta, with 50 g (2 oz) flour, 1 egg yolk, 50 g (2 oz) Parmesan, seasoning and nutmeg.

3 Using floured hands carefully shape heaped teaspoons of mixture into rounds. Cook the gnocchi in batches: drop into a large pan of simmering water and cook until they float on the surface, 3–4 minutes.

4 Lift out, drain and place in a lightly greased flameproof dish. Spoon over the sauce and sprinkle with the remaining Parmesan. Place under a hot grill until golden. Serve immediately garnished with parsley.

NOTE: If fresh spinach isn't available, use 225 g (8 oz) frozen chopped spinach, thawed and well drained.

❖ Spinach ❖ and Feta Cheese Puffs

SERVES 4

PREPARATION TIME
15 minutes
COOKING TIME
15 minutes
FREEZING
Not suitable

- ½ onion, peeled
- 25 g (1 oz) butter
- 125 g (4 oz) fresh spinach leaves, or 75 g (3 oz) frozen leaf spinach, thawed
- freshly grated nutmeg
- pepper

- two 20 cm (8 inch) ready-rolled squares puff pastry, thawed
- 50–75 g (2–3 oz) feta cheese, sliced
- beaten egg, to glaze

330 CALS/SERVING

1 Finely chop the onion. Melt the butter in a saucepan and sauté the onion for 2 minutes or until softened. Add the spinach with plenty of nutmeg. Cook for 3–4 minutes; or 2 minutes if using frozen spinach; stirring until the spinach is soft and the juices have evaporated. Season with pepper and cool slightly.
2 Cut each pastry square in half diagonally. Divide the spinach mixture into 4 portions and place on one half of each triangle. Top with feta cheese. Dampen the edges of the pastry, fold over and seal well. Brush with beaten egg to glaze.
3 Place on a baking sheet and cook at 200°C (400°F) mark 6 for about 15 minutes or until cooked through and golden brown. Serve immediately, with a mixed salad.

NOTE: Don't use too much filling or it will ooze out on cooking.

❖ Cheese and Potato Cake ❖

SERVES 3

PREPARATION TIME
20 minutes, plus
cooling
COOKING TIME
15 minutes
FREEZING
Not suitable

- *900 g (2 lb) waxy potatoes*
- *salt and pepper*
- *50 g (2 oz) smoked streaky bacon, derinded*
- *2 spring onions*
- *15 ml (1 tbsp) olive oil*
- *1 garlic clove, crushed*
- *30 ml (2 tbsp) chopped parsley*
- *75 g (3 oz) Jarlsberg or mozzarella cheese*

440 CALS/SERVING

1 Cook the potatoes in their skins in boiling salted water until just tender. Drain and leave until cold. Chop the bacon; finely chop the onions.

2 Heat the oil in a 20 cm (8 inch) non-stick frying pan. Add the bacon, garlic and spring onions and fry until the bacon is cooked.

3 Meanwhile, peel and coarsely grate the cold potatoes. Add to the pan and cook for 2 minutes, stirring to mix well and seasoning with pepper and a little salt.

4 Pat the mixture into a flat cake, so that it begins to stick together. Continue cooking over a medium heat for about 10 minutes or until the underside is well browned.

5 Sprinkle the parsley over the potato cake then, using a cheese slicer, cut the cheese into thin slices directly over the top. Cook under a hot grill until well browned and bubbling. Serve in wedges straight from the pan, with a crisp green salad.

NOTE: It is essential to use waxy potatoes, such as Charlotte or Belle de Fontenay, for this recipe; floury ones are unsuitable.

❖ Soufflé Welsh Rarebits ❖

SERVES 4

PREPARATION TIME
10 minutes
COOKING TIME
20 minutes
FREEZING
Not suitable

- *4 slices wholemeal bread*
- *about 25 g (1 oz) butter*
- *15 ml (1 tbsp) poppy seeds*
- *15 ml (1 tbsp) plain flour*
- *150 ml (¼ pint) semi-skimmed milk*
- *5 ml (1 tsp) Dijon mustard*
- *5 ml (1 tsp) Worcestershire sauce*
- *125 g (4 oz) Edam or Gouda cheese, grated*
- *2 eggs, separated*
- *parsley sprigs, to garnish*

280 CALS/SERVING

1 Spread the slices of bread lightly with butter. Sprinkle with poppy seeds and bake at 190ºC (375ºF) mark 5 for 5 minutes.
2 Melt 15 g (½ oz) butter in a saucepan, stir in the flour and cook for 1 minute. Gradually stir in the milk and bring to the boil, stirring. Cook, stirring, over a low heat until thickened.
3 Remove from the heat and beat in the mustard, Worcestershire sauce, grated cheese and egg yolks.
4 Whisk the egg whites until stiff, then fold into the cheese mixture.
5 Spoon the mixture on top of the bread slices and return to the oven for a further 15 minutes or until puffed and golden. Serve immediately, garnished with parsley sprigs.

❖ Chèvre en Croûte ❖

SERVES 6

PREPARATION TIME
minutes
OOKING TIME
2 minutes
EEZING
ot suitable

125 CALS/SERVING

- ½ short baguette
- 15–30 ml (1–2 tbsp) hazelnut oil
- 1 small garlic clove, crushed
- 125 g (4 oz) chèvre log, about 2.5 cm (1 inch) in diameter
- paprika, for sprinkling
- 6 thyme sprigs

Cut six 1 cm (½ inch) thick slices from the baguette. Brush oth sides of the slices with hazelnut oil mixed with the garlic. lace on a baking sheet and bake at 180°C (350°F) mark 4 for bout 5 minutes.

Cut the chèvre into six slices, place one on each baguette slice nd top with a sprinkling of paprika and a sprig of thyme.

Return the croûtes to the oven for a further 7 minutes, or until e cheese is soft and spongy. Serve warm, with a salad.

❖ Mozzarella and ❖ Tomato Toasts

SERVES 6

REPARATION TIME
) minutes
OKING TIME
minutes
EEZING
ot suitable
)LOUR INDEX
age 47

- 1 small baguette
- 225 g (8 oz) mozzarella cheese
- 175 g (6 oz) ripe tomatoes
- 60 ml (4 tbsp) black olive paste (tapenade) or finely chopped, pitted black olives
- 75 g (3 oz) thinly sliced salami, cooked ham or pastrami
TOMATO VINAIGRETTE:
- 30 ml (2 tbsp) red wine vinegar
- 75 ml (5 tbsp) olive oil
- 10 ml (2 tsp) tomato purée
- 15 ml (1 tbsp) finely chopped red onion
- few drops of Tabasco sauce
- pinch of caster sugar
- salt and pepper
TO SERVE:
- basil leaves
- celery tops
- marinated olives

405 CALS/SERVING

1 Cut the baguette into about 12 slices. Lightly toast on both sides. Slice the mozzarella and tomatoes.

2 Spread one side of each slice of bread with olive paste. Wrap a slice of mozzarella and a slice of tomato in two slices of salami and place on top of the bread.

3 Whisk together the ingredients for the dressing.

4 Arrange the toasts on a bed of basil, celery tops and olives. Serve the dressing separately.

❖ Cheese and ❖ Vegetable Croûtes

SERVES 4

PREPARATION TIME
15 minutes, plus marinating
COOKING TIME
20 minutes
FREEZING
Not suitable
COLOUR INDEX
Page 47

- 1 small aubergine
- 1 medium courgette
- 1 small bulb Florence fennel
- 1 small red pepper
- 1 small yellow pepper
- 2 garlic cloves
- 150 ml (¼ pint) olive oil
- 5 ml (1 tsp) chopped thyme or 2.5 ml (½ tsp) dried
- salt and pepper
- 4 large thick slices white crusty bread
- 125 g (4 oz) Halloumi or feta cheese, sliced

380 CALS/SERVING

1 Thinly slice the aubergine; cut the courgette into 1 cm (½ inch) slices; cut the fennel into large pieces; cut each pepper into eight pieces, discarding the core and seeds.

2 Crush the garlic and mix with the oil and herbs; season well. Stir in the vegetables, cover and leave to marinate for at least 15 minutes, preferably longer.

3 Preheat the grill and spread the vegetables over a foil-lined grill pan. Grill for 15 minutes, turning at least three times and basting with the oil. Cover and keep warm.

4 Brush the bread on both sides with olive oil from the grill pan and toast lightly on both sides. Place a layer of cheese on each slice of toast, pile the vegetables on top and finish with the remaining cheese. Grill for 2–3 minutes until bubbling. Serve at once.

VEGETABLES

Never has the choice of vegetables been so good. Modern methods of production, transportation and refrigeration ensure that a constant supply reaches the shops no matter what the season. The influence of other cultures and cuisines brings us 'exotic vegetables' such as yams, bamboo shoots and water chestnuts and genetic engineering brings us more and more hybrids and baby vegetables.

Traditionally vegetables are categorised into family groups. First are the *brassicas*, the cabbage family, which include Brussels sprouts, kohlrabi, cauliflower, broccoli and curly kale, as well as the many varieties of cabbage. *Roots and tubers* are the vegetables that grow underground, such as carrot, potato, turnip, beetroot, parsnip, Jerusalem artichoke and salsify. *Pods and seeds* takes in the many varieties of bean, along with peas, mangetout and sweetcorn. *Vegetable fruits* include the tomato, okra, aubergine and cucumber. Some would also put the avocado pear in this category but strictly it is a fruit rather than a vegetable. *Leafy vegetables* include the many varieties of salad leaves, which are described in more detail in the next chapter.

Other categories are *stalks and shoots* – celery, asparagus, fennel and chard; *squashes* – marrow, pumpkin and courgette; and of course the much loved family of *onions* comprising garlic, leek and shallot, as well as red, white, Spanish and spring onion. Finally come *mushrooms* in all their many varieties and *thistles* – notably the globe artichoke – the thistle with the delicately flavoured heart.

With all this variety and choice it is no surprise that the vegetable has been lifted from its previously underrated position, to something other than a mere accompaniment. Nutritionally vegetables are, of course, excellent. They are low in fat and cholesterol and high in vitamins, minerals and fibre. However to retain the maximum nutrients they should be eaten as fresh as possible; tough old vegetables have a much lower vitamin content than those that have been freshly picked.

When choosing vegetables look for a good bright colour, and crisp, firm leaves. Avoid those that show signs of discolouration or bruising, or that look shrivelled. Always look for firm root vegetables; those that are wrinkled and flabby have lost flavour and goodness. Don't buy potatoes with a green tinge, as these are unfit for eating. At home, always store potatoes in the dark or the exposure to light will turn them green. Resist buying the largest vegetables, particularly when choosing roots, since as they swell and enlarge they become tough and woody. Generally the younger and smaller the vegetable the sweeter and more tender it will be, although you may find that some of the baby vegetables lack flavour because they are so immature.

Store all vegetables in a cool, dark, well-ventilated place, preferably in a rack or in the bottom of the refrigerator. It is important that they are kept in the dark because light destroys vitamins B and C. Paper bags are preferable to plastic for wrapping; pierce holes in plastic bags and loosen or remove cling film to increase ventilation. Root vegetables should stay fresh for 5–6 days, and green vegetables for 3–4 days. Most vegetables freeze well if blanched beforehand. They are best used within 6 months, and cooked from frozen.

❖ Organic Fruit and Vegetables ❖

The demand for organic produce – obtained by farming methods which do not utilize artificial fertilizers or pesticides – is increasing. There is a growing awareness of the possible health risks of these chemicals and consumers are responding accordingly. Many supermarket chains now stock a reasonably good range of organic produce, but it tends to be rather expensive. This is because organic farming is labour intensive, yields are relatively low and there is a high demand for a restricted supply.

❖ Preparing Vegetables ❖

If vegetables are incorrectly prepared they may not cook through in the stated time or they may spoil the appearance of the finished dish, so do pay attention to instructions given in recipes. Unless stated otherwise, in this book the weight of vegetables given relates to the unprepared weight, in other words the amount you should be buying.

Cleaning

Always shake or brush off loose earth before washing. With the exception of mushrooms, all vegetables must be thoroughly washed before cooking. To ensure that leeks are thoroughly cleaned, slit the green part in half lengthways and wash under cold running water to remove any accumulated grit inside. Brush or wipe mushrooms, rather than wash them, or they will soak up water and become spongy.

Vegetables with inedible skins, such as onion, thick-skinned roots and tubers, and large squash, must be peeled. If you're particularly worried about residual contamination from pesticides, peel vegetables with edible skins too – washing alone is not enough to remove all traces.

Peeling and Cutting

A vegetable peeler or small paring knife is best for peeling. A really sharp knife and a good, heavy chopping board are essential for slicing and chopping. Some recipes call for a specific method of preparation, such as a julienne or chiffonade. To cut into juilienne the aim is to cut the vegetable into neat evenly sized pieces the shape of a matchstick. Simply cut into thin slices (which are the width of a matchstick), trim into 5 cm (2 inch) lengths, then stack the slices and cut lengthways again into strips. To make a chiffonade (usually of lettuce, rocket or basil) stack several leaves on top of each other, roll tightly then slice across the roll into fine strips.

Turned vegetables are popular on restaurant menus and are the hallmark of many classic French dishes, although at home they're best reserved for special occasions since they are wasteful and rather labour intensive. The aim is to 'turn' or carve chunks of vegetable into an elongated baton shape, usually with seven sides. A sharp paring knife is essential. Choose firm vegetables like carrots, courgettes, squash and turnips. Cut the vegetable into 5 cm (2 inch) lengths and trim off any sharp edges. Then working from the top to the bottom make a series of curved cuts around the vegetable, turning as you cut.

Avoiding Discolouration

Some vegetables, notably celeriac, artichoke bottoms, Jerusalem artichokes and salsify, rapidly discolour once they are cut. To prevent this, peel and cut these vegetables with a stainless steel knife and drop them into acidulated water immediately. To acidulate water, simply add the juice of 1 lemon to each 600 ml (1 pint) water.

Dégorging

Vegetables such as aubergine, cucumber and gourd contain bitter juices which some people like to remove before cooking to improve the flavour of the finished dish and to reduce the amount of oil absorbed if the vegetable is to be fried. The French term for this technique is known as *dégorger*. Slice the vegetable (or prepare according to the recipe), then spread out in a large shallow dish or colander and sprinkle generously with salt. Leave for about 30 minutes to let the salt draw out the juices, then rinse very thoroughly and pat dry.

Blanching

Vegetables are blanched before further cooking, so that they are slightly softened, or before freezing, to inhibit enzyme action. Since the cooking times are so short, different types of vegetables should be blanched separately, although the water may be reused. To blanch, bring a large pan of water to a rapid boil, drop in the vegetables (using a wire basket to make speedy retrieval easy) and cook according to the recipe – usually for just a minute or two. Drain and refresh under cold running water or in a large bowl of iced water to prevent further cooking and to retain the colour. Blanched green vegetables, such as French beans, broad beans and mangetouts, make good additions to salads.

Parboiling is much the same as blanching although the vegetables are generally cooked until almost, but not quite tender. Root vegetables which are to be roasted, baked or cooked *au gratin* and vegetables intended for stuffing, are usually parboiled to speed up the final cooking.

❖ Cooking Vegetables ❖

Once peeled, the vegetables begin to lose their vitamins. To reduce vitamin losses, don't prepare vegetables hours in advance and leave them soaking in water. Leave the skins on whenever you can. Cook with the minimum amount of water until just tender and use the cooking water in sauces, gravies and soups. Never add bicarbonate of soda to the cooking water as it destroys vitamin C, and try to get into the habit of using less salt. Vitamin losses continue after cooking, particularly when warm foods are left waiting around, so eat as soon as possible once cooked.

Most vegetables are best cooked until crisp and crunchy but no longer hard, however this is a matter of personal taste and many people still prefer them to be cooked until soft. Test during cooking with the point of a knife or preferably by tasting. Always test well before the estimated cooking time since vegetables are easily overcooked and ruined.

Although many vegetables can be cooked simply and enjoyed with little adornment – perhaps a knob of butter and a sprinkling of herbs – they may also be cooked and flavoured in numerous ways.

Boiling

In most households this is still probably the most popular method of cooking vegetables. Green vegetables should be dropped straight into boiling water, while roots should be added to cold water and brought up to boiling point. Cook green vegetables with the lid off the pan so that volatile acids from the vegetables don't get trapped in the pan and cause discolouration. The vegetables should be barely covered with water. Do not fill the pan to the brim. To retain vitamins, boil potatoes in their skins and peel after cooking.

Serve boiled vegetables tossed in butter or olive oil and a few chopped fresh herbs. Alternatively flavour the butter or oil with garlic or aromatic spices, such as coriander or cumin. White sauce – either plain or flavoured with cheese, onion, egg or herbs – is also delicious with boiled vegetables. To make a tasty supper dish, coat the vegetables in a sauce of your choice, sprinkle with cheese and breadcrumbs and cook under a hot grill until browned and bubbling. Add strips of cooked ham, bacon or chicken for a really substantial dish.

If making a vegetable purée ensure that the vegetables are well drained after boiling, or you will end up with an unpleasantly watery purée. Season generously with salt, pepper and a little cayenne or nutmeg. Moisten with cream or milk and melted butter or olive oil, or yogurt or fromage frais if you're watching your weight.

A food processor takes much of the effort out of puréeing but it is unsuitable for starchy vegetables, particularly potatoes, as it tends to pulverise them into a 'gluey' mess. Sieve vegetables which have fibres, strings or skin for an absolutely smooth purée. Vegetable purées are ideal for entertaining since they can be made well in advance and reheated later in the oven or microwave.

Steaming

If practised correctly, steaming will retain more nutrients than boiling. Use a metal or bamboo steamer, or a collapsible steamer fitted in a large saucepan. Cut vegetables into uniform sizes so that they cook evenly. Bring a 5 cm (2 inch) depth of water to the boil in the saucepan, then add the vegetables to the steamer in a single layer. Set the steamer about 5 cm (2 inches) above the water and cover with a lid. Steaming often takes longer than boiling since the vegetables are not in direct contact with the water. As with boiling, use the water for gravies and sauces. Serve in the same way as boiled vegetables.

Sautéeing

To sauté vegetables you will need a sauté pan or a large, preferably non-stick, heavy-based frying pan. Use olive oil, butter, bacon fat or even lard. Heat the oil or fat in the pan until it is really hot, then add the vegetables and shake the pan vigorously over a high heat until they begin to brown, then lower the heat and cook until tender. Aim for a dark golden brown, crisp crust and a soft succulent inside. Tough root vegetables should be parboiled before sautéeing.

Stir-frying

Stir-frying differs from sautéeing in that it is traditionally done in a wok, although if you haven't got a wok a large deep frying pan can be used. Vegetables are usually cut into small evenly sized pieces, added to a little hot oil in the wok and cooked vigorously over a high heat so that they remain crisp and retain their colour. Slower-cooking vegetables, such as baby corn, carrots and onions, are added first, followed by fast-cooking vegetables, such as courgettes, mangetouts and mushrooms.

Peanut oil is sometimes used to give an authentic flavour, but a lightly flavoured oil such as sunflower may also be used. If you like, you can sprinkle a few drops of distinctively flavoured sesame oil on to the vegetables before serving.

Flavourings such as garlic, chilli, ginger, five-spice powder and lemon grass are often stir-fried with the vegetables to add interest. For a moist stir-fry add a little soy sauce, sherry, oyster sauce or black bean sauce. Try sprinkling the cooked vegetables with a few sesame seeds, fried cashew nuts or toasted almonds before serving.

Deep-frying

There is something irresistible about chips, however calorific they may be! Potatoes are still the most commonly deep-fried vegetable but many others, including mushrooms, broccoli, onions, peppers and courgettes, are suitable. A light batter or a coating of breadcrumbs is essential to protect the vegetables from the hot oil. As with all deep-frying the correct temperature is vital. Most vegetables are deep-fried at around 190°C (375°F) but follow directions in individual recipes. If possible determine the exact temperature of the oil with a thermometer. Drain deep-fried vegetables on crumpled absorbent kitchen paper as soon as they are cooked and serve immediately.

Roasting

This is another favourite way to cook the ubiquitous potato, but most root vegetables can be roasted. For roast potatoes with really crunchy skins and light fluffy insides, parboil, drain thoroughly then shake the potatoes vigorously in the pan to roughen all the cut sides. Tip into a pan of really hot dripping, olive or vegetable oil, white vegetable fat or lard. Turn frequently during roasting so that the potatoes cook evenly.

Roast garlic – cooked until tender and delicately flavoured – makes a delicious accompaniment to roast meat. Alternatively it can be used to flavour the gravy. Simply put whole cloves, with the papery skins still attached, in the tin with the meat. To eat simply pop the succulent interior out of the crisp skin.

Braising

A comforting wintry method of cooking vegetables in the oven, usually with aromatic herbs or spices and a little liquid. The vegetables are often left whole or just halved so that they can be cooked slowly and retain their shape. Traditional choices for braising are chicory, leeks, cabbage, onions and celery. Delicately flavoured braised vegetables make good accompaniments to grilled or roast meats, sausages and game.

Grilling

The influence of Mediterranean cooking has brought grilled vegetables onto numerous restaurant menus. They are colourful, tasty and easy to prepare – making them the perfect starter. Halved radicchio and chicory are delicious grilled and flavoured with lemon juice. Peppers are grilled until the skins blacken and char, then left to cool so that the skins can be peeled off. Courgettes and aubergines are usually cut into fairly thick slices before grilling. Brush vegetables with olive oil as they cook. Serve warm or cold tossed in a little extra olive oil flavoured with garlic or fresh herbs, such as basil.

❖ Baked Artichokes ❖

SERVES 6

PREPARATION TIME
10 minutes
COOKING TIME
45–50 minutes
FREEZING
Not suitable

• 6 small globe artichokes
• salt and pepper
• 90 ml (6 tbsp) extra-virgin olive oil

TO GARNISH:
• lemon slices
• chervil or parsley sprigs

110 CALS/SERVING

1 Trim the artichoke stalks close to the base. Bring a large pan of salted water to the boil.

2 Add the artichokes and simmer, covered, for about 30 minutes or until you can pull away a base leaf easily. Drain and refresh under cold water.

3 Halve the artichokes lengthways. With a small spoon, remove the 'hairy' choke.

4 Place the artichokes cut side uppermost on a baking sheet. Drizzle with olive oil and season. Bake at 200°C (400°F) mark 6 for about 15–20 minutes. Alternatively grill for 20 minutes, basting occasionally with olive oil. Serve garnished with lemon slices and herbs.

❖ Jerusalem Artichoke ❖ and Chive Bake

SERVES 4

PREPARATION TIME
15 minutes
COOKING TIME
40 minutes
FREEZING
Not suitable

• 900 g (2 lb) Jerusalem artichokes
• salt and pepper
• dash of lemon juice
• 2 eggs, separated
• 15 ml (1 tbsp) chopped chives
• 50 g (2 oz) Cheddar cheese, grated
• snipped chives, to garnish

190 CALS/SERVING

1 Scrub the artichokes; leave whole or cut into large chunks about the size of a golf ball.
2 Place in a saucepan and cover with salted water, acidulated with lemon juice. Bring to the boil, cover and simmer for about 12 minutes, until the artichokes are quite tender.
3 Drain and rinse under cold running water. Peel off the skins, then mash the flesh until almost smooth, retaining a few small pieces of artichoke to add texture to the bake. Return the purée to the pan and stir over a moderate heat to drive off excess moisture; cool slightly. (The purée will discolour a little.)
4 Stir the egg yolks into the purée with the chives and seasoning. Whisk the egg whites until stiff, then fold into the mixture. Turn into a greased 1.1 litre (2 pint) shallow ovenproof dish. Sprinkle with the cheese. Bake at 190°C (375°F) mark 5 for 25–30 minutes or until lightly set and golden brown. Serve immediately, sprinkled with chives.

✤ Asparagus with ✤ Beurre Blanc

3 Meanwhile make the beurre blanc. Finely dice the shallots. Cut the butter into tiny dice and chill. Place the vinegar and wine in a small non-aluminium saucepan with the shallots. Boil until reduced to 15 ml (1 tbsp).

4 Quickly whisk in the butter until it is all absorbed; do this on and off a gentle heat, but don't let it get too hot or the butter will become greasy; the process takes about 2 minutes. Season and stir in the chopped herbs.

5 Drain the cooked asparagus thoroughly. Serve garnished with herbs if wished, and accompanied by the beurre blanc sauce.

SERVES 6

PREPARATION TIME
5 minutes
COOKING TIME
about 10 minutes
FREEZING
Not suitable

- *900 g (2 lb) asparagus*
- *salt and pepper*
- *dash of lemon juice*
- *herb sprigs, to garnish (optional)*

BEURRE BLANC:
- *2 small shallots, about 50 g (2 oz)*
- *225 g (8 oz) unsalted butter, chilled*
- *15 ml (1 tbsp) white wine vinegar*
- *45 ml (3 tbsp) dry white wine*
- *30 ml (2 tbsp) chopped chives*
- *30 ml (2 tbsp) chopped chervil or parsley*

593 CALS/SERVING

NOTE: If you use white asparagus spears you will need to allow 12–15 minutes' cooking time.

✤ Sautéed Aubergines ✤ and Courgettes

SERVES 8

PREPARATION TIME
15 minutes, plus standing
COOKING TIME
6–8 minutes
FREEZING
Not suitable
COLOUR INDEX
Page 48

- *4 small aubergines*
- *salt and pepper*
- *450 g (1 lb) small courgettes*
- *45 ml (3 tbsp) olive oil*
- *15 ml (1 tbsp) toasted sesame seeds*
- *oregano or marjoram sprigs, to garnish*

105 CALS/SERVING

1 Break off the woody ends of the asparagus and discard. Trim the asparagus stalks to the same lengths. Tie them in four equal bundles and stand up upwards in a large saucepan of boiling salted water, to which the lemon juice has been added.

2 Cover the pan with a lid or dome of foil and simmer for about 10 minutes or until tender, depending on the size of the spears.

1 Cut the aubergines lengthways into 2.5 cm (1 inch) slices. Cut the slices across into 1 cm (½ inch) wide fingers. Put the aubergines in a colander and sprinkle generously with salt. Leave to dégorge for at least 30 minutes.
2 Rinse the aubergines and dry thoroughly. Trim the courgettes and cut into pieces about the same size as the aubergine.
3 Heat the oil in a large heavy-based frying pan and sauté the aubergines for 3 minutes. Add the courgettes and continue cooking for 3–4 minutes or until just tender but not soft. Season with salt and pepper. Sprinkle with the sesame seeds and garnish with oregano or marjoram.

❖ Spiced Aubergines ❖ with Yogurt

SERVES 4–6

PREPARATION TIME
15 minutes
COOKING TIME
20 minutes
FREEZING
Not suitable
COLOUR INDEX
Page 48

- 3 medium aubergines, about 900 g (2 lb) total weight
- 60 ml (4 tbsp) oil
- 30 ml (2 tbsp) black mustard seeds, ground
- 2.5 ml (½ tsp) chilli powder

- 60 ml (4 tbsp) chopped coriander
- 1.25 ml (¼ tsp) salt
- 300 ml (½ pint) natural yogurt
- coriander to garnish

215–145 CALS/SERVING

1 Cook the aubergines under a hot grill, turning occasionally, for 15 minutes until the skins are charred and the flesh is soft.
2 Leave the aubergines until just cool enough to handle, then peel the skins off and discard. Chop the flesh roughly.
3 Heat the oil in a heavy-based frying pan, add the ground mustard seeds, chopped aubergine and chilli powder. Stir over a moderate heat for about 5 minutes, then add the coriander.
4 Stir the salt into the yogurt, then stir into the aubergine mixture. Serve immediately, garnished with coriander.

❖ Broccoli Stir-fry ❖

SERVES 6

PREPARATION TIME
10 minutes
COOKING TIME
6–8 minutes
FREEZING
Not suitable

- 30 ml (2 tbsp) red wine vinegar
- 30 ml (2 tbsp) soy sauce
- 15 ml (1 tbsp) sesame oil
- 10 ml (2 tsp) cornflour
- 5 ml (1 tsp) sugar

- 900 g (2 lb) broccoli
- 45 ml (3 tbsp) oil
- 1 garlic clove, crushed
- 30 ml (2 tbsp) sesame seeds
- pepper

160 CALS/SERVING

1 In a large bowl, whisk together the first 5 ingredients.
2 Cut the broccoli into medium florets, discarding any coarse stalks. Blanch in boiling water for 2–3 minutes or until almost tender. Drain well and toss in the soy sauce mixture.
3 Heat the oil in a wok or large frying pan. Add the garlic and sesame seeds. Stir in the broccoli mixture and fry, stirring, for 4–5 minutes until piping hot. Adjust the seasoning to serve.

❖ Broad Beans with ❖ Artichokes and Cumin

SERVES 6

PREPARATION TIME
10 minutes
COOKING TIME
20 minutes
FREEZING
Not suitable
COLOUR INDEX
Page 49

- 450 g (1 lb) shelled small broad beans
- salt and pepper
- 1 onion, peeled
- 400 g (14 oz) can artichoke hearts, drained
- 75 g (3 oz) sliced raw cured ham, such as jamón serrano, or prosciutto
- 30 ml (2 tbsp) olive oil
- 2 garlic cloves, crushed

- 5 ml (1 tsp) ground cumin
- 2 bay leaves
- pinch of powdered saffron
- 60 ml (4 tbsp) dry white wine
- 45 ml (3 tbsp) chopped parsley

115 CALS/SERVING

1 Cook the broad beans in boiling salted water until just tender; drain.

2 Meanwhile, chop the onion; halve the artichoke hearts; slice the ham into small pieces.

3 Heat the oil in a large sauté pan. Add the onion and garlic and fry until beginning to brown. Stir in the cumin and cook for 1 minute.

4 Mix in the artichokes, broad beans, bay leaves, saffron and seasoning. Pour in the wine with 100 ml (4 fl oz) water. Cover and allow to simmer for 5 minutes.

5 Stir in the ham and chopped parsley, then simmer for 2–3 minutes. Check the seasoning and serve immediately.

❖ French Beans with ❖ Tomatoes and Herbs

SERVES 6

PREPARATION TIME
15 minutes
COOKING TIME
About 20 minutes
FREEZING
Not suitable

- 400 g (1 lb) tomatoes
- 1 large onion
- 700 g (1½ lb) French beans
- salt and pepper
- 30 ml (2 tbsp) olive oil
- 1 garlic clove, crushed
- 15 ml (1 tbsp) each chopped parsley and basil

90 CALS/SERVING

1 Skin and roughly chop the tomatoes. Peel and chop the onion. Halve the French beans and cook in boiling salted water for 2–3 minutes only; drain.

2 Heat the oil in a saucepan. Add the onion and fry until beginning to colour. Stir in the tomatoes with the garlic. Cook, covered, for about 5 minutes.

3 Mix in the beans, re-cover and cook gently for a further 10 minutes, or until the beans are tender and the sauce is reduced. Stir in the herbs and season with salt and pepper to taste.

❖ French Beans with ❖ Feta and Sun-dried Tomatoes

SERVES 4

PREPARATION TIME
10 minutes
COOKING TIME
9 minutes
FREEZING
Not suitable
COLOUR INDEX
Page 49

- 350 g (12 oz) fine French beans
- salt and pepper
- 50 g (2 oz) sun-dried tomatoes in oil, drained
- 125 g (4 oz) feta or Wensleydale cheese
- 15 ml (1 tbsp) olive oil

120 CALS/SERVING

1 Halve the French beans. Cook in boiling salted water for about 6 minutes. Drain well.

2 Meanwhile, cut the sun-dried tomatoes into slices lengthways. Crumble the cheese.

3 Toss the beans while still hot with the sun-dried tomatoes, cheese and olive oil. Season to taste, remembering that feta is salty. Serve immediately.

❖ Chestnut and Brussels ❖ Sprout Sauté

SERVES 8

PREPARATION TIME
30 minutes
COOKING TIME
About 40 minutes
FREEZING
Not suitable
COLOUR INDEX
Page 49

- 900 g (2 lb) fresh chestnuts
- 600 ml (1 pint) chicken stock
- 900 g (2 lb) Brussels sprouts
- salt and pepper
- 450 g (1 lb) small onions, peeled
- 225 g (8 oz) celery
- 50 g (2 oz) butter
- finely grated rind of 1 lemon

325 CALS/SERVING

1 Nick the outer chestnut skins with a sharp knife. Immerse in boiling water for 10 minutes. Lift the chestnuts out a few at a time, then peel off both the brown and inner skins. Put the chestnuts in a saucepan, cover with the stock and simmer for 20 minutes or until tender. Drain well.

2 Meanwhile trim the sprouts and with a sharp knife, make a cross in the stalk end of each. Cook in boiling salted water for 3–4 minutes only; drain.

3 Cut the onions into wedges and separate out the layers. Cut the celery into 2.5 cm (1 inch) pieces.

4 Melt the butter in a large frying pan or flameproof casserole and sauté the onions and celery with the lemon rind for 2–3 minutes until softened.

5 Add the cooked chestnuts, Brussels sprouts and salt and pepper to taste. Sauté for a further 2–3 minutes until heated through. Serve immediately.

NOTE: In place of fresh chestnuts, you can use an 880 g (1 lb 15 oz) can whole chestnuts. Drain well and add at stage 5.

❖ Citrus Leeks ❖ with Sugar Snap Peas

SERVES 6

PREPARATION TIME
10 minutes
COOKING TIME
5–6 minutes
FREEZING
Not suitable

- *700 g (1½ lb) trimmed leeks*
- *450 g (1 lb) sugar snap peas or mangetouts*
- *20–30 ml (1½–2 tbsp) olive oil*
- *salt and pepper*
  DRESSING:
- *45 ml (3 tbsp) olive oil*
- *15 ml (1 tbsp) balsamic vinegar*

- *2.5 ml (½ tsp) light soft brown sugar*
- *10–15 ml (2–3 tsp) lemon juice*
- *2.5 ml (½ tsp) Dijon mustard*
- *finely grated rind and juice of ½ orange*

150 CALS/SERVING

1 Cut the leeks into 1 cm (½ inch) slices. Trim the sugar snap peas.

2 Heat the oil in a large sauté pan, add the leeks and sauté gently for 5–6 minutes or until just tender.

3 Meanwhile cook the sugar snap peas in boiling salted water for 5 minutes. Drain, then mix with the leeks. Whisk together all the ingredients for the dressing and season with salt and pepper to taste. Pour over the hot vegetables and toss to mix. Serve immediately.

❖ Marrow with ❖ Tomato and Onion

SERVES 4–6

PREPARATION TIME
20 minutes
COOKING TIME
30 minutes
FREEZING
Not suitable

- *1 medium marrow*
- *2 onions, peeled*
- *6 large tomatoes*
- *25 g (1 oz) butter or margarine*
- *1 garlic clove, crushed*
- *30 ml (2 tbsp) tomato purée*

- *30 ml (2 tbsp) chopped mixed herbs or 10 ml (2 tsp) dried*
- *salt and pepper*
- *parsley sprigs, to garnish*

100–65 CALS/SERVING

1 Peel the marrow, cut in half lengthways and scoop out the seeds. Cut the flesh into 2.5 cm (1 inch) cubes. Chop the onions, skin and chop the tomatoes.
2 Melt the butter in a large saucepan and gently fry the onions and garlic for 5 minutes, until soft. Add the marrow and cook for a further 5 minutes.
3 Stir in the tomatoes, tomato purée and herbs. Cover and simmer for 20 minutes, until the vegetables are tender. Season to taste. Serve at once, garnished with parsley.

❖ Baked Mushrooms ❖ with Parsley

SERVES 4–6

PREPARATION TIME
10 minutes
COOKING TIME
30 minutes
FREEZING
Not suitable
COLOUR INDEX
Page 51

- *550 g (1¼ lb) large flat mushrooms*
- *1 garlic clove, crushed*
- *30 ml (2 tbsp) chopped parsley*

- *salt and pepper*
- *olive oil, for basting*
- *parsley sprig, to garnish*

55–35 CALS/SERVING

1 Thickly slice the mushrooms and arrange in a greased ovenproof dish. Sprinkle with the garlic, parsley, and seasoning to taste. Drizzle over enough oil to moisten the mushrooms.
2 Bake at 200°C (400°F) mark 6 for about 30 minutes. Serve hot, garnished with parsley.

❖ Mushrooms Sautéed ❖ with Thyme and Garlic

SERVES 4–6

PREPARATION TIME
10 minutes

COOKING TIME
10 minutes

FREEZING
Not suitable

- 900 g (2 lb) mixed mushrooms, such as open cup, oyster and button
- 45 ml (3 tbsp) olive oil
- 1 large garlic clove, crushed
- few thyme sprigs or 1.25 ml (¼ tsp) dried
- juice of ½ small lemon
- salt and pepper
- 60 ml (4 tbsp) crème fraîche
- 2.5 ml (½ tsp) Dijon mustard
- lemon rind shreds, to garnish

145–95 CALS/SERVING

1 To clean the mushrooms, wipe them with a clean cloth or brush or pick off any lumps of dirt; do not wash them or they will become waterlogged. Slice any large mushrooms, but try to leave some whole.

2 Heat the oil in a large, heavy-based frying pan, preferably non-stick. Add the mushrooms and sauté over a high heat until slightly softened, shaking the pan occasionally.

3 Add the garlic, thyme, lemon juice, and plenty of seasoning. Reduce the heat and simmer gently until the mushrooms are tender. Blend the crème fraîche with the mustard and add to the pan. Let bubble for 1–2 minutes to reduce. Serve hot, garnished with lemon rind shreds.

❖ Spinach and ❖ Mushroom Bhaji

SERVES 8

PREPARATION TIME
15 minutes

COOKING TIME
45 minutes

FREEZING
Suitable

- 2 garlic cloves
- 2.5 cm (1 inch) piece fresh root ginger
- 15 ml (1 tbsp) black mustard seeds
- 10 ml (2 tsp) coriander seeds
- 5 ml (1 tsp) cumin seeds
- 45 ml (3 tbsp) oil or ghee
- 2 large onions, peeled and thinly sliced
- 10 ml (2 tsp) turmeric
- 5–10 ml (1–2 tsp) chilli powder, to taste
- 450 g (1 lb) button mushrooms, thickly sliced
- 400 g (14 oz) can chopped tomatoes
- 900 g (2 lb) spinach leaves
- salt and pepper
- about 60 ml (4 tbsp) toasted shredded coconut, to garnish

120 CALS/SERVING

1 Roughly chop the garlic and ginger. Put the mustard, coriander and cumin seeds in a large heavy-based pan and dry-fry over moderate heat for 2–3 minutes, stirring all the time. Remove the spices from the pan and crush with the garlic and ginger using a mortar and pestle.
2 Heat the oil in the pan, add the onions and cook gently, stirring frequently, for about 10 minutes until softened and golden. Add the spice paste, turmeric and chilli powder and cook gently, stirring all the time, for 5 minutes.
3 Add the mushrooms and stir well, then add the tomatoes and bring to the boil, stirring. Simmer for 10 minutes, stirring occasionally.
4 Roughly shred the spinach and add to the pan. Stir well, then season with salt and pepper to taste. Lower the heat, cover and simmer for 15 minutes, stirring frequently to blend in the spinach as it cooks down. Check the seasoning and sprinkle with the coconut to serve.

NOTE: Frozen spinach can be used for this recipe. You will need 450 g (1 lb) frozen leaf spinach, thawed and well drained.

SALADS

The days when a salad consisted of tired lettuce leaves, a sliced tomato and a limp piece of cucumber are over – or at least they should be. Market stalls, greengrocers and supermarkets now positively abound with brilliant displays of fruit and vegetables.

To start with, cast your eye over the varieties of salad leaves now on offer. Although leafy salad plants have been grown the world over for centuries the number of varieties produced commercially has until recently been disappointing. But now, new interesting well-flavoured leaves are appearing all the time, from the russet coloured loose-leafed Oak Leaf, frilly Lollo Rosso and Biondo to the delicate, lacy frisée and slightly bitter but hardier curly endive. Use them alone or in combination and look out for ready-prepared bags of mixed salad leaves in supermarkets; although these tend to be expensive they keep well and may work out cheaper than buying four or five different items. Other varieties worth looking out for are Batavia, Quattro Stagioni and dark red radicchio which has robust, tightly packed leaves and a strong bitter flavour. Use radicchio sparingly in salads, combined with other leaves.

Lamb's lettuce, also known as corn salad or mâche, is now a popular salad leaf. It is not a true lettuce, but a weed native to Europe which is now cultivated mainly in France. It has a mild delicate flavour, making it a good foil for strong flavours, and the dainty, brightly coloured leaves are a useful garnish.

Chinese leaves are particularly crunchy but rather bland in flavour. They are best teamed with spicy, aromatic dressings, for example – garlic and ginger – or they may be stir-fried.

Rocket (or roquette) has a delicious peppery taste and although it is expensive a little will add a distinctive flavour to a mixture of other leaves. Rocket is also extremely easy to grow. Serve it as a delicious salad on its own tossed with a little vinaigrette and sprinkled with shavings of freshly grated Parmesan. Sorrel tastes similar to rocket but it is much stronger. Use a little in conjunction with other leaves or use to encase delicate fish mousses or rolled fish fillets.

Tender, baby spinach leaves are irresistible in salads. They are particularly good tossed with croûtons, crumbled blue cheese and crispy bacon. Chicory has a tightly packed head and elegant long leaves. It adds crunch and bitterness to a mixed salad or it can be braised or grilled.

With all these new varieties on offer it's easy to overlook the more familiar Cos (Romaine), Iceberg (Crisphead), Webb's Wonder, Butterhead and Little Gem. Cos with its large, crisp, mildly flavoured leaves is as essential to a Caesar Salad as eggs and Parmesan cheese. While an authentic 'BLT' (Bacon, Lettuce and Tomato Sandwich) would be incomplete without the crunch of Iceberg lettuce. The French know how to make the most of Butterhead and Little Gem lettuces by braising them with peas and onion for the classic *petits pois à la française*.

When choosing salad plants look for fresh, crisp leaves and a tightly packed head where appropriate. Avoid wilted or damaged specimens. Limp leaves can sometimes be crisped if immersed in a bowl of iced water. Store salad leaves in the refrigerator, loosely wrapped in the salad drawer. Lettuces with very delicate leaves will only remain fresh for a couple of days while the more robust varieties will keep for up to a week.

To prepare, pull off and discard any damaged outer leaves and wash thoroughly in several changes of water to remove all traces of earth and insect life. Drain thoroughly and dry in a clean tea towel or salad shaker.

❖ Salad Herbs and Flowers ❖

Fresh herbs are an indispensable addition to any summer salad. Chives, basil, tarragon, mint and, of course, parsley and dill all have a particular affinity with salad ingredients. Break into delicate sprigs or chop roughly. Fresh basil may be shredded. Alternatively, chop the herbs finely and use to flavour the dressing.

To store fresh herbs, put them in a plastic bag; then, holding the bag in two hands by the opening corners, rotate it vigorously in the air to aerate and seal it simultaneously; knot the ends together then store in the refrigerator. This creates an environment in the bag which keeps the herbs fresh for several days. (Salad leaves may be stored in the same way.) If the herbs have long stems, treat them like flowers, placing them in a jug of water. They should keep like this for several days after which they will begin to lose their colour. Limp herbs may be revived by immersing in a bowl of iced water.

During the summer months a few edible flowers such as nasturtiums, violas, pansies, chive flowers and dandelions make a pretty addition to most salads. Fish and seafood salads are especially good with flowers of all kinds. Courgette flowers are much prized since they are large enough to stuff and deep-fry or bake; they make a delicious starter. Other more pungent flowers like roses and violets are usually crystallised and used to decorate cakes; these are really too overpowering to be used in salads.

Always pick flowers on a warm, dry day and choose those that are open but not full blown. Make sure that they are free from insects and contamination from pesticides. Although previously available only to those who grew them at home, edible flowers can now be found in supermarkets, greengrocers and delicatessens. Finally, it goes without saying that you should not pick wild flowers: some are protected by law but even those that are not protected are best left. Buying from a greengrocer or growing them in your garden ensures too that what you are sprinkling on your salad is edible.

❖ Summer ❖ Leafy Herb Salad

SERVES 8

PREPARATION TIME
10 minutes
FREEZING
Not suitable
COLOUR INDEX
Page 54

- *few large handfuls of mixed salad and herb leaves, such as spinach, rocket, sorrel, lamb's lettuce, dandelion, salad burnet*
- *handful of chervil sprigs*
- *handful of parsley sprigs*
- *few edible flowers, such as violas, marigold petals (optional)*

DRESSING:
- *15 ml (1 tbsp) mustard*
- *10 ml (2 tsp) thin honey*
- *60 ml (4 tbsp) lemon juice*
- *2.5 ml (½ tsp) paprika*
- *60 ml (4 tbsp) sunflower oil*
- *30 ml (2 tbsp) walnut oil*
- *salt and pepper*

120 CALS/SERVING

1 Roughly shred the leaves using your hands and place them in a bowl with the chervil and parsley sprigs. Sprinkle the herb flowers over the top.
2 To make the dressing, blend the mustard with the honey until smooth. Add the lemon juice, paprika, sunflower and walnut oils, and seasoning; mix well.
3 Pour the dressing over the salad and toss lightly to serve.

❖ Summer Salad Bowl ❖

SERVES 6

PREPARATION TIME
15 minutes
COOKING TIME
45 minutes
FREEZING
Not suitable

- *125 g (4 oz) each carrots, sugar snap peas, green beans, yellow beans, patty-pan squash, baby corn cobs*
- *1 small cauliflower*
- *50 g (2 oz) green lentils*
DRESSING:
- *100 ml (4 fl oz) grapeseed oil*

- *25 ml (1 fl oz) sesame oil*
- *30 ml (2 tbsp) white wine vinegar*
- *2.5 ml (½ tsp) caster sugar*
- *30 ml (2 tbsp) toasted sesame seeds*
- *salt and pepper*

305 CALS/SERVING

1 Bring a large saucepan of water to the boil. Halve any larger vegetables, such as patty-pan squash. Divide the cauliflower into small florets.

2 Cook each vegetable separately until just tender, using the same water. Remove with a slotted spoon and put into a large bowl of ice-cold water.

3 Finally, cook the green lentils in the vegetable water for about 15 minutes or until just tender; drain well.

4 Whisk together all the ingredients for the dressing, seasoning to taste. Drain the vegetables thoroughly and toss together with the dressing and lentils to serve.

NOTE: You can vary the vegetables. Use the freshest, cheapest and most colourful ones available – you'll need about 1 kg (2 lb).

❖ Mixed Leaf Salad ❖

SERVES 4

PREPARATION TIME
10 minutes
FREEZING
Not suitable
COLOUR INDEX
Page 54

- *1 small head radicchio*
- *1 small bunch lamb's lettuce*
- *½ head oak leaf lettuce*
- *½ head frisée*
- *25–50 g (1–2 oz) alfalfa sprouts*
- *25 g (1 oz) pine nuts, toasted*

DRESSING:
- *45 ml (3 tbsp) grapeseed oil*
- *30 ml (2 tbsp) white wine vinegar*
- *10 ml (2 tsp) thin honey*
- *salt and pepper*

155 CALS/SERVING

1 Roughly shred the salad leaves, using your hands.
2 To make the dressing, whisk together the grapeseed oil, wine vinegar and honey. Season with salt and pepper to taste.
3 Toss the salad leaves, alfalfa sprouts, pine nuts and dressing together in a large salad bowl. Serve immediately.

NOTE: For the crispest salad, toss the leaves and dressing together at the last minute.

❖ French Bean ❖ and Fennel Salad

SERVES 8	• 450 g (1 lb) French	• 200 ml (7 fl oz)
PREPARATION TIME	beans, halved	Vinaigrette (page 273)
20 minutes	• salt and pepper	• about 12 black olives
COOKING TIME	• 1 bulb Florence fennel	
4–5 minutes	• 1 cucumber	
FREEZING	• 1 avocado	
Not suitable		**220 CALS/SERVING**

1 Blanch the French beans in boiling salted water for 3–4 minutes until tender but crisp. Drain; refresh under cold running water.

2 Remove the feathery tops from the fennel and reserve. Thinly slice the fennel; blanch in boiling water for 1 minute. Drain and refresh under cold running water.

3 Peel, halve and thickly slice the cucumber and place in a salad bowl with the French beans and fennel.

4 Peel, halve and stone the avocado; slice thickly and add to the dressing. Add to the salad with the olives, toss gently and serve immediately, garnished with the reserved fennel tops.

❖ Cauliflower, Broccoli ❖ and Pepper Salad

SERVES 6	• 225 g (8 oz) broccoli	• 90 ml (6 tbsp) lemon
PREPARATION TIME	• 225 g (8 oz) cauliflower	juice
10 minutes	• 1 small yellow pepper	• salt and pepper
COOKING TIME	• 1 small red pepper	TO GARNISH:
3 minutes	DRESSING:	• sesame seeds
COLOUR INDEX	• 1 garlic clove, crushed	
Page 54	• 60 ml (4 tbsp) tahini	**85 CALS/SERVING**

1 Divide the broccoli and cauliflower into florets and blanch in boiling water for 3 minutes, then drain and leave to cool.

2 Halve, core and thinly slice the peppers, discarding the seeds. Place in a salad bowl with the broccoli and cauliflower.

3 For the dressing, whisk the garlic, tahini, lemon juice, 60 ml (4 tbsp) water and seasoning together in a small bowl. Pour the dressing over the salad and toss gently. Chill before serving sprinkled with sesame seeds.

❖ Spinach and Watercress ❖ Salad with Bacon

SERVES 4	• 125 g (4 oz) smoked	• 10 ml (2 tsp) white
PREPARATION TIME	streaky bacon rashers	wine vinegar
10 minutes	• 125 g (4 oz) young	• 7.5 ml (1½ tsp)
COOKING TIME	spinach leaves	wholegrain mustard
5 minutes	• 1 bunch watercress	• salt and pepper
FREEZING	DRESSING:	
Not suitable	• 40 ml (2½ tbsp) olive	
	oil	
	• 7.5 ml (1½ tsp)	
	hazelnut oil	**155 CALS/SERVING**

1 Grill the streaky bacon until really crisp. Drain on absorbent kitchen paper to absorb any excess oil. Snip into small pieces, discarding the rind.

2 Remove any coarse stalks from the spinach and shred any large leaves. Trim the watercress and divide into sprigs. Place in a salad bowl with the spinach and bacon.

3 To make the dressing, whisk together the oils, vinegar, mustard and seasoning. Just before serving, pour the dressing over the salad and toss lightly.

❖ Pasta Salad ❖

SERVES 6

PREPARATION TIME
10 minutes
COOKING TIME
10–15 minutes
FREEZING
Not suitable
COLOUR INDEX
Page 56

- 225 g (8 oz) dried small pasta, such as rice-shaped puntalette, shells or twists
- salt and pepper
- 225 g (8 oz) thin asparagus spears
- 225 g (8 oz) courgettes
- 125 g (4 oz) Gruyère cheese
- 125 g (4 oz) feta cheese

DRESSING:
- 150 ml (¼ pint) olive oil
- 30 ml (2 tbsp) white wine vinegar
- 2.5 ml (½ tsp) sugar
- 10 ml (2 tsp) Dijon mustard
- 30 ml (2 tbsp) chopped parsley

510 CALS/SERVING

1 Cook the pasta in boiling salted water until *al dente* (just tender). Drain and rinse under cold running water, then drain thoroughly.

2 Cut the asparagus into finger length pieces. Cook in boiling salted water for 5–7 minutes or until just tender. Drain and rinse as in step 1.

3 Coarsely grate the courgettes or cut into julienne strips. Grate the Gruyère cheese. Dice the feta.

4 Whisk together all the ingredients for the dressing and season with salt and pepper.

5 Toss all the salad ingredients together with the dressing. Serve immediately, or cover and keep in the refrigerator for up to 1 day. Stir well before serving.

NOTE: The secret of successful pasta (and rice) salads is to include plenty of extras – such as herbs, nuts and vegetables – and to be generous with the dressing.

❖ Mustardy Potato Salad ❖

SERVES 4

PREPARATION TIME
5 minutes
COOKING TIME
10 minutes
FREEZING
Not suitable

- 700 g (1½ lb) very small potatoes, scrubbed
- salt and pepper

DRESSING:
- 225 ml (8 fl oz) fromage frais
- 75 ml (5 tbsp) mayonnaise

- 30 ml (2 tbsp) wholegrain mustard
- 10 ml (2 tsp) Dijon mustard

TO GARNISH:
- parsley sprigs

375 CALS/SERVING

1 Cook the potatoes in their skins in boiling salted water for about 10 minutes or until tender. Meanwhile, mix together the ingredients for the dressing and season to taste with salt and pepper.

2 When the potatoes are cooked, drain them well and add them to the dressing, tossing well so they are completely coated in the dressing. Leave to cool before serving, garnished with parsley.

NOTE: French smooth-skinned potato varieties, such as La Ratte, Cornichon or Belle de Fontenay, make excellent potato salads. Alternatively, the English Pink Fir Apple variety is equally delicious and well worth looking out for.

❖ Roasted ❖ New Potato Salad

SERVES 6

PREPARATION TIME
8–10 minutes
COOKING TIME
About 40 minutes
FREEZING
Not suitable
COLOUR INDEX
Page 56

- 700 g (1½ lb) small new potatoes
- salt and pepper
- 50 ml (2 fl oz) olive oil
- 3–4 rosemary sprigs

DRESSING:
- 125 g (4 oz) pancetta or rindless smoked streaky bacon rashers
- 50 g (2 oz) mushrooms, preferably brown cap

- 30 ml (2 tbsp) dry red wine
- 15 ml (1 tbsp) red wine vinegar
- 30 ml (2 tbsp) pine nuts or cashew nuts, toasted

TO GARNISH:
- rosemary sprigs

280 CALS/SERVING

Parboil the potatoes in boiling salted water for 1–2 minutes; drain well. Place in a roasting tin with the oil and rosemary and turn to coat with the oil. Cook at 200°C (400°F) mark 6 for 35–40 minutes or until tender, turning once during cooking.

Meanwhile, chop the bacon and slice the mushrooms. Sauté the bacon with the mushrooms in a non-stick frying pan for 2–3 minutes until the mushrooms have softened. Remove from the heat and add the wine, vinegar and pine nuts. Season to taste.

Transfer the hot cooked potatoes and roasting oil to a large heatproof bowl, discarding the rosemary sprigs. Reheat the bacon dressing if necessary and pour over the potatoes. Stir together well. Serve warm or cold, garnished with fresh rosemary sprigs.

NOTE: This is a good salad with barbecued or grilled meats.

❖ Spiced Potato Salad ❖

SERVES 6
PREPARATION TIME
5 minutes, plus
cooling
COOKING TIME
10–12 minutes
FREEZING
Not suitable

- 900 g (2 lb) small new potatoes
- salt and pepper
- 30 ml (2 tbsp) chopped coriander or parsley
DRESSING:
- 150 ml (¼ pint) Greek-style yogurt
- 1.25 ml (¼ tsp) ground coriander
- 1.25 ml (¼ tsp) ground cumin

`145 CALS/SERVING`

Lightly scrub the potatoes and cook in boiling salted water for 10–12 minutes until tender.

In a large bowl, whisk together the yogurt and spices. Season with salt and pepper to taste.

Drain the potatoes and immediately stir into the dressing; leave to cool. Just before serving, stir in the chopped coriander or parsley. Serve at room temperature.

NOTE: Don't peel the potatoes or you'll remove valuable fibre and vitamins – just lightly scrub them. Warm potatoes will absorb the spicy dressing better than cold ones.

❖ Wild Rice ❖ and Thyme Salad

SERVES 6–8
PREPARATION TIME
15 minutes, plus
standing
COOKING TIME
35 minutes
FREEZING
Not suitable
COLOUR INDEX
Page 56

- 150 g (5 oz) French beans
- salt and pepper
- 150 g (5 oz) shelled broad beans
- 50 g (2 oz) wild rice
- 175 g (6 oz) long-grain white rice
- 50 ml (2 fl oz) sunflower oil
- 50 g (2 oz) chanterelles, trompette de mort or small button mushrooms, roughly sliced
- 30 ml (2 tbsp) chopped thyme
- 25 ml (1 fl oz) walnut oil
- 30 ml (2 tbsp) white wine vinegar
- 15 ml (1 tbsp) Dijon mustard

`275–210 CALS/SERVING`

1 Halve the French beans and cook in boiling salted water for 10–12 minutes or until just tender. Drain, refresh under cold running water and set aside to cool completely.

2 Cook the broad beans in boiling salted water for 5–7 minutes. Drain and refresh under cold running water, slipping off their outer skins if wished, and set aside to cool completely.

3 Cook the wild rice in a large pan of boiling salted water for 20 minutes, then add the long-grain white rice. Boil together for a further 15 minutes or until both are just tender. Drain and refresh under cold running water. Stir together the French beans, broad beans and rice in a large mixing bowl.

4 Heat the sunflower oil in a small frying pan and fry the mushrooms with the thyme for 2–3 minutes, stirring. Remove from the heat and stir in the walnut oil, vinegar, mustard and seasoning. Add to the rice mixture; stir well. Check the seasoning. Cover and leave to stand for at least 30 minutes before serving.

NOTE: If fresh broad beans are out of season, use frozen instead, or replace them with any cooked beans of your choice.

VEGETARIAN DISHES

An ever increasing number of people are choosing to eat more and more meatless meals based on ingredients like pasta, rice, pizza and vegetables. Many others – sometimes known as the 'demi-veggies' – choose to exclude red meat from their diet completely but still eat the occasional meal containing fish, shellfish or chicken. As for vegetarians, there are as many types of vegetarian diet as there are reasons for being one. Vegans are very strict vegetarians, who won't eat any animal product whatsoever and that includes gelatine and in some cases honey. Less strict vegetarians eat cheese, butter and milk. Some also eat eggs.

The reasons for becoming vegetarian are numerous. Some look to it as a healthier way of eating; current research seems to suggest that many so-called 'diseases of Western civilization' such as heart disease, strokes, obesity and high blood pressure are related to a diet that's high in animal fats. Others are influenced by their religion or choose to avoid meat because they're concerned about animal welfare. Many vegetarians are worried about the environment and believe that a vegetarian diet is a more economical method of food production in terms of the world's limited resources.

❖ Balancing a Vegetarian Diet ❖

Many people make the mistake of assuming that a vegetarian diet is automatically healthier than a carnivore's. This isn't always the case. It is not enough simply to stop eating meat; the nutrients that would have been obtained from meat must be derived from other sources. It's quite common for vegetarians to rely too heavily on dairy products – like cheese – which are high in saturated fats and calories.

As with any diet, variety is important. If a wide range of foods is eaten, a vegetarian diet is no more likely to be lacking nutritionally than any other diet. There are lots of good vegetable sources of protein such as beans, grains, nuts, tofu, quorn and TVP as well as dairy products. Animal proteins contain almost all of the essential amino acids and are regarded as 'complete protein' foods. With the exception of soya products, vegetable proteins are lacking or low in one or more of the essential amino acids. However, by eating certain foods together at the same meal any deficiency is overcome. This isn't as complicated as it sounds and tends to happen automatically when menu planning. For example, cereals should be eaten with dairy products, pulses or nuts: muesli with yogurt or milk; chilli beans with rice; nut roast

made with breadcrumbs. Pulses and nuts should also be eaten with dairy products: dhal with raita; nut burgers with a cream-based sauce; bean stew with cheese topping; for example.

Vegetarians and vegans should be careful to regulate their intake of vitamins B12 and D, although contrary to popular belief a deficiency of either is unlikely. Both are found in dairy products and fortified products such as breakfast cereals. Anaemia or a lack of dietary iron is often discussed in relation to a vegetarian diet because meat and liver are commonly believed to be the best sources of iron. In fact, iron is found in a wide range of foods including leafy green vegetables, cereals, pulses, nuts, eggs and dried fruits – especially apricots. The absorption of iron is greatly increased if vitamin C rich foods are eaten at the same meal. It is decreased by the presence of tannin, which is found in large amounts in tea – so don't drink tea at meal times!

❖ The Vegetarian Storecupboard ❖

Vegetarian alternatives to ingredients of animal origin are becoming increasingly available. You can now buy a wide range of cheeses produced using vegetarian rennet, for example. Other useful products include Agar-Agar and Gelazone which are alternatives for gelatine. Certain foods are particularly significant in a vegetarian diet; these are described below.

Pulses

The term pulse covers all the various beans, peas and lentils which have been preserved by drying. Pulses are an important source of protein, carbohydrate and fibre in a vegetarian diet.

Pulses should be stored in airtight containers in a cool, dark place. They keep well, but after about 6 months their skins toughen and they take increasingly longer to cook, so buy them from a supplier with a fast turnover.

Before cooking, with the exception of lentils and split peas, all pulses should be soaked overnight in a large bowl of cold water. In the morning, drain them, bring to the boil in fresh water and boil rapidly for 10 minutes to destroy any toxins present. Although fast-boiling is not strictly necessary for all types of pulse it does them no harm and saves the problem of remembering which ones require it. After fast-boiling, lower the heat, cover and simmer until tender. The flavour can be subtly enhanced by adding a couple of bay leaves or garlic cloves, or an onion studded with a few cloves, to the cooking water. Add salt approximately

15 minutes before the end of the cooking time. Salt added at the beginning of cooking tends to toughen the skins.

To save time the quick soak method works just as well. Put the beans into a saucepan, cover with cold water and bring to the boil. Boil rapidly for 10 minutes. Cover the pan and leave the beans to soak in the same water for 2 hours. Drain and cook in fresh water for the usual time (see chart below).

The weight of dried pulses approximately doubles during cooking, so if a recipe calls for 225 g (8 oz) cooked beans you will need to start with 125 g (4 oz) dried beans. Drained, cooked pulses will keep for several days in a covered container in the refrigerator. Alternatively, freeze them in usable quantities. Thaw overnight and use as freshly cooked beans.

❖ COOKING PULSES IN A PRESSURE COOKER This cuts down on lengthy cooking times (see chart below). Overnight soaking is unnecessary: just cover the beans with boiling water and leave to soak for 1 hour. Drain, then weigh and transfer to the pressure cooker, adding 600 ml (1 pint) water for every 225 g (8 oz) soaked beans. The cooker must not be more than one-third full.

Bring to the boil, then skim off any scum that's risen to the surface. Lower the heat so that the beans are simmering gently, then put the lid on the pan. Bring up to pressure and cook for the time suggested below. Reduce the pressure slowly. Season with salt while warm.

Do not cook mixtures of different types of pulse at the same time. This is potentially dangerous as overcooked beans can rise up in the pan and block the safety valves and air vents.

❖ Cooking Dried Pulses ❖

These times are approximate depending on the age of the pulse and the length of soaking time.

TYPE ❖	COOKING TIME ❖	PRESSURE COOKING TIME (HIGH/15 LB PRESSURE) ❖
Aduki beans	30–60 minutes	12 minutes
Black beans	1½ hours	20 minutes
Black-eye beans	1½ hours	12 minutes
Borlotti beans	1 hour	17 minutes
Butter beans	1½ hours	17 minutes
Cannellini beans	1 hour	25 minutes
Chick peas	1½–2 hours	20 minutes
Flageolet beans	1 hour	15 minutes
Haricot beans	1–1½ hours	20 minutes
Lentils	30–60 minutes	15 minutes
Mung beans	40 minutes	12 minutes
Red kidney beans	1–1½ hours	20 minutes
Soya beans	3–4 hours	30 minutes
Split peas	45–60 minutes	15 minutes

Canned Beans

Canned beans are a good quick alternative to cooking your own. It's a good idea to empty them straight into a sieve and rinse under cold running water before use. They tend to be rather soft but some brands are definitely firmer and better than others, so shop around. Nevertheless they are all much softer than home-cooked beans so always add them towards the end of the recipe cooking time or they will disintegrate.

As a guide, a 425 g (15 oz) can of beans, drained, is roughly equivalent to 225 g (8 oz) cooked beans, or 125 g (4 oz) dried (uncooked) beans.

Tofu

Also known as soya bean curd, tofu is made from a paste of soya beans which has been pressed into blocks. It is virtually tasteless but readily absorbs flavours when marinated in tasty dressings. It's really worth experimenting with tofu, since it is an excellent source of vegetable protein and contains no fat.

Silken tofu is soft and creamy and is useful for dressings, cheesecakes, sauces and dips. It adds bulk and texture, increases the nutritional value of these foods and takes on the flavours of the other ingredients. Firm tofu has been pressed for longer and can be cut into chunks for frying, grilling and inclusion in stews and curries, or it can be grated or chopped and made into burgers and roasts.

Tofu should be stored in the refrigerator. Once the packet is opened, keep the tofu immersed in a bowl of cold water in the refrigerator and it should remain fresh for up to 1 week if the water is changed daily.

TVP (Textured Vegetable Protein)

TVP forms the bulk of most veggie burgers, and veggie mince and banger mixes. It's made from a mixture of soya flour, flavourings and liquid, which is cooked, then extruded under pressure and cut into chunks or small pieces to resemble mince. Unlike tofu it has a slightly chewy, meat-like texture which makes it unappetising to some vegans and vegetarians; although for the same reason it may appeal to new vegetarians who miss the texture of meat. It is worth keeping a packet in the cupboard for emergencies because it's quite versatile, keeps well, and like tofu it is an excellent source of low-fat protein.

Quorn

Quorn is a relatively new product; a myco-protein derived from a distant relative of the mushroom. It has a chicken-like texture and is very low in fat and calories, yet high in fibre and protein. Although unsuitable for vegans, because it contains egg albumen, quorn is a good source of complete protein for vegetarians. As it has a bland flavour quorn benefits from being marinated before cooking, but it cooks in a matter of minutes.

Available from the chilled cabinet, quorn is usually sold in 225–300 g (8–10 oz) packets, which is enough to serve 4 people. It will keep in the refrigerator for 3 days and can be frozen for up to 3 months. Quorn can also be used straight from the freezer in very moist dishes; otherwise, thaw it overnight in the refrigerator and use within 24 hours.

❖ Jerusalem ❖ Artichoke Gratin

3 Heat 50 g (2 oz) butter with the oil in a heavy-based pan, add the onions and garlic and sauté for 2–3 minutes. Add the wine, stock and nutmeg. Bring to the boil, cover and simmer for 10 minutes.

4 Add the artichokes, leeks and peas and simmer for 5 minutes or until all the vegetables are tender. With a slotted spoon, transfer the vegetables to a flameproof gratin dish.

5 Boil the cooking liquid until reduced by about half. Lower the heat and stir in the cream and half of the two cheeses; stir until melted.

6 Pour the sauce over the vegetables. Sprinkle with the remaining cheese and bread-crumbs; dot with remaining butter. Bake at 220°C (425°F) mark 7 for about 10 minutes.

SERVES 4

PREPARATION TIME
5 minutes
COOKING TIME
5 minutes
FREEZING
Not suitable

- *900 g (2 lb) Jerusalem artichokes*
- *salt and pepper*
- *225 g (8 oz) button onions*
- *75 g (3 oz) butter or margarine*
- *15 ml (1 tbsp) olive oil*
- *2 garlic cloves, crushed*
- *150 ml (¼ pint) dry white wine*
- *150 ml (¼ pint) vegetable stock*
- *1.25 ml (¼ tsp) freshly grated nutmeg*
- *3 leeks, thickly sliced*
- *225 g (8 oz) shelled fresh or frozen peas*
- *150 ml (¼ pint) double cream*
- *75 g (3 oz) Gruyère cheese, grated*
- *75 g (3 oz) Cheddar cheese, grated*
- *50 g (2 oz) fresh white breadcrumbs*
- *bay leaves, to garnish*

735 CALS/SERVING

1 Parboil the Jerusalem artichokes in salted water for 10 minutes. Remove with a slotted spoon and leave until cool enough to handle. Peel off the skins and slice the flesh thickly.

2 Add the button onions to the water and boil for 2 minutes, then remove with a slotted spoon. Peel off the skins, leaving the root ends intact so that the onions remain whole.

❖ Vegetable Bake with Cheese ❖

SERVES 6

PREPARATION TIME
15 minutes
COOKING TIME
About 1¼ hours
FREEZING
Not suitable
COLOUR INDEX
Page 57

- *450 g (1 lb) carrots*
- *225 g (8 oz) turnips*
- *225 g (8 oz) parsnips*
- *2 onions*
- *25 g (1 oz) butter or margarine*
- *1 large garlic clove, crushed*
- *45 ml (3 tbsp) chopped parsley*
- *salt and pepper*
- *15 ml (1 tbsp) flour*
- *300 ml (½ pint) vegetable stock*
- *15 ml (1 tbsp) coarse-grained mustard*
- *75 g (3 oz) Cheddar cheese*

160 CALS/SERVING

1 Peel and thinly slice the carrots, turnips, parsnips and onions.
2 Heat the butter in a shallow flameproof dish, add the onions and fry, stirring, for about 10 minutes until lightly browned.
3 Stir in the remaining vegetables with the garlic, parsley and seasoning. Stir in the flour. Mix the stock with the mustard and pour over the vegetables, stirring.
4 Cover tightly and bake at 180°C (350°F) mark 4 for about 1¼ hours, or until the vegetables are just tender. Sprinkle the cheese over the top and bake at 200°C (400°F) mark 6 for a further 20–30 minutes. Serve immediately.

❖ Mixed Lentil Casserole ❖

PREPARATION TIME
20 minutes
COOKING TIME
About 1 hour
FREEZING
Not suitable

- 5 ml (1 tsp) cumin seeds
- 15 ml (1 tbsp) coriander seeds
- 5 ml (1 tsp) mustard seeds
- 3 onions, peeled
- 450 g (1 lb) carrots, peeled
- 350 g (12 oz) leeks
- 350 g (12 oz) mooli (white radish), peeled
- 450 g (1 lb) button mushrooms

- 45 ml (3 tbsp) olive oil
- 2 garlic cloves, crushed
- 25 g (1 oz) fresh root ginger, peeled and grated
- 1.25 ml (¼ tsp) turmeric
- 175 g (6 oz) split red lentils
- 50 g (2 oz) brown or green lentils
- salt and pepper
- 60 ml (4 tbsp) chopped coriander

240 CALS/SERVING

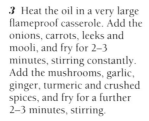

1 Crush the cumin, coriander and mustard seeds in a mortar with a pestle (or strong bowl with the end of a rolling pin).

2 Slice the onions, carrots and leeks. Roughly chop the mooli; halve the mushrooms if large.

3 Heat the oil in a very large flameproof casserole. Add the onions, carrots, leeks and mooli, and fry for 2–3 minutes, stirring constantly. Add the mushrooms, garlic, ginger, turmeric and crushed spices, and fry for a further 2–3 minutes, stirring.

4 Stir in the lentils with 750 ml (1¼ pints) boiling water. Season with salt and pepper and return to the boil. Cover and cook at 180°C (350°F) mark 4 for about 45 minutes or until the vegetables and lentils are tender. Stir in the chopped coriander before serving.

❖ Winter Vegetable Casserole ❖

PREPARATION TIME
20 minutes
COOKING TIME
1 hour
FREEZING
Not suitable

- 450 g (1 lb) carrots, peeled
- 450 g (1 lb) parsnips, peeled
- 2 onions, peeled
- 350 g (12 oz) celeriac
- squeeze of lemon juice
- 25 g (1 oz) butter or margarine
- 2 garlic cloves, crushed

- 350 g (12 oz) button mushrooms
- 450 ml (¾ pint) vegetable stock
- salt and pepper
- 60 ml (4 tbsp) single cream
- 30 ml (2 tbsp) chopped parsley

130 CALS/SERVING

1 Cut the carrots and parsnips into 5 mm (¼ inch) slices. Thinly slice the onions. Chop the celeriac into chunks and immediately drop into a bowl of cold water lightly acidulated with lemon juice.
2 Melt the butter in a large flameproof casserole. Add the onions and garlic and fry for 2–3 minutes or until beginning to soften, stirring constantly. Stir in the carrots, parsnips and mushrooms and fry for a further 4–5 minutes, stirring. Add the stock and seasoning. Bring to the boil, cover and cook at 170°C (325°F) mark 3 for 50 minutes or until the vegetables are tender.
3 Meanwhile, remove the celeriac from the acidulated water and cook in boiling salted water for about 35 minutes or until very tender. Drain and purée in a blender or food processor with a little of the casserole juices.
4 Stir the celeriac purée into the casserole, reheat and check the seasoning. Stir in the cream and parsley just before serving.

❖ Root Vegetable ❖ and Tahini Stew

SERVES 4

PREPARATION TIME
5 minutes
COOKING TIME
40–45 minutes
FREEZING
Suitable (stage 3)
COLOUR INDEX
Page 57

- 225 g (8 oz) carrots, peeled
- 225 g (8 oz) parsnips, peeled
- 2 onions, peeled
- 225 g (8 oz) old potatoes, peeled
- 225 g (8 oz) swede, peeled
- 30 ml (2 tbsp) oil
- 60 ml (4 tbsp) tahini
- 450 ml (¾ pint) vegetable stock

- 2 bay leaves
- 175 g (6 oz) French beans, halved
- 150 ml (¼ pint) soured cream or fromage frais
- 45 ml (3 tbsp) sesame seeds, toasted
- salt and pepper

355 CALS/SERVING

Slice the carrots and parsnips; chop the onions; roughly chop the potatoes and swede.

2 Heat the oil in a large heavy-based frying pan or flameproof casserole over a high heat. Add all the vegetables, except the French beans, and fry for 4–5 minutes or until they are just beginning to brown and soften.

Stir the tahini into the vegetable stock, then pour over the vegetables. Add the bay leaves. Bring to the boil, then lower the heat, cover and simmer for 15 minutes. Add the French beans, re-cover and simmer for a further 20–25 minutes or until all the vegetables are tender.

4 Stir in the soured cream and sesame seeds. Season with salt and pepper and serve immediately.

❖ Red Kidney Bean Hot Pot ❖

SERVES 4–6

PREPARATION TIME
20 minutes, plus soaking
COOKING TIME
About 1¾ hours
FREEZING
Not suitable

- 225 g (8 oz) dried red kidney beans, soaked overnight in cold water
- 2 onions, peeled
- 225 g (8 oz) celery
- 225 g (8 oz) carrots, peeled
- 50 g (2 oz) butter or margarine
- 30 ml (2 tbsp) plain flour
- 600 ml (1 pint) vegetable stock

- salt and pepper
- 225 g (8 oz) French beans, halved
- 225 g (8 oz) courgettes, sliced
- 30 ml (2 tbsp) chopped parsley
- 50 g (2 oz) fresh wholemeal breadcrumbs
- 75 g (3 oz) Cheddar cheese, grated

455–305 CALS/SERVING

1 Drain the kidney beans and place in a large saucepan. Cover with plenty of fresh cold water, bring to the boil and boil rapidly for 10 minutes. Lower the heat, cover and simmer for about 1½ hours, until the beans are tender.

2 Meanwhile, slice the onions, celery and carrots. Melt the butter in a large saucepan, add the onions and fry gently for about 5 minutes until softened. Add the celery and carrots, cover and cook gently for 5 minutes.

3 Add the flour and cook gently, stirring, for 1–2 minutes. Remove from the heat and gradually blend in the stock. Bring to the boil, stirring constantly, then simmer for 5 minutes. Season with salt and pepper to taste.

4 Add the French beans and simmer for 5 minutes, then add the courgettes and parsley. Cook for a further 5 minutes or until the vegetables are just tender. Drain the kidney beans, add to the vegetables and heat through. Taste and adjust the seasoning, then turn into a deep flameproof dish.

5 Mix the breadcrumbs and cheese together. Sprinkle on top of the bean mixture and place under a hot grill until the topping is crisp and brown. Serve hot, with brown rice or wholemeal bread, and a crisp green salad.

❖ Vegetable Chilli ❖

SERVES 8

PREPARATION TIME
20 minutes
COOKING TIME
About 1 hour
FREEZING
Suitable

- 30 ml (2 tbsp) oil
- 2 onions, peeled and chopped
- 2 large garlic cloves, crushed
- 1–2 green chillies, deseeded and chopped
- 1 bay leaf
- 1 cinnamon stick
- 4 cloves
- 15 ml (1 tbsp) paprika
- 10 ml (2 tsp) ground cumin
- 2.5 ml (½ tsp) chilli powder, or to taste
- 5 ml (1 tsp) dried marjoram
- 30 ml (2 tbsp) tomato purée
- 225 g (8 oz) button mushrooms, sliced
- 1 large green pepper, cored, deseeded and chopped
- 900 g (2 lb) mixed vegetables, including carrots, aubergines, parsnips, potato and celery, prepared and cut into chunks
- two 400 g (14 oz) cans chopped tomatoes
- two 425 g (15 oz) cans red kidney beans, drained and rinsed
- pinch of sugar
- 5 ml (1 tsp) vinegar
- 45 ml (3 tbsp) chopped coriander
- salt and pepper

`225 CALS/SERVING`

1 Heat the oil in a large heavy-based saucepan. Add the onions, garlic and chillies and fry, stirring, for 3–4 minutes. Add the bay leaf, all the spices, the marjoram and tomato purée, and cook for a further 2 minutes, stirring.

2 Add all the fresh vegetables and cook, stirring for 1–2 minutes. Add the tomatoes. Bring to the boil, stirring occasionally. Add enough water just to cover the vegetables, half cover the pan and simmer for 35–45 minutes.

3 Add the kidney beans with the sugar, vinegar and half the coriander. Add extra chilli powder, if liked, and season with salt and pepper. Bring to the boil, lower the heat and simmer for 10 minutes, stirring occasionally. If there is too much liquid, leave the lid off during this time. If dry, add a little water and cover.

4 Stir in the remaining coriander, then leave to stand for 5 minutes. Taste and adjust the seasoning, if necessary. Serve with plain boiled rice.

NOTE: This is delicious served with grated cheese and topped with soured cream or Greek yogurt. If preferred, use cooked dried kidney beans; you will need 225 g (8 oz) dried weight.

❖ Bean Goulash ❖

SERVES 6

PREPARATION TIME
15 minutes, plus soaking
COOKING TIME
1¼–1½ hours
FREEZING
Suitable (stage 3)
COLOUR INDEX
Page 58

- 450 g (1 lb) dried beans, such as black-eye beans, kidney beans and haricot beans, soaked overnight in cold water
- 450 g (1 lb) onions, peeled
- 450 g (1 lb) waxy potatoes, such as Maris Bard or Wilja, peeled
- 30 ml (2 tbsp) oil
- 2.5 ml (½ tsp) caraway seeds, crushed
- 60 ml (4 tbsp) tomato purée
- 15 ml (1 tbsp) paprika
- 5 ml (1 tsp) sugar
- 30 ml (2 tbsp) plain flour
- 1 litre (1¾ pints) vegetable stock
- 300 ml (½ pint) soured cream or Greek yogurt
- 30 ml (2 tbsp) chopped parsley
- salt and pepper

`505 CALS/SERVING`

1 Drain the beans and put them in a saucepan. Add enough fresh water to cover, bring to the boil and boil rapidly for 10 minutes.

2 Meanwhile, roughly chop the onions and potatoes. Heat the oil in a large flameproof casserole and fry the onions and potatoes for about 10 minutes or until golden brown. Add the caraway seeds, tomato purée, paprika and sugar and cook, stirring, for 1–2 minutes. Add the flour and cook for 1 minute, then gradually add the stock. Bring to the boil, stirring.

3 Drain the beans and add to the casserole. Bring back to the boil, cover and simmer for 1–1½ hours or until the beans are tender.

4 Stir in the cream or yogurt and parsley. Season with salt and pepper and serve immediately.

❖ Vegetable Couscous ❖

4 Place over the cooking vegetables, cover and cook for 5 minutes or until the vegetables are tender, the sauce is well reduced and the couscous is piping hot. Check the seasoning. Spoon the couscous onto a serving dish and pile the vegetables and juices on top to serve.

❖ Boston Baked Beans ❖

SERVES 6–8	
PREPARATION TIME 10 minutes, plus soaking	• 450 g (1 lb) dried haricot beans, soaked overnight in cold water
COOKING TIME 5 hours	• 2 onions, peeled and chopped
FREEZING Suitable	• 30 ml (2 tbsp) Dijon mustard
COLOUR INDEX Page 58	• 30 ml (2 tbsp) dark soft brown sugar

- • 450 g (1 lb) dried haricot beans, soaked overnight in cold water
- • 2 onions, peeled and chopped
- • 30 ml (2 tbsp) Dijon mustard
- • 30 ml (2 tbsp) dark soft brown sugar
- • 75 ml (5 tbsp) black treacle
- • 450 ml (¾ pint) tomato juice
- • 450 ml (¾ pint) lager
- • 60 ml (4 tbsp) tomato purée
- • 60 ml (4 tbsp) Worcestershire sauce
- • 30 ml (2 tbsp) chilli sauce
- • 1 garlic clove, crushed
- • salt and pepper

335–250 CALS/SERVING

1 Drain the beans. Put them in a large heavy-based saucepan and add enough fresh cold water to cover. Bring to the boil and boil rapidly for 10 minutes, then cover and simmer for 45 minutes. Drain and place in a casserole dish. Add all the remaining ingredients, including seasoning, and mix together thoroughly.
2 Cover with a tightly fitting lid and cook at 150°C (300°F) mark 2 for 4 hours or until the beans are very tender, stirring occasionally during cooking and adding a little extra tomato juice or water, if necessary. Check the seasoning before serving.

❖ Hot Spiced Chick Peas ❖

SERVES 4	
PREPARATION TIME 5 minutes	• 15 ml (1 tbsp) oil
COOKING TIME 10–15 minutes	• 1 onion, peeled and chopped
FREEZING Not suitable	• 10 ml (2 tsp) turmeric
COLOUR INDEX Page 58	• 15 ml (1 tbsp) cumin seeds

- • 15 ml (1 tbsp) oil
- • 1 onion, peeled and chopped
- • 10 ml (2 tsp) turmeric
- • 15 ml (1 tbsp) cumin seeds
- • 450 g (1 lb) tomatoes, roughly chopped
- • two 425 g (15 oz) cans cooked chick peas, drained
- • 15 ml (1 tbsp) lemon juice
- • 60 ml (4 tbsp) chopped coriander
- • salt and pepper
- • coriander leaves, to garnish

345 CALS/SERVING

1 Heat the oil in a saucepan, add the onion and cook for 5–10 minutes until golden brown, stirring constantly.
2 Add the turmeric and cumin seeds and cook, stirring, for 1–2 minutes. Add the remaining ingredients, including seasoning. Cook for 1–2 minutes, stirring frequently.
3 Serve garnished with coriander and accompanied by baked potatoes or rice, or wholemeal bread.

SERVES 4	
PREPARATION TIME 10 minutes	• 225 g (8 oz) quick-cook couscous
COOKING TIME 15 minutes	• 225 g (8 oz) aubergine
FREEZING Not suitable	• 175 g (6 oz) courgettes

- • 225 g (8 oz) quick-cook couscous
- • 225 g (8 oz) aubergine
- • 175 g (6 oz) courgettes
- • 175 g (6 oz) carrots, peeled
- • 1 large onion, peeled
- • 15 ml (1 tbsp) oil
- • 2 garlic cloves, crushed
- • 10 ml (2 tsp) ground cumin
- • 2.5 ml (½ tsp) mild chilli seasoning
- • 2.5 ml (½ tsp) ground ginger
- • 60 ml (4 tbsp) tomato purée
- • 1 bay leaf
- • 175 g (6 oz) canned chick peas drained, or frozen broad beans
- • 750 ml (1¼ pints) vegetable stock
- • salt and pepper

260 CALS/SERVING

1 Soak the couscous according to packet instructions. Cut the aubergine, courgettes and carrots into chunks. Chop the onion. Heat the oil in a saucepan (over which a steamer, sieve or colander fits). Add the onion, garlic and spices and cook gently for 1 minute, stirring occasionally.

2 Add the tomato purée, bay leaf, vegetables and chick peas, with the stock. Cover and bring to the boil, then uncover and boil rapidly for 8 minutes.

3 Meanwhile, fork the couscous to break up any lumps and spread in a steamer, metal sieve or colander lined with a double thickness of muslin.

❖ Vegetable Tempura ❖

SERVES 4

PREPARATION TIME
20 minutes
COOKING TIME
About 15 minutes
FREEZING
Not suitable
COLOUR INDEX
Page 59

BATTER:
- 125 g (4 oz) plain flour
- 30 ml (2 tbsp) cornflour
- 30 ml (2 tbsp) arrowroot
- salt and pepper

DIPPING SAUCE:
- 25 g (1 oz) fresh root ginger, peeled and grated
- 60 ml (4 tbsp) sake or dry sherry
- 45 ml (3 tbsp) soy sauce

VEGETABLES:
- 125 g (4 oz) cauliflower florets
- 2 large carrots
- 16 button mushrooms
- 2 courgettes
- 2 red peppers
- 30 ml (2 tbsp) plain flour
- oil for deep-frying

TO GARNISH:
- coriander sprigs

610 CALS/SERVING

1 To make the batter, sift the plain flour, cornflour and arrowroot into a large bowl with a pinch each of salt and pepper. Gradually whisk in 300 ml (½ pint) ice cold water to form a smooth, thin batter. Chill in the refrigerator. To make the dipping sauce, put the ginger in a bowl and add the sake or sherry, soy sauce and 200 ml (7 fl oz) boiling water. Stir well to mix, then set aside.

2 To prepare the vegetables, divide the cauliflower into tiny sprigs, discarding any thick, woody stalks. Peel the carrots and cut into thin sticks. Trim the mushroom stalks if necessary. Slice the courgettes. Cut the red peppers in half, remove the cores and seeds and slice the flesh into thin strips.

3 Toss the vegetables in the flour. Heat the oil in a wok or deep-fat fryer to 190°C (375°F) or until a cube of bread dropped into the hot oil will brown in 40 seconds.

4 Cook the vegetables in batches. Dip in the batter, then remove with a slotted spoon, taking up a lot of the batter with the vegetables, and add to the hot oil. Deep-fry for 3–5 minutes or until crisp and golden.

5 Remove the vegetables with a slotted spoon and drain on absorbent kitchen paper. Keep hot while cooking the remaining batches. Serve immediately, garnished with coriander and accompanied by the dipping sauce.

❖ Stir-fried Vegetables ❖

SERVES 4–6

PREPARATION TIME
15 minutes
COOKING TIME
10 minutes
FREEZING
Not suitable

- 60 ml (4 tbsp) oil
- 2 garlic cloves, crushed
- 2.5 cm (1 inch) piece fresh root ginger, peeled and sliced
- 1–2 fresh chillies, deseeded and chopped (optional)
- 125 g (4 oz) cashew nuts, peanuts or almonds
- 900 g (2 lb) mixed vegetables, prepared as necessary and cut into thin strips or slices (see note)

- 15 ml (1 tbsp) light soy sauce
- 15 ml (1 tbsp) dry sherry
- 5 ml (1 tsp) sugar
- 5 ml (1 tsp) five-spice powder (optional)

440–290 CALS/SERVING

1 Heat the oil in a wok or large deep frying pan. Add the garlic, ginger and chillies if using, and stir-fry for 1–2 minutes. Add the nuts and cook for 2 minutes, stirring all the time. Remove the nuts with a slotted spoon and set aside.

2 Add slower-cooking vegetables to the oil remaining in the wok. Cook over a very high heat for 3–4 minutes, stirring all the time. Add the remaining vegetables and cook for a further 2–3 minutes or until heated through but still very crisp.

3 Add the soy sauce, sherry, sugar and five-spice powder, if using. Cook for a further 1 minute, then transfer to a warmed serving dish, sprinkle with the nuts and serve immediately.

NOTE: Vegetable stir-fries are delicious made with whatever vegetables you have to hand, though it's important to cut them into pieces of a similar size. First add tougher, slower-cooking vegetables, such as baby corn, carrots, spring onions, celery, fennel and radish. Delicate fast-cooking vegetables, such as bean sprouts, Chinese leaves, mangetouts, courgettes and mushrooms, need only 2–3 minutes. When cooked, the vegetables should be served right away, so make sure accompanying noodles or rice are almost cooked when you begin stir-frying.

4 Place the pastry cases on a baking sheet and divide the vegetables between them. Spoon the cheese mixture over the vegetables. Protect the filo edges with foil and place under a hot grill for about 30 seconds to glaze the vegetables. Serve immediately, as a light meal, snack or starter.

❖ Glazed Vegetable Pastries ❖

SERVES 4 OR 8	
PREPARATION TIME 15 minutes	
COOKING TIME About 10 minutes	
FREEZING Not suitable	
COLOUR INDEX Page 59	

- 24 filo pastry squares, each 10 × 10 cm (4 × 4 inches)
- 40 g (1½ oz) butter, melted
- 500 g (1 lb 2 oz) mixed baby vegetables, such as carrots, corn cobs, courgettes and mangetouts
- salt and pepper
- 90 ml (6 tbsp) Lemon Mayonnaise (page 273)
- 15–30 ml (1–2 tbsp) chopped mixed herbs, such as chives, parsley and chervil
- 75 g (3 oz) fresh soft goat's cheese
- a little single cream

250 CALS/PASTRY

1 Layer the filo pastry squares over a buttered upturned Yorkshire pudding tin, brushing liberally with melted butter, to make 4 baskets. Bake at 190°C (375°F) mark 5 for 7–8 minutes until crisp and golden. Carefully lift each pastry basket off the tin and place on a wire rack.

2 Meanwhile, steam or cook the vegetables in boiling salted water until just tender; drain well.

3 In a bowl, beat the mayonnaise with the herbs and goat's cheese until evenly blended. Add enough cream to give a coating consistency and season with salt and pepper to taste.

❖ Vegetable Kebabs ❖ with Tofu Sauce

SERVES 2–4	
PREPARATION TIME 15 minutes	
COOKING TIME 10 minutes	
FREEZING Not suitable	

- 300 g (10 oz) silken tofu
- 30 ml (2 tbsp) olive oil
- 20 ml (4 tsp) soy sauce
- about 30 ml (2 tbsp) lemon juice
- 1–2 garlic cloves, crushed
- 15 ml (1 tbsp) sesame oil (optional)
- salt and pepper
- 4 small courgettes
- 6 baby corn cobs
- 16 button mushrooms
- 12 cherry tomatoes or 3 medium tomatoes, quartered
- 12 bay leaves
- 30 ml (2 tbsp) sesame seeds

480–240 CALS/SERVING

1 Put the tofu in a blender or food processor with 15 ml (1 tbsp) oil, 10 ml (2 tsp) soy sauce, the lemon juice, garlic and sesame oil if using. Work until evenly combined, then add salt and pepper to taste and more lemon juice, if liked. Pour into a jug and chill.

2 Cut each courgette into 3 chunks. Blanch in boiling salted water for 1 minute, then drain. Halve the corn cobs diagonally. Thread the vegetables and bay leaves on to oiled skewers.

3 Mix the remaining oil and soy sauce with the sesame seeds. Brush over the kebabs and grill for about 10 minutes, turning and brushing frequently. Serve hot, on a bed of boiled rice, if liked, with the tofu sauce handed separately.

✦ Aubergine Cannelloni ✦

SERVES 6

PREPARATION TIME
45 minutes
COOKING TIME
45 minutes
FREEZING
Not suitable
COLOUR INDEX
Page 60

SAUCE:
- 2 shallots, peeled
- 900 g (2 lb) ripe tomatoes
- 30 ml (2 tbsp) olive oil
- 2 garlic cloves, crushed
- 300 ml (½ pint) vegetable stock or water
- 15 ml (1 tbsp) tomato purée
- 2.5 ml (½ tsp) caster sugar
- salt and pepper
- 30 ml (2 tbsp) dry white wine

CANNELLONI:
- 4 aubergines, about 250 g (9 oz) each
- 150 ml (¼ pint) olive oil
- 450 g (1 lb) ricotta or curd cheese
- 125 g (4 oz) Parmesan cheese, freshly grated
- 30 ml (2 tbsp) finely shredded basil

TO SERVE:
- freshly grated Parmesan cheese
- basil sprigs

540 CALS/SERVING

1 To make the sauce, chop the shallots; skin, deseed and chop the tomatoes. Heat the oil in a heavy-based saucepan, add the shallots and cook gently, stirring frequently, for 5–7 minutes. Add the tomatoes and garlic, cover and cook gently, stirring occasionally, for 10 minutes. Add the stock, tomato purée, sugar and seasoning. Half cover and simmer for 30 minutes, stirring often. Press through a sieve, add the wine and set aside.

2 Meanwhile, make the cannelloni. Cut the aubergines lengthways into thin slices, discarding the ends and side pieces. Heat 30–45 ml (2–3 tbsp) oil in a large non-stick frying pan. Fry the aubergine slices in batches in a single layer until light golden on both sides. Add a little more oil between batches as necessary. Drain the slices on absorbent kitchen paper.

3 Mix the ricotta and Parmesan cheeses together with the basil and seasoning; beat well. Lay the aubergine slices on a clean surface; if small, overlap two slices so they will roll up as one (you will need 24 cannelloni). Spoon the cheese mixture along the aubergines slices.

4 Roll up the slices to enclose the filling. Place, seam-side down, in a single layer in an ovenproof dish. Bake at 190°C (375°F) mark 5 for 10–15 minutes until hot. Reheat the tomato sauce and spoon over the cannelloni. Sprinkle lightly with Parmesan and garnish with basil to serve.

✦ Tian de Courgettes ✦

SERVES 3–4

PREPARATION TIME
25 minutes
COOKING TIME
35–40 minutes
FREEZING
Not suitable

- 2 thick slices white bread
- 300 ml (½ pint) milk
- 125 g (4 oz) long-grain rice
- salt and pepper
- 2 eggs, beaten
- 45 ml (3 tbsp) olive oil
- 50 g (2 oz) Gruyère cheese, grated
- 1 garlic clove, crushed
- 700 g (1½ lb) small courgettes, thinly sliced
- 15–30 ml (1–2 tbsp) freshly grated Parmesan cheese (optional)
- snipped chives, to garnish

575–435 CALS/SERVING

1 Remove the crusts from the bread and discard. Tear the bread into small pieces and place in a large bowl. Pour over the milk and leave to soak. Meanwhile, cook the rice in boiling salted water until tender. Drain well.

2 Beat the eggs and 30 ml (2 tbsp) olive oil into the bread mixture with about a quarter of the cheese and the garlic. Season generously with salt and pepper.

3 Carefully fold the courgettes and rice into the milk and bread mixture, and pour into a greased gratin dish. Sprinkle with the remaining Gruyère cheese and a little Parmesan, if using. Drizzle with a little extra olive oil. Bake at 200°C (400°F) mark 6 for 35–40 minutes or until golden brown and firm to the touch. Sprinkle with chives and serve with a tomato salad.

❖ Vegetable and Nut Roast ❖

SERVES 4-6

PREPARATION TIME
40 minutes
COOKING TIME
1–1¼ hours
FREEZING
Not suitable
COLOUR INDEX
Page 60

- 175 g (6 oz) long-grain brown rice
- salt and pepper
- 1 onion, peeled
- 125 g (4 oz) mushrooms
- 2 carrots, peeled
- 15 g (½ oz) butter or margarine
- 1 garlic clove, crushed
- 125 g (4 oz) fresh wholemeal breadcrumbs
- 125 g (4 oz) nuts, finely chopped (see note)
- 125 g (4 oz) mature Cheddar cheese, grated
- 2 eggs, beaten
- 30 ml (2 tbsp) chopped parsley (optional)
- Tomato Sauce (page 93) or chutney, to serve

620–415 CALS/SERVING

1 Cook the rice in boiling salted water for 30–35 minutes or until tender. Drain well. Meanwhile finely chop the onion and mushrooms; grate the carrots.

2 Heat the butter in a frying pan and fry the onion, garlic and carrots for 3–4 minutes. Add the mushrooms and cook for about 5 minutes or until the vegetables are softened, stirring frequently.

3 Remove from the heat, then stir in the breadcrumbs, nuts, cooked rice, cheese and eggs. Stir in the parsley if using. Season with salt and pepper and mix thoroughly.

4 Pack the mixture into a greased 1.1 litre (2 pint) loaf tin and bake at 180°C (350°F) mark 4 for 1–1¼ hours or until firm to the touch and brown on top. Serve sliced, hot or cold, with fresh tomato sauce or chutney and a crisp salad.

NOTE: Any chopped nuts can be used, for example almonds, Brazils or unsalted peanuts, but it's worth buying mature Cheddar to add a mouth-watering depth of flavour.

❖ Lentil Loaf ❖

SERVES 4-6

PREPARATION TIME
30 minutes, plus standing
COOKING TIME
1¼ hours
FREEZING
Not suitable

- 175 g (6 oz) split red lentils
- 450 ml (¾ pint) vegetable stock or water
- 1 bay leaf
- 1 medium onion, peeled
- 2 celery sticks
- 125 g (4 oz) mushrooms
- 1 red pepper
- 15 ml (1 tbsp) oil
- 1 garlic clove, chopped (optional)
- 225 g (8 oz) fresh wholemeal breadcrumbs
- 30 ml (2 tbsp) chopped parsley
- 15 ml (1 tbsp) lemon juice
- 175 g (6 oz) farmhouse Cheddar cheese, grated
- salt and pepper
- 1 egg, beaten
- Tomato Sauce (page 93), to serve

525–350 CALS/SERVING

1 Put the lentils, stock or water and bay leaf in a saucepan, bring to the boil, then lower the heat, cover and simmer gently for 15–20 minutes or until the lentils are very soft.

2 Meanwhile, grease and line a 1.1 litre (2 pint) loaf tin. Finely chop the onion, celery and mushrooms; halve, core and deseed the pepper, then chop finely.

3 Heat the oil in a large saucepan, add all the vegetables and the garlic, if using, and fry for 2–3 minutes, stirring all the time. Reduce the heat, cover and cook for 10 minutes or until the vegetables are softened.

4 Mix the vegetables with the lentil mixture, discarding the bay leaf. Add the breadcrumbs, parsley, lemon juice and half of the cheese. Season generously with salt and pepper. Stir in the beaten egg; the mixture should be moist but not sloppy.

5 Spoon into the prepared tin and bake at 180°C (350°F) mark 4 for about 1 hour or until firm to the touch in the centre. Sprinkle over the remaining cheese. Increase the temperature to 200°C (400°F) mark 6 and bake for 8–10 minutes until the cheese melts. Cool in the tin for 10 minutes before turning out.

6 Serve hot or cold, thickly sliced and accompanied by fresh tomato sauce and a crisp salad.

❖ Stuffed Peppers ❖

4 Stir in the nuts and soy sauce. Check the seasoning. Use this mixture to fill the pepper cavities.

5 Replace the lids, then stand the peppers in a deep ovenproof dish and pour over the oil. Cover with foil and bake at 190°C (375°F) mark 5 for 30 minutes or until tender. Serve with crusty bread.

SERVES 6

PREPARATION TIME
30 minutes
COOKING TIME
30 minutes
FREEZING
Not suitable

- 6 red peppers
- 1 onion, peeled
- 2.5 cm (1 inch) piece fresh root ginger, peeled
- 50 g (2 oz) butter or margarine
- 1 garlic clove, crushed
- 125 g (4 oz) long-grain rice
- 450 ml (¾ pint) vegetable stock
- 15 ml (1 tbsp) tomato purée
- 125 g (4 oz) mushrooms, sliced
- 75 g (3 oz) pine nuts or flaked almonds, toasted
- 10 ml (2 tsp) soy sauce
- salt and pepper
- 30 ml (2 tbsp) oil

230 CALS/SERVING

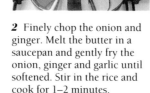

1 Cut a 2.5 cm (1 inch) lid from the stem end of each pepper. Scoop out the core and seeds. Blanch the shells and lids in boiling water for about 2 minutes; drain and cool.

2 Finely chop the onion and ginger. Melt the butter in a saucepan and gently fry the onion, ginger and garlic until softened. Stir in the rice and cook for 1–2 minutes.

3 Add the stock, tomato purée and mushrooms. Bring to the boil and simmer for 13–15 minutes or until the rice is tender and all the stock has been absorbed.

❖ Imam Bayildi ❖

SERVES 6

PREPARATION TIME
20 minutes, plus standing
COOKING TIME
1½ hours
FREEZING
Not suitable
COLOUR INDEX
Page 60

- 6 small aubergines
- salt and pepper
- 200 ml (7 fl oz) olive oil
- 450 g (1 lb) onions, peeled and finely sliced
- 3 garlic cloves, crushed
- 400 g (14 oz) can tomatoes, drained, or 450 g (1 lb) tomatoes, skinned and chopped
- 60 ml (4 tbsp) chopped parsley
- 2.5 ml (½ tsp) ground allspice
- 5 ml (1 tsp) sugar
- 30 ml (2 tbsp) lemon juice
- chopped parsley, to garnish

220 CALS/SERVING

1 Halve the aubergines lengthways. Scoop out the flesh, leaving substantial shells so they do not disintegrate on cooking. Chop the flesh and set aside.
2 Sprinkle the insides of the aubergine shells with salt and invert on to a plate. Leave to degorge for 30 minutes.
3 Heat 45 ml (3 tbsp) olive oil in a saucepan, add the onions and garlic and fry gently for about 15 minutes or until soft but not coloured. Add the tomatoes, reserved aubergine flesh, parsley and allspice. Season with salt and pepper. Simmer gently for about 20 minutes or until the mixture has reduced.
4 Rinse the aubergine shells and pat dry with absorbent kitchen paper. Spoon the filling into the aubergines and place them side by side in a shallow ovenproof dish; they should fit quite closely together.
5 Mix the remaining oil with 150 ml (¼ pint) water, the sugar, lemon juice and seasoning. Pour around the aubergines, cover and bake at 150°C (300°F) mark 2 for about 1 hour or until tender.
6 Leave to cool, then chill in the refrigerator for at least 2 hours before serving. Garnish with parsley and serve with crusty bread or toasted pitta bread, and perhaps a Greek Salad (page 278).

NOTE: This traditional Turkish dish is usually served cold, but it could be served lukewarm if you prefer.

❖ Catalan Red Peppers ❖

SERVES 4	
PREPARATION TIME 20 minutes	• 4 red peppers
COOKING TIME 15–20 minutes	• oil for brushing
FREEZING Not suitable	• 175 g (6 oz) mixed long-grain and wild rice
COLOUR INDEX Page 60	• salt and pepper

- 4 red peppers
- oil for brushing
- 175 g (6 oz) mixed long-grain and wild rice
- salt and pepper
- 8 tomatoes
- 8 spring onions, chopped
- few pitted olives, chopped
- 30 ml (2 tbsp) capers
- 90 ml (6 tbsp) olive oil
- 30 ml (2 tbsp) white wine vinegar
- 1 large garlic clove, crushed

340 CALS/SERVING

1 Put the peppers on a baking sheet and brush lightly with oil. Bake at 220°C (425°F) mark 7 for 15–20 minutes or until just tender. Cool, halve and remove the core and seeds. (The skin can also be removed, if wished, but the pepper will not hold its shape so well.) Pat dry with absorbent kitchen paper.

2 Meanwhile, cook the rice in boiling salted water according to the packet instructions or until tender. Drain and rinse under cold running water, then drain well again. Quarter the tomatoes, discard the seeds and roughly chop the flesh. Mix into the rice with the spring onions, olives and capers.

3 Whisk together the olive oil, vinegar and garlic, and season with salt and pepper. Stir into the rice mixture.

4 Pile the rice into the pepper halves and arrange on serving plates. Cover and chill for 30 minutes before serving.

NOTE: These peppers are also delicious served hot. Keep the peppers warm while assembling the filling and use boiling water to rinse the rice.

❖ Bulgar-stuffed Tomatoes ❖

SERVES 4	
PREPARATION TIME 20 minutes, plus soaking	• 125 g (4 oz) bulgar wheat
FREEZING Not suitable	• 4 large beefsteak tomatoes, about 175 g (6 oz) each
COLOUR INDEX Page 60	• 25 g (1 oz) nuts, such as hazelnuts, peanuts or cashews, toasted and chopped

- 125 g (4 oz) bulgar wheat
- 4 large beefsteak tomatoes, about 175 g (6 oz) each
- 25 g (1 oz) nuts, such as hazelnuts, peanuts or cashews, toasted and chopped
- 50 g (2 oz) pitted black olives, roughly chopped
- 30 ml (2 tbsp) Pesto (page 310)
- 45 ml (3 tbsp) chopped basil
- salt and pepper
- TO SERVE:
- natural yogurt
- Pesto (page 310) or Guacamole (page 115)
- chopped basil

230 CALS/SERVING

1 Put the bulgar wheat in a bowl and pour over 150 ml (¼ pint) boiling water. Leave to soak for 30 minutes or until the water has been absorbed and the bulgar has softened.

2 Cut the tops off the tomatoes and reserve. Scoop out the tomato centres with a spoon and finely chop half the tomato flesh. (Use the remainder for another dish.)

3 Add the chopped tomato to the bulgar wheat with the nuts, olives, pesto and basil. Mix well and season with salt and pepper. Use to fill the tomato shells.

4 To serve, top each tomato with a spoonful of yogurt and a little pesto or a spoonful of guacamole. Sprinkle with basil and replace the tomato tops.

❖ Jacket Potatoes ❖

SERVES 4	
PREPARATION TIME 10 minutes	• 4 large potatoes, about 175 g (6 oz) each
COOKING TIME About 1½ hours	• oil for coating (optional)
FREEZING Not suitable	• salt and pepper
COLOUR INDEX Page 60	HOT CHILLI BEAN FILLING:

- 4 large potatoes, about 175 g (6 oz) each
- oil for coating (optional)
- salt and pepper
- HOT CHILLI BEAN FILLING:
- 400 g (14 oz) can chopped tomatoes
- 10 ml (2 tsp) tomato purée
- 2 garlic cloves, crushed
- 2.5 ml (½ tsp) chilli powder
- 2.5 ml (½ tsp) dried oregano
- 400 g (14 oz) can red kidney beans, drained and rinsed
- 30 ml (2 tbsp) chopped coriander or parsley
- TO GARNISH:
- coriander sprigs

300 CALS/SERVING

1 Scrub the potatoes and prick all over with a fork. If you prefer baked potatoes with softish skins, put the potatoes into the oven while still wet. For crunchy skins, rub them all over with a little oil and sprinkle with salt.

2 Bake the potatoes at 200°C (400°F) mark 6 for about 1½ hours or until the potatoes feel soft when gently squeezed, turning them over once during cooking.

3 Meanwhile make the filling. Put all the ingredients in a saucepan, season with salt and pepper, and bring to the boil. Cook vigorously for 15–20 minutes or until reduced and thickened.

4 When the potatoes are cooked, cut them in half and mash the flesh lightly with a fork. Pile the filling on top. Serve garnished with coriander and accompanied by a mixed salad.

Variations

Omit the chilli bean filling and serve the potatoes topped with grated cheese, ratatouille, or soured cream mixed with chives.

PASTA

It's difficult to remember what we did for fast, satisfying meals before pasta became readily available. Because it keeps well and is quick to cook, cheap and tasty, pasta has become one of our most popular foods. Nutritionally speaking pasta is high in fibre and low in fat and calories – it's the sauce that makes pasta dishes fattening. If you're watching your weight use low-calorie ingredients like vegetables, skimmed milk and low- or medium-fat cheese to replace full-fat equivalents, and keep the use of ingredients like olive oil, butter, olives and salami to a minimum.

❖ Fresh and Dried Pasta ❖

Fresh pasta is now widely available in a good range of shapes and flavours, in supermarkets as well as delicatessens. It cooks in a matter of minutes and is considered superior to dried pasta. Of course, you can make your own at home following our recipe overleaf – homemade pasta is incomparable. The best flour to use is a very fine-textured soft wheat flour known as 'type 00'. This yields a dough which is easier to stretch by hand. Durum or hard wheat semolina flour is only really suitable if you are using a pasta machine which flattens, rather than stretches the dough. Both types of flour are available from Italian delicatessens.

If you make pasta frequently, it is probably a good idea to invest in a pasta machine to do the rolling and cutting for you. One of these machines will take all the hard work out of rolling and get the dough really thin. It will also ensure that the dough is cut into neat, uniform shapes, so that it cooks evenly.

Dried pastas are available in a bewildering range of sizes, shapes and flavours. The best are made from 100% durum wheat (*pasta di semola di grano duro*); some include eggs (*all'uovo*).

Shapes, Sizes and Flavours

The choice of shape and size is a matter of personal taste but it's worth bearing in mind that some varieties – such as conchiglie (shells) – are particularly suited to holding lots of sauce, while other chunkier shapes – such as penne – are good with robust vegetable-based sauces. Fine spaghetti and noodles are excellent with delicate fish sauces, while tiny ditalini are perfect for soups and young children's meals. There are the classic recipes, such as macaroni cheese, spaghetti bolognese and spaghetti alla carbonara, but do experiment with your own combinations.

Coloured and flavoured pastas (fresh and dried) can add a new twist to a familiar meal. These are coloured with puréed vegetables; although the colours are fun the flavours are rarely pronounced. If you're looking for extra flavour choose those flavoured with garlic and herbs. Wholemeal pasta is made with wholemeal flour and has a rather heavy chewy texture. If you're trying to increase your intake of dietary fibre you may prefer to eat plain pasta with a high fibre vegetable-based sauce.

Quantities

It is difficult to give specific quantity guidelines for pasta since it really depends on how rich the sauce is, and even on the size and shape of the pasta – some are easier and quicker to eat than others! Of course appetites, particularly for pasta, vary enormously, too. As a very rough guide allow about 75–125 g (3–4 oz) uncooked weight, per person.

❖ Cooking Pasta ❖

All pasta, fresh and dried, should be cooked until *al dente* – firm to the bite, definitely not soft, and without a hard, uncooked centre. The most important thing to remember is that pasta requires lots of fast-boiling salted water; a small pan containing insufficient water will produce unevenly cooked stodgy pasta. Some cooks add a little olive oil to the water in the belief that it will prevent sticking, but this is not necessary. Fresh pasta will cook in a few minutes, while dried pasta usually takes around 8–12 minutes. Whether you're cooking fresh or dried pasta the time will depend on the size and shape; obviously thin shapes like capellini (angel's hair) will cook more quickly than chunky or filled shapes. Manufacturers' recommended cooking times vary too. The only accurate way to determine when pasta is cooked is by tasting.

❖ Serving Suggestions ❖

Toss cooked pasta with the chosen sauce or butter as soon as it is cooked, or it will stick together as it cools. Always have warm plates or bowls ready as it quickly loses heat. If cooking pasta to serve cold, drain and rinse with cold water to prevent further cooking and rinse away surface starch. Toss with dressing while still slightly warm for optimum flavour. If you store the salad in the refrigerator, bring it to room temperature before serving.

Parmesan cheese is a must for serving with hot pasta – although some seafood pasta dishes are better without it. Do buy a piece of Parmesan; the taste is far superior to the 'soapy' ready-grated alternatives sold in tubs and packets. A well wrapped piece of Parmesan will keep in the refrigerator for several weeks. Rather than grating it on the fine side of the grater, try using a cheese slice or swivel potato peeler to shave off large flakes of cheese. But, dieters be warned, just one tablespoonful (15 ml) of grated Parmesan adds an extra 70 calories!

Should you find yourself with leftovers, the only satisfactory method of reheating pasta is in the microwave. Both dressed and plain pasta can be reheated in this way without loss of texture or flavour. To reheat plain pasta, toss with a little olive oil, cover and cook on HIGH for about 2 minutes. Alternatively, toss plain leftover pasta with a well flavoured dressing and salad ingredients and serve as a salad.

❖ Pesto ❖

SERVES 4–6
PREPARATION TIME
5–10 minutes
FREEZING
Not suitable

- 50 g (2 oz) basil leaves
(weighed without stalks)
- 2 garlic cloves, skinned
- 30 ml (2 tbsp) pine
nuts
- salt and pepper

- 120 ml (4 fl oz) olive
oil
- 50 g (2 oz) freshly
grated Parmesan cheese

75 CALS/15 ML (1 TBSP)

1 Put the basil, garlic, pine nuts, salt, pepper and olive oil in a
mortar and pound with a pestle, or place in a blender or food
processor and blend at high speed until very creamy.
2 Transfer the mixture to a bowl, fold in the cheese and mix
thoroughly. Store for up to 2 weeks in a screw-topped jar in the
refrigerator.

❖ Spaghetti alla Carbonara ❖

SERVES 4
PREPARATION TIME
5 minutes
COOKING TIME
About 10 minutes
FREEZING
Not suitable

- 1 onion, peeled
- 6 pancetta or unsmoked
streaky bacon rashers
- 30 ml (2 tbsp) olive oil
- 1 garlic clove, crushed
- 400 g (14 oz) dried
spaghetti or other long
thin pasta
- salt and pepper

- 3 eggs
- 60 ml (4 tbsp) freshly
grated Parmesan cheese
- 30 ml (2 tbsp) single
cream
- 30 ml (2 tbsp) chopped
parsley

720 CALS/SERVING

1 Finely chop the onion.
Remove the rind from the
pancetta or bacon, then cut
into thin strips. Heat the oil in
a pan, add the onion and fry
gently for 5 minutes until soft
but not coloured. Add the
garlic and cook for a further
1 minute.

2 Cook the spaghetti in a
large pan of boiling salted
water for 8–10 minutes or
until *al dente* (tender but still
firm to the bite). Meanwhile,
add the bacon to the onion
and fry for 2 minutes over
high heat.

3 In a bowl, lightly beat the
eggs with the Parmesan,
cream, chopped parsley and
salt and pepper to taste.

4 Drain the spaghetti and
return to the pan with the
bacon and onion mixture. Stir
well over a moderate heat for
1 minute.

5 Remove from the heat and
pour in the egg mixture,
mixing well; the heat from the
spaghetti will cook the egg.
Turn into a warmed serving
dish and serve immediately.

❖ Pasta with Bacon Sauce ❖

SERVES 4
PREPARATION TIME
10 minutes
COOKING TIME
15 minutes
FREEZING
Not suitable
COLOUR INDEX
Page 61

- 350 g (12 oz) dried
pasta, such as vermicelli,
spaghetti or penne
- salt and pepper
- 125 g (4 oz) black
olives (preferably the
wrinkly variety), pitted
- 225 g (8 oz) rindless
smoked streaky bacon
- 60 ml (4 tbsp) olive oil

- 2 garlic cloves, crushed
- two 400 g (14 oz) cans
chopped tomatoes
- 60 ml (4 tbsp) chopped
herbs, such as basil,
marjoram or parsley
- chopped herbs, to
garnish

720 CALS/SERVING

1 Cook the pasta in a large pan of boiling salted water for about
10 minutes until *al dente* (tender but still firm to the bite).
2 Meanwhile, roughly chop the olives and bacon. Heat 30 ml
(2 tbsp) oil in a frying pan and fry the garlic and bacon until
golden. Stir in the tomatoes, olives and herbs and heat through
for 2–3 minutes until piping hot. Adjust the seasoning.
3 Drain the pasta and toss with the remaining oil. Add the bacon
sauce and toss well. Leave, covered, for 1 minute, then toss again
and serve immediately, garnished with chopped herbs.

❖ Seafood Spaghetti ❖

3 Drain the spaghetti, toss with the seafood sauce and season to taste. Serve immediately, garnished with plenty of chopped parsley.

❖ Spaghetti with Garlic ❖

SERVES 4–6
PREPARATION TIME
15 minutes
COOKING TIME
About 25 minutes
FREEZING
Not suitable

- 900 g (2 lb) mussels
- 2 leeks
- 1 onion, peeled
- 30 ml (2 tbsp) olive oil
- 1 garlic clove, crushed
- large pinch of saffron strands
- 350 g (12 oz) dried spaghetti
- salt and pepper
- 200 ml (7 fl oz) dry white wine

- 150 ml (¼ pint) double cream
- 45 ml (3 tbsp) chopped parsley
- 225 g (8 oz) large cooked peeled prawns
- 175 g (6 oz) scallops, cleaned (optional)
- chopped parsley, to garnish

745–495 CALS/SERVING

1 Clean the mussels (see page 134). Thinly slice the leeks; finely chop the onion. Heat the oil in a large saucepan, add the leeks, onion, garlic and saffron and sauté for 3–4 minutes, stirring all the time. Cover the pan, lower the heat and cook for about 10 minutes or until the vegetables are really soft.

2 Cook the spaghetti in a large pan of boiling salted water for 8–10 minutes or until *al dente* (tender but still firm to the bite). Meanwhile, add the wine, cream and parsley to the leek mixture. Bring to the boil and boil for a few minutes to reduce slightly. Add the seafood, re-cover and cook for 2–3 minutes, shaking the pan frequently, until the mussels have opened; discard any that stay closed.

SERVES 4–6
PREPARATION TIME
5 minutes
COOKING TIME
8–10 minutes
FREEZING
Not suitable

- about 450 g (1 lb) dried spaghetti
- salt and pepper
- 75 ml (5 tbsp) virgin olive oil
- 2 garlic cloves, crushed
- 1 chilli, deseeded and chopped

- 30 ml (2 tbsp) chopped parsley, coriander or basil (optional)
- freshly grated Parmesan cheese, to serve (optional)

560–370 CALS/SERVING

1 Cook the spaghetti in a large pan of boiling salted water for 8–10 minutes or until *al dente* (tender but still firm to the bite).
2 Meanwhile, heat the oil in a heavy-based saucepan, add the garlic and chilli and fry for 2–3 minutes, stirring occasionally. Don't let the garlic and chilli become too brown or the oil will taste bitter. Remove from the heat and set aside until the pasta is cooked.
3 Drain the pasta thoroughly. Reheat the oil over a very high heat for 1 minute, then pour over the pasta with the herbs, if using. Season with salt and pepper and serve immediately, with Parmesan if preferred.

NOTE: Increase or decrease the quantity of garlic and chilli used in this recipe according to taste. It's an intensely flavoured dish, best served with a crisp mixed leaf and watercress salad dressed lightly with a sharp vinaigrette.

✦ Spinach and ✦ Ricotta Cannelloni

3 Lay the lasagne sheets on a work surface and divide the spinach mixture between them. Roll up the sheets to enclose the filling.

4 Arrange, seam-side down in a single layer, in a greased ovenproof dish. Pour the sauce over and sprinkle with Parmesan cheese and breadcrumbs. Bake at 200°C (400°F) mark 6 for 30 minutes. Serve with a salad.

NOTE: It's much easier to make cannelloni using sheets of lasagne than it is to make them with cannelloni tubes. If you cannot buy sheets of fresh lasagne, use dried, but cook them first according to packet instructions and reduce the final cooking time to about 20 minutes.

SERVES 4–6

PREPARATION TIME
20 minutes
COOKING TIME
About 1 hour
FREEZING
Not suitable

- 60 ml (4 tbsp) olive oil
- 2 small onions, peeled and finely chopped
- 30 ml (2 tbsp) tomato purée
- 5 ml (1 tsp) mild paprika
- two 400 g (14 oz) cans chopped tomatoes
- pinch of dried oregano
- 300 ml (½ pint) dry red wine or vegetable stock
- large pinch of sugar
- salt and pepper

- 450 g (1 lb) frozen leaf spinach, thawed
- 1 garlic clove, crushed
- 450 g (1 lb) ricotta cheese
- freshly grated nutmeg
- 18 small sheets fresh lasagne
- 30 ml (2 tbsp) freshly grated Parmesan cheese
- 30 ml (2 tbsp) fresh white breadcrumbs

645–430 CALS/SERVING

1 To make the sauce, heat half the oil in a heavy-based saucepan, add half the onion and fry for 5–10 minutes or until very soft. Add the tomato purée and paprika and cook for 2–3 minutes. Add the tomatoes, oregano, red wine or stock and sugar, and season with salt and pepper. Simmer for 20 minutes.

2 Meanwhile drain the spinach thoroughly and chop finely. Heat the remaining oil in a large saucepan, add the garlic and remaining onion and cook for 5 minutes, stirring frequently. Add the spinach and cook for 2 minutes. Cool slightly, then add the ricotta cheese. Season with nutmeg, salt and pepper.

✦ Lasagne ✦

SERVES 4–6

PREPARATION TIME
15 minutes, plus making sauce
COOKING TIME
45 minutes
FREEZING
Suitable (stage 1)
COLOUR INDEX
Page 63

- 1 quantity Bolognese Sauce (page 309)
- about 350 g (12 oz) fresh lasagne, or 225 g (8 oz) oven-ready dried (12–15 sheets)
- 900 ml (1½ pints) Béchamel Sauce (page 92)

- 45 ml (3 tbsp) freshly grated Parmesan cheese

465–310 CALS/SERVING

1 Spoon one third of the Bolognese sauce into the base of a 2.5 litre (4 pint) ovenproof dish. Cover with a layer of lasagne, then spread over enough Béchamel sauce to cover the pasta. Repeat these layers twice more, finishing with a layer of Béchamel sauce to cover the lasagne completely.

2 Sprinkle the Parmesan cheese over the top and stand the dish on a baking sheet. Bake at 180°C (350°F) mark 4 for about 45 minutes or until well browned and bubbling. Leave to stand for about 5 minutes before cutting.

NOTE: Sheets of fresh lasagne are available in the chilled cabinet of most supermarkets these days. If using oven-ready dried lasagne, add a little extra stock or water to the sauce. You will find it easiest to use a large rectangular or square ovenproof dish.

❖ Vegetable Lasagne ❖

3 Add the remaining vegetables to the pan with the tomatoes, tomato purée, bay leaves and seasoning. Bring to the boil, then reduce the heat, cover and simmer for about 30 minutes.

4 Spread a small amount of the tomato sauce in the base of a 2.8 litre (5 pint) ovenproof dish. Cover with a layer of lasagne and top with a layer of Béchamel sauce. Continue layering in this way.

5 Finish with a layer of Béchamel sauce and sprinkle with the cheese, if using. Bake at 190°C (375°F) mark 5 for 45–50 minutes or until the lasagne is piping hot and well browned. Leave to stand for 5 minutes before serving, with a crisp salad.

SERVES 6

PREPARATION TIME
30 minutes
COOKING TIME
about 1½ hours
FREEZING
suitable (stage 4)

- 1 carrot, peeled
- 1 large onion, peeled
- 1 red pepper
- 1 large aubergine
- 225 g (8 oz) button mushrooms
- 2 large courgettes
- 30 ml (2 tbsp) olive oil
- 1 garlic clove, crushed
- 15 ml (1 tbsp) mild paprika
- 10 ml (2 tsp) dried oregano or marjoram
- two 400 g (14 oz) cans chopped tomatoes
- 30 ml (2 tbsp) tomato purée

- 2 bay leaves
- salt and pepper
- about 350 g (12 oz) fresh lasagne or 225 g (8 oz) oven-ready dried
- 900 ml (1½ pints) Béchamel Sauce (page 92)
- 45 ml (3 tbsp) freshly grated Parmesan or Cheddar cheese (optional)

365 CALS/SERVING

❖ Prawn and ❖ Leek Pasta Shells

SERVES 4

PREPARATION TIME
15 minutes
COOKING TIME
About 15 minutes
FREEZING
Not suitable
COLOUR INDEX
Page 63

- 125 g (4 oz) conchiglioni rigate (about 20 large dried pasta shells)
- salt and pepper
- 15 g (½ oz) butter
- 30 ml (2 tbsp) plain flour
- 450 ml (¾ pint) milk
- 25 g (1 oz) freshly grated Parmesan cheese
- 10 ml (2 tsp) oil

- 350 g (12 oz) leeks, thinly sliced
- 125 g (4 oz) cooked peeled prawns
- 10 ml (2 tsp) lemon juice
- 125 g (4 oz) cottage cheese

365 CALS/SERVING

1 Cook the pasta in a large pan of boiling salted water for 12–15 minutes or until *al dente* (tender but still firm to the bite).
2 Meanwhile melt the butter in a pan, stir in the flour and cook, stirring, for 1 minute. Off the heat, gradually stir in the milk. Bring to the boil, stirring, until the sauce thickens. Simmer for 1–2 minutes. Stir in the Parmesan cheese. Keep warm.
3 Heat the oil in a large frying pan. Add the leeks and cook for 2–3 minutes until soft and golden brown. Stir in the prawns and lemon juice. Sauté for a further 1–2 minutes until all excess moisture is driven off. Remove from the heat and stir in the cottage cheese and seasoning to taste.
4 Drain the pasta thoroughly and fill the pasta shells with the leek mixture. Spoon the Parmesan sauce over the pasta shells and grill until golden brown and bubbling. Serve immediately.

Chop the carrot; slice the onion. Halve, core and deseed the pepper, then chop. Cut the aubergine into large chunks; slice the mushrooms and courgettes.

2 Heat the oil in a large saucepan. Add the garlic, carrot, onion and pepper and fry for 1–2 minutes or until beginning to soften. Add the paprika, herbs and aubergine and fry for 1–2 minutes.

RICE, GRAINS & NOODLES

Rice is one of our staple foods. It contains protein and B vitamins, but no fat, and it is cheap and quick to cook. There are many types of rice, each with its own characteristics, and for many dishes it is important to choose the correct variety.

❖ Types of Rice ❖

Brown rice is the whole grain with only the tough outer husk removed. Like other unrefined grains it is higher in fibre, B vitamins and protein than its refined counterpart. Because the bran is retained, the rice has a chewy texture and nutty flavour, and it takes longer to cook than white varieties.

Long-grain white rice is brown rice that has been further milled to remove the bran and germ. When cooked the grains should be separate, quite dry and fluffy. Varieties include Patna and Carolina.

Basmati rice is a wonderfully aromatic long-grain rice which was originally harvested mainly in the foothills of the Himalayas. It is the perfect accompaniment to curries and other spicy dishes, and is used to make a pilaf. Brown basmati rice is also available.

Thai rice is a newcomer to our supermarkets. The large plump grains are extremely fragrant with a slightly sweet flavour. Try it flavoured with chopped chillies and fresh coriander, as an accompaniment to spicy foods.

Arborio rice is a special short-grain variety from Italy which is essential for an authentic risotto. It has the unique ability to absorb a lot of liquid during cooking without turning mushy.

Glutinous rice is another Asian variety which is also known as sticky rice. It has oval cream-coloured grains which cook into a sticky mass. It is a vital ingredient in Japanese sushi.

Short-grain pudding rice is indispensable for a rice pudding. The small grains absorb lots of liquid during cooking, softening in the process to produce the characteristic creamy result.

Cooking Rice

Contrary to popular belief, cooking rice isn't difficult. Some of the 'speciality rices' are cooked in specific ways: the liquid is usually added gradually to arborio for a risotto; pudding rice is usually baked slowly in a low oven; glutinous rice is steamed; but in general long-grain rice varieties can be treated in the same way.

Many cooks like to wash or rinse the rice before cooking to remove excess starch. With some varieties this is not necessary, but others – particularly basmati – tend to be very starchy and may contain small pieces of grit so washing is advisable. Simply put the rice in a sieve and wash under cold running water until the water runs clear, shaking the sieve and picking out any bits of grit.

To cook the rice you will need a large saucepan and plenty of fast-boiling salted water. Sprinkle the rice into the boiling water and keep the heat high until the water returns to the boil. Stir once with a fork to loosen any rice grains that have sunk to the bottom, lower the heat and cook, uncovered, fairly vigorously. As long as you have sufficient water the rice will not stick.

There are so many varieties of long-grain rice on the market that it is impossible to give exact cooking times. Most varieties take a minimum of 10 minutes; to test, pick out a few grains and taste. As soon as the rice is cooked, drain in a sieve and rinse with boiling water to remove excess starch. Fluff up the grains with a fork and tip into a heated serving dish or warmed plates.

The alternative method relies on accurately estimating the volume of liquid to that of rice (usually double liquid to rice). It is a little trickier because the rice has a habit of sticking to the base of the pan, so you need to use a pan with a really solid base, and control the heat carefully. Always keep a careful watch on the time and resist lifting the lid during cooking because this lets precious steam escape. Rice can also be cooked by this method in the oven, usually at about 180°C (350°F) mark 4, but it will take much longer. If converting a white rice recipe to use brown rice, don't forget to add extra liquid and increase the cooking time.

Rice may be cooked in advance, stored in the refrigerator and reheated in the microwave or in the oven – in a well-buttered covered dish. Cooked rice can also be frozen, but takes ages to thaw, so freeze it in portion sizes to reduce defrosting time.

❖ Grains and Noodles ❖

The interest in wholefood and healthy eating means that a better range of grains can be found in supermarkets than ever before. Grains are high in vitamins. They are also extremely versatile and can be used for making all sorts of dishes or at the very least as a change from rice or potatoes as an accompaniment.

One of the most delicious and expensive grains is wild rice. It is not as the name suggests a rice but the seed of an aquatic grass. It is dark brown in colour and has a strong, nutty flavour. Because of its cost, wild rice is usually mixed with other grains or rice. Look out for commercially prepared mixtures. Other useful grains include bulgar wheat, couscous, barley and maize, which is used for making polenta.

Noodles are derived from soya beans, such as cellophane noodles; rice flour, as in rick stick noodles; and of course from pasta. Some varieties need to be soaked before cooking. Like rice and grains, noodles are often served as an accompaniment.

❖ Special Fried Rice ❖

SERVES 4

PREPARATION TIME
15 minutes
COOKING TIME
15 minutes
FREEZING
Not suitable
COLOUR INDEX
Page 64

- 225 g (8 oz) long-grain rice
- salt and pepper
- 75 g (3 oz) bean sprouts
- 1 large carrot, peeled
- 4 spring onions
- 50 g (2 oz) frozen cooked peeled prawns, thawed

- 15–30 ml (1–2 tbsp) oil
- 1 garlic clove, crushed
- 75 g (3 oz) frozen peas, thawed
- 20 ml (4 tsp) light soy sauce
- 5 ml (1 tsp) sesame oil

325 CALS/SERVING

1 Cook the rice in boiling salted water for about 10 minutes until almost tender. Drain, then rinse with boiling water. Spread out on a large tray and leave to cool.

2 Meanwhile, soak the bean sprouts in sufficient cold water to cover for 10 minutes. Coarsely grate the carrot. Thinly slice the spring onions diagonally. Drain the beansprouts; thoroughly drain the prawns.

3 Heat the oil in a wok or large frying pan. Add the carrot and garlic and stir-fry for 2 minutes. Add the prawns, peas and bean sprouts and stir-fry for 1 minute.

4 Stir in the rice and spring onions; stir-fry for 3 minutes. Stir in the soy sauce and seasoning. Transfer the rice to a serving dish. Sprinkle with the sesame oil and serve at once.

❖ Egg Fried Rice ❖

SERVES 6

PREPARATION TIME
10 minutes
COOKING TIME
12–15 minutes
FREEZING
Not suitable
COLOUR INDEX
Page 64

- 450 g (1 lb) long-grain rice
- salt
- 1 large onion, peeled
- 1 green chilli
- 2 large carrots, peeled
- 1 green pepper
- about 30 ml (2 tbsp) oil
- 4 spring onions, chopped

- 50 g (2 oz) unsalted cashew nuts or peanuts (optional)
- 2 eggs, beaten
- 5 ml (1 tsp) sugar
- 30 ml (2 tbsp) light soy sauce

405 CALS/SERVING

1 Cook the rice in boiling salted water for 10 minutes or until just tender; do not overcook or the fried rice will be mushy. Drain the rice, rinse with boiling water, then spread out on a tray while cooking the vegetables.

2 Chop the onion; deseed and chop the chilli; coarsely grate the carrots. Halve, core and finely chop the green pepper, discarding the seeds.

3 Heat the oil in a wok or very large frying pan. Add the onion, chilli, carrots and green pepper and stir-fry for 3–4 minutes or until the vegetables are softened. Add the spring onions and nuts, if using, and stir-fry for 1 minute.

4 Pour in the egg in a thin stream, stirring all the time so that it breaks up into small pieces. When all of the egg has set, add the rice, sugar and soy sauce and continue cooking, stirring all the time, until the rice is heated through. Add a little extra oil if the rice starts to stick. Serve immediately.

❖ Fragrant Coconut Rice ❖

SERVES 4–6

PREPARATION TIME
5 minutes
COOKING TIME
About 15 minutes
FREEZING
Not suitable

- 25 g (1 oz) creamed coconut, chopped
- 5 ml (1 tsp) salt
- 2.5 ml (½ tsp) freshly grated nutmeg
- pepper
- 2 cloves
- 1 cinnamon stick

- 1 piece lemon grass, split
- 1 bay leaf
- 2 slices dried galangal
- 350 g (12 oz) basmati rice

335–225 CALS/SERVING

1 Put all the ingredients, except the rice, in a heavy-based saucepan with 600 ml (1 pint) water. Bring slowly to the boil. Add the rice, stir with a fork, then cover and simmer gently for 15 minutes or until all liquid is absorbed and the rice is tender.

2 Leave to stand for 2 minutes before serving.

NOTE: Lemon grass lends a unique flavour and aroma to anything it's cooked with. If you cannot find any in the shops, add the finely grated rind of 1 lemon instead. This is not comparable, but adds a delicious flavour of its own. Galangal is a root that looks very similar to ginger. If you're lucky enough to find fresh galangal in an oriental shop, use it in this recipe.

❖ Fragrant Saffron Pilaf ❖

3 Add 600 ml (1 pint) water, the saffron, sugar and seasoning. Bring to the boil, stirring. Reduce the heat, cover tightly and cook very gently for 15 minutes, or until all the liquid is absorbed and the rice is tender.

4 Taste and adjust the seasoning. Fluff up the rice with a fork before serving.

NOTE: Fresh or dried morels add a delicious rich flavour to this pilaf. Soak dried ones overnight and use some of the liquor to cook the rice.

SERVES 6		
PREPARATION TIME minutes, plus soaking	• *350 g (12 oz) basmati rice*	• *1 stick cassia bark or cinnamon*
COOKING TIME 5–20 minutes	• *225 g (8 oz) button mushrooms or morels*	• *2.5 ml (½ tsp) saffron strands*
FREEZING Not suitable	• *60 ml (4 tbsp) oil*	• *5 ml (1 tsp) sugar*
	• *3 cloves*	• *salt and pepper*
	• *6 green cardamom pods*	

275 CALS/SERVING

1 Wash the rice in several changes of cold water to remove excess starch. Place in a bowl, cover with cold water and leave to soak for 30 minutes. Drain and rinse in a sieve under cold running water until the water runs clear.

2 Slice the mushrooms. Heat the oil in a large pan, add the mushrooms, cloves, cardamom pods, cassia bark or cinnamon, and rice. Cook, stirring, over moderate heat for 1–2 minutes.

❖ Mixed Rice Pilaf ❖

SERVES 6		
PREPARATION TIME 5 minutes	• *350 g (12 oz) long-grain brown rice*	• *50 g (2 oz) pine nuts, toasted*
COOKING TIME 35–50 minutes	• *50 g (2 oz) wild rice*	• *chopped parsley, to serve*
FREEZING Not suitable	• *salt and pepper*	
	• *60 ml (4 tbsp) olive oil*	

365 CALS/SERVING

1 Cook the brown and wild rice in boiling salted water until tender: they can be cooked together but check the packet instructions as some varieties of wild rice take longer to cook than brown rice; these will have to be started off first.
2 Drain the rice in a sieve and rinse with boiling water. Drain thoroughly and transfer to a heated serving dish.
3 Stir in the oil and season with salt and pepper to taste. Stir in the toasted pine nuts and plenty of chopped parsley to serve.

❖ Thai Fried Rice ❖

SERVES 4

PREPARATION TIME
10 minutes
COOKING TIME
15 minutes
FREEZING
Not suitable

- 225 g (8 oz) basmati rice
- salt
- 1 hot red chilli
- 2 spring onions
- 45 ml (3 tbsp) oil
- 10 ml (2 tsp) nam pla fish sauce
- 1 large egg, beaten (optional)
- 15 ml (1 tbsp) soy sauce
- 5 ml (1 tsp) brown sugar

335 CALS/SERVING

1 Cook the rice in boiling salted water for about 10 minutes until almost tender. Drain, then rinse with boiling water. Spread out on a tray and leave to cool while cooking the vegetables.
2 Deseed and chop the chilli; chop the spring onions. Heat the oil in a wok, then add the fish sauce, chilli and spring onions and stir-fry for 1–2 minutes to flavour the oil.
3 Add the egg, if using, and stir-fry until the egg scrambles, stirring all the time so that the egg sets in small pieces rather than one large lump.
4 Stir the rice with a fork to separate the grains, then tip into the hot oil. Stir-fry with the eggs until thoroughly heated through. Mix the soy sauce with the sugar, then stir into the rice mixture. Serve immediately.

❖ Basmati Pilaf ❖

SERVES 4

PREPARATION TIME
10 minutes, plus
soaking
COOKING TIME
25 minutes
FREEZING
Not suitable
COLOUR INDEX
Page 65

- 225 g (8 oz) basmati rice
- 4 cardamom pods, split
- 4 black peppercorns
- 3 whole cloves
- 2.5 cm (1 inch) cinnamon stick
- 7.5 ml (1½ tsp) cumin seeds
- 30 ml (2 tbsp) oil
- 1 small onion, peeled and finely chopped
- 5 ml (1 tsp) turmeric
- 2 curry leaves or bay leaves, torn into pieces
- salt and pepper
- 25–50 g (1–2 oz) pistachio nuts, roughly chopped
- 25 g (1 oz) raisins (optional)

365 CALS/SERVING

1 Wash the rice in several changes of cold water to remove excess starch. Place in a bowl, cover with cold water and leave t soak for 30 minutes. Drain off the water, transfer the rice to a sieve and rinse under cold running water until the water runs clear.
2 Put the cardamom pods, peppercorns, cloves, cinnamon stick and cumin seeds in a large, heavy flameproof casserole and dry-fry over moderate heat for 2–3 minutes, stirring all the time unt the seeds pop and release their flavour. Add the oil and stir unti hot, then add the onion and turmeric and cook gently, stirring frequently, for 10 minutes until the onion is softened.
3 Add the rice and stir until coated in the spiced onion mixture then slowly pour in 1.1 litres (2 pints) boiling water. (Take care as the water may sizzle and splash.) Add the curry or bay leaves and seasoning, bring to the boil and stir well. Lower the heat, cover and cook very gently for 10 minutes, without lifting the lid. Remove from the heat and leave to stand for 10 minutes to allow the flavours to develop.
4 Uncover the rice, add half the pistachio nuts, and the raisins using, and gently fork through to fluff up the grains. Taste and adjust the seasoning. Spoon the pilaf on to a warmed serving platter and sprinkle with the remaining pistachio nuts to serve.

❖ Asparagus Risotto ❖

SERVES 4

PREPARATION TIME
30 minutes
COOKING TIME
30–35 minutes
FREEZING
Not suitable

- 1 litre (1¾ pints) vegetable stock
- 150 ml (¼ pint) dry white wine
- 450 g (1 lb) thin green asparagus
- 1 onion, peeled
- 75 g (3 oz) butter
- 350 g (12 oz) arborio rice
- pinch of saffron stran
- salt and pepper
  TO SERVE:
- 50 g (2 oz) freshly shredded Parmesan cheese

455 CALS/SERVIN

Bring the stock and wine to [th]e boil in a large saucepan [an]d keep at barely simmering [po]int. Meanwhile, cut off the [ti]ps of the asparagus and set [as]ide. Peel the asparagus [st]alks and cut into 5 cm [2] inch) lengths.

2 Finely chop the onion. Melt 25 g (1 oz) butter in a large heavy-based saucepan. Add the onion and fry gently for 5 minutes or until soft. Add the asparagus stems and the arborio rice to the pan and stir over a low heat for 2–3 minutes until the rice is well coated with the butter.

Add a ladleful of stock to [th]e pan and cook gently, [sti]rring occasionally, until the [sto]ck is absorbed. Stir in more [sto]ck as soon as each ladleful [is] absorbed.

4 When the rice becomes creamy, sprinkle in the saffron with salt and pepper to taste. Continue adding stock and stirring until the risotto is thick and creamy, tender but not sticky. This process should take 20–25 minutes; it must not be hurried. You may not need to add all of the stock.

5 Meanwhile, steam the asparagus tips until just tender. Just before serving the risotto, add the asparagus tips with the remaining butter. Check the seasoning and serve sprinkled with the Parmesan cheese.

❖ Mushroom Risotto ❖

SERVES 4

PREPARATION TIME
15 minutes
COOKING TIME
20–25 minutes
FREEZING
Not suitable

- *1 onion, peeled*
- *1 lemon*
- *175 g (6 oz) flat mushrooms*
- *225 g (8 oz) broccoli florets*
- *175 g (6 oz) French beans*
- *salt and pepper*
- *1 litre (1¾ pints) vegetable stock*
- *30 ml (2 tbsp) olive oil*
- *350 g (12 oz) arborio rice*
- *pinch of saffron strands (optional)*
- *60 ml (4 tbsp) dry white wine*
- *freshly grated Parmesan cheese, to serve*

420 CALS/SERVING

1 Finely chop the onion. Finely pare the rind from the lemon in one piece, then squeeze the juice from the lemon. Slice the mushrooms.

2 Break the broccoli into small florets; halve the French beans. Blanch the beans and broccoli together in boiling salted water for about 4 minutes. Drain and refresh under cold running water.

3 Bring the stock to the boil in a large saucepan and keep at barely simmering point.

4 Heat the oil in a large heavy-based saucepan, add the onion and cook for about 2–3 minutes until beginning to soften. Stir in the rice and saffron, if using, season well and add the wine, pared lemon rind, 30 ml (2 tbsp) lemon juice and a ladleful of stock. Cook gently, stirring occasionally until the stock is absorbed. Continue adding the stock, a ladleful at a time as each addition is absorbed.

5 When most of the stock has been added and the rice is creamy (after about 15 minutes), stir in the mushrooms, broccoli, French beans and a little more stock. Cover and simmer for a further 5 minutes, or until the rice is just tender and most of the liquid absorbed. Remove the lemon rind and check the seasoning. Serve the risotto with freshly grated Parmesan.

❖ Buttered Saffron Couscous ❖

SERVES 6

PREPARATION TIME
10 minutes
COOKING TIME
35 minutes
FREEZING
Not suitable

- 250 g (9 oz) couscous
- 2.5 ml (½ tsp) saffron strands
- 75 g (3 oz) pine nuts, toasted
- 45 ml (3 tbsp) chopped parsley
- 75 g (3 oz) butter
- salt and pepper

265 CALS/SERVING

1 Put the couscous in a bowl and pour on 350 ml (12 fl oz) cold water. Leave for 10 minutes or until the water is absorbed.

2 Put the saffron in a small bowl and add 15 ml (1 tbsp) boiling water. Stir the saffron and liquid into the couscous.

3 Spoon into a wire sieve lined with muslin. Set over a pan of boiling water; cover with foil. Steam for 35 minutes.

4 Fork the couscous to remove any lumps, then mix in the pine nuts, parsley and butter. Season and serve.

NOTE: Look out for quick-cook couscous, which only needs to be moistened slightly and steamed for 2 minutes.

❖ Lemon Couscous ❖ with Mushrooms

SERVES 2

PREPARATION TIME
10 minutes
COOKING TIME
5 minutes
FREEZING
Not suitable

- 125 g (4 oz) quick-cook couscous
- grated rind and juice of 1 lemon
- salt and pepper
- 75 g (3 oz) butter or margarine
- 225–275 g (8–10 oz) flat or cup mushrooms, sliced
- 10 ml (2 tsp) Dijon mustard
- 25 g (1 oz) pine nuts

TO GARNISH:
- shredded lemon rind
- parsley sprigs

520 CALS/SERVING

1 Put the couscous in a bowl and pour on 150 ml (¼ pint) boiling water. Add the lemon rind, season with salt and pepper and leave to soak for about 5 minutes, stirring occasionally.
2 Heat 50 g (2 oz) of the butter in a frying pan, add the mushrooms and fry quickly until softened. Remove from the heat and stir in the mustard and 10 ml (2 tsp) lemon juice. Taste and adjust the seasoning.
3 Meanwhile, heat the remaining butter in a separate frying pan. Add the pine nuts and couscous and cook over a high heat, stirring occasionally, until piping hot. Season with salt and pepper. Serve topped with the mushrooms and garnished with shredded lemon rind and parsley.

❖ Hot Noodles ❖ with Sesame Dressing

SERVES 6

PREPARATION TIME
5 minutes
COOKING TIME
About 5 minutes
FREEZING
Not suitable
COLOUR INDEX
Page 65

- 350 g (12 oz) Chinese egg noodles or other noodles
- salt and pepper
- 1 small green chilli
- 45 ml (3 tbsp) toasted sesame seeds
- 45 ml (3 tbsp) oil
- 30 ml (2 tbsp) sesame oil
- 1 clove garlic, crushed
- 60 ml (4 tbsp) soy sauce
- 60 ml (4 tbsp) chopped coriander or parsley

320 CALS/SERVING

1 Cook the noodles in boiling salted water, according to the packet instructions.

2 Meanwhile, deseed and finely chop the chilli, wearing rubber gloves to avoid skin irritation. Mix with the sesame seeds, oils, garlic and soy sauce.

3 Drain the noodles well and toss in the sesame dressing and chopped coriander. Adjust the seasoning and serve immediately.

❖ Singapore Noodles ❖

SERVES 4

PREPARATION TIME
10 minutes
COOKING TIME
about 5 minutes
FREEZING
Not suitable

- 250 g (8 oz) Chinese egg noodles or rice stick noodles
- salt
- 1 onion, peeled
- 2.5 cm (1 inch) piece fresh root ginger
- 1 green chilli
- 2 carrots, peeled
- handful of mustard greens, pak choi or 2 Chinese leaves
- 60 ml (4 tbsp) oil
- 2 garlic cloves, crushed
- 125 g (4 oz) mangetouts
- 4 spring onions, chopped
- 5 ml (1 tsp) curry powder
- 30 ml (2 tbsp) light soy sauce
- 30 ml (2 tbsp) hoisin sauce

440 CALS/SERVING

1 Cook the noodles in boiling salted water following the instructions on the packet. Meanwhile chop the onion; peel and chop the ginger; deseed and chop the chilli. Thinly slice the carrots; shred the greens. Drain the noodles and toss in 15 ml (1 tbsp) of the oil.

2 Heat the remaining oil in a wok or very large frying pan. Add the garlic, onion, ginger and chilli and stir-fry for 2–3 minutes.

3 Add the vegetables and sprinkle with the curry powder. Stir-fry for 3–4 minutes or until the vegetables are softened but still crisp. Add the noodles with the soy sauce and hoisin sauce and stir-fry for 1–2 minutes until hot.

Variation

Try using other vegetables, such as broccoli, green beans, baby corn cobs, water chestnuts and mooli.

❖ Toasted Polenta ❖

SERVES 6

PREPARATION TIME
15 minutes, plus chilling
COOKING TIME
20 minutes
FREEZING
Not suitable
COLOUR INDEX
Page 65

- 5 ml (1 tsp) salt
- 200 g (7 oz) polenta
- 25 g (1 oz) butter or margarine
- 1 garlic clove, crushed (optional)
- pepper

150 CALS/SERVING

1 Pour 1.1 litres (2 pints) cold water into a large saucepan and bring to the boil. Add the salt, then pour in the polenta in a very fine stream, stirring vigorously all the time with a wooden spoon. Simmer for about 15 minutes or until the polenta is very thick and no longer grainy, stirring occasionally to prevent it from sticking.

2 Remove the pan from the heat and stir in the butter, garlic if using, and pepper.

3 Turn out on to a wooden board or a plate and spread to a thickness of about 1–2 cm (½–¾ inch). Cool, cover and chill in the refrigerator for at least 1 hour. Cut into 5 cm (2 inch) pieces.

4 When ready to serve, toast the polenta squares under a hot grill for 3–4 minutes each side. Serve at once or cover loosely and keep warm.

NOTE: Polenta, or ground corn, is a staple of northern Italian cooking. It's often eaten hot, like porridge, but it can also be cooled, cut into squares and then fried or grilled as here. Different types require varying cooking times; always ensure the mixture is tender and the liquid well reduced. The polenta squares can be prepared the day before you wish to serve them. Serve as an accompaniment to casseroles, stews or grilled vegetables or meat.

PIES, FLANS
& PIZZAS

The art of successful pastry making lies in light careful handling and accurate measuring. Except when making choux pastry, the golden rule is to keep everything cool – the kitchen, work surface, utensils, ingredients and yourself!

There are three main types of pastry: shortcrust, puff and choux. Flan pastry and the classic French *pâte sucrée* are similar to shortcrust, though they are richer and *pâte sucrée* is mixed differently. (Recipes for these sweet pastries are on page 354.)

For most pastries, plain white flour is the best, as it gives a light, crisp result. Self-raising flour produces a soft spongy pastry, while using all wholemeal flour tends to give a heavy pastry. For wholemeal pastry it is best to use half wholemeal and half plain white flour.

Puff pastry is made with strong flour which contains extra gluten to strengthen the dough and enable it to be rolled and folded intensively. A little lemon juice is usually added to puff pastry to soften the gluten and make the dough more elastic.

Traditionally shortcrust pastry is made with a mixture of lard and either butter or margarine, but more often nowadays white vegetable fat replaces lard, or all butter or margarine is used instead. For a rich flavour, butter is undoubtedly the best, although for savoury pastries margarine gives good results. Generally the firmer block margarine should be used in preference to soft-tub margarine.

Be careful when adding the water to the dough: too much will make the cooked pastry tough while too little will make a dry dough that's hard to handle and is crumbly when cooked.

❖ Mixing Pastry ❖

Most pastries involve rubbing the fat into the flour. To do this, cut the fat into small cubes then tip them into the flour and salt. Mix them round briefly to evenly coat the exposed surfaces with flour, then using your fingertips and picking up small amounts at a time, rub the fat and flour together until the fat breaks down into small pieces. Try to do this as quickly and lightly as possible and don't use the palms of your hands or you will end up with a sticky mess.

Sprinkle the water evenly over the mixture and stir it in with a round-bladed knife. You may need to add a little more or a little less than stated in the recipe since the absorbency of different flours varies, so don't add the liquid all at once. Collect the dough into a ball and knead lightly for a few seconds. If it feels very sticky, simply sprinkle with a little extra flour.

❖ Using a Food Processor ❖

Shortcrust pastry can be made very quickly and successfully in a food processor. It's important to pulse the machine or turn it on in short bursts only so that the dough doesn't get overworked. Don't try to make too much pastry at one time, or you will overload the machine.

❖ Ready-made Pastries ❖

If you haven't the time or inclination to make your own pastry, choose from the good range of ready-made pastries now available – both frozen and from the chilled cabinet. Ready-made wholemeal and plain, shortcrust, puff, flaky and filo pastries are widely available. For real time saving look out for ready-rolled sheets of puff pastry, and before buying check the quantity required (see below).

❖ Pastry Quantities ❖

It is important to note that where a recipe specifies a weight of pastry, the quantity refers to the weight of flour rather than the combined weight of the ingredients. For example, if a recipe calls for 225 g (8 oz) shortcrust pastry you will need this amount of flour and 110 g (4 oz) fat because the correct proportion of flour to fat is 2:1.

When buying ready-made pastry remember that the weight specified on the packet is the combined weight of the ingredients and not the flour weight. As a guide, a 375 g (13 oz) packet of shortcrust pastry is approximately equivalent to homemade pastry made with 225 g (8 oz) flour. Two 375 g (13 oz) packets of ready-made puff pastry are roughly equivalent to homemade pastry made with 450 g (1 lb) flour.

❖ Rolling Out Pastry ❖

Dust the work surface and the rolling pin – never the pastry – with as little flour as possible. Roll the dough lightly and evenly in one direction only. Always roll away from you, using light, firm strokes and rotate the pastry frequently to keep an even shape and thickness. Roll it out until it is quite thin; very thick pastry is unpleasant to eat, but avoid over-rolling or stretching the pastry as you roll or it will shrink badly during cooking.

✧ Lining a Flan Case ✧

Loose-based metal flan tins are ideal because they transfer heat rapidly and pastry tends to cook better in these than in china dishes. The removable base makes it easier to transfer the baked flan to a serving plate. Alternatively use a flan ring placed on a baking sheet, a sandwich tin or a fluted china flan dish. If cooked in a china dish the flan is generally served from the dish.

1 Roll out the pastry until it is about 5 cm (2 inches) larger than the flan tin all round. Use the rolling pin to help you lift the pastry over the tin.

2 Lift the edges of the pastry so that it falls down into the tin, then gently press the pastry against the edges of the flan tin so that there are no gaps between the pastry and the tin.

3 Turn any surplus pastry outwards over the rim and trim the edges with a sharp knife.

✧ Baking Blind ✧

If a recipe instructs you to bake blind, it means that you should bake the pastry case (or cases) without any filling. The pastry may be partially cooked before adding the filling, or it may be completely cooked if the filling doesn't require further cooking.

Fully baked pastry cases will keep for several days in an airtight tin or they may be frozen.

1 Line the flan tin or dish with pastry. If you have time, chill the pastry case in the refrigerator for 20–30 minutes to rest the pastry and help reduce shrinkage during cooking. Prick the pastry base with a fork, then line with a large piece of greaseproof paper or foil.

2 Fill with ceramic baking beans or dried pulses. Small pastry cases don't need lining; it should be sufficient to prick these with a fork.

3 For partially baked cases, bake at 200°C (400°F) mark 6 for 10–15 minutes until the case looks 'set'. Carefully remove the paper or foil and the beans and bake for a further 5 minutes until the base is firm to the touch and lightly coloured. Pastry cases which need complete baking should be returned to the oven for about 15 minutes until firm and golden brown.

✧ Covering a Pie Dish ✧

1 Using the inverted pie dish as a guide, roll out the pastry until 5 cm (2 inches) larger than the pie dish. Cut a 2.5 cm (1 inch) strip from the outside of the pastry. Place on the moistened rim of the pie dish and brush with water.

2 Fill the dish generously, so that the surface of the filling is slightly rounded; use a pie funnel if insufficient filling is available. Use the rolling pin to help lift the pastry lid into position. Press the edges together to seal.

3 Using a sharp knife held at a slight angle away from the dish, trim off excess pastry. Knock up the edges and finish as desired (see right).

❖ Finishing Touches ❖

Decorative edges and applied pastry shapes look attractive. Remember to glaze the decoration as well as the pie or flan.

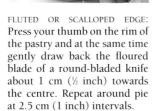

KNOCK UP: This seals the edges and prevents the filling leaking out. Press your index finger along the rim and holding a knife horizontally, tap the edge of the pastry sharply with the blunt edge of the knife to give a 'flaky' appearance.

FLUTED OR SCALLOPED EDGE: Press your thumb on the rim of the pastry and at the same time gently draw back the floured blade of a round-bladed knife about 1 cm (½ inch) towards the centre. Repeat around pie at 2.5 cm (1 inch) intervals.

CRIMPED EDGE: Push your forefinger into the rim of the pastry and using the thumb and forefinger of the other hand gently pinch the pastry that is pushed up by this action. Continue around the edge of the pie.

FORKED EDGE: Simply press all around the edge of the pie with the back of a floured fork.

LEAVES: Cut 2.5 cm (1 inch) strips from pastry trimmings, then cut these diagonally into diamonds. Use the back of a knife to mark veins.

OTHER DECORATIONS: Although leaves are the traditional decoration for pies, different shapes can be cut freehand or using cutters as desired. Holly leaves and berries are ideal for festive pies.

❖ Shortcrust Pastry ❖

This plain short pastry is probably the most widely used of all pastries. If preferred, omit the white fat and use 110 g (4 oz) butter or margarine. For shortcrust pastry, the proportion of flour to fat is 2:1, or twice the quantity. Therefore, for a recipe using quantities of shortcrust pastry other than 225 g (8 oz), simply use half the quantity of fat to the flour weight specified.

MAKES 225 G (8 OZ)
PREPARATION TIME 10 minutes
FREEZING Suitable

- 225 g (8 oz) plain flour
- pinch of salt
- 50 g (2 oz) butter or margarine, chilled and diced
- 50 g (2 oz) lard or white vegetable fat, chilled and diced

175 CALS/25 G (1 OZ)

1 Mix flour and salt together in a bowl. Add the fat to the flour. Using your fingertips, rub the fat lightly into the flour until the mixture resembles fine breadcrumbs.

2 Add 45–60 ml (3–4 tbsp) chilled water, sprinkling it evenly over the surface. (Uneven addition may cause blistering when the pastry is cooked.)

3 Stir in with a round-bladed knife until the mixture begins to stick together in large lumps. With one hand, collect the dough mixture together to form a ball.

4 Knead lightly for a few seconds to give a firm, smooth dough; do not overhandle the dough. Wrap in cling film or greaseproof paper and chill in the refrigerator for about 30 minutes.

5 To roll out the pastry, sprinkle a very little flour on a work surface and the rolling pin (not on the pastry) and roll out the dough evenly in one direction only, turning it occasionally. The usual thickness is 3 mm (⅛ inch). Do not pull or stretch the pastry.

Variations

❖ **WHOLEMEAL PASTRY:** Follow the recipe for Shortcrust Pastry, replacing half of the white flour with plain wholemeal flour. You may need a little extra water due to the absorbency of wholemeal flour.

❖ **NUT PASTRY:** Follow the recipe for Shortcrust Pastry, stirring in 40 g (1½ oz) very finely chopped, shelled walnuts, cashew nuts, hazelnuts or almonds before adding the water.

❖ **CHEESE PASTRY:** Follow the recipe for Shortcrust or Wholemeal Pastry, stirring in 125 g (4 oz) finely grated Cheddar or other hard cheese, or 45 ml (3 tbsp) freshly grated Parmesan cheese, and a pinch of mustard powder before adding the water.

❖ **SESAME PASTRY:** Follow the recipe for Shortcrust or Wholemeal Pastry, stirring in 40 g (1½ oz) toasted sesame seeds before adding the water.

❖ **POPPY SEED PASTRY:** Follow the recipe for Shortcrust or Wholemeal Pastry, stirring in 15 g (½ oz) poppy seeds before adding the water.

❖ **HERB PASTRY:** Follow the recipe for Shortcrust or Wholemeal Pastry, stirring in 45 ml (3 tbsp) chopped mixed herbs before adding the water.

❖ **OLIVE PASTRY:** Follow the recipe for Shortcrust or Wholemeal Pastry, stirring in 60 ml (4 tbsp) finely chopped stoned black olives before adding the water.

NOTE: Shortcrust pastry can be baked straight away, but it is better if allowed to 'rest' in the refrigerator for about 30 minutes before baking. Bake at 200°C (400°F) mark 6, except where otherwise specified, until lightly browned.

❖ Using a Food Processor ❖

A food processor makes shortcrust pastry very quickly and gives good results. It is most important not to overmix the dough as a food processor works in seconds not minutes. For even 'rubbing in', turn the machine on in short bursts rather than let it run continuously. Never overload the processor bowl; if making a large quantity of pastry, make it in two batches.

1 Mix the flour and salt together in the bowl of the food processor. Add the fat to the flour. Mix for a few seconds until the mixture resembles fine breadcrumbs.
2 Add 45–60 ml (3–4 tbsp) chilled water through the funnel and process briefly until the mixture forms a smooth dough. Roll out and use as for shortcrust pastry.

❖ Puff Pastry ❖

The richest of all the pastries, puff requires patience, practice and very light handling. Whenever possible it should be made the day before use. It is not practical to make in a quantity with less than 450 g (1 lb) flour weight. This quantity is equivalent to two 375 g (13 oz) packets.

MAKES 450 G (1LB)

PREPARATION TIME 40 minutes, plus 'resting'
FREEZING Suitable

- 450 g (1 lb) strong plain flour
- pinch of salt
- 450 g (1 lb) butter or margarine, chilled
- 15 ml (1 tbsp) lemon juice

270 CALS/25 G (1 OZ)

1 Mix the flour and salt together in a bowl. Cut off 50 g (2 oz) of the butter and flatten the remaining butter with a rolling pin to a slab 2 cm (¾ inch) thick.

2 Cut the 50 g (2 oz) butter into small pieces, add to the flour and rub in. Using a round-bladed knife, stir in the lemon juice and about 300 ml (½ pint) chilled water or sufficient to make a soft, elastic dough.

3 Quickly knead the dough until smooth and shape into a round. Cut through half the depth in the shape of a cross. Open out to form a star.

4 Roll out, keeping the centre four times as thick as the flaps. Place the slab of butter in the centre of the dough.

5 Fold the flaps envelope-style and press gently with a rolling pin. Roll out to a rectangle measuring about 40 × 20 cm (16 × 8 inches).

6 Fold bottom third up and top third down, keeping the edges straight. Seal edges. Wrap in greaseproof paper and 'rest' in the refrigerator for 30 minutes.

7 Put the pastry on a lightly floured work surface with the folded edges to the sides, then repeat the rolling, folding and resting sequence 5 times.

1 To make the pastry, mix the flour and a pinch of salt together in a bowl. Rub in the butter until the mixture resembles fine breadcrumbs. Stir in the Parmesan. Make a well in the centre, then add the egg and about 30 ml (2 tbsp) cold water or enough to bind the dough together. Knead lightly, then wrap and chill for about 30 minutes.

2 Meanwhile, make the filling. Cut the potato, leeks and parsnips into chunks. Bring 600 ml (1 pint) salted water to the boil in a saucepan. Add the bouquet garni, potato, leeks, parsnips and red pepper. Cover and simmer for about 10 minutes or until the vegetables are all tender, drain in a colander; reserve the liquid and make up to 600 ml (1 pint) with water if necessary. Discard the bouquet garni.

NOTE: Shape the pastry as required, then leave to 'rest' in the refrigerator for 30 minutes before baking. Brush with beaten egg before baking at 220°C (425°F) mark 7, unless otherwise stated.

❖ Vegetable Pie ❖

3 Melt the butter in a saucepan and fry the garlic for 1 minute. Off the heat, stir in the flour. Cook for 2 minutes, stirring. Gradually add the reserved liquid, then bring to the boil and simmer for 2–3 minutes, stirring. Add the Gruyère, cooked vegetables, courgettes, chives and seasoning. Spoon into a 1.4 litre (2½ pint) pie dish.

4 On a lightly floured surface, roll out the pastry to a round or oval 5 cm (2 inches) larger than the pie dish. Cut a strip from the outside edge of the pastry. Moisten the rim of the pie dish with water and position the strip on the rim. Brush with water.

5 Position the pastry lid and press edges together to seal; trim and knock up. Decorate with leaves cut from the pastry trimmings. Brush with egg. Bake at 190°C (375°F) mark 5 for 45–50 minutes until the pastry is crisp and golden brown, covering with foil after 30 minutes if necessary.

SERVES 4–6

PREPARATION TIME
45 minutes
COOKING TIME
45–50 minutes
FREEZING
Suitable

PASTRY:
• 225 g (8 oz) plain white flour
• salt and pepper
• 110 g (4 oz) butter or margarine
• 50 g (2 oz) freshly grated Parmesan cheese
• 1 egg, beaten
FILLING:
• 225 g (8 oz) potato, peeled
• 225 g (8 oz) leeks
• 225 g (8 oz) parsnips, peeled
• bouquet garni

• 1 red pepper, deseeded and sliced
• 50 g (2 oz) butter or margarine
• 1 garlic clove, crushed
• 50 g (2 oz) plain white flour
• 75 g (3 oz) Gruyère cheese, grated
• 2 small courgettes, thinly sliced
• 30 ml (2 tbsp) chopped chives
• beaten egg, to glaze

655–440 CALS/SERVING

❖ Mediterranean Tartlets ❖

SERVES 6

PREPARATION TIME
35 minutes, plus
'resting'
COOKING TIME
15 minutes
FREEZING
Not suitable
COLOUR INDEX
Page 66

PASTRY:
• 175 g (6 oz) plain white flour
• salt and pepper
• 85 g (3 oz) butter
• 45 ml (3 tbsp) freshly grated Parmesan cheese
• 1 egg yolk

FILLING:
• 450 g (1 lb) onions
• 30 ml (2 tbsp) oil
• 5 ml (1 tsp) dark brown sugar

• 50 g (2 oz) sun-dried tomatoes in oil, drained
• 125 g (4 oz) feta cheese
• 30 ml (2 tbsp) chopped basil

TO GARNISH:
salad leaves

350 CALS/SERVING

1 To make the pastry, sift the flour into a bowl with a pinch of salt, then rub in the butter until the mixture resembles fine breadcrumbs. Stir in the Parmesan cheese. Make a well in the centre and add the egg yolk with 45–60 ml (3–4 tbsp) water; mix to a firm dough.

2 Roll out the pastry thinly on a lightly floured surface and use to line six individual loose-based 10 cm (4 inch) fluted flan tins. Cover and chill for about 20 minutes. Bake blind (see page 328) at 200°C (400°F) mark 6 for about 15 minutes or until crisp and light golden brown.

3 Meanwhile peel and finely slice the onions. Heat the oil in a large frying pan, add the onions and sauté over a high heat, stirring, until they begin to brown, about 5–6 minutes. Stir in the brown sugar and cook for a further 3–4 minutes until the onions caramelise. Allow to cool slightly.

4 Roughly chop the sun-dried tomatoes, crumble the feta cheese and mix together with the onions. Divide the filling between the tartlet cases and sprinkle with chopped basil. Season with pepper. Serve immediately, garnished with salad leaves.

❖ Goat's Cheese ❖ and Watercress Tart

SERVES 4–6

PREPARATION TIME
15 minutes, plus
pastry and 'resting'
COOKING TIME
45–50 minutes
FREEZING
Not suitable
COLOUR INDEX
Page 67

• Shortcrust Pastry made with 175 g (6 oz) flour (page 329)
• 1 shallot or small onion, peeled
• 1 bunch watercress
• 25 g (1 oz) butter
• 1 garlic clove, crushed
• 175 g (6 oz) fresh soft goat's cheese

• 5 ml (1 tsp) Dijon mustard
• pinch of freshly grated nutmeg
• 2 eggs
• 150 ml (¼ pint) single cream
• salt and pepper

555–370 CALS/SERVING

1 Roll out the pastry on a lightly floured surface and use to line a loose-based 23 cm (9 inch) fluted flan tin. Cover and chill in the refrigerator for 30 minutes. Bake blind (see page 328) at 200°C (400°F) mark 6 for 15–20 minutes until set and golden.
2 Meanwhile, finely chop the shallot. Roughly chop the watercress. Melt the butter in a sauté pan and sauté the shallot with the garlic for 3–4 minutes until golden. Add the watercress and sauté for a further 1 minute until just wilted.
3 Turn the watercress mixture into a bowl and beat in the goat's cheese, mustard, nutmeg, eggs, cream and seasoning.
4 Spoon the filling into the prepared flan case and cook at 180°C (350°F) mark 4 for about 30 minutes or until puffed and golden. Serve the tart warm or cold, with a salad.

❖ Plaice and ❖ Spinach Flan

SERVES 4–6

PREPARATION TIME
25 minutes, plus
pastry and 'resting'
COOKING TIME
45–50 minutes
FREEZING
Not suitable
COLOUR INDEX
Page 67

• Shortcrust Pastry made with 175 g (6 oz) flour (page 329)
• 2 plaice, skinned and filleted, about 450 g (1 lb) filleted weight
• 300 ml (½ pint) milk
• few black peppercorns
• 1 bay leaf
• 125 g (4 oz) spinach leaves or 50 g (2 oz) frozen chopped spinach

• 25 g (1 oz) butter
• 20 g (¾ oz) plain white flour
• 50 g (2 oz) Brie, derinded and roughly chopped
• 2 eggs, size 4 or 5
• salt and pepper
• 15 ml (1 tbsp) freshly grated Parmesan cheese

620–415 CALS/SERVING

1 Roll out the pastry on a lightly floured surface and use to line a 34 × 11 cm (13½ × 4½ inch) loose-based fluted tranche tin or a 23 cm (9 inch) round flan tin. Chill for about 30 minutes. Place the tin on a baking sheet and bake blind (see page 328) at 200°C (400°F) mark 6 for 20 minutes or until just cooked through.
2 Meanwhile, halve the plaice fillets lengthways and roll up, skinned side out. Place in a saucepan into which they will just fit and pour over the milk. Add the peppercorns and bay leaf. Cover and bring slowly to the boil, then simmer for about 2 minutes or until the fillets are just cooked. Remove with a slotted spoon and dry on absorbent kitchen paper. Strain and reserve the liquid.
3 If using fresh spinach place in a saucepan with just the water clinging to the leaves after washing. Cover and cook over a gentle heat for 3–4 minutes or until wilted. Drain well. Squeeze out any excess liquid and finely chop.

4 Melt the butter in a saucepan. Stir in the flour and cook, stirring, for 1–2 minutes. Gradually stir in 200 ml (7 fl oz) of the reserved poaching liquid and bring to the boil. Simmer for 2–3 minutes until thickened and smooth. Off the heat, beat in the Brie, eggs and spinach. Add frozen spinach at this stage, stirring until evenly blended. Season.

5 Arrange the poached fish down the centre of the prepared flan tin. Spoon over the sauce and sprinkle with the Parmesan. Bake at 180°C (350°F) mark 4 for 25–30 minutes or until the filling is lightly set. Serve warm.

❖ Smoked Salmon Quiche ❖

SERVES 6

PREPARATION TIME
15 minutes, plus pastry and 'resting'

COOKING TIME
1–1¼ hours

FREEZING
Not suitable

- Shortcrust or Olive Pastry made with 175 g (6 oz) flour (page 330)
- 1 large onion, peeled
- 15 ml (1 tbsp) oil
- 125 g (4 oz) smoked salmon trimmings
- 2 eggs
- 175 g (6 oz) low-fat soft cheese
- 25 g (1 oz) fresh soft goat's cheese
- 300 ml (½ pint) single cream
- 15 ml (1 tbsp) chopped thyme or dill
- pepper

425 CALS/SERVING

1 Roll out the pastry on a lightly floured surface and use to line a 23 cm (9 inch) fluted deep flan tin or ring, about 4 cm (1½ inches) deep, placed on a baking sheet. Cover and chill in refrigerator for about 30 minutes, then bake blind (see page 328) at 200°C (400°F) mark 6 for about 20 minutes until golden.

2 Meanwhile, finely chop the onion. Heat the oil in a small pan and sauté the onion until soft and golden; cool slightly. Roughly chop the smoked salmon trimmings. Whisk the eggs and cheeses together until almost smooth, then whisk in the cream, herbs and pepper.

3 Scatter the onion and smoked salmon over the base of the flan case and pour over the egg mixture. Bake at 170°C (325°F) mark 3 for 45–55 minutes until lightly set. Serve warm or cold.

❖ Spanakhopitas ❖

SERVES 6–8

PREPARATION TIME
25 minutes

COOKING TIME
30 minutes

FREEZING
Suitable (stage 4)

COLOUR INDEX
Page 67

- 1 onion, peeled
- about 150 ml (¼ pint) olive oil
- 10 ml (2 tsp) ground cumin
- 2 garlic cloves, crushed
- 450 g (1 lb) frozen chopped spinach, thawed and well drained
- 125 g (4 oz) feta cheese, crumbled
- 125 g (4 oz) full-fat soft cheese or curd cheese
- pepper
- 400 g (14 oz) packet filo pastry, containing 48×25 cm (19×10 inch) sheets

545–410 CALS/SERVING

1 Chop the onion very finely. Heat 30 ml (2 tbsp) olive oil in a frying pan, add the onion and cook gently, until softened. Sprinkle in the cumin and stir for 2 minutes, then stir in the garlic and spinach. Remove from heat and stir in the two cheeses and pepper to taste.

2 Brush a 30×23 cm (12×9 inch) baking dish with olive oil. Place 1 sheet of filo pastry in the dish, bringing it up the sides and letting the short edges hang over at either end. Brush the pastry in the dish with oil, then layer half of the filo sheets in this way.

3 Spread the spinach and cheese mixture over the filo, then cover with the remaining sheets, brushing olive oil between them as before.

4 Trim the overhanging edges of filo, then tuck in the edges to seal. Brush the top with oil. With a sharp knife, cut through the layers to make 16 squares.

5 Bake at 190°C (375°F) mark 5 for 30 minutes. Leave to cool for about 10 minutes, then cut into the marked squares and remove from the dish. Serve hot or warm.

❖ Raised Game Pie ❖

For this impressive pie, hot water crust pastry encases a mixture of game, herbs and dried fruit. Hot water crust is a pliable dough which must be moulded while warm. The cooked texture is different from other pastries in that it is doughy inside. Make the pie the day before you wish to serve it.

SERVES 8–10

PREPARATION TIME
1¼ hours, plus
'resting' and
chilling
COOKING TIME
1 hour 55 minutes
FREEZING
Suitable (stage 9)

HOT WATER CRUST
PASTRY:
• *275 g (10 oz) plain
white flour*
• *1.25 ml (¼ tsp) salt*
• *65 g (2½ oz) white
vegetable fat*
PIE FILLING:
• *225 g (8 oz) rabbit
joints, skinned*
• *225 g (8 oz) shoulder
venison*
• *1.1 litres (2 pints)
brown stock*
• *225 g (8 oz) pork
sausagemeat*
• *½ onion, finely chopped*
• *2 garlic cloves, crushed*

• *60 ml (4 tbsp) Madeira*
• *2.5 ml (½ tsp) ground
mace*
• *salt and pepper*
• *125 g (4 oz) no-soak
dried apricots*
• *4 no-soak dried prunes*
• *2 pheasant or chicken
breasts, boned and
skinned, about 225 g
(8 oz) total weight*
• *8 large sage leaves or
5 ml (1 tsp) dried sage*
• *beaten egg, to glaze*
• *5 ml (1 tsp) powdered
gelatine*

440–355 CALS/SERVING

1 For the filling, remove the flesh from the rabbit joints, Cut the rabbit and venison into small pieces. Place in a saucepan and cover with the stock. Bring to the boil, cover and simmer for 25 minutes, or until tender; drain and cool. Reduce stock by boiling to 150 ml (¼ pint).

2 Base-line a 25×7.5 cm (10×3 inch) loose-sided pie mould with non-stick baking parchment. Mix together the cooled meats, sausagemeat, onion, garlic, Madeira, mace and seasoning. Cover and refrigerate.

3 To prepare the hot water crust pastry, sift the flour and salt into a bowl and make a well in the centre. Heat the fat and 100–125 ml (4–5 fl oz) water gently together until the fat melts, then bring to the boil and pour into the well.

4 Gradually lap the flour into the liquid, then beat together. Lightly knead against the side of the bowl until smooth. Immediately wrap the pastry in a tea towel. (If exposed to the air, it will become dry and impossible to use.) Leave for up to 30 minutes; no longer. Use warm.

5 On a lightly floured surface roll out three quarters of the pastry to an oblong 20×35 cm (8×14 inches), turning to keep an even shape and thickness. Use rolling pin to help lift pastry over the tin. (Keep remaining pastry covered on a plate placed over warm water.)

6 Ease pastry into corners and press evenly up the sides of the tin. Trim off excess pastry. Line with baking parchment and beans and bake blind at 200°C (400°F) mark 6 for 15–20 minutes, until golden brown and set. Remove paper and beans. Allow to cool.

7 Spoon half the meat mixture into the pastry case. Scissor-snip half the apricots and 2 prunes into the tin. Place the pheasant or chicken breasts end to end over the fruit. Place the sage leaves on top. Repeat the fruit and meat layers.

8 Roll out the remaining pastry to a 28 × 10 cm (11 × 4 inch) oblong and use to top the pie. Seal well, then trim and flute the edges. Make a small hole in the centre of the pie, and two more near the edge. Shape the pastry trimmings into leaf and berry shapes. Arrange on top of the pie, half covering the holes.

9 Place the pie on an edged baking sheet and glaze with egg. Bake at 200°C (400°F) mark 6 for 20 minutes, then reduce the temperature to 180°C (350°F) mark 4 and cook for a further 1¼ hours, covering the top lightly with foil if necessary. To test, insert a skewer gently through the centre hole – the meat should feel tender. Ease away the sides of the tin and bake the pie for a further 20 minutes to brown the sides. Cool.

1 Roll out pastry on a lightly floured surface to a 1 cm (½ inch) thickness. Using a 9 cm (3½ inch) pastry cutter, or a sharp knife and a ramekin as a guide, cut out 8 rounds.

2 Place on a dampened baking sheet. Using a 6 cm (2½ inch) cutter or a sharp knife, cut an inner oval or round halfway through the pastry and 1 cm (½ inch) in from the edge.

10 Soak the gelatine in 20 ml (4 tsp) water, then dissolve in the stock. Chill until beginning to set. Place the pie on a large edged plate, easing off the base gently. Gradually pour in the stock through the holes. Cover loosely, then refrigerate overnight.

3 Lightly score a lattice on the surface of the pastry. Brush the tops with egg. Chill for 30 minutes. Bake at 230°C (450°F) mark 8 for 10 minutes, then at 200°C (400°F) mark 6 for about 10–15 minutes until well risen and golden brown.

4 Cut around the lids, lift off and scoop out the soft dough inside. Return to the oven lightly covered with foil for a further 10 minutes or until dried out and crisp. Keep warm, covered, in a low oven while making the filling.

❖ Mushroom and Pepper ❖ Vol-au-Vents

Make these with ready-made puff pastry if preferred. Use two 375 g (13 oz) packets and roll out more thinly – to a 5 mm (¼ inch) thickness – to allow for the extra rise.

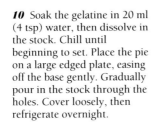

MAKES 8

PREPARATION TIME
40 minutes, plus pastry and 'resting'
COOKING TIME
30–35 minutes
FREEZING
Suitable (stage 2)
COLOUR INDEX
Page 68

- 450 g (1 lb) Puff Pastry (page 330)
- beaten egg, to glaze
FILLING:
- 2 yellow peppers
- 2 red peppers
- 75 g (3 oz) shallots
- 700 g (1½ lb) mixed mushrooms, such as chanterelles, brown cap, button
- 60 ml (4 tbsp) olive oil
- 1 large garlic clove, crushed

- 90 ml (6 tbsp) white wine
- 90 ml (6 tbsp) double cream
- 15 ml (1 tbsp) chopped tarragon or 5 ml (1 tsp) dried
- salt and pepper
- herbs and salad leaves, to garnish

770 CALS/SERVING

5 For the filling halve, core and deseed the peppers. Place under a hot grill, skin-side uppermost, until soft and well charred, about 15 minutes. Peel off the skin under cold running water. Pat the peppers dry on absorbent kitchen paper and slice thinly. Finely chop the shallots. Thickly slice the mushrooms.

6 Heat the oil in a large pan and sauté shallots and garlic for 1–2 minutes. Add the wine and boil to reduce by half. Add mushrooms and sauté for 5 minutes. Add peppers and cream. Bring to the boil and bubble for 2–3 minutes. Add the tarragon and seasoning. Spoon into the cases and replace the lids. Garnish and serve.

❖ Sausage Rolls ❖

MAKES 28

PREPARATION TIME
25 minutes
COOKING TIME
30 minutes
FREEZING
Suitable
COLOUR INDEX
Page 67

- 450 g (1 lb) Puff Pastry (page 330)
- 450 g (1 lb) pork sausagemeat
- flour, for dusting
- a little milk
- beaten egg, to glaze

230 CALS/ROLL

1 On a lightly floured surface roll out half the pastry to a 40 × 20 cm (16 × 8 inch) oblong. Cut lengthways into 2 strips. Divide the sausagemeat into 4 pieces, dust with flour and form into rolls the length of the pastry. Lay a sausagemeat roll on each pastry strip.

2 Repeat with remaining pastry and sausagemeat rolls. Brush the pastry edges with a little milk, fold one side of the pastry over the sausagemeat and press the two long edges firmly together to seal.

3 Brush the pastry with egg then cut each roll into 5 cm (2 inch) lengths. Place on a baking sheet and bake at 220°C (425°F) mark 7 for 15 minutes. Reduce the temperature to 180°C (350°F) mark 4 and cook for a further 15 minutes. Serve hot or cold.

❖ Gougère ❖

SERVES 4

PREPARATION TIME
25 minutes
COOKING TIME
45–50 minutes
FREEZING
Not suitable
COLOUR INDEX
Page 68

CHOUX PASTRY:
- 125 g (4 oz) plain white flour
- large pinch of salt
- large pinch of cayenne
- 75 g (3 oz) butter
- 3 eggs, lightly beaten
- 75 g (3 oz) mature Cheddar cheese, grated
- 30 ml (2 tbsp) chopped parsley
FILLING:
- 25 g (1 oz) butter
- 1 onion, peeled and chopped

- 1 garlic clove, crushed
- 125 g (4 oz) mushrooms, sliced
- 300 ml (½ pint) thick Béchamel sauce (page 91)
- 350 g (12 oz) cooked boneless chicken, chopped
- 30 ml (2 tbsp) chopped parsley
- salt and pepper
- 15–30 ml (1–2 tbsp) fresh breadcrumbs
- 30 ml (2 tbsp) freshly grated Parmesan cheese

780 CALS/SERVING

1 To make the filling, melt the butter in a saucepan and fry the onion and garlic until softened. Add the mushrooms and cook for 2–3 minutes until softened. Stir in the Béchamel sauce. Leave to cool.

2 To make the choux pastry, sift the flour, salt and cayenne onto a piece of paper. Melt the butter with 200 ml (7 fl oz) water in a saucepan, then quickly bring to the boil. Off the heat, immediately tip in all the flour and beat vigorously with a wooden spoon.

3 Return to the heat and continue beating until the mixture is smooth and leaves the sides of the pan clean to form a 'ball'; do not over-beat. Let cool for 1–2 minutes.

4 Gradually beat in the eggs, a little at a time, adding just enough to give a dropping consistency. The choux pastry should be smooth and shiny. Fold in the cheese and parsley.

5 Spoon the mixture around the edge of a greased gratin dish. Bake at 200°C (400°F) mark 6 for about 25 minutes until well risen and golden brown. Meanwhile add the chicken to the cold sauce with the parsley and seasoning.

6 Pile the filling in the centre of the choux ring. Sprinkle with the breadcrumbs and Parmesan and bake for a further 15 minutes or until the filling is hot. Serve immediately.

Variation

VEGETABLE GOUGERE: Replace the filling with stir-fried mixed vegetables. Sprinkle with toasted cashew nuts to serve.

PIZZAS

Fast-action dried yeast has revolutionised pizza making. It is mixed straight into the flour without any pre-blending and the dough only needs to be left to rise once. Packet bread or pizza mix also makes a good, speedy pizza base; as a guide one 284 g (10 oz) packet is roughly equivalent to a pizza dough made with 225 g (8 oz) flour. When making up the mix, substitute a little olive oil for some of the liquid to improve the flavour. Included below is a recipe for a quick scone-like alternative base that doesn't need proving.

❖ Pizza Toppings ❖

Before the toppings are added, the dough is usually covered with a layer of tomato. This may be homemade tomato sauce, canned chopped tomatoes, bottled passata or even sliced tomatoes. The golden rule here is to make sure that the tomato mixture isn't too wet or it will make the base soggy. If using homemade tomato sauce ensure it is well reduced and thick; drain excess juice from canned tomatoes. Tomato purée has an intense, almost bitter, flavour and is best avoided. If you don't like tomatoes in any form, brush the dough with a well flavoured olive oil instead.

The sky's the limit when it comes to toppings! All manner of ingredients can be arranged on the tomato base. Uncooked meat and most vegetables need to be cooked first, as they will not cook through sufficiently on the pizza. In addition to the main ingredients, don't forget flavourings such as garlic, herbs, chillies, olives and capers. Try the following suggestions:

VEGETABLE: Almost any vegetable is good on a pizza. Try steamed fresh spinach (or well drained frozen leaf spinach); roasted, skinned and sliced peppers; sliced canned artichoke hearts; or mushrooms, aubergine, courgettes or baby onions, cut into chunks or sliced and sautéed in olive oil.

SPICY SAUSAGE: Scatter sliced chorizo, chopped salami or other spicy sausage over the pizza(s) before cooking.

CHEESE: Most firm cheeses with good melting properties are suitable for topping pizzas. Mozzarella is traditional, but try Bel Paese, Fontina, Taleggio, Gruyère or Parmesan.

❖ Quick Pizza Dough ❖

MAKES 1 LARGE PIZZA BASE	• 200 g (7 oz) plain white flour	• 15 ml (1 tbsp) olive oil
PREPARATION TIME 5 minutes	• 1.25 ml (¼ tsp) salt	• 1 egg
FREEZING Suitable	• 5 ml (1 tsp) baking powder	• 75 ml (3 fl oz) milk
	• 40 g (1½ oz) butter or margarine	310 CALS/SERVING

1 In a bowl, stir together the flour, salt and baking powder. Rub in the butter until the mixture resembles breadcrumbs.
2 Whisk together the olive oil, egg and milk in a bowl. Make a well in the centre of the dry ingredients and add the liquid.
3 Stir the mixture quickly by hand until it forms a soft dough. (Cover if not using immediately – while making up the topping.)
4 Turn out the dough on to a well floured surface and knead for about 30 seconds; do not overwork. Place a lightly oiled flat baking sheet in a hot oven at 220°C (425°F) mark 7 to heat.

5 Roll out the dough to a circle roughly 25 cm (10 inches) in diameter. Place on the heated baking sheet and press up the edges. Complete and bake with your choice of toppings.

❖ Basic Pizza Dough ❖

MAKES 1 LARGE PIZZA BASE	• 175 g (6 oz) strong plain white flour	• 15 ml (1 tbsp) olive oil
PREPARATION TIME 1 hour	• 1.25 ml (¼ tsp) salt	
FREEZING Suitable	• 5 ml (1 tsp) fast-action dried yeast	185 CALS/SERVING

1 In a warm bowl, mix the flour, salt and yeast. Make a well in the centre and add 150 ml (¼ pint) warm water and the olive oil.

2 Stir the mixture by hand or with a wooden spoon until it forms a wet dough. Beat for a further 2–3 minutes.

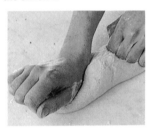

3 Turn out the dough on to a well floured surface and knead for about 5 minutes, or until smooth and elastic. Place in a bowl, cover and leave in a warm place until doubled in size, about 45 minutes.

4 Turn out the dough on to a floured surface and knead again for 2–3 minutes. Place a lightly oiled flat baking sheet in a hot oven at 220°C (425°F) mark 7 to heat.

5 Roll out the dough to a circle roughly 25 cm (10 inches) in diameter. Place on the heated baking sheet and press up the edges. The pizza dough is now ready to complete and bake with your choice of toppings.

NOTE: Each of these pizza dough recipes makes a large enough base to serve 4, if the topping is generous.

❖ Pizza Niçoise ❖

4 Make a hollow in the centre of the ingredients on the pizza and carefully crack the egg into it. Season with pepper.

5 Arrange the mozzarella around the egg. Sprinkle with Parmesan. Bake at 220°C (425°F) mark 7 for 20–25 minutes until well risen and golden. Garnish and serve.

❖ Wild Mushroom ❖ and Hollandaise Pizza

SERVES 4	
PREPARATION TIME 15 minutes, plus pizza dough	• 1 quantity Pizza Dough (page 339) • 125 g (4 oz) French beans
COOKING TIME 20–25 minutes	• salt and pepper • 1 quantity Tomato Sauce (page 93)
FREEZING Not suitable	• 200 g (7 oz) can tuna fish in brine, drained • 6 green olives, stoned • 6 black olives, stoned

- 15 ml (1 tbsp) chopped basil
- 6 anchovy fillets, halved
- 1 egg
- 125 g (4 oz) mozzarella cheese, thinly sliced
- 10 ml (2 tsp) freshly grated Parmesan cheese
- basil sprigs, to garnish

460 CALS/SERVING

1 Prepare either of the pizza doughs to the end of stage 3. Cook the French beans in boiling salted water until just tender. Drain thoroughly.

2 Knead and shape the dough as directed in stages 4–5 of your chosen recipe. Using a knife or spoon, spread the tomato sauce evenly over the surface of the dough, right to the edges.

3 Sprinkle the beans, tuna fish, olives and basil over the sauce. Arrange the anchovy fillets on top.

SERVES 4	
PREPARATION TIME 15 minutes, plus pizza dough	• 1 quantity Pizza Dough (page 339) • 1 egg yolk
COOKING TIME 20 minutes	• 150 g (5 oz) unsalted butter or margarine • grated rind of 1 lemon
FREEZING Not suitable	• 15 ml (1 tbsp) lemon juice • 30 ml (2 tbsp) chopped coriander • salt and pepper

- 275 g (10 oz) mixed wild mushrooms, such as chanterelles, trompettes-des-morts, oyster mushrooms, fairy-ring mushrooms
- 1 garlic clove, crushed
- coriander sprigs, to garnish

488 CALS/SERVING

1 Prepare either of the pizza doughs to the end of stage 3.
2 Meanwhile, place the egg yolk in a small heatproof bowl over a pan of gently simmering water. Beat well with a wooden spoon. Cut 125 g (4 oz) butter into small dice. Gradually beat the butter into the egg yolk, beating all the time; the finished sauce should have the consistency of mayonnaise. Beat in the lemon rind and juice, and the coriander. Season to taste.

3 Slice the mushrooms. Heat the remaining butter with the garlic in a sauté pan and sauté the mushrooms over a high heat for about 1 minute until just cooked. Allow to cool.

4 Knead and shape the dough as directed in stages 4–5 of your chosen recipe. Prick all over with a fork. Bake at 220°C (425°F) mark 7 for about 20 minutes, or until golden brown and cooked. Check the dough halfway through cooking; if it is rising, press down with a fork.

5 Fold the mushroom mixture into the hollandaise sauce. Spread over the cooked pizza dough, right to the edges. Place under a hot grill for 2–3 minutes, until golden and bubbling. Garnish with coriander to serve.

❖ Chorizo, Feta ❖ and Aubergine Pizza

SERVES 2

PREPARATION TIME
10 minutes
COOKING TIME
15–20 minutes
FREEZING
Not suitable

- 2 long-life pizza bases, about 22 cm (8½ inches) in diameter
- 50 ml (2 fl oz) olive oil
- 450 g (1 lb) tomatoes
- 175 g (6 oz) aubergine
- 150 g (5 oz) chorizo or other spicy sausage
- 125 g (4 oz) feta cheese, crumbled
- 15 ml (1 tbsp) roughly chopped oregano
- pepper
- oregano leaves, to garnish

900 CALS/SERVING

1 Place the pizza bases on baking sheets and brush lightly with olive oil. Slice the tomatoes and scatter over the bases to the edges.

2 Cut the aubergine into wafer-thin slices and tuck the slices between the tomatoes.

3 Cut the chorizo into chunks and scatter over the pizzas. Top with the crumbled feta and sprinkle with oregano. Season with pepper only, as feta is salty.

4 Drizzle with the remaining olive oil and bake at 220°C (425°F) mark 7 for 15–20 minutes. Serve immediately, garnished with oregano leaves.

NOTE: Vacuum-packed pizza bases make this a very quick recipe. If you have time, make your own pizza bases.

❖ Smoked Salmon ❖ and Avocado Pizza

SERVES 4

PREPARATION TIME
15 minutes, plus pizza dough
COOKING TIME
20–25 minutes
FREEZING
Not suitable
COLOUR INDEX
Page 68

- 1 quantity Pizza Dough (see page 339)
- 2 small ripe avocados
- 10 ml (2 tsp) olive oil
- 5 ml (1 tsp) lemon juice
- 150 ml (¼ pint) soured cream
- 5 ml (1 tsp) chopped dill
- 1 egg yolk
- 5 ml (1 tsp) wholegrain mustard
- grated rind of 1 lemon
- 125 g (4 oz) thinly sliced smoked salmon

TO GARNISH:
- dill sprigs
- caviar (optional)
- lemon wedges

415 CALS/SERVING

1 Prepare either of the pizza doughs to the end of stage 3. Halve, stone and thinly slice the avocados; gently toss them with the olive oil and lemon juice to prevent discolouration.

2 Whisk together the soured cream, dill, egg yolk, mustard and lemon rind.

3 Knead and shape the dough as directed in stages 4–5 of your chosen recipe.

4 Neatly arrange the avocado slices over the surface of the dough, right to the edges. Distribute the smoked salmon evenly over the top.

5 Spoon the soured cream mixture on top of the smoked salmon and spread evenly to cover completely. Bake at 220°C (425°F) mark 7 for 20–25 minutes, until well risen and the topping is lightly browned. Serve warm, garnished with dill, caviar if using, and lemon wedges.

DESSERTS

Few of us can resist something sweet at the end of a meal. No matter how full we might feel, somehow there always seems to be room for a refreshing fruit sorbet, a feather-light mousse or meringue, or a creamy, fragrant custard. Texture and weight are all-important, so always choose a dessert that balances the rest of the meal. Complement a rich, cream-based main course with a crisp and tangy fruit tart; follow a substantial stew or pie with an airy soufflé; supplement a light fish dish with a satisfying steamed pudding.

At one time season dictated choice, but now ingredients like soft fruits are available virtually all year round (at premium prices), so it is possible to serve strawberries and cream midwinter if you wish. But imported soft fruits tend to lack the flavour of home-produced summer berries, so they are generally best avoided. Instead you can opt for traditional autumn and winter fare like fruit crumble or bread and butter pudding; these old-fashioned favourites are enjoying a revival. But bear in mind that winter puddings don't have to be hearty: there are many lighter alternatives, using seasonal home-produced fruits and other readily available ingredients.

Counting Calories

It's the traditional hot puddings that have given desserts a bad name as far as weight watching is concerned. Of course, not all desserts are so fattening, and there are various guidelines you can follow to cut down on calories still further.

In summer, make fruit salads with fresh soft fruits and fragrant exotic fruits; in winter, poach apples and plums and serve as warm compotes. Don't steep the fruit in sugary syrup: instead, use natural fruit juices – preferably homemade, though there are now plenty of commercially prepared varieties to choose from; and try adding extra interest with a vanilla pod, a little grated fresh ginger, or some lemon, lime or orange rind. Leave the fruit to macerate in the juice for at least an hour before serving, to let the full flavours develop.

As a change from fruit salad, try pears poached in red wine, served warm in winter and chilled in summer. Sweeter but still fruity alternatives include sorbets, mousses and pies (pastry on top only). Serve these with low-fat crème fraîche or natural bio yogurt. (Greek yogurt is surprisingly high in fat, though not as rich as double cream.)

❖ Adding the Finishing Touches ❖

Attractive presentation can turn a simple dessert into something quite irresistible. A generous dusting of icing sugar transforms pies and pastries, while chocolate curls (shaved with a potato peeler) add texture to mousses and creams. Fresh fruits can be relied on to give a touch of colour and interest; strawberries always look good, but for something a little more extravagant try Cape gooseberries (with the papery calyxes peeled back to reveal the gleaming orange berries inside) or tiny, sparkling bundles of seedless grapes (frosted by dipping in egg white and caster sugar).

Don't forget dried fruits either: dip whole fruits in both dark and light chocolate, to create a spectacular effect. Chopped or flaked nuts are another way to add texture and colour: toast them first under the grill or in the oven to enhance the flavour.

❖ Some Key Ingredients ❖

Sugar, cream, eggs, fruit and of course chocolate all play leading roles in the creation of delectable desserts. The one thing all desserts have in common is a varying degree of sweetness.

❖ VANILLA SUGAR: One of those ingredients that's well worth keeping in the cupboard, vanilla sugar can be used to flavour not only custards and ice creams but also meringues and pastry. It adds a subtle sophistication to whatever it touches. Don't buy the overpriced commercially prepared type. Make your own at home by burying a whole vanilla pod in a jar of caster sugar; leave it for about two weeks before using. Whenever vanilla itself is called for, always use a pod or pure vanilla essence in preference to synthetic vanilla flavouring.

❖ CREAM: When choosing cream, look for real fresh cream and not sugar-loaded synthetic substitutes. Don't be misled by some of these products. Although they do contain less calories than cream, many are still high in saturated fat, and they don't taste nearly as good as the real thing. So unless you are following a strict calorie-controlled diet it's probably better to use real cream but eat a smaller portion.

❖ CHOCOLATE: Many of the most tempting desserts are based on chocolate. Don't spoil them by using cheap brands with a low cocoa solids content or, worse still, chocolate-flavoured imitations of the real thing. Instead, buy intensely flavoured, almost bitter brands with less sugar and more cocoa solids. Read the labels: look for at least 50 per cent cocoa solids. Good delicatessens offer expensive French and Belgian brands, but some of the best supermarkets now stock quite acceptable 'luxury' chocolate.

❖ EGGS: Many classic desserts – including mousses, soufflés, ice creams and sorbets – are prepared with raw eggs. Others, such as egg custards, are based on lightly cooked eggs. There is a very slight risk of salmonella if raw or undercooked eggs are eaten, which most people choose to ignore. However if you are in the at-risk group (see page 435) you should avoid these desserts.

FRUIT DESSERTS

Soft or crisp fleshed, juicy or firm, fruits make perfect desserts. Simply washed, peeled and freed from any stems, stones or cores, many make a refreshing dessert served on their own or with yogurt, cream or ice cream; others are first lightly poached in syrup, wine or fruit juice.

FROSTED FRUITS AND FLOWERS: These make a pretty decoration for fruit desserts, gâteaux and mousses. Whisk 1 egg white and 10 ml (2 tsp) cold water together to give a frothy mixture. Using a small paintbrush, brush onto small firm fruits and flowers. Dip in caster sugar, shake off any excess, then spread out on greaseproof paper. Leave to dry for at least 24 hours.

❖ Oranges in Caramel ❖

SERVES 6	• 225 g (8 oz) granulated sugar	CARAMEL CHIPS:
PREPARATION TIME 25 minutes, plus chilling	• 6 large oranges	• 75 g (3 oz) granulated sugar
COOKING TIME 25–30 minutes	• 30–45 ml (2–3 tbsp) Grand Marnier or other orange-flavoured liqueur	
FREEZING Not suitable		

265 CALS/SERVING

1 Put the sugar and 50 ml (2 fl oz) water in a saucepan and heat gently until dissolved, brushing down the sides of the pan with hot water. Bring to the boil, then boil until the syrup turns a golden caramel.

2 Immediately plunge the base of the pan into cold water to prevent further cooking. Carefully pour 300 ml (½ pint) boiling water into the pan. Reheat gently until the caramel has completely dissolved.

3 Meanwhile, thinly pare the rind from two of the oranges, taking care not to remove the white pith. Cut the rind into very fine shreds and set aside. Using a very sharp knife, remove the skin and white pith from all the oranges.

4 Add the oranges and shredded rind to the caramel, cover and cook very gently for 25–30 minutes, turning frequently until the oranges are tender; do not overcook – they must retain a good shape Transfer the oranges and syrup to a large serving dish. Add the liqueur and leave to cool. Cover and chill.

5 To make the caramel chips, dissolve the sugar in 75 ml (3 fl oz) water in a pan over low heat. Increase heat and boil rapidly, without stirring, to a rich brown caramel. Pour into a greased shallow tin; leave until set. Crush with a rolling pin and sprinkle over oranges just before serving.

❖ Peaches in Spiced Wine ❖

SERVES 6	• 450 ml (¾ pint) red wine	• finely pared rind and juice of 1 orange
PREPARATION TIME 15 minutes, plus chilling	• 2 cinnamon sticks	• 6 ripe peaches
COOKING TIME 4–6 minutes	• 3 cloves	
FREEZING Not suitable	• 45 ml (3 tbsp) caster sugar	
COLOUR INDEX Page 69		

100 CALS/SERVING

1 Put the red wine and 50 ml (2 fl oz) water into a saucepan and add the spices, sugar, orange rind and juice. Heat gently for 4–6 minutes, then transfer to a non-metallic bowl.

2 Halve, stone and quarter the peaches. Place them skin side uppermost in the spiced wine and baste with the liquid. Cover and leave to macerate in a cool place, but not the refrigerator, for 3–4 hours or overnight, stirring occasionally.

3 Divide the fruit and wine between individual serving dishes, discarding the cinnamon, cloves and orange rind. Serve with cream or yogurt.

NOTE: You could also include a few raspberries, blueberries, strawberries or redcurrants – adding them to the spiced wine with the peaches.

❖ Pears in Red Wine ❖

SERVES 4

PREPARATION TIME
15 minutes

COOKING TIME
20–35 minutes

FREEZING
Not suitable

COLOUR INDEX
Page 69

- *4 large firm, ripe Comice pears*
- *25 g (1 oz) blanched split almonds*
- *50 g (2 oz) caster sugar*
- *300 ml (½ pint) red wine*
- *2 cloves*

180 CALS/SERVING

1 Peel the pears, leaving the stalks attached. Spike the pears with the almonds.

2 Put the sugar, wine and cloves in a saucepan just large enough to hold the pears and heat gently until the sugar has dissolved. Add the pears, standing them upright in the pan. Cover and simmer gently for 20–35 minutes until the pears are just tender, basting them from time to time with the liquid. The cooking time will depend on the ripeness of the pears.

3 Using a slotted spoon, transfer the pears to a serving dish. Boil the liquid in the pan until reduced by half, then pour over the pears. Serve hot or cold with thick yogurt or clotted cream.

❖ Fragrant Fruit Salad ❖

SERVES 8

PREPARATION TIME
25 minutes, plus
chilling

COOKING TIME
5 minutes

FREEZING
Not suitable

- *2 pieces preserved stem ginger (in syrup)*
- *50 g (2 oz) caster sugar*
- *grated rind and juice of 1 lemon*
- *60 ml (4 tbsp) ginger wine*
- *700 g (1½ lb) lychees*
- *3 ripe mangoes*
- *450 g (1 lb) fresh pineapple or 425 g (15 oz) can in natural juice*
- *4 ripe kiwi fruit, peeled*
- *50 g (2 oz) Cape gooseberries, to decorate (optional)*

160 CALS/SERVING

1 Finely chop the ginger. Put the sugar in a pan with 150 ml (¼ pint) water and the lemon rind and juice. Heat gently to dissolve, bring to the boil and simmer for 1 minute. Off the heat, stir in the ginger and wine. Pour into a bowl; cool.

2 Peel the lychees, cut in half and remove the shiny stones. Peel the mangoes and cut the flesh away from the stones. Cut the flesh into cubes.

3 If using fresh pineapple, peel, slice and remove core. Cut into cubes. Slice the kiwi fruit. Add the fruit to the syrup and stir gently. Cover and chill for several hours.

4 If using Cape gooseberries, peel back each calyx to form a 'flower'. Clean the orange berries by wiping with a damp cloth. Arrange on top of the fruit salad to serve.

❖ Soft Fruit ❖
in Summer Sauce

SERVES 8

PREPARATION TIME
10 minutes, plus
chilling

COOKING TIME
5 minutes

FREEZING
Not suitable

COLOUR INDEX
Page 69

- *900 g (2 lb) mixed soft summer fruit, such as raspberries, strawberries and blueberries*

  SAUCE:
- *225 g (8 oz) redcurrants*
- *450 g (1 lb) raspberries*
- *125 g (4 oz) caster sugar*
- *60 ml (4 tbsp) Kirsch*

125 CALS/SERVING

1 First make the sauce. Strip the redcurrants from their stalks and place in a saucepan with the raspberries and sugar. Add 45 ml (3 tbsp) water and heat gently until the juices begin to run, stirring occasionally.

2 Transfer to a food processor and blend until smooth. Push through a nylon sieve to remove the pips. Allow to cool.

3 Prepare the fresh fruit as necessary and divide between individual serving bowls. Stir the Kirsch into the cooled sauce, then pour over the fruit. Chill before serving, with single cream.

❖ Red Fruit Terrine ❖

SERVES 6

PREPARATION TIME
50 minutes, plus
chilling
COOKING TIME
3 minutes
FREEZING
Not suitable
COLOUR INDEX
Page 69

- 65 g (2½ oz) caster sugar
- 250 ml (9 fl oz) medium-dry white wine
- 45 ml (3 tbsp) lemon juice
- 20 ml (4 tsp) powdered gelatine
- 225 g (8 oz) redcurrants

- 225 g (8 oz) medium ripe strawberries, hulled
- 225 g (8 oz) raspberries
- 6 mint leaves
TO DECORATE:
- redcurrant sprigs

100 CALS/SERVING

1 Put the sugar and 250 ml (9 fl oz) water in a heavy-based saucepan. Dissolve over a low heat, then bring to the boil and let bubble for 1 minute. Pour into a bowl, cool, then add the wine and lemon juice.

2 Sprinkle gelatine over 60 ml (4 tbsp) water in a small bowl and leave to soak for 2–3 minutes. Stand the bowl over a pan of gently simmering water for 2–3 minutes until gelatine is dissolved. Add to syrup; cool.

3 Strip redcurrants off stalks. Slice strawberries. Place a 1.1 litre (2 pint) non-stick loaf tin in a roasting tin containing ice cubes and cold water to come halfway up sides of tin. Place a layer of redcurrants in the tin; spoon over liquid jelly to cover. Leave to set.

4 Layer the remaining fruit in the tin, with the mint leaves. Carefully spoon over the jelly to fill. Leave the mould in the roasting tin until the jelly is just set. Transfer to the refrigerator and leave until set completely – at least 3 hours or preferably overnight.

5 Fill a large bowl with hot water. Dip the loaf tin in the water for 3–4 seconds. Immediately invert onto a flat platter, gently shaking the tin to release the jelly. Lift off the tin. Decorate the fruit terrine with tiny sprigs of redcurrants. Slice and serve with single cream or yogurt.

❖ Strawberry ❖ and Champagne Jelly

SERVES 6

PREPARATION TIME
10 minutes, plus
chilling
COOKING TIME
3 minutes
FREEZING
Not suitable
COLOUR INDEX
Page 69

- 125 g (4 oz) caster sugar
- thinly pared rind and juice of 1 lemon
- 20 ml (4 tsp) powdered gelatine
- 450 ml (¾ pint) pink champagne

- 175 g (6 oz) small strawberries or fraise du bois, hulled
- mint sprigs, to decorate

160 CALS/SERVING

1 Put the sugar, lemon rind and 300 ml (½ pint) water in a saucepan. Heat gently until the sugar has dissolved. Leave to cool, then discard the lemon rind.
2 Sprinkle the gelatine over the lemon juice in a small bowl and leave to soak for 2–3 minutes or until sponge-like. Stand the bowl over a pan of gently simmering water for about 2–3 minutes until the gelatine has dissolved. Pour into the sugar syrup and add the champagne.
3 Divide most of the strawberries between 6 serving glasses. Carefully pour over enough of the liquid jelly to cover and chill until set. When the jelly has set, pour in the remaining liquid jelly. Chill in the refrigerator for 2–3 hours or until set.
4 Decorate with the reserved strawberries and mint sprigs.

❖ Summer Pudding ❖

SERVES 8

PREPARATION TIME
20 minutes, plus
chilling
COOKING TIME
10 minutes
FREEZING
Suitable

- 175 g (6 oz) redcurrants, stalks removed
- 350 g (12 oz) blackcurrants, stalks removed
- 225–275 g (8–10 oz) granulated sugar
- thinly pared rind of 1 large orange

- 225 g (8 oz) raspberries, hulled
- 225 g (8 oz) loganberries, hulled
- 12 thick slices white bread, about 2 days old, crusts removed

250 CALS/SERVING

1 Place the redcurrants, blackcurrants, sugar and orange rind in a large saucepan. Cover and cook gently until the juices flow and the sugar has dissolved. Add the raspberries and loganberries, and continue cooking for about 5 minutes until they are softened. Remove from the heat and leave to cool.

2 Cut a round from one of the slices of bread, large enough to fit in the base of a 1.7 litre (3 pint) pudding basin. Place the round in the basin, then line the sides of the basin with slightly overlapping slices of bread; reserve the rest for the centre and top.

3 Remove the orange rind from the fruit. Spoon half of the fruit and juice into the bread-lined basin, then place a layer of bread on top. Add the remaining fruit and juice, then cover completely with the remaining bread, trimmed to fit if necessary.

4 Cover the pudding with a small plate or saucer which just fits inside the basin. Place some heavy weights on top of the plate. Chill overnight.

5 To serve, gently loosen the pudding from the sides of the basin with a palette knife, then turn out on to a flat serving plate. Serve with cream or Greek yogurt.

Variation

AUTUMN PUDDING: Replace the summer fruits with 900 g (2 lb) mixed autumn fruits such as apples, blackberries, plums. Put the fruit, 90 ml (6 tbsp) water and 50 g (2 oz) sugar in a saucepan. Cover and cook as above.

❖ Gooseberry Fool ❖

SERVES 4–6

PREPARATION TIME
30 minutes, plus
chilling
COOKING TIME
10 minutes
FREEZING
Suitable

• 900 g (2 lb) fresh or frozen gooseberries
• 90–125 g (3–4 oz) caster sugar, to taste
• 15 ml (1 tbsp) powdered gelatine

• 150 ml (¼ pint) double cream
• mint sprigs or lemon geranium leaves, to decorate

360–240 CALS/SERVING

1 Top and tail the gooseberries and place in a saucepan with the sugar and 60 ml (4 tbsp) water. Cover tightly and simmer gently for about 10 minutes until the fruit is soft and pulpy. Cool slightly, then press the fruit through a nylon sieve to remove the pips; there should be about 800 ml (1⅓ pints) purée.
2 Spoon 45 ml (3 tbsp) water into a small bowl. Sprinkle over the gelatine and leave to soak for 2–3 minutes or until sponge-like. Stand the bowl over a pan of gently simmering water for 2–3 minutes until the gelatine is dissolved. Stir into the gooseberry purée; cool.
3 Whip the double cream until it just holds its shape – it should be of a similar consistency to the gooseberry purée. Gently fold the cream through the cold gooseberry purée.
4 Spoon into serving glasses, cover and chill in the refrigerator for about 2 hours until set. Decorate with mint or lemon geranium leaves to serve.

Variations

APRICOT AND GINGER FOOL: Replace the gooseberries with apricots; add a little finely chopped stem ginger.

PEAR AND CINNAMON FOOL: Replace the stewed gooseberries with poached pears. Sweeten the puréed pears with brown sugar and a pinch of ground cinnamon to taste.

❖ Cinnamon Fruit Wafers ❖

3 To make the filling, halve, stone and thickly slice the peaches. Place the caster sugar, cinnamon and orange rind in a saucepan with 300 ml (½ pint) water. Heat gently until the sugar has dissolved, then bring to the boil. Let bubble for 2 minutes, then add the peaches and redcurrants. Simmer for 2–3 minutes or until just tender.

4 With a slotted spoon, transfer the fruit to a bowl and add the strawberries. Return the liquid to the heat, bring to the boil and bubble for 4–5 minutes or until reduced and syrupy. Discard the orange rind. Add the strained orange juice and cool.

SERVES 8

PREPARATION TIME
25 minutes, plus
cooling
COOKING TIME
15 minutes
FREEZING
Not suitable

WAFERS:
• 75 g (3 oz) butter, softened
• 75 g (3 oz) caster sugar
• few drops of vanilla essence
• pinch of freshly grated nutmeg
• 2 egg whites
• 75 g (3 oz) plain flour
FILLING:
• 6 peaches
• 175 g (6 oz) caster sugar

• 1 cinnamon stick
• pared rind and juice of 1 orange
• 225 g (8 oz) redcurrants, stalks removed
• 225 g (8 oz) strawberries, hulled
• 300 ml (½ pint) double cream
• 150 ml (¼ pint) soured cream
TO FINISH:
• icing sugar, for dusting

465 CALS/SERVING

5 Whip the double cream until it just holds its shape, then fold in the soured cream. Layer up the wafers with the cream and spiced fruits, allowing three wafers for each portion. Dust the tops with icing sugar. Serve immediately with the fruit sauce.

❖ Baked Stuffed Apples ❖

SERVES 4

PREPARATION TIME
10 minutes
COOKING TIME
45–50 minutes
FREEZING
Not suitable
COLOUR INDEX
Page 70

• 4 cooking apples, each about 225 g (8 oz)
• 60–90 ml (4–6 tbsp) Mincemeat (page 430)

• knob of butter or margarine

175 CALS/SERVING

1 Wipe the apples and remove the cores with an apple corer. Make shallow vertical cuts through the skin around each apple. Fill the centres with the mincemeat, packing down firmly.
2 Stand the apples in an ovenproof dish in which they fit snugly and pour 60 ml (4 tbsp) water around them. Top each apple with a small knob of butter.
3 Bake at 200°C (400°F) mark 6 for about 45–50 minutes, until the apples are soft. Serve with single cream.

Variation
Replace the mincemeat with chopped dates flavoured with grated orange rind and soft brown sugar.

1 To make the wafers, cream together the butter and sugar until very soft and light. Add the vanilla essence and nutmeg. Gradually beat in the lightly whisked egg whites. Fold in the flour.

2 Drop heaped teaspoons of the mixture onto greased baking sheets, allowing space to spread. Bake at 200°C (400°F) mark 6 for 6–7 minutes or until set and pale golden around the edges. Remove from the baking sheet and cool on a wire rack.

STEAMED & BAKED PUDDINGS

Steamed puddings are made by gently cooking in a bowl in a steamer or saucepan of boiling water. Follow the rules below and the result will always be soft and moist. These puddings are turned out and often served with a sauce. Baked puddings are cooked in the oven and served from the dish.

GENERAL RULES FOR STEAMING

* Half fill the bottom of the steamer with water and heat so that it is boiling by the time the pudding is made. If you do not have a steamer, fill a large saucepan with water to come halfway up the pudding basin. Cover and bring to the boil.
* Grease the pudding basin well.
* Cut a double thickness of greaseproof paper or a piece of foil to cover the pudding basin and grease well. Put a pleat in the paper or foil to allow the pudding to rise.
* Fill the basin not more than two thirds full.
* Cover the basin tightly with paper or foil to prevent steam or water entering. Secure with string and make a string handle to life the basin in and out of the pan.
* Keep the water in the steamer boiling rapidly all the time and have a kettle of boiling water ready to top it up regularly, or the steamer will boil dry. If using a saucepan, put an old saucer or metal pastry cutter in the base to keep the basin off the bottom.

❖ *Steamed Fruit Pudding* ❖

SERVES 4

PREPARATION TIME
5–20 minutes

COOKING TIME
½ hours

FREEZING
Not suitable

* 450 g (1 lb) fruit, prepared and stewed, or drained canned fruit
* 125 g (4 oz) butter or margarine
* 125 g (4 oz) caster sugar
* few drops of vanilla essence
* 2 eggs, beaten
* 175 g (6 oz) self-raising flour
* a little milk, to mix

580 CALS/SERVING

1 Half fill a steamer or large saucepan with water and put it on to boil. Grease a 900 ml (1½ pint) pudding basin and spoon the fruit into the bottom.

2 Cream the butter and sugar together in a bowl until pale and fluffy. Stir in the vanilla essence. Add the eggs, a little at a time, beating well after each addition.

3 Using a metal spoon, fold in half the flour, then fold in the rest, with enough milk to give a dropping consistency. Spoon the mixture into the prepared pudding basin.

4 Cover with greased greaseproof paper or foil and secure with string. Steam for 1½ hours. Serve with custard.

Variations

For all of these variations, omit the stewed fruit.

SUET PUDDING: Put 30 ml (2 tbsp) jam in the bottom of the basin. Mix together 175 g (6 oz) self-raising flour, a pinch of salt, 75 g (3 oz) shredded suet, 50 g (2 oz) caster sugar and 150 ml (¼ pint) milk. Cook as above for 1½–2 hours.

SYRUP OR JAM PUDDING: Put 30 ml (2 tbsp) golden syrup or jam into the bottom of the basin instead of the fruit.

INDIVIDUAL DRIED FRUIT PUDDINGS: Add 75 g (3 oz) dried mixed fruit to the basic mixture. Spoon into greased dariole moulds and steam as for Steamed castle puddings (see below).

MINCEMEAT PUDDING: Line the bottom and sides of the basin with a thin layer of mincemeat and fill with the sponge mixture. When the pudding is cooked, turn it out carefully so that the outside remains completely covered with the mincemeat.

CHOCOLATE PUDDING: Blend 60 ml (4 tbsp) cocoa powder with 30 ml (2 tbsp) hot water, then gradually beat into the creamed mixture before adding the eggs.

STEAMED CASTLE PUDDINGS: Spoon a little jam in the bottom of greased dariole moulds and two-thirds fill with the sponge mixture. Cover each mould with greased foil and secure with string. Steam for 30–45 minutes (depending on size).

❖ Christmas Pudding ❖

SERVES 10

PREPARATION TIME
30 minutes, plus
standing
COOKING TIME
8 hours, plus 4
hours reheating
FREEZING
Suitable, after
maturing

- 50 g (2 oz) each
shelled almonds, pecan
and brazil nuts
- 75 g (3 oz) carrot
- 75 g (3 oz) pitted
no-soak prunes
- 350 g (12 oz) mixed
seedless raisins, currants
and sultanas
- 25 g (1 oz) chopped
mixed peel
- 125 g (4 oz) butter
- finely grated rind of
1 lemon
- 125 g (4 oz) dark soft
brown sugar

- 2 eggs, beaten
- 50 g (2 oz) fresh
brown breadcrumbs
- 125 g (4 oz) plain
wholemeal flour
- 50 g (2 oz) plain flour
- 15 ml (1 tbsp) ground
mixed spice
- 200 ml (7 fl oz)
Guinness
- 30 ml (2 tbsp) brandy
- 30 ml (2 tbsp) black
treacle
- brandy, to flame

445 CALS/SERVING

1 To skin almonds immerse
in boiling water for 5–10
minutes. Drain, then slip off
the skins. Roughly chop all
nuts. Peel and coarsely grate
the carrot. Snip the prunes
into small pieces. Place these
ingredients in a large bowl
with the raisins, currants,
sultanas and mixed peel.

2 In another bowl, beat the
butter, lemon rind and sugar
together until light and fluffy.
Gradually beat in the eggs.
Spoon this mixture into the
bowl of fruit and nuts. Add all
the remaining ingredients, and
mix thoroughly. Cover and
leave in a cool place (not the
refrigerator) overnight.

3 Beat the pudding mixture
well. Take a piece of muslin,
measuring about 51 × 102 cm
(20 × 40 inches), and fold into
a 51 cm (20 inch) square. Dust
liberally with flour. Spoon the
pudding mixture in the centre.
Bring the edges of the muslin
over the pudding, moulding
it into a round. Tie securely
with string, leaving a length.

4 Take a large pan – ideally a
preserving pan – and lay a
wooden spoon across the top.
Tie on the pudding so that it i
suspended in the pan. Pour in
boiling water to come just
below the bottom of the
pudding. Cover pan with foil.
Steam the pudding for about &
hours, topping up with boiling
water to prevent boiling dry.

5 Drain the water from the
pan and leave the pudding
suspended until quite cold.
Remove the wet muslin and
carefully retie in clean, dry,
well-floured muslin. Overwrap with foil. Store in the
refrigerator for up to 1 month.

6 On the day, steam the
pudding for about 4 hours. If
necessary, re-shape. Unwrap
and place on a heatproof plate
Warm about 60 ml (4 tbsp)
brandy in a pan. Pour over the
pudding, then set alight. Serve
with Brandy Butter (below).

NOTE: Alternatively the pudding mixture can be steamed in
a 1.5 litre (2¼ pint) pudding basin.

❖ Brandy Butter ❖

SERVES 10

PREPARATION TIME
10 minutes
FREEZING
Suitable

- 125 g (4 oz) unsalted
butter
- 125 g (4 oz) icing
sugar
- 25 g (1 oz) ground
almonds

- 60 ml (4 tbsp) double
cream
- 45 ml (3 tbsp) brandy

190 CALS/SERVING

1 In a bowl, beat the butter until really soft, then gradually beat
in the sugar and ground almonds. Gently work in the cream.
2 Beat in the brandy, 15 ml (1 tbsp) at a time; if mixture shows
signs of curdling, beat really vigorously. Cover and refrigerate.
3 Remove from the refrigerator at least 30 minutes before serving

❖ Old-fashioned Rice Pudding ❖

SERVES 4–6	• 75 g (3 oz) short-grain	• 50 g (2 oz) caster
PREPARATION TIME	pudding rice	sugar
minutes	• 900 ml (1½ pints)	• knob of butter
COOKING TIME	milk	• stewed fruit, to serve
bout 2½ hours	• 1 bay leaf	
FREEZING	• freshly grated nutmeg	
Not suitable		375–250 CALS/SERVING

Lightly grease a 1.4 litre (2½ pint) shallow ovenproof dish. Add the rice, milk, bay leaf, sugar and a little nutmeg; stir gently.

2 Dot the surface of the pudding with a little butter. Stand the dish on a baking sheet and bake at 170°C (325°F) mark 3 for about 30 minutes. Stir the pudding mixture.

3 Return to the oven for a further 2 hours or until most of the milk has been absorbed and a golden brown skin has formed on top of the pudding; cover loosely with foil towards the end of the cooking time if necessary. Serve warm with freshly stewed fruit.

❖ Lemon Caramel Rice ❖

SERVES 4	• 50 g (2 oz) ground rice	• 30 ml (2 tbsp) lemon
PREPARATION TIME	• 600 ml (1 pint) milk	curd
0 minutes	• 50 g (2 oz) caster	• icing sugar, for dusting
COOKING TIME	sugar	
0–55 minutes	• finely grated rind of	
FREEZING	2 lemons	
Not suitable	• 2 eggs, separated	
COLOUR INDEX		
Page 71		250 CALS/SERVING

Lightly grease a 1.4 litre (2½ pint) soufflé dish.

2 Put the rice, milk, sugar and lemon rind in a pan and simmer or about 10 minutes, stirring all the time until thickened.

3 Off the heat, beat in the egg yolks then cool slightly. Whisk the egg whites until stiff but not dry and gently fold into the rice mixture. Spoon into the prepared dish. Bake at 170°C (325°F) mark 3 for about 50–55 minutes or until golden and firm.

4 Mix the lemon curd with 15 ml (1 tbsp) water to a pouring consistency. Drizzle over the cooked pudding. Sift a little icing sugar over the surface and caramelise under a hot grill.

❖ St Clement's Pudding ❖

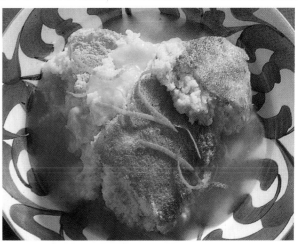

SERVES 4	• 50 g (2 oz) butter or	• 2 eggs, separated
PREPARATION TIME	margarine	• 50 g (2 oz) self-raising
15–20 minutes	• 125 g (4 oz) caster	flour
COOKING TIME	sugar	• 300 ml (½ pint) milk
About 45 minutes	• 1 orange	
FREEZING	• 2 small lemons	
Not suitable		335 CALS/SERVING

1 Lightly grease a 1.1 litre (2 pint) deep ovenproof dish.

2 In a bowl, beat the butter with the sugar and the grated rinds of the orange and 1 lemon until pale and fluffy. Add the egg yolks and flour; beat well. Stir in the milk, 45 ml (3 tbsp) strained lemon juice and 30 ml (2 tbsp) strained orange juice.

3 Whisk the egg whites until they hold soft peaks, then fold into the mixture with a large metal spoon. Pour into the dish.

4 Stand the dish in a roasting tin containing enough water to come halfway up the side of the dish. Cook at 190°C (375°F) mark 5 for about 45 minutes or until spongy to the touch.

❖ Queen of Puddings ❖

SERVES 4	• 4 eggs	• 45–60 ml (3–4 tbsp)
PREPARATION TIME	• 600 ml (1 pint)	raspberry jam or black
15 minutes, plus	milk	cherry conserve
standing	• 75 g (3 oz) fresh	• 75 g (3 oz) caster
COOKING TIME	breadcrumbs	sugar
About 1¼ hours		
FREEZING		
Not suitable		
COLOUR INDEX		
Page 71		240 CALS/SERVING

1 Separate 3 eggs. Beat together the 3 egg yolks and whole egg. Add to the milk in a bowl and mix well. Stir in the breadcrumbs.

2 Spread the jam on the base of a pie dish. Pour over the milk mixture and leave for 30 minutes, then bake in the oven at 150°C (300°F) mark 2 for 1 hour until set.

3 Whisk the egg whites in a bowl until stiff. Fold in the sugar.

4 Pile the meringue on top of the custard and return to the oven for a further 15 minutes or until the meringue is set.

❖ Bread and Butter Pudding ❖

SERVES 6

PREPARATION TIME
15 minutes, plus
standing
COOKING TIME
50–55 minutes
FREEZING
Suitable
COLOUR INDEX
Page 71

- 750 ml (1¼ pints) milk
- finely grated rind of 1 lemon
- 65 g (2½ oz) butter
- 6 thick slices white bread
- 50 g (2 oz) no-soak dried apricots
- 50 g (2 oz) sultanas
- 50 g (2 oz) currants
- 3 eggs
- 50 g (2 oz) caster sugar
- 30 ml (2 tbsp) brandy
- 2.5 ml (½ tsp) rosewater
- 15 ml (1 tbsp) demerara sugar
- 5 ml (1 tsp) ground cinnamon

360 CALS/SERVING

1 Heat the milk in a saucepan with the grated lemon rind to the boil. Turn off the heat and leave to infuse for 20 minutes. Meanwhile, butter the slices of bread and cut into triangles. Roughly chop the apricots.

2 Mix together the sultanas, currants and apricots. Place three quarters of the mixed fruit in the base of a 1.4 litre (2½ pint) shallow ovenproof dish.

3 Arrange the bread neatly overlapping on top of the mixed fruit, with the points uppermost, then sprinkle on the remaining fruit.

4 Beat together the eggs, caster sugar, brandy, rosewater and flavoured milk. Spoon the mixture over the bread and leave to soak for 5 minutes. Gently push the bread down into the custard.

5 Dust the top with demerara sugar and cinnamon. Place in a roasting tin containing enough hot water to come halfway up the side of the dish. Bake at 180°C (350°F) mark 4 for about 50–55 minutes or until the custard is lightly set and the top is golden brown.

❖ Rich Pear Sponge ❖

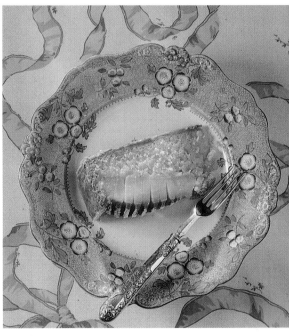

SERVES 10–12

PREPARATION TIME
15 minutes, plus
pastry
COOKING TIME
1–1¼ hours
FREEZING
Not suitable

- 1¼ quantity Shortcrust Pastry (see page 329)
  FILLING:
- 150 g (5 oz) butter or margarine
- 150 g (5 oz) caster sugar
- few drops of almond essence
- 3 eggs
- 125 g (4 oz) self-raising flour
- 75 g (3 oz) cornflour
- 5 ml (1 tsp) baking powder
- 75 g (3 oz) ground almonds
- 30 ml (2 tbsp) milk
- 3 small ripe, even-size pears
  TO FINISH:
- icing sugar, for dusting

555–465 CALS/SERVING

1 Lightly grease a 24 cm (9½ inch) round spring-release cake tin. Roll out the pastry on a lightly floured surface and use to line the tin. Chill the pastry case in the refrigerator while making the filling.

2 To make the filling, cream the butter and sugar together in a bowl until pale and fluffy. Beat in a few drops of almond essence, then add the eggs, one at a time, beating well. Sift the flours, baking powder and ground almonds together, then fold into the beaten mixture, using a large metal spoon. Fold in the milk. Spoon the sponge mixture into the pastry case and level the surface.

3 Peel, halve and core the pears. Make a series of parallel cuts across the width of each pear half, but do not cut right through. Arrange the pear halves, rounded sides up, on top of the filling.

4 Bake at 190°C (375°F) mark 5 for 1–1¼ hours or until a skewer inserted into the centre of the sponge comes out clean. Cool in the tin for 15 minutes, then carefully remove the sides of the tin. Serve warm or cold, dusted with icing sugar.

❖ Blueberry Crumble ❖

3 Spoon the crumble mixture on top of the berries and press down lightly. Bake at 190°C (375°F) mark 5 for about 30–35 minutes or until golden brown. Serve warm or cold, with custard or cream.

Variation

SPICED APPLE AND PLUM CRUMBLE: For the filling, use 450 g (1 lb) plums, halved and stoned; 700 g (1½ lb) cooking apples, peeled, quartered, cored and sliced; 50 g (2 oz) sugar and 5 ml (1 tsp) ground mixed spice. Cook the apples with the sugar and spice in a covered pan over a low heat for 15 minutes. Stir in the plums, transfer to a pie dish and continue as above.

❖ Rhubarb and Orange ❖ Crumble Cake

SERVES 8	• 125 g (4 oz) butter or margarine	CRUMBLE TOPPING:
PREPARATION TIME 20 minutes	• 125 g (4 oz) caster sugar	• 50 g (2 oz) butter or margarine
COOKING TIME 45–55 minutes	• 125 g (4 oz) self-raising flour	• 125 g (4 oz) plain flour
FREEZING Not suitable	• 2 eggs, beaten	• 30 ml (2 tbsp) granulated sugar
COLOUR INDEX Page 71	• finely grated rind of 1 orange	• 2.5 ml (½ tsp) ground cinnamon
	• two 540 g (1¼ lb) cans rhubarb, well drained	• icing sugar, for dusting

405 CALS/SERVING

1 Grease a 23 cm (9 inch) spring-release cake tin and line the base with greaseproof paper. To make the cake, beat the butter, caster sugar, self-raising flour, eggs and orange rind together in a bowl until well mixed and smooth. Spoon into the tin.
2 Spoon the rhubarb over the cake mixture. To make the crumble mixture, rub the butter into the flour in a bowl, then stir in the granulated sugar and cinnamon.
3 Sprinkle the crumble mixture over the rhubarb. Bake at 190°C (375°F) mark 5 for 45–55 minutes or until firm to the touch and golden brown. Serve warm, dredged with icing sugar.

Variations

Add a few chopped nuts or sunflower seeds, or a little desiccated coconut to the topping. Use stewed fresh rhubarb or other poached or canned fruit, as desired.

SERVES 6–8	• 900 g (2 lb) blueberries (or a mixture of blackberries and blueberries)	CRUMBLE TOPPING:
PREPARATION TIME 5 minutes	• 125 g (4 oz) plain flour	
COOKING TIME 30–35 minutes	• 45 ml (3 tbsp) light soft brown sugar	• 125 g (4 oz) butter
FREEZING Suitable, before baking	• 30 ml (2 tbsp) plain flour	• 125 g (4 oz) light soft brown sugar
	• 15 ml (1 tbsp) lemon juice	• 75 g (3 oz) rolled oats
		• 50 g (2 oz) pecan or walnut halves, chopped and toasted
		• freshly grated nutmeg (optional)

500–375 CALS/SERVING

1 To make the filling, mix the blueberries with the sugar, flour and lemon juice in a 1.4 litre (2½ pint) pie dish.

2 To make the crumble topping, sift the flour into a bowl and rub in the butter. Stir in the brown sugar, rolled oats and nuts. Flavour with a little grated nutmeg, if liked.

SWEET FLANS, PIES & PASTRIES

Fruit-filled flans and pies are an ideal way of making the most of fruits in season. For perfect results follow the guidelines for pastry-making on pages 327–330. Pâte Sucrée is the classic French rich short pastry used for sweet flans; it is thin and crisp, yet melting in texture. Flan pastry is an enriched sweetened shortcrust pastry, which is quick and easy to make. Both of these pastries benefit from being left to rest in the refrigerator for at least 30 minutes before rolling out.

✦ Pâte Sucrée ✦

Pâte sucrée keeps its shape: it shrinks very little and does not spread during baking. Although it can be made in a bowl, the classic way to make this pastry is on a flat, cold surface, preferably marble.

MAKES 100 G (4 OZ) PASTRY

PREPARATION TIME
10 minutes, plus resting
FREEZING
Suitable

- 100 g (4 oz) plain flour
- pinch of salt
- 50 g (2 oz) butter (at room temperature)
- 2 egg yolks
- 50 g (2 oz) caster sugar

255 CALS/25 G (1 OZ)

1 Sift the flour and salt onto a work surface. Make a well in the centre and add the butter, egg yolks and sugar.

2 Using the fingertips of one hand, pinch and work the sugar, butter and egg yolks together until well blended.

3 Gradually work in all the flour to bind the mixture together.

4 Knead lightly until smooth, then wrap the pastry in foil or cling film and leave to rest in the refrigerator or a cool place for at least 30 minutes. Roll out as for Shortcrust Pastry (see page 329).

✦ Flan Pastry ✦

This is made by the same rubbing-in method as shortcrust pastry, but beaten egg is used instead of water. It is usually sweetened with sugar and is ideal for flan cases and small tarts.

MAKES 100 G (4 OZ) PASTRY

PREPARATION TIME
10 minutes, plus resting
FREEZING
Suitable

- 100 g (4 oz) plain flour
- pinch of salt
- 75 g (3 oz) butter or margarine, chilled and diced
- 5 ml (1 tsp) caster sugar
- 1 egg, beaten

250 CALS/25 G (1 OZ)

1 Sift the flour and salt into a bowl. Rub in the fat until the mixture resembles fine breadcrumbs. Stir in the sugar.

2 Add the egg, stirring with a round-bladed knife until the ingredients begin to stick together in large lumps.

3 With one hand, collect the mixture together and knead lightly for a few seconds to give a firm, smooth dough. Wrap the pastry in foil or cling film and leave to rest in the refrigerator or a cool place for at least 30 minutes. Roll out as for Shortcrust Pastry (see page 329).

✦ Mince Pies ✦

MAKES 18

PREPARATION TIME
15 minutes, plus pastry
COOKING TIME
15–20 minutes
FREEZING
Suitable
COLOUR INDEX
Page 73

- 1 quantity Shortcrust Pastry (page 329)
- 350–450 g (¾–1 lb) Mincemeat (page 430)
- a little egg white, beaten, to glaze
- caster sugar, for sprinkling

145 CALS/PIE

1 Roll out the pastry on a lightly floured surface. Cut out 18 rounds with a 7.5 cm (3 inch) fluted cutter and 18 smaller rounds with a 5.5 cm (2¼ inch) fluted cutter.
2 Line 6 cm (2½ inch) patty tins with the larger rounds and fill with mincemeat. Dampen the edges of the small rounds with water and place firmly on top. Make a slit in the top of each.
3 Bake at 200°C (400°F) mark 6 for 10 minutes. Brush with egg white and sprinkle with caster sugar. Return to the oven for 5–10 minutes, until light golden brown. Leave to cool on a wire rack. Serve dusted with a little more sugar.

❖ Bakewell Tart ❖

SERVES 6
EPARATION TIME
 minutes, plus
astry
OKING TIME
 minutes
EEZING
itable

- 1½ quantity Flan Pastry (page 354)
- 60 ml (4 tbsp) strawberry or raspberry jam

FILLING:
- 125 g (4 oz) ground almonds
- 125 g (4 oz) caster sugar

- 50 g (2 oz) butter
- 3 eggs, beaten
- 1.25 ml (¼ tsp) almond essence

TO FINISH:
- icing sugar, for dusting
- toasted slivered almonds (optional)

590 CALS/SERVING

Roll out the pastry on a lightly floured work surface and use
 line a 23 cm (9 inch) shallow pie plate.

Knock up the edge of the pastry with the back of a knife and
ark the rim with the prongs of a fork. Spread the jam over the
ase. Chill while making the filling.

To make the filling, beat the ground almonds, sugar, butter,
gs and almond essence together in a bowl. Pour the filling over
e jam and spread evenly.

Bake at 200°C (400°F) mark 6 for 30 minutes or until the
lling is set. Dust with icing sugar, and decorate with toasted
monds if desired. Serve warm or cold, with cream or custard.

❖ Apple Pie ❖

SERVES 6
EPARATION TIME
 minutes, plus
stry
OKING TIME
-40 minutes
EEZING
itable
LOUR INDEX
ge 72

- 1½ quantity Shortcrust Pastry (page 329)

FILLING:
- 700 g (1½ lb) cooking apples
- finely grated rind and juice of ½ lemon
- 50 g (2 oz) granulated sugar
- 50 g (2 oz) dark soft brown sugar
- 15 ml (1 tbsp) flour
- pinch of freshly grated nutmeg

- 1.25 ml (¼ tsp) ground cinnamon
- finely grated rind and juice of ½ orange
- 50 g (2 oz) sultanas
- 15–25 g (½–1 oz) butter or margarine

TO FINISH:
- caster sugar, for sprinkling

550 CALS/SERVING

1 Roll out two thirds of the pastry on a lightly floured work
surface and use to line a 23 cm (9 inch) pie dish. Chill in the
refrigerator for 30 minutes, together with the remaining dough
wrapped in cling film.
2 Meanwhile to make the filling, peel, quarter and core the
apples, then slice them thickly into a bowl of cold water to
which the lemon juice has been added.
3 Mix the sugars, flour, nutmeg, cinnamon, lemon and orange
rinds together and sprinkle a little of this onto the pastry lining.
4 Cover the base of the pastry lining with half the sliced apples,
then sprinkle with half the sultanas and half the remaining
sugar mixture. Repeat, using all the apples, sultanas and sugar.
Sprinkle the fruit with the orange juice and dot with the butter.
5 Roll out the remaining pastry and use to cover the pie, sealing
the edges well. Slash the top twice to let steam escape.
6 Cut leaves and berries from the pastry trimmings. Brush the
top of the pie with water and position the decorations. Dredge
with caster sugar. Bake at 190°C (375°F) mark 5 for 35–40
minutes until the fruit is tender and the top is golden brown.
Serve warm, with custard or cream.

❖ Apricot and Cardamom Flan ❖

SERVES 6
PREPARATION TIME
30 minutes, plus
pastry and soaking
COOKING TIME
35 minutes
FREEZING
Not suitable
COLOUR INDEX
Page 72

- 1½ quantity Pâte Sucrée (page 354)

FILLING:
- 125 g (4 oz) no-soak dried apricots
- 6 green cardamom pods, split
- 2 bay leaves
- 150 ml (¼ pint) single cream

- 1 egg
- 1 egg yolk
- 25 g (1 oz) caster sugar

TO GLAZE:
- 60 ml (4 tbsp) apricot jam

405 CALS/SERVING

1 To begin preparing the filling, place the apricots, split
cardamoms and bay leaves in a bowl. Add sufficient cold water
to cover completely and leave to soak overnight.
2 Roll out the pastry on a lightly floured surface and use to line
a 34 × 11 cm (13½ × 4½ inch) loose-based fluted tranche tin or a
deep 22 cm (8½ inch) round fluted flan tin. Chill in the
refrigerator for 15 minutes.
3 Place on a baking sheet and bake blind (see page 328) at
190°C (375°F) mark 5 for about 20 minutes until pale golden.
4 Drain the apricots, discarding the bay leaves and cardamoms.
Cut the apricots in half and pat dry with absorbent kitchen
paper.
5 In a bowl, whisk the cream, whole egg, egg yolk and sugar
together. Arrange the apricots, cut-side down, in the pastry case,
then pour the cream mixture over them.
6 Bake at 180°C (350°F) mark 4 for 35 minutes or until the
filling is set. Place under a hot grill for 1–2 minutes to brown the
top if desired. Allow to cool slightly before removing from the
flan tin.
7 Heat the apricot jam with 15 ml (1 tbsp) water in a small pan
over a low heat. Bring to the boil, sieve, then brush evenly over
the warm flan to glaze. Serve warm or cold.

NOTE: A tranche tin is a French-style, loose-based rectangular
metal flan tin, with a fluted edge.

❖ Glazed Nut Flan ❖

SERVES 6–8

PREPARATION TIME
35 minutes, plus
pastry
COOKING TIME
35 minutes
FREEZING
Not suitable
COLOUR INDEX
Page 72

- 1½ quantity Pâte Sucrée (page 354)
  FILLING:
- 50 g (2 oz) hazelnuts
- 25 g (1 oz) pistachio nuts
- 1 egg
- 25 g (1 oz) caster sugar
- finely grated rind and juice of 1 lemon
- 25 g (1 oz) butter, melted

- pinch of freshly grated nutmeg
- 60 ml (4 tbsp) golden syrup
- 15 ml (1 tbsp) plain flour
- 75 g (3 oz) walnut pieces
- 75 g (3 oz) brazil nuts
- 50 g (2 oz) pecan nuts

665–500 CALS/SERVING

1 Roll out the pastry on a lightly floured surface and use to line a 22 cm (8½ inch) loose-based fluted flan tin. Chill in the refrigerator for 15 minutes, then bake blind (see page 328) at 190°C (375°F) mark 5 for 15–20 minutes until pale golden.

2 Meanwhile to make the filling, brown the hazelnuts under a hot grill. Place in a clean tea towel and rub well to remove the skins. Dip the pistachio nuts in boiling water for 1 minute; drain and remove the skins.

3 Using an electric whisk, beat the egg and sugar together in a bowl until very thick and pale; about 5 minutes. Quickly stir in the lemon rind, melted butter, nutmeg and 30 ml (2 tbsp) golden syrup. Fold in the flour, then fold in all of the nuts.

4 Spoon the nut mixture into the pastry case. Bake at 180°C (350°F) mark 4 for about 35 minutes or until golden brown and firm to the touch. Leave to cool for 10–15 minutes.

5 Heat the remaining golden syrup and 30 ml (2 tbsp) lemon juice together in a pan. Boil for 2–3 minutes until syrupy. Brush over the warm flan. Leave the flan in the tin for 10–15 minutes before removing to a wire rack to cool. Serve warm or cold.

❖ Pineapple Tarte Tatin ❖

SERVES 6

PREPARATION TIME
35 minutes, plus
cooling
COOKING TIME
25 minutes
FREEZING
Not suitable
COLOUR INDEX
Page 72

- 50 g (2 oz) caster sugar
- 175 g (6 oz) butter or margarine
- 2 egg yolks
- 125 g (4 oz) self-raising flour
- 125 g (4 oz) granulated sugar

- 60 ml (4 tbsp) double cream
- 900 g (2 lb) fresh pineapple
- 15 ml (1 tbsp) Kirsch (optional)
- mint sprigs, to decorate

380 CALS/SERVING

1 In a bowl, beat together the caster sugar and 50 g (2 oz) of the butter until pale and light. Beat in the egg yolks, then fold in the flour. Knead lightly to form a smooth dough. Wrap and chill in the refrigerator for 30 minutes.

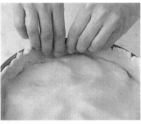

2 In a small pan, slowly heat the remaining butter with the granulated sugar until melted. Bring to the boil, then simmer for 3–4 minutes, beating continuously until the mixture is smooth, dark and fudge-like. Take off the heat, cool for 1 minute, then stir in the cream, beating until smooth. If necessary, warm gently, stirring, until completely smooth. Spoon into a 22 cm (8½ inch) non-stick sandwich tin.

4 Roll out the dough to a 25 cm (10 inch) round. Place over the pineapple, tucking and pushing the edges down the side of the tin. Stand the tin on a baking sheet.

3 Peel, core and thinly slice the pineapple. Arrange neatly in overlapping circles on the fudge mixture. Drizzle with Kirsch if wished.

5 Bake at 200°C (400°F) mark 6 for about 20 minutes or until the pastry is a deep golden brown. Run the blade of a knife around the edge of the tin to loosen the pastry. Leave to cool for 2–3 minutes then invert onto a heatproof serving dish. Cook under a hot grill for 2–3 minutes to caramelise the top. Serve decorated with mint sprigs, and accompanied by Ginger Cream (see below) or whipped cream.

GINGER CREAM: Simply stir together equal quantities of whipped cream and Greek yogurt. Gently fold in a few pieces of finely chopped stem ginger and sugar to taste.

❖ Deep-dish Apple Flan ❖

SERVES 8
PREPARATION TIME
0 minutes, plus
astry
OKING TIME
5 minutes
EEZING
ot suitable
OLOUR INDEX
age 72

- 1½ quantity Flan Pastry (page 354)
  FILLING:
- 1.4 kg (3 lb) cooking apples
- 50 g (2 oz) butter
- 75 g (3 oz) caster sugar
- 5 ml (1 tsp) ground mixed spice

- 1 cinnamon stick
  TO FINISH:
- beaten egg, to glaze
- flaked almonds, for sprinkling
- demerara sugar, for sprinkling
- icing sugar, for dusting

330 CALS/SERVING

Roll out two thirds of the pastry on a lightly floured surface nd use to line a deep 22 cm (8½ inch) loose-based fluted flan n. Chill in the refrigerator for 30 minutes, together with the emaining dough wrapped in cling film.

To make the filling, peel, quarter, core and thickly slice the pples. Put half of the apple slices in a saucepan with the butter, aster sugar, mixed spice and cinnamon. Cook, stirring, over a igh heat until the apples are soft. Remove from heat, discard e cinnamon, then add the remaining apples. Cool slightly.

Spoon the apple mixture into the pastry case. Make pastry aves from the trimmings. Arrange these interlocking in an ttractive pattern over the apple filling and brush lightly with eaten egg. Sprinkle with almonds and demerara sugar.

Bake at 180°C (350°F) mark 4 for 35 minutes or until golden nd crisp. Leave for 10 minutes before removing from the tin. erve warm, dusted with icing sugar.

❖ Pear Tart ❖

SERVES 6
EPARATION TIME
0 minutes, plus
astry
OKING TIME
5–20 minutes
EEZING
ot suitable
LOUR INDEX
age 72

- ½ quantity Flan Pastry (page 354)
  FILLING:
- 120 ml (8 tbsp) apricot jam
- 30 ml (2 tbsp) Calvados or brandy

- 30 ml (2 tbsp) lemon juice
- 7 medium firm ripe red-skinned pears, about 1.1 kg (2½ lb) total weight

415 CALS/SERVING

Roll out the pastry on a lightly floured surface and use to line 23 cm (9 inch) loose-based fluted flan tin. Bake blind (see page 28) at 200°C (400°F) mark 6 for 15–20 minutes until the pastry cooked through. Cool. Meanwhile warm the jam with 15 ml tbsp) each of Calvados and lemon juice, then sieve.

Set aside the three best pears. Peel, quarter and core the emainder, then place in a food processor with 15 ml (1 tbsp) ich of Calvados and lemon juice. Blend until smooth, then oon the pear purée into the flan case.

Peel, halve and core the remaining pears; thinly slice length-ise, leaving the stalk end intact; place on the fruit purée.

Reheat the glaze, then brush it carefully over the pears and oon over the pear purée. Leave for 30 minutes to allow the aze to set before serving. Accompany with single cream.

ariation

s an alternative, simply quarter, core and thickly slice the maining pears and scatter over the pear purée.

❖ Mille Feuilles ❖

SERVES 4
PREPARATION TIME
40 minutes, plus
pastry (if making)
and cooling
COOKING TIME
10–15 minutes
FREEZING
Not suitable

- ½ quantity Puff Pastry (page 330) or a 370 g (14 oz) packet ready-made puff pastry
  FILLING:
- 450 g (1 lb) plums
- 75 g (3 oz) caster sugar, plus 15 ml (1 tbsp)
- 1.25 ml (¼ tsp) ground cinnamon

- 300 ml (½ pint) double cream
- 1 egg white
  TO DECORATE:
- icing sugar, for dusting
  TO SERVE:
- 300 ml (½ pint) Nutmeg Crème Anglaise (page 95)

700 CALS/SERVING

1 To make the mille feuilles, roll out the pastry on a lightly floured surface to a 3 mm (⅛ inch) thickness. Using a 7.5 cm (3 inch) plain cutter, cut out 6 rounds. Using the back of a round-bladed knife, make horizontal cuts into the edges to encourage the layers to form. Place on a dampened baking sheet.

2 Prick the pastry rounds all over with a fork. Chill for about 15 minutes, then bake at 230°C (450°F) mark 8 for 10–15 minutes or until well risen and golden brown. Cool on a wire rack. Split each round into two layers to give 12 rounds.

3 Meanwhile, make the filling. Halve and stone the plums and place in a pan with 75 g (3 oz) sugar, the cinnamon and 15 ml (1 tbsp) water. Cook over a low heat until the plums begin to soften but still hold their shape. Increase the heat and reduce the liquid to a syrup. Cool.

4 To assemble the mille feuilles, whisk the cream until it just holds its shape. Whisk the egg white until stiff, add 15 ml (1 tbsp) caster sugar; then whisk again until stiff. Fold into the cream. On individual plates, layer up the pastry rounds in threes, with the cream and plums, ending with a pastry layer.

5 Sift a generous covering of icing sugar over the top of each round. Heat a skewer over a gas flame or electric ring until red-hot. Holding the skewer in a cloth or oven glove, press it into the icing sugar; it will bubble and caramelise. Use the skewer to make a lattice pattern in the sugar, reheating when necessary. Pour some nutmeg crème anglaise around each mille feuille; serve the remaining sauce separately.

❖ Peach and ❖ Nectarine Croustade

SERVES 8

PREPARATION TIME
35 minutes
COOKING TIME
About 30 minutes
FREEZING
Not suitable

- 100 g (4 oz) butter
- 50 g (2 oz) caster sugar
- 1 egg, beaten
- 50 g (2 oz) self-raising flour
- finely grated rind of 1 orange
- 6 large sheets of filo pastry
- 1 ripe peach
- 2 ripe nectarines
- icing sugar, for dusting
- 60 ml (4 tbsp) clear honey
- 30 ml (2 tbsp) lemon juice
- 30 ml (2 tbsp) pistachio nuts
- a little Armagnac (optional)

215 CALS/SERVING

1 Cream together 50 g (2 oz) of the butter with the caster sugar until very light and pale. Gradually beat in the egg. Lightly fold in the flour and orange rind.

2 Melt the remaining butter. Cut nine 25 cm (10 inch) rounds from the filo pastry sheets; keep covered with a damp tea towel. Place one filo round on a large baking sheet and brush lightly with melted butter. Add another two rounds, brushing each with butter. Spread the creamed mixture on the pastry, leaving a 2.5 cm (1 inch) clear edge.

3 Halve, stone and thickly slice the fruits. Scatter over the mixture and around the pastry edges. Cover the fruit with three more pastry rounds, brushing with melted butter between each layer.

4 Scrunch up the remaining three rounds and place on top of the pie. Drizzle the remaining butter over the top and dust with icing sugar. Bake at 200°C (400°F) mark 6 for about 30 minutes, until the filling is cooked and the pastry is golden brown and crisp, covering with foil if necessary to prevent overbrowning.

5 Heat together the honey, lemon juice and nuts. Spoon over the hot croustade and drizzle with Armagnac, if wished. Serve warm or cold, with cream or custard.

❖ Individual Fruit Flans ❖

MAKES 10

PREPARATION TIME
20 minutes, plus
pastry and crème
pâtissière
COOKING TIME
20–25 minutes
FREEZING
Not suitable
COLOUR INDEX
Page 73

- double quantity Pâte Sucrée (page 354)
- 300 ml (½ pint) Crème Pâtissière (see page 359)

APRICOT GLAZE:
- 225 g (8 oz) apricot jam
- 15 ml (1 tbsp) kirsch

FILLING:
- selection of seasonal fruits, such as raspberries, strawberries, blueberries, figs, grapes, kiwi fruit

385 CALS/FLAN

1 Roll out the pastry on a lightly floured surface and cut out ten 12 cm (5 inch) circles with a plain cutter. Use to line individual 10 cm (4 inch) loose-based fluted flan tins. Prick the bases with a fork, then chill for 30 minutes.

2 Bake blind (see page 328) at 190°C (375°F) mark 5 for about 20 minutes until golden and crisp. Allow the flan cases to cool a little in the tins, then carefully remove to a wire rack to cool.

3 To make the apricot glaze, put the jam and kirsch in a saucepan with 15 ml (1 tbsp) water and heat gently until melted. Simmer for 1 minute, then sieve. Brush the inside of each pastry case evenly with glaze.

4 Spread a generous layer of crème pâtissière in each pastry case. Arrange the sliced or whole fruit on top.

5 Reheat the remaining apricot glaze, then carefully brush over the fruits to glaze evenly. Serve as soon as possible.

❖ Profiteroles ❖

3 Beat in the eggs, a little at a time, adding only just enough to give a piping consistency. It is important to beat the mixture vigorously at this stage to incorporate as much air as possible.

4 Put the choux pastry in a piping bag fitted with a 1 cm (½ inch) plain nozzle. Pipe about 20 small bun shapes on 2 dampened baking sheets. Alternatively simply spoon the mixture into small mounds.

5 Bake at 220°C (425°F) mark 7 for 20–25 minutes until well risen and golden brown. Reduce the oven temperature to 180°C (350°F) mark 4. Make a hole in the side of each bun, then return to the oven for 5 minutes to dry out completely. Leave to cool on a wire rack.

6 For the chocolate sauce, melt the chocolate, butter, 30 ml (2 tbsp) water, the golden syrup and vanilla essence in a small saucepan over a very low heat. Stir until smooth and well blended.

SERVES 4

PREPARATION TIME
30 minutes
COOKING TIME
40–25 minutes
FREEZING
Suitable (unfilled choux buns and sauce separately)

CHOUX PASTRY:
• 65 g (2½ oz) plain or strong plain flour
• 50 g (2 oz) butter or margarine
• 2 eggs, lightly beaten
CHOCOLATE SAUCE:
• 125 g (4 oz) plain chocolate
• 15 g (½ oz) butter or margarine

• 30 ml (2 tbsp) golden syrup
• 2–3 drops of vanilla essence
TO FINISH:
• 150 ml (¼ pint) double cream or Crème Pâtissière (below)
• icing sugar, for dusting

575 CALS/SERVING

7 Whip the cream until it just holds its shape. Spoon into a piping bag, fitted with a medium nozzle and use to fill the choux buns through the hole in the sides. Alternatively simply split the buns and spoon in the cream. Dust with icing sugar and serve with the chocolate sauce spooned over.

1 To make the choux pastry, sift the flour onto a plate or piece of paper. Put the butter and 150 ml (¼ pint) water in a saucepan. Heat gently until the butter has melted, then bring to the boil. Remove pan from heat and immediately tip in the flour. Beat thoroughly with a wooden spoon.

2 Continue beating over a low heat until the mixture is smooth and forms a ball in the centre of the pan (take care not to overbeat or the mixture will become fatty). Remove from the heat and leave to cool for 1–2 minutes.

CRÈME PÂTISSIÈRE: Heat 300 ml (½ pint) milk with a split vanilla pod almost to the boil; set aside to infuse. Whisk 3 egg yolks and 50 g (2 oz) caster sugar together in a bowl until pale and thick. Whisk in 30 ml (2 tbsp) each plain flour and cornflour. Strain in milk, whisking constantly. Return to pan, bring to the boil and cook, whisking, for 2–3 minutes until thickened. Pour into a bowl and cool, with a circle of damp greaseproof paper on top to prevent a skin forming. When cool, fold in 1 stiffly whisked egg white.

CHEESECAKES

Cheesecakes are made from full-fat or low-fat soft cheese, curd cheese or cottage cheese. Full-fat soft cheese gives a superbly smooth texture. Low-fat soft cheese is an alternative, but will not give such a rich texture and flavour. Curd cheese has the most pronounced flavour; its texture is slightly grainy. Cottage cheese is lighter, but has a lumpy texture, mild flavour and is rather moist; it is best sieved and drained of any excess whey before it is added to the mixture.

Both baked and chilled gelatine-set cheesecakes are best made in spring-release cake tins to ease turning out. If you do not have a spring-release tin, a loose-based cake tin works almost as well.

❖ Baked Cheesecake ❖ with Red Fruit Sauce

SERVES 8

PREPARATION TIME
25 minutes, plus chilling
COOKING TIME
About 1 hour
FREEZING
Suitable (undecorated cheesecake and sauce separately)
COLOUR INDEX
Page 73

BASE:
• *175 g (6 oz) digestive biscuits, crushed*
• *50 g (2 oz) ground almonds*
• *75 g (3 oz) butter or margarine, melted*
FILLING:
• *225 g (8 oz) full-fat soft cheese*
• *225 g (8 oz) curd cheese or well-drained cottage cheese*
• *60 ml (4 tbsp) double cream*
• *2 eggs, separated*
• *1 egg yolk*
• *15 ml (1 tbsp) cornflour*
• *finely grated rind and juice of 3 lemons*

• *125 g (4 oz) caster sugar*
SAUCE:
• *350 g (12 oz) strawberries, hulled*
• *350 g (12 oz) raspberries, hulled*
• *40 g (1½ oz) icing sugar*
• *90 ml (6 tbsp) orange-flavoured liqueur or fresh orange juice*
TO DECORATE:
• *whipped cream*
• *frosted rose petals (see page 344) or raspberries*
• *icing sugar, for dusting*

495 CALS/SERVING

3 Whisk the egg whites until stiff but not dry. Whisk in 30 ml (2 tbsp) of the caster sugar, then whisk again until stiff and shiny. Fold in the remaining caster sugar. Gently fold the egg whites into the cheese mixture.

4 Spoon into the tin and spread evenly. Sprinkle the remaining biscuit mixture on top. Bake at 180°C (350°F) mark 4 for 1 hour or until a skewer inserted into the centre comes out clean; cover with foil if necessary during cooking. Leave to cool in the tin. Chill for at least 1 hour.

5 To make the sauce, blend the fruit, icing sugar and liqueur together in a blender or food processor. Sieve to remove pips. Chill. Carefully remove the tin from the sides of the cheesecake, then transfer to a flat serving plate. Decorate with whipped cream and rose petals or raspberries. Dust with icing sugar and serve with the chilled red fruit sauce.

❖ Hot Chocolate Cheesecake ❖

SERVES 8–10

PREPARATION TIME
25 minutes
COOKING TIME
1½ hours
FREEZING
Not suitable
COLOUR INDEX
Page 73

CHOCOLATE PASTRY:
• *150 g (5 oz) plain flour*
• *75 g (3 oz) butter or margarine*
• *30 ml (2 tbsp) cocoa powder, sifted*
• *30 ml (2 tbsp) caster sugar*
• *25 g (1 oz) ground hazelnuts*
• *1 egg yolk*
FILLING:
• *2 eggs, separated*
• *75 g (3 oz) caster sugar*

• *350 g (12 oz) curd cheese*
• *40 g (1½ oz) ground hazelnuts*
• *150 ml (¼ pint) double cream*
• *25 g (1 oz) cocoa powder, sifted*
• *10 ml (2 tsp) dark rum*
• *icing sugar, for dusting*

405–325 CALS/SERVING

1 Grease the base and sides of a 20 cm (8 inch) spring-release cake tin and line with greaseproof paper. To make the base, stir the crushed biscuits and ground almonds into the melted butter and blend well. Press half the mixture into the base of the prepared tin.

2 To make the filling, blend the cheeses, double cream, the 3 egg yolks, cornflour, lemon rind and 60 ml (4 tbsp) lemon juice together in a blender or food processor, then transfer to a bowl. Alternatively, beat the ingredients together in a bowl until smooth.

1 Grease a 20 cm (8 inch) loose-based cake tin. To make the chocolate pastry, put the flour in a bowl and rub in the butter until the mixture resembles fine breadcrumbs. Stir in the cocoa powder, sugar and hazelnuts. Add the egg yolk and sufficient water to give a soft dough.

Roll out the pastry on a lightly floured work surface and use to line the prepared tin. Chill while making the filling.

To make the filling, whisk the egg yolks and sugar together in a bowl until thick enough to leave a trail on the surface when the whisk is lifted. Whisk in the curd cheese, ground hazelnuts, cream, cocoa powder and rum until blended.

Whisk the egg whites until stiff, then fold into the cheese mixture. Pour into the pastry case and fold the edges of the pastry over the filling.

Bake at 170°C (325°F) mark 3 for 1½ hours until risen and just firm to the touch. Carefully remove from the tin and dust icing sugar over the top. Serve while still hot.

❖ Lemon Cheesecake ❖

2 To make the filling, make up the juice from the lemons to 150 ml (¼ pint) with water. Sprinkle the gelatine over the lemon juice and water in a bowl and leave to soak for 2–3 minutes. Place the bowl over a pan of simmering water until the gelatine is dissolved. Leave to cool slightly.

3 Whisk the cheese, yogurt and honey together in a bowl. Stir in the grated lemon rind and dissolved gelatine. Whisk the egg whites until stiff, then fold into the mixture. Pour into the tin and level the surface. Chill for at least 4 hours until set. Remove cheesecake from tin and decorate with lemon rind to serve.

❖ Raspberry Cheesecake ❖

SERVES 10–12

PREPARATION TIME
25 minutes, plus
chilling
FREEZING
Not suitable
COLOUR INDEX
Page 73

BASE:
• 25 g (1 oz) blanched almonds
• 225 g (8 oz) almond butter biscuits, crushed
• 100 g (4 oz) butter or margarine, melted
• few drops of almond essence
FILLING:
• 450 g (1 lb) raspberries

• 300 ml (½ pint) Greek yogurt
• 150 g (5 oz) low-fat soft cheese
• 15 ml (1 tbsp) powdered gelatine
• 2 egg whites
• 50 g (2 oz) icing sugar
TO DECORATE:
• mint leaves

275–230 CALS/SERVING

1 Grease a 2.5 litre (4 pint) loose-based heart-shaped cake tin or a 22 cm (8½ inch) spring-release cake tin.

2 To make the base, lightly toast the almonds, then finely chop. Mix with the biscuits and butter. Add the almond essence. Spoon the mixture into the base of the prepared tin and pack down with the back of a spoon. Chill while making the filling.

3 To make the filling, purée 225 g (8 oz) of the raspberries in a blender or food processor, then press through a sieve. Pour three quarters of the purée into a bowl and reserve. Return the remaining purée to the blender or processor, add the yogurt and cheese and process until well blended. Transfer to a bowl.

4 Sprinkle the gelatine over 30 ml (2 tbsp) water in a small bowl and leave to soak for 2–3 minutes. Place the bowl over a pan of simmering water until the gelatine is dissolved.

5 In a bowl, whisk the egg whites with the icing sugar until very thick and shiny. Fold into the cheese mixture.

6 Arrange half of the reserved raspberries over the biscuit base. Pour the cheese mixture into the tin. Spoon in reserved purée and swirl with a knife to make a marbled pattern. Sprinkle with the remaining raspberries. Chill for 3–4 hours or until set. To serve, carefully remove from the tin and top with mint leaves.

SERVES 6

PREPARATION TIME
5 minutes, plus
chilling
FREEZING
suitable

BASE:
• 175 g (6 oz) digestive biscuits, crushed
• 75 g (3 oz) butter or margarine, melted
FILLING:
• finely grated rind and juice of 2 lemons
• 15 ml (1 tbsp) powdered gelatine
• 225 g (8 oz) low-fat soft cheese

• 150 ml (¼ pint) natural yogurt
• 60 ml (4 tbsp) clear honey
• 2 egg whites
TO DECORATE:
• shredded lemon rind, blanched

315 CALS/SERVING

1 Grease a 20 cm (8 inch) spring-release cake tin. To make the base, stir the crushed biscuits into the melted butter and mix well. Press the mixture over the base of the prepared tin. Chill to set while making the filling.

MERINGUES

The light, crisp texture of meringues is the perfect foil to creamy fillings and soft fruit. Meringues are made with whisked egg whites into which sugar is incorporated.

To make a meringue suisse, the egg whites must be whisked until they are very stiff and will hold an unwavering peak. The sugar can then be whisked in a little at a time; or part whisked, part folded into the whites.

To make meringue cuite, the unwhisked egg whites and sugar are put in a bowl, then whisked over a pan of gently simmering water until stiff and thick. As soon as the mixture becomes thick, the bowl should be removed from the heat. This meringue has a smooth texture and wonderful gloss. It also holds its shape well.

❖ Meringues with Grand ❖ Marnier and Chocolate Sauce

SERVES 8

PREPARATION TIME
35 minutes, plus cooling
COOKING TIME
About 2 hours
FREEZING
Suitable (unfilled meringues and sauce separately)

MERINGUES:
• 4 egg whites
• 225 g (8 oz) caster sugar
FILLING AND SAUCE:
• 150 g (5 oz) sultanas, roughly chopped
• 45 ml (3 tbsp) Grand Marnier or Cointreau

• 300 ml (½ pint) double cream
• 200 g (7 oz) plain chocolate
• icing sugar, for dusting

485 CALS/SERVING

1 Put the sultanas and Grand Marnier in a small bowl, and leave to soak for at least 4 hours. To make the meringues, line 2 baking sheets with non-stick baking parchment. Whisk the egg whites in a bowl until stiff. Whisk in 25 g (1 oz) sugar, keeping the mixture stiff, then fold in the remaining sugar.

2 Spoon the meringue into a piping bag fitted with a 1 cm (½ inch) plain nozzle and pipe ovals onto the prepared baking sheets, making about 32 meringues. Bake at 100°C (200°F) mark low for about 2 hours or until the meringues are well dried out; switch the baking trays around halfway through the cooking time. Cool on wire racks.

3 About 2 hours before serving, whip all but 45 ml (3 tbsp) of the cream in a bowl until it holds its shape, then fold in the sultanas and Grand Marnier. Sandwich the meringues together with the cream mixture and pile into a serving dish. Grate over a little chocolate and dust with icing sugar. Cover and chill until required.

4 To make the sauce, break the remaining chocolate into a saucepan and add the cream and 150 ml (¼ pint) water. Warm gently until chocolate melts, stirring occasionally. Simmer gently for about 3 minutes, stirring frequently, until slightly thickened. Serve with the meringues.

❖ Brown Sugar and ❖ Hazelnut Meringues

MAKES 18

PREPARATION TIME
30 minutes, plus cooling
COOKING TIME
2–3 hours
FREEZING
Suitable (unfilled)
COLOUR INDEX
Page 74

MERINGUES:
• 25 g (1 oz) hazelnuts
• 3 egg whites
• 175 g (6 oz) light soft brown sugar

FILLING:
• 300 ml (½ pint) ice cream or whipping cream, whipped

110 CALS/MERINGUE

1 Line 2 large baking sheets with non-stick baking parchment. Toast the hazelnuts under the grill until golden brown. Tip onto a clean tea towel and rub off the loose skins. Chop roughly.
2 Whisk the egg whites in a bowl until stiff. Whisk in the sugar, 15 ml (1 tbsp) at a time. Spoon the meringue mixture into a piping bag fitted with a large star nozzle and pipe about 36 small swirls on the prepared baking sheets. Sprinkle with the nuts.
3 Bake at 110°C (225°F) mark ¼ for 2–3 hours or until dry; swap the positions of the sheets halfway through cooking. Let cool.
4 Sandwich the meringues together in pairs with ice cream or whipped cream to serve.

❖ Meringue Basket ❖

4 Use the remaining egg white and sugar to make the meringue as before. Remove the cooked meringue rings from the paper and layer up on the base, piping a ring of fresh meringue between each. Return to the oven for a further 1½–2 hours.

5 Leave to cool, then peel off the base paper. Place on a flat serving plate. To make the filling, lightly whip the cream and fold in the kirsch. Spoon half into the meringue basket and cover with fruit. Top with the remaining cream and fruit. Serve as soon as possible.

Variation

INDIVIDUAL MERINGUE BASKETS: Prepare the baking sheets as above, but draw eight 10 cm (4 inch) circles on the paper. Make the meringue as above, using 3 egg whites and 175 g (6 oz) icing sugar. Pipe a continuous coil of meringue on each circle to make the bases, then pipe a ring on top of each circle. Bake as in step 3 above for 2½ hours to dry out.

SERVES 6–8

PREPARATION TIME
35 minutes, plus
cooling
COOKING TIME
4–5 hours
FREEZING
Suitable (unfilled)

MERINGUE:
• 4 egg whites
• 225 g (8 oz) icing sugar, sifted
FILLING:
• 300 ml (½ pint) whipping cream

• 30 ml (2 tbsp) kirsch
• 450 g (1 lb) prepared fresh fruit in season, such as strawberries, raspberries and blueberries

375–280 CALS/SERVING

1 Line 3 baking sheets with non-stick baking parchment and draw a 19 cm (7½ inch) circle on each. Turn the paper over so that the pencilled circle does not come into contact with the meringues.

2 To make the meringue, place 3 egg whites and 175 g (6 oz) of the icing sugar in a large bowl set over a pan of simmering water. Whisk until the mixture stands in stiff peaks; do not allow the bowl to get too hot or the meringue will crust around the edges.

3 Using a piping bag fitted with a large star nozzle, pipe rings of meringue inside two of the circles. From the centre, pipe a continuous coil of meringue on the third circle, for the base. Bake at 100°C (200°F) mark low for 2½–3 hours until dry; swap the positions to ensure even cooking.

❖ Snow Eggs ❖

SERVES 6

PREPARATION TIME
25 minutes, plus
chilling
COOKING TIME
30 minutes
FREEZING
Not suitable
COLOUR INDEX
Page 74

• 10 ml (2 tsp) coffee beans
• 3 eggs, separated
• 75 g (3 oz) caster sugar
• 450 ml (¾ pint) milk

• 50 g (2 oz) milk chocolate
• 30 ml (2 tbsp) whisky
• blackberries, to decorate (optional)

200 CALS/SERVING

1 Toast the coffee beans under the grill for a few minutes.

2 To make the meringue, whisk the egg whites until stiff but not dry. Add half the sugar and continue whisking until the mixture is firm and shiny.

3 Put the milk in a large deep frying pan. Bring to the boil, then reduce the heat to a gentle simmer. Drop five or six spoonfuls of the meringue mixture into the milk and poach for about 5 minutes, turning once. Remove with a slotted spoon and drain on absorbent kitchen paper. Repeat until all the mixture is used: there should be about 18 meringues.

4 Whisk the egg yolks and remaining sugar into the poaching milk, then add the coffee beans. Stir over a very gentle heat for 10–12 minutes or until slightly thickened, making sure it does not boil. Strain the coffee custard into a serving dish and arrange the meringues on top.

5 Melt the chocolate with 15 ml (1 tbsp) water in a heatproof bowl over a pan of hot water until smooth, then stir in the whisky. Drizzle over the meringues. Chill for 15–20 minutes before serving, decorated with blackberries if wished.

❖ Pavlova ❖

1 Roll out the pastry on a lightly floured surface and use to line a 23 cm (9 inch) fluted flan tin. Prick the base with a fork. Chill for 30 minutes.

2 Bake blind (see page 328) at 190°C (375°F) mark 5 for 25–30 minutes until cooked and lightly browned. Meanwhile to make the filling, put the lemon rind and 600 ml (1 pint) water in a saucepan. Bring to the boil, remove from the heat and leave to stand for 30 minutes.

SERVES 8	MERINGUE:	• 2 kiwi fruit

PREPARATION TIME
30 minutes, plus cooling
COOKING TIME
1¼–1½ hours
FREEZING
Not suitable

MERINGUE:
• *3 egg whites*
• *175 g (6 oz) caster sugar*
• *5 ml (1 tsp) cornflour*
• *5 ml (1 tsp) vinegar*
• *2.5 ml (½ tsp) vanilla essence*
FILLING:
• *2 passion fruit*

• *2 kiwi fruit*
• *225 g (8 oz) strawberries*
• *225 g (8 oz) fresh pineapple*
• *300 ml (½ pint) double cream or Greek yogurt and double cream, mixed*

220 CALS/SERVING

1 Line a baking sheet with non-stick baking parchment.
2 To make the meringue, whisk the egg whites in a large bowl until stiff. Whisk in the sugar a third at a time, whisking well between each addition until stiff and very shiny. Fold in the cornflour, vinegar and vanilla essence.
3 Pile the meringue in a 23 cm (9 inch) round onto the baking sheet, making sure there is a substantial hollow in the centre.
4 Bake at 130°C (250°F) mark ½ for 1¼–1½ hours or until pale brown and dry but a little soft in the centre; press lightly with a finger to test. Leave to cool slightly, then peel off the paper. At this stage the meringue will probably crack and sink a little.
5 To make the filling, halve the passion fruit and scoop out the pulp. Peel and slice the kiwi fruit. Halve the strawberries. Slice the pineapple, discard skin and core, and chop the flesh. Whip cream until thick and, if using, mix with the yogurt. Spoon onto the Pavlova and top with the fruit. Serve as soon as possible.

3 Discard the lemon rind, then stir in the lemon juice. Blend the cornflour with a little of the lemon liquid to form a smooth paste, pour it into the pan and stir well. Bring the lemon mixture to the boil, stirring continuously. Reduce the heat and cook, stirring, until thickened. Remove from the heat. Stir in the sugar to taste, then beat in the egg yolks. Pour the lemon filling into the pastry case.

4 To make the meringue, whisk the egg whites in a bowl until stiff but not dry. Gradually whisk in the sugar, a little at a time, whisking well between each addition, until very stiff and shiny.

❖ Lemon Meringue Pie ❖

SERVES 6–8	• *1 quantity Pâte Sucrée*	• *3 egg yolks*

PREPARATION TIME
20 minutes, plus pastry and cooling
COOKING TIME
30–40 minutes
FREEZING
Not suitable
COLOUR INDEX
Page 74

• *1 quantity Pâte Sucrée (page 354)*
FILLING:
• *finely pared rind and juice of 2–3 lemons*
• *65 g (2½ oz) cornflour*
• *50–75 g (2–3 oz) caster sugar*

• *3 egg yolks*
MERINGUE:
• *3 egg whites*
• *175 g (6 oz) caster sugar*

395–295 CALS/SERVING

5 Spoon the meringue over the filling and shape into swirls with a palette knife. Bake in the oven at 190°C (375°F) mark 5 for 5–10 minutes until very lightly browned. Leave to cool before serving.

❖ Hazelnut Meringue Gâteau ❖

SERVES 6-8

PREPARATION TIME
30 minutes, plus
cooling
COOKING TIME
1½ hours
FREEZING
Suitable (meringue
rounds only)
COLOUR INDEX
Page 74

MERINGUE:
• 50 g (2 oz) hazelnuts
• 3 egg whites
• 175 g (6 oz) caster
sugar
FILLING:
• 300 ml (½ pint) double
cream
• 350 g (12 oz)
raspberries, hulled

TO FINISH:
• icing sugar, for dusting
• finely chopped
pistachio nuts, to
decorate

415-310 CALS/SERVING

5 Arrange the raspberries on
top of the cream, then place
the second meringue on top.
Sift icing sugar over the top of
the gâteau, then sprinkle
with the nuts. Serve the gâteau
as soon as possible.

1 Line 2 baking sheets with
non-stick baking parchment,
then draw a 20 cm (8 inch)
circle on each one, using a
plate as a guide. Turn the
paper over. Toast the
hazelnuts under the grill.
Turn onto a clean tea towel
and rub off the loose skins,
then chop finely.

2 To make the meringue,
whisk the egg whites in a bowl
until stiff but not dry.
Gradually whisk in the sugar,
a little at a time, whisking well
between each addition until
stiff and very shiny. Carefully
fold in the chopped hazelnuts.

3 Divide the meringue
equally between the prepared
baking sheets, then spread
neatly into rounds. With a
palette knife, mark the top of
one of the rounds into swirls –
this will be the top meringue.
Bake at 140°C (275°F) mark 1
for about 1½ hours until dry;
switch the baking sheets
around halfway through to
ensure even cooking. Turn the
oven off, and allow the
meringues to cool in the oven.

4 To make the filling, whip
the cream until it will hold
soft peaks. Carefully remove
the meringues from the
baking paper. Place the
smooth meringue round on a
large flat serving plate, then
spread with the cream.

❖ Chocolate Chestnut Vacherin ❖

SERVES 10

PREPARATION TIME
35 minutes, plus
cooling
COOKING TIME
1¼-1½ hours
FREEZING
Suitable (meringue
rounds only)

MERINGUE:
• 75 g (3 oz) hazelnuts
• 6 egg whites
• 350 g (12 oz) caster
sugar
FILLING AND TOPPING:
• 175 g (6 oz) plain
chocolate, in pieces

• 500 g (1.1 lb) can
sweetened chestnut purée
• 400 ml (14 fl oz)
double cream
• cocoa powder, for
dusting

505 CALS/SERVING

1 Line 3 baking sheets with non-stick baking parchment and
draw a 20 cm (8 inch) circle on each. Turn the paper over. Toast
the hazelnuts under the grill. Turn onto a clean tea towel and
rub off the loose skins, then grind to a coarse powder.
2 In a bowl, whisk the egg whites until stiff, then gradually
whisk in the sugar a little at a time, whisking well until the
meringue is stiff and shiny. Very lightly fold in the hazelnuts.
3 Divide the meringue equally between the marked circles and
spread neatly into rounds. Bake at 140°C (275°F) mark 1 for
1¼-1½ hours or until dried out. Change the positions of the
baking sheets during cooking so the meringues cook evenly.
Leave to cool, then carefully remove the lining papers.
4 To make the filling, melt the chocolate in a heatproof bowl set
over a pan of hot water. Soften the chestnut purée in a bowl and
stir in the melted chocolate. Lightly whip the cream until soft
peaks form and fold three quarters into the chestnut mixture.
5 To assemble the vacherin, sandwich the meringues together
with a little of the chestnut cream; cover the top and sides with
the remainder. Spread the remaining whipped cream thinly on
top of the gâteau and dust with cocoa powder to serve.

SOUFFLÉS & MOUSSES

A hot soufflé always looks spectacular. It's made by combining a flavoured sauce or purée with whisked egg whites. The air trapped within the egg whites expands on heating causing the soufflé to rise dramatically. A cold soufflé is really a mousse set high in a soufflé dish with gelatine. For soufflés and mousses follow these guidelines:

❖ Make sure egg whites are whisked in a clean, dry bowl. Any trace of fat, egg yolk or moisture will adversely affect whisking.
❖ Don't overwhisk the egg whites. They should just flop over at the tip when ready to fold in.
❖ Don't open the oven door while a soufflé is cooking. Towards the end, check it in the oven, gently opening and closing the door.
❖ For a cold soufflé the preparation of the dish is important. Do not tie the collar so tightly as to flute the paper.
❖ For gelatine-set cold soufflés and mousses, before adding the gelatine make sure it is properly dissolved in a little liquid. Sprinkle the gelatine into the liquid (not the other way round). Leave to soak for 2–3 minutes until sponge-like, then dissolve over a pan of simmering water until transparent. Always add gelatine to a mixture which is at room temperature or lukewarm. If added to a cold mixture it will set on contact in fine threads.

❖ Kirsch and Almond Soufflés ❖

SERVES 6	• 50 g (2 oz) amaretti biscuits	• 50 g (2 oz) caster sugar
PREPARATION TIME 25 minutes COOKING TIME 15–20 minutes FREEZING Not suitable	• 450 g (1 lb) ripe plums • 120 ml (8 tbsp) Kirsch • 50 g (2 oz) butter • 40 g (1½ oz) plain flour • 300 ml (½ pint) milk	• 50 g (2 oz) ground almonds • 5 eggs, size 2, separated

360 CALS/SERVING

1 Grease six 300 ml (½ pint) soufflé dishes. Roughly crush the biscuits; sprinkle three quarters over the insides of the dishes.
2 Halve, stone and slice the plums and sprinkle with 30 ml (2 tbsp) Kirsch. Divide between the dishes.
3 Melt the butter in a large saucepan. Stir in the flour and cook for 1 minute. Off the heat, gradually blend in the milk. Bring to the boil, stirring, and cook for 1–2 minutes, stirring. Cool slightly. Beat in the sugar, ground almonds and remaining 90 ml (6 tbsp) Kirsch. Beat in the egg yolks one at a time.

4 Whisk the egg whites until they stand in soft peaks. Beat one spoonful into the sauce mixture to lighten it, then carefully fold in the remaining egg whites.
5 Gently pour the soufflé mixture into the prepared dishes and sprinkle the remaining crushed biscuits on top.
6 Bake at 190°C (375°F) mark 5 for 15–20 minutes or until golden and just firm to the touch. Serve at once.

❖ Hot Chocolate Soufflé ❖

SERVES 4	• 75 g (3 oz) plain chocolate, in pieces	• 5 eggs, size 2, separated
PREPARATION TIME 20 minutes COOKING TIME 35–45 minutes FREEZING Not suitable COLOUR INDEX Page 75	• 300 ml (½ pint) milk, plus 15 ml (1 tbsp) • 50 g (2 oz) butter or margarine • 40 g (1½ oz) plain flour • 2.5 ml (½ tsp) ground cinnamon	• 25 g (1 oz) caster sugar • icing sugar, for dusting

380 CALS/SERVING

1 Tie a double strip of grease-proof paper around a 1.4 litre (2½ pint) soufflé dish to make a 7.5 cm (3 inch) collar. Brush the inside of the dish and paper with melted butter.

2 Place the chocolate in a heatproof bowl with the 15 ml (1 tbsp) milk. Stand the bowl over a pan of simmering water and heat gently until the chocolate melts.

3 Melt the butter in a large saucepan. Stir in the flour and cook for 1 minute, then off the heat gradually blend in the remaining milk and cinnamon. Bring to the boil, stirring, and cook for 1–2 minutes, stirring. Cool slightly, then beat in the egg yolks, one by one. Beat in the sugar and melted chocolate until smooth.

4 Whisk the egg whites until they stand in soft peaks. Beat one spoonful into the sauce mixture to lighten it, then carefully fold in the remaining egg whites.

5 Gently pour the soufflé mixture into the prepared dish. Level the top with a palette knife and stand the dish on a baking sheet.

6 Bake at 190°C (375°F) mark 5 for about 35–45 minutes or until well risen, and just set. Remove the paper and dust lightly with icing sugar. Serve at once.

2 Whisk the lemon rind, egg yolks and 75 g (3 oz) of the caster sugar together in a bowl until pale and creamy. Pour 105 ml (7 tbsp) lemon juice into a small bowl, sprinkle in the gelatine and leave to soak for 2–3 minutes. Place bowl over a pan of simmering water until the gelatine is dissolved. Stir into the whisked mixture.

3 Lightly whip 450 ml (¾ pint) of the cream until it just begins to hold its shape. Place the whisked egg yolk mixture over a bowl of iced water and stir until the mixture is just beginning to thicken. Remove the bowl from the iced water and fold in the cream.

❖ Chilled Lemon Soufflé ❖

4 Whisk the egg whites in a large bowl until they stand in soft peaks. Add the remaining caster sugar and whisk again until standing in firm peaks. Stir a spoonful into the egg yolk mixture to loosen it. Then quickly and carefully fold in the rest of the whites until evenly mixed.

5 Gently pour the mixture into the prepared dish. Chill for at least 4 hours until set. Meanwhile, melt granulated sugar slowly in a small pan until bubbling and golden brown. Stir in the nuts. Immediately pour onto the oiled baking sheet and leave to cool.

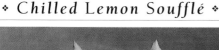

SERVES 6–8

PREPARATION TIME 0 minutes, plus chilling

FREEZING Suitable (chilled, undecorated)

- finely grated rind and juice of 3 lemons
- 6 eggs, size 2, separated
- 125 g (4 oz) caster sugar
- 30 ml (2 tbsp) powdered gelatine
- 600 ml (1 pint) whipping cream
- 125 g (4 oz) granulated sugar
- 75 g (3 oz) pistachio nuts
- star fruit, to decorate

715–535 CALS/SERVING

1 Tie a double strip of greaseproof paper around a 900 ml (1½ pint) soufflé dish to make a 7.5 cm (3 inch) collar. Lightly brush the inside of the paper with oil. Lightly oil a baking sheet.

6 Whip the remaining cream until it holds its shape. Chop the pistachio praline. When the soufflé is set, carefully ease the paper collar away with a knife dipped in hot water.

7 Spread a thin layer of cream around the edge of the soufflé and press on the pistachio praline. Decorate the top with piped cream whirls and slices of star fruit. Serve at once.

❖ Chocolate Orange Soufflé ❖

SERVES 6–8

PREPARATION TIME
20 minutes, plus
chilling
COOKING TIME
About 10 minutes
FREEZING
Suitable (stage 5)
COLOUR INDEX
Page 75

- 450 ml (¾ pint) milk
- 150 g (5 oz) plain chocolate, in pieces
- 3 eggs, size 2, separated, plus 1 egg white
- 75 g (3 oz) caster sugar
- 15 ml (1 tbsp) powdered gelatine
- finely grated rind and juice of 1 orange
- 300 ml (½ pint) whipping cream

TO DECORATE:
- whipped cream
- grated chocolate

475–360 CALS/SERVING

1 Tie a double strip of greaseproof paper around a 900 ml (1½ pint) soufflé dish to make a 7.5 cm (3 inch) collar. Lightly brush the inside of the paper with oil.

2 Put the milk and chocolate in a saucepan and heat gently until the chocolate melts, then heat until almost boiling.

3 Whisk the egg yolks and sugar together in a bowl until pale and thick. Gradually pour on the chocolate milk, stirring. Return to the pan and cook for about 10 minutes, stirring continuously, until thick enough to coat the back of the spoon; do not boil.

4 Sprinkle the gelatine over 45 ml (3 tbsp) water in a small bowl and leave to soak for 2–3 minutes. Place the bowl over a pan of simmering water until the gelatine is dissolved. Stir into the custard with the orange rind and juice. Leave to cool.

5 Whip the cream until it just holds its shape, then fold into the cold mixture. Whisk egg whites until they stand in soft peaks, then fold in. Pour into the prepared dish and chill until set.

6 Carefully ease away the paper collar just before serving. Decorate the soufflé with cream and grated chocolate.

❖ Lemon Mousse ❖

SERVES 4–6

PREPARATION TIME
25 minutes, plus
chilling
FREEZING
Suitable
COLOUR INDEX
Page 75

- finely grated rind and juice of 3 lemons
- 3 eggs, size 1, separated
- 75 g (3 oz) caster sugar
- 15 ml (1 tbsp) powdered gelatine
- 300 ml (½ pint) whipping cream

TO DECORATE:
- whipped cream
- chopped pistachio nuts

435–290 CALS/SERVING

1 Put the lemon rind, egg yolks and sugar in a bowl and whisk until pale and creamy.

2 Measure 75 ml (5 tbsp) lemon juice into a small bowl. Sprinkle in the gelatine and leave to soak for 2–3 minutes. Stand the bowl over a saucepan of gently simmering water until the gelatine is dissolved, then stir into the whisked egg mixture.

3 Stand the bowl over a larger bowl of iced water and stir frequently until the mixture is just beginning to thicken. Lightly whip the cream until it just holds its shape, then fold into the egg mixture.

4 Whisk the egg whites in a large bowl until they stand in soft peaks. Stir a spoonful of whisked egg white into the lemon mixture to lighten it. Using a large metal spoon, lightly fold in the rest of the egg whites until evenly mixed.

5 Spoon into serving dishes or glasses and chill for 2–3 hours until set. Serve decorated with cream and pistachio nuts.

❖ Summer Fruit Mousse ❖

SERVES 6–8

PREPARATION TIME
20 minutes, plus
cooling
COOKING TIME
3–4 minutes
FREEZING
Suitable

- 450 g (1 lb) mixed soft fruits, such as strawberries, raspberries, blackberries and redcurrants
- 15 ml (1 tbsp) powdered gelatine
- 15 ml (1 tbsp) cornflour
- 2 egg yolks
- 75 g (3 oz) caster sugar
- 150 ml (¼ pint) milk
- 30 ml (2 tbsp) Grand Marnier or Cointreau
- 300 ml (½ pint) double cream

TO DECORATE:
- frosted fruits (see page 344)
- mint leaves

360–270 CALS/SERVING

1 Prepare the soft fruit as necessary, then purée in a food processor or blender. Sieve to remove pips.

2 In a small bowl, sprinkle the gelatine over 45 ml (3 tbsp) water and leave to soak while making the custard.

3 Whisk the cornflour, egg yolks, sugar and a little of the milk together in a bowl until thick and pale. Heat remaining milk until almost boiling, then gradually pour on to the egg yolk mixture, stirring. Return to the pan and cook, stirring, over a low heat until thickened.

4 Remove from the heat and stir in the softened gelatine until completely dissolved. Transfer to a large bowl; cool slightly. Stir in the fruit purée and liqueur and leave to cool until on the point of setting.

5 Whip the cream until it just holds its shape; fold into the mousse. Leave for several minutes until on the point of setting. Pile into serving dishes. Top with frosted fruits and mint. Serve with crisp biscuits.

1 For the praline, toast nuts until golden brown, stirring occasionally. Dissolve sugar in 15 ml (1 tbsp) water in a heavy-based pan over a low heat. Stir in the nuts and boil until the syrup starts to brown. Immediately pour onto a lightly oiled baking sheet. Leave until cold, then roughly crush with a rolling pin.

2 Grease and line a 1.1 litre (2 pint) loaf tin with cling film. To make the mousses, melt each chocolate separately in a small heatproof bowl set over a pan of simmering water. Stir until smooth. Cool slightly.

❖ Dark and Light ❖ Chocolate Terrine

3 To make the dark chocolate mousse, cream the butter with half the sugar until pale; beat in the cocoa. In another bowl, beat egg yolks with remaining sugar; stir in rum. Whip cream until it holds its shape. Beat the chocolate into the creamed butter; stir into yolk mixture, then fold in cream.

4 To make the white chocolate mousse, beat the butter into the melted white chocolate. Stir in the egg yolks and 30 ml (2 tbsp) crushed praline. Whip the cream until it just holds its shape, then fold into the chocolate mixture.

SERVES 6–8

PREPARATION TIME
45 minutes, plus chilling
COOKING TIME
10 minutes
FREEZING
Not suitable

PRALINE:
• 225 g (8 oz) blanched almonds or skinned hazelnuts
• 125 g (4 oz) granulated sugar
DARK CHOCOLATE MOUSSE:
• 175 g (6 oz) plain chocolate, in pieces
• 75 g (3 oz) unsalted butter
• 75 g (3 oz) caster sugar
• 30 ml (2 tbsp) cocoa powder, sifted
• 3 egg yolks

• 30 ml (2 tbsp) rum or brandy
• 300 ml (½ pint) whipping cream
WHITE CHOCOLATE MOUSSE:
• 175 g (6 oz) white chocolate, in pieces
• 50 g (2 oz) unsalted butter, softened
• 2 egg yolks
• 200 ml (7 fl oz) whipping cream
TO DECORATE:
• seasonal fruits

1210–910 CALS/SERVING

5 Drop large spoonfuls of each mousse alternately into the prepared tin until full; tap to level. Cover and chill for at least 4 hours or preferably overnight until very firm.

6 To serve, turn out and peel off cling film. Press remaining praline over top and sides. Chill for 30 minutes until firm, then serve in slices, decorated with fruits.

CRÊPES

Crêpes – or pancakes – are made from a pouring batter which has a consistency similar to single cream. If you have time, leave the batter to rest for about 20 minutes to allow the starch grains time to swell and soften. This gives a lighter batter. To freeze crêpes, interleave with freezer tissue and wrap in foil.

If necessary filled crêpes can be warmed through in the oven at 190°C (375°F) mark 5 for 15–20 minutes.

❖ Plain Crêpes ❖

MAKES 8

PREPARATION TIME
10 minutes
COOKING TIME
About 15 minutes
FREEZING
Suitable

- 125 g (4 oz) plain flour
- pinch of salt
- 1 egg
- 300 ml (½ pint) milk
- oil, for frying

100 CALS/CRÊPE

1 Sift the flour and salt into a bowl and make a well in the centre. Add the egg and whisk well with a balloon whisk. Gradually beat in the milk, drawing in the flour from the sides to make a smooth batter. Cover and leave to stand if possible, for 20 minutes.

2 Heat the minimum of oil in an 18 cm (7 inch) heavy-based pancake pan or frying pan. Pour in just enough batter to thinly coat the base of the pan. Cook over a moderately high heat for about 1 minute until golden brown. Turn or toss and cook the second side for ½–1 minute until golden.

3 Transfer the crêpe to a plate and keep hot. Repeat with the remaining batter, stacking the cooked crêpes on top of each other with greaseproof paper in between; keep warm in the oven while cooking the remainder. Serve as soon as they are all cooked, sprinkled with sugar and lemon juice.

Variations

BUCKWHEAT CRÊPES: Replace half the flour with buckwheat flour and add an extra egg white.

ORANGE, LEMON OR LIME CRÊPES: Add the finely grated rind of 1 lemon, ½ an orange or 1 lime with the milk.

CHOCOLATE CRÊPES: Replace 15 g (½ oz) of the flour with sifted cocoa powder.

CREOLE PANCAKES: Put the grated rind and juice of 1 lime in a saucepan with 50 g (2 oz) butter, 50 g (2 oz) demerara sugar, 60 ml (4 tbsp) dark rum and 2.5 ml (½ tsp) ground cinnamon. Heat gently until dissolved, then add 3–4 bananas, sliced; cook gently for 5 minutes. Remove the banana slices with a slotted spoon and arrange on the pancakes. Fold the pancakes over the filling to enclose and pour over the hot sauce to serve.

ORANGE AND NECTARINE CRÊPES: Make the grated rind and juice of 2 oranges up to 150 ml (¼ pint) with water. Place in a saucepan, add 50 g (2 oz) sugar and heat gently until dissolved, then boil for 1 minute. Add 4 nectarines, skinned, stoned and chopped. Simmer for 3–4 minutes, then remove the fruit with a slotted spoon and divide between the crêpes. Fold to enclose filling. Add 45 ml (3 tbsp) Grand Marnier or Cointreau to the syrup and pour over the crêpes to serve.

❖ Crêpes Suzette ❖

SERVES 4–6

PREPARATION TIME
5 minutes, plus
crêpes
COOKING TIME
10 minutes
FREEZING
Not suitable
COLOUR INDEX
Page 76

- 105 ml (7 tbsp) Grand Marnier or Cointreau
- 1 quantity crêpe batter (see left)
- 125 g (4 oz) unsalted butter
- 125 g (4 oz) caster sugar
- finely grated rind and juice of 1 large orange

TO DECORATE:
- finely shredded orange rind, blanched (optional)
- mint sprigs

630–420 CALS/SERVING

1 Stir 15 ml (1 tbsp) liqueur into the crêpe batter. Make 8–12 crêpes (see left). Heat the butter and sugar in a large heavy-based frying pan until thick and syrupy. Add 30 ml (2 tbsp) liqueur with the orange rind and juice and heat through.

2 Fold the crêpes into triangle shapes by folding each one in half, then in half again. Place them in the frying pan and spoon over the sauce to coat evenly.

3 Heat the remaining liqueur gently in a ladle or separate small pan. Pour over the crêpes and set alight, basting until the flames die down. Serve at once, topped with orange rind shreds if desired, and mint sprigs to decorate.

CREAMY DESSERTS

Real egg custard forms the basis of many creamy desserts, such as crème caramel and bavarois. Always cook custard in a heavy-based saucepan or in the top of a double boiler over a very low heat, until slightly thickened – just enough to coat the back of the spoon lightly.

❖ Crème Caramel ❖

SERVES 4–6

PREPARATION TIME
15 minutes, plus cooling
COOKING TIME
20–30 minutes
FREEZING
Not suitable
COLOUR INDEX
Page 76

CARAMEL:
- *175 g (6 oz) granulated sugar*
CUSTARD:
- *1 vanilla pod or few drops of vanilla essence*

- *600 ml (1 pint) milk*
- *4 eggs*
- *4 egg yolks*
- *50–65 g (2–2½ oz) caster sugar, to taste*

470–310 CALS/SERVING

1 To make the caramel, slightly warm 6 ramekin dishes. Put the granulated sugar in a heavy-based saucepan over a low heat and heat gently until it is dissolved, brushing any sugar down from the side of the pan to help it dissolve.

2 Bring to the boil and boil rapidly for a few minutes until the syrup begins to turn pale brown, gently swirling the pan to ensure even browning. When the caramel is a rich golden brown colour, dip the base of the pan in cool water to prevent further cooking.

3 Pour a little caramel into each of the warmed ramekins and quickly rotate to coat the bottom and part way up the sides with caramel. Leave to cool.

4 To make the custard, split vanilla pod to expose seeds. Place in a pan with the milk and heat until almost boiling; if using vanilla essence, add after heating the milk. Meanwhile, beat the eggs, egg yolks and caster sugar until well mixed. Stir in the milk. Strain, then pour into the ramekins.

5 Place ramekins in a roasting tin containing enough hot water to come halfway up sides of dishes. Bake at 170°C (325°F) mark 3 for 20–30 minutes until just set and a knife inserted in centre comes out clean. Remove from tin. Cool.

6 To turn out, free the edges by pressing with the fingertips then run a knife around the edge of each custard. Place a serving dish over the top and invert. Lift off the ramekin. The caramel will have formed a sauce around the custard.

❖ Crème Brûlée ❖

SERVES 6

PREPARATION TIME
15 minutes, plus chilling
COOKING TIME
1 hour
FREEZING
Not suitable

- *600 ml (1 pint) double cream*
- *1 vanilla pod, split or 2.5 ml (½ tsp) vanilla essence*

- *4 egg yolks*
- *125 g (4 oz) caster sugar*

570 CALS/SERVING

1 Put the cream and vanilla pod if using in a heatproof bowl over a pan of hot water and heat gently; do not boil.
2 Meanwhile, beat the egg yolks with 50 g (2 oz) of the caster sugar and the vanilla essence if using. Stir in the cream.
3 Strain the custard and divide equally between 6 ramekins. Stand in a roasting tin containing enough hot water to come halfway up the sides of the dishes. Bake at 150°C (300°F) mark 2 for about 1 hour or until set. Remove from the tin and allow to cool, then chill for at least 4 hours, preferably overnight.
4 Sprinkle each crème brûlée with the remaining sugar to form a layer and put under a hot grill for 2–3 minutes until the sugar melts and caramelizes. Allow to cool for 2–3 hours until the caramel layer is firm and crisp, before serving.

❖ Zabaglione ❖

1 Line 4–6 small heart-shaped perforated moulds with muslin.

2 Press the cheese through a nylon sieve into a bowl. Lightly whip the crème fraîche, vanilla essence and sugar together in another bowl then lightly mix into the cheese.

3 Whisk the egg whites until stiff, then fold into the cheese mixture. Turn the mixture into the prepared moulds, set on a tray. Cover and leave to drain overnight in the refrigerator. To serve, turn each mould out onto a serving plate and decorate with strawberries.

SERVES 6	• 4 egg yolks	• 100 ml (4 fl oz)
PREPARATION TIME 10 minutes COOKING TIME 10 minutes FREEZING Not suitable	• 65 g (2½ oz) caster sugar	Marsala

100 CALS/SERVING

1 Beat the egg yolks and sugar together in a large heatproof bowl. Beat in the Marsala.
2 Place the bowl over a saucepan of simmering water and heat gently, whisking the mixture until it is very thick and creamy.
3 Pour the zabaglione into 6 serving glasses and serve immediately, with crisp biscuits.

❖ Coeurs à la Crème ❖

SERVES 4–6	• 225 g (8 oz) curd or ricotta cheese	• 2 egg whites
PREPARATION TIME 15 minutes, plus chilling FREEZING Not suitable COLOUR INDEX Page 76	• 300 ml (½ pint) crème fraîche • few drops of vanilla essence • 25 g (1 oz) caster sugar	• strawberries, to decorate

195–130 CALS/SERVING

❖ Vanilla Bavarois ❖

SERVES 8	• 450 ml (¾ pint) milk • 450 ml (¾ pint) single cream	FRUIT PURÉE: • 225 g (8 oz) blackcurrants
PREPARATION TIME 40 minutes, plus chilling COOKING TIME 20–25 minutes FREEZING Suitable (bavarois and fruit purée separately) COLOUR INDEX Page 76	• 1 vanilla pod, split, or few drops of vanilla essence • 1 cinnamon stick • 6 egg yolks, size 2 • 125 g (4 oz) caster sugar • 20 ml (4 tsp) powdered gelatine • 300 ml (½ pint) double cream	• 225 g (8 oz) raspberries • 75 g (3 oz) caster sugar TO FINISH: • selection of soft fruits, such as strawberries, redcurrants, blueberries • herb sprigs, such as chervil, to decorate

475 CALS/SERVING

1 Lightly oil a 1.4 litre (2½ pint) ring mould. Put the milk and single cream in a saucepan with the vanilla pod and cinnamon stick. Heat gently until almost boiling, then remove from the heat. Cover and leave to infuse for 30 minutes, then strain.

2 Meanwhile, beat the egg yolks with the sugar until thick and pale. Stir in the milk. Add the vanilla essence, if using. Return to the pan. Cook gently, stirring all the time, until thickened enough to coat the back of the spoon; this will take about 10–12 minutes; do not boil. Strain into a large bowl, cover the surface with damp greaseproof paper and allow to cool.

3 Put 60 ml (4 tbsp) water in a small bowl and sprinkle over the gelatine. Leave to soak for 3–4 minutes until sponge-like in texture. Stand over a pan of simmering water until the gelatine is dissolved. Stir into the cooled custard. Set bowl in a roasting tin of iced water and stir until the custard thickens to resemble lightly whipped cream; about 15 minutes. Remove from iced water.

Variations

ORANGE BAVAROIS: Substitute the thinly pared rind of 2 oranges for the vanilla and cinnamon stick.

CHOCOLATE BAVAROIS: At stage 1, gently heat 125g (4 oz) plain chocolate with the milk and cream until melted. At stage 2, beat the egg yolks with 50 g (2 oz) sugar, then strain on the chocolate milk.

❖ Petits Pots de ❖ Crème au Chocolat

Working quickly, whip the cream until it is the same consistency as the custard, then lightly fold in.

5 Pour the custard into the prepared mould and chill for at least 4 hours until set.

SERVES 6-8	• 600 ml (1 pint) single cream	• 25 g (1 oz) caster sugar
PREPARATION TIME 15 minutes, plus chilling	• 2.5 ml (½ tsp) vanilla essence	TO DECORATE: • whipped cream
COOKING TIME About 1 hour	• 225 g (8 oz) plain chocolate, in pieces	• cocoa powder, for dusting
FREEZING Not suitable	• 1 egg	
	• 5 egg yolks	

475–355 CALS/SERVING

Meanwhile to make the fruit purée, place the fruit in a saucepan with the sugar and 300 ml (½ pint) water. Heat gently until the sugar dissolves then bring to the boil. Cover and simmer for 10 minutes. Cool, then purée in a blender or food processor. Sieve into a bowl.

7 To turn out the bavarois, ease the edges away from the tin. Place a dampened plate over the tin, invert and shake gently to release the bavarois. Spoon the fruit into the centre of the bavarois, moistening with a little fruit purée. Pour purée around the bavarois and decorate with herbs.

1 Put the cream, vanilla essence and chocolate into a heavy-based saucepan over a low heat and heat gently, stirring, until the chocolate melts and the mixture is smooth.
2 Lightly mix together the whole egg, egg yolks and caster sugar, then stir in the chocolate cream. Strain the mixture into eight 75 ml (3 fl oz) custard pots, or six ramekins. Cover with lids or small rounds of foil.
3 Stand the custard pots or ramekins in a roasting tin, containing enough hot water to come halfway up the sides of the dishes. Cook at 150°C (300°F) mark 2 for about 1 hour until lightly set and the centres are still slightly soft.
4 Remove from the tin and allow to cool. Chill before serving, topped with a spoonful of cream and dusted with cocoa powder.

❖ Tiramisu ❖

SERVES 8

PREPARATION TIME
20 minutes, plus
chilling
FREEZING
Not suitable
COLOUR INDEX
Page 77

- _four 250 g (9 oz) cartons mascarpone cheese_
- _40 g (1½ oz) caster sugar_
- _3 eggs, separated_
- _250 ml (8 fl oz) kahlua or other coffee-flavoured liqueur_
- _425 ml (14 fl oz) very strong cold black coffee_
- _about 30 savoiardi (Italian sponge fingers)_
- _cocoa powder, for sprinkling_

700 CALS/SERVING

1 Put the mascarpone cheese, sugar and egg yolks in a bowl and beat with an electric mixer until evenly blended and creamy.

2 Whisk the egg whites until standing in stiff peaks. Fold into the mascarpone mixture until evenly incorporated. Spoon one quarter into the base of a glass serving bowl.

3 Mix the liqueur and coffee together in a shallow dish. One at a time, dip one third of the savoiardi in this mixture for 10–15 seconds, turning once, then place on top of the mascarpone in the bowl, in a single layer to cover.

4 Cover the savoiardi with one third of the remaining mascarpone, then dip another third of the savoiardi in the liqueur and coffee mixture and layer them in the bowl as before. Repeat with another layer of mascarpone and savoiardi.

5 Spread the remaining mascarpone over the top and swirl with a palette knife. Sift cocoa powder liberally all over the top. Cover the bowl and chill in the refrigerator for 24 hours. Serve chilled.

❖ Old English Syllabub ❖

SERVES 4

PREPARATION TIME
15 minutes, plus
standing and
chilling
FREEZING
Not suitable
COLOUR INDEX
Page 77

- _1 clove_
- _1 allspice berry_
- _2.5 cm (1 inch) piece cinnamon stick_
- _little freshly grated nutmeg_
- _50 g (2 oz) caster sugar_
- _finely grated rind and juice of 1 lemon_
- _90 ml (6 tbsp) pale cream sherry_
- _300 ml (½ pint) double cream_
- _24 ratafia biscuits_

450 CALS/SERVING

1 Very finely grind the clove, allspice and cinnamon stick with a pestle and mortar, then sift through a fine sieve.
2 Put the ground spices, nutmeg, sugar, lemon rind, lemon juice and sherry into a bowl. Stir well until the sugar dissolves, then cover and leave to stand for 1 hour.
3 Strain the sherry mixture through a fine nylon sieve into a clean bowl. Pour in the cream in a continuous stream, whisking all the time. Whip the cream mixture until it is just thick enough to hold a trail when the whisk is lifted.
4 Place 4 ratafias in each of 4 serving glasses, then cover with the syllabub. Chill for about 1 hour. Top with remaining ratafias.

❖ Trifle ❖

SERVES 8

PREPARATION TIME
35 minutes, plus
chilling
COOKING TIME
15–20 minutes
FREEZING
Not suitable

- _10 trifle sponges or 1 large Madeira cake, 400 g (14 oz) weight_
- _225 g (8 oz) strawberry or raspberry jam or jelly_
- _75 ml (5 tbsp) sherry_
- _75 ml (5 tbsp) brandy_
- _450 g (1 lb) fresh or frozen raspberries, blackberries or strawberries_
- _600 ml (1 pint) creamy milk_
- _1 vanilla pod, split_
- _8 eggs_
- _175 g (6 oz) caster sugar_
- _150 ml (¼ pint) double cream_
- _glacé fruits or toasted nuts, to decorate_

625 CALS/SERVING

1 Split the trifle sponges in two and lay the bottom halves over the base of a deep glass bowl. Warm the jam or jelly until just melted, sieve if necessary and spoon over the trifle sponges. Top with the remaining sponges. (Use Madeira cake sliced thinly.)
2 Mix the sherry and brandy together and spoon evenly over the sponges, making sure they are saturated. Scatter over the fruit, halving some of the berries if wished. Cover and chill for 1 hour.
3 Heat the milk with the vanilla pod and bring almost to the boil. Take off the heat; cover and infuse for about 20 minutes.
4 Using an electric whisk, whisk the eggs and sugar in a bowl until pale and foaming. Strain on the milk, stirring.
5 Return to the pan and stir the custard over a low heat until it begins to thicken; this will take about 15–20 minutes; do not allow to boil or it will curdle. When the custard is thick enough to lightly coat the back of the spoon, pour into a bowl and leave to cool. (It will thicken up quite considerably when chilled.)
6 Lightly whisk the cool custard, then pour over the fruit. Cover and chill for several hours, preferably overnight.
7 Whip the double cream until it just holds its shape. Carefully spread this over the custard and decorate with the fruits or nuts.

ICE CREAMS & SORBETS

There is nothing to beat the rich flavour and creamy texture of homemade ice cream, or the mouthwatering tang of a real fruit sorbet. The key to success when making smooth frozen desserts is to ensure that no large ice crystals form during freezing. If you do not own an ice cream machine, it is necessary to periodically whisk the freezing mixture by hand.

TO FREEZE ICE CREAM BY HAND

❖ Set the freezer to maximum or fast-freeze about 1 hour before you intend to freeze the mixture.

❖ Pour the ice cream into a shallow non-metal, freezerproof container. Cover and freeze for about 3 hours or until just frozen all over. It will have a mushy consistency.

❖ Spoon into a bowl and mash with a fork or flat whisk to break down the ice crystals, working quickly so that the ice cream does not melt completely. Return the mixture to the shallow container and freeze again for about 2 hours or until mushy.

❖ Mash again as above, folding in any other ingredients, such as nuts, at this stage. Freeze for about 3 hours or until firm.

❖ Remove from the freezer and leave at room temperature for 20–30 minutes to soften before serving.

USING AN ICE CREAM MACHINE

An ice cream machine will freeze an ice cream or sorbet mixture and churn it at the same time, giving a smooth, even-textured result and eliminating the physical effort.

❖ Always follow the manufacturer's instructions carefully and clean the machine thoroughly after use.

❖ When making ice cream this way, cream doesn't need to be whisked before it is added.

❖ When making sorbet, any egg white should be lightly whisked with a fork and added at the start of the churning process.

❖ Freezing time is usually about 20–30 minutes. The ice cream or sorbet should then be transferred to the freezer for 1–2 hours to allow the flavours to develop before serving. Soften slightly at room temperature before serving.

❖ *Vanilla Ice Cream* ❖

SERVES 4–6

PREPARATION TIME
25 minutes, plus
freezing
COOKING TIME
15 minutes
COLOUR INDEX
Page 77

- 1 vanilla pod or 2.5 ml (½ tsp) vanilla essence
- 300 ml (½ pint) milk
- 3 egg yolks
- 50–75 g (2–3 oz) caster sugar
- 300 ml (½ pint) double cream

480–320 CALS/SERVING

1 Split the vanilla pod to reveal the seeds. Put the milk and vanilla pod into a heavy-based saucepan and bring almost to the boil. Remove from the heat, cover and leave to infuse for about 20 minutes.

2 Beat the egg yolks and sugar together in a bowl until well blended. Stir in the milk and strain back into the pan. Cook the custard over a gentle heat, stirring all the time, until it thickens just enough to lightly coat the back of the spoon. Do not boil or it will curdle. Pour into a bowl and leave to cool.

3 Whisk the cream into the cold custard mixture, with the vanilla essence, if using. Freeze the ice cream mixture by hand or in an ice cream machine (see left). Leave at cool room temperature for 20–30 minutes to soften before serving.

Variations

FRUIT ICE CREAM: Add 300 ml (½ pint) fruit purée, sweetened to taste, to the cooled custard.

CHOCOLATE ICE CREAM: Gently heat the milk in a pan with 125 g (4 oz) plain chocolate until the chocolate melts, then cook over a high heat until almost boiling. Continue as above.

CHOCOLATE FLAKE ICE CREAM: Crumble 2 large chocolate flakes. Stir half into the cooled custard with the cream. Continue as above. Stir in remaining flake just before the ice cream freezes.

COFFEE ICE CREAM: Add 150 ml (¼ pint) cold strong fresh coffee to the cooled custard or 10 ml (2 tsp) instant coffee granules to the milk instead of the vanilla pod.

COCONUT ICE CREAM: Finely chop 175 g (6 oz) creamed coconut. Add to the milk and warm until dissolved, whisking until smooth, then add 30 ml (2 tbsp) lemon juice. Complete as above, omitting the vanilla.

❖ Raspberry Rose Ice Cream ❖

SERVES 6

PREPARATION TIME
20 minutes, plus
freezing
COOKING TIME
5 minutes
COLOUR INDEX
Page 77

- 15 ml (1 tbsp) custard powder
- 15 ml (1 tbsp) caster sugar
- 300 ml (½ pint) milk
- 450 g (1 lb) raspberries
- 15 ml (1 tbsp) rose-water (optional)
- 300 ml (½ pint) double cream

295 CALS/SERVING

1 Blend the custard powder and sugar to a paste with 15–30 ml (1–2 tbsp) milk. Heat the remaining milk until boiling, then pour onto the blended mixture, stirring.
2 Return the mixture to the pan and bring to the boil, stirring continuously. Cook for 1–2 minutes after the mixture has thickened to make a smooth, glossy sauce. Cover the surface of the custard with damp greaseproof paper and leave to cool.
3 Meanwhile, mash the raspberries then push through a nylon sieve to make a purée. Stir in the rosewater, if using.
4 Whisk the cream into the cold custard mixture, then stir in the raspberry purée. Pour into a shallow non-metal, freezerproof container. Cover and freeze for about 3 hours.
5 Spoon into a bowl and mash with a fork to break down the ice crystals. Return to the container and freeze again for about 2 hours until mushy.
6 Mash again as step 5, then return to the freezer for a further 3 hours or until firm.
7 Remove from the freezer and leave at room temperature for 20–30 minutes to soften before serving.

SORBETS

For each of the following sorbets you will need 350 ml (12 fl oz) sugar syrup. To make this, put 125 g (4 oz) granulated sugar in a heavy-based saucepan. Add 300 ml (½ pint) water and heat gently until the sugar dissolves. Do not stir the ingredients but occasionally loosen the sugar from the base of the pan to help it dissolve. Bring to the boil and boil for 2 minutes. Cool and use as required.

To freeze sorbets in an ice cream machine, see page 375.

❖ Lemon Sorbet ❖

SERVES 3–4

PREPARATION TIME
10 minutes, plus
freezing
COLOUR INDEX
Page 77

- 350 ml (12 fl oz) sugar syrup (see above)
- finely pared rind and juice of 3 lemons
- 1 egg white

170–130 CALS/SERVING

1 Prepare the sugar syrup as far as dissolving the sugar. Add the pared lemon rinds and simmer gently for about 10 minutes. Leave to cool completely.

2 Stir in the lemon juice and strain into a shallow non-metal, freezerproof container. Cover and freeze for about 3 hours until mushy.

3 Whisk the egg white until stiff. Turn the sorbet into a bowl and beat gently to break down the ice crystals.

4 Fold in the egg white. Return to the container, cover and freeze for 4 hours or until firm. Leave in the refrigerator for about 40 minutes to soften slightly before serving.

Variations

ORANGE OR LIME SORBET: Make as above, using the pared rind and juice of 2 oranges or 5 limes instead of the lemons.

❖ Raspberry Sorbet ❖

SERVES 6

PREPARATION TIME
10 minutes, plus
freezing
COLOUR INDEX
Page 77

- 450 g (1 lb) raspberries
- 30 ml (2 tbsp) lemon juice
- 30 ml (2 tbsp) kirsch
- 350 ml (12 fl oz) sugar syrup (see left)
- 2 egg whites

120 CALS/SERVING

1 Purée the raspberries with the lemon juice and kirsch in a blender or food processor. Press through a nylon sieve.
2 Add to the sugar syrup. Freeze as for Lemon Sorbet, adding the egg whites as directed.

❖ Mango Sorbet ❖

SERVES 8

PREPARATION TIME
10 minutes, plus
freezing
COLOUR INDEX
Page 77

- 2 large ripe mangoes
- 350 ml (12 fl oz) sugar syrup (see left)
- juice of 1 large lime
- 1 egg white

90 CALS/SERVING

1 Peel the mangoes and remove the flesh from the stones. Purée the flesh in a blender or food processor. Press through a sieve. Mix with the sugar syrup and lime juice.
2 Freeze as for Lemon Sorbet, adding the egg white as directed. Serve straight from the freezer.

❖ Marsala Macaroon Parfait ❖

SERVES 8

PREPARATION TIME
0 minutes, plus
eezing
OOKING TIME
minutes
OLOUR INDEX
age 77

- 1 vanilla pod or 1.25 ml (¼ tsp) vanilla essence
- 225 g (8 oz) caster sugar
- 6 egg yolks
- 50 ml (2 fl oz) Marsala
- 300 ml (½ pint) double cream
- 150 ml (¼ pint) Greek yogurt
- 75 g (3 oz) ratafia, amaretti or macaroon biscuits, crushed

390 CALS/SERVING

Soak the vanilla pod in a ttle warm water for minutes to soften. Split nd scrape out the seeds into saucepan. Add the sugar nd 100 ml (3½ fl oz) water. eat gently until the sugar issolves. Increase the heat nd boil rapidly for 2–3 ninutes. Strain.

2 Working quickly, beat the egg yolks with the Marsala in a bowl, then pour the syrup onto the yolks in a steady stream, whisking all the time. Continue whisking for 6–8 minutes until the mixture has doubled in volume and is thick and foamy. Leave to cool slightly.

Whip the cream until it just olds its shape. Gently fold to the yolk mixture with the ogurt and the crushed ratafia iscuits.

4 Pour into a freezerproof container and freeze until firm, about 3–4 hours. Meanwhile line 2 baking sheets with foil and place in the freezer to chill.

5 Working quickly, scoop the parfait into balls and place on the chilled baking trays. Cover and freeze until firm. To serve, pile the parfait balls into a chilled serving bowl. Serve immediately, accompanied by caramelised or poached fruit and crisp biscuits.

❖ Individual Coffee Bombes ❖ with Truffle Centres

SERVES 6

PREPARATION TIME
40 minutes, plus
ice cream and
freezing
COLOUR INDEX
Page 77

- 1½ quantity Coffee Ice Cream (page 375)

FILLING:
- 25 g (1 oz) cake crumbs
- 25 g (1 oz) ground almonds
- 50 g (2 oz) plain chocolate, in pieces
- 45 ml (3 tbsp) double cream
- 30 ml (2 tbsp) rum or brandy
- chocolate leaves or curls, to decorate

615 CALS/SERVING

1 Put six 175 ml (6 fl oz) individual freezerproof pudding moulds in the freezer to chill. Leave the ice cream at room temperature for 20 minutes or until soft enough to spread.

2 Meanwhile, to make the filling, mix the cake crumbs and ground almonds together in a bowl. Put the chocolate and cream in a small bowl over a pan of simmering water; stir until melted. Stir into the crumb mixture with the rum.

3 Spread the softened ice cream around the base and sides of the moulds, leaving a cavity in the centre. Freeze for 1 hour or until firm.

4 Fill the centre of each mould with the truffle mixture and level the surface. Cover and freeze for 1 hour or until firm.

5 To serve, dip the moulds briefly in hot water, then unmould onto serving plates. Return to the freezer for 10 minutes to firm up. Decorate with chocolate leaves or curls to serve.

CAKES & BISCUITS

Once in a while there's something wonderfully uplifting about baking a cake, a spectacular gâteau or a batch of scones. However health-conscious we may be, few can resist the aroma of a freshly baked cake or tray of cookies. Try one of the deliciously moist fresh fruit cakes, such as Raspberry and Apple Cake (page 393). The following notes should help you to achieve perfect results with your home baking.

❖ Essential Ingredients ❖

The following ingredients are commonly used in baking recipes, in addition to a wide variety of flavourings, including spices, essences, nuts, dried fruit, and chocolate. Remember to check the use-by dates on these items before use.

❖ FAT: Butter gives a rich flavour and colour which many prefer, but the flavour of margarine has improved enormously in recent years. Soft-tub margarine, which can be used straight from the fridge, is ideal for all-in-one methods. If you are using butter (or one of the hard 'block' margarines) bring it to room temperature first. Alternatively microwave on LOW for about 1 minute, but watch carefully – if it melts you'll have to start again.

Avoid using low-fat spreads: many contain high proportions of water and, although they look like margarine, they do not behave identically during cooking. Oil can be used in suitably proportioned recipes only.

❖ SUGAR AND SWEETENERS: Sugar is needed for texture and volume as well as flavour. Caster sugar is generally the best choice since it has small regular granules which dissolve easily. Granulated sugar can be used for rubbed-in cakes but, like icing sugar, it is unsuitable for creamed or whisked mixtures. Other sugars lend a particular effect: demerara makes a delicious crunchy topping, while dark barbados sugar imparts a rich colour and distinctive flavour. Golden syrup, honey, treacle and malt extract are generally added for flavour only and are used in addition to sugar. Sugar substitutes and artificial sweeteners cannot be substituted for sugar in cakes.

❖ EGGS: Avoid using eggs straight from the refrigerator – a cake mixture is much more likely to curdle if it's made with cold eggs. Eggs act as a raising agent in many cakes so it's important to select the right size – use size 2 eggs in these recipes unless otherwise stated. Using the wrong size could result in failure.

❖ FLOUR: Self-raising flour is used in many cake recipes as it conveniently includes a raising agent. Plain flour can be converted to self-raising, by blending it with baking powder. To every 225 g (8 oz) plain flour, use 15 ml (1 level tbsp) baking powder for scones; 10 ml (2 level tsp) for a plain cake mixture; and 5 ml (1 level tsp) for a rich fruit cake mixture. Cake flour is now widely available; its slightly lower gluten content is deemed to produce lighter cakes, but in practice the difference is minimal.

Wholemeal flour is nutritionally preferred to white flour but produces cakes with a darker colour and denser texture. If you wish to use wholemeal flour, a mixture of white and wholemeal with a little extra baking powder works best. If you sieve it don't forget to tip in the bran from the sieve or valuable fibre and nutrients will be wasted.

❖ Cake-making Methods ❖

The following standard mixing methods employ different techniques which largely determine the texture of the cake. Some recipes use more than one method – for example, creamed cakes sometimes have whisked egg whites folded in.

❖ CREAMING: This is the traditional method used to make a classic Victoria sandwich. Softened fat makes creaming considerably easier, as does a hand-held whisk or a mixer. As soon as the fat and sugar are creamed to a pale-coloured mixture, fluffy and light in texture, you can start adding the beaten egg. Don't be tempted to add it all at once or the mixture will curdle, producing a dense cake. If the mixture looks as if it is about to curdle, add a spoonful of the sifted flour. Finally fold in all of the flour with a large metal spoon.

❖ ALL-IN-ONE: For speedy last-minute cakes, this is the ideal method. Simply throw all the ingredients together in a bowl and beat thoroughly. If using a food processor, don't over-process or you will beat out all the air. Soft-tub margarine or softened butter are the best fats to use. It's prudent to add a little extra raising agent to compensate for the lack of creaming.

❖ WHISKING: This is the method used to produce the classic fat-less sponge. Because the cake relies on the volume of air trapped in the egg mixture to make it rise, the eggs must be beaten really thoroughly. This is virtually impossible unless you use an electric hand-held whisk, an electric table-top mixer or a good rotary whisk plus strong arms and a lot of patience! Standing the bowl over a pan of simmering water helps to increase volume and stabilise the foamy mass. Keep the the bottom of the bowl clear of the water or you will end up with scrambled eggs! The whisked mixture is ready for the flour when you can lift the beaters and write the numeral 8 on the surface with the trail of mixture.

A Genoese sponge is a whisked sponge that's enriched with melted butter. It is probably the most difficult of all cakes to perfect, but well worth the effort since it is rich yet light, and keeps much better than a fatless sponge. The tricky part is getting the butter to the correct consistency – it should be melted but cooled until almost cold. Add the butter gradually by pouring a small amount around the edge of the bowl. Fold this in and then add a little more, but take your time.

❖ MELTING: Cakes made by this method usually contain a high proportion of treacle, golden syrup, honey or malt extract and it is vital that they are measured accurately; if you add too much the cake will be dense and it will probably sink in the middle. If the measurements are given in tablespoons, use a warmed measuring spoon, preferably metal. Alternatively put the saucepan on the scales, set the dial to zero then spoon in the required amount.

This measured syrup or treacle is then heated gently with fat and sugar until melted; cool slightly before mixing with the dried ingredients. The mixture should have the consistency of a thick batter; it should find its own level when poured into the tin. For best results wrap these cakes in greaseproof paper, then overwrap with foil and store for 1–2 days before cutting.

❖ RUBBING-IN: As the name suggests these cakes are made in the same way as shortcrust pastry, by rubbing the fat into the flour with the fingertips. Once you have rubbed in the fat, add the liquid carefully – too much will result in a heavy doughy cake, while too little will make it dry. Remember that flour absorbencies vary; use the recipe as a fairly accurate guide but don't be afraid to add a little more or a little less. In general, for large cakes the mixture should be soft enough to drop from a spoon; for small buns it should be a little stiffer. Because rubbed-in cakes are comparatively low in fat they stale quickly and are best eaten on the day of making.

Cake Tins

Using the correct size tin can make all the difference between success and failure. It goes without saying that if you put a cake mixture in a tin that's too big you will end up with a pancake and if the tin is too small the mixture will spill out over the top. Because tins come in a confusing array of sizes – particularly loaf tins – a volume measurement is sometimes given as well. To check the capacity of a tin, simply fill with water from a measuring jug, noting how many litres (or pints) it will hold.

Grease tins and base-line with lightly greased greaseproof paper, or non-stick baking parchment which does not require greasing. We advise doing this even when using non-stick cake tins, to ease turning out. For rich mixtures and fruit cakes, line the sides of the tin, too. For large rich fruit cakes, stand the tin on a double thickness of brown paper and tie a band of brown paper around the outside of the tin to prevent the outside overcooking.

What Went Wrong?

Unfortunately it's not always easy to determine why a cake hasn't come out looking like the picture. It is important to measure everything accurately – using scales and measuring spoons – and to use the right size tin. Once the cake is in the oven resist the temptation to open the door until at least three quarters of the cooking time has elapsed – a sudden gush of cold air will make it sink in the middle. If your cake appears to be browning too quickly, cover it with greaseproof paper towards the end of cooking. Here are some other common problems and possible causes:

CLOSE, DENSE TEXTURE
❖ Too much liquid.
❖ Too little raising agent, or raising agent past its use-by date.
❖ Insufficient creaming of the fat and sugar.
❖ Creamed mixture curdled.
❖ Flour folded in too vigorously.

PEAKED AND CRACKED TOP
❖ Oven too hot, or the cake was too near the top of the oven.
❖ Not enough liquid.
❖ Tin too small.

SUNKEN FRUIT
❖ Fruit too sticky or too wet.
❖ Mixture too soft to support the weight of the fruit.

SUNK IN THE MIDDLE
❖ Wrong size tin.
❖ Inaccurately measured ingredients (gingerbread in particular).
❖ Oven too hot or too cool, or cooking time too short.
❖ Oven door opened too soon.

Storing Cakes

Make sure that the cake is completely cold before you put it into a cake tin or plastic airtight container. If you haven't a large enough container, wrap in a double layer of greaseproof paper and overwrap with foil. Avoid putting rich fruit cakes in direct contact with foil; the fruit may react with it. Most cakes freeze well; they are best frozen undecorated. If you want to freeze a finished gâteau, open freeze, then pack in a rigid container.

❖ Biscuits and Scones ❖

Biscuits are quick and easy to make, taste much better than many commercial varieties, and they're cheaper too! Exaggerate the fact that they are homemade by using interesting or quirky cutters; you'll find a wide range in most cookshops. Don't be alarmed if the biscuits seem soft when you have baked them; some, particularly those containing syrup or honey, crisp as they cool. Homemade biscuits freeze well and thaw in a matter of minutes, so it's a good idea to make double quantities and freeze some.

Homemade scones are delicious served warm from the oven. To ensure a good rise, avoid heavy handling, or rolling the dough too thinly: it should be at least 2 cm (¾ inch) thick. Remember too that the raising agent begins to work as soon as it is mixed with liquid, so put the scones into a hot oven as quickly as possible.

❖ Peanut and Raisin Cookies ❖

MAKES 30	
PREPARATION TIME	• 125 g (4 oz) butter or margarine, softened
15 minutes	• 150 g (5 oz) caster sugar
COOKING TIME	• 1 egg
15 minutes	• 150 g (5 oz) plain white flour
FREEZING	
Suitable	

• 125 g (4 oz) butter or
margarine, softened
• 150 g (5 oz) caster
sugar
• 1 egg
• 150 g (5 oz) plain
white flour
• 2.5 ml (½ tsp) baking
powder
• pinch of salt
• 125 g (4 oz) crunchy
peanut butter
• 175 g (6 oz) raisins

110 CALS/BISCUIT

1 Put all the ingredients except the raisins in a bowl and beat together until well blended. Stir in the raisins.
2 Spoon large teaspoonfuls of the mixture onto lightly greased baking sheets, leaving room for spreading.
3 Bake at 190°C (375°F) mark 5 for about 15 minutes, or until golden brown around the edges. Allow to cool slightly before lifting onto a wire rack to cool completely.

Variations

CHOCOLATE NUT COOKIES: Omit the peanut butter and raisins and add 5 ml (1 tsp) vanilla essence. Stir in 175 g (6 oz) chocolate drops and 75 g (3 oz) roughly chopped walnuts.

COCONUT AND CHERRY COOKIES: Omit the peanut butter and raisins, reduce the sugar to 75 g (3 oz) and stir in 50 g (2 oz) desiccated coconut and 125 g (4 oz) rinsed, dried and roughly chopped glacé cherries.

OAT AND CINNAMON COOKIES: Omit the peanut butter and raisins and add 5 ml (1 tsp) vanilla essence. Stir in 5 ml (1 tsp) ground cinnamon and 75 g (3 oz) rolled oats.

❖ Inverness Gingernuts ❖

MAKES 36	
PREPARATION TIME	20 minutes
COOKING TIME	20–25 minutes
FREEZING	Suitable
COLOUR INDEX	Page 78

• 225 g (8 oz) plain
white flour
• 10 ml (2 tsp) ground
ginger
• 5 ml (1 tsp) ground
mixed spice
• 75 g (3 oz) fine
oatmeal
• 75 g (3 oz) caster
sugar
• 2.5 ml (½ tsp)
bicarbonate of soda
• 175 g (6 oz) treacle
• 50 g (2 oz) butter

75 CALS/BISCUIT

1 Put the flour, ginger, spice, oatmeal, sugar and bicarbonate of soda in a bowl and mix together.
2 Heat the treacle and butter in a pan until melted. Pour onto the dry ingredients and mix to a smooth dough. Knead well.
3 Roll out to about a 5 mm (¼ inch) thickness. Prick with a fork and cut out 6 cm (2½ inch) rounds with a plain cutter. Place on greased baking sheets. Bake at 170°C (325°F) mark 3 for 20–25 minutes, until firm to the touch. Transfer to wire racks to cool.

❖ Caraway Biscuits ❖

MAKES 24	
PREPARATION TIME	20 minutes
COOKING TIME	10 minutes
FREEZING	Suitable
COLOUR INDEX	Page 78

• 225 g (8 oz) plain
white flour
• 75 g (3 oz) butter,
diced
• 75 g (3 oz) caster
sugar
• 1 egg, beaten
• 1 egg white, beaten, to
glaze
• caraway seeds, for
sprinkling

70 CALS/BISCUIT

1 Sift the flour into a bowl and rub in the butter until the mixture resembles fine breadcrumbs. Stir in the sugar. Add the egg and mix to a stiff paste.
2 Roll out on a lightly floured surface, until 5 mm (¼ inch) thick. Prick with a fork and cut into rounds with a 5 cm (2 inch) plain cutter. Brush with egg white and sprinkle on a few caraway seeds.
3 Place on greased baking sheets. Bake at 180°C (350°F) mark 4 for 10 minutes or until lightly browned. Cool on wire racks.

❖ Shrewsbury Biscuits ❖

MAKES 24	
PREPARATION TIME	20 minutes
COOKING TIME	15 minutes
FREEZING	Suitable
COLOUR INDEX	Page 78

• 125 g (4 oz) butter or
block margarine
• 150 g (5 oz) caster
sugar
• 2 egg yolks
• 225 g (8 oz) plain flour
• finely grated rind of
1 lemon or orange
• 50 g (2 oz) chopped
dried fruit (optional)

100 CALS/BISCUIT

1 Cream the butter and sugar together in a bowl until pale and fluffy. Add the egg yolks and beat well. Stir in the flour, grated lemon rind and dried fruit if using. Mix to a fairly firm dough with a round-bladed knife.
2 Turn out onto a lightly floured surface and knead lightly. Roll out to a 5 mm (¼ inch) thickness and cut out rounds with a 6 cm (2½ inch) fluted cutter. Place on lightly greased baking sheets.
3 Bake at 180°C (350°F) mark 4 for 15 minutes, or until golden.

❖ Coconut Macaroons ❖

MAKES 24
PREPARATION TIME
20 minutes
COOKING TIME
25 minutes
FREEZING
Suitable

- 2 egg whites
- 100 g (4 oz) icing sugar, sifted
- 100 g (4 oz) ground almonds
- few drops of almond essence
- 100 g (4 oz) desiccated coconut
- 30 ml (2 tbsp) shredded coconut

70 CALS/BISCUIT

1 Line 2 baking sheets with non-stick baking parchment. Whisk the egg whites in a bowl until stiff but not dry. Lightly fold in the icing sugar.

2 Gently stir in the ground almonds, almond essence and desiccated coconut until the mixture forms a sticky dough.

3 Spoon walnut-sized pieces of mixture onto the lined baking sheets. Press a few strands of shredded coconut on the top of each one.

4 Bake at 150°C (300°F) mark 2 for about 25 minutes; the outer crust should be golden and the inside soft. Cool on a wire rack.

❖ Easter Biscuits ❖

MAKES 30
PREPARATION TIME
20 minutes
COOKING TIME
15 minutes
FREEZING
Suitable
COLOUR INDEX
Page 78

- 100 g (4 oz) butter
- 75 g (3 oz) caster sugar
- 1 egg, separated
- 200 g (7 oz) plain white flour
- pinch of salt
- 2.5 ml (½ tsp) ground mixed spice
- 2.5 ml (½ tsp) ground cinnamon
- 50 g (2 oz) currants
- 15 ml (1 tbsp) chopped mixed peel
- 15–30 ml (1–2 tbsp) brandy or milk
- caster sugar, for sprinkling

65 CALS/BISCUIT

1 Cream the butter and sugar together in a bowl until pale and fluffy, then beat in the egg yolk. Sift the flour, salt and spices together over the mixture. Stir well, then add the fruit and mixed peel, with enough brandy or milk to give a fairly soft dough.
2 Knead lightly on a lightly floured surface and roll out to a 5 mm (¼ inch) thickness. Cut into 5 cm (2 inch) rounds using a fluted cutter. Place on lightly greased baking sheets.
3 Bake at 200°C (400°F) mark 6 for 10 minutes, then brush with the lightly beaten egg white and sprinkle with a little caster sugar. Return to the oven for a further 5 minutes, or until golden brown. Transfer to wire racks to cool.

❖ Shortbread ❖

MAKES 8
PREPARATION TIME
20 minutes
COOKING TIME
About 40 minutes
FREEZING
Suitable
COLOUR INDEX
Page 79

- 150 g (5 oz) plain white flour
- 45 ml (3 tbsp) rice flour
- 50 g (2 oz) caster sugar
- 100 g (4 oz) butter, at room temperature
- caster sugar, for dredging

200 CALS/PIECE

1 Sift the flours into a bowl and add the sugar. Work in the butter with your fingertips – keep it in one piece and gradually work in the dry ingredients. Knead well.
2 Pack into a floured shortbread mould, then turn out onto a baking sheet. Alternatively, pack into an 18 cm (7 inch) sandwich tin, prick well with a fork and pinch up the edges decoratively with finger and thumb.
3 Bake at 170°C (325°F) mark 3 for about 40 minutes, until firm and pale golden. Mark into 8 triangles while still hot. Cool slightly before transferring to a wire rack.
4 When cool, dredge with sugar. Serve cut into wedges.

NOTE: Traditional Scottish shortbread moulds are made with a thistle design in the centre. These can be bought at cookshops, but are not essential; an ordinary sandwich tin will do the job just as well. Be sure to use a good-quality butter. The flavour of shortbread relies heavily on the butter in the mixture, and margarine is no substitute.

❖ Florentines ❖

MAKES 20–24
PREPARATION TIME
0 minutes, plus
ooling
OOKING TIME
0 minutes
REEZING
uitable (stage 3)

- *100 g (3½ oz) butter or margarine*
- *125 g (4 oz) caster sugar*
- *125 g (4 oz) flaked almonds, roughly chopped*
- *25 g (1 oz) sultanas*
- *5 glacé cherries, chopped*
- *25 g (1 oz) chopped mixed peel*
- *15 ml (1 tbsp) single cream*
- *225 g (8 oz) plain or white chocolate, in pieces*

165–140 CALS/BISCUIT

1 Line 3 baking sheets with non-stick baking parchment. Melt the butter in a saucepan over a low heat. Add the sugar and heat gently until dissolved, then boil for 1 minute. Remove from the heat and add the remaining ingredients, except the chocolate, stirring well to mix.

2 Drop the mixture in small, well-rounded heaps onto the prepared baking sheets, allowing enough room between each for the mixture to spread. Bake at 180°C (350°F) mark 4 for 10 minutes or until golden brown.

3 Remove from the oven and press around the edges of the biscuits with the blade of a knife to neaten the shape. Leave on the baking sheets for 5 minutes until beginning to firm, then lift onto a wire rack. Allow to cool for 20 minutes.

4 Melt the chocolate in a heatproof bowl over a pan of simmering water. Stir until smooth, then leave to cool for 10–15 minutes until beginning to set. Spread over the back of the biscuits and mark wavy lines with a fork. Leave to set.

❖ Gingerbread Men ❖

MAKES 10–12
PREPARATION TIME
20 minutes
COOKING TIME
12–15 minutes
FREEZING
Suitable
COLOUR INDEX
Page 79

- *350 g (12 oz) plain white flour*
- *5 ml (1 tsp) bicarbonate of soda*
- *10 ml (2 tsp) ground ginger*
- *100 g (4 oz) butter or block margarine*
- *175 g (6 oz) light soft brown sugar*
- *60 ml (4 tbsp) golden syrup*
- *1 egg, beaten*
- *currants, to decorate*

300–250 CALS/BISCUIT

1 Sift the flour, bicarbonate of soda and ginger into a bowl. Rub in the butter until mixture resembles fine crumbs. Stir in the sugar. Beat the syrup with the egg, then stir in.

2 Mix to form a dough and knead until smooth. Divide in half and roll out each piece on a lightly floured surface to a 5 mm (¼ inch) thickness.

3 Using suitable cutters, cut out gingerbread figures and place them on lightly greased baking sheets. Decorate with currants to represent eyes and buttons. Bake at 190°C (375°F) mark 5 for 12–15 minutes, until golden. Cool slightly, then transfer to a wire rack to cool completely.

❖ Brandy Snaps ❖

MAKES 12–16

PREPARATION TIME
25 minutes
COOKING TIME
8–10 minutes
FREEZING
Suitable (unfilled)

- 75 g (3 oz) butter or block margarine
- 75 g (3 oz) caster sugar
- 45 ml (3 tbsp) golden syrup
- 75 g (3 oz) plain white flour
- 5 ml (1 tsp) ground ginger
- 30 ml (2 tbsp) brandy
- 15 ml (1 tbsp) lemon juice

TO SERVE:
- 150 ml (¼ pint) double cream, whipped (optional)

165–125 CALS/BISCUIT

1 Lightly oil the handles of several wooden spoons and line 2–3 baking sheets with non-stick baking parchment.

2 Place the butter, sugar and golden syrup in a heavy-based pan and warm gently until evenly blended. Allow to cool for 2–3 minutes. Stir in the flour and ginger sifted together, the brandy and lemon juice.

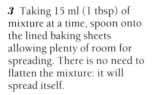

3 Taking 15 ml (1 tbsp) of mixture at a time, spoon onto the lined baking sheets allowing plenty of room for spreading. There is no need to flatten the mixture: it will spread itself.

4 Bake at 190°C (375°F) mark 5 for about 8–10 minutes or until the brandy snaps have spread considerably and are golden brown – the texture will be open and lacy. Remove from oven and leave to firm up slightly – about 15 seconds only. Loosen with a palette knife and roll them around the spoon handles.

5 Place on a wire rack and leave until set, then twist gently to remove and leave to cool completely and crisp up. Just before serving, fill with whipped cream, if desired, using a piping bag fitted with a 1 cm (½ inch) fluted nozzle.

NOTE: If the biscuits set too hard to roll while on the baking sheet, return to the oven for a few moments to soften.

Variations

LACY TUILES: Instead of using wooden spoon handles, curve the brandy snap rounds over a lightly oiled large rolling pin. These biscuits take their name from the French *tuile* meaning roof tile, which they resemble.

LACY PETALS: Allow the biscuits to cool on the baking sheets until beginning to set, then carefully lift off and pinch 2 edges together to form a point. The biscuits will then resemble petals.

❖ Pistachio Rings ❖

MAKES 20

PREPARATION TIME
30 minutes
COOKING TIME
8–10 minutes
FREEZING
Suitable
(undecorated)
COLOUR INDEX
Page 79

- 175 g (6 oz) butter, softened
- 50 g (2 oz) caster sugar
- 225 g (8 oz) plain white flour, sifted
- 15 ml (1 tbsp) milk

ICING:
- 125 g (4 oz) icing sugar, sifted
- 15–30 ml (1–2 tbsp) fresh lime juice
- 40 g (1½ oz) shelled pistachio nuts, skinned and chopped

150 CALS/BISCUIT

1 Cream the butter and sugar together until light and creamy. Stir in the flour and milk and mix to form a fairly soft dough. Put the mixture into a piping bag fitted with a 1 cm (½ inch) star nozzle.

4 Spread the chocolate and hazelnut spread evenly over the base in the tin. Cover with the cake mixture. Bake at 180°C (350°F) mark 4 for 45–50 minutes or until golden, covering loosely with foil if necessary.
5 Leave in the tin for about 10 minutes before turning out onto a wire rack to cool. Cut into bars and store in an airtight container for up to 2 days.

? Pipe the mixture into 5.5 m (2¼ inch) diameter rings, paced well apart, on greased aking sheets. Bake at 180°C 350°F) mark 4 for 8–10 minutes until lightly golden nd cooked through.

3 Transfer the biscuits to wire racks to cool slightly. Meanwhile, blend the icing sugar with enough lime juice to make a thin icing. Brush the icing over the rings while still warm, to glaze.

4 Sprinkle at once with chopped nuts. Leave to set before serving.

❖ Fruit and Nut Bars ❖

❖ Chocolate Pecan Bars ❖

MAKES 25		
PREPARATION TIME 5 minutes COOKING TIME about 1 hour FREEZING suitable COLOUR INDEX age 80	BASE: • 125 g (4 oz) plain white flour • 25 g (1 oz) icing sugar • 65 g (2½ oz) butter, in pieces • 1 egg yolk CAKE: • 125 g (4 oz) self-raising white flour • 5 ml (1 tsp) baking powder • 125 g (4 oz) caster sugar	• 3–4 drops of vanilla essence • 2 eggs • 150 g (5 oz) butter, softened • 150 g (5 oz) milk chocolate chips • 75 g (3 oz) pecan nuts TO ASSEMBLE: • 90 ml (6 tbsp) chocolate and hazelnut spread

200 CALS/BAR

Grease and base-line a 4 cm (1½ inch) deep baking tin measuring 26 × 16 cm (10¼ × 6½ inches).
To make the base, put the flour, icing sugar and butter in a ood processor and work the mixture until crumb-like in xture. Add the egg yolk and blend for 10–15 seconds or until e mixture begins to come together. Turn into the tin and press to a thin layer. Bake at 200°C (400°F) mark 6 for 15 minutes r until golden.
Meanwhile, prepare the cake mixture. Put the flour, baking owder, sugar, vanilla essence, eggs and butter in the food rocessor and blend for 15 seconds or until smooth. Turn into a owl and fold in the chocolate chips and pecan nuts.

MAKES 12		
PREPARATION TIME 20 minutes COOKING TIME About 40 minutes FREEZING Not suitable	• 450 g (1 lb) eating apples • 75 ml (5 tbsp) unsweetened fruit juice • 225 g (8 oz) mixed dried fruit, such as no-soak dried apricots, dates, sultanas, chopped if necessary • 125 g (4 oz) chopped mixed nuts • 75 g (3 oz) rolled oats	• 75 g (3 oz) self-raising wholemeal flour • 25 g (1 oz) desiccated coconut • 50 g (2 oz) pumpkin seeds • 30 ml (2 tbsp) oil • 30 ml (2 tbsp) pear and apple spread, or apricot conserve

235 CALS/BAR

1 Grease and base-line a 20 cm (8 inch) square tin. Peel, core and chop the apples and place in a heavy-based saucepan with the fruit juice. Cover and cook gently for 10–15 minutes or until the apples are very soft, shaking the pan occasionally (don't remove the lid). Beat thoroughly to make a smooth purée.
2 Add all the remaining ingredients except the spread or conserve, and beat well. Spoon the mixture into the prepared tin. Bake at 180°C (350°F) mark 4 for about 40 minutes or until firm to the touch.
3 Leave in the tin for 5 minutes, then turn out onto a wire rack. Brush with the spread or conserve while still warm and mark into 12 bars. Leave to cool, then cut through into bars.

❖ Vanilla Crumble Bars ❖

MAKES 25

PREPARATION TIME
15 minutes
COOKING TIME
50–55 minutes
FREEZING
Suitable

CRUMBLE TOPPING:
• 75 g (3 oz) butter, softened
• 75 g (3 oz) caster sugar
• 125 g (4 oz) plain white flour
CAKE:
• 175 g (6 oz) butter
• 175 g (6 oz) caster sugar

• 175 g (6 oz) self-raising white flour
• finely grated rind of 1 lemon
• 3 eggs
• 7.5 ml (1½ tsp) vanilla essence

160 CALS/BAR

1 Grease and base-line a 4 cm (1½ inch) deep baking tin, measuring 26 × 16 cm (10¼ × 6½ inches).
2 To make the crumble topping, put the butter and sugar in a food processor and blend until smooth. Add the plain flour and blend for 8–10 seconds to a very rough crumb mixture; remove and set aside.
3 To make the cake, place the butter, sugar, self-raising flour, grated lemon rind, eggs and vanilla essence in the food processor and blend for about 15 seconds or until smooth. Pour into the prepared tin.
4 Sprinkle the crumble topping over the surface of the mixture to cover and press down lightly.
5 Bake at 180°C (350°F) mark 4 for 50–55 minutes, covering loosely with foil if necessary. Leave in the tin for 5 minutes before turning out onto a wire rack to cool. Cut into bars. Store in an airtight container for up to 3 days.

Cherry and Coconut Crumble Bars
Make the base as above, adding 50 g (2 oz) desiccated coconut at the end of stage 2. Fold in 225 g (8 oz) rinsed, dried and quartered glacé cherries at the end of stage 3. Cook as above.

❖ Lemon and Almond Bars ❖

MAKES 25

PREPARATION TIME
15 minutes
COOKING TIME
About 1 hour
FREEZING
Suitable
COLOUR INDEX
Page 80

BASE:
• 125 g (4 oz) plain white flour
• 25 g (1 oz) icing sugar
• 65 g (2½ oz) butter, in pieces
• 1 egg yolk
CAKE:
• 125 g (4 oz) self-raising white flour
• 5 ml (1 tsp) baking powder
• 2.5 ml (½ tsp) ground nutmeg
• 125 g (4 oz) caster sugar

• 1.25 ml (¼ tsp) almond essence
• 2 eggs
• 150 g (5 oz) butter, softened
• 150 g (5 oz) flaked almonds
TO ASSEMBLE:
75 ml (5 tbsp) lemon curd
• icing sugar, for dusting

170 CALS/BAR

1 Grease and base-line a 4 cm (1½ inch) deep baking tin, measuring 26 × 16 cm (10¼ × 6½ inches).
2 To make the base, put the flour, icing sugar and butter in a food processor and blend until crumb-like in texture. Add the egg yolk and blend for 10–15 seconds or until the mixture begins to come together. Turn into the prepared tin and press into a thin layer. Bake at 200°C (400°F) mark 6 for 15 minutes or until golden.
3 Meanwhile, prepare the cake mixture. Put the flour, baking powder, nutmeg, sugar, almond essence, eggs and butter in the food processor and blend for 15 seconds or until smooth. Turn into a bowl and fold in two thirds of the flaked almonds; set aside.
4 Spread the lemon curd evenly over the base in the tin. Cover with the cake mixture and sprinkle with the remaining almonds. Bake at 180°C (350°F) mark 4 for 45–50 minutes or until golden, covering loosely with foil if necessary.
5 Leave in the tin for about 10 minutes before turning out onto a wire rack to cool. Cut into bars and store in an airtight container for up to 2 days. Dust with icing sugar to serve.

Date and Banana Bars
Omit the lemon curd, almond essence and almonds. Instead, place 175 g (6 oz) chopped dates in a small saucepan with the grated rind and juice of 1 lemon and 30 ml (2 tbsp) water. Simmer very gently for about 4 minutes or until tender; there should be very little liquid left. Leave to cool slightly. Blend 1 roughly chopped banana with the mixture in step 3. Fold in the date mixture. Finish as above, omitting the icing sugar.

❖ Chocolate Brownies ❖

4 Pour into the prepared tin and bake at 190°C (375°F) mark 5 for 40–45 minutes or until just firm to the touch in the centre. Leave to cool in the tin, then turn out. Trim off the edges and cut into squares.

NOTE: Do not overcook or the gooey texture will be ruined.

MAKES 24	
PREPARATION TIME	• 550 g (1¼ lb) plain chocolate
0.minutes	• 225 g (8 oz) butter
OOKING TIME	• 3 eggs
0–45 minutes	• 30 ml (2 tbsp) freshly made strong coffee
FEEZING	• 225 g (8 oz) caster sugar
uitable	

- 75 g (3 oz) self-raising white flour
- 1.25 ml (¼ tsp) salt
- 175 g (6 oz) walnut halves, chopped
- 5 ml (1 tsp) vanilla essence

300 CALS/CAKE

Grease and line a baking tin easuring 22 × 29 cm 8½ × 11½ inches) across top d 19×27 cm (7½×10½ inches) ross the base. (Or use a milar-sized tin.)

2 Using a sharp knife, roughly chop 225 g (8 oz) of the chocolate and set aside. Melt the remaining chocolate with the butter in a heatproof bowl over a pan of simmering water. Leave to cool slightly.

3 Mix the eggs, coffee and sugar together in a large bowl until smooth, then gradually beat in the melted chocolate mixture. Fold in the flour, salt, walnuts, vanilla essence and chopped chocolate.

❖ Madeleines ❖

MAKES 24	
PREPARATION TIME	• 3 eggs
20 minutes	• 150 g (5 oz) caster sugar
COOKING TIME	• 150 g (5 oz) plain white flour
12 minutes	
FREEZING	• 2.5 ml (½ tsp) baking powder
Suitable	
COLOUR INDEX	• pinch of salt
Page 79	

- finely grated rind of 1 lemon
- 150 g (5 oz) butter, melted and cooled
- icing sugar, for dusting

120 CALS/CAKE

1 Brush two trays of Madeleine moulds with melted white vegetable fat, then dust with flour, shaking off any excess.
2 Beat the eggs and sugar together in a bowl until rich and creamy. Sift in the flour with the baking powder and salt. Add the lemon rind and beat well. Pour in the melted butter and fold in until blended.
3 Half-fill the Madeleine moulds with the mixture and leave to stand for 10 minutes. Bake at 220°C (425°F) mark 7 for about 12 minutes or until well risen and golden. Ease out of the tins and cool on a wire rack. Serve dusted with icing sugar.

NOTE: If you have only 1 Madeleine tray, bake in 2 batches.

❖ Queen Cakes ❖

MAKES 16	
PREPARATION TIME	• 100 g (4 oz) butter
15 minutes	• 100 g (4 oz) caster sugar
COOKING TIME	
15–20 minutes	• 2 eggs, beaten
FREEZING	
Suitable	
COLOUR INDEX	
Page 79	

- 100 g (4 oz) self-raising white flour
- 50 g (2 oz) sultanas

110 CALS/CAKE

1 Put 16 paper cases into a tray of bun tins.
2 Cream the butter and sugar together until pale and fluffy. Gradually beat in the eggs, a little at a time, beating well after each addition. Fold in the flour, then the fruit.
3 Half-fill the paper cases. Bake at 190°C (375°F) mark 5 for 15–20 minutes, until golden. Transfer to a wire rack to cool.

Variations
Replace the sultanas with: 50 g (2 oz) chopped dates; 50 g (2 oz) chopped glacé cherries; or 50 g (2 oz) chocolate chips.
FAIRY CAKES: Omit sultanas. Ice the cakes with Glacé Icing (page 410).

❖ Oven Scones ❖

MAKES 8

PREPARATION TIME
15 minutes
COOKING TIME
About 10 minutes
FREEZING
Suitable

- *225 g (8 oz) self-raising white flour*
- *pinch of salt*
- *5 ml (1 tsp) baking powder*
- *40 g (1½ oz) butter or margarine*
- *about 150 ml (¼ pint) milk*
- *beaten egg or milk, to glaze (optional)*

140 CALS/SCONE

1 Sift the flour, salt and baking powder together into a bowl. Rub in the butter until the mixture resembles fine breadcrumbs. Stir in enough milk to give a fairly soft, light dough.

2 On a lightly floured surface, lightly roll out the dough to a 2 cm (¾ inch) thickness and cut into rounds with a 6 cm (2½ inch) plain cutter.

3 Place on a greased baking sheet and brush the tops with beaten egg or milk. Bake at 220°C (425°F) mark 7 for about 10 minutes until golden brown and well risen. Cool on a wire rack. Serve warm, split and filled with jam and cream.

Variations

WHOLEMEAL SCONES: Replace half of the white flour with wholemeal flour.

FRUIT SCONES: Add 50 g (2 oz) currants, sultanas, raisins or chopped dates (or a mixture) to the dry ingredients.

CHEESE AND HERB SCONES: Sift 5 ml (1 tsp) mustard powder with the dry ingredients. Stir 50 g (2 oz) finely grated Cheddar cheese into the mixture before adding the milk. After glazing, sprinkle a little cheese on top of each scone.

❖ Drop Scones ❖

MAKES 15–18

PREPARATION TIME
10 minutes
COOKING TIME
12–18 minutes
FREEZING
Suitable
COLOUR INDEX
Page 80

- *100 g (4 oz) self-raising flour*
- *30 ml (2 tbsp) caster sugar*
- *1 egg, beaten*
- *150 ml (¼ pint) milk*

40–35 CALS/SCONE

1 Mix the flour and sugar together in a bowl. Make a well in the centre and stir in the egg, with enough of the milk to make a batter the consistency of thick cream; the mixing should be done as quickly and lightly as possible.

2 Cook the mixture in batches: drop spoonfuls onto a greased hot griddle or heavy-based frying pan.

3 Keep the griddle at a steady heat and when bubbles rise to the surface of the scone and burst, after 2–3 minutes, turn over with a palette knife. Continue cooking for a further 2–3 minutes, until golden brown on the other side.

4 Place the cooked drop scones on a clean tea towel and cover with another towel to keep in the steam and prevent the scones from becoming dry. Serve warm, with butter, or cream and jam.

❖ Pecan and Raisin Muffins ❖

MAKES 12

PREPARATION TIME
15 minutes
COOKING TIME
25 minutes
FREEZING
Suitable
COLOUR INDEX
Page 80

- *350 g (12 oz) plain white flour*
- *15 ml (1 tbsp) baking powder*
- *pinch of salt*
- *125 g (4 oz) caster sugar*
- *2 eggs*
- *150 ml (¼ pint) milk*
- *60 ml (4 tbsp) corn oil*
- *1.25 ml (¼ tsp) vanilla essence*
- *75 g (3 oz) pecan nuts roughly chopped*
- *75 g (3 oz) raisins*

270 CALS/MUFFIN

1 Line 12 deep bun tins with paper cases, or thoroughly grease 12 muffin tins.

2 Sift the flour, baking powder and salt into a bowl. Mix in the sugar and make a well in the centre.

3 Lightly beat the eggs with the milk, oil and vanilla essence and pour into the well. Mix quickly to blend into the dry ingredients; do not over-mix. Lightly stir in the nuts and raisins.

4 Divide the mixture equally between the paper cases or muffin tins. Bake at 190°C (375°F) mark 5 for 25 minutes or until well risen, golden brown and cooked through. Leave in tins for a few minutes, then transfer to a wire rack to cool. Serve warm or cold

❖ Mixed Fruit Teabread ❖

14 SLICES
PREPARATION TIME
15 minutes, plus
soaking
COOKING TIME
1¼ hours
FREEZING
Suitable
COLOUR INDEX
Page 80

- 175 g (6 oz) raisins
- 125 g (4 oz) sultanas
- 50 g (2 oz) currants
- 175 g (6 oz) soft brown sugar
- 300 ml (½ pint) strained cold black tea
- 1 egg, beaten

- 225 g (8 oz) plain wholemeal flour
- 7.5 ml (1½ tsp) baking powder
- 2.5 ml (½ tsp) ground mixed spice

175 CALS/SLICE

1 Put the dried fruit and sugar in a bowl. Pour over the tea and soak overnight. Grease and base-line a 1.1 litre (2 pint) loaf tin.
2 The next day, add the egg, flour, baking powder and mixed spice to the fruit and tea mixture. Beat thoroughly with a wooden spoon until all the ingredients are evenly combined. Spoon into the prepared tin and level the surface.
3 Bake at 180°C (350°F) mark 4 for about 1¼ hours or until well risen and a skewer inserted in the centre comes out clean.
4 Turn out and cool on a wire rack. Wrap in greaseproof paper and foil; store in an airtight container for 1–2 days before slicing.

❖ Marmalade Teabread ❖

8–10 SLICES
PREPARATION TIME
15 minutes
COOKING TIME
1¼ hours
FREEZING
Suitable
COLOUR INDEX
Page 80

- 200 g (7 oz) plain white flour
- 5 ml (1 tsp) ground ginger
- 5 ml (1 tsp) baking powder
- 50 g (2 oz) light soft brown sugar

- 50 g (2 oz) butter
- 60 ml (4 tbsp) marmalade
- 1 egg, beaten
- 75 ml (3 tbsp) milk
- 25 g (1 oz) candied peel, chopped

195–155 CALS/SLICE

Grease and base-line a 900 ml (1½ pint) loaf tin. Sift the flour, ginger and baking powder into a bowl and stir in the sugar. Rub in the butter.

2 Mix the marmalade with the egg and most of the milk. Add to the dry ingredients. Mix to a soft dough, adding more milk, if necessary.

3 Turn the mixture into the prepared tin, level the surface and press the candied peel on top. Bake at 170°C (325°F) mark 3 for about 1¼ hours or until well risen and firm to the touch. Turn out onto a wire rack to cool. Serve sliced and spread with butter.

❖ Sticky Gingerbread ❖

10 SLICES
PREPARATION TIME
20 minutes
COOKING TIME
1 hour
FREEZING
Suitable (without icing)

- 75 g (3 oz) butter or margarine
- 75 g (3 oz) light soft brown sugar
- 125 g (4 oz) black treacle
- 125 g (4 oz) golden syrup
- 175 g (6 oz) plain white flour
- 5 ml (1 tsp) ground ginger
- 2.5 ml (½ tsp) ground mixed spice
- 2.5 ml (½ tsp) ground cinnamon
- finely grated rind of 1 lemon

- 1 egg, beaten
- 75 ml (5 tbsp) milk
- 2.5 ml (½ tsp) bicarbonate of soda
- 25 g (1 oz) preserved stem ginger in syrup, drained and chopped

TOPPING:
- 50 g (2 oz) icing sugar, sifted
- 5–10 ml (1–2 tsp) lemon juice
- preserved stem ginger slices, to decorate

250 CALS/SLICE

1 Grease and base-line a 1.1 litre (2 pint) loaf tin. Melt the butter with the sugar, treacle and syrup in a saucepan over a low heat and stir until evenly blended; cool slightly.
2 Sift together the flour and ground spices into a bowl and make a well in the centre. Add the grated lemon rind with the treacle mixture, egg and milk. Beat well to mix, whisking if necessary, until smooth.
3 Dissolve the bicarbonate of soda in 15 ml (1 tbsp) hot water. Add to the gingerbread mixture with the chopped ginger; stir well. Pour into the prepared tin.
4 Bake at 170°C (325°F) mark 3 for about 1 hour, or until a skewer inserted in the centre comes out clean. Leave to cool in the tin for 5 minutes, then turn out onto a wire rack and leave until cold.
5 For the topping, mix the icing sugar with enough lemon juice to form a smooth thin glacé icing. Drizzle over the gingerbread and top with slices of ginger. Once set, store in an airtight container for up to 1 week.

❖ Marbled Chocolate Teabread ❖

14 SLICES
PREPARATION TIME
20 minutes
COOKING TIME
1¼–1½ hours
FREEZING
Suitable
COLOUR INDEX
Page 81

- *225 g (8 oz) butter or margarine*
- *225 g (8 oz) caster sugar*
- *3 eggs, beaten*
- *125 g (4 oz) self-raising white flour*
- *finely grated rind of 1 large orange*
- *30 ml (2 tbsp) orange juice*
- *few drops of orange flower water (optional)*
- *75 g (3 oz) plain chocolate*
- *15 ml (1 tbsp) cocoa powder*
- *125 g (4 oz) self-raising wholemeal flour*
- *15 ml (1 tbsp) milk*

290 CALS/SLICE

1 Grease a 1.1 litre (2 pint) loaf tin and line the base and sides with greaseproof paper.

2 Cream the fat and sugar together in a bowl until pale and fluffy, then gradually beat in the eggs, beating well after each addition.

3 Transfer half of the mixture to another bowl and beat in the white flour, orange rind, juice and orange flower water, if using.

4 Break the chocolate into pieces, put into a small bowl and place over a pan of simmering water. Stir until the chocolate melts. Stir into the remaining cake mixture with the cocoa powder, wholemeal flour and milk.

5 Put alternate spoonfuls of the two mixtures into the prepared tin. Use a knife to swirl through the mixtures to make a marbled effect, then level the surface. Bake at 180°C (350°F) mark 4 for 1¼–1½ hours, until well risen and firm to the touch. Turn out onto a wire rack to cool.

❖ Victoria Sandwich Cake ❖

8 SLICES
PREPARATION TIME
20 minutes
COOKING TIME
20 minutes
FREEZING
Suitable (unfilled)

- *175 g (6 oz) butter or margarine, softened*
- *175 g (6 oz) caster sugar*
- *3 eggs, size 3, beaten*
- *175 g (6 oz) self-raising white flour*

TO FINISH:
- *45–60 ml (3–4 tbsp) jam*
- *caster sugar, for dredging*

370 CALS/SERVING

1 Grease and base-line two 18 cm (7 inch) sandwich tins. Beat the butter and sugar together until pale and fluffy.

2 Add the eggs, a little at a time, beating well after each addition.

3 Fold in half the flour using a metal spoon, then fold in the rest.

4 Divide evenly between the tins and level the surface. Bake at 190°C (375°F) mark 5 for 20 minutes until well risen, firm to touch and beginning to shrink from sides of tins.

5 Turn out and leave to cool on a wire rack. When the cakes are cool, sandwich them together with jam and sprinkle the top with sugar.

Variations

CHOCOLATE: Replace 45 ml (3 tbsp) flour with 45 ml (3 tbsp) cocoa powder. Sandwich the cakes with Chocolate Butter Cream (page 410).

COFFEE: Add 10 ml (2 tsp) instant coffee powder, dissolved in a little warm water, to the creamed butter and sugar mixture with the eggs, or use 10 ml (2 tsp) coffee essence. Sandwich the cakes with Coffee Butter Cream (page 410).

ORANGE OR LEMON: Add the finely grated rind of an orange or lemon to the mixture. Sandwich the cakes with Orange or Lemon Butter Cream (page 410).

ALL-IN-ONE CAKE: Add 5 ml (1 tsp) baking powder to the basic recipe. Simply put all the ingredients in a large bowl or food processor and beat until smooth and glossy.

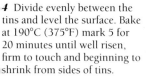

❖ Orange and Poppy Seed Cake ❖

12 SLICES		
PREPARATION TIME 10 minutes COOKING TIME 50–55 minutes FREEZING Suitable (without icing) COLOUR INDEX Page 81	• 225 g (8 oz) butter or margarine • 175 g (6 oz) golden caster sugar • 3 eggs • 350 g (12 oz) self-raising wholemeal flour • 5 ml (1 tsp) baking powder • pinch of salt	• finely grated rind and juice of 2 oranges • 50 g (2 oz) poppy seeds TOPPING: • 75 g (3 oz) icing sugar • 10–15 ml (2–3 tsp) orange juice • shredded orange rind, to decorate

335 CALS/SLICE

1 Grease and line a 1.4 litre (2½ pint) loaf tin. Put all the cake ingredients except the poppy seeds in a food processor and process until smooth and well mixed. Fold in the poppy seeds.
2 Spoon the mixture into the prepared tin and level the surface. Bake at 180°C (350°F) mark 4 for 50–55 minutes or until well risen and firm to the touch. Turn out and cool on a wire rack.
3 For the topping, mix the icing sugar with enough orange juice to form a smooth coating consistency. Spread over the top of the cake and decorate with orange rind shreds.

❖ Madeira Cake ❖

12 SLICES		
PREPARATION TIME 20 minutes COOKING TIME About 1 hour FREEZING Suitable COLOUR INDEX Page 81	• 100 g (4 oz) plain white flour • 100 g (4 oz) self-raising white flour • 175 g (6 oz) butter or block margarine, softened • 175 g (6 oz) caster sugar	• 5 ml (1 tsp) vanilla essence • 3 eggs, beaten • 15–30 ml (1–2 tbsp) milk (optional) • 2–3 thin slices citron peel

245 CALS/SLICE

1 Grease and line a deep 18 cm (7 inch) round cake tin. Sift the plain and self-raising flours together.
2 Cream the butter and sugar together in a bowl until pale and fluffy, then beat in the vanilla essence. Add the eggs, a little at a time, beating well after each addition.
3 Fold in the sifted flours with a metal spoon, adding a little milk if necessary to give a dropping consistency.
4 Spoon the mixture into the tin and level the surface. Bake at 180°C (350°F) mark 4 for 20 minutes. Lay the citron peel on top of the cake and bake for a further 40 minutes until firm. Turn out and cool on a wire rack.

❖ Honey Cake ❖

12–16 SLICES		
PREPARATION TIME 20 minutes COOKING TIME 1¼ hours FREEZING Suitable COLOUR INDEX Page 81	• 225 ml (8 fl oz) thin honey • 75 g (3 oz) butter • 350 g (12 oz) plain wholemeal flour • pinch of salt • 5 ml (1 tsp) ground mixed spice • 5 ml (1 tsp) bicarbonate of soda • 50 g (2 oz) glacé cherries, halved • 50 g (2 oz) chopped mixed peel	• 3 eggs • 45 ml (3 tbsp) milk • grated rind of 1 large lemon • 25 g (1 oz) flaked almonds TO FINISH: • 45 ml (3 tbsp) thin honey

250–185 CALS/SLICE

1 Grease and line a deep 20 cm (8 inch) square cake tin. Put the honey in a saucepan, add the butter and heat gently, stirring, until smooth.
2 Sift the flour, salt, spice and bicarbonate of soda into a large bowl, stirring in any bran left in the sieve. Add the cherries and peel.
3 Beat the eggs and milk together and stir into the honey mixture with the lemon rind. Pour gradually onto the dry ingredients, beating well after each addition, until well blended.
4 Turn the mixture into the prepared tin and sprinkle with the flaked almonds. Bake at 170°C (325°F) mark 3 for about 1¼ hours, until the cake is firm to the touch and a skewer inserted in the centre comes out clean.
5 Keeping the cake in the tin, prick the top all over with a skewer and spoon over the honey. Leave in the tin for a further 5 minutes, then turn out and place the cake the right way up on a wire rack. Allow to cool. Do not remove the greaseproof lining paper until the cake is cold.

❖ Spiced Apple Cake ❖

10 SLICES

PREPARATION TIME
20 minutes
COOKING TIME
1½ hours
FREEZING
Suitable
COLOUR INDEX
Page 81

- 125 g (4 oz) butter or margarine
- 175 g (6 oz) dark soft brown sugar
- 2 eggs, beaten
- 225 g (8 oz) plain wholemeal flour
- 5 ml (1 tsp) ground mixed spice
- 5 ml (1 tsp) ground cinnamon
- 10 ml (2 tsp) baking powder

- 450 g (1 lb) cooking apples, peeled, cored and chopped
- 45–60 ml (3–4 tbsp) milk

TOPPING:
- 15 ml (1 tbsp) thin honey
- 15 ml (1 tbsp) light demerara sugar

260 CALS/SLICE

1 Grease and line a deep 18 cm (7 inch) round cake tin.
2 Cream the butter and sugar together in a bowl until pale and fluffy. Add the eggs, a little at a time, beating well after each addition. Add the flour, spices and baking powder and mix well. Fold in the apples and milk to yield a soft dropping consistency.
3 Turn the mixture into the prepared tin and bake at 170°C (325°F) mark 3 for 1½ hours or until well risen and firm to the touch. Turn out onto a wire rack to cool.
4 When cold, brush with honey and sprinkle with the sugar.

❖ Carrot Cake ❖

10–12 SLICES

PREPARATION TIME
25 minutes
COOKING TIME
1¼–1½ hours
FREEZING
Suitable (without topping)
COLOUR INDEX
Page 81

- 225 g (8 oz) butter
- 225 g (8 oz) light soft brown sugar
- 4 eggs, separated
- finely grated rind of ½ orange
- 15 ml (1 tbsp) lemon juice
- 175 g (6 oz) self-raising white flour
- 5 ml (1 tsp) baking powder
- 50 g (2 oz) ground almonds

- 125 g (4 oz) walnut pieces, chopped
- 350 g (12 oz) young carrots, peeled and grated

TOPPING:
- 225 g (8 oz) full-fat soft cheese
- 10 ml (2 tsp) thin honey
- 5 ml (1 tsp) lemon juice
- 40 g (1½ oz) walnut pieces

600–500 CALS/SLICE

1 Grease and line a deep 20 cm (8 inch) round cake tin.
2 Cream the butter and sugar together in a bowl until pale and fluffy. Beat in the egg yolks, then stir in the orange rind and lemon juice.
3 Sift in the flour with the baking powder and fold into the mixture, then fold in the ground almonds and walnuts.
4 Whisk the egg whites until stiff and fold into the cake mixture with the carrots. Pour into the prepared tin and hollow the centre slightly.
5 Bake at 180°C (350°F) mark 4 for 1¼–1½ hours, covering the top with foil towards the end of cooking if necessary. Leave in the tin for 5 minutes, then turn out onto a wire rack to cool.
6 For the topping, beat together the soft cheese, honey and lemon juice. Spread on top of the cake and sprinkle with walnuts.

❖ Warm Lemon Syrup Cake ❖

12 SLICES

PREPARATION TIME
20 minutes, plus soaking
COOKING TIME
1 hour
FREEZING
Suitable

- 65 g (2½ oz) candied lemon peel (optional)
- 225 g (8 oz) butter or margarine, softened
- finely grated rind of 2 lemons
- 225 g (8 oz) caster sugar
- 4 eggs, size 2, beaten

- 225 g (8 oz) self-raising white flour
- 30 ml (2 tbsp) lemon juice

SYRUP:
- 175 g (6 oz) caster sugar
- juice of 3 lemons, strained

360 CALS/SLICE

1 Grease and base-line a 22 cm (8½ inch) base measurement moule à manqué tin (see note). Finely chop the candied peel, if using.
2 Cream the butter and lemon rind together in a bowl. Gradually beat in the caster sugar, followed by the eggs. Fold in the flour, candied peel and lemon juice.
3 Spoon the mixture into the prepared tin and level the surface. Bake at 180°C (350°F) mark 4 for about 1 hour or until well browned.
4 Meanwhile, prepare the syrup. Place the sugar, lemon juice and 75 ml (3 fl oz) water in a saucepan. Heat gently until the sugar dissolves, then bring to the boil and let bubble for 1 minute. Cool.
5 As soon as the cake is cooked, turn out onto an edged dish and immediately spoon over the syrup. Leave for about 30 minutes for the syrup to soak in. Serve warm, with lightly poached fruit if desired. Alternatively cool completely and store in an airtight tin for up to 3–4 days.

NOTE: A moule à manqué tin is a deep cake tin with sloping sides; if unavailable, use a deep round cake tin of a similar diameter instead.

❖ Dundee Cake ❖

16 SLICES

PREPARATION TIME
20 minutes
COOKING TIME
2–2¼ hours
FREEZING
Suitable
COLOUR INDEX
Page 82

- 100 g (4 oz) currants
- 100 g (4 oz) raisins
- 50 g (2 oz) blanched almonds, chopped
- 100 g (4 oz) chopped mixed peel
- 275 g (10 oz) plain white flour
- 225 g (8 oz) butter or margarine

- 225 g (8 oz) light soft brown sugar
- finely grated rind of 1 lemon
- 4 eggs, beaten
- 50–75 g (2–3 oz) split almonds, to decorate

335 CALS/SLICE

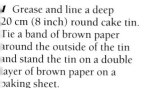

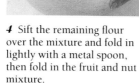

1 Grease and line a deep 20 cm (8 inch) round cake tin. Tie a band of brown paper around the outside of the tin and stand the tin on a double layer of brown paper on a baking sheet.

2 Combine the fruit, chopped nuts and mixed peel in a bowl. Sift in a little flour and stir until the fruit is evenly coated.

3 Cream the butter and sugar together in a bowl until pale and fluffy, then beat in the lemon rind. Add the eggs to the creamed mixture a little at a time, beating well after each addition.

4 Sift the remaining flour over the mixture and fold in lightly with a metal spoon, then fold in the fruit and nut mixture.

5 Turn the mixture into the prepared tin and make a slight hollow in the centre with the back of a metal spoon. Arrange the almonds on top.

6 Bake at 170°C (325°F) mark 3 for 2–2¼ hours until a skewer inserted in the centre comes out clean. If necessary cover with foil towards end of cooking. Leave in the tin for 15 minutes, then turn out onto a wire rack to cool. Wrap in greaseproof paper and foil. Let mature for at least 1 week.

❖ Raspberry and Apple Cake ❖

8–10 SLICES

PREPARATION TIME
20 minutes
COOKING TIME
1–1¼ hours
FREEZING
Not suitable

- 225 g (8 oz) self-raising white flour
- large pinch of salt
- 175 g (6 oz) butter or margarine
- 50 g (2 oz) ground almonds
- 125 g (4 oz) caster sugar
- 225 g (8 oz) eating apples, peeled, cored and chopped

- 2 eggs, beaten
- 45 ml (3 tbsp) milk
- 225 g (8 oz) firm but ripe raspberries, or frozen raspberries
- 50 g (2 oz) flaked almonds
- icing sugar, for dusting

440–350 CALS/SLICE

1 Grease and base-line a 20 cm (8 inch) spring-release cake tin.
2 Sift the flour and salt into a large bowl. Rub in the butter until the mixture resembles fine breadcrumbs. Stir in the ground almonds, sugar and apples, using a wooden spoon. Beat in the eggs and milk, then carefully fold in half of the raspberries.
3 Spoon the mixture carefully into the tin and level the surface. Sprinkle over the remaining raspberries and the flaked almonds. Bake at 180°C (350°F) mark 4 for about 1–1¼ hours or until well risen, golden brown and firm to the touch in the centre.
4 Dust with icing sugar and serve warm or cold, on its own or with yogurt, cream or crème fraîche.

NOTE: If using frozen raspberries, add while still frozen.

❖ Whisked Sponge ❖

4 Pour the mixture into the tins, tilting the tins to spread the mixture evenly. Do not use a palette knife or spatula to smooth the mixture as this would crush the air bubbles.

5 Bake at 190°C (375°F) mark 5 for 20–25 minutes, until well risen, firm to the touch and beginning to shrink from sides of tins. Turn out and cool on a wire rack. When cold, sandwich together with jam and cream, if using; dredge with sugar.

NOTE: This classic fatless sponge does not keep well and should be eaten on the day of making.

To make two 20 cm (8 inch) sponges, use 4 eggs, 100 g (4 oz) caster sugar and 100 g (4 oz) plain flour.

8 SLICES	
PREPARATION TIME 25 minutes	• 3 eggs
COOKING TIME 20–25 minutes	• 100 g (4 oz) caster sugar
FREEZING Suitable (unfilled)	• 75 g (3 oz) plain white flour

• 120 ml (4 fl oz) whipping cream, whipped (optional)
• caster or icing sugar, for dredging

TO FINISH:
• 60 ml (4 tbsp) straw-berry or apricot jam

190 CALS/SLICE

❖ Swiss Roll ❖

Make the sponge mixture as for Whisked Sponge (left) but use 100g (4 oz) flour and fold in with 15 ml (1 tbsp) hot water.

1 Grease and base-line two 18 cm (7 inch) sandwich tins, then dust with a mixture of flour and caster sugar.

2 Put the eggs and sugar in a large heatproof bowl over a pan of hot water and whisk until the mixture has doubled in volume and is thick enough to leave a trail on the surface when whisk is lifted. Remove bowl from pan and whisk for 5 minutes, or until cool.

1 Pour into a lined 33 × 23 cm (13 × 9 inch) Swiss roll tin. Tilt the tin to spread the mixture in an even layer. Bake at 200°C (400°F) mark 6 for 10–12 minutes until golden brown, well risen and firm.

2 Meanwhile, place a sheet of greaseproof paper on a damp tea towel. Dredge the paper with caster sugar. Quickly turn out the cake onto the paper, trim off the crusty edges and spread with jam.

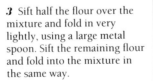

3 Sift half the flour over the mixture and fold in very lightly, using a large metal spoon. Sift the remaining flour and fold into the mixture in the same way.

3 Roll up the cake with the aid of the paper. Make the firs[t] turn firmly so that the whole cake will roll evenly and have a good shape when finished, but roll more lightly after this initial turn.

4 Place seam-side down on a wire rack and dredge with sugar.

CHOCOLATE SWISS ROLL: Make the sponge as for Swiss Roll (left), but replace 15 ml (1 tbsp) flour with 15 ml (1 tbsp) cocoa powder. Turn out the cooked sponge and trim as above, then cover with a sheet of greaseproof paper and roll with the paper inside. When cold, unroll and remove the paper. Spread with whipped cream and re-roll. Dust with icing sugar.

4 Gradually fold in the remaining butter and flour alternately. Fold in very lightly or the butter will sink and result in a heavy cake.

5 Pour into the prepared tin. Bake at 180°C (350°F) mark 4 for 35–40 minutes until well risen, firm to the touch and beginning to shrink from sides of tin. Turn out and cool on a wire rack. Serve dusted with icing sugar, or split and filled with fruit and cream.

❖ Genoese Cake ❖

12–14 SLICES	
PREPARATION TIME 25 minutes	
COOKING TIME 35–40 minutes	
FREEZING Suitable (unfilled)	

- 75 g (3 oz) butter
- 6 eggs
- 175 g (6 oz) caster sugar
- 150 g (5 oz) plain flour
- 30 ml (2 tbsp) cornflour

TO FINISH:
- icing sugar, for dredging

- fresh fruit, such as raspberries, blueberries and sliced strawberries (optional)
- 150 ml (¼ pint) whipping cream, whipped (optional)

250–215 CALS/SLICE

❖ Dark Chocolate Cake ❖

SERVES 10	
PREPARATION TIME 35 minutes	
COOKING TIME 45–50 minutes	
FREEZING Suitable (without icing)	

- 200 g (7 oz) plain chocolate, in pieces
- 125 g (4 oz) unsalted butter
- 3 eggs, separated
- 125 g (4 oz) dark soft brown sugar
- 50 ml (2 fl oz) brandy
- 2.5 ml (½ tsp) vanilla essence
- 75 g (3 oz) plain flour
- 50 g (2 oz) ground almonds

ICING:
- 175 g (6 oz) plain chocolate, in pieces
- 25 g (1 oz) unsalted butter
- 175 g (6 oz) icing sugar, sifted

TO DECORATE:
- 300 ml (½ pint) double cream, stiffly whipped
- grated chocolate

655 CALS/SLICE

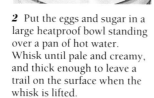

1 Grease and line a 23 cm (9 inch) spring-release cake tin. Put the butter into a saucepan and heat gently until melted, then remove from the heat and leave for a few minutes to cool slightly.

2 Put the eggs and sugar in a large heatproof bowl standing over a pan of hot water. Whisk until pale and creamy, and thick enough to leave a trail on the surface when the whisk is lifted.

3 Remove from the heat and whisk until cool. Sift the flour and cornflour together into a bowl. Fold half the flour into the egg mixture with a metal spoon. Pour half the cooled butter around the edge of the mixture and lightly fold in.

1 Grease, base-line and flour a deep 20 cm (8 inch) round cake tin. Melt the chocolate and butter in a heatproof bowl over a pan of hot water. Remove from heat and stir until smooth.
2 Whisk the egg yolks and sugar in a large heatproof bowl standing over a pan of hot water until very pale and creamy, and thick enough to leave a trail on the surface when the whisk is lifted. Remove from the heat and whisk until cool.
3 Add the brandy and vanilla essence and whisk in the melted chocolate mixture. Add the sifted flour and ground almonds and fold in gently. Whisk the egg whites until stiff, then lightly fold into the mixture a little at a time.
4 Pour the mixture into the tin and bake at 180°C (350°F) mark 4 for 45–50 minutes or until firm to the touch. Leave in the tin for 10 minutes, then turn out onto a wire rack to cool.
5 To make the icing, melt the chocolate and butter in a bowl over a pan of hot water. Off the heat, gradually stir in the icing sugar and 45 ml (3 tbsp) warm water to make a thick icing.
6 Cut the cake in half and spread one third of the icing over one half; cool, then top with one third of the cream. Put the other cake half on top. Spoon the rest of the icing over the cake and swirl quickly with a knife to coat the top and sides. Leave to set, then decorate with remaining cream and grated chocolate.

❖ Black Forest Gâteau ❖

SERVES 10

PREPARATION TIME
40 minutes, plus
caraque
COOKING TIME
40 minutes
FREEZING
Suitable
(undecorated)

- *75 g (3 oz) butter*
- *6 eggs*
- *175 g (6 oz) caster sugar*
- *125 g (4 oz) plain white flour*
- *50 g (2 oz) cocoa powder*
- *2.5 ml (½ tsp) vanilla essence*

- *two 425 g (15 oz) cans stoned black cherries*
- *60 ml (4 tbsp) kirsch*
- *600 ml (1 pint) whipping cream*
- *125 g (4 oz) Chocolate Caraque (see right)*
- *5 ml (1 tsp) arrowroot*

600 CALS/SERVING

1 Line and grease a deep 23 cm (9 inch) round cake tin. Put the butter in a bowl over a pan of warm water; beat until very soft.
2 Whisk the eggs and sugar together in a large bowl standing over a pan of simmering water until pale and creamy, and thick enough to leave a trail on the surface when the whisk is lifted. Remove from the heat and whisk until cool.
3 Sift the flour and cocoa together, then lightly fold into the egg mixture. Fold in the vanilla essence and softened butter. Turn into the prepared tin and tilt to spread evenly.
4 Bake at 180°C (350°F) mark 4 for about 40 minutes until well risen, firm to the touch and beginning to shrink away from the sides of the tin. Turn out onto a wire rack covered with grease-proof paper, and leave to cool. Cut the cake into three layers.
5 Place one layer on a flat plate. To make the filling, drain the cherries, reserving the syrup. Mix 75 ml (5 tbsp) of the cherry syrup and the kirsch together. Spoon 45 ml (3 tbsp) over the cake layer. Whip the cream until it holds its shape, then spread a thin layer over the soaked sponge. Reserve a third of the cherries for decoration; scatter half the remainder over the cream.
6 Repeat the layers of sponge, syrup, cream and cherries. Top with the third cake round and spoon over the remaining kirsch-flavoured syrup.
7 Spread a thin layer of cream around the side of the cake. Press on the chocolate caraque, reserving some. Pipe whirls of cream around the edge of the cake and top each with a chocolate curl.
8 Fill the centre with the reserved cherries. Blend the arrowroot with 45 ml (3 tbsp) cherry syrup. Place in a small pan, bring to the boil and boil, stirring, for a few minutes until the mixture is clear. Brush the glaze over the cherries.

❖ Chocolate Mousse Gâteau ❖

SERVES 12–16

PREPARATION TIME
30 minutes, plus
cake
FREEZING
Not suitable
COLOUR INDEX
Page 82

- *23 cm (9 inch) Genoese cake (page 395)*
FILLING:
- *175 g (6 oz) plain chocolate, in pieces*
- *30 ml (2 tbsp) brandy*
- *2 eggs, separated*
- *300 ml (½ pint) double cream*

- *5 ml (1 tsp) powdered gelatine*
CHOCOLATE CARAQUE:
- *275 g (10 oz) plain or white chocolate*
TO DECORATE:
- *150 ml (¼ pint) double cream*
- *icing sugar, for dusting*

640–480 CALS/SERVING

1 To make the filling, melt the chocolate in a heatproof bowl standing over a pan of simmering water. Remove from the heat and stir in the brandy and egg yolks. Whip the cream until it stands in soft peaks, then fold in.

2 Sprinkle the gelatine over 15 ml (1 tbsp) water in a small bowl and leave to soak for 2–3 minutes, then dissolve over a pan of simmering water. Cool, then stir into the chocolate mixture. Whisk the egg whites until stiff, then fold in.

3 Cut the cake into two layers. Put one layer of sponge back in the cake tin. Pour the mousse filling on top. Put the second layer of sponge on top. Leave in a cool place to set.

4 To make the chocolate caraque, melt the chocolate as in step 1. Spread out thinly on a marble slab or clean work surface. Leave to set until no longer sticky to touch.

5 Holding a large knife with both hands, push the blade across the surface to shave off long chocolate curls. Adjust the angle of the blade to get the best curls. Alternatively, use a clean wallpaper scraper as shown.

6 When the mousse is set, whip the cream until it holds its shape. Release the side of the tin and carefully ease the cake out. Place on a serving plate. Cover with the cream. Coat completely with the chocolate curls and dust lightly with icing sugar.

❖ Chocolate Roulade ❖

SERVES 8–10

PREPARATION TIME
35 minutes
COOKING TIME
20–25 minutes
FREEZING
Suitable (unfilled and rolled with lining paper)
COLOUR INDEX
Page 83

- 125 g (4 oz) plain chocolate, in pieces
- 4 eggs, separated
- 125 g (4 oz) caster sugar
FILLING:
- 150 ml (¼ pint) double cream
- 225 g (8 oz) strawberries or raspberries, sliced

- 15 ml (1 tbsp) icing sugar
- 150 ml (¼ pint) Greek yogurt
TO DECORATE:
- icing sugar, for dusting
- strawberries or raspberries

395–315 CALS/SERVING

1 Grease a 33 × 23 cm (13 × 9 inch) Swiss roll tin, line with greaseproof paper and grease the paper. Melt the chocolate in a bowl set over a pan of simmering water.

2 Whisk the egg yolks with the sugar until very thick and pale in colour. Beat in the chocolate. Whisk the egg whites until stiff, then fold into the chocolate mixture.

3 Pour into the prepared tin and spread out evenly. Bake at 180°C (350°F) mark 4 for 20–25 minutes until well risen and firm to the touch.

4 Turn the sponge out onto a sheet of greaseproof paper generously sprinkled with caster sugar. Carefully peel off the lining paper. Cover the roulade with a warm, damp tea towel and leave to cool.

5 For the filling, softly whip the cream. Mash half of the strawberries with the icing sugar; fold into the cream with the yogurt. Fold in the remaining sliced strawberries. Spread the cream over the roulade. Starting from one of the narrow ends, carefully roll it up, using the paper to help.

6 Dust the roulade generously with icing sugar. Decorate with strawberries. Serve with a fruit Coulis (page 95), if desired.

NOTE: Don't worry if the roulade cracks as you are rolling – this is usual and adds to the appearance!

❖ Sachertorte ❖

SERVES 8–10

PREPARATION TIME
30 minutes
COOKING TIME
40–45 minutes
FREEZING
Suitable (without icing)
COLOUR INDEX
Page 83

- 150 g (5 oz) plain chocolate, in pieces
- 125 g (4 oz) unsalted butter or margarine, softened
- 125 g (4 oz) caster sugar
- 125 g (4 oz) ground almonds
- 4 eggs, separated

- 50 g (2 oz) fresh brown breadcrumbs
- 30 ml (2 tbsp) apricot jam, melted
ICING:
- 200 g (7 oz) plain chocolate, in pieces
- 200 ml (7 fl oz) double cream

690–550 CALS/SERVING

1 Grease a 23 cm (9 inch) spring-release cake tin, line with greaseproof paper and grease the paper.
2 Melt the chocolate in a bowl standing over a pan of simmering water. Remove from the heat.
3 Cream the butter and sugar together until light and fluffy. Stir in the almonds, egg yolks, breadcrumbs and melted chocolate and beat until well combined.
4 Whisk the egg whites until stiff and fold half into the chocolate mixture, then fold in the other half. Pour into the prepared tin and level the surface. Bake at 180°C (350°F) mark 4 for 40–45 minutes until firm to the touch.
5 Cover with a damp tea towel, leave for 5 minutes to cool slightly, then unclip the sides of the tin and invert on to a wire rack. Remove the base. Turn the cake the right way up, cover and leave to cool. When cold, brush the top with the jam.
6 To make the icing, put the chocolate and cream in a heatproof bowl over a pan of simmering water until the chocolate has melted and evenly blended with the cream. Cool for a few minutes until the icing just coats the back of a spoon.
7 Pour the icing over the cake and gently shake the cake to spread the icing evenly; use a palette knife, if necessary, to ensure that the sides are completely covered. Leave to set in a cool place, but do not refrigerate or the icing will lose its shine.

✦ Red Fruit Gâteau ✦

SERVES 10

PREPARATION TIME
40 minutes
COOKING TIME
35–40 minutes
FREEZING
Suitable (sponge
only)

- *50 g (2 oz) unsalted butter*
- *4 eggs, size 4*
- *125 g (4 oz) caster sugar*
- *125 g (4 oz) plain white flour*
- *few drops of vanilla essence (optional)*

FRUIT SAUCE:
- *700 g (1½ lb) mixed red summer fruit, such as raspberries, strawberries, redcurrants, loganberries*
- *caster sugar, to taste*

- *45 ml (3 tbsp) lemon juice*
- *15 ml (1 tbsp) rosewater (optional)*

FILLING AND TOPPING:
- *1 egg white*
- *450 g (1 lb) mixed red summer fruit*
- *few pink or red rose petals*
- *a little caster sugar*
- *300–450 ml (½–¾ pint) double cream*

310 CALS/SERVING

1 Grease and base-line a 25 cm (10 inch) spring-release cake tin with non-stick baking parchment. Dust out the tin with flour. Melt the butter and cool slightly.

2 Whisk the eggs and sugar in a large bowl standing over a pan of simmering water for 10 minutes, or until the mixture is thick, pale and mousse-like. Remove from heat and whisk until cool.

3 Sift half of the flour over the egg mixture and carefully fold in. Pour the cooled, melted butter around the edge of the bowl and gently fold in. Add the vanilla essence if using, then sift over the remaining flour and fold in.

4 Pour the mixture into the prepared tin. Bake at 180°C (350°F) mark 4 for 35–40 minutes until golden brown, and shrunk slightly from the sides of the tin. Leave in the tin for 5 minutes, then turn out onto a wire rack to cool.

5 To make the fruit sauce, put all the ingredients into a pan and heat gently until the juice starts to run from the fruit and the sugar melts. Add a little water and press through a nylon sieve, or purée in a blender, then sieve. Cool and chill.

6 Prepare the frosted decoration. Lightly beat the egg white. Brush a few fruits and rose petals with a thin coating of egg white. Sprinkle with caster sugar and lay on non-stick baking parchment to dry. Pick over the remaining fruit.

7 Whip the cream until it just holds its shape; chill briefly.

5 To assemble the cake, using a long serrated knife, carefully cut the cake into two layers. Sandwich together with some of the fruit sauce and the prepared fruit. Spread the cream evenly over the top and sides of the cake. Decorate with the frosted fruit and petals. Serve the remaining fruit sauce separately.

✦ Coffee Gâteau ✦

SERVES 8

PREPARATION TIME
40 minutes, plus
icing
COOKING TIME
10–12 minutes
FREEZING
Suitable (sponge
only)

- *75 g (3 oz) caster sugar*
- *3 eggs*
- *100 g (3½ oz) plain white flour*
- *1½ quantity Coffee Crème au Beurre (page 410)*

PRALINE:
- *50 g (2 oz) unblanched almonds*
- *50 g (2 oz) caster sugar*

350 CALS/SERVING

1 Grease a 33 × 23 cm (13 × 9 inch) Swiss roll tin and line with greaseproof paper. Grease the paper.

2 Whisk the sugar and eggs in a bowl over a pan of simmering water, using an electric whisk, until pale and creamy and thick enough to leave a trail on the surface when the whisk is lifted. Remove the bowl from the heat and whisk until cool.

3 Sift the flour over the mixture and fold in lightly using a metal spoon. Turn the mixture into the prepared tin and gently level the surface. Bake at 190°C (375°F) mark 5 for 10–12 minutes until well risen and golden brown.

4 Turn out onto a sheet of greaseproof paper, sprinkled with caster sugar. Remove the lining paper and leave to cool.

5 To make the praline, gently heat the almonds and sugar in a non-stick frying pan until the sugar melts and turns a rich dark golden brown. Carefully pour onto a well buttered baking sheet. Quickly coat 8 almonds and leave to set individually. Leave the rest of the praline to cool and set, then roughly crush in a blender, or between two sheets of greaseproof paper with a rolling pin.

6 Cut the sponge crossways into 3 equal strips. Sandwich them together with half of the crème au beurre. Spread more crème au beurre over the top and sides of the gâteau. Cover the sides with the crushed praline. Put the remaining crème au beurre into a piping bag fitted with a small star nozzle and pipe on top of the gâteau. Decorate with the caramel-coated almonds.

❖ *Lemon Gâteau* ❖

SERVES 8

PREPARATION TIME
50 minutes, plus
chilling
COOKING TIME
20–25 minutes
FREEZING
Suitable
(undecorated)

- 2 eggs, separated
- 65 g (2½ oz) caster sugar
- grated rind of 1 lemon
- 15 ml (1 tbsp) ground almonds
- 30 ml (2 tbsp) fine semolina
- 30 ml (2 tbsp) plain white flour
- 15 ml (1 tbsp) lemon juice

MOUSSE:
- grated rind and juice of 2 lemons

- 10 ml (2 tsp) powdered gelatine
- 3 eggs, separated
- 125 g (4 oz) caster sugar
- 150 ml (¼ pint) double cream

TO DECORATE:
- icing sugar, for dusting
- raspberries

270 CALS/SERVING

1 Grease and base-line a 20 cm (8 inch) spring-release cake tin with non-stick baking parchment. Dust the tin with caster sugar and flour. Whisk the egg yolks and sugar with the lemon rind in a bowl over a pan of simmering water until thick, pale and mousse-like in texture. Fold in the ground almonds, semolina and flour with the lemon juice.

2 Whisk the egg whites until soft peaks form. Stir a small spoonful of egg white into the yolk mixture to lighten it, then fold in the remainder. Spoon into the cake tin. Bake at 180°C (350°F) mark 4 for about 20–25 minutes or until golden, firm, and beginning to shrink slightly from the edges of the tin.

3 Turn on to a wire rack lined with non-stick baking parchment. Cool completely. Carefully slice into two thin rounds. Rinse and dry the tin. Line the base and sides with non-stick baking parchment, dabbing melted fat around the edge to attach the paper to the sides. Place one half of the cake in the base of the tin.

5 Dissolve gelatine by placing the bowl over a pan of simmering water; whisk into the egg yolk mixture. Whip cream until it just holds its shape, then fold into the egg mixture.

7 Pour the mousse over the cake in the tin; level the surface if necessary. Cover and refrigerate until lightly set, about 45 minutes. Carefully place the second cake layer on top of the mousse; re-cover. Refrigerate until set, at least 4 hours, preferably overnight.

4 For the mousse, put 45 ml (3 tbsp) lemon juice in a small bowl with 15 ml (1 tbsp) water. Sprinkle on the gelatine and leave to soak until sponge-like in texture. Meanwhile, in a bowl, whisk together the egg yolks, sugar and lemon rind until thick and mousse-like. Gradually whisk in the remaining lemon juice.

6 Whisk the egg whites until soft peaks form. Stir a small spoonful of egg white into the mousse to lighten the mixture, then gently fold in the remainder.

8 To serve, remove the sides of the tin and carefully peel away the paper. Place a flat plate on top of the gâteau and quickly invert. Ease off the bottom of the tin. Dust the gâteau generously with sifted icing sugar and decorate with raspberries.

❖ Celebration Cake ❖

SERVES 20

PREPARATION TIME
30 minutes, plus
standing
COOKING TIME
1–1¼ hours
FREEZING
Suitable (sponge
only)

- 225 g (8 oz) butter or
margarine, softened
- 225 g (8 oz) caster
sugar
- 4 eggs, lightly beaten
- 225 g (8 oz) self-
raising white flour
- grated rind and juice of
1 lemon
TO DECORATE:
- red, blue or yellow food
colouring

- three 225 g (8 oz)
packets ready-to-roll
fondant icing
- 300 ml (½ pint) double
cream
- 120 ml (8 tbsp) black
cherry conserve or 50 g
(2 oz) sliced strawberries
- ribbon and fresh
flowers, to decorate

315 CALS/SERVING

1 Grease and base-line a 23 cm (9 inch) round cake tin.
2 Cream the butter and sugar together until pale and fluffy. Add
the eggs a little at a time, beating well after each addition, and
adding a little flour if the mixture begins to curdle.
3 Sift the flour over the mixture and fold in with the lemon rind
and juice. Spoon into the prepared tin and level the surface.
4 Bake at 180°C (350°F) mark 4 for about 1–1¼ hours or until
golden and firm to the touch. Cover the top with greaseproof
paper, if necessary, towards the end of the cooking time. Turn
out onto a wire rack to cool.
5 Meanwhile tint the ready-to-roll icing a pale shade by
kneading in a little colouring until evenly blended. Wrap tightly
in greaseproof paper.
6 Split the cake in half horizontally. Whip the cream until it just
holds its shape. Sandwich the cake layers together with conserve
or fruit and all but 45 ml (3 tbsp) cream. Place on a serving
plate. Spread the reserved cream thinly around the sides and
over the top of the cake.
7 Dust the work surface lightly with icing sugar and roll out the
icing to a circle large enough to cover the cake completely. Lift
the icing over a rolling pin and carefully onto the cake; gently
smooth the sides. Trim the excess icing from the base of the
cake.
5 Decorate with a ribbon and fresh flowers just before serving.

❖ Teddy Bear Cake ❖

SERVES 20

PREPARATION TIME
About 2 hours
COOKING TIME
1¼ hours
FREEZING
Suitable

- 400 g (14 oz) butter or
margarine, softened
- 400 g (14 oz) caster
sugar
- 6 eggs, lightly beaten
- 450 g (1 lb) self-
raising flour
- 50 g (2 oz) cocoa
powder
- 10 ml (2 tsp) baking
powder

TO DECORATE:
- 1.6 kg (3½ lb) regalice
or ready-to-roll fondant
icing
- blue, brown, yellow,
red and green food
colourings
- 45 ml (3 tbsp) apricot
jam, sieved

555 CALS/SERVING

1 Grease and base-line a 1.4
litre (2½ pint) and a 600 ml
(1 pint) pudding basin. Place
3 paper cake cases in a bun
tin. Cream together the butter
and sugar in a bowl. Gradually
beat in the eggs, adding a
little flour if the mixture begins
to curdle. Sift the remaining
flour with the cocoa and
baking powder and fold in.
Half fill the paper cake cases; divide remaining mixture between
the pudding basins. Bake at 170°C (325°F) mark 3, allowing
15 minutes for the paper cases, 45 minutes for the small basin
and 1–1¼ hours for the large basin. Test by inserting a skewer
into the centre: it should come out clean. Leave in the basins
and cake cases for 15 minutes, then turn out onto a wire rack
to cool completely.

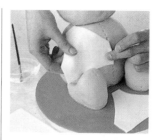

2 Trim off top edges from basin cakes to give rounded shapes. Cut one small cake in half for ears. Make two sloping cuts on remaining small cakes to shape feet.

3 Cut a slice from one side of the large cake to make a firm base when the cake is lifted on its side. Cut another slice from the opposite side to support the head. Cut a slice from one side of the small basin cake.

8 To make waistcoat, thinly roll 50 g (2 oz) of the reserved white icing. Cut 2 front sections of waistcoat, each 9 cm (3½ inches) from neck to waist and 10 cm (4 inches) from centre front to sides. Cut away V neck and armholes and secure to cake. Re-roll trimmings and cut out back of waistcoat, about 10 cm (4 inches) deep and 23 cm (9 inches) wide. Cut away armholes and shape around back of teddy, easing to fit.

9 To make the arms, halve the remaining brown icing and roll out 2 sausage shapes, each 10 cm (4 inches) long and slightly thicker in the middle. Secure to sides of teddy, letting ends rest on the legs or down sides. Mark stitching lines with teaspoon.

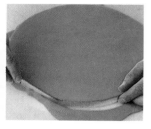

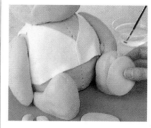

4 Colour 225 g (8 oz) of the icing blue and roll out thinly on a surface dusted with cornflour and use to cover a 28 cm (11 inch) dampened board. Smooth out using hands dusted with cornflour; trim off excess icing around edge. Mix the jam with 15 ml (1 tbsp) boiling water; spread over the round cakes.

5 Reserve 225 g (8 oz) of the icing; colour remainder pale brown. Thinly roll a generous third of the brown icing to a 28 cm (11 inch) round. Lift over the large cake. Using hands dusted with cornflour, smooth icing around sides to eliminate creases and folds. Tuck excess icing under the base. Position cake on board.

10 Colour another 125 g (4 oz) white icing yellow, adding a little brown colour to tone down if preferred. Roll half into a ball, then flatten into a snout shape and secure to cake. Use remainder to shape feet, paw and ear pads. Press into position.

11 Colour a little of the remaining icing red and use to shape small round buttons, a semi-circle for the mouth and a neck tie; secure in place. Shape and position 2 small rounds of white icing for eyes. Colour remaining icing dark brown and use to shape nose and mouth; secure to cake. To finish cake, use diluted colours to paint centres of eyes and candy stripes on waistcoat. Leave to dry and harden in a cool place, preferably for 2 days.

6 Use another 225 g (8 oz) brown icing to cover the smaller round cake and sit it on top of the large cake. Using the tip of a teaspoon impress 'stitching' lines around head, front and sides of teddy.

7 To make each leg, roll out 75 g (3 oz) brown icing. Lay one small cake in the centre. Mould icing around cake and shape excess into foot. Press into position on cake. Mark stitching lines. Use 50 g (2 oz) brown icing to cover ears and position. Mark stitching lines.

NOTE: As you work, keep any icing not in use wrapped in cling film otherwise it will dry out and become difficult to use. The cake can be stored in a cool place for 2–3 weeks. Alternatively you could freeze it for longer, but the icing will develop a moist sheen. Apply any painted-on colour once the cake has thawed.

✦ Dinosaur Cake ✦

SERVES 16

PREPARATION TIME
About 2 hours,
plus standing
COOKING TIME
1¼ hours
FREEZING
Suitable

- 225 g (8 oz) butter or margarine, softened
- 225 g (8 oz) caster sugar
- 4 eggs, lightly beaten
- 300 g (10 oz) self-raising white flour
- 5 ml (1 tsp) baking powder
- grated rind of 1 orange
- 15 ml (1 tbsp) orange juice

- ½ quantity Buttercream (page 410)

TO DECORATE:
- 1.6 kg (3½ lb) regalice or ready-to-roll fondant icing
- brown, green, yellow, red and blue food colourings

580 CALS/SERVING

1 Line and grease a 20 cm (8 inch) round cake tin. Cream together the butter and sugar. Gradually beat in the eggs, with a little flour if needed. Sift flour with baking powder; fold in with orange rind and juice. Turn into the tin. Bake at 170°C (325°F) mark 3 for 1–1¼ hours. Leave in tin for 15 minutes, then cool on a wire rack. Halve cake vertically and sandwich together with one third of the buttercream. With cut sides down, trim cake edges to shape dinosaur's underside.

2 Roughly knead brown food colouring into 350 g (12 oz) of the icing until streaked with colour. Roll out thinly on a surface dusted with cornflour and use to cover a dampened 30 cm (12 inch) cake board. Smooth out icing using hands dusted with cornflour, then trim off excess around edge.

3 Reserve 50 g (2 oz) of the icing. Colour the remainder green. Take 125 g (4 oz) of the green icing and roll out to a thick sausage, about 11 cm (4½ inches) long and thicker at one end. Cut a slice off the thick end. Press a 'neck' 4 cm (1½ inches) from the rounded end, then bend icing to create the head.

4 Using a sharp knife cut a 1 cm (½ inch) slice through rounded end to form the mouth, curving cut upwards at ends to create 'smiling' expression. Take a pea-sized piece of green icing and cut in half. Press on to the top of the head to shape eye sockets. Press 2 small holes into icing, just above mouth, to make nostrils. Thread a wooden skewer through icing as far as neck. Transfer to a sheet of baking parchment or foil and leave to harden for 1–2 days.

5 Once head has hardened, push skewer into cake to secure head to body. Place on cake board and spread body with remaining buttercream. Brush lower end of neck with water. Reserve 550 g (1¼ lb) of the green icing. Colour another 75 g (3 oz) a darker shade of green and reserve. Roll out remainder to a 28 cm (11 inch) round. Make a 7.5 cm (3 inch) cut from edge towards centre. Lift icing over cake so the slit falls around neck of dinosaur. Using hands dusted with cornflour, smooth icing eliminating as many creases and folds as possible. Smooth icing around the neck until join barely shows. Trim off excess at base.

6 To shape tail take another 225 g (8 oz) green icing and roll out to a sausage, about 5 cm (2 inches) thick at one end and tapering to a point at other end. Dampen thick end and attach to cake, letting tail bend round front of board. Using fingers, smooth the icing onto dinosaur body until join barely shows.

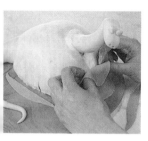

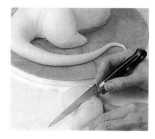

7 Colour 40 g (1½ oz) reserved white icing with an equal quantity of yellow and brown colour. Thinly roll and press on to front of dinosaur and around base of sides.

8 To shape each hind leg, roll 125 g (4 oz) green icing and mould into a pear shape. Bend the thin end of the pear shape around the back of a knife. Gently press against side of cake. Halve remaining green icing and roll each piece to a 9 cm (3½ inch) sausage tapering slightly at one end. Bend icing around back of knife, then press into position for front legs. Use a cocktail stick to make markings on feet and crease lines at leg joints.

9 Roll out the dark green icing as thinly as possible. Cut 30–40 strips of icing, varying in length from 12 cm (5 inches) to 2.5 cm (1 inch) and tapering to a point at each end. Lay over the back of dinosaur. Continue adding strips, decreasing in size as you work towards head and tail ends. (Use strips to cover any visible joins where neck and tail meet body.) Re-roll trimmings and use to shape spikes. Position along back, again decreasing in size towards head and tail ends.

10 Colour a little icing red and shape a small pointed tongue; press into mouth. Roll 2 small balls of white icing and press into eye sockets. Paint centres of eyes blue. Shape small claws from remaining white icing and secure to feet. Finish cake by painting brown streaks between the dark green markings down the dinosaur's back. Remove the skewer before cutting the cake.

NOTE: Always keep any icing not in use tightly wrapped in cling film. This cake stores well for 2–3 weeks in a cool place. It can be frozen for longer, but the icing will develop a moist sheen. If freezing, painted-on colour should be added once thawed.

❖ Simnel Cake ❖

SERVES 20

PREPARATION TIME
40 minutes
COOKING TIME
About 2½ hours
FREEZING
Suitable
(undecorated)
COLOUR INDEX
Page 84

- 175 g (6 oz) butter or block margarine, softened
- 175 g (6 oz) caster sugar
- 3 eggs, lightly beaten
- 225 g (8 oz) plain white flour
- pinch of salt
- 2.5 ml (½ tsp) ground cinnamon
- 2.5 ml (½ tsp) grated nutmeg
- 125 g (4 oz) glacé cherries, washed, dried and cut into quarters
- 50 g (2 oz) chopped mixed peel
- 250 g (9 oz) currants
- 125 g (4 oz) sultanas
- finely grated rind of 1 lemon
- 15–30 ml (1–2 tbsp) milk (if necessary)
- 450 g (1 lb) Almond Paste (page 411)

TO DECORATE:
- 1 egg white, lightly beaten
- ribbon
- fresh or crystallized flowers

345 CALS/SERVING

1 Line and grease an 18 cm (7 inch) round cake tin.

2 Cream the butter and sugar together until pale and fluffy. Gradually beat in the eggs.

3 Sift in the flour, salt and spices and fold into the mixture with a metal spoon. Add all the fruit and the lemon rind, folding in to give a smooth dropping consistency. If a little too firm add 15–30 ml (1–2 tbsp) milk.

4 Divide the almond paste in half. Lightly dust a surface with icing sugar and roll out one half to a 16 cm (6½ inch) circle.

5 Spoon half of the cake mixture into the prepared tin. Place the round of almond paste on top and cover with the remaining cake mixture. Press down gently with the back of a spoon to level the surface.

6 Tie a double thickness of brown paper around the outside of the tin. Bake at 150°C (300°F) mark 2 for about 2½ hours. When cooked the cake should be a rich brown colour, and firm to the touch.

7 Cool in the tin for about 1 hour, then turn out and leave to cool completely on a wire rack.

8 Divide the remaining almond paste in two. Roll out one half to a 17 cm (7½ inch) circle and the rest into 11 small balls. Brush the top of the cake with egg white. Place the circle of almond paste on top, crimp the edges and, with a little of the egg white, fix the balls around the top edge of the cake.

9 Brush the almond paste with the remaining egg white and place under a hot grill for 1–2 minutes until the paste is well browned. Tie ribbon around the cake and decorate with flowers.

Variation

Before grilling, apply a rope edging of almond paste around the top edge of the cake. When cool, cover the top of the cake with a layer of white Glacé Icing (page 410).

CELEBRATION CAKES

You need to make celebration cakes well ahead to allow time for them to mature. Cake decorating tools and equipment are available from specialist suppliers, often by mail order.

❖ *Christmas Cake* ❖

25–30 SLICES
PPREPARATION TIME
About 3 hours, plus standing
COOKING TIME
3–3½ hours
FREEZING
Suitable (cake only)
COLOUR INDEX
Page 84

- 175 g (6 oz) glacé cherries
- 175 g (6 oz) seeded raisins, such as lexia
- 75 g (3 oz) seedless raisins
- 75 g (3 oz) currants
- 150 g (5 oz) sultanas
- 50 g (2 oz) chopped candied peel
- 75 ml (5 tbsp) brandy
- 225 g (8 oz) butter, softened
- finely grated rind of 1 lemon
- 225 g (8 oz) light muscovado sugar
- 4 eggs (size 3), beaten
- 30 ml (2 tbsp) black treacle
- 225 g (8 oz) plain white flour
- 5 ml (1 tsp) ground mixed spice
- 125 g (4 oz) brazil nuts, roughly chopped
- 50 g (2 oz) ground almonds
TO MATURE:
- 30 ml (2 tbsp) brandy
TO COVER:
- Apricot Glaze (page 411)

- 225 g (8 oz) white Almond Paste (page 411)
- 450 g (1 lb) ready-to-roll or Fondant Icing (page 412)
TO DECORATE:
- a little Royal Icing (page 413)
CHRISTMAS ROSES:
- about 75 g (3 oz) petal paste
- lemon-yellow dusting powder
- about 35 double-headed yellow stamens
HOLLY LEAVES AND BERRIES:
- about 75 g (3 oz) ready-to-roll or Fondant Icing (page 412)
- green mint and Christmas red food colouring paste
TO FINISH:
- 1½ metres (5 ft) red ribbon, 6–7.5 cm (2½–3 inches) wide

410–345 CALS/SLICE

1 Rinse the cherries under cold water to remove all syrup; drain and pat dry with kitchen paper; quarter each cherry. Roughly chop the seeded raisins. Place the cherries, all the raisins, currants, sultanas and candied peel in a bowl; mix well. Spoon over the brandy, cover and leave to soak for 3–4 hours.

2 Meanwhile, line a 20 cm (8 inch) round deep cake tin with a double thickness of greaseproof paper.

3 In a large mixing bowl, beat the butter with the grated lemon rind until very soft and pale in colour. Gradually beat in the sugar until well blended. Beat in the eggs, a little at a time. Beat in the treacle until evenly blended.

4 Sift the flour and spice together and stir half into the creamed ingredients with the chopped brazil nuts and the ground almonds. Gently fold in all of the fruit, followed by the remaining flour. Spoon into the prepared cake tin and level the surface. Tie a band of brown paper around the outside of the tin.

5 Bake at 150°C (300°F) mark 2 for 3–3½ hours or until a fine skewer inserted into the centre comes out clean. If necessary, lay a sheet of brown paper over the cake tin after about 2 hours cooking to prevent overbrowning.

6 Leave the cake to cool in the tin for about 1 hour then turn out onto a wire rack to cool completely. Prick the surface with a fine skewer and spoon over the brandy. Leave for about 1 hour to allow the brandy to soak in.

7 When completely cold, wrap in greaseproof paper and overwrap with foil. Leave in a cool, dry place to mature for at least 2 weeks or up to 3 months, before applying the icing.

8 About 1 week before the cake is required, cover the top with almond paste; refer to page 412 for step-by-step instructions.

9 Roll out the ready-to-roll icing on a surface dusted with cornflour to a circle slightly larger than the top of the cake. Position on top of the almond paste; smooth and neaten the edges. To store for 1–2 days, secure a strip of foil around the exposed side of the cake.

To Decorate the Cake

You will need about 7 roses on the cake, but it is wise to make a few extra to allow for breakages. The roses and holly leaves can be prepared ahead and stored in an airtight container for up to 2 months.

To make the decorations, you will need the following items of equipment: medium rose-petal cutter; sponge block; holly-leaf cutter; fine paintbrushes.

CHRISTMAS ROSES
1 Lightly dust the work surface or small board with cornflour or icing sugar. Roll out a small piece of petal paste very thinly. Keep the rest of the paste tightly covered with cling film.

2 Dust the petal cutter with icing sugar and cut out 5 petals. Gently roll a cocktail stick over the round edge of the petal to a make a thinner, slightly frilled edge.

3 Place each petal on the sponge block and gently curl each one to give a shallow cup shape, using your fingertips. Cover each petal loosely with some cling film to prevent it drying out.

4 Brush one side of the first petal with water, then put the next petal in position, overlapping the edges. Repeat, adding 2 more petals. Cup the half-assembled flower, first dusting your fingers with cornflour or icing sugar. Put the last petal in position so that it overlaps the fourth petal and tucks under the first to form the rose. Repeat to make about 9 more roses. Leave to dry for about 1 hour.

TO FINISH

9 Using a little royal icing, attach the Christmas roses, holly leaves and berries to the top of the cake. Leave to dry in a cool, dry place. Tie the ribbon around the cake and finish with a large bow.

5 Using a dry brush, carefully dust the inside of the flowers with the lemon-yellow dusting powder. Brush from the centre outwards to obtain a graduated effect.

6 Using the end of a teaspoon, place a small blob of royal icing in the centre of one flower. Cut 4–5 stamens in half to give 8–10 heads, trim to size and then position them in the icing. Leave to dry for about 2 hours. Repeat with the remaining roses.

❖ White Christmas Cake ❖

16–20 SLICES	
PREPARATION TIME 1¼ hours, plus soaking	
COOKING TIME 2 hours	
FREEZING Not suitable	
COLOUR INDEX Page 84	

- 300 g (10 oz) mixed dried peaches, pears and apples
- 75 ml (5 tbsp) brandy
- 125 g (4 oz) no-soak dried apricots
- 125 g (4 oz) brazil nuts
- 200 g (7 oz) butter or margarine, softened
- 200 g (7 oz) caster sugar
- 3 eggs, lightly beaten
- 225 g (8 oz) plain white flour
- 2.5 ml (½ tsp) ground allspice
- 5 ml (1 tsp) vanilla essence
- 225 g (8 oz) candied citrus fruits, in pieces

TO DECORATE:
- 45 ml (3 tbsp) apricot jam, sieved
- 700 g (1½ lb) Almond Paste (page 411)
- 2 egg whites
- 900 g (2 lb) icing sugar, sifted (approximately)
- gold and white ribbon
- sugared almonds

595-476 CALS/SLICE

1 Roughly chop the dried peaches, pears and apples in a food processor and transfer to a bowl. Stir in the brandy and leave to soak for about 3 hours, until absorbed. Grease and line a 20 cm (8 inch) round deep cake tin.

2 Chop the apricots and brazil nuts. Cream together the butter and sugar. Gradually beat in the eggs, adding a little of the flour if the mixture begins to curdle.

3 Sift the remaining flour with the allspice and fold into the mixture with the vanilla essence. Fold in all the fruit and nuts, except the pieces of candied citrus fruit. Spoon half the mixture into the prepared tin. Press the citrus fruit over the surface in a single layer. Spread with the remaining cake mixture and level.

4 Bake in the centre of the oven at 140°C (275°F) mark 1 for 2 hours or until a skewer inserted into the centre comes out clean. Leave to cool in the tin for 1 hour, then transfer to a wire rack to cool completely.

5 Place the cake on a 25 cm (10 inch) cake board. Spread the top and sides with the jam. Roll out the almond paste on a surface dusted with icing sugar to a round, 30 cm (12 inches) in diameter. Lay the almond paste over the cake and ease to fit around the sides. Trim off any excess paste around base.

6 Lightly beat the egg whites in a large bowl, gradually beating in the icing sugar until the icing stands in soft peaks. Add a little extra icing sugar if necessary. Using a palette knife, spread the icing over the top and sides of the cake until evenly covered. Lightly 'peak' the icing using the tip of the knife.

7 Decorate the top with loops of ribbon and sugared almonds.

HOLLY LEAVES AND BERRIES
7 Set aside a small quantity of icing for berries. Add a little green paste to the rest of the icing; blend by kneading between fingers and thumbs. Repeat until a good colour is obtained. Repeat with the red paste and reserved icing. Lightly dust a work surface or board with icing sugar. Roll out the green icing thinly and cut out about 12 holly leaves, using the cutter.

8 Mark central and small veins lightly, with a cocktail stick. Twist the leaves a little and dry over the handle of a wooden spoon for 24 hours to create a curved shape. Roll about 15 berries from red icing.

✦ Christening Cake ✦

To give the cake time to mature, make it at least 1 month ahead, longer if possible.

4 Spoon the cake mixture into the prepared tin and spread evenly. Tie a double thickness band of brown paper around the outside of the tin.
5 Bake at 150°C (300°F) mark 2 for 1 hour, then reduce the temperature to 140°C (275°F) mark 1 and bake for a further 3–3½ hours. To test, insert a skewer into the centre of the cake; if the cake is cooked it should come out clean.
6 Cool in the tin for 1 hour then turn out onto a wire rack to cool completely. Prick the surface all over with a fine skewer and spoon over the brandy. Leave to soak for about 1 hour.
7 When completely cold, wrap the cake in greaseproof paper and overwrap with foil. Leave in a cool, dry place to mature for at least 2 weeks, or up to 2 months.
8 About 10–14 days before the cake is required, cover with almond paste; refer to page 412 for step-by-step instructions.
9 Cover the cake with royal icing; refer to page 413 for step-by-step instructions. Apply 3 coats in total.

To Decorate the Cake

You only need 3 swans, but it is advisable to make a few extra to allow for breakages. Trace the body and wing outlines (below) onto a piece of paper. Use this way up for right-hand pieces, invert the paper for left-hand pieces. Add a few drops of acetic acid to the royal icing to ensure the decorations harden.

ABOUT 50 SLICES

PREPARATION TIME
4–5 hours, plus
standing
COOKING TIME
4–4½ hours
FREEZING
Suitable (cake
only)

- 350 g (12 oz) glacé cherries
- 550 g (1¼ lb) sultanas
- 450 g (1 lb) currants
- 450 g (1 lb) raisins
- 125 g (4 oz) chopped mixed peel
- finely grated rind of 1 orange
- finely grated rind of 1 lemon
- 45 ml (3 tbsp) Grand Marnier
- 250 g (9 oz) butter
- 125 g (4 oz) soft light brown sugar
- 150 g (5 oz) muscovado sugar
- 7 eggs, size 2
- 125 g (4 oz) ground almonds

- 275 g (10 oz) plain flour
TO MATURE:
- 60 ml (4 tbsp) brandy or rum
TO COVER:
- Apricot Glaze (page 411)
- 900 g (2 lb) Almond Paste (page 411)
- 1 kg (2¼ lb) Royal Icing (page 413)
TO DECORATE:
- 450 g (1 lb) Royal Icing (page 413), plus a few drops of acetic acid
- narrow white and broad coloured ribbons

395 CALS/SLICE

1 Rinse the cherries under cold water to remove the syrup; drain and pat dry with kitchen paper, then cut into quarters. Place in a large mixing bowl with the sultanas, currants, raisins, mixed peel and orange and lemon rinds. Add the Grand Marnier and mix well. Cover and leave to soak for 2–3 hours.
2 Meanwhile line a 25 cm (10 inch) round deep cake tin with a double thickness of greaseproof paper.
3 Beat the butter with the sugars until very light, soft and fluffy. Beat in the eggs, one at a time, beating well between each addition. Fold in the ground almonds and flour. Add the soaked fruit and mix together thoroughly.

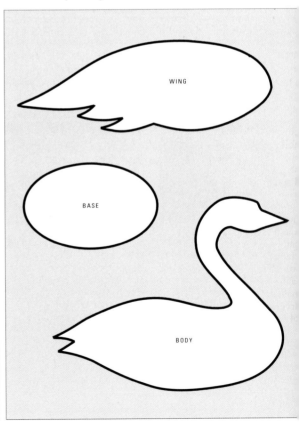

WING

BASE

BODY

1 Cut several squares of non-stick baking parchment just large enough to cover the swan outlines. Put a little icing into a small icing bag, and cut a small hole in the bottom. Place a piece of the paper over a swan body. Trace the outline.

2 Fill the outline in completely with icing. To smooth it out, gently rub a palette knife from side to side under the paper, holding the paper firmly. Make 4–5 more right-hand body pieces. Make an equal number of left-hand pieces. Lay on a flat tray to dry.

5 Pipe a good blob of icing at either side of the body, then place the wings in position – angling the wings out slightly.

6 To support the swan until the icing has set hard, stand it on a flat tray and place a ball of foil at each side, just behind each wing – this will take the weight and prevent the swan falling over. Repeat with the other swans.

3 To make the wings, thicken a little of the icing by beating in a little extra sifted icing sugar until the icing holds its shape. Put into a new paper piping bag and cut a small hole in the bottom. Making one wing at a time, place a piece of the paper over a wing diagram, then start to pipe from the top of the wing in a continuous line from side to side across the wing, each line touching the other. Make a pair of wings for each swan. Place on the tray with the swan bodies. Make a base for each swan in the same way as making the bodies. Leave to dry in a cool place for at least 24 hours.

4 To assemble the swans, carefully sandwich the left-hand and right-hand body pieces in pairs, joining them together with a little icing. Pipe small blobs of icing on one of the base pieces, then place a swan body on top and position carefully. Repeat with the remaining swans.

7 To decorate the cake, use a template and a pin to mark a row of evenly spaced scallops around the side of the cake, so that they end just about halfway down the side. Put a little icing into a small paper piping bag and cut a small hole in the bottom of the bag.

8 Pipe continuous squiggly lines in the scallops to give a filigree effect. Put some more icing into a paper piping bag fitted with a small star nozzle, then pipe a star edge to each scallop. Tie a ribbon around the side of the cake, just under the scallops, ending with a neat bow. Secure another ribbon around the edge of the cake board.

9 Decorate the top edge of the cake with 2 rows of stars, then pipe a row of stars around the bottom edge. To complete the cake, make 3 pretty bows with thin ribbon and tie one around each swan neck. Place the swans on top of the cake.

Wedding Cake

ABOUT 125 SLICES

PPREPARATION TIME
About 12–15 hours, plus standing
COOKING TIME
7–9 hours
FREEZING
Suitable (cakes only)

- *375 g (13 oz) seeded raisins, such as lexia*
- *250 g (9 oz) glacé cherries*
- *200 g (7 oz) shelled almonds*
- *550 g (1¼ lb) seedless raisins*
- *450 g (1 lb) currants*
- *700 g (1½ lb) sultanas*
- *250 g (9 oz) chopped candied peel*
- *250 g (9 oz) ground almonds*
- *105 ml (7 tbsp) brandy*
- *175 g (6 oz) plain chocolate, in pieces*
- *700 g (1½ lb) butter or margarine*
- *700 g (1½ lb) soft dark brown sugar or muscovado sugar*
- *finely grated rind of 3 large lemons*
- *13 eggs*
- *800 g (1 lb 12 oz) plain white flour*
- *7.5 ml (1½ tsp) ground cinnamon*
- *7.5 ml (1½ tsp) grated nutmeg*
- *60 ml (4 tbsp) black treacle*

TO MATURE:
- *105 ml (7 tbsp) brandy*

TO COVER:
- *Apricot Glaze (page 411)*
- *about 1.9 kg (4½ lb) Almond Paste (page 411)*
- *about 1.9 kg (4½ lb) Fondant Icing (page 412)*

TO DECORATE:
- *about 450 g (1 lb) Royal Icing (page 413)*

SUGAR-PASTE FLOWERS:
- *about 450 g (1 lb) petal paste*
- *lemon-yellow dusting powder*
- *about 72 white stamens (double-headed)*

TO FINISH:
- *ribbon or board edging*
- *fresh flowers*

325 CALS/SLICE

1 Use 15 cm (6 inch), 20 cm (8 inch) and 28 cm (11 inch) round deep cake tins. Line the 3 cake tins with a double thickness of greaseproof paper. Tie a double thickness band of brown paper around the outside of the tin. To mix the ingredients for all 3 cakes together, use a very large bowl. Alternatively you may find it easier to mix the cakes separately (see chart for quantities).

2 Prepare the fruit and nuts: chop the seeded raisins; wash, dry and halve the cherries; blanch and shred the almonds. In a large bowl, mix these together with the seedless raisins, currants, sultanas, peel, ground almonds and brandy.

3 Melt the chocolate in a heatproof bowl over a pan of simmering water; allow to cool.

4 In a separate bowl, cream the fat, sugar and lemon rind until pale and fluffy. Add the eggs one at a time, beating well.

5 Sift the flour with the spices. Fold half carefully into the creamed mixture. Add the other half to the fruit; mix well and add to the creamed mixture with the chocolate and treacle. Stir.

6 Divide the mixture among the 3 tins, taking care to make the largest cake slightly deeper than the others.

7 Bake the two small cakes together first. Spoon the cake mixture into the large tin, cover and put in a cool, dry place until ready to cook. Bake at 150°C (300°F) mark 2 for the first hour then reduce to 140°C (275°F) mark 1. Cook the small cake for a further 1–1½ hours, the medium cake for a further 1½–2 hours and the large cake 3½–5 hours longer. (If the cakes are cooked together they will take considerably longer.) After 2 hours' cooking, cover with greaseproof paper. Cool in the tins, then transfer to wire racks.

8 Pierce the cakes at regular intervals with a fine skewer, spoon a little brandy over each and leave for several hours to soak in. Wrap in greaseproof paper, then overwrap with foil and leave to mature in a cool, dry place for 1–3 months, impregnating with a little brandy at regular intervals.

9 Cover the cakes with almond paste; refer to page 412.

10 Cover the cakes with fondant icing; refer to page 412.

Wedding Cake Quantities

INGREDIENTS	15 CM (6 INCH) ROUND	20 CM (8 INCH) ROUND	28 CM (11 INCH) ROUND
seeded raisins (lexia)	*50 g (2 oz)*	*125 g (4 oz)*	*200 g (7 oz)*
glacé cherries	*40 g (1½ oz)*	*60 g (2½ oz)*	*150 g (5 oz)*
whole almonds	*25 g (1 oz)*	*50 g (2 oz)*	*125 g (4 oz)*
seedless raisins	*75 g (3 oz)*	*175 g (6 oz)*	*300 g (11 oz)*
currants	*50 g (2 oz)*	*125 g (4 oz)*	*275 g (10 oz)*
sultanas	*125 g (4 oz)*	*200 g (7 oz)*	*375 g (13 oz)*
chopped candied peel	*40 g (1½ oz)*	*60 g (2½ oz)*	*150 g (5 oz)*
ground almonds	*40 g (1½ oz)*	*60 g (2½ oz)*	*150 g (5 oz)*
brandy	*15 ml (1 tbsp)*	*30 ml (2 tbsp)*	*60 ml (4 tbsp)*
plain chocolate	*25 g (1 oz)*	*50 g (2 oz)*	*75 g (3 oz)*
margarine/butter	*75 g (3 oz)*	*200 g (7 oz)*	*400 g (14 oz)*
soft dark brown sugar	*75 g (3 oz)*	*200 g (7 oz)*	*400 g (14 oz)*
lemons	*½*	*1*	*2*
eggs	*1½*	*4*	*7½*
plain white flour	*150 g (5 oz)*	*225 g (8 oz)*	*425 g (15 oz)*
ground cinnamon	*1.25 ml (¼ tsp)*	*2.5 ml (½ tsp)*	*3.75 ml (¾ tsp)*
grated nutmeg	*1.25 ml (¼ tsp)*	*2.5 ml (½ tsp)*	*3.75 ml (¾ tsp)*
black treacle	*7.5 ml (1½ tsp)*	*15 ml (1 tbsp)*	*30 ml (2 tbsp)*
ALMOND PASTE	*350 g (12 oz)*	*550 g (1¼ lb)*	*1 kg (2¼ lb)*
FONDANT ICING	*350 g (12 oz)*	*700 g (1½ lb)*	*1 kg (2¼ lb)*

To Decorate the Cake

The three-tiered cake is decorated with about 24 sugar-paste azaleas and 180 cut-out flowers. To make these you will need the following special equipment: a set of 3 blossom cutters, with ejector; small and medium 5-point calyx cutters; medium 8-petal daisy cutter; set of rose-petal cutters; a sponge block, a ball modelling tool and fine paintbrushes.

MAKING SMALL FLOWERS
1 Break off a piece of sugar paste about the size of a large pea. (Keep the remaining paste tightly covered to prevent it from drying out.) Roll out the paste as thinly as possible using a little cornflour or icing sugar (the thinner it is, the better the flower).

2 Using the blossom, calyx and daisy cutters, cut out flowers. The blossom cutters with ejector are easiest to use – depress the plunger over the sponge and the paste is automatically cupped in the shape of a flower. For the cutters without ejectors, use the ball modelling tool to cup the paste; leave to dry.

3 Knead a little yellow dusting powder into some of the sugar paste. Repeat as above until you have about 80 flowers in all. When dry, pipe a small dot of royal icing into the centre of each flower. Leave to dry.

MAKING AZALEAS
4 Roll out a small piece of yellow sugar paste very thinly, keeping the rest well covered. Cut out 5 petals, using the large rose-petal cutter.

5 Gently mark the centre vein of each petal with a cocktail stick and 2 veins on either side. Create the frilled edge by gently rolling a cocktail stick along the curved edge of the petal. Place the petal against a wooden spoon handle to curve into shape. Repeat with the remaining 4 petals.

6 Line 2–3 large piping nozzles with foil. Brush one side of the petal with water; place the next petal in position, overlapping the edges. Repeat until all 5 petals are in position, using the nozzles to hold in shape; dry. Repeat using various cutters until you have 12 large, 6 medium and 6 small azaleas.

APPLYING DECORATIONS
8 Make the templates: cut a strip of paper to fit around the side of each cake. Fold into 6 equal portions. Cut out a semi-circle making sure the folds are linked. Transfer the outline using pin pricks.

7 Dust the outside of the flowers lightly with the lemon colour. Dampen a fine brush with water and paint small spots of dust inside each azalea. Pipe a dot of royal icing into the centre of each flower. Cut 3 stamens in half to give 6 heads, cut to size and position in the icing. Leave to dry.

9 Using the pin pricks as a guide, attach the sugar-paste flowers with a dot of royal icing. Attach 1 or 2 azaleas on top of the cake where each loop forms a point. Attach 2 small cut-out flowers to neaten the back of the azaleas.

10 Using a No 14 star or No 5 rope nozzle, pipe shells of royal icing along the bottom edge of each cake.

To Assemble the Cake

You need 8 round 7.5 cm (3 inch) hollow cake pillars and 8 wooden skewers for assembling – in situ, of course. Mark the position of the pillars on the bottom 2 tiers of the cake. Place in position and insert the skewers carefully into the cake until the point reaches the cake board. Mark the skewers 3 mm (⅛ inch) above the top of the pillar. Remove and cut to size. Replace skewers and assemble the cake. Finish with flowers.

❖ Buttercream ❖

MAKES 350 G (12 OZ)	• 125 g (4 oz) butter, softened	• few drops of vanilla essence
PREPARATION TIME 5 minutes	• 225 g (8 oz) icing sugar, sifted	• 15–30 ml (1–2 tbsp) milk
FREEZING Suitable		130 CALS/25 G (1 OZ)

1 Cream the butter until soft. Gradually beat in the icing sugar, adding the vanilla essence and milk, to form a smooth icing.

NOTE: This quantity is sufficient to coat the top and sides of a 20 cm (8 inch) cake.

Variations

ORANGE OR LEMON BUTTERCREAM: Omit the vanilla and add a little finely grated orange or lemon rind and a little of the juice, beating well to avoid curdling the mixture.

COFFEE BUTTERCREAM: Omit the vanilla and milk. Add 10 ml (2 tsp) instant coffee powder dissolved in 15–30 ml (1–2 tbsp) hot water; cool before adding.

CHOCOLATE BUTTERCREAM: Flavour by adding 25–40 g (1–1½ oz) melted chocolate, omitting 15 ml (1 tbsp) of the milk.

MOCHA BUTTERCREAM: Dissolve 5 ml (1 tsp) cocoa powder and 10 ml (2 tsp) instant coffee powder in a little hot water; cool before adding to the mixture.

❖ Crème au Beurre ❖

MAKES 275 G (10 OZ)	• 75 g (3 oz) caster sugar	• 175 g (6 oz) butter, softened
PREPARATION TIME 15 minutes	• 2 egg yolks, beaten	
COOKING TIME 5 minutes		
FREEZING Not suitable		155 CALS/25 G (1 OZ)

1 Place the sugar in a heavy-based saucepan with 60 ml (4 tbsp) water and dissolve over a low heat. When completely dissolved, bring to boiling point and boil steadily for 2–3 minutes until a temperature of 107°C (225°F) is registered on a sugar thermometer.
2 Put the egg yolks in a deep bowl and pour on the syrup in a thin stream, whisking all the time. Continue to whisk until the mixture is thick and cold.
3 In another bowl, cream the butter until very soft, then gradually beat in the egg yolk mixture to make a smooth icing.

Variations

CHOCOLATE CRÈME AU BEURRE: Melt 50 g (2 oz) plain chocolate with 15 ml (1 tbsp) water. Cool slightly and beat into the crème au beurre.

ORANGE OR LEMON CRÈME AU BEURRE: Add a little freshly grated citrus rind and a little juice to taste.

COFFEE CRÈME AU BEURRE: Beat 15–30 ml (1–2 tbsp) coffee essence into the crème au beurre.

❖ Glacé Icing ❖

MAKES 100–175 G (4–6 OZ)	• 125–175 g (4–6 oz) icing sugar	• flavouring (optional) • colouring (optional)
PREPARATION TIME 5 minutes		
FREEZING Not suitable		100 CALS/25 G (1 OZ)

1 Sift the icing sugar into a bowl, then gradually mix in 15–30 ml (1–2 tbsp) warm water until the icing is thick enough to coat the back of a spoon.
2 Stir in any flavouring. If necessary, add more sugar or water to obtain the correct consistency. Add a few drops of colouring, if required. Use at once.

NOTE: This quantity is sufficient to cover the top of a 20 cm (8 inch) cake or about 8 small cakes.

Variations

EXTRA-SMOOTH GLACÉ ICING: Place the icing sugar, water, flavouring and colouring in a small pan and heat gently, stirring, until the mixture is warm; do not allow it to get too hot. The icing should coat the back of a wooden spoon and look smooth and glossy.

ORANGE OR LEMON GLACÉ ICING: Substitute 15–30 ml (1–2 tbsp) strained orange or lemon juice for the water.

CHOCOLATE GLACÉ ICING: Blend 10 ml (2 tsp) cocoa powder in a little hot water and use to replace the same amount of measured water.

COFFEE GLACÉ ICING: Flavour with either 5 ml (1 tsp) coffee flavouring or 10 ml (2 tsp) instant coffee powder dissolved in a little of the measured and heated water.

MOCHA GLACÉ ICING: Flavour with 5 ml (1 tsp) cocoa powder and 10 ml (2 tsp) instant coffee powder, dissolved in a little of the measured and heated water.

❖ Coffee Fudge Frosting ❖

MAKES 400 G (14 OZ)	• 50 g (2 oz) butter or margarine	• 30 ml (2 tbsp) single cream or milk
PREPARATION TIME 5 minutes	• 125 g (4 oz) light soft brown sugar	• 200 g (7 oz) icing sugar, sifted
COOKING TIME 5 minutes	• 45 ml (3 tbsp) coffee essence	
FREEZING Not suitable		105 CALS/25 G (1 OZ)

1 Put the butter, brown sugar, coffee essence and cream in a saucepan and heat gently until the sugar dissolves. Boil briskly for 3 minutes.
2 Remove from the heat and gradually stir in the icing sugar. Beat with a wooden spoon until smooth, then continue to beat for 2 minutes until the icing is thick enough to spread. Use immediately, spreading with a wet palette knife.

Variation

CHOCOLATE FUDGE FROSTING: Replace the coffee essence with 75 g (3 oz) plain chocolate.

❖ American Frosting ❖

MAKES 225 G (8 OZ)
PREPARATION TIME
15 minutes
COOKING TIME
5 minutes
FREEZING
Not suitable

- 1 egg white
- 225 g (8 oz) caster or granulated sugar
- pinch of cream of tartar

225 CALS/25 G (1 OZ)

1 Whisk the egg white in a bowl until stiff. Put the sugar in a heavy-based saucepan with 60 ml (4 tbsp) water and the cream of tartar. Heat gently, stirring until dissolved. Then without stirring, bring to the boil and boil to a temperature of 120°C (240°F), as registered on a sugar thermometer.
2 Remove the syrup from the heat and as soon as the bubbles subside, pour it onto the egg white in a thin stream, beating constantly. Allow to cool slightly.
3 When the mixture begins to appear dull around the edges and is almost cold, pour quickly over the cake and spread evenly with a palette knife.

❖ Chocolate Ganache ❖

MAKES 200 ML (7 FL OZ)
PREPARATION TIME
10 minutes, plus cooling
FREEZING
Suitable

- 150 ml (¼ pint) double cream
- 125 g (4 oz) plain or milk chocolate, in pieces

165 CALS/25 ML (1 FL OZ)

1 Pour the cream into a small pan and bring to the boil. Remove from the heat and add the chocolate; stir gently until the chocolate has melted and the mixture is smooth.
2 Return the mixture to the heat. Bring to the boil, remove from the heat and allow to cool. Use at room temperature: the mixture should be the consistency of softened butter.

❖ Apricot Glaze ❖

MAKES 150 ML (¼ PINT)
PREPARATION TIME
5 minutes
COOKING TIME
5 minutes
FREEZING
Suitable

- 125 g (4 oz) apricot jam

55 CALS/25 ML (1 FL OZ)

1 Place the jam and 30 ml (2 tbsp) water in a small pan. Heat gently, stirring, until the jam begins to melt. Bring to the boil and simmer for 1 minute.
2 Strain the jam through a nylon sieve. Use while warm.

❖ Almond Paste ❖

Almond paste or marzipan is applied to rich fruit cakes to create a smooth foundation for the icing. It is therefore important to apply it neatly.

You can either make your own almond paste, following the recipe below, or buy it ready-made. When buying ready-made choose the white variety, rather than the yellow one, as it is less likely to discolour the icing. The flavour of homemade almond paste is, however, better than either ready-made alternative.

If royal icing a cake, cover the cake with almond paste 1 week before applying the first coat of icing, to allow the almond paste to dry. Homemade almond paste takes longer to dry out than the ready-made variety.

MAKES ABOUT 450 G (1 LB)
PREPARATION TIME
10 minutes
FREEZING
Suitable

- 225 g (8 oz) ground almonds
- 125 g (4 oz) caster sugar
- 125 g (4 oz) icing sugar
- 1 egg
- 5 ml (1 tsp) lemon juice
- 5 ml (1 tsp) sherry
- 1–2 drops vanilla essence

135 CALS/25 G (1 OZ)

1 Place the ground almonds, caster sugar and icing sugar in a bowl and mix together. In a separate bowl, whisk the egg with the remaining ingredients and add to the dry mixture.
2 Stir well to mix, pounding gently to release some of the oil from the almonds. Knead with your hands until smooth.

NOTE: If you wish to avoid using raw egg to bind the almond paste, mix the other liquid ingredients with a little water instead.

❖ Almond Paste Quantity Guide ❖

SQUARE TIN ❖	ROUND TIN ❖	ALMOND PASTE ❖
12 cm (5 inch)	15 cm (6 inch)	350 g (12 oz)
15 cm (6 inch)	18 cm (7 inch)	450 g (1 lb)
18 cm (7 inch)	20 cm (8 inch)	550 g (1¼ lb)
20 cm (8 inch)	23 cm (9 inch)	800 g (1¾ lb)
23 cm (9 inch)	25 cm (10 inch)	900 g (2 lb)
25 cm (10 inch)	28 cm (11 inch)	1 kg (2¼ lb)
28 cm (11 inch)	30 cm (12 inch)	1.1 kg (2½ lb)
30 cm (12 inch)	33 cm (13 inch)	1.4 kg (3 lb)
33 cm (13 inch)	35 cm (14 inch)	1.6 kg (3½ lb)

❖ Covering a Cake ❖ with Almond Paste

For recommended quantities, see the chart on page 411. You will need to make up a quantity of Apricot Glaze (page 411) before applying the almond paste.

1 If the cake has an uneven top, cut it level. Turn the cake over so the flat bottom becomes the top. Sift some icing sugar onto a clean work surface.

2 Roll out half the almond paste slightly larger than the top of the cake. Using the cake tin as a guide, cut the paste to fit. Brush the top of the cake with warm apricot glaze.

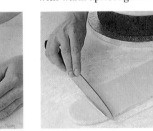

3 Lift the almond paste onto the cake and smooth over, neatening the edges. Place on a cake board, which should be 5 cm (2 inches) larger than the cake.

4 Cut a piece of string the same height as the cake with its almond paste top, and another to fit around the side of the cake. Roll out the remaining almond paste and, using the string as a guide, trim the paste to size. Brush the sides of the cake and the almond paste rim with apricot glaze.

5 Roll up the almond paste strip loosely. Place one end against the side of the cake and unroll to cover the sides of the cake. Use a palette knife to smooth over the sides and joins of the paste. Flatten the top lightly with a rolling pin. Leave the cake in a cool, dry room to dry out thoroughly for about 2 days before applying the icing.

❖ Fondant Icing ❖

Fondant icing – or moulding icing – provides an easy to apply covering. It is also used to mould decorations. Ready-to-roll icing (ready-made fondant) is used in the same way.

MAKES ABOUT 450 G (1 LB)	• 400 g (14 oz) icing sugar	• 50 g (2 oz) liquid glucose (available from chemists)
PREPARATION TIME 15 minutes	• 1 egg white	
FREEZING Not suitable		

95 CALS/25 G (1 OZ)

1 Sift the icing sugar in a large bowl. Make a well in the centre and add the egg white and glucose. Beat these ingredients with a clean wooden spoon, gradually pulling in the icing sugar.
2 When the mixture becomes stiff, turn onto a surface sprinkled with icing sugar. Knead thoroughly to a smooth paste.
3 If necessary, store tightly wrapped in cling film in a cool place.

❖ Covering a Cake ❖ with Fondant Icing

For recommended quantities, see chart (right).

1 First, cover the cake with almond paste and allow to dry. Sprinkle a clean work surface with cornflour and dredge your rolling pin. Roll out the icing until it is 12–15 cm (5–6 inches) larger than the cake top.

2 Supporting the icing on a rolling pin, place it centrally over the top of the cake, allowing the icing to drape over the sides. Press the icing onto the sides of the cake.

3 Work it with your hands sprinkled with cornflour or icing sugar, from the centre of the cake; gently ease the icing down the sides to give an even covering.

4 Trim excess icing from the base. Smooth icing, using a circular movement with the fingers. Leave for about 2 days to dry before decorating.

❖ Royal Icing ❖

Omit the glycerine from the recipe if the icing is to cover a tiered cake, as a very hard surface is required to support the tiers.

MAKES 450 G (1 LB)

PREPARATION TIME
20 minutes
FREEZING
Not suitable

• *2 egg whites or albumen powder equivalent*
• *10 ml (2 tsp) liquid glycerine*

• *450 g (1 lb) icing sugar*

100 CALS/25 G (1 OZ)

1 If using the egg whites with the glycerine, place them in a bowl and stir just enough to break up the egg whites. If using albumen powder, mix according to manufacturer's instructions.
2 Using a clean wooden spoon, add a little sieved icing sugar and start mixing gently, to incorporate as little air as possible.
3 Add a little more icing sugar as the mixture becomes lighter. Continue to add the sugar, stirring gently but thoroughly until the mixture is stiff and stands in soft peaks. If required for coating, it should form soft peaks; for piping it should be a little stiffer. Transfer to an airtight container, cover the icing closely with cling film to exclude air and prevent the surface of the icing drying out, then seal. When required, stir the icing slowly.

❖ Flat Icing a ❖ Cake with Royal Icing

Always apply royal icing over a layer of almond paste.

1 Put a large spoonful of icing onto the centre of the cake and spread out, using a palette knife in a paddling motion; this helps to eliminate air bubbles.

2 Draw an icing ruler across the top of the cake towards you, applying an even pressure and keeping the ruler at an angle of about 30°. Remove surplus icing by running a palette knife around the edge, at right angles to the cake.

3 To cover the sides, for best results, place a round cake on a turntable. Spread icing onto the sides using the same paddling motion. Hold a cake scraper at an angle of about 45° and draw it around the side, then pull it off quickly to leave only a slight mark. Dry in a cool place for 24 hours. Store the remaining icing as above.

4 The next day, scrape away any rough icing from the top edge with a small sharp knife. Clean fine sandpaper can be used to achieve a very smooth finish. Brush off loose icing with a clean pastry brush. Apply 2 or 3 further coats, allowing each coat to dry overnight before applying the next. Leave to dry overnight before applying decorations.

Quantity Guide

The table below indicates the amount of royal icing needed to cover various-sized square and round, almond-pasted cakes. Multiply the recipe as appropriate. Remember that it is better not to make up more than 900 g (2 lb) at a time as smaller quantities of icing keep better. The chart below will give you enough icing for 2–3 coats (depending on how skillful you are). It is difficult to give an accurate guide as to the amount of icing needed for piping work – allow approximately 450 g (1 lb) royal icing to elaborately pipe a 30 cm (12 inch) cake.

❖ Fondant and Royal Icing ❖ Quantity Guide

SQUARE TIN ❖	ROUND TIN ❖	FONDANT ICING ❖	ROYAL ICING (SUGAR WEIGHT) ❖
12 cm (5 inch)	15 cm (6 inch)	350 g (12 oz)	450 g (1 lb)
15 cm (6 inch)	18 cm (7 inch)	450 g (1 lb)	550 g (1¼ lb)
18 cm (7 inch)	20 cm (8 inch)	700 g (1½ lb)	700 g (1½ lb)
20 cm (8 inch)	23 cm (9 inch)	800 g (1¾ lb)	900 g (2 lb)
23 cm (9 inch)	25 cm (10 inch)	900 g (2 lb)	1 kg (2¼ lb)
25 cm (10 inch)	28 cm (11 inch)	1 kg (2¼ lb)	1.1 kg (2½ lb)
28 cm (11 inch)	30 cm (12 inch)	1.1 kg (2½ lb)	1.4 kg (3 lb)
30 cm (12 inch)	33 cm (13 inch)	1.4 kg (3 lb)	1.6 kg (3½ lb)
33 cm (13 inch)	35 cm (14 inch)	1.6 kg (3½ lb)	1.8 kg (4 lb)

BREADS & YEAST BAKING

There really is nothing quite like the aroma and taste of homemade bread. Unfortunately bread-making is one of those traditional tasks that many believe to be difficult, but in fact it's never been easier. Fast-action dried yeast is now readily available and simple to use; it speeds up bread-making dramatically. You will also find that many supermarkets and healthfood shops now stock a good range of bread flours.

Once you've mastered the basic techniques there is nothing to stop you baking your own creations and imitations of commercially produced speciality breads at a fraction of the cost. Look to the recipes here for inspiration but don't be shy of creating your own combinations: flavour savoury doughs with cheese, fresh herbs, olives, or sun-dried tomatoes; sweet doughs with vanilla sugar or scented spices like cinnamon, as well as dried fruits and nuts.

Yeast

Yeast is one of those fantastic ingredients with unique properties. Although not difficult to use, it is a living organism and must be handled in the right way in order to work effectively. When you buy yeast it is alive, but inactive. Only when it is mixed with a warm liquid does it become active and release the gases that should make the dough rise. Yeast is available in a number of different forms which are interchangable in recipes, providing that the method is adjusted accordingly.

❖ FRESH YEAST: Although good healthfood shops continue to stock fresh yeast, it is becoming more and more difficult to buy. Should you manage to find a supplier, check that the yeast is firm, moist and creamy coloured with a good 'yeasty' smell. If it is dry and crumbly with discoloured brown patches then it is probably stale and it won't work. Fresh yeast is easy to use – simply blend with a little of the liquid specified in the recipe, add the remaining liquid, then mix into the flour. It will only stay fresh for about 3 days if stored in the refrigerator, but it freezes well – freeze in usable quantities for up to 3 months.

❖ FAST-ACTION DRIED YEAST: Also called easy-blend dried yeast, this product has revolutionised bread-making. It is sprinkled directly into the flour and the liquid is mixed in afterwards. After kneading, the dough can be shaped straight away and only requires one rising. However, for enriched doughs – particularly heavily fruited ones – better results are obtained if the dough is given the traditional two rises. Always make sure you adhere to the use-by date on the packet – fast-action dried yeast won't work if it's stale.

❖ DRIED YEAST: Because fast-action yeast works so well, it largely seems to have replaced 'ordinary' dried yeast in the shops. If, however, you use 'ordinary' dried yeast for any of the recipes in this chapter, blend it with the liquid (see below) and leave it in a warm place for about 15 minutes or until a frothy head (similar to the head on a pint of Guinness) develops. This shows that the yeast is active. If it refuses to froth, then it is probably past its use-by date; discard and start again with a fresh packet of yeast.

❖ SOURDOUGH STARTER: This is one of those old-fashioned methods that has regained popularity in recent years. A mixture of yeast, flour and water is left to ferment for several days before it is added to the dough. It produces a close-textured loaf with a distinctive flavour. If you make bread regularly, a sourdough starter is a convenient way of leavening.

Simply blend 15 g (½ oz) fresh yeast (or its equivalent) with 450 ml (¾ pint) warm water and about 225 g (8 oz) strong white flour or enough to make a thick pourable batter. Cover the bowl with a damp cloth and leave at room temperature for 3–5 days to ferment and develop the sourdough flavour. Use 125 ml (4 fl oz) of the starter to replace each 15 g (½ oz) fresh yeast called for in a recipe, then make the bread in the usual way. Providing the starter is nourished with a paste made from at least 25 g (1 oz) strong flour mixed with water every 4 days it will keep for several weeks and always be on hand ready to use. If you do not use it for a few days, store it in the refrigerator.

❖ YEAST QUANTITIES: As a rough guide, 15 g (½ oz) fresh yeast, a 7 g sachet (1½ tsp) fast-action (easy-blend) dried yeast, or 15 ml (1 tbsp) dried yeast is enough to rise 750 g (1½ lb) flour. If you add more than this, the dough will not rise any higher and the bread is likely to have an unpleasant yeasty taste. However, if the dough is enriched with fruit, sugar, butter or nuts, the rise is more difficult and you will usually need more yeast – be guided by the recipes. Because fast-action dried yeast seems to be the most readily available dried form, it is used in the recipes in this chapter; should you wish to use 'ordinary' dried yeast simply adjust the quantity and method accordingly.

Liquid

Ordinary dried yeast (not the fast-action type) needs sugar to activate it. If using milk the natural sugars present in the milk will be enough; if using water add a pinch of sugar. No matter which variety of yeast you are using, the liquid should be just warm or tepid: it should feel slightly warm to the fingertips. If it is too hot it could kill the yeast; if too cold the yeast will not begin to work. Always regard any quantity of liquid specified in a recipe as a guide because flour absorbency varies from brand to brand.

Flour

A variety of different flours is used for bread-making. 'Strong' flours give the best results because they are high in gluten – the substance which stretches the dough and traps air in it as it cooks, to give an open texture. Ordinary plain flour can be used for bread-making, but because it is lower in gluten it produces a close-textured crumbly loaf. Bread made with wholemeal flour has a distinctive flavour and texture; it is also an excellent source of fibre. It is, however, heavier than white bread. If you want a high fibre, lighter loaf use brown (wheatmeal) flour, or half wholemeal and half white flour.

Stoneground flour takes its name from the specific grinding process – between stones – which heats the flour and gives it a slightly roasted, nutty flavour. Both stoneground wholemeal and brown flours are available. Granary flour is a strong brown flour, with added malted wheat flakes, which give it a distinctive flavour. Rye and buckwheat flours also make interesting breads, but as these are both low in gluten, they should be mixed with a strong flour for best results.

Other Ingredients

Salt improves the flavour of bread, but it also slows down the action of yeast, so don't add too much. Use the amount specified in the recipe as a guide – if you are trying to reduce your salt intake use less, or a low-sodium salt instead.

Some recipes call for a little fat to be rubbed into the flour before the yeast is added. This helps the keeping quality of the bread and imparts extra flavour, but too much fat will slow down the action of the yeast.

Mixing and Kneading the Dough

Some recipes recommend warming the flour and mixing bowl in advance. If using fresh or 'ordinary' dried yeast or if you are working in a very cold room this helps speed things up a little, but otherwise it isn't really necessary. After mixing the yeast and liquid into the dry ingredients to make a soft dough, the dough must be kneaded. Vigorous kneading is required to strengthen the gluten in the flour, make the dough elastic and ultimately to achieve a good rise. If you omit this stage, the dough will not rise. There's nothing difficult about kneading and it doesn't take long – 5–10 minutes should be enough.

Turn the dough onto a floured surface, fold it firmly towards you, then quickly and firmly push it down and away from you with the heel of your hand. Give it a quarter turn and continue kneading until the dough feels elastic and smooth: it shouldn't be sticky.

As an alternative to kneading by hand, you can use a mixer with a dough hook attachment, or a food processor. In both cases it is essential to avoid overloading the machine; follow the manufacturer's instructions for quantities.

Rising

Put the kneaded dough into a clean bowl and cover with a clean tea towel, an oiled polythene bag or oiled cling film to prevent a skin forming. Leave in a warm place until the dough has doubled in size and springs back when pressed. The time it takes to rise will depend on the surrounding temperature. If you put the bowl near a warm oven or in an airing cupboard, rising can take as little as 30 minutes, while at cooler temperatures it may take over an hour. Don't be tempted to put it somewhere hot to speed things up; you will end up with a badly shaped, uneven-textured loaf, or you could even kill the yeast. For a slower rise, leave the dough in the refrigerator overnight; bring it to room temperature in the morning before shaping.

Knocking Back and Proving

The risen dough is 'knocked back' to smooth out any large pockets of air. A brief kneading is sufficient, just 2–3 minutes before shaping as required. Leave the shaped dough once again in a warm place until it has doubled in size and springs back when pressed. This proving stage is quicker than the first rising.

Baking

Bread is baked in a hot oven to kill the yeast and halt its action. If the bread shows signs of browning too quickly, cover with foil. When cooked, the bread should be well risen, firm to the touch and golden brown; if you turn it over and tap it on the bottom the loaf should sound hollow. To crisp large loaves all over, return them to the oven upside down for about 10 minutes. Always remove bread from the tins before cooling on wire racks.

Storing Bread

Bread which contains lots of fat or sugar should keep well for 3–4 days, but ordinary plain bread stales fairly quickly. It is best stored in a dry, well ventilated bread bin. If stored in the refrigerator, bread will stale more quickly. Bread freezes well for a short time – up to 1 month – after which the crust begins to deteriorate and lift off. Frozen or slightly stale bread can be freshened in a warm oven.

Quick yeastless breads – leavened with baking powder or bicarbonate of soda rather than yeast – tend to stale quickly. They are invariably at their best eaten fresh and warm from the oven.

❖ Wholemeal Bread ❖

MAKES 1

PREPARATION TIME
15 minutes, plus
rising

COOKING TIME
about 35 minutes

FREEZING
Suitable

COLOUR INDEX
Page 85

- 15 g (½ oz) fresh yeast or 7 g sachet (1½ tsp) fast-action dried yeast
- 150 ml (¼ pint) tepid milk
- 450 g (1 lb) plain wholemeal flour
- 5 ml (1 tsp) salt
- 5 ml (1 tsp) caster sugar
- 25 g (1 oz) butter or margarine

1700 CALS/LOAF

If using fresh yeast, blend with the milk. Mix the flour, salt and sugar in a bowl, and stir in the fast-action dried yeast if using. Rub in butter. Make a well in the centre; pour in the yeast liquid or milk and about 175 ml (6 fl oz) tepid water. Mix to a soft dough.

2 Turn out the dough onto a lightly floured surface and knead for about 10 minutes until smooth and elastic. If using fresh yeast, place in an oiled bowl and cover with oiled cling film. Leave to rise until doubled in size and sponge-like in texture.

Knock risen dough down, then knead again on a lightly floured surface for 3–4 minutes until smooth. The dough is now ready for shaping (see right). After shaping it can be lightly scored to produce a pattern on the crust.

4 Cover the shaped dough with oiled cling film and leave in a warm place to rise. Free-shaped dough will double in size, dough in tins should rise to the rims; this takes about 45 minutes depending on size and room temperature.

5 Glaze and finish (see page 418). Bake at 220°C (425°F) mark 7 for 20 minutes. Reduce the temperature to 180°C (350°F) mark 4 and remove bread from tin if using. Bake for a further 15 minutes. To test, tap the bottom crust; the bread should sound hollow. Cool on a wire rack.

Variations

LIGHT WHOLEMEAL BREAD: Use 225 g (8 oz) strong plain white flour and 225 g (8 oz) plain wholemeal flour with about 150 ml (¼ pint) tepid milk and 150 ml (¼ pint) tepid water.

SOFT WHITE BREAD: Use all strong plain white flour with 200 ml (7 fl oz) tepid milk and 90 ml (3 fl oz) tepid water.

NUTTY WHOLEMEAL BREAD: Use 425 g (15 oz) Granary flour with 25 g (1 oz) oatmeal. For additional texture add 75 g (3 oz) mixed sesame and sunflower seeds. Mix with about 150 ml (¼ pint) tepid milk and 200 ml (7 fl oz) tepid water.

Shaping

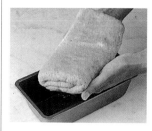

TRADITIONAL TIN LOAF: Flatten the dough to an oblong the length of a 900 g (2 lb) loaf tin but three times as wide. Fold the bottom third up over the centre and the top third down. Press down well. Turn over, then place in the lightly greased tin.

ROUND: Shape the dough into a ball. For a smooth top, knead the edges of the round repeatedly into the centre and press down. Turn over and place seam-side down on a lightly greased baking sheet or in a deep 15–18 cm (6–7 inch) greased cake tin.

BATONS: Divide the dough in half and shape each piece into a long roll with tapering ends, about 35 cm (14 inches) long.

PLAIT: Divide the dough into three. Shape each piece into a roll 30 cm (12 inches) long. Pinch ends together and plait loosely. Pinch the other ends.

COTTAGE LOAF: Cut one third off the dough. Knead both pieces well and shape into rounds. Place the smaller round on top of the larger one, on a baking sheet. Push the handle of a wooden spoon down through the middle. Brush with salt water to glaze before baking.

Rolls

With the exception of the tray rolls, bake these at 220°C (425°F) mark 7 for about 20 minutes.

ROUNDS: Divide the dough into 8-10 pieces. Place on a very lightly floured surface and roll each into a ball.

TRAY ROLLS: Shape the dough into rounds as above. Arrange to fit exactly into a lightly greased shallow 20 cm (8 inch) round cake tin. Bake as for Wholemeal Bread (page 417).

COTTAGE ROLLS: Divide the dough into 8 pieces, then shape the rolls as for cottage loaf (page 417).

PLAITS: Divide the dough into 8 pieces, then shape as for plaited loaf (page 417).

Glazing

For a deep golden, shiny finish brush with beaten egg. Brushing with water gives a crisp crust, while milk produces a soft, golden crust. Whole grains, nuts, seeds, coarse salt or grated Parmesan cheese can be sprinkled over the dough before baking.

4 Wrap one end of the dough over the other and pinch with your fingers to form a circle. Transfer the dough to a greased baking sheet and cover loosely with a clean tea towel. Leave in a warm place for about 20 minutes until doubled in size.

5 Remove the tea towel and, with a sharp pair of scissors, snip around the top of the loaf to make a zig-zag pattern. Brush with water and bake at 230°C (450°F) mark 8 for 15 minutes. Reduce temperature to 190°C (375°F) mark 5 and bake for a further 20–25 minutes or until the loaf sounds hollow when tapped on the base. Cool on a wire rack.

❖ Olive Sourdough Bread ❖

MAKES 1		
PREPARATION TIME 25 minutes, plus rising	• 400 g (14 oz) strong plain white flour	• 200 ml (7 fl oz) Sourdough Starter (page 415)
COOKING TIME 35–40 minutes	• 75 g (3 oz) rye flour	• 45 ml (3 tbsp) virgin olive oil
FREEZING Suitable	• 75 g (3 oz) strong wholemeal flour	• 225 g (8 oz) mixed stoned black and green
COLOUR INDEX Page 85	• 5 ml (1 tsp) salt • 45 ml (3 tbsp) chopped mixed herbs	olives, roughly chopped
		3375 CALS/LOAF

1 Put the flours, salt and herbs in a bowl and mix together. Add the sourdough starter, the olive oil and 225 ml (8 fl oz) tepid water, or enough to mix to a soft dough.

2 On a lightly floured surface, knead for 10 minutes or until smooth and elastic. Place in a large oiled bowl, cover and let rise in a warm place for 1 hour or until doubled in size.

3 Knock back the dough on a lightly floured surface, then carefully knead in the olives. Shape into a long sausage, then curl it round to form a circle.

❖ Cornbread ❖

MAKES 2		
PREPARATION TIME 25 minutes, plus rising	• 15 g (½ oz) fresh yeast or 7 g sachet fast-action dried yeast	• 75 g (3 oz) light soft brown sugar
COOKING TIME About 25 minutes	• about 375 ml (13 fl oz) tepid milk	• 10 ml (2 tsp) salt • 50 g (2 oz) butter or margarine
FREEZING Suitable	• 350 g (12 oz) cornmeal	• corn or maize meal, for sprinkling
COLOUR INDEX Page 85	• 450 g (1 lb) strong plain white flour	
		1650 CALS/LOAF

1 If using fresh yeast, blend with the milk.
2 Put the cornmeal, flour, sugar and salt in a bowl. Add the fast action dried yeast, if using. Rub in the butter. Make a well in the centre, then pour in the yeast liquid – or 375 ml (13 fl oz) tepid milk if using fast-action dried yeast – and mix to a soft dough, adding a little more milk if necessary. Knead on a floured surface for 10 minutes or until smooth and elastic.
3 If using fresh yeast, put the dough in an oiled bowl, cover with a clean tea towel and leave to rise in a warm place for about 1 hour until doubled in size. Turn the dough on to a floured surface and knead for 5 minutes. (If fast-action dried yeast has been used, this stage is not necessary.)
4 Divide the dough into two, shape each piece into a 15 cm (6 inch) round and place on 2 greased baking sheets. Cover and leave in a warm place until doubled in size.
5 Using a sharp knife, mark the top of each loaf in squares. Brush with water, then sprinkle generously with corn or maize meal. Bake at 220°C (425°F) mark 7 for 10 minutes, then reduce the temperature to 190°C (375°F) mark 5 and bake for a further 15 minutes or until well risen and the loaves sound hollow if tapped on the bottom. Cool on a wire rack.

❖ Potted Herb Bread ❖

4 Cut the dough into six pieces. Shape the pieces into elongated balls and drop them into the prepared pots. Alternatively, shape into rounds and place on a baking sheet. Leave in a warm place until risen to the tops of the pots, or doubled in size.

5 Brush the loaves with salt water. Bake at 200°C (400°F) mark 6 for 10 minutes. Lower temperature to 180°C (350°F) mark 4 and bake for a further 20 minutes. Turn loaves out of pots and bake for 5 minutes to crisp the sides. Cool on a wire rack. Serve warm.

MAKES 6
REPARATION TIME
0 minutes, plus
ising
OOKING TIME
5 minutes
REEZING
uitable

- white vegetable fat, melted, for greasing
- 15 g (½ oz) fresh yeast or one 7 g sachet fast-action dried yeast
- 450 g (1 lb) strong plain white or wholemeal flour
- 7.5 ml (1½ tsp) salt
- 50 g (2 oz) butter or margarine
- 150 ml (10 tbsp) finely chopped herbs, such as basil, parsley or thyme

400 CALS/LOAF

Soak 6 terracotta flowerpots, cm (3½ inch) in diameter, in old water overnight. Dry, hen brush with melted fat. If using fresh yeast, blend with 00 ml (½ pint) tepid water.

2 In a large bowl, mix together the flour and salt. Add the fast-action dried yeast, if using. Rub in the butter and stir in the herbs. Make a well in the centre.

3 Pour in the yeast liquid, or 300 ml (½ pint) tepid water if using fast-action dried yeast. Mix well (adding a little extra water if needed). Turn on to a floured surface. Knead for 10 minutes or until smooth. If using fresh yeast, put the dough in a large oiled bowl, cover and leave to rise in a warm place for about 1 hour until doubled in size; knead again for 2–3 minutes.

❖ Soda Bread ❖

MAKES 1
PREPARATION TIME
10 minutes
COOKING TIME
35–40 minutes
FREEZING
Suitable

- 450 g (1 lb) plain wholemeal flour
- 125 g (4 oz) plain white flour
- 50 g (2 oz) rolled oats
- 5 ml (1 tsp) salt
- 5 ml (1 tsp) bicarbonate of soda
- about 450 ml (¾ pint) buttermilk

2190 CALS/LOAF

1 Put the flours, oats, salt and bicarbonate of soda in a large bowl and mix together. Add enough buttermilk to mix to a soft dough.
2 Knead very lightly, then shape into a large round and place on a greased baking sheet. Cut a deep cross in the top.
3 Bake at 230°C (450°F) mark 8 for 15 minutes, then reduce the temperature to 200°C (400°F) mark 6 and bake for a further 20–25 minutes or until the loaf sounds hollow when tapped on the bottom. Cool on a wire rack. Eat while still warm.

❖ Rustic Walnut Bread ❖

MAKES 2

PREPARATION TIME
25 minutes, plus
rising
COOKING TIME
35 minutes
FREEZING
Suitable

- *15 g (½ oz) fresh yeast
or 7 g sachet fast-action
dried yeast*
- *600 g (1 lb 5 oz)
strong plain white flour*
- *5 ml (1 tsp) salt*
- *25 g (1 oz) butter or
margarine*
- *125 g (4 oz) walnuts,
roughly chopped*

1080 CALS/LOAF

1 If using fresh yeast, blend it with 350 ml (12 fl oz) tepid water.

2 Mix the flour and salt together in a large bowl. Rub in the butter, then stir in the fast-action dried yeast if using, and the chopped walnuts.

3 Make a well in the centre of the flour mixture and pour in the yeast liquid, or 350 ml (12 fl oz) tepid water if using fast-action dried yeast. Mix to a smooth dough, then turn out onto a lightly floured surface and knead for 10 minutes until smooth and elastic, adding a little more flour if the dough becomes too sticky.

4 If using fresh yeast, put the dough in a large oiled bowl and cover with oiled cling film. Leave to rise in a warm place for about 1 hour until doubled in size. Turn out and knead the dough again for 2–3 minutes. (If fast-action dried yeast has been used, this stage is not necessary.)

5 Divide the dough in half and shape each piece into a roll. Place on oiled baking sheets, cover with a damp tea towel, and leave to rise in a warm place for about 1 hour, or until doubled in size.

6 Uncover the loaves and slash the tops with a sharp knife. Bake at 220°C (425°F) mark 7 for 10 minutes. Reduce the oven temperature to 190°C (375°F) mark 5 and bake for a further 25

❖ Schiacciata ❖

12 SLICES

PREPARATION TIME
25 minutes, plus
rising
COOKING TIME
30–35 minutes
FREEZING
Not suitable
COLOUR INDEX
Page 86

- *5 ml (1 tsp) fast-action
dried yeast*
- *450 g (1 lb) strong
plain white flour*
- *about 125 ml (4 fl oz)
extra-virgin olive oil*
- *1 large rosemary sprig*
- *coarse salt, for
sprinkling*

180 CALS/SLICE

1 In a large bowl, mix together the yeast and flour. Make a well in the centre and pour in 300 ml (½ pint) tepid water and 75 ml (5 tbsp) olive oil. Mix well to a soft dough.

2 Turn out onto a lightly floured surface and knead for 10 minutes until smooth and elastic. Place in an oiled bowl cover and leave to rise in a warm place for about 1 hour until doubled in size.

3 Knead the dough again for 2–3 minutes, then roll out to a large rectangle about 1 cm (½ inch) thick. Place on an oiled baking sheet and cover with oiled cling film. Leave to rise again for about 20–25 minutes.

4 Strip the leaves from the rosemary sprig. Prick the rise dough all over with a fork. Brush the surface with more oil and sprinkle with the rosemary leaves and salt.

5 Bake at 220°C (425°F) mark 7 for 30–35 minutes or until golden brown. Cool on wire rack, brushing with mor olive oil as it cools to soften the crust.

NOTE: This flat, pizza-type bread originated from Tuscany.

❖ Quick Cheese and ❖ Apple Bread

8 SLICES

PREPARATION TIME
20 minutes
COOKING TIME
45 minutes
FREEZING
Not suitable

- 225 g (8 oz) self-raising white flour
- 1.25 ml (¼ tsp) ground black pepper
- 25 g (1 oz) butter
- 1 small crisp eating apple, about 125 g (4 oz)
- 125 g (4 oz) mature Cheddar cheese, coarsely grated
- 50 g (2 oz) roasted salted peanuts, chopped
- 1 egg
- 60–75 ml (4–5 tbsp) milk

225 CALS/SLICE

1 Mix the flour and pepper together in a large bowl and rub in the butter.

2 Peel, quarter, core and chop the apple, then stir into the dry ingredients with the cheese and chopped nuts. Make a well in the centre.

3 Whisk together the egg and milk, then pour into the well and mix to a soft dough.

4 Turn out onto a lightly floured surface and knead quickly into a small neat round, about 15–18 cm (6–7 inches) in diameter. Mark a lattice on top of the round.

5 Place on a lightly greased baking sheet and bake at 190°C (375°F) mark 5 for about 40 minutes or until well risen and golden brown. Turn the bread over and cook for a further 5 minutes. Cool on a wire rack.

NOTE: This bread is best eaten on the day of making. For a richer flavour, try using a smoked Cheddar cheese.

❖ Brioche ❖

SERVES 10

PREPARATION TIME
20 minutes
COOKING TIME
15–20 minutes
FREEZING
Suitable
COLOUR INDEX
Page 86

- 15 g (½ oz) fresh yeast or 7 g sachet fast-action dried yeast
- 225 g (8 oz) strong plain white flour
- pinch of salt
- 15 ml (1 tbsp) caster sugar
- 2 eggs, size 1, beaten
- 50 g (2 oz) butter, melted and cooled
- beaten egg, to glaze

140 CALS/SERVING

1 Oil a 1.1 litre (2 pint) brioche mould. If using fresh yeast, blend with 30 ml (2 tbsp) tepid water. Mix flour, salt and sugar in a bowl. Stir in fast-action dried yeast, if using.

2 Make a well in the centre and pour in the yeast liquid (or 30 ml (2 tbsp) tepid water, if using fast-action dried yeast), the eggs and melted butter. Work to a soft dough.

3 Turn out onto a floured surface and knead for about 5 minutes, until smooth and elastic. Put the dough in a large oiled bowl, cover with oiled cling film and leave in a warm place for about 1 hour until doubled in size.

4 Knead the dough well on a lightly floured surface. Shape three quarters of it into a ball and place in the mould. Press a hole through the centre. Shape the remaining dough into a 'knob', place on top and press down lightly.

5 Cover with oiled cling film and leave in a warm place until the dough is light and puffy and nearly reaches the top of the mould. Brush lightly with beaten egg and bake at 230°C (450°F) mark 8 for 15–20 minutes, until golden. Turn out and serve at once, or cool on a wire rack.

NOTE: For individual brioches, divide the dough into 12 pieces. Shape as above. Bake in individual tins, for 10 minutes.

❖ Mini Hot Cross Buns ❖

MAKES 25

PREPARATION TIME
30 minutes, plus
rising
COOKING TIME
15–18 minutes
FREEZING
Suitable
COLOUR INDEX
Page 86

- 15 g (½ oz) fresh yeast
or 7 g sachet fast-action
dried yeast
- about 175 ml (6 fl oz)
tepid milk
- 350 g (12 oz) strong
plain white flour
- 5 ml (1 tsp) salt
- 5 ml (1 tsp) ground
mixed spice
- 5 ml (1 tsp) ground
cinnamon
- 5 ml (1 tsp) ground
nutmeg

- 50 g (2 oz) butter
- finely grated rind of
1 lemon
- 25 g (1 oz) caster
sugar
- 75 g (3 oz) currants
- 25 g (1 oz) chopped
mixed peel
- 1 egg, beaten
- 75 g (3 oz) ready-
made shortcrust pastry
- beaten egg, to glaze

95 CALS/SERVING

1 If using fresh yeast, blend with the milk. Sift the flour, salt and spices into a bowl and rub in the butter. Stir in the lemon rind, sugar, currants, mixed peel and fast-action dried yeast if using. Make a well in the centre; add yeast liquid or milk and egg. Beat to form a soft dough, adding a little more milk if necessary.

2 Turn out the dough onto a floured surface and, with floured hands, knead for about 8–10 minutes or until the dough is elastic and almost smooth. Place in a large, lightly oiled bowl. Cover with oiled cling film and leave in a warm place until doubled in size; this usually takes 1½–2 hours.

3 Knock down the dough and knead lightly for 1–2 minutes. Divide the dough into about 25 equal-sized pieces and knead each one into a small ball. Place on buttered baking sheets, seam-side down, and flatten slightly with the heel of your hand.

4 Roll out the pastry and cut into narrow strips. Brush the buns with egg to glaze and top each one with a pastry cross. Glaze again. Leave in a warm place until doubled in size; about 30 minutes. Bake at 190°C (375°F) mark 5 for 15–18 minutes until they sound hollow when tapped. Cool on wire racks.

❖ Stollen ❖

SERVES 10

PREPARATION TIME
40 minutes, plus
rising
COOKING TIME
About 40 minutes
FREEZING
Suitable

- 15 g (½ oz) fresh yeast
or 7 g sachet fast-action
dried yeast
- about 175 ml (6 fl oz)
tepid milk
- 350 g (12 oz) strong
plain white flour
- 5 ml (1 tsp) salt
- 3.75 ml (¾ tsp) ground
mixed spice
- 50 g (2 oz) butter
- finely grated rind of
1 lemon
- 25 g (1 oz) caster
sugar

- 50 g (2 oz) currants
- 75 g (3 oz) raisins or
sultanas
- 25 g (1 oz) chopped
mixed peel
- 40 g (1½ oz) flaked
almonds
- 1 egg, beaten
- melted butter, for
brushing
- 175 g (6 oz) Almond
Paste (page 411)
- icing sugar, for dusting

325 CALS/SERVING

1 If using fresh yeast, blend with the milk. Sift the flour, salt and spice into a bowl and rub in the butter. Stir in the lemon rind, sugar, currants, raisins, mixed peel, almonds and fast-action dried yeast if using. Make a well in the centre of the dry ingredients and add the yeast liquid or milk and egg. Beat to form a soft dough, adding a little more milk if necessary.

2 Turn out the dough onto a floured surface and, with floured hands, knead for 8–10 minutes until the dough is elastic and almost smooth. Place in an oiled bowl. Cover with oiled cling film and leave in a warm place until doubled in size; 1½–2 hours.

3 Using floured hands, knock down the dough, then place on a lightly floured work surface and knead for 1–2 minutes only. Roll out the dough to a 25 cm (10 inch) square. Brush lightly with melted butter. Knead and roll out the almond paste to a strip about 23 × 10 cm (9 × 4 inches) and place down the centre of the dough. Fold the dough over the almond paste so that it just overlaps itself, sealing well.

4 Pinch the ends together to enclose the almond paste. Place, seam-side down, on a buttered baking sheet. Make a few shallow slits across the top with a sharp knife. Cover and leave in a warm place to prove and double in size; about 30–45 minutes.

5 Bake at 190°C (375°F) mark 5 for 40 minutes or until sounding hollow when tapped. Cool on a wire rack. Dust with icing sugar

❖ Chelsea Buns ❖

MAKES 12

PREPARATION TIME
30 minutes, plus
rising
COOKING TIME
25–30 minutes
FREEZING
Suitable (unglazed)
COLOUR INDEX
Page 86

• 15 g (½ oz) fresh yeast
or 7 g sachet fast-action
dried yeast
• about 200 ml (7 fl oz)
tepid milk
• 450 g (1 lb) strong
plain white flour
• 5 ml (1 tsp) salt
• 125 g (4 oz) butter
• 50 g (2 oz) caster
sugar
• 1 egg, size 1, beaten
• 3.75 ml (¾ tsp) ground
mixed spice

• grated rind of 1 orange
or lemon
• 50 g (2 oz) sultanas
• 50 g (2 oz) currants
• 50 g (2 oz) pistachios,
almonds or hazelnuts,
roughly chopped
GLAZE:
• 50 g (2 oz) caster
sugar
• 5 ml (1 tsp) orange
flower water (optional)

300 CALS/BUN

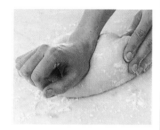

1 If using fresh yeast, blend with the milk. Sift the flour and salt into a large bowl. Mix in the fast-action dried yeast, if using. Rub in half the butter; stir in half the sugar. Make a well in the centre. Stir the egg into the yeast liquid or milk; pour into the well. Mix to a soft dough, using a round-bladed knife, adding a little more milk if necessary.

2 Turn out onto a floured surface; knead well for about 5 minutes until smooth and elastic. Place dough in a large oiled bowl. Cover with oiled cling film and leave to rise in a warm place until doubled in size, about 1–2 hours. Turn out the dough onto a floured surface and knead lightly until smooth. Roll out to a 30 cm (12 inch) square.

3 Cream remaining butter with half remaining sugar and dot over the dough, leaving a 2.5 cm (1 inch) border. Fold in half and roll out to the same size as before. Scatter remaining sugar, spice, citrus rind, dried fruit and nuts over the dough, leaving a border, then roll up like a Swiss roll.

4 Cut the roll into 12 slices. Arrange cut-side up in a greased 23 × 28 cm (9 × 11 inch) baking tin. Cover with oiled cling film and leave to prove in a warm place until the pieces are doubled in size and touching each other, about 15–20 minutes.

5 Bake at 200°C (400°F) mark 6 for 25–30 minutes. Transfer to a wire rack. For the glaze, dissolve the sugar in 75 ml (3 fl oz) water over a low heat, then boil for 2–3 minutes until syrupy. Stir in orange flower water, if using. Brush over the warm buns. Pull apart and serve warm.

❖ Savarin ❖

SERVES 6

PREPARATION TIME
20 minutes, plus
rising
COOKING TIME
40 minutes
FREEZING
Suitable

• 15 g (½ oz) fresh yeast
or 7 g sachet fast-action
dried yeast
• 45 ml (3 tbsp) milk
• 100 g (4 oz) plain
white flour
• 15 ml (1 tbsp) caster
sugar
• 25 g (1 oz) desiccated
coconut
• 2 eggs, lightly beaten

• 50 g (2 oz) butter,
melted and cooled
TO FINISH:
• 90 ml (6 tbsp)
redcurrant jelly
• 75 ml (5 tbsp) lemon
juice
• 450 g (1 lb)
strawberries, hulled

250 CALS/SERVING

1 Lightly oil a 1.3 litre (2¼ pint) savarin tin or ring mould.
2 If using fresh yeast, blend with the tepid milk. Mix together the flour, sugar and coconut in a bowl. Stir in the fast-action dried yeast, if using. Make a well in the centre and add the eggs, butter and yeast liquid (or milk if using fast-action dried yeast). With a wooden spoon, beat thoroughly to a thick smooth batter.
3 Turn into the tin, cover with oiled cling film and leave in a warm place for 30 minutes or until nearly doubled in size.
4 Bake at 190°C (375°F) mark 5 for 35–40 minutes until golden. Turn out on to a wire rack placed over a large plate. Melt the redcurrant jelly with the lemon juice in a pan over a low heat. Spoon over the warm savarin to glaze, allowing any excess to collect on the plate. Transfer the savarin to a serving plate.
5 Return excess glaze to the pan and stir in the strawberries. Allow to cool for 15–20 minutes, then spoon into the middle of the savarin. Serve warm or cold, with soured cream.

PRESERVES

There can be no finer or more satisfying sight than a pantry stacked full of homemade jams, jellies, chutneys and pickles. These preserved delights can bring to life the most mundane or humble meal and they're infinitely superior to and cheaper than commercially prepared equivalents. Once you've mastered the basic principles, the recipes here can be adapted to cope with almost any produce from a glut of fruit in the garden to a harvest picked from a local hedgerow.

❖ Preserving Equipment ❖

If you make a lot of preserves, it's worth investing in a proper preserving pan: the sloping sides help maintain a fast boil and reduce the chances of everything boiling over. Choose a pan made from stainless steel, tin-lined copper or lined aluminium. Don't use unlined aluminium, particularly when cooking acidic fruits or pickles, because aluminium has been linked with Alzheimer's disease and research suggests that acidic substances encourage transference.

If you don't have a preserving pan use a large heavy-based saucepan instead. Note that if you are using a saucepan rather than a preserving pan the preserve will take much longer to reach the setting point or potting stage owing to the reduced surface area.

For jelly making, you will need a jelly bag for straining the juice from the cooked fruit. Although you can improvise with a large piece of muslin, a jelly bag is a worthwhile investment because it makes things easier. Whatever you use, it should be scalded with boiling water before use. If the jelly bag doesn't have a stand, suspend it from the legs of an upturned chair or stool. Leave until the dripping has stopped. Don't be tempted to squeeze the bag: if you do, the finished jelly will be cloudy.

❖ Preserving Ingredients ❖

❖ PECTIN is naturally present in fruit, and reacts with sugar and acid to set jams, jellies, marmalades and conserves. Some fruits such as cooking apples, lemons, Seville oranges, gooseberries and damsons are high in natural pectin and acid; eating apples, raspberries, blackberries, apricots and plums have a medium pectin and acid content; while cherries, grapes, peaches, rhubarb and strawberries score low on both counts.

Fruits with a low or medium pectin content should be cooked with a fruit high in pectin to achieve a set. Lemon juice is most commonly used since it is rich in both pectin and acid; 30 ml (2 tbsp) lemon juice to 1.8 kg (4 lb) fruit should be enough. Alternatively use 'sugar with pectin' (see below) or commercially produced bottled pectin to ensure a good set.

❖ SUGAR acts as a preservative as well as helping to achieve a set, so it is important to use the amount stated in the recipe. Granulated sugar is fine for most preserves. Caster sugar or brown sugar can also be used, but brown sugar will lend a

distinctive flavour and darker colour that are more suited to chutneys and pickles. Perfectionists insist that preserving sugar gives a clearer more sparkling finish to jams, jellies and marmalades, so you may prefer to use it. 'Sugar with pectin' contains apple pectin and tartaric acid. Preserves made with this should reach setting point in just 4 minutes (providing they are kept at a fast rolling boil).

❖ VINEGAR acts as a preservative in pickles and some chutneys. Virtually any vinegar is suitable – red, white, or flavoured providing that the acetic acid content is 5 per cent or more (as in most vinegars on the market today).

❖ Testing for a Set ❖

Jams, jellies, marmalades and conserves are cooked sufficiently when setting point is reached. There are various tests to determine this. Remove the pan from the heat while you are testing, to prevent overcooking.

❖ TEMPERATURE TEST: The preserve is ready when the temperature registers 105°C (221°F) on a sugar thermometer.

❖ SAUCER TEST: Drop a spoonful of the preserve onto a chilled saucer and leave to cool. Push your finger through the jam: if the surface wrinkles, the preserve is ready.

❖ FLAKE TEST: Using a wooden spoon, lift a little of the preserve out of the pan. Let it cool slightly then tip the spoon so that the preserve drops back into the pan; if the drips run together and fall from the spoon in a 'flake' rather than as drips, it is ready.

There is no accurate test for chutneys and pickles, because they are not cooked to a setting point. Instead, be guided by the consistency and cooking time specified in the recipe; they are ready when no excess liquid remains and the mixture is very thick.

❖ Yields and Potting Preserves ❖

It is difficult to give accurate yields since they vary from batch to batch. Jelly yields are particularly difficult to estimate since so much depends on the time allowed for dripping and the quality and ripeness of the fruit. So that you can have enough jars prepared, we have given a rough guide wherever possible.

All preserves should be potted into scrupulously clean containers. Wash jars or bottles in really hot soapy water, rinse thoroughly, then dry in a warm oven. Stand them upside down on a clean tea towel until the preserve is ready. Aim to pour hot jam or marmalade into the jars while they are still warm, to reduce the chances of the glass cracking, and fill them almost to the top. If potting jam, jelly, marmalade or conserve, cover with a waxed disc while the preserve is piping hot or else completely cold, then seal with a dampened clear disc secured with an elastic band. If you seal while the preserve is warm, mould will grow on the surface. Chutneys and pickles are covered in the same way. For long-term storage, cover the jar with a screw top as well.

❖ Raspberry Jam ❖

MAKES ABOUT 3 KG (6½ LB)	• 1.8 kg (4 lb) raspberries	• 1.8 kg (4 lb) sugar • knob of butter
PREPARATION TIME 10 minutes COOKING TIME About 1 hour		40 CALS/15 ML (1 TBSP)

1 Put the fruit in a preserving pan and simmer very gently in its own juice for about 20 minutes, stirring carefully from time to time, until the fruit is really soft.

2 Remove the pan from the heat and add the sugar, stirring until dissolved, then add the butter.

3 Boil rapidly for about 30 minutes or until setting point is reached.

4 Remove any scum with a slotted spoon, then pot and cover in the usual way.

❖ Gooseberry ❖ and Elderflower Jam

MAKES ABOUT 4.5 KG (10 LB)	• 2.7 kg (6 lb) gooseberries (slightly under-ripe)	• 2.7 kg (6 lb) sugar • knob of butter
PREPARATION TIME 20 minutes COOKING TIME 50 minutes COLOUR INDEX Page 87	• 20 elderflower heads, cut close to the stem	40 CALS/15 ML (1 TBSP)

1 Top and tail the gooseberries. Wash the elderflowers and tie in a piece of muslin. Put the gooseberries in a preserving pan with 1.1 litres (2 pints) water and the elderflower bundle. Simmer gently for about 30 minutes or until the fruit is really soft and reduced, mashing it to a pulp with a wooden spoon and stirring from time to time to prevent sticking.
2 Remove the pan from the heat, add the sugar and stir until dissolved, then add the butter. Bring to the boil and boil rapidly for about 10 minutes or until setting point is reached.
3 Remove any scum with a slotted spoon. Remove the muslin bag, then pot and cover in the usual way.

NOTE: Elderflowers impart a delicious flavour but they may be omitted if unavailable.

❖ Blackberry Jam ❖

MAKES ABOUT 1.6 KG (3½ LB)	• 1 kg (2¼ lb) blackberries (not over-ripe), washed	• 1 kg (2.2 lb) 'sugar with pectin' • knob of butter
PREPARATION TIME 10 minutes COOKING TIME About 35 minutes	• juice of ½ lemon	40 CALS/15 ML (1 TBSP)

1 Put the blackberries in a preserving pan with the lemon juice and 120 ml (4 fl oz) water. Simmer very gently for about 30 minutes or until the blackberries are very soft and are well reduced.

2 Remove the pan from the heat, add the sugar, stir until dissolved, then add the butter. Bring to the boil and boil rapidly for 4 minutes or until setting point is reached.

3 Remove any scum with a slotted spoon, then pot and cover in the usual way.

❖ Apricot Jam ❖

MAKES ABOUT 3 KG (6½ LB)
- *1.8 kg (4 lb) apricots*
- *juice of 1 lemon*
- *1.8 kg (4 lb) sugar*
- *knob of butter*

PREPARATION TIME
20 minutes
COOKING TIME
About 40 minutes

40 CALS/15 ML (1 TBSP)

1 Halve the apricots and remove the stones. Crack a few of the apricot stones with a weight, nutcracker or mallet; take out the kernels and blanch them in boiling water for 1 minute, then drain.

2 Put the apricots, lemon juice, apricot kernels and 450 ml (¾ pint) water in a preserving pan and simmer for about 15 minutes or until the fruit is soft and the contents of the pan are well reduced.

3 Take the pan off the heat and add the sugar, stirring until dissolved. Add the butter and boil rapidly for about 15 minutes or until setting point is reached.

4 Remove any scum with a slotted spoon, then pot and cover in the usual way.

❖ Strawberry Jam ❖

MAKES ABOUT 1.8 KG (4 LB)
- *900 g (2 lb) strawberries, hulled*
- *1 kg (2.2 lb) 'sugar with pectin'*
- *juice of ½ lemon*

PREPARATION TIME
10 minutes, plus standing
COOKING TIME
About 10 minutes
COLOUR INDEX
Page 87

35 CALS/15 ML (1 TBSP)

1 Put the strawberries in a preserving pan with the sugar and lemon juice. Heat gently, stirring until the sugar has dissolved.

2 Bring to the boil and boil steadily for about 4 minutes or until setting point is reached.

3 Remove from the heat and remove any scum with a slotted spoon. Leave to stand for 15–20 minutes.

4 Stir the jam gently, then pot and cover in the usual way.

❖ Strawberry Conserve ❖

MAKES ABOUT 1.4 KG (3 LB)
- *1.4 kg (3 lb) strawberries, hulled*
- *1.4 kg (3 lb) sugar*

PREPARATION TIME
15 minutes, plus standing
COOKING TIME
About 20 minutes
COLOUR INDEX
Page 87

65 CALS/15 ML (1 TBSP)

1 Put the strawberries in a large bowl in layers with the sugar. Cover and leave for 24 hours.

2 Put the strawberries and sugar in a preserving pan. Heat gently, stirring until the sugar dissolves. Bring to the boil and boil rapidly for 5 minutes.

3 Return the mixture to the bowl, cover and leave in a cool place for a further 2 days. Return to the pan.

4 Boil rapidly for 10 minutes. Leave to cool for 15 minutes. Pot and cover in the usual way.

❖ Apple and Mint Jelly ❖

PREPARATION TIME
30 minutes, plus
standing
COOKING TIME
About 1¼ hours
COLOUR INDEX
Page 87

- 2.3 kg (5 lb) cooking apples, such as Bramleys
- few large mint sprigs
- 1.1 litres (2 pints) distilled white vinegar
- sugar (see method)
- 90–120 ml (6–8 tbsp) chopped mint
- few drops of green food colouring (optional)

35–40 CALS/15 ML (1 TBSP)

1 Remove any bruised parts from the apples, then roughly chop into chunks without peeling or coring. Put the apples in a preserving pan with 1.1 litres (2 pints) water and the mint sprigs.

2 Bring to the boil, then simmer gently for about 45 minutes or until soft and pulpy, stirring from time to time to prevent sticking. Add the vinegar and boil for a further 5 minutes.

3 Spoon the apple pulp into a jelly bag suspended over a large bowl and leave to drip through for at least 12 hours.

4 Discard pulp remaining in jelly bag. Measure extract and return to the preserving pan with 450 g (1 lb) sugar for each 600 ml (1 pint) extract.

5 Heat gently, stirring, until the sugar has dissolved, then boil rapidly for about 10 minutes or until setting point is reached. Remove any scum with a slotted spoon.

6 Stir in the chopped mint and colouring, if using. Cool slightly, stir well to distribute the mint, then pot and cover in the usual way. Serve with roast lamb or pork.

❖ Rosehip Jelly ❖

PREPARATION TIME
25 minutes, plus
standing
COOKING TIME
About 1¼ hours
COLOUR INDEX
Page 87

- 900 g (2 lb) cooking apples
- 450 g (1 lb) ripe rosehips
- sugar (see method)

35–40 CALS/15 ML (1 TBSP)

1 Remove any bruised or damaged portions from the apples, then roughly chop without coring or peeling.

2 Put the apples and rosehips in a preserving pan with just enough water to cover. Bring to the boil, then simmer gently for about 45 minutes or until the fruit is soft and pulpy, stirring from time to time to prevent sticking.

3 Spoon the fruit pulp into a jelly bag suspended over a large bowl and leave to drip through for at least 12 hours.

4 Discard the pulp remaining in the jelly bag. Measure the extract and return to the preserving pan with 450 g (1 lb) sugar for each 600 ml (1 pint) extract.

5 Heat gently, stirring, until the sugar has dissolved, then bring to the boil and boil rapidly for about 15 minutes or until setting point is reached. Remove any scum with a slotted spoon, then pot and cover in the usual way.

❖ Lime Marmalade ❖

MAKES ABOUT 2.3 KG (5 LB)

PREPARATION TIME
20 minutes, plus
standing
COOKING TIME
2–2½ hours

- 700 g (1½ lb) limes
- 1.4 kg (3 lb) sugar

35 CALS/15 ML (1 TBSP)

1 For this recipe, weigh the empty preserving pan or large saucepan before you start.

2 Put the limes in the preserving pan with 1.7 litres (3 pints) water and bring to the boil. Cover with a tight-fitting lid and simmer for 1½–2 hours or until the fruit is very soft.

3 Remove the fruit from the pan with a slotted spoon and slice very thinly (using a knife and fork), discarding the pips and reserving any juice. Return the sliced fruit and juice to the pan and weigh it. If necessary, boil the mixture, uncovered, until reduced to about 1.1 kg (2½ lb).

4 Add the sugar and stir until it has dissolved, then bring to the boil and boil rapidly for about 15 minutes or until setting point is reached. Remove any scum with a slotted spoon, leave the marmalade to stand for about 15 minutes, then stir gently to distribute the fruit. Pot and cover in the usual way.

❖ Seville Orange Marmalade ❖

MAKES ABOUT 4.5 KG (10 LB)

PREPARATION TIME
30 minutes
COOKING TIME
About 2½ hours

- *1.4 kg (3 lb) Seville oranges*
- *juice of 2 lemons*
- *2.7 kg (6 lb) sugar*

35 CALS/15 ML (1 TBSP)

1 Halve the oranges and squeeze out the juice and pips. Tie the pips, and any membrane that has come away during squeezing, in a piece of muslin. Slice the orange peel thinly or thickly, as preferred, and put it in a preserving pan with the fruit juices, muslin bag and 3.4 litres (6 pints) water.

3 Bring to the boil and boil rapidly for about 15 minutes until setting point is reached.

2 Simmer gently for about 2 hours or until the peel is really soft and the liquid reduced by about half. Remove the muslin bag, squeezing it well and allowing the juice to run back into the pan. Add the sugar. Heat gently, stirring until the sugar has dissolved.

4 Remove any scum with a slotted spoon. Leave to stand for 15 minutes, then stir to distribute the peel. Pot and cover in the usual way.

❖ Lemon Curd ❖

MAKES ABOUT 700 G (1½ LB)

PREPARATION TIME
20 minutes
COOKING TIME
About 25 minutes
COLOUR INDEX
Page 88

- *grated rind and juice of 4 medium ripe, juicy lemons*
- *4 eggs, beaten*
- *125 g (4 oz) butter, cut in small pieces*
- *350 g (12 oz) caster sugar*

55 CALS/15 ML (1 TBSP)

1 Place all the ingredients in a heatproof bowl over a pan of simmering water. Stir until the sugar has dissolved. Heat gently, without boiling, for 20 minutes or until thick enough to coat the back of the spoon.

2 Strain the lemon curd and pour into jars. Cover in the usual way. Store in the refrigerator and use within 2–3 weeks.

Variation

LIME CURD: Replace the lemons with the grated rind and juice of 5 large ripe, juicy limes.

❖ Mincemeat ❖

MAKES ABOUT 2.5 KG (5½ LB)

PREPARATION TIME
15 minutes, plus
standing
COLOUR INDEX
Page 88

- *1.6 kg (3½ lb) mixed dried fruit*
- *225 g (8 oz) cooking apples*
- *125 g (4 oz) blanched almonds, chopped*
- *450 g (1 lb) dark soft brown sugar*
- *175 g (6 oz) shredded suet*
- *5 ml (1 tsp) freshly grated nutmeg*
- *5 ml (1 tsp) ground cinnamon*
- *grated rind and juice of 1 lemon*
- *grated rind and juice of 1 orange*
- *300 ml (½ pint) brandy or sherry*

55 CALS/15 ML (1 TBSP)

1 Put the dried fruit in a large bowl. Peel, quarter and core the apples, then grate and add to the bowl with the chopped almonds.

2 Add the sugar, suet, spices, lemon and orange rind and juice, and brandy or sherry, then mix all the ingredients together thoroughly.

3 Cover the mincemeat and leave to stand for 2 days. Stir well, put into jars and cover (as for jam). Allow at least 2 weeks to mature before using.

NOTE: Vegetarian 'suet' is available and can be substituted for beef suet in this recipe.

For mincemeat that will keep well, use a firm, hard type of apple, such as Wellington; juicy apples, such as Bramleys, may make the mixture too moist.

❖ Brandied Cherries ❖

MAKES ABOUT 450 G (1 LB)

PREPARATION TIME
15 minutes
COOKING TIME
About 15 minutes
COLOUR INDEX
Page 88

- *450 g (1 lb) cherries*
- *225 g (8 oz) sugar*
- *1 cinnamon stick*
- *about 150 ml (¼ pint) brandy*

50 CALS/15 ML (1 TBSP)

1 Prick the cherries all over with a sterilised fine skewer. Put 125 g (4 oz) of the sugar and 300 ml (½ pint) water in a saucepan and dissolve over a low heat to make a light syrup.

2 Add the cherries and cinnamon stick and poach gently for 4–5 minutes.

3 Remove the pan from the heat and drain the cherries, reserving the syrup but removing the cinnamon stick. Cool, then arrange the fruit in jars.

4 Add the remaining sugar to the reserved syrup and dissolve it slowly. Bring to the boil and boil to 110°C (230°F), then allow to cool.

5 Measure the syrup and add an equal quantity of brandy. Pour over the cherries. Cover and store for about 1 month before eating.

Variation

BRANDIED PEACHES: Replace the cherries with peaches. Omit the cinnamon. Plunge the peaches briefly into boiling water, then remove and peel off the skins. Halve the peaches and remove the stones. Continue as above, from step 1.

❖ Pickled Pears with Ginger ❖

MAKES ABOUT 1.6 KG (3½ LB)

PREPARATION TIME
20 minutes
COOKING TIME
About 1¼ hours

- *1.8 kg (4 lb) firm pears*
- *squeeze of lemon juice*
- *1 cinnamon stick*
- *25 g (1 oz) piece fresh root ginger, peeled and sliced*
- *3–4 whole cloves*
- *600 ml (1 pint) white wine vinegar*
- *800 g (1¾ lb) sugar*

30 CALS/15 ML (1 TBSP)

1 Peel, halve and core pears; quarter if large. Immerse in a saucepan of water with the lemon juice added. Simmer gently for about 1 hour until just tender. Put the remaining ingredients in a preserving pan. Heat gently, until sugar is dissolved. Bring to the boil and simmer for 5 minutes.

2 Carefully lift the pears from the water and place in the spiced vinegar syrup. Simmer for 15 minutes or until the pears look translucent and are very tender.

3 Lift out the pears using a slotted spoon and pack into jars. Boil syrup for 5 minutes to thicken, then pour over pears to cover completely. Cover and seal in the usual way.

❖ Mustard Pickle ❖

3 Put the sugar, mustard, turmeric, ginger and crushed peppercorns in a stainless steel saucepan. Add enough of the remaining vinegar to blend the ingredients to a smooth paste, then stir in the remainder. Bring to the boil.

4 Pour the spiced vinegar over the vegetables in the preserving pan. Bring to the boil, then reduce the heat and simmer for about 5 minutes, stirring occasionally, until the vegetables are only just tender. Drain, reserving liquid.

5 Pack the vegetables into jars to within 1 cm (½ inch) of the rim. Stir the cornflour paste into the reserved liquid. Return to the preserving pan. Heat gently, stirring, until it boils and thickens. Pour at once over the vegetables to cover completely. Cover and seal in the usual way.

MAKES ABOUT 1.8 KG (4 LB)

PREPARATION TIME
25 minutes, plus marinating
COOKING TIME
About 8 minutes

- ½ cucumber
- 450 g (1 lb) fine green beans
- 4 green peppers
- 4 red peppers
- 225 g (8 oz) button or pickling onions
- 225 g (8 oz) green tomatoes
- 225 g (8 oz) cauliflower
- 125 g (4 oz) carrots
- 275 g (10 oz) coarse sea salt
- 50 g (2 oz) cornflour

- 1 litre (1¾ pints) white wine vinegar
- 400 g (14 oz) sugar
- 60 ml (4 tbsp) mustard powder
- 10 ml (2 tsp) turmeric
- 5 ml (1 tsp) ground ginger
- 2.5 ml (½ tsp) black peppercorns, lightly crushed

15 CALS/15 ML (1 TBSP)

1 Peel or trim all vegetables as appropriate and cut into bite-sized pieces, about 2 cm (¾ inch) long. Place in a large bowl and mix in the coarse salt. Cover and leave in a cold place for 24 hours.

2 Rinse the vegetables thoroughly. Drain and dry well and put into a preserving pan. In a small bowl, blend the cornflour with 75 ml (3 fl oz) of the vinegar; set aside.

❖ Summer Pickle ❖

MAKES ABOUT 1.8 KG (4 LB)

PREPARATION TIME
25 minutes, plus marinating
COOKING TIME
About 8 minutes
COLOUR INDEX
Page 88

- 225 g (8 oz) each celery, carrots, cucumber, red peppers and red onions
- 125 g (4 oz) each green beans, baby corn cobs and button mushrooms
- 600 ml (1 pint) distilled malt vinegar
- 6 allspice berries
- 6 black peppercorns
- 1 mace blade
- 1 bay leaf

- 2 cloves
- pinch of powdered saffron or turmeric
- 30 ml (2 tbsp) chopped dill
- 90 ml (6 tbsp) light soft brown sugar
- salt and pepper
- 125 g (4 oz) cherry tomatoes
- 90 ml (6 tbsp) walnut oil

15 CALS/15 ML (1 TBSP)

1 Thickly slice the celery. Peel and thinly slice the carrots. Halve the cucumber lengthways and thickly slice. Deseed the peppers and cut into similar-sized pieces. Trim the onions, leaving the root intact, and cut into 8 'wedges' each. Top and tail the green beans and corn cobs; trim the mushrooms.
2 Combine all the ingredients, except the cherry tomatoes and walnut oil, in a preserving pan or large saucepan. Bring to the boil and simmer, stirring gently, for 5 minutes.
3 Stir in the cherry tomatoes and walnut oil, then transfer to a non-metallic bowl. Cool, cover with a plate and leave to marinate overnight.
4 Pack the pickle into jars, cover and seal in the usual way.

❖ Hot Mango Chutney ❖

MAKES ABOUT 1.4 KG (3 LB)

PREPARATION TIME
25 minutes
COOKING TIME
About 1 hour
COLOUR INDEX
Page 88

- *1.1 kg (2½ lb) firm mangoes, just starting to ripen (about 2 large ones)*
- *25 g (1 oz) piece fresh root ginger*
- *2–3 small red or green chillies*
- *1 large onion, peeled*
- *1 garlic clove, skinned*
- *450 g (1 lb) cooking apples*

- *15 ml (1 tbsp) salt*
- *600 ml (1 pint) white wine vinegar*
- *2.5 ml (½ tsp) ground cinnamon*
- *225 g (8 oz) demerara sugar*
- *225 g (8 oz) granulated sugar*

30 CALS/15 ML (1 TBSP)

1 Peel the mangoes and cut into 2.5 cm (1 inch) pieces. Peel and finely chop the ginger. Deseed and finely chop the chillies, wearing rubber gloves to avoid skin irritation. Roughly chop the onion and garlic. Peel, core and roughly chop the apples.

2 Put all the ingredients, except the sugars, in a preserving pan. Bring to the boil and simmer gently for about 10 minutes or until the fruits are beginning to soften.

3 Add the demerara and granulated sugars and heat gently, stirring until dissolved, then bring to the boil. Reduce the heat and simmer, uncovered, for about 45 minutes, stirring occasionally, until thick. Cool the chutney slightly, then pot, cover and seal in the usual way.

❖ Marrow and ❖ Tomato Chutney

MAKES 1.6–1.8 KG (3½–4 LB)

PREPARATION TIME
20 minutes
COOKING TIME
About 1 hour
COLOUR INDEX
Page 88

- *1.4 kg (3 lb) marrow*
- *450 g (1 lb) ripe tomatoes*
- *2 onions, peeled*
- *2 garlic cloves, skinned*
- *10 ml (2 tsp) black peppercorns*
- *10 ml (2 tsp) allspice berries*

- *30 ml (2 tbsp) salt*
- *10 ml (2 tsp) ground ginger*
- *700 g (1½ lb) sugar*
- *750 ml (1¼ pints) cider vinegar*

30 CALS/15 ML (1 TBSP)

1 Peel the marrow, halve lengthwise and remove the seeds and any coarse fibres. Cut the flesh into 1 cm (½ inch) chunks. Skin and roughly chop the tomatoes. Roughly chop the onions and garlic.
2 Finely crush the peppercorns and allspice with a pestle and mortar, or use the end of a rolling pin in a bowl.
3 Put all the ingredients in a large saucepan. Heat gently, stirring until the sugar has dissolved. Bring to the boil and boil steadily, stirring occasionally to prevent sticking, for about 50 minutes or until reduced by half. (This will be a little more liquid than most chutneys.)
4 Cool the chutney slightly, then pot, cover and seal in the usual way.

❖ Green Tomato Chutney ❖

MAKES ABOUT 1.4 KG (3 LB)

PREPARATION TIME
20 minutes
COOKING TIME
About 2 hours

- *450 g (1 lb) cooking apples*
- *2 onions, peeled*
- *1.4 kg (3 lb) green tomatoes*
- *225 g (8 oz) sultanas*
- *225 g (8 oz) demerara sugar*
- *10 ml (2 tsp) salt*

- *450 ml (¾ pint) malt vinegar*
- *4 small pieces dried root ginger*
- *2.5 ml (½ tsp) cayenne pepper*
- *5 ml (1 tsp) mustard powder*

20 CALS/15 ML (1 TBSP)

1 Peel, quarter and core the apples. Finely grate the apples and onions. Thinly slice the tomatoes.
2 Place all the ingredients in a large saucepan. Bring to the boil, reduce the heat and simmer gently for about 2 hours, stirring occasionally, until the ingredients are tender and reduced to a thick consistency, and no excess liquid remains. Discard ginger.
3 Spoon the chutney into jars, cover and seal in the usual way.

FOOD SAFETY

Correct food storage and preparation is important for preventing food poisoning. It also helps extend the life of food and ensures that food remains as nutritious and flavourful as possible.

❖ General Kitchen Hygiene ❖

Following a few simple guidelines will help make your kitchen a safe and hygienic place for food preparation and storage:
❖ Wash down and dry surfaces regularly with a mild detergent solution or multi-surface cleaner.
❖ Use rubber gloves for washing up, so that water can be hotter than hands can bear. Leave dishes to drain if possible; this is more hygienic than using a drying-up cloth.
❖ Change drying-up cloths and cleaning cloths regularly.
❖ Use plastic chopping boards for preparing food. These are more hygienic than wooden ones as they can be washed in a dishwasher or in very hot water with a mild solution of bleach or sterilising solution.
❖ Ideally, keep separate chopping boards for different foods, such as raw meat, fish, vegetables and cooked foods. Wooden chopping boards cannot be cleaned as thoroughly as plastic ones; if you prefer to use them, scrub thoroughly after use and allow to dry thoroughly before storing.
❖ Always wash your hands before handling food and again between handling different types of food, such as raw and cooked meat where you could transfer bacteria from one to the other.
❖ Always wash knives and other kitchen utensils in between preparing raw and cooked foods.
❖ Never put cooked or ready-to-eat foods on to a surface which has just had raw food on it.
❖ Use disposable kitchen paper to wipe up spills from meat or poultry juices.
❖ Never handle food with an uncovered cut. Keep wounds covered with a clean, sterile dressing.
❖ Try not to leave milk bottles standing on the doorstep. Discard any that have been pecked by birds as they can be carriers of food poisoning bacteria. (Also milk left out in direct sunlight loses its vitamin B2.)
❖ Keep pets out of the kitchen, or at least discourage them from walking or sitting on work surfaces.

❖ Buying Food ❖

❖ When you are shopping, always be guided by the use-by, or best-before date. Foods with a longer shelf life have a best-before date; more perishable foods have a use-by date. It is now illegal to sell food that is past its use-by date. Certain foods – such as salt, sugar and alcoholic drinks – do not require a date mark. Date marks are only valid if the food is stored in accordance with the manufacturer's instructions; they do not apply once the packaging has been opened.
Apply the following guidelines whenever you are shopping for food:
❖ Shop at a reliable source; avoid shops that appear unclean.
❖ Avoid packs that are damaged or look dirty or dusty.
❖ Beware of chilled or frozen food display cabinets which are overfilled.
❖ Before you buy, look at the dates on the goods and make sure that they are still within their best-before or use-by date. Check that food will still be within this date when you are intending to use it.
❖ If you are buying chilled or frozen foods make sure they can be stored correctly straight away. If you shop in your lunch hour, don't allow chilled or frozen foods to remain in a warm office or in the boot of your car all afternoon.
❖ Pack all chilled or frozen foods together in an insulated cool bag or box at the checkout.
❖ Pack fresh food separately from cooked food.
❖ As soon as you get home, put perishable food in the refrigerator or freezer immediately.

❖ Safe Storage ❖

Always check the label to see if the manufacturer has given any storage advice; this is important even with familiar foods. As manufacturers have started to remove some of the additives from foods and reduce levels of sugar and salt, storage requirements may have changed. For instance, once opened, reduced-sugar jam needs to be kept in the fridge.
Apply the following guidelines to food storage:
❖ keep your cupboards, fridge, and freezer clean. Spilt food, drips and broken packets can spread bacteria and attract flies, ants and mice.
❖ Cupboards or shelves used to store food should be cool, dry and well ventilated.
❖ Use cupboard stocks efficiently, using older packs first.
❖ Do not use cans that are swollen, rusty, leaking or badly dented.
❖ Once opened, canned foods should be treated as though they are fresh. Transfer contents to a clean container, cover and keep in the fridge.
❖ Transfer dry goods such as sugar, rice and pasta into moistureproof containers. Old supplies should be used up before new ones are started, and containers washed out and dried thoroughly before refilling.

❖ Refrigerator Storage ❖

When choosing a fridge make sure you buy one that is large enough for your needs. Some fridges have a frozen food compartment for storing ready frozen food. Only those which carry the four star symbol **** can be used for freezing fresh food. Appliances with a lower star rating are only suitable for storing ready frozen food as follows:

* up to 1 week
** up to 1 month
*** up to 3 months

❖ Refrigerator Storage Times ❖

Providing food is in good condition when you put it into the fridge and that your fridge is working properly a rough guide to recommended maximum storage times is as follows:

RAW MEAT
❖

joints	3 days
poultry	2 days
raw sliced meat	2 days
minced meat	1 day
offal	1 day
sausages	3 days
bacon	7 days
vacuum-packed bacon	2–3 weeks
fish	eat on day of purchase

VEGETABLES
❖

salad leaves	2–3 days
green vegetables	3–4 days

COOKED MEAT
❖

joints	3 days
casseroles/stews	2 days
sliced meat	2 days
ham	2 days
pies	2 days
vacuum-packed meat	1–2 weeks

DAIRY FOODS
❖

milk (pasteurised/ homogenised)	4–5 days
cheese, soft	2–3 days
cheese, hard	1–2 weeks
eggs (pointed end down)	2 weeks

❖ Use a fridge thermometer to check that your fridge is operating at the correct temperature. These are inexpensive and can be bought at most supermarkets and kitchenware departments. Domestic fridges should operate at temperatures between 1-5°C (34-41°F). To check the temperature of your fridge, place the thermometer in the middle of the top shelf, usually the warmest part. Leave for a couple of hours then check the temperature. If the temperature is above 5°C (41°F) the fridge is too hot; adjust the temperature control dial accordingly.
❖ To avoid bacterial cross-contamination do not allow raw food to come into contact with cooked food. Store cooked and raw foods on separate shelves in the fridge. Place cooked foods on the top shelf. Make sure that food is always well covered.
❖ Never put hot food into the fridge as this will cause the fridge temperature to rise. Cool food quickly and thoroughly first.
❖ Do not leave the fridge door open longer than necessary.
❖ Avoid overfilling your fridge as this restricts the circulation of air and prevents the fridge from working properly. Bear this in mind around Christmas and when you are catering for parties.
❖ Clean your fridge regularly with a weak solution of bicarbonate of soda: 15 ml (1 tbsp) to 1 litre (1¼ pints) water.
❖ Defrost your fridge regularly.

❖ Freezer Storage ❖

❖ Use a freezer thermometer to check that your freezer is operating at the correct temperature which is -18°C (0°F).
❖ Do not buy frozen food if it looks battered or old; it may have been in the shop for too long, or it may have partially thawed and then refrozen.
❖ Pack and seal food for the freezer with care. If cold air or moisture gets into the food, it will deteriorate; there is also a risk of cross-flavouring.
❖ Keep your freezer as full as possible. If necessary add loaves of bread to fill up spaces. Empty spaces require more energy to keep cool.
❖ Try to defrost the freezer when stocks are low. While defrosting keep any remaining stocks as cold as possible – in a cold box or wrapped in newspaper.
❖ Never freeze more than one tenth of your freezer's capacity in any 24 hours or put warm food into the freezer as either action will cause the internal temperature to rise.
❖ When freezing large quantities of food always use the fast-freeze option.
❖ Do not store food above the load line in chest freezers.
❖ Do not re-freeze food once it has been thawed, unless it has been subsequently cooked.
❖ Always wrap non-packaged food before storing in the freezer.
❖ Make sure food is clearly labelled and dated. Keep a record of the contents of your freezer and use old stocks first.

❖ Freezer Storage Times ❖

Always follow manufacturer's instructions for storage. A rough guide to recommended maximum storage times is as follows:

DAIRY PRODUCE
❖

cream	6–8 months
butter, salted	3–4 months
butter, unsalted	6–8 months
cheese, hard	4–6 months
cheese, soft	3–4 months
ice cream	3–4 months

FISH
❖

white fish	6–8 months
oily fish	3–4 months
fish portions	3–4 months
shell fish	2–3 months

FRUIT & VEGETABLES
❖

fruit, stewed	8–10 months
fruit juice	4–6 months
most vegetables	10–12 months
mushrooms and tomatoes	6–8 months
vegetable purées	6–8 months

MEAT & POULTRY
❖

beef and lamb	4–6 months
pork and veal	4–6 months
offal	3–4 months
sliced bacon/ other cured meat	2–3 months
ham and bacon joints	3–4 months
chicken and turkey	4–6 months
duck and goose	4–6 months
venison	4–6 months
rabbit	4–6 months
sausages, sausagemeat	2–3 months
minced beef	3–4 months

PREPARED FOODS
❖

cakes	4–6 months
bread	2–3 months
sandwiches	2–3 months
bread dough	2–3 months
pastries	3–4 months

Freezer Emergencies

In the case of a power cut or someone inadvertently turning the freezer off, don't panic. Food in a chest freezer should be safe for about 48 hours without power. Food in an upright freezer should remain frozen for about 30 hours.

❖ In the event of a power failure, do not open the freezer door. Cover the freezer with a blanket or rug to increase insulation, but do not cover the condenser and pipes.

❖ If you have advance warning of a power failure, turn on the fast-freeze switch, having made sure the freezer is completely full. Use old towels or rolled up newspapers to fill any gaps.

❖ In the case of a long period without power, salvage what you can of the contents. Raw items can be cooked, then frozen again afterwards. Other items can be cooked and consumed. Throw away any food that you suspect may have deteriorated.

❖ Only re-freeze food if it is still full of ice crystals and firm in the centre. Some foods, like ice cream and uncooked baked goods, will not retain their quality if re-frozen.

❖ Thawing Food ❖

Freezing does not kill bacteria. Once food is thawed bacteria will start multiplying again, so thawing must be done properly.

❖ Do not thaw food in a warm environment as this provides ideal breeding conditions for bacteria to multiply. Choose a cool place, such as a larder or in the refrigerator.

❖ Cover food loosely while it is thawing.

❖ Make sure food is completely defrosted before cooking. This is particularly important with large joints of meat and poultry. The legs of poultry should be able to move freely and there should be no ice crystals present.

❖ Cook food as soon as possible after thawing.

❖ Throw away the liquid which drains from thawing meat and poultry. Do not allow it to drip on to other food.

Thawing Food in the Microwave

Follow the defrosting instructions in your microwave manufacturer's manual.

❖ Only thaw food in the microwave if it's going to be cooked or eaten immediately.

❖ Always defrost on the LOW or DEFROST setting.

❖ Cooking and Reheating Food ❖

❖ Never re-heat food more than once.

❖ Cool leftover food quickly, then cover and place in the fridge or freezer. Leftover food should be stored in the fridge for no longer than 2 days.

❖ To kill any food poisoning bacteria present, food needs to reach a temperature of 70°C (158°F) and cook at that temperature for at least 2 minutes.

❖ Never eat undercooked poultry. Test the thickest part of the leg with a skewer: the juices should run clear when the bird is cooked. When cooking large joints or birds use a meat thermometer.

❖ Always reheat food until it is piping hot.

❖ When reheating food in the microwave follow the manufacturer's instructions.

❖ If food is to be left for any length of time before serving, make sure that it is kept piping hot at 63°C (145°F) or over.

❖ Cooked food should be cooled thoroughly and as quickly as possible before placing it in the fridge or freezer. Small quantities should cool quite quickly but larger quantities are better divided into smaller portions, or transferred to a container with a large surface area. During warm weather place the container in a bowl of iced water. Do not cover the food while it is cooling. Ensure the food is cooled within a maximum of 1½ hours.

❖ Food Poisoning ❖

Although food poisoning is rarely life-threatening, it can be very unpleasant and may cause serious illness in vulnerable groups. These 'at risk groups' are as follows:

❖ babies and infants under 2 years

❖ pregnant women

❖ elderly people

❖ anyone who is already ill or convalescing

❖ anyone with an impaired immune system

❖ anyone taking drugs which suppress their body's natural defences, such as transplant patients, people receiving chemotherapy or anyone taking large doses of steroids.

Raw Eggs and Salmonella

Raw or lightly cooked eggs will not have been cooked sufficiently to kill any salmonella which may be present. As eggs can sometimes be a source of salmonella it is recommended that raw or lightly cooked eggs and products made from them should be avoided. In practice the chances of eggs being infected with salmonella are very small and as a result many fit and healthy people choose to ignore this advice. However it is obviously important for vulnerable groups to adhere firmly to this advice. The following guidelines apply:

❖ Hard-boiled eggs should be cooked for at least 7 minutes.

❖ Fried eggs should be cooked for 3 minutes on each side.

❖ Scrambled eggs should be cooked until they have a firm solid texture.

❖ The following should be avoided unless made using pasteurised egg: mayonnaise; egg custard; Hollandaise sauce; meringues; ice creams and sorbets; soufflés and mousses; royal icing.

Listeria

To reduce the risk of listeriosis, pregnant women and all others in the vulnerable group should avoid the following products:

❖ soft ripened cheeses, such as Brie, Camembert and all cheeses made from goat's or sheep's milk

❖ pâté

❖ raw or undercooked meat products

❖ unpasteurised milk and products made from it.

In addition:

❖ All fruit and vegetables, even ready-prepared salads, should be washed thoroughly.

❖ Cook-chilled meals should be reheated until piping hot through to the centre.

GLOSSARY

A brief guide to cooking methods, terms and ingredients.

Agar-agar A tasteless white powder, made from seaweed, which has useful gelling properties and can be used as a vegetarian substitute for gelatine.

Antipasto Italian phrase for a varied selection of hot or cold foods served as an appetiser.

Arrowroot Can be used as an alternative to cornflour as a thickening agent in liquids, such as sauces and glazes. Arrowroot gives a clear gloss, unlike cornflour which produces an opaque sauce.

Aspic jelly Savoury jelly used for setting and garnishing savoury dishes.

Au gratin Describes a dish which has been coated with sauce, sprinkled with breadcrumbs or cheese and finished by browning under the grill or in the oven. Low sided gratin dishes are used.

Bain-marie A low-sided container which is half filled with water kept just below boiling point. Containers of food are placed in it to keep warm or cook without overheating. A bain-marie is used for cooking custards and other egg dishes and keeping sauces warm. No special container is needed; a roasting tin will do. The term is also sometimes applied to a double boiler.

Baking Cooking in the oven by dry heat.

Baking blind The method used for cooking flans and tarts without their fillings.

Baking powder A raising agent consisting of an acid, usually cream of tartar and an alkali, such as bicarbonate of soda which react to produce carbon dioxide. This expands during baking and makes cakes and breads rise.

Barding Covering dry meat or the breast of poultry or game birds with pieces of bacon or fat to prevent the flesh drying out during roasting.

Basting Spooning the juices and melted fat over meat, poultry or game during roasting to keep it moist. The term is also used to describe spooning over a marinade.

Bean curd Also known as tofu and widely used in vegetarian and oriental cooking. It is made from a pressed purée of soya beans and sold fresh, dried and in cans.

Beating A method of incorporating air into an ingredient or mixture by agitating it vigorously with a spoon, fork, whisk or electric mixer. Also used to soften ingredients.

Béchamel Classic French white sauce, which is used as the basis for other sauces and a variety of savoury dishes.

Beurre manié Equal parts of flour and butter kneaded together to form a paste. Used for thickening soups, stews and casseroles. It is whisked into the hot liquid a little at a time at the end of cooking.

Bicarbonate of soda Sometimes used in baking to act as a raising agent.

Blanching Immersing food briefly in boiling water to whiten it, as in sweetbreads, or to remove the skin, such as peaches and tomatoes. Vegetables which are to be frozen and kept for a certain length of time are blanched to destroy enzymes and preserve the colour, flavour and texture.

Blanquette Stew usually made from white meat, such as veal or poultry, cooked in a white sauce enriched with cream and egg yolk.

Blender An electric machine usually consisting of a goblet with rotating blades in the base. Used for puréeing wet mixtures and grinding dry ingredients. Ideal for making fresh breadcrumbs.

Boning Removing the bones from meat or poultry, cutting the flesh as little as possible, so that it can be rolled or stuffed.

Bottling The term used for preserving food or preserves in glass jars under sterile conditions.

Bouquet garni Small bunch of herbs – usually a mixture of parsley stems, thyme and a bay leaf – tied in muslin and used to flavour stocks, soups and stews.

Braising A slow cooking method used for cuts of meat, poultry and game which are too tough to roast. It is also good for some vegetables. A pan or casserole with a tight-fitting lid should be used so that little liquid is lost through evaporation. The meat is first browned, then cooked on a bed of chopped vegetables (called a *mirepoix*), with just enough liquid to cover the vegetables. It may be cooked on the hob or in the oven.

Brining A method of preserving by immersing food in a salt and water solution.

Brioche An enriched yeast dough mixture baked in the shape of a cottage loaf. French in origin and usually eaten warm for breakfast.

Brochette Fish, meat or vegetables, cooked on a skewer or spit.

Broth The liquid produced by boiling meat or fish bones in water for a long time. Also sometimes called stock.

Brûlée A French term, literally meaning 'burnt' used to refer to a dish with a crisp coating of caramelised sugar.

Calorie A scientific term used in dietetics to measure the heat and energy producing quality of food.

Canapé Small appetisers, usually served with drinks and often consisting of a topping on a bread or pastry base.

Candying Method of impregnating pieces of fruit or peel with sugar to preserve them.

Caramel Substance obtained by heating sugar syrup very slowly to a rich brown colour.

Carbonade Rich stew or braise of meat which includes beer.

Casserole Strictly speaking, a dish with a tight-fitting lid used for cooking meat and vegetables. Now applied to the food cooked in this way.

Celsius Also known as Centigrade. A scale for measuring temperature in which the freezing point of water is 0° and the boiling point 100°. Now used for the oven settings on electric cookers, replacing the Fahrenheit scale which is gradually becoming obsolete.

Chantilly A classic French whipped cream which is slightly sweetened and may be flavoured with vanilla.

Charcuterie The French term for cooked pork products, such as hams, sausages and terrines.

Charlotte A hot or cold moulded dessert. For a hot charlotte the mould is lined with bread and for a cold charlotte it is lined with sponge fingers.

Chasseur Literally translated means 'hunter-style'. Describes dishes cooked with mushrooms, shallots and white wine.

Chaudfroid A cold dish of jellied fish, poultry or game that is coated in a thick Béchamel based or brown sauce, set under a layer of aspic.

Chilling Cooling food without freezing.

Chining Applied to joints of meat, this means severing the rib bones from the backbone by sawing through the ribs close to the spine. Joints such as loin or neck of lamb, veal or pork are best chined as this makes them easier to carve into chops or cutlets after cooking.

Chorizo Spanish sausage made of smoked pork and pimiento. Sold ready cooked.

Chowder An American dish somewhere between a soup and a stew, usually based on fish, eg clam chowder.

Citric acid A mild acid which occurs naturally in citrus fruit. Commercially produced citric acid is used mainly for preserving soft fruit drinks and in home wine making.

Clarifying Process of removing sediment or impurities from a food. Butter and dripping may be clarified so that they can be used for frying at higher temperatures.

To clarify butter, heat until melted and all bubbling stops. Remove from the heat and stand until the salt and sediment have sunk to the bottom, then gently pour off the fat, straining it through muslin. Chill and use as required. Clarified butter is also known as ghee.

To clarify dripping, melt the fat, then strain it to remove any particles. Pour over two to three times its volume of boiling water and allow to cool. The fat will rise to the top and become firm. Lift it off and wipe the underside with absorbent kitchen paper to remove any sediment.

Clarifying also means to clear a liquid or jelly, such as consommé, usually by adding egg white. The coagulation of the egg white throughout the liquid gathers up all the impurities and forms a scum on the surface which can be discarded.

Clotting A gentle heat applied to cream which produces the thick clotted cream of the south-west of England.

Cocotte Small earthenware, ovenproof container of single portion size. Also called a ramekin.

Coddling Method of soft boiling eggs.

Colander Perforated metal or plastic draining basket.

Compote Mixture of fruit stewed in sugar syrup. Served hot or cold.

Concasser A French term used to describe food that is finely or roughly chopped. It is most often applied to skinned, seeded and chopped tomatoes.

Conserve Whole fruit jam.

Consistency Term used to describe the texture of a mixture, eg firm, dropping or soft.

Consommé Concentrated stock which has been clarified.

Cornstarch American name for cornflour.

Coulis A French term applied to a purée of vegetables, fish, poultry or fruit.

Court bouillon Seasoned liquid in which meat, poultry, fish or vegetables are boiled or poached.

Couscous Processed semolina in tiny pellets. Staple food in North African countries.

Crackling The crisp skin on roasted pork.

Cream of tartar (tartaric acid) A raising agent which is an ingredient of baking powder and self-raising flour.

Creaming Beating together fat and sugar until the mixture is pale and fluffy and resembles whipped cream in texture and colour. Used in cakes and puddings which contain a high proportion of fat and require the incorporation of a lot of air.

Crêpe French term for a pancake.

Crimping Decorating the edges of a pie, tart or shortbread by pinching it at regular intervals to give a fluted effect. The term may also refer to trimming cucumber, radishes, etc with a canelle knife or fork to produce a deckled-cut finish.

Croquette Mixture of meat, fish, poultry, cooked potatoes or vegetables bound together and formed into roll or cork shapes, coated with egg and breadcrumbs and shallow or deep-fried.

Croûte A circle or rectangle of fried or toasted bread on which game and some main dishes and savouries are served. The term may also refer to a pastry crust, usually crescent shaped, served with savoury dishes.

Croûtons Small pieces of fried or toasted bread which are served with salads and soup.

Curd The parts of milk which coagulate when natural fermentation takes place, or when a curdling agent, such as rennet or an acid is added. The term also refers to a creamy preserve made from fruit (usually lemon or orange) and sugar, eggs and butter.

Curdle To separate fresh milk or a sauce either by adding acid (such as lemon juice) or by heating excessively. Also used to refer to creamed mixtures which have separated when the egg has been beaten in too quickly.

Cure To preserve fish, meat or poultry by salting, drying or smoking.

Daube Braising meat or vegetables in stock, often with wine or herbs.

Deglaze To heat stock, wine or other liquid with the cooking juices left in the pan after roasting or sautéeing meat, stirring to dissolve the sediment.

Dégorge To draw out moisture from food, eg salting aubergines to remove bitter juices.

Dhal The Indian collective term for pulses.

Dice To cut food into small cubes.

Dough A thick mixture of uncooked flour and liquid, usually combined with other ingredients. The term is used to refer to mixtures such as pastry, scones and biscuits as well as those made with yeast.

Drawing Removing the entrails from poultry and game.

Dredging Sprinkling food with flour, sugar or other powdered coating. Fish and meat are often dredged with flour before frying, while cakes, biscuits and pancakes may be sprinkled with caster or icing sugar after cooking.

Dressing Plucking, drawing and trussing poultry and game. The term is also used to describe garnishing a dish, and coating a salad.

Dripping Fat obtained from roasting meat or pieces of fat which are rendered down deliberately (see also Rendering).

Dropping consistency Term used to describe the correct texture of a cake or pudding mixture just before cooking. Test for it by taking a spoonful of the mixture and holding the spoon on its side above the bowl. The mixture should fall off of its own accord within 5 seconds.

Drying Preserving food by dehydration. This is usually done commercially for foods such as rice, pasta and pulses, but it is possible to dry herbs and fruit at home.

Dust: To sprinkle lightly with flour, cornflour or icing sugar.

Egg and crumbing Method of coating fish, rissoles, croquettes, etc before frying or baking.

Emulsion A mixture of two liquids which do not automatically dissolve into each other, eg oil and water. They can be made to emulsify by vigorous beating or shaking together, as when combining oil and vinegar in a French Dressing.

En croûte Term describing food which is wrapped in pastry before cooking.

En papillote A French term applied to food which is baked in baking parchment or greaseproof paper for a brief period and served in the parcel.

Enzyme Substances present in all foods which have not been subjected to processing. They work within foods continuously and are responsible for changes in food condition. Most enzymes are killed by cooking (see also Blanching).

Escalope A thin slice of meat, such as veal, turkey or pork, cut from the top of the leg and often egged and crumbed, then fried or grilled.

Espagnole Classic French rich brown sauce, used as the basis for other sauces.

Extract Concentrated flavouring which is used in small quantities, eg meat extract, yeast extract.

Fahrenheit System of measuring temperature which is being replaced with Celsius. Its freezing point is 32° and boiling point 212°.

Farce Alternative French term for stuffing.

Fermenting Term used to denote chemical changes deliberately or accidentally brought about by fermenting agents, such as yeast or bacteria. The process is utilised for making bread, yogurt and wine.

Fillet A term used for the undercut of a loin of beef, veal, pork or game; boned breasts of birds; and boned sides of fish.

Fines herbes Classic French mixture of chopped herbs, ie parsley, tarragon, chives and chervil.

Flambé Flavouring a dish with alcohol, usually brandy or rum, which is then ignited so that the actual alcohol content is burned off. Christmas Pudding and Crêpes Suzette are traditionally flambéed.

Folding in Method of combining a whisked or creamed mixture with other ingredients by cutting and folding so that it retains its lightness. Used mainly for meringues, soufflés and certain cake mixtures. Use a large metal spoon.

Fondue Dish cooked at the table over a fondue burner into which the diners dip food speared on long pronged fondue forks.

Fool Cold dessert consisting of puréed fruit with whipped cream or custard blended into it.

Forcemeat Stuffing for meat, fish or vegetables.

Fricassée White stew of chicken, rabbit, veal or vegetables, finished with cream and egg yolks.

Frosting American term for icing cakes. Also refers to the decorating of fruits, flowers and the rims of glasses, by coating with a fine layer of sugar.

Frothing Dredging the surface of roast meat, usually game, with flour and heating to a brown colour in a hot oven.

Frying Method of cooking food in hot fat or oil. There are various methods: shallow-frying in a little fat in a shallow pan; deep-frying where the food is totally immersed in oil; dry-frying in which fatty foods, such as bacon and sausages, are cooked in a non-stick pan without extra fat; see also Stir-frying.

Galantine A dish of white meat which has been boned, sometimes stuffed, then rolled, cooked, pressed and glazed with aspic to be served cold.

Garnish A decoration, usually edible, such as parsley or lemon, which is added to a savoury dish to enhance its appearance.

Gelatine An animal-derived gelling agent sold in powdered form in sachets, and as leaf gelatine.

Genoese Sponge cake made with a whisked egg mixture enriched with melted butter.

Ghee Clarified butter widely used in Indian cookery (see also Clarifying).

Glacé French word meaning iced or glossy.

Glaze Food used to give a glossy coating to sweet and savoury dishes to improve their appearance and sometimes flavour. Ingredients for glazes include beaten egg, egg white, milk and syrup.

Gluten A protein constituent of wheat and other cereals. The amount present in flours varies and accounts for the different textures of cakes and breads.

Grating Shredding cheese, carrots and other hard foods with a grater or food processor attachment.

Griddle A flat, heavy, metal plate used on top of the cooker for cooking scones, crumpets etc.

Grinding Reducing foods to small particles in a food mill, pestle and mortar, electric grinder or food processor. Foods ground include coffee beans, nuts and spices.

Grissini Long, slim, brittle Italian bread sticks.

Gut To clean out the inside of a fish, removing all the entrails.

Hanging Leaving meat or game suspended in a cool, dry place to allow air to circulate around it to tenderise the flesh and develop the flavour.

Hors d'oeuvre Often used as a term for a starter but, strictly speaking, means a selection of cold foods served together as an appetiser.

Hulling Removing the calyx from soft fruits, eg strawberries.

Infusing Method of imparting flavour to a liquid. Flavourings, such as aromatic vegetables, herbs, spices, vanilla pod or coffee beans, are added to milk or water, sometimes brought to the boil, then left to soak.

Jardinière Refers to dishes garnished with mixed fresh spring vegetables or green peas and sprigs of cauliflower.

Jugged Traditional method of cooking hare in a tall covered pot until very tender and rich dark brown in colour. The blood is added at the end of the cooking time.

Julienne Vegetables or fruit rind cut into very fine strips to use as a garnish or ingredient.

Kebab General name for a dish comprising cubes of meat, fish, shellfish, fruit and vegetables which are cooked on skewers under a grill or on a barbecue.

Knead To work dough by pummelling with the heel of the hand.

Knock back To knead a yeast dough for a second time after rising, to ensure an even texture.

Kosher Food prepared according to orthodox Jewish laws.

Kugelhopf A sweetened yeast cake which contains dried fruit and is baked in a special deep fluted tin.

Langues de chats Literally means cats' tongues. Small thin flat crisp biscuits served with ice creams and mousses.

Larding Inserting small strips of fat bacon into the flesh of game birds, poultry and dry meat before cooking. It is done with a special larding needle.

Leaven The raising agent in dough, usually yeast or baking powder.

Liaison Term used to describe any combination of ingredients which is used for thickening or binding. The ingredients of a liaison are usually flour, cornflour, arrowroot, rice or potato flour, or egg yolk.

Macédoine The French term for a mixture of fruit or vegetables cut into even-sized dice. Usually used as a garnish.

Macerate To soften and flavour raw or dried foods by soaking in a liquid.

Marinate To soak meat, poultry or game in a mixture of oil, wine, vinegar and flavourings to tenderise it and add flavour. The mixture, which is known as a marinade, may also be used to baste the food during cooking.

Marmite A French metal or earthenware pot used for long slow cooking of casseroles on top of the stove or in the oven.

Medallions French term for small rounds of meat, usually beef or veal.

Meunière A French term which refers to food cooked in butter, seasoned with salt, pepper and lemon juice and finished with parsley. Usually applied to fish dishes.

Milling Reducing to a powder or paste (see also Grinding).

Mincing Chopping or cutting food into very small pieces. It may be done with a knife, a manual mincing machine or in a food processor.

Mirepoix A mixture of cut vegetables, usually carrot, celery and onion, with a little added ham or bacon, used as a bed on which to braise meat.

Mocha A term which has come to mean a blend of chocolate and coffee.

Monosodium glutamate (MSG) A powder with little flavour of its own, but which enhances the flavour of ingredients it is added to. A principal ingredient in processed foods and Chinese cookery.

Noisettes Neatly trimmed and tied boneless pieces of lamb, not less than 1 cm (½ inch) thick, cut from the loin or best end of neck.

Panada A thick roux-based sauce used for binding croquettes and similar mixtures.

Parboiling A term used to describe boiling food for part of its cooking time before finishing it by another method.

Paring Thinly peeling and trimming vegetables or fruit.

Pasteurising Sterilising milk by heating to 60-92°C (140-180°F) to destroy bacteria.

Pâte The French word for pastry, familiar in *pâte sucrée*, a sweet flan pastry.

Pâté A savoury mixture made from minced meat, flaked fish and/or vegetables cooked to form a solid mass. Smoked fish pâtés are rarely cooked.

Paunching Removing the stomach and intestines of a rabbit or hare.

Paupiettes Slices of meat or fish rolled around a stuffing, usually braised or fried.

Pectin A naturally occuring substance found in most fruit and some vegetables which is necessary for setting jams and jellies.

Pickling Preserving raw fresh or lightly cooked food in vinegar.

Piping Forcing cream, icing, mashed potato, cake mixtures or meringue through a nozzle fitted into the end of a nylon or greaseproof paper piping bag.

Pith White lining under the rind of citrus fruit.

Plucking Removing feathers from poultry and game.

Poaching Cooking food gently in liquid at simmering point, so that the surface of the liquid is just trembling.

Pot roasting A method of cooking meat slowly in a covered pan with fat and a little liquid.

Potage The French term for a thick soup.

Praline Almonds caramelised in sugar, then crushed and used to flavour sweet dishes.

Preserving Keeping food in edible condition by freezing, canning, pickling, crystallising, irradiation, drying, smoking etc.

Pressure cooking Cooking food quickly in steam under pressure.

Prosciutto Italian raw smoked ham.

Proving The term used for leaving bread dough to rise after shaping.

Pulses The generic name given to all dried peas, beans and lentils. These are valued for their high protein and fibre content.

Purée Fruit, vegetable, meat or fish which has been pounded, sieved or liquidised to a smooth pulp. Purées often form the basis for soups and sauces.

Quenelles Fish, meat or poultry which has been blended to a fine forcemeat, shaped into rounds or ovals, then cooked in liquid and served either as a garnish for soup or as a main course.

Ramekin Individual round ovenproof dish.

Réchauffé French term for reheated leftovers.

Reducing Fast-boiling a liquid in an uncovered pan to evaporate water and produce a more concentrated flavour.

Refresh To pour cold water over blanched and drained vegetables to set the colour and stop the cooking process.

Rendering Extracting fat from meat trimmings by cutting them into small pieces and heating in a cool oven at 150°C (300°F) mark 2 until the fat runs out and can be strained.

Rennet A substance extracted from a calf's stomach which will curdle or coagulate milk. The process is also used for junket and cheese-making. Vegetarian rennet is also available.

Rice paper Edible paper made from the pith of a Chinese tree. Used as an edible base for sticky baked goods such as macaroons.

Roasting Cooking meat by dry heat in an oven or over an open flame.

Roulade Meat, cake or soufflé mixture rolled around a filling.

Roux A mixture of equal amounts of fat and flour cooked together to form the basis of many sauces.

Rubbing in Method of incorporating fat into flour when a short texture is required. It is used for pastry, cakes, scones and biscuits.

Salmis A stew made from game birds; the bird is partly roasted and then cooked with wine or port.

Salting A method of preserving food in dry salt or a brine solution.

Sautéeing Cooking food in a small quantity of fat in a sauté pan (a frying pan with straight sides and a wide base), which browns the food quickly.

Scalding Pouring boiling water over food to clean it, loosen hairs or remove the skin. Food should not be left in boiling water or it will begin to cook. It is also the term used for heating milk to just below boiling point, to retard souring or to infuse it with another flavour.

Scalloping Decorating the double edge of a pastry pie with small horizontal cuts which are pulled up with the back of a knife to produce a scalloped effect.

Scoring To cut narrow parallel lines in the surface of food to improve its appearance or help it cook more quickly.

Searing Browning meat quickly in a little hot fat before grilling or roasting.

Seasoned flour Flour mixed with a little salt and pepper, for dusting meat and fish before frying.

Seasoning Adding salt, pepper, herbs and spices to a dish to enhance flavour.

Shredding Grating cheese or slicing raw vegetables into very fine pieces or strips.

Sieving Pushing food through a perforated sieve to get a soft, even texture.

Sifting Shaking dry ingredients through a sieve to remove lumps.

Simmering Keeping a liquid just below boiling point.

Singeing Using a flame to burn off any residual traces of feather on plucked game or poultry.

Skimming Removing froth, scum or fat from the surface of stock, gravy, stews and jam. Use either a skimmer, a spoon or absorbent kitchen paper.

Smoking The process of curing food by exposure to wood smoke.

Souring Adding acid, often in the form of lemon juice, to cream to give it a sour taste.

Sousing Pickling in brine or vinegar.

Spit Rotating rod on which meat, poultry or game is cooked either in the oven or over a fire.

Steaming Cooking food in the steam of rapidly boiling water.

Steeping Covering food with hot or cold water and leaving it to stand, either to soften it or extract its flavour and/or colour.

Sterilising Destroying bacteria in foods by heating.

Stewing Long, slow cooking method where food is placed in liquid which is kept at simmering point. Good for tenderising tougher cuts of meat.

Stir-frying Quick method of frying in shallow fat. The food must be cut into small, even-sized pieces and moved around constantly until cooked. Stir-fried food is usually cooked in a wok.

Stock The liquid produced when meat, bones, poultry, fish or vegetables are simmered in water with herbs and flavourings for several hours to extract their flavour.

Suet Hard fat found around the kidneys in beef or mutton. Sold in packets. Used in pastry and steamed puddings. A vegetarian alternative is available.

Sweating Gently cooking food (usually vegetables) in melted fat in a covered pan, until the juices run.

Syrup A concentrated solution of sugar in water, used in making sorbets, drinks and fruit juices.

Tenderising Beating raw meat with a spiked mallet or rolling pin to break down the fibres and make it more tender for grilling or frying.

Tepid The term used to describe temperature at approximately blood heat, ie 37°C (98.7°F).

Terrine China or earthenware dish used for pâtés. Also used to refer to the food cooked in it.

Texturised vegetable protein (TVP) Meat substitute made from vegetables, usually soya beans. It generally takes on the flavour of anything it is cooked with.

Truffle Rare black or white fungus of the same family as the mushroom. Due to the cost, truffles are used mainly for garnishing.

Trussing Tying or skewering into shape before cooking. Applied mainly to poultry and game.

Unleavened Bread without a raising agent.

Vanilla sugar Sugar in which a vanilla pod has been stored to release its flavour.

Vol-au-vent A round or oval puff pastry case which is filled with diced meat, poultry, fish or vegetables in sauce.

Whipping (whisking) Beating air rapidly into a mixture either with a manual or electric whisk.

Wok Chinese pan used for stir-frying. The food cooks on the sloping sides of the pan as well as in the rounded base.

Zest The coloured outer layer of citrus fruit which contains essential oil.

INDEX

❖ D ❖

❖ E ❖